Human Sexuality

Human Sexuality: Biological, Psychological, and Cultural Perspectives is a unique textbook that provides a broad analysis of this crucial basic aspect of life. Utilizing viewpoints across cultural and national boundaries, and incorporating evolutionary and psychological perspectives, four major lines of evidence and knowledge are comprehensively discussed, including: evolutionary theory, primatology, the cross-cultural record and contemporary issues, and emphasizing anthropological contributions while incorporating psycho-social perspectives.

Taking into account the evolution of human anatomy, sexual behavior, attitudes, and beliefs, this far-reaching resource goes beyond what is found in U.S. society to present a wide diversity of beliefs, attitudes, and behaviors found globally. In addition to providing a rich array of photographs, illustrations, tables, an extensive bibliography, and a helpful glossary of terms, topics discussed include:

- modern human male and female anatomy and physiology.
- pregnancy and childbirth as a bio-cultural experience.
- life-course issues related to gender identity, sexual orientations, behaviors, and lifestyles.
- influences on socioeconomic, political, historical, and ecological systems of sexual behavior.
- evolutionary history of human sexuality.
- early childhood sexuality, puberty and adolescence.
- human sexual response.
- birth control, fertility, conception, and sexual differentiation.
- HIV infection, AIDS, AIDS globalization, and sex work.

Fusing biological, socio-psychological, and cultural influences to offer an original perspective to understanding human sexuality, its development over millions of years of evolution, and how sexuality is embedded in specific socio-cultural contexts, this is an important text for educators and students in a variety of human sexuality courses.

Human Sexuality
Biological, Psychological, and Cultural Perspectives

Anne Bolin, PhD
Elon University

Patricia Whelehan, PhD
SUNY-Potsdam

NEW YORK AND LONDON

First published 2009
by Routledge
270 Madison Ave, New York, NY 10016

Simultaneously published in the UK
by Routledge
2 Park Square, Milton Park, Abingdon, Oxon OX14 4RN

*Routledge is an imprint of the Taylor & Francis Group,
an informa business*

© 2009 Taylor & Francis

Typeset in Sabon by
Integra Software Services Pvt. Ltd, Pondicherry, India
Printed and bound in the United States of America on acid-free paper
by Edwards Brothers, Inc.

Library of Congress Cataloging in Publication Data
A catalog record has been requested for this book

Every effort has been made to contact copyright holders for their
permission to reprint material in this book. The publishers would be
grateful to hear from any copyright holder who is not here
acknowledged and will undertake to rectify any errors or omissions
in future editions of this book.

ISBN10: 0–7890–2671–6 (hbk)
ISBN10: 0–7890–2672–4 (pbk)
ISBN10: 0–2038–8923–1 (ebk)

ISBN13: 978–0–7890–2671–2 (hbk)
ISBN13: 978–0–7890–2672–9 (pbk)
ISBN13: 978–0–2038–8923–7 (ebk)

This book is dedicated to Jose Andres Gonzalez del Valle (August 4, 1963–September 9, 1991) who taught me to love without fear and who enhanced the lives of everyone who knew him. We miss you.

Pat

For my mother, Vivian Bolin (April 23, 1912–March 21, 1998).
I still miss you so very much.

Anne

Contents

Illustrations

Tables

About the authors

Anne Bolin received her Ph.D. in Anthropology from the University of Colorado. She is a Professor of Anthropology in the Department of Sociology and Anthropology at Elon University, Elon, North Carolina and is the recipient of the Elon University Distinguished Scholar Award. She has presented and published extensively in the research areas of women and gender, human sexuality, the body, gender identity, and gender variance. Her publications include several books and numerous articles in journals, books, and scholarly encyclopedias. Her book, *In Search of Eve: Transsexual Rites of Passage* (Bergin and Garvey), received a CHOICE Magazine Award  for an Outstanding Academic Book for 1988–1989. With co-author, Patricia Whelehan, she has published *Perspectives on Human Sexuality* (State University of New York Press, 1999.) In 2003, she authored *Athletic Intruders: Women, Culture and Exercise*, with Jane Granskog (State University of New York Press). Her latest book with co-author Patricia Whelehan is titled *Human Sexuality: Biological, Psychological and Cultural Perspectives*, (Routledge/Taylor and Francis, 2009). Her current research is focused on gender and embodiment including ethnographic research with physique competitors as well as ongoing research on gender identity and gender variance. She is a Diplomate with the American Board of Sexology, a certified sex researcher, Fellow of the Society for Applied Anthropology, former co-chair/co-founder and currently Steering Committee member of the Human Sexuality and Anthropology Interest Group.

Patricia Whelehan is Professor of Anthropo-
logy and the campuses' AIDS Education
Coordinator at SUNY-Potsdam. She is the
editor of *Women and Health: Cross-Cultural
Perspectives* (Bergin and Garvey/Greenwood
Publishers, 1988), co-author of *Perspectives
on Human Sexuality* with Anne Bolin (SUNY-
Press, 1999) and *Human Sexuality: Biolo-
gical, Psychological and Cultural Perspectives*
(Routledge/Taylor and Francis, 2009); and
author of *An Anthropological Perspective on
Prostitution: The World's Oldest Profession*
(Edwin Mellen Press, 2001). In 2007, she
received the President's Award for Excellence
in Service. In 1999 and 2008, she received the Phi Eta Sigma award for
Outstanding Teacher of the year, and in 2008 she was inducted into
Phi Kappa Phi, a national honor's society that recognizes scholarly distinction. Her textbook, *The Anthropology of AIDS: A Global Perspective*
with the University Press of Florida is expected to be released in 2009.

About the contributors

Georgina S. Hammock is a social psychologist who specializes in the study of violence. She received her doctorate from the University of Georgia. Since that time she has studied violence between strangers, violence between intimates, conflict in intimate relationships, and the perception of violent encounters. She has published and presented this work both nationally and internationally. Most recently she has focused on the study of intimate violence with a concentration in the new area of psychological aggression. Her work in this area can be found in the journals *Violence and Victims, Aggression and Violent Behavior; Aggressive Behavior, Journal of Applied Social Psychology,* and the *International Review of Social Psychology.* She also worked recently with her colleague, Deborah Richardson, to edit a special issue on nondirect aggression for the *International Review of Social Psychology.* Presently, she is an assistant professor at Augusta State University.

Wenda Trevathan is Regents Professor of Anthropology at New Mexico State University, where she has been on the faculty since 1983. She received her PhD in anthropology from the University of Colorado and is a biological anthropologist whose research focuses on the evolutionary and biocultural factors underlying human reproduction including childbirth, maternal behavior, sexuality, and menopause. She is the recipient of the Margaret Mead Award from the American Anthropological Association and the Society for Applied Anthropology (1990) and is the author of *Human Birth: An Evolutionary Perspective* (1987). She also publishes in the area of evolutionary medicine, most significantly the two edited books (with E. O. Smith and J. J. McKenna) *Evolutionary Medicine* (1999) and *Evolutionary Medicine and Health: New Perspectives* (2007), published by Oxford University Press. She is a co-author on a series of textbooks in physical anthropology published by Wadsworth Press (Jurmain et al.). Awards she has received include the New Mexico Professor of the Year, awarded by the Carnegie Foundation for the Advancement of Teaching (1994), the Westhafer Award for Excellence in Research at New Mexico State University (1998), and the Donald

C. Roush Excellence in Teaching Award, also from New Mexico State University (1999). She was a Fulbright Senior Scholar to the University of San Carlos in the Philippines in 1999–2000. Her current research includes cortisol in mother-infant interaction and stress, sexuality, and mood during the menopause transition.

Preface

This preface is a welcome to all our potential readers—students, professors, and researchers—of human sexuality. For those of you who teach or conduct research in human sexuality, you may be wondering why there is the need for yet *another* undergraduate human sexuality text, especially since there are several fine books on the market dealing with current United States sexual behavior and attitudes (e.g., Kelly's *Sexuality Today: The Human Perspective*; Tiefer's *Sex Is Not a Natural Act and Other Essays*; Westheimer and Lopater's *Human Sexuality: A Psychosocial Perspective*; and McCammon, Knox, and Schact's *Choices in Sexuality*).

We believe that since most of the current undergraduate texts are *not* written by anthropologists, there are dimensions of human sexuality that are not covered by these. Most noticeably, *Human Sexuality: Biological, Psychological, and Cultural Perspectives* does *not* focus on a view of sexuality as anchored in Euro-American behaviors; nor do we wish to inculcate a view of nonindustrialized peoples as "exotic others." Euro-American behaviors and beliefs are as exotic and alien to people in other cultures as theirs are to us, or even to people of previous generations in our own culture, as their behaviors are to us. This book incorporates an anthropological perspective that is unique and different from most of the available literature. For those unfamiliar with anthropology, this perspective is intrinsically an interdisciplinary one emphasizing the intersections of biological, psychological, and cultural aspects of human sexuality, hence the title. Specifically, *Human Sexuality: Biological, Psychological, and Cultural Perspectives* integrates evolutionary, cross-cultural, and bio-cultural dimensions of human sexuality. We examine patterns of sexuality as they occur in a variety of cultures, including our own, as opposed to a conflict/issues approach of many late-twentieth-century United States sexuality texts.

Translated, this means that we look at modern human sexual behavior as having evolved from a primate heritage. It has changed through time and space physically and behaviorally as a means of adapting to our specific needs as a large-brained, upright organism which depends on learning as its primary survival (adaptive) strategy. We compare ourselves to our nearest relatives—the nonhuman primates—and to other human groups to gain a better understanding and insight into what we share as a human species, as well as carryovers from our primate heritage. We integrate, as much as possible, the biological and learned aspects of sexuality through the life cycle from conception through old age.

The twenty-first century brings us daunting challenges as a species, members of groups, and as individuals. HIV infection and AIDS are global, pandemic health concerns that governments and health agencies realize are ongoing concerns. HIV infection cross-culturally and in the United States is spread primarily through sexual contact. There is neither a cure nor a vaccine available in this, the third decade of the pandemic, although vaccine trials continue. Thus, prevention of infection through education coupled with behavior and attitude changes which are geared to the specific needs, perceptions, and values of people at risk and groups seriously impacted by the disease continue to be important. Interventions need to occur at the individual, societal, and global level. They necessitate a cross-cultural, holistic, and relativistic anthropological approach.

We are a human community. Twenty-first century technology that includes computers and satellite communication, as well as industrialized societies' medical technology, which can be available on a worldwide basis, makes diversity (i.e., a variety of value systems, behaviors, and perceptions) a reality of United States and international life. To survive, we need to appreciate, understand, and accept difference and use it to enhance our humanity as individuals, groups, and a species. Meeting these challenges also involves a cross-cultural, comparative anthropological perspective. Therefore, our approach in this book has both theoretical as well as applied dimensions in trying to understand ourselves as sexual beings.

To do this, however, we have recognized certain limits to this text. One, we do not cover every aspect of modern U.S. sexuality. Two, this is not a book on twenty-first-century U.S. sexual behavior. Although we include U.S. sexuality as part of human sexuality, we do not focus primarily on it. Simultaneously, we include sexual behaviors and attitudes of nonindustrialized people through time and space. We try to incorporate sexuality as part of their worldview and socio-cultural life—as integrated and related to political, economic, and social structures.

Those sexual behaviors and aspects of the life cycle that we discuss are those which are human (found in all human groups) although arranged, defined, and constructed according to the specific demands of a given group. For example, fertility issues, pregnancy, and childbirth are pan-human concerns. We discuss how the United States and other societies culturally define and manage these life cycle issues. Childhood sexuality is also part of human sexuality. So, we examine how various cultures, including our own, channel and regard childhood sexuality as a prelude to adult sexuality. The transgendered social identity includes socio-sexual roles found cross-culturally and in the United States. They are defined, structured, and responded to very differently in the United States than in the nonindustrialized and international societies in which they occur.

On the other hand, fetishes and paraphilias (focusing exclusively on particular objects or body parts as the primary or only means of sexual arousal) appear not to be particularly widespread cross-culturally. They are *not* dealt with in this book. While they are not dealt with specifically, we do provide an important framework for furthering the understanding of such Euro-American-based categories, or "culture-bound" syndromes. We aim for a better understanding of human sexuality—that which we share as a species and not exclusively what occurs in middle-class U.S. society.

Given this interdisciplinary perspective, instructors, researchers, and students may use *Human Sexuality* in a variety of ways. It can be used as a basic text with supplemental or recommended readings in U.S. sexuality courses. Or, it may be used as a supplemental text for those most comfortable in dealing with human sexuality as it occurs in the United States in this relatively new century. It can also serve as a resource for researchers and teachers who want to incorporate evolutionary or cross-cultural data as part of their writing and teaching.

We hope the approach taken here will be of use and value to you in your understanding of this highly varied and data-rich topic of human sexuality. By understanding human sexuality, we have a greater appreciation of and may be able to develop a broader tolerance of the diversity that comprises our species.

One final *caveat* is in order that relates to the speed with which science progresses. There is a necessary time lag in the publication of a manuscript, so that when a book comes into print it cannot, by virtue of the production process, contain the most recent findings in the months prior to its publication date. Scientific research surges forward at a rapid rate in our postmodern world. As a consequence, we would like our readers to be aware that new scientific evidence will continue to occur as *Human Sexuality: Biological, Psychological, and Cultural Perspectives* is published.

New evidence is likely to occur in relation to Chapter 11, "Topics in adult sexuality: human sexual response," which examines cultural aspects of sexual response; Chapter 12; "Topics in adult sexuality: birth control," which discusses the context of birth control; Chapter 13; "Topics in adult sexuality: life course issues related to gender identity, gender roles, and aging," which emphasizes issues related to aging and sexuality; and Chapter 15 which focuses on HIV infection and AIDS. We encourage the reader to check with his or her physician and/or contact The Association of Reproductive Health Professionals, 2401 Pennsylvania Avenue NW Suite #350, Washington, DC 20037, telephone: (202) 466-3825, www.arhp.org; Planned Parenthood Federation of America, 810 Seventh Avenue, New York, NY 10019, telephone: (800) 230-7526, www.plannedparenthood.org, for any new developments in sexual response treatments and birth control methods in the recent months preceding and encompassing the production and publication of this book. For the latest information on the topics of aging and hormone/drug therapies check with your physician and or contact the North American Menopause Society, Post Office Box 94527, Cleveland, OH 44101, telephone: (440) 442-7550, www.menopause.org; the American Psychological Association Committee on Aging, 750 First Street, NE, Washington, DC 20002, telephone: (202) 336-6050, www.apa.org/pi/aging/cona01.html; the American Urological Association, 1000 Corporate Blvd., Linthicum, MD 21090, telephone: (866) 746-4282, www.auanet.org, among other resources on aging and sexuality. We encourage you to explore the "New View of Women's Sexuality" website, www.fsd-alert.org, for a nonmedical interpretation of women's sexuality across the life span.

New treatments for HIV infection and AIDS occur rapidly. The availability of HAART (Highly Active Antiretroviral Therapy) for people living with HIV/AIDS (PLWH/A) in industrialized countries, particularly the United States, since 1996 has resulted in reduced death rates from the disease, and increased health and functioning. Although these new drugs offer optimism and hope for people infected in industrialized societies, the situation is not as optimistic in nonindustrialized societies, most notably sub-Saharan Africa, where only 17 to 27 percent of the people who need the drugs receive them. For the most recent information on HIV infection and AIDS, we recommend contacting the Centers for Disease Control and Prevention Division of Sexually Transmitted Diseases, 1600 Clinton Road, Atlanta, GA 30329. In addition, numerous sources for information on HIV/AIDS are available, among them are the National AIDS Hotline, telephone: (800) 342-2437; the ACLU AIDS Project, telephone: (212) 944-9800, ext. 545; the National AIDS Clearing House, telephone: (800) 458-5231; American Foundation for AIDS Research, telephone: (212) 682-7440; and the National Lesbian and Gay Health Foundation, telephone: (202) 797-3578.

This text, *Human Sexuality: Biological, Psychological, and Cultural Perspectives*, is radically different from our previous book in a number of ways. For example, it is interdisciplinary and global in scope; it includes contributions from psychologist Georgina Hammock and biological anthropologist Wenda Trevathan and addresses "Globalization and sexuality: the meaning and issues of 'sex work'." Sex work in all of its expressions (male, female, and transgendered prostitution, media-based and written pornography, sex tourism) is a multibillion dollar industry. This chapter looks at the cultural-historical basis for sex work and the sharp cultural contrasts in its expression depending on whether it occurs in industrialized or nonindustrialized societies.

Your authors and contributors hope that this book presents new data and approaches on important topics such as birth control, sexual response, and HIV/AIDS. It is our wish that you find this book interesting, informative, and of value to your understanding of sexuality.

Acknowledgments

While we recognize and accept the importance of formally acknowledging those of you who have helped us write and publish this text, we also know this statement merely touches the surface of what you have given us. We would both like to thank The Haworth Press and Routledge, Taylor and Francis for adopting our book as one of their publications and to offer our gratitude to Eli Coleman for his thoughtful comments, editorial skill and vision for this new human sexuality book. Each of us will thank our respective sources of support.

Patricia Whelehan wants to express her appreciation and gratitude to a number of people. I would like to thank: Ms. Kathy LaDue of the Anthropology Department, SUNY Potsdam, for her invaluable help since 1992 with this book; students Mary Bailey, for whom this is the second book she's helped me with, and Myra Tramazzo whose eye for detail helped with the revisions and updates for this book. Interns Amanda Pryce and Stacy Pople reread chapters and worked on the bibliography in the fall 2005. Intern Carol Michelfelder compiled the final bibliography during the fall 2006 semester. The Human Sexuality 1 and 2 classes at SUNY Potsdam since the spring of 2004 have offered valuable criticisms and suggestions for improving this book. I'd also like to thank my daughter, Rachel Galgoul, for her insights and contributions, as well as Mr. Currie Nunnery, Ms. Joyce Rice and Ms. Linda Nelson, Ms. Sylvia Macey, and Dr. Ed Hosley. Your willingness to read and comment on manuscripts on an ongoing basis is invaluable. Ms. Linda Martindale has proofread and reviewed the entire manuscript. Thank you for the time and care you have given each version.

To all of you in the sexual subcultures and the HIV communities in New York, California, the Dominican Republic, and Lima, Peru, I wish to express my appreciation for your acceptance. I hope I have accurately represented your points of view in this book.

Anne Bolin wants to thank Elon University's Faculty Research and Development Committee for a sabbatical in the fall 2003 to work on this book. I am grateful to a number of colleagues both at Elon and elsewhere for their support of this project. Tom Henricks, who has served as chair of the Sociology and Anthropology Department during the life course of this book, has provided encouragement of this project and support of research and writing as integral to the life of teacher-scholars as well as tweaking my thinking on issues of sexuality and gender. I am also indebted to my colleague Larry Basirico, Dean of the Isabella Cannon Centre for International Studies. Larry gave me valuable feedback, advice, and generous gifts of joy and laughter. Special thanks are due to Paul Shankman of the University of Colorado who has taught me so much during the course of my career as an anthropologist. His dedication to scholarship and rigor has remained an invaluable touchstone for me since my graduate school days.

Linda Martindale of Elon University played an essential role in this book since 2005. I offer her my gratitude for her expertise in manuscript preparation, working her computer magic, her exquisite editorial skills and insightful suggestions, especially those regarding popular culture. Words cannot express my thanks to her for her enormous contribution to the birthing of this book. The students in my spring 2005 Anthropology of Sex course deserve special mention as well for their encouragement and enthusiasm for this book. In addition, SUNY Potsdam student Myra Tramazzo offered comments for my chapters as well as research for the contraception portions of the text. During the fall of 2005, Elon student and honors fellow Virginia Rodgers became my trusty sidekick; she offered superb skills as a research assistant for all phases of the revision process including editing, research on controversial issues and was a wonderful sounding board. Research intern Alyssa Morley offered a keen eye on checking details in the bibliography as well as worked on creating and representing data in graphs and tables. The Elon University library staff were helpful in locating resources with special thanks to Randall Bowman for his expertise in library research. I am especially grateful to Kim Eke, Senior Instructional Designer and Morgan Lasater, Multimedia Developer, for their help with designing several figures for the book. Greg Babcock, my spouse, high school sweetheart and partner, has provided me an environment in which to write that is filled with love and harmony. My family has always been an important source of emotional and intellectual support for my academic efforts. My deepest appreciation is given to my mother, Vivian Bolin, who instilled in me a sense of *joie de vivre*. And finally my thanks are given to the transgender community who have given so freely of their time and shared their most personal experiences. You have taught me so much about gender.

1 Introduction

CHAPTER OVERVIEW

1 Introduces human sexuality from a biological, psychological, and cultural perspective.
2 Discusses how the social control of human sexuality forms the fundamental basis for the functioning of human groups and group life.
3 Discusses ethnographic and comparative approaches to the cultural patterning of human sexuality. Highlights anthropologists such as Malinowski, Benedict, Mead, Ford and Beach, Martin and Voorhies, and Frayser.

THE ANTHROPOLOGICAL PERSPECTIVE

In one ruling by the Supreme Court, *sex* has been declared as "a great and mysterious motive force in human life [that] has indisputably been a subject of absorbing interest" (in Demac, 1988: 41). As children, we have heard our parents speak euphemistically about the "birds and the bees" and as adolescents we may have shared late-night discussions with our friends about the "secrets" of intimacy; as adult North Americans, our concerns are expressed in an array of new "self-help" books on the subject, which flood the market every year. Problems with **human sexuality** such as **sexual addictions** and **sexual desire disorders** (lack of interest in sex) have captured the imagination of the television, radio, and Internet news media, as well as the *Diagnostic and Statistical Manual of Mental Disorders-IV-TR* (2000), the "Bible" of diagnostic criteria for mental health professionals in the United States since 1968 (Tiefer, 2004: 133). Obviously, the subject enthralls more than *Dr. Phil* and *Oprah;* controversies abound around sex-related issues such as same-sex marriage and abortion in the United States. In addition, questions arise concerning the impact of rising HIV rates globally, and how access to sexually charged content through the Internet will affect human sexual expression today and in the future.

Our intent is to offer a unique way of understanding ourselves as sexual beings through the perspective of **anthropology**. Some of our readers may not be familiar with what anthropology entails and might be wondering what exactly Speilberg's *Raiders of the Lost Ark* or Holland's *Krippendorf's Tribe* has to do with a serious anthropological approach to sex. For those of you unfamiliar with anthropology, we welcome and invite you to explore an exciting new viewpoint that you will find very interdisciplinary in approach. Anthropology is probably the most interdisciplinary of all the fields engaged in studying sexuality (also referred to as sexology). **Sexology** spans the social and biological sciences as well as the humanities. For those of you majoring or minoring in anthropology, we hope that our book inspires you to conduct further research on the subject of human sexuality.

Sex as biology, psychology, and culture

Confusion about what anthropology is stems from the interdisciplinary nature of the field. An anthropological approach is one that incorporates an understanding of humans as both biological and cultural beings. The term **bio-cultural** is often used to describe this perspective. However, we are not suggesting that these are the only two dimensions for interpreting sex; indeed, sex has a very important psychological component as well. As anthropologists, we regard the psychological component as part of how culture shapes our personalities in characteristic ways, yet also allows for the diversity of individuals as unique **genetic entities**. There is a feedback relationship between culture, psychology, and the individual.

Therefore, to express the complexity of the relationship between biology and culture to human beings, we have added the psychological dimension to our mix, thereby highlighting the contributions of psychology and psychological anthropology to the study of human sexuality. This accentuates the importance of the individual in society by emphasizing her/his relationship to the cultural context including personality, motives, attitudes, values, perceptions, and emotions. It is because of these individual differences that cultures are so dynamic and ever-changing. Human beings are not just robots blindly enacting their cultural scripts; they innovate, invent, resist, subvert, rebel, and negotiate just as they may **reproduce** and subscribe to aspects of their cultures (Basirico and Bolin, 2002). We have reframed our bio-cultural terminology as "biological, psychological and cultural" to better reflect the role of individuals within society. (See Figure 1.1. For further discussion see Chapter 2.)

Although a **biological, psychological,** and **cultural approach** in anthropology may not be appropriate for all the subjects anthropologists might research, such a view lends a fuller and more complete understanding for a number of topics. Biological, psychological and cultural perspectives are

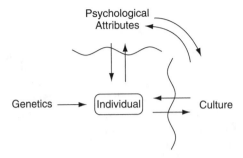

Figure 1.1 The individual in society. (*Source:* Anne Bolin with Elon University Department of Instructional and Campus Technologies, 2006.)

widespread in fields such as medical anthropology, biological anthropology, the anthropology of sex and gender, psychological anthropology, and clinical anthropology.

The interweaving of biology, psychology, and culture into a bio-psycho-cultural perspective is the distinguishing feature of this book and the theme that unifies the diversity of studying human sexuality through an anthropological lens. The term "sex" has many meanings. Sex is part of our biology. It is a behavior that involves a choreography of endocrine functions, muscles, and phases of physical change. It is expressed through the "biological sex" of people classified as male or female (Katchadourian, 1979). Despite this physiological component, the act of sex cannot be separated from the psychological and cultural context in which it occurs, thereby incorporating meanings, symbols, myths, ideals, and values. Sex expresses variation across and within cultures and among individuals.

An anthropological definition of sex is necessarily broad, and includes the cultural, psychological, and biological aspects of sex. We shall offer you a definition of sex, but urge you to remember that defining sex is far more complex than our definition suggests. For example, our definition cannot limit sex to only those behaviors resulting in **penile-vaginal intercourse**; in doing so, we would eliminate a variety of **homosexual, bisexual,** and **heterosexual** behaviors that are obviously sexual but not **coital.** Therefore, we shall define **sex** as those behaviors, sentiments, emotions, and perceptions related to and resulting in sexual arousal as defined by the society or culture in which it occurs. We qualified our definition by referring to cultural definitions of **sexual behaviors** since these differ a great deal among ethnic groups and cross-culturally. For example, "petting" as we know it in industrialized societies is not universal; that is, it is not necessarily considered a form of arousal among all other peoples of the world. As you read this book, you will begin to broaden your understanding of yourself, your own society, and the multicultural world in which we live.

Anthropological perspectives on human sexuality

The study of human sexuality is cross-disciplinary. Six major perspectives dominate the study of human sexuality. They include: the biological with a focus on physiology, hormones, and anatomy; the psychosocial that emphasizes the developmental aspects of sexuality and the interaction of the effect of cognitive and affective states with social variables on the individual; the behavioral that stresses behavior over cognitive and emotional states; the clinical concern with sexual problems and dysfunctions; the sociological, with a focus on social structures and the impact of institutions and socioeconomic status factors on sexual behavior; and the anthropological which includes evolutionary and cultural approaches with emphases on sexual meanings and behaviors within the cultural context. **Culture** is the shared reality of people that includes both ideas and patterned behaviors within a group, community (geographical and ideological), and/or region. Therefore, by culture we mean: the skills, attitudes, beliefs, and values underlying behavior as well as the behaviors themselves. These are learned by observation, imitation, and social learning. This preliminary definition is elaborated upon further in this chapter and Chapter 2.

In today's global community, it is increasingly important for us to incorporate multicultural perspectives in our knowledge base. Since this approach is at the heart of anthropology, we offer a brief historical overview of some of the more well-known cultural anthropologists who have shaped the study of human sexuality. The contributions of anthropologists studying the evolution of human sexuality are discussed in Chapter 3.

Anthropology as a discipline developed in the nineteenth century. From its inception, anthropologists have been interested in the role of human sexuality in **evolution** and the organization of culture. Darwin, most well-known for the biological theory of evolution (see Chapter 2 for definition and Chapter 3 for discussion), also formulated theories on culture that included ideas on human sexuality. These were presented in *The Descent of Man and Selection in Relation to Sex* (1874 [1871]). Darwin argued that morality is what separates humans from animals. In his theory of morality, Darwin regarded the regulation of sexuality as essential to its development. According to Darwin, marriage was the means for controlling sexual jealousy and competition among males. In the course of moral evolution, restrictions on sexuality were first required of married females, then later all females; finally males restricted their own sexuality to monogamy. Darwin's approach incorporated notions of male sexuality and assertiveness, and female asexuality. These views reflected Darwin's own cultural beliefs about sex and gender (Martin and Voorhies, 1975: 147–149).

Other nineteenth-century anthropologists also produced theories of social evolution that included the regulation of sexuality. John McLennan (1865), John Lubbock (1870) and Louis Henry Morgan (1870) conceived of societies as having evolved through stages. These stages represented increasing restrictions on sexuality as societies progressed from alleged "primitive" stages of **promiscuity** to modern "civilization" characterized by **monogamy** and **patriarchy** (Martin and Voorhies, 1975: 150). These theories were flawed in that they regarded European culture as superior and viewed social evolution as an unwavering linear trend of "progress."

The twentieth century brought new approaches to the study of human sexuality as anthropology shifted from grand evolutionary schemes with little rigor to empirically oriented studies. This transition led to a new methodology for which anthropology has gained acclaim. Bronislaw Malinowski is the acknowledged parent of this anthropological research method known as **ethnography.** Ethnography is the research method of **participant-observation** in which the anthropologist becomes entrenched in the lives of people in their research community. The ethnographic method serves as the basis for an ethnography, the detailed study of the culture of a particular group of people. Malinowski is known for his analysis of sex as part of the ethnographic context. His groundbreaking work titled *The Sexual Life of Savages in North-Western Melanesia: An Ethnographic Account of Courtship, Marriage and Family Life Among the Natives of the Trobriand Islands, British New Guinea* was first published in 1929. Although others in the 1920s wrote about the subject of indigenous peoples and their sexuality, their approaches, unlike Malinowski, were not based on firsthand research but rather on missionary and travelers' reports or short-term field projects (Weiner, 1987: xiii–xiv). Malinowski's two-year term living with the Melanesian Trobriand Islanders and his scientific and systematic methods of data collection left an important legacy for the field of anthropology and the study of human sexuality.

Malinowski was interested in the relationship of institutions such as **kinship** to cultural customs including sexual behaviors. His perspective stressed the importance of the cultural context and emphasized how social rules ordered sexuality among the Trobriand Islanders. What appeared to Europeans as unrestrained sexuality were in fact highly structured premarital sex rules and taboos based on kinship classification (Weiner, 1987: xvii). Malinowski seriously challenged the dominant nineteenth-century cultural evolutionism of McLennan, Lubbock, and Morgan. He rejected the notion that early human life was represented by sexual promiscuity. The Trobriand Islanders illustrated that even the most non-technologically complex peoples regulated their desires through systems of kinship. Rather than promiscuity as a prior condition, Malinowski focused on the patterning of sexual relations in creating the family (Weiner, 1987: xxv–xxvi).

Malinowski was also influenced by another trend impacting anthropology: that of **psychoanalysis.** He was impressed with the psychoanalytic openness to the study of sex, but was critical of Sigmund Freud's theory of the **incest taboo** and the **Oedipus complex.** In a nutshell, Freud's argument is that little boys unconsciously experience a desire to marry/have sex with their mothers and want to murder their fathers whom they regard as rivals. In *Sex and Repression in Savage Society* (1927), Malinowski "argued that Freud's theory of the universality of the Oedipus complex needed revision because it was culturally biased. Freud based his theory on the emotional dynamics within the patriarchal western family" (Weiner, 1987: xxi). This resulted in a heated debate with psychoanalyst Ernest Jones. Malinowski again argued that the Oedipus complex was a result of the European patriarchal family complex. The Trobrianders presented quite a different picture from the European **nuclear family**; the Trobriand culture is a matrilineal one—that is, people traced their ancestral descent through their mother's family. This produced different family dynamics leading Malinowski to conclude that the Trobrianders were free of the Oedipus complex. Unfortunately, his work did not influence the psychoanalytic position to any great degree. For a more detailed discussion see Chapter 9.

Ruth Benedict and Margaret Mead loom large in the history of anthropology and in their respective contributions to the study of sex. Both were students of Franz Boas, the parent of U.S. anthropology. Benedict's contribution continues to be felt today. Her perspective, in revised form, is embedded in contemporary anthropology in the concepts of **ethos** (the "approved style of life") and worldview (the "assumed structure of reality") (Geertz, 1973: 126–141). Benedict's *Patterns of Culture*, published in 1934, offered an approach in which cultures were regarded as analogous to personalities. She stressed how each culture produced a unique and integrated configuration. This was known as the configurational approach and was popular in the school of thought known as culture and personality (Benedict, 1959: 42–45).

Benedict was deeply committed to diversity and to those relegated to the margins of society. This was demonstrated in her concluding chapter where she reiterated points from her paper, "Anthropology and the Abnormal" (1934). She was concerned with individuals whose temperaments did not match their cultural configuration and the psychic costs to those such as homosexually oriented people who were "not supported by the institutions of their civilization" (in Bock, 1988: 52). She proposed that "abnormality" was not constant but rather is culturally constituted. She suggested what, at that time, was a radical view: tolerance for non-normative sexual practices such as homosexuality. Implicit in her view is that sexuality is no different than any other social behavior; it is culturally patterned. Benedict argued that "in a society that values trance, as in India, they will have supernormal experience. In a society that institutionalizes homosexuality, they will be homosexual" (in Singer, 1961: 25). Benedict challenged prevailing notions of homosexuality as pathology. In 1939, she concluded in *Sex in Primitive Society*, "that homosexuality was primarily social in nature, shaped by the meanings of gender and sex roles" (Dickermann, 1990: 7).

For the study of human sexuality, Benedict's major contribution was that sex—which is a part of culture—is patterned, fitting into the larger society, the cultural whole, or the **gestalt**. The configurational approach was certainly not without flaws and anthropology has moved beyond regarding cultures as personalities. However, Benedict has left an important legacy for anthropology in her emphasis on patterning, cultural holism, and sensitivity to difference. For the field of sexology, Benedict was bold and unafraid in her perspective on sexual variation.

Margaret Mead was also an important and powerful figure in anthropology and sexology. Before her death in 1978 she was more widely recognized for her work than any other anthropologist in the world. In numerous books and articles, Mead addressed the subject of sex and gender. Although her contributions are many, we shall focus on her first book, *Coming of Age in Samoa* (1961 [1928]), investigated when she was not yet 24 years old.

Mead was a proponent of **cultural constructionist** explanations for understanding human behavior. She explained this approach by saying:

It was simple—a very simple point—to which our materials were organized in the 1920's, merely the documentation over and over of the fact that human nature is not rigid and unyielding, not an unadaptable plant which insists on flowering or becoming stunted after its own fashion, responding only quantitatively to the social environment, but that it is extraordinarily adaptable, that cultural rhythms are strong and more compelling than the physiological rhythms which, they overlay and distort. . . . We had to present evidence that human character is built upon a biological base which is capable of enormous diversification in terms of social standards. (in Singer, 1961: 16)

In *Coming of Age in Samoa,* her commentary addressed female adolescence in Samoa as well as in the United States. She proposed that the turbulence of U.S. girls' adolescence was not typical of adolescence throughout the world. Mead was responding to a popular biological theory of adolescent "stress and storm" believed to be caused by the changes in hormones during puberty (not unlike the "raging hormones" view of adolescence and of PMS popular in today's media). Her study of Samoan adolescence provided a very different picture. Unlike U.S. adolescence, the Samoan youth did not experience a period of turbulence and high emotion. Based on evidence of a carefree Samoan adolescence, Mead reasoned that the conflict experienced by the U.S. teenagers was due to cultural influences rather than hormones. The latter part of *Coming of Age in Samoa* explained the strife of U.S. adolescence as a cultural phenomenon. Mead offered explanations that emphasized the importance of culture in shaping behavior. For example, she identified the importance of rapid culture change in U.S. society as contributing to the turmoil so typical of adolescence.

In contrast, Mead argued, the Samoan girls' adolescence was conflict free. This was due to Samoan culture which was relatively homogeneous and casual. So casual that according to Mead the young woman:

> defers marriage through as many years of casual love-making as possible... The adolescent girl's total interest is expended on clandestine sex adventures... to live with as many lovers as possible and then to marry into one's village... (Mead, 1961 [1928]: 157)

Samoan society was one in which extremes in emotion were culturally discouraged. It was characterized by casualness in a number of spheres including sexuality, parenting, and responsibility. In contrast to industrialized culture, a young Samoan woman's sexuality was experienced without guilt. She concluded that the foundation of this nonchalant approach to sex and conflict-free adolescence could be explained by the following:

- a dearth of deep feeling between relatives and peers,
- a liberal attitude toward sex and education for life,
- an absence of conflicting alternatives, and
- a lack of emphasis on individuality.

In this work, she established the importance of the study of women when little information was available (Howard, 1993: 69). She also challenged notions of **biological reductionism** that even today are still too often used to support status quo politics.

Despite the magnitude of Margaret Mead's contribution to anthropology, and her recognition as a public figure who brought anthropology out of the halls of academia into mainstream U.S.A, she was not without her detractors. Since her death in 1978, *Coming of Age in Samoa* has been at the center of a heated debate in anthropology launched by Australian anthropologist Derek Freeman in his book *Margaret Mead and Samoa: The Making and Unmaking of an Anthropological Myth* in 1983 and his subsequent 1999 book *The Fateful Hoaxing of Margaret Mead: A Historical Analysis of Her Samoan Research*. Derek Freeman argued strongly for a very different Samoa from the one studied by Mead. Based on his own research in Samoa from 1940–1943 and extensive subsequent research in the 1960s, Freeman took issue with the picture of the easygoing family life, low affect, and positively sanctioned **premarital sex**, citing punitive family relationships, competition and aggression, sexual jealousy, and a stormy puberty. His explanations are in direct opposition to those of Mead; he weighed in on the "biology is destiny" spectrum arguing for instinctive and innate interpretations of his findings. Freeman, however, did not disagree with Mead's depiction of adolescent casual attitudes toward adolescent sex (in Barnouw, 1985: 98–99). In his second attack, he argued that Mead's two key informants deliberately lied to her. Just as Freeman has critiqued

Mead, other anthropologists have found much lacking in Freeman's evidence (Cote, 2000; Ember, 1985; Holmes, 1987), yet others have argued that they were both partially correct (Abramson, 1987; Shankman, 1996; Ember and Ember, 1994).

The different conclusions can be attributed to several factors, including the gender of the fieldworker, which can have a decided effect on developing rapport and on the kind of data collected (Holmes, 1987). There was also a fourteen-year gap in time between when Mead finished her research in 1926 and Freeman started his in 1940. Samoan culture had changed a great deal since the 1920s with the impact of missionization, colonialism, increasing Euro-American contact, globalization, and the expansion of capitalism, which undoubtedly affected Freeman's interpretation of Samoan adolescent behavior (Ember, 1985: 88; Shankman, 1996; Ember and Ember, 1994). Mead worked primarily with adolescent girls while Freeman's main sources were senior men whose knowledge of what teenage girls were experiencing was undoubtedly limited. Abramson's research supports the view that adults opposed premarital sex, but in spite of this, Samoan adolescents had frequent premarital sex (in Bates and Fratkin, 2003: 65–66). Not only did Mead and Freeman rely on different populations for research, but they also studied on different islands whose history of colonization varied as well. Mead studied in American Samoa while Freeman worked mostly in the Independent State of Samoa (Ember, 1985: 87). Shankman has argued that the disagreement may lie in the vantage point of comparison. Thus, compared with the United States at the time, Samoan premarital sexuality may have indeed been more common and open (Ember and Ember, 1994). In addition, Freeman has criticized Mead for too heavy a reliance on her two key informants and not collecting enough divergent views. However, Cote (2000) and Shankman (1996: 564) have critiqued Freeman's research on the same grounds; that he has selectively used information that supports his stance, while ignoring evidence which substantiated Mead's claims.

The general consensus by anthropologists is that Mead may have overstressed the homogeneity of Samoan culture and adolescent experiences, but her general stance, that culture is a *tour de force* in shaping the expression of gender and influencing biological differences in the sexes to a very strong degree, is supported by the huge range of variation in the expression of gender found cross-culturally. Finally, Freeman claims to "Unmake... an Anthropological Myth" by focusing his critique on one of her earliest works undertaken when she was just 24 years old and by ignoring an entire lifetime of research publications. As such, this is a rather extreme claim. Indeed, this ongoing debate confirms one of our favorite quotes by Margaret Mead: "Sooner or later I am going to die, but I'm not going to retire" (Brainy Quotes).

[Margaret Mead and Ruth Benedict's] view of culture as a pattern or configuration of homogenous and integrated elements, often linked with a unified theme, lacks the dimensions of contemporary theories. Now Anthropologists think that culture is never simple, uniform or well integrated. It is a messy, complicated, and often contradictory set of differences or oppositions that may exist side by side within the same group claiming the same territory, history, or worldview. This is why, today, we can talk of a female culture and a male culture with complex and contradictory ethnic, national and world cultures. (Ward and Edelstein, 2006: 62)

Although the approaches of Malinowski, Benedict, and Mead contributed to the creation of the ethnographic study of sexuality with an emphasis on the cultural, Clellan S. Ford and Frank A. Beach's *Patterns of Sexual Behavior* deserves credit in 1951 for offering the first synthetic study that incorporated biological, cross-cultural, and evolutionary considerations. Their work is distinctive for its inclusion of homosexual and **lesbian** data; a trend continued in Gregerson's 1994 *The World of Human Sexuality: Behaviors, Customs and Beliefs*. According to Miracle and Suggs (1993: 3), Ford and Beach's book is "[t]he single most important and provocative work on sexuality to date...It also provided the intellectual—if not the methodological—foundation for the subsequent work of Masters and Johnson." (See Chapter 11 for a discussion of Masters and Johnson.) *Patterns of Sexual Behavior* integrated information from 190 different cultures as well as provided comparative data on different **species** with an emphasis on the **primates** (humans, apes, and monkeys). Their work includes an encyclopedic collection of sexual behavior cross-culturally. For example, Ford and Beach offer discussion and information on sexual positions, length (time) of intercourse, locations for intercourse, orgasm experiences, types of foreplay, courting behaviors, frequencies of intercourse, methods of attracting a partner, among numerous other topics.

Ford and Beach's study of human sexuality employed the cross-cultural correlational method. This is a statistical method for comparing attributes (variables) in large samples of diverse cultures (Cohen and Eames, 1982: 419). This approach is valuable for testing hypotheses about human sexuality, establishing patterns and trends, and formulating generalizations. Their study relied on ethnographic data that is collected and coded in the **Human Relations Area Files (HRAF Files)**. HRAF is a rigorous classification scheme for information on the world's societies containing descriptive ethnographic data. Categories of information for 350 societies, based on a 900,000-page database of more than 7,000 books and articles are coded and available to researchers. These data are in the process of being digitized (Bernard, 1994: 343). A caveat for the student researcher is that the HRAF data for a particular society may not take into account historical context and culture change, particularly the more recent impact of globalization (Scupin and DeCorse, 1998: 307).

The cross-cultural correlational statistical method was subsequently used by Martin and Voorhies in *Female of the Species* (1975). Like Ford and Beach, Martin and Voorhies included evolutionary and biological issues. Their focus was broader in that they were interested in the relationship of human sexuality to gender status/roles, social organization, and type of subsistence (how people make a living). Martin and Voorhies tested hypotheses to arrive at generalizations about the relationships of these factors. In a sample of fifty-one foraging societies, Martin and Voorhies found that 30 percent of them allowed premarital sexual experimentation (1975: 188–189). This pattern was related to matrilineality (where descent is traced through the mother's side of the family) and **matrilocality** (where the couple resides in the community of the wife's mother). Their studies of horticultural groups also revealed a statistical correlation between matrilineal societies and sexual permissiveness toward premarital sex, while patrilineal (tracing descent through the father's side) societies tended to control female premarital sexual behavior (1975: 246–247).

There are many research applications for this methodological approach to sexological research. For example, Schlegel and Barry in *Adolescence: An Anthropological Inquiry* (1991) report that premarital restrictiveness occurs in societies in which a dowry is given (wealth from the bride's family is included in the marriage transaction). They conclude that "[f]amilies guard their daughters' chastity in dowry-giving societies in order to protect their property (dowry) against would-be social climbers and to ensure that they can use their daughters' dowries to attract the most desirable sons-in-law" (Schlegel and Barry, 1991: 116). Chastity rules guard against a lower-status man impregnating a higher-status woman and thereby making claim on her dowry and inheritance by trapping her into marriage. In this way, property exchange and status considerations are factors in restricting premarital sexuality (Schlegel and Barry, 1991: 117–118). Davis and Whitten report that the general pattern found in HRAF studies such as these is that sexual restrictions tend to be associated with complex societies (1987: 74).

Frayser's *Varieties of Sexual Experience* (1985) continues the tradition spawned by Ford and Beach, incorporating the cross-cultural correlational approach with biological and evolutionary concerns. Frayser presents an integrated model in which human sexuality is regarded as "a system in its own right, related to but not subsumed by social, cultural, psychological, and biological factors" (Frayser and Whitby, 1987: 351). For Frayser, although the cross-cultural record reveals an almost infinite variety in sexual expression, there is continuity with our evolutionary past. In regard to evolution, Frayser examines cross-species sexuality, particularly that of our close relatives, the nonhuman primates. For example, she points out that human sexuality is distinguished by unique sexual and reproductive attributes, including the potential for sexual arousal that is not limited to estrus ("heat") and the evolution of the female orgasm. These capabilities are present in our relatives to a limited extent, but emerge full blown in humans and are linked to extraordinary amounts of nonreproductive sexual behavior among humans in comparison with other animals.

Frayser has distinguished the social and cultural aspects of human sexuality in terms of the social system defined as "patterned interactions." The **social system** is contrasted to the **cultural system** which Frayser defined as the "patterned beliefs and meanings" that influence sexual expression (Frayser, 1985: 7). This model is one in which the biological, the social, and the cultural system converge to influence the sexual system. It is a valuable approach for understanding sexual patterning and for recording the continuities and heterogeneity within and between cultures. However, it should be noted that anthropologists' definitions for the social and cultural system are often quite divergent. For example, many anthropologists do not limit their definition of the cultural system to the ideological realm, but include behaviors as well. Others define the social system functionally as "institutions," recurrent patterns that fulfill human needs such as the family and religion (Bates and Fratkin, 2003: 45). See the last section of this chapter, "The Patterning of Human Sexuality," for a more detailed discussion of the culture concept.

Sex as culture

The regulation of human sexual expression as to "when, where, how, and who" may serve diverse socio-cultural goals. George Peter Murdock's pioneering study, *Social Structure* (1949), offers us a classic approach to the different ways that the regulation of sexuality contributes to the organization of cultures. In all societies, sexual access among members of a society is regulated. The most obvious example of this is the incest taboo. With an almost universal prevalence, the incest taboo prohibits sexual access between siblings and between siblings and their parents. Even in those societies that have allowed incest, regulations surround it that are integrated in the wider social organization and belief system. The exceptions include Hawaiian royalty, the ancient Egyptian pharaohs and nobility, and Inca emperors. These elites, usually brothers and sisters, were regarded as so powerful and sacred that only their very close relatives had the equivalent status to qualify as a mate and to perpetuate the lineage. Such sexual unions and marriages were not allowed, however, for the population at large (Murdock, 1949: 13).

Rules for sexual access also extend beyond the immediate **nuclear family**. **Exogamy** is a rule requiring that people marry outside their group, while **endogamy** specifies marriage within the group, but not the immediate family. These rules create **kin groups** through different kinds of restrictions on sexual access. Rules of exogamy and endogamy are defined by reference to marriage. This illustrates how sexual ideologies are integrated in the social organization of kin groups; but one should not make the error of thinking that sex and marriage are always equated. This is a mistake often found in the literature on human sexuality, but one seldom made by the people involved in extramarital affairs. "**Marriage** is a publicly recognized union between two or more people that creates economic rights and obligations within the group . . . and guarantees their offspring rights of inheritance" (Crapo, 1987: 148). It is regarded as an enduring relationship and includes sexual rights (Ember and Ember, 1988: 13). Murdock (1949: 8) offers clarification:

> Sexual unions without economic co-operation are common, and there are relationships between men and women involving a division of labor without sexual gratification, e.g., between brother and sister, master and maidservant, or employer and secretary [sic], but marriage exists only when the economic and the sexual are united in one relationship, and this combination occurs only in marriage.

Ford and Beach's pioneering *Patterns of Sexual Behavior* (1951) proposed that sexual partnerships consist of two types: **mateships** defined in the same way as marriages; and **liaisons**, "less stable partnerships in which the relationship is more exclusively sexual" (1951: 106). Sexologists and anthropologists generally subdivide human liaisons on the basis of their premarital or extramarital character (Ford and Beach, 1951: 106).

The regulation of **sexual partnerships** makes it possible to define groups of people by relationships based on offspring and kinship. These kin relationships are formalized through marriage systems. **Sexual prohibitions** function to "minimize competition among relations and to increase the bonds of cooperation and friendship between neighboring groups" (Crapo, 1987: 61). Because descent is important for a number of reasons such as inheritance, obligations, and affiliations, we can regard sexual unions as having the potential to shape kin group formation; sexual access therefore defines kin groups. The importance of sexuality is socially recognized through marriage as an institution with sexual rights and obligations. But it should be kept in mind that there is a great deal of sexual activity that occurs prior to and outside marriage, including sexual activities between people of the same sex, ritual and ceremonial sex, as well as a host of other encounters including affairs, "one-night stands," and "hooking up."

Societies differ as to their tolerance of premarital and extramarital activities and the conditions under which they are acceptable and/or prohibited. According to Broude and Greene's (1976) survey of the cross-cultural record, in 69 percent of the societies studied, men **commonly participated** in extramarital sex, and in 57 percent of the societies women did so as well. This leads us to another thorny issue for sex researchers, the contrast between **ideal** and **real** culture. The ideal culture or normative expectation is that 54 percent of the societies surveyed **allow** only men to have extramarital sex, while 11 percent allow it for women. But the data suggest that many more people worldwide actually violate this ideal, particularly in the case of women.

In summary, human sexuality is a central force in the origin of kin groups. In Murdock's words: "All societies have faced the problem of reconciling the need of controlling sex with that of giving it adequate expression" (1949: 261). The regulation of sexual relations is the basis for descent and inheritance, critical factors for human societies in the maintenance of social groups. Yet sex and marriage do not necessarily "go together" like a horse and carriage. Sex is not the central factor in the bonding of two individuals through marriage. To think so is to engage in a bias shaped by recent modern U.S. views of marriage. Sex is indeed critical for kin groups and their perpetuation; although sex is a right and an obligation in marriage, it is not necessarily the basis upon which marriages are made. Economic cooperation emerges as an important factor in marriage both in evolutionary terms and in the cross-cultural record. This will become more evident in our discussion of "The patterning of human sexuality."

The patterning of human sexuality: the biological, psychological, and cultural perspective

This section emphasizes the relationship between biology, psychology, and culture. These three dimensions necessarily have a psychological component as well. As stated earlier, the psychological theme emphasizes the importance of individuals' relationship to their cultural context. And from a biological perspective each person has a unique genetic heritage (with the exception of identical twins). This aspect is elaborated upon more in Chapter 2. Human sexuality has a foundation in human biology which provides us with certain inherited potentialities. "The inherited aspects of sex seem to be nearly formless." It is only through culture that sex assumes form and meaning (Davenport, 1977: 161). (See Figure 1.1.)

Our human biological wiring is very different from what we think of as animal instinct. For example, the drive for food that allows us to survive is fulfilled through learning how to get food; in some cultures people collect food, some fish and yet others go to the grocery store. The desire for sex is also shaped by culture and is very unlike a mating instinct. When a female animal comes into heat, she naturally and necessarily (through hormonal mechanisms) becomes sexually responsive and follows her mating instinct. Humans, however, may ignore their drives and or desires. For example, Buddhist monks traditionally deny their sexuality in order to live in celibacy as required by their religion (Ruan and Lau, 2004: 187). Others delay sexuality until marriage which may not occur until their twenties or later. For example, in the Irish community of Inis Beag, Messenger, whose research spanned 1958–1966, found that the average age of marriage for men was thirty-six and for women twenty-five (Messenger, 1971).

Human biological predispositions are not "rigidly determined... They may orient us in particular directions in pursuing certain goals, but they do not determine our behavior in a mechanical fashion without learned experiences" (Scupin and DeCorse, 1992: 164). This biological underpinning to our sexuality and other behaviors is part of what is called an **open biogram**, "an extremely flexible genetic program that is shaped by learning experiences" (Scupin and DeCorse, 1992: 164). Humans acquire their culture through the process of socialization. This capacity to learn and to adapt to one's environs is a part of our unique bio-cultural and psychological evolution as humans. We can say that our biology sustains us as cultural beings by providing us with an unusual aptitude for learning.

Sexual behavior is culturally patterned; it is not accidental or random but is interconnected and/or integrated to varying degrees (this itself is of interest to anthropologists) within the broader context of culture and is intermeshed in a web of other cultural features as we have seen in our discussion of sex, marriage, and kinship. A number of cultural characteristics are associated with patterns of human sexuality. These may include: the level of technology, population size, religion, economics, political organization, medical practices, kinship structure, degree of acculturation and culture change, gender roles, power and privilege (stratification). Consequently, larger cultural patterns are important in shaping reproductive and nonreproductive sexual behaviors and values in a society. Sexuality is patterned across cultures in relation to these variables as well as within a culture. Davenport suggests that sex is molded by the "internal logic and consistency of the total culture. As one sector of culture changes, all other sectors that articulate must undergo adjustments (1975: 162). However, as we noted, cultural systems are never simple and the interconnections between the elements of culture are often intertwined with oppositions and contradictions.

Cultures are systems that exist within particular environmental and historical contexts. We have discussed the biological basis of human sexuality; we offer now an overview of the cultural basis of human sexuality. To comprehend how sexuality is embedded in culture necessitates an understanding of the culture concept. We can think of culture in terms of architecture[1] (see Figure 1.2).

In Figure 1.2 the basement represents our biology as humans, including our evolution and physiology. The floor in Figure 1.2 is the foundation for understanding that cultural variation rests in how humans have adapted to their environments. This includes how people make a living, their technologies, and economics. There are a number of ways people have found to survive in the world. Anthropologists have classified societies in terms of foraging, horticulture, agriculture, pastoral (herding), industrial, and postindustrial adaptations.

Adaptation to the environment impacts the social system including **social organization** and **social structures**, which may be likened to the frame of a house. The social system is the means that people adapt to one another.

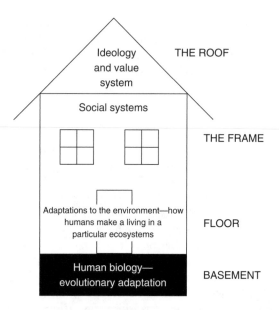

Figure 1.2 Culture as architecture. (*Source:* Anne Bolin with Elon University Department of Instructional and Campus Technologies, 2006.)

It includes social organization and its elements including kinship and marriage, and various institutions and structures such as religion and political organization. The social system is influenced by how people make a living through demographics, the relations of work such as age, gender, and kinship; who controls the means of production, and the power relations of society. Societies have been classified in terms of their social systems as bands, tribes, chiefdoms, preindustrial states, and nation states.

The roof of our building may be conceptualized as the ideological **value system**. This is the system of meanings and beliefs in a culture. It includes expressive elements of culture like art, music, rituals, myths, folklore, and cosmology. It is the meanings and beliefs behind and sustaining the patterning of cultures such as marriage norms, gender roles, courtship, etc. The foundation, the frame, and the roof are all interrelated parts of the cultural whole.

Human sexuality is part of that cultural whole. We may first encounter it in the basement in terms of our evolution and our unique human physiology. To grasp human sexuality as part of a cultural matrix we may locate it in any of our architectural levels. For example, in investigating beliefs about human sexuality, we might begin with our roof (ideology and the value system). We may observe that a particular culture has very few restrictions on premarital sex. In this culture, premarital sex among adolescents may be regarded as an amusement (Schlegel and Barry, 1991: 21), as part of an experiential kind of sex education, or perhaps as a way to find a marriage partner. In short, there are numerous meanings and beliefs around premarital permissiveness among cultures which allow and encourage its practice.

In order to see how the meanings behind premarital sex are part of the interconnections within a cultural system, we will want to investigate how premarital sex relates to the broader social system. As we saw earlier, Martin and Voorhies (1975) found a correlation between matrilineal social organization and premarital permissiveness, while patrilineal social organization was correlated with restrictions on female premarital sexuality. From this correlation, explanations may be proposed. After reading about the relationship between premarital sexuality and matrilineality/patrilineality, what explanation can you think of to account for this difference?

To be even more rigorous in our investigation of premarital sexual permissiveness requires an analysis of the foundation of culture: adaptation to the environment or how people make a living and survive in a particular locale. For example, agricultural systems are associated with higher populations, stratification, and greater social complexity. Earlier we noted in the work of Davis and Whitten (1987: 74) that the greater the sociocultural complexity, the more likely there are to be premarital restrictions on sexuality. Since subsistence type is associated with complexity, it has been argued that foragers and matrilineal horticulturalists are more likely to be sexually permissive than agriculturalists (Martin and Voorhies, 1975). This approach allows us to see the connections between sexual practices, kinship, social organization, and how people make a living. To understand how permissiveness or restrictions influence individuals and their sexuality, the psychological dimension may be brought in. Ethnographic studies often provide insights into how the cultural system influences individuals in terms of motives, emotions, and feelings. For example, the Mead (1961 [1928]) and Freeman (1983, 1999) debate includes this psychological dimension. Individual expressions of jealousy and casual affect (feelings) toward sexual encounters were emphasized by Mead and contested by Freeman.

Our analysis could go even further and include the biological. For example, research into premarital permissiveness among foragers will reveal that **adolescent sterility** may be a variable to be considered (see Chapter 10). Adolescent sterility is a period of infertility among young females after the onset of menarche. They are not fertile until their late teens or early twenties. If premarital sex is allowed in societies in which this occurs, young people may explore their sexuality without the consequences of pregnancy and responsibilities of parenthood.

We offer this architectural approach to culture and sex to illustrate that culture is a complex whole in which the parts are interrelated. One can begin anywhere in our biological, psychological, and cultural architecture and explore human sexuality. Some researchers prefer limiting their research to one area; for example, Masters and Johnson's investigations of human sexual response have focused on the biological. Others, such as the anthropologists cited, may be more interested in the relationship between beliefs and premarital sex practices and how these are related to social organization. Yet others may want a bigger picture and explore how premarital sex norms are related to the types of subsistence adaptation.

In offering this overview of culture, it should be remembered that what the ethnographic study reveals represents a particular point in time. Cultures are not static entities, and change is ongoing. Immigration has been going on for two million years ever since *homo erectus* (one of our hominid ancestors) left Africa and went as far as China carrying with her/him tool traditions and cultural practices. Anthropologists no longer assume that tribal peoples lived unchanging isolated lives for thousands of years.

The indigenous Australian people of Arnhem Land had a long history of contact with Macassan (Indonesians from Sulawesi) mariners. The Arnhem Land aboriginal people learned to make sea-going dugouts from the Macassans who came to fish for trepang (sea slugs). In exchange for their help collecting the trepang, they were given cloth, iron, glass, and pottery. This exchange occurred for hundreds of years, beginning around 1720 (some suggest possibly three hundred years earlier) and continually occurred until 1906 when government regulations ended it. This cultural encounter left a cultural legacy in terms of art, oral history, development of a trading language, and the exchange of genes. Some went willingly with the Macassans, while others, such as Yolgnu women, were abducted, and others were forcibly traded (Nannup, n.d.; Singh, et al., 2001: 69; Wikipedia).

Thus, cultures are dynamic and even the most traditional culture does not remain static. This is due to a number of factors. Because individuals are not all the same, they actively negotiate their culture through lived experiences and consequently change occurs. In addition, as humans modify their environments, their populations may grow, and the demand for technologies to solve new problems caused by the changing circumstances occurs. Human groups have never lived in isolation, and contact with other peoples leads to culture change as well. Culture is a dynamic and ever-changing process. However, a strong argument can be made that the rate of change has been dramatically increased as a result of colonialism, and more recently globalization with the expansion of capitalism worldwide. Indigenous and tribal peoples have been particularly impacted by globalization. In terms of human sexuality, culture change, colonialism and globalization have huge implications for issues in sexuality, particularly as these are related to women. In the barred text, Yolgnu women were abducted and traded (this is referred to as **trafficking**). For further discussion of the globalization of sex and trafficking see Chapter 16.

These are the kinds of opportunities for understanding human sexuality offered by a biological, psychological, and cultural perspective. We hope this approach will allow students and other readers a greater awareness of themselves as sexual beings, a greater understanding of themselves as cultural creatures, and an appreciation of our evolutionary past and biological heritage.

SUMMARY

1 Human sexuality is a biological, psychological, and cultural experience and phenomenon.

2 Human sexuality is a means used by human groups to achieve sociocultural goals such as the creation of kin groups.

3 A variety of anthropological perspectives and their proponents were introduced including: Malinowski, Benedict, Mead, Ford and Beach, Martin and Voorhies, and Frayser.

4 We concluded that human sexuality has several components, one in human biology which provides us with certain potentials and limitations, and the other in culture, wherein our sexuality is learned and integrated in the broader cultural context.

5 Emphasis was placed on the importance of the individual in society through her/his relationship to the cultural context including motives, personality, attitudes, values, perceptions, and emotions. It is because of these individual differences that cultures are so dynamic and ever-changing.

6 We discussed the value of a biological, psychological, and cultural perspective for understanding human sexuality.

7 We offered discussion of the culture concept, including discussion of the dynamic elements of culture and introduced the importance of culture change for understanding human sexuality.

Thought-provoking questions

1 After reading this chapter, reflect on how your views about human sexuality have been affirmed, challenged, or expanded.

2 What did you learn about human sexuality in this chapter that was unexpected?

3 What makes anthropological perspectives on human sexuality unique?

4 What are some of the ways in which human sexuality is shaped by culture? Can you think of any sexual or related behavior that is completely natural? Would you regard breastfeeding as completely natural without any cultural influences?

SUGGESTED RESOURCES

Books

Holmes, Lowell Don. 1987. *The Quest for the Real Samoa: The Mead/Freeman Controversy and Beyond.* South Hadley: Bergin and Garvey.

LaFont, Suzanne, (ed.). 2003. *Constructing Sexualities: Readings in Sexuality, Gender and Culture.* Upper Saddle River: Prentice Hall.

Web sites

American Anthropological Association (http://www.aaanet.org)
International Academy of Sex Research (http://www.iasr.org/)
National Sexuality Resource Center (http://www.nsrc.sfsu.edu)
Public Anthropology (http://www.publicanthropology.org/index.htm)
Society for the Scientific Study of Sexuality (http://www.sexscience.org)

2 Biological, psychological, and cultural approaches

Georgina Hammock, PhD

CHAPTER OVERVIEW

1   Compares and contrasts psychological, sociological, and biological perspectives of human sexuality.
2   Presents anthropological concepts, terms, and definitions. Specific examples from the fields of physical anthropology and cultural anthropology that are relevant to our understanding of sexology are offered.
3   Provides a definition of and discusses the scope of human sexuality.
4   Offers the importance of a relativistic perspective of human sexual expression.

Human behavior is an incredibly complicated phenomenon. Indeed, it is arguably one of the most complicated topics that science has tried to understand and explain. Many factors and variables influence human behavior and identifying all of the various sources of influence is quite difficult. Therefore, it is not surprising that different disciplines are devoted to the study of human behavior. Human sexual behavior is no different. In Chapter 1, various perspectives were discussed that shape the study of human sexual behavior. These perspectives cross several different disciplines including the biological, psychosocial, behavioral, clinical, and sociological, with an emphasis on anthropological factors in the explanation of sexual behavior. All of these perspectives are important to developing a thorough understanding of the various forces and factors that influence sexual behavior and the many different viewpoints that must be considered.

In this chapter we present an in-depth discussion of the anthropological perspective. Further, anthropology is contrasted with the disciplines of biology, sociology, and psychology in order to highlight its unique contribution to the study of human sexuality. In addition, key **sexological** terms and definitions are presented.

ANTHROPOLOGICAL PERSPECTIVES IN CONTRAST

Because of its interdisciplinary nature, the anthropological perspective incorporates psychological, sociological, and biological views into a holistic approach. **Holism** is defined as an all-embracing outlook that "refers to the study of the whole of the human condition; past, present, and future; biology, society, language and culture" (Kottak, 2002: 4). Because of its interdisciplinary nature, the anthropological approach incorporates psychological, sociological, and biological views but is not limited to any one viewpoint. It is precisely because of anthropology's interdisciplinary nature and its **holistic approach** with its interest in spanning great periods of time and vast distances, that it includes, but varies from the strictly biological, sociological, and psychological approaches to human sexuality. These latter approaches tend to emphasize contemporary twenty-first-century (Euro-United States) sexuality and to focus on only one dimension (i.e., the biological, sociological, or psychological). For anthropology, our scope is all of humankind. We study and compare a wide range of peoples and societies from the ancient to the contemporary whose technologies vary from simple to complex, along multiple dimensions including the biological, psychological, and the sociocultural.

Biological

The biological perspective focuses on the physiological basis of sexual behavior. Biological perspectives on human sexuality stress what are referred to as **essentialist** views of human sexuality. Essentialist views look at instinct as an "essential" attribute of sexuality and regard reproduction as the core of that instinct. Katchadourian and Lunde (1975: 2–3) have challenged this perspective of human sexuality and counter that:

> The incentive is in the act itself, rather than in its possible consequences [reproduction]. Sexual behavior in this sense arises from a psychological "drive," associated with sensory pleasure, and its reproductive consequences are a by-product (though a vital one)...[O]ur sexual behavior involves certain physical "givens," including sex organs, hormones, intricate networks of nerves, and brain centers.

To reduce human sexuality to an instinct to reproduce ignores the importance of other variables such as symbolic, cognitive, and affective factors in motivating sexual behaviors. In addition, such a perspective ignores the role of the group and shared cultural meanings in the survival of the species.

The biological view is, however, important for our understanding of human sexuality. As females and males, the physiology of our sex (and this is far more complex and continuous than might be expected) serves as the basis for our discussion of the endocrinology and anatomy of sex in Chapters 4, 5, and 6, *but even these biological features must be placed in a cultural context.* For example, we might ask if the sexual cycle of people in the United States, which is believed to peak in males around eighteen or nineteen years of age and in females between the ages thirty-five and forty, is not shaped by cultural factors. Evidence suggests that this is the case (see Hyde, 1982: 342, 353). The perspective of anthropology is one that regards biology and culture as tandem developments in human history. Anthropology emphasizes the importance of cultural systems and learning as central features in human evolution.

Sociological

The sociological tradition in sexual science is characterized by research that focuses on contemporary sexuality in Europe and the United States and/or usually emphasizes industrialized nations. It looks at the importance of "social learning, social rules and role playing" in the expression of human sexuality (Musaph, 1978: 84) and stresses patterns of social interaction. The survey method remains the most popular sociological research technique used for collecting sexological data (Katchadourian, 1985: 11). Sociological research has provided a valuable contribution to sexology through its attention to the intersection of class, status group, and the sexual experience. This approach is evident in such classic works as Komarovsky's *Blue Collar Marriage* (1962) and Rubin's *Worlds of Pain* (1976).

Anthropology and sociology are very compatible perspectives. There are, in fact, a number of anthropologists whose sexological interests are primarily in studying U.S. culture. The anthropologist, in contrast to the sociologist, is trained to maintain a comparative and bio-cultural view with reference to the cross-cultural record regardless of the research topic; whether it is studying childbirth or middle-aged women (Brown and Kerns, 1985; Jordan, 1993; Trevathan, 1987). Although the sociological perspective tends to focus on the importance of social structure and patterns of interaction, the anthropological one additionally integrates the significance of beliefs in understanding human behavior. This is essential in overcoming our own industrial society's cultural biases about sex which can creep into research. It is therefore useful in the study of sexology in the United States to sustain a broader frame of reference including structure, meaning, and cultural variation internally and cross-culturally. For the anthropologist, this may also include an evolutionary understanding as well. Generally speaking, however, anthropology and sociology are very closely related disciplines and it is often impossible to distinguish between the works of anthropologists and sociologists.

Psychological

Psychology addresses sexuality from the perspective of the individual and the individual's environment. In general, psychology's approach to sexuality focuses on the motives behind sexual behavior and factors that influence that motivation. To understand this process, psychologists study many different facets of the human experience. Indeed, there is perhaps no one psychological perspective, but several different thrusts within a general concern with cognitive, emotional, behavioral, and some physiological components of human sexuality.

On the theoretical level, psychologists have approached human sexuality from many different angles. Some rather infamous theories within psychology have focused on the critical role of sexuality in the development of personality. Freud's rather complex theory proposes that the sex instinct *(eros)* along with the death instinct *(thanatos)* were driving forces in the development of an individual's personality (Hyde, 1982: 6). Thus, Freud places biology at the root of the individual's psychosexuality. Developmental aspects of sexuality are considered part of our physiological inheritance. As individuals develop, they encounter various stages in which sexuality and conflict are characteristic and shape the personality that individuals will have as adults.

Other theories, such as social learning theory (Bandura, 1986), emphasize the role of observational learning in the acquisition of behavior. From this perspective, other people serve as models (e.g., a parent, friend, or a person in the media) that help us to learn what behaviors are acceptable and unacceptable in our society. When we see these models rewarded for their behaviors, we are more likely to behave like the model and when we see the models punished for their behavior, we are less likely to behave like the model. For example, social learning has a powerful role in shaping our gender roles. In U.S. culture, females and males learn to present themselves in specific ways to be accepted and valued. These lessons are learned from many different sources from an early age onward. These models include parents, teachers, the media, and peers. Even Halloween costumes serve to reinforce these roles. Boys are traditionally dressed in action-oriented outfits that emphasize violence and death. Girls, on the other hand, are dressed as brides and princesses and when they are presented as villains, they are eroticized—even at the ages of six and seven (Nelson, 2000).

In addition to theories important to human sexual behavior, psychology researchers are also interested in the impact of individuals and their environments on other aspects of sexual functioning. For example, research on the male sex hormone testosterone is an interesting case. Research in this area has found that numerous situational factors are related to changes in the levels of testosterone in males. Males who have lost a competition, whether physical or mental, (Mazur, Booth, and Dabbs, 1992), whose sports' teams have lost (Fielden, Lutter, and Dabbs as cited in

Mazur and Booth, 1998) and who have been degraded in the context of a military officer training program (Thompson, Dabbs and Frady, 1990) show decreases in their testosterone levels. These relationships suggest a reciprocal relationship between societal or cultural events and biological responses and highlight the importance of socio-cultural variables to physiological functions.

Developmental psychologists are interested in the relationship of aging and human sexuality. The number of processes involved in the development of an individual's sexuality across childhood, adolescence, early and late adulthood is quite large. For example, researchers have studied the influence of parents and peers on adolescents' sexual activity. Others have looked at the effectiveness of school sex education courses on the initiation of sexual activity and the use of safer sex behaviors. Still others investigate the motivation behind sexual infidelity.

Social and personality psychologists are interested in the significance of variables associated with the person (e.g., religious attitudes, self-esteem, mood, love for one's partner) and the environment (e.g., the media, perceived friends' behavior, attractiveness of the partner) in understanding sexual motivation and behavior. One major area of study for these psychologists is intimate relationships. For example, research on the initiation of relationships shows that some of the most important variables in attraction are physical attractiveness, similarity, and physical proximity. Other research focuses on the dynamics of relationships and factors that influence whether individuals will stay or leave a relationship. Another area of relationship research deals with the darker side of relationships—violence and jealousy. Finally, other researchers in this area study the impact of erotica and pornography on perceptions of partners and violence against women.

Another area of psychology deals with the study and treatment of sexual dysfunction and "pathologies." Research in this area is devoted to uncovering the various explanations for sexual difficulties and finding effective means of treating those difficulties. The goal of these treatments is to help those with difficulties to function more effectively. For those whose behavior is considered undesirable or unwanted or detrimental to society, such as rapists and pedophiles, the goal is to shape the behavior so that it no longer harms other members of society.

As you can see, the scope of psychological studies covers extensive areas, including sexual motivation, familial and peer influence, self-esteem issues, and a number of other subject areas as far ranging as gender identity and gender differences in sexual response. Although the topics may vary, the approach is usually focused on the psychology of the individual and his/her environment in the development of sexuality. The predominant trend in psychology is to focus on a far smaller or micro-level analysis than that undertaken by anthropologists. Though psychological anthropologists may be interested in the mental and emotional structures behind the expression of human sexuality in individuals, the cultural context remains an important feature for their analysis. Psychological anthropologists specifically, and anthropologists generally, are more likely to be interested in the impact of culture on family dynamics, childrearing practices, or in the cultural patterning of sexual dysfunction within society. For example, the psychological perspective locates dysfunction within the individual and the family milieu, in contrast to an anthropological perspective which locates its source in society. Like anthropology, psychology emphasizes the role of learning; however, unlike anthropology it does not usually consider it within a cross-cultural framework. Nor does it emphasize a culture's childrearing practices which can influence adult personality (Katchadourian, 1985: 11; Kottak, 2002: 21). A relatively recent point of connection between psychology and anthropology has been the increasing popularity of evolutionary perspectives in psychology, a major theoretical perspective often taken in anthropology. See Chapter 3 for further discussion.

Interdisciplinary approaches

Hopefully, by this point, it is clear that while each discipline views and investigates sexuality with a different focus, each contributes to a more complete understanding of the behavior. The case of studying the issues associated with sexuality and aging is illustrative of this point. A biologist might address the developmental process of aging by studying the impact of elevated or reduced levels of hormonal changes on the different sexual organs at adolescence and old age. A sociologist might look at different types of sexual behaviors that are expressed at different ages—childhood, adolescence, adulthood and late adulthood—and how these differ as a function of race and class. A psychologist might study the impact of aging on the individual's perception of their sexual attractiveness to others and an anthropologist might question the evolutionary advantage of sexuality at the various stages of the **life cycle** and how different cultures might respond to these behaviors. All of these points are important aspects of the relationship between aging and sexuality.

Not only do the different perspectives provide different pieces to the puzzle that is human behavior, they also often enjoy a certain amount of "cross-pollination." There are scientists who are trained as physical anthropologists, social psychologists, and psychological anthropologists. In other words, often scientists are interested in the crossover of information from one discipline to another. The physical anthropologist must be knowledgeable about both anatomy and anthropology, the social psychologist looks at the intersection of sociology and psychology, and the psychological anthropologist studies the influence of culture on psychological phenomena. Therefore, it is often difficult at times to determine what the perspective of the researcher might be. Imagine that you have read about research that was conducted on the occurrence of violence in dating relationships. In this study, the research looked at variables such as the impact of personality (e.g., self-esteem, neuroticism, the willingness to trust others) and the environment (e.g., your partner's level of aggression) on the use of aggression. In addition, they report on the prevalence of the behavior and how males and females differ in its use. What would the perspective of that researcher be? What if you also find out that his/her colleagues have looked at whether the rates of aggression differ across regions of this country? Would you assume that the researcher was a sociologist, a psychologist or an anthropologist? Actually the research mentioned here was done by social psychologists (Hammock, 2003; White and Koss, 1991).

As you can see, it is often difficult to imagine what the perspective of the researcher might be. Is the person who studies the influence of social class, cultural norms, and beliefs about women on the incidence of date rape a psychologist, a sociologist or an anthropologist? Is the researcher studying safer sex behavior in sex workers a sociologist or an anthropologist? Is the researcher investigating the impact of the family on the use of violence in intimate relationships a psychologist or sociologist? Is the work on the supportive function of transgender support groups on transgender communities conducted by an anthropologist, sociologist or psychologist? In other words, the borders between the different disciplines and their perspectives are often fuzzy and allow for a great deal of sharing of interdisciplinary research to be conducted.

Similarly, you often find that teams of researchers representing different perspectives often come together to conduct research on sexual behavior. A recent article on romantic love provides an excellent case in point. In this study, the researchers studied different regions of the brain to determine whether areas of the brain associated with reward and motivation systems are related to reports of being intensely in love with a romantic partner. The study used MRI images taken while the participants were looking at a picture of the beloved and of a familiar individual. Their results support the relationship of love with certain regions of the brain. Further, their research argues that romantic love is quite complex and might actually be a motivational state that leads to specific types of emotions and a focusing on the beloved (Aron et al., 2005). This fascinating research was accomplished by a team of individuals trained as psychologists, anthropologists, and neurologists.

The bottom line is that all of the different disciplines are critical to obtaining a complete understanding of human sexuality. Though the primary focus of this book is on the anthropological perspective, in the following chapters you will see how each of these perspectives has contributed to the topics studied. This will result in a biological, psychological, and cultural approach that examines how biological, psychological and cultural variables influence sexual behavior. But before we can look at individual behaviors, several critical terms and theories must be understood.

Anthropological concepts

Having compared and contrasted the anthropological perspective with biological, sociological, and psychological ones, specific concepts from anthropology must be introduced to help further the understanding of the anthropological approach to human sexuality. We have selected four key terms and related concepts that will be useful. These are: evolution, the culture concept, ethnocentrism, and cultural relativism. We have been very selective in our choice of these four terms; there are numerous others that are important in anthropological approaches to human sexuality. These are introduced in subsequent chapters and may be found in the glossary at the end of the text. Anthropological terms and concepts are discussed in greater depth than other terms because of their importance. Other anthropological terms of particular relevance for understanding the perspective of this textbook are: society, primates, bonding, ethnological, ethnographic, comparative, cross-cultural, and genetic fitness. These are presented in the glossary at the end of the text and are interspersed throughout the various chapters of this book.

Evolution

The modern theory of **evolution** challenged the prevailing view of the seventeenth and eighteenth centuries that all species were separate and divine creations. Through his famous travels on the *HMS Beagle*, Charles Darwin formulated his theory of natural selection. Naturalist Alfred Russell Wallace, during this same period, independently arrived at a similar conclusion: species are not separate creations but have evolved through a process of natural selection. In 1858 Darwin and Wallace together rocked the meetings of the Linnaean Society of London, and in 1859 Darwin published *The Origin of Species,* documenting and detailing the theory of natural selection (Ember, Ember and Peregrine, 2005).

The central tenants of natural selection are straightforward. Natural selection is a mechanism of evolution that involves long periods of time. Those individuals who are better adapted to their environments will be more likely to reproduce surviving offspring than those who are not. Those individuals who reproduce themselves are more likely to pass on the traits they possess than those who are not so well adapted to their environments. This has been referred to as **survival of the fit** and is calculated in terms of reproduction, not life span of the individual. Since environments do not remain stable over time, different characteristics may emerge as more adaptive so that what was adaptive in one environment at one time is no longer adaptive at another time. **Adaptation** is defined as "a process by which organisms achieve a beneficial adjustment to an available environment, and the results of that process" (Haviland, 1989: 59).

Though Darwin knew that traits were inherited, he could not explain how new variation in populations occurred. It was Gregor Mendel, an Austrian monk, who pioneered the study of genetics. His findings were incorporated into the theories of the scientific community in the early 1900s. Studies of genetics are now an essential component in the study of evolution (Ember, Ember and Peregrine, 2005).

The culture concept

The culture concept developed at the end of the nineteenth century. Sir Edward Burnett Tylor, considered the parent of anthropology, provided the first clear definition. In 1897 he defined culture as "that complex whole which includes the knowledge, belief, art, morals, law, custom and any other capabilities and habits acquired by man...[and woman]...as a member of society." By 1952 Kroeber and Kluckhohn, in reviewing the anthropological literature, found 164 different definitions of culture (Lett, 1987: 54–55).

With so many definitions available for the culture concept, we will be using the following definition by Boyd and Richerson (1989: 28) for the purpose of this book: "[Culture is the]...information—skills, attitudes, beliefs, values—capable of affecting individual's behavior, which they acquire from others by teaching, imitation, and other forms of social learning." We have selected this definition because of its thrust on the mental or cognitive dimension of culture, i.e., what an individual knows, both consciously and unconsciously, about her or his culture. This aspect, borrowing from a linguistic model of language in anthropology, may be thought of as **competence**. It is all the rules you need to know to act like a native of "x" group. Spradley (1987: 17) calls this "cultural knowledge" and notes that it has two dimensions: explicit and tacit. **Explicit culture** is the knowledge we can easily communicate about, for example, knowing what our genealogies are or that we practice monogamy, albeit serial, in our marriage systems. **Tacit culture** is "outside our awareness." Hall's classic work on nonverbal communication, *The Hidden Dimension* (1966), has described a number of spatially oriented rules about how close to stand next to someone and when to touch or not touch that are examples of tacit culture. We tend to be aware of these rules only when they are violated (Spradley, 1987: 22–24) as in the case of when someone "violates your space" or "gets in your face."

But culture is not just floating around in our heads; culture is behavior too. It includes **performance**, our socially acquired life ways and our patterned interactions, the things humans do and make. For the most part, it can be observed and this is what makes research into sex so difficult. Human sexuality, except in certain cases of public and ritualized religious events, is private and not readily observable. In order to understand observable patterns of behavior or performance we need to know about competence, the values and beliefs underlying the behaviors.

Culture has certain characteristics that anthropologists have identified:

- Culture is shared in that it is composed of a group of people who experience a common culture although they need not embrace all the attributes of the culture.
- Culture is learned and transmitted. The process of learning one's culture in a society is "enculturation" (Ember, Ember and Peregrine, 2005).
- Culture is symbolic. Thus, culture can be seen as the making of meaning where meaning is arbitrarily assigned to behaviors, events, and the world in general.

Related to the issue of cultural meanings are two additional concepts incorporated by anthropologists in their research on culture and sexuality; these are **emic** and **etic** perspectives. Emic approaches take the perspective of the participant's point of view, seeing the world from the standpoint of the insider. Ethnographers are dedicated to acquiring this emic perspective, before they can undertake an etic analysis. Etic perspectives are those based on a scientific outsider's ways of knowing and understanding the world. This includes a "set of epistemological and theoretical principles and methodologies acquired during a more or less rigorous and lengthy training period" (Harris, 1999: 33).

Ethnocentrism

According to Bernstein (1983: 183), **ethnocentrism** is "unreflectively imposing alien standards of judgment and thereby missing the point of the meaning of a practice." It is "the attitude that other societies' customs and ideas can be judged in the context of one's own culture" (Ember and Ember, 1990: 510) and "that one's own culture is superior in every way to all others" (Haviland, 1989: 296). As a discipline, anthropology has rejected this view as a result of the method of participant-observation; early on anthropologists came to know that "savages" were as human as those peoples living in industrialized societies and that their behavior could only be understood as part of their culture (Haviland, 1989: 296). To fully comprehend the meaning and danger of ethnocentrism, it is important to adopt the anthropological stance of cultural relativism.

Cultural relativism

According to Ember and Ember (1990: 510), relativism is "the attitude that a society's customs and ideas should be viewed within the context of that society's problems and opportunities." Thus, "there is no single scale of values applicable to all societies" (Winick, 1970: 454). Anthropologists find it crucial to remain relativistic in order to describe, explain and to discover meaning without the biases of their home society. For example, it is obvious that U.S. cultural biases against homosexuality could impact a scientific understanding of the subject. Herdt (1981, 1987, 1988, 2006) and Williams (1986) have written about tribal people's homosexual practices and Blackwood (1984a, 1984b, 2005a, 2005b) on indigenous lesbian behavior. They offer a relativistic and nonjudgmental view of the subject. It is evident from their writings that even the terminology such as "homosexual" and "lesbian" are so loaded and culturally specific that they cannot be directly translated into the meaning given to, for example, boy-inseminating rites among Sambia of Highland New Guinea (Herdt, 1987, 2006 among others). The "homosexual" behavior of these peoples is simply not commensurable with our Euro-American concept of homosexuality or gay (Herdt, 2006).

At some point in adopting a culturally relativistic perspective, you might be faced with a clash of values. How far to take cultural relativism and where to draw the line are questions often asked by students; however, it is one that concerns anthropologists as well. In fact, *Ethos*, the journal of the Society for Psychological Anthropology, devoted an entire issue to the question of moral relativism (1990: 131–223). The introduction begins with:

> What sort of theory of human values can be devised which encompasses and accords legitimacy to the obvious cultural and historical diversity in moral systems, without being so open that "anything goes"? That is a core problem of moral (ethical) relativism... (Fiske and Mason, 1990: 131)

As we live in an ever shrinking world, cultural differences are increasingly apparent through tourism, immigration, international education, the Internet, and a host of other issues that bring moral relativism into play. These issues are significant particularly around topics directly affecting the lives of college-age students. Often it is easier to be relativistic regarding behavior or beliefs of people so geographically or even temporally distant. Both Bolin and Whelehan maintain a stance that it is more difficult to be relativistic in one's own culture, especially when encountering nonnormative behaviors and values which vary from the ideals of the U.S. middle class that currently dominate U.S. ideological systems. For example, homosexuality is only one of several possibilities for sexual orientations, yet in several areas of the southern United States these sexual practices were considered illegal and participants were prosecuted under ethnocentric and inhumane laws. On June 26, 2003, in *Lawrence & Garner v. State of Texas*, the U.S. Supreme Court ruled 6–3 that sodomy laws are unconstitutional and unenforceable when applied to noncommercial consenting adults in private (Sodomy Laws, 2006).

But what about other behaviors such as incest, rape, or abortion? Does a culturally relativistic stance mandate that these are acceptable? No, it does not. Rape and incest are most clearly "crimes" in the industrialized society's view. Abortion, though, presents something of a quandary. Once a crime, abortion now is considered a choice by the individual until that legally granted choice is removed. Where you draw the line is ultimately your decision on many of these issues. While you may choose to take the stance that it is an individual's choice on abortion, others may find this problematic and challenge you. In the case of rape and in most incest situations, the participants are clearly victims of crimes and have no choice. In keeping with a feminist perspective on the abortion issue, we take the position that it is the right of the woman to choose. Cultural relativism does not require that you agree with or like a certain behavior or belief system. Rather, it requires that you are able to suspend judgment and place that behavior or belief system within the context of the culture in which it is found. Cultural relativism is therefore a method and an approach to the world that asks that you temporarily suspend judgment. It does not demand that you forsake all values or beliefs in human rights. "Thus, after an understanding generated by a culturally relativistic stance may come an ethical positioning which for many of us includes a humanistic concern for all human rights" (Basirico and Bolin, 2000: 88).

DEFINITIONS OF HUMAN SEXUALITY

So how do you define human sexuality? We turn now to this definition. In keeping with the anthropological perspective, human sexuality should be viewed through a wide lens and understood from a relativistic perspective. Defining human sexuality is no simple task. It is impossible to set narrow boundaries for what is included within the category we call sex.

Katchadourian (1979: 8–34) has described the many meanings of the word "sex." According to Katchadourian's research, the English word, derived from the Latin *sexus,* can be traced back to the fourteenth-century (1979: 9). The term "sex" has undergone a variety of permutations and grammatical uses in popular culture over time in U.S. society. This is particularly evident in the changing metaphors for sex in the lyrics of songs. Compare the lyrics that Elvis Presley sang in 1955:

Play house with me

with Sinatra's lyrics from 1966:

We'd be sharing love,
Before the night was through

with Def Leppard's refrains:

c'mon fire me up,
I'm hot, sticky sweet from my head to my feet yeah.

I want to taste you

and Justin Timberlake's lyrics in "Future Sex" (2006):

She's hopped upon me,
I think she's ready to blow

Lyrics in some contemporary genres of music have dispensed altogether with the use of metaphors and are keenly explicit. Sex commonly refers to what people "do," is usually termed "sexual behavior," and often is described as erotic (Katchadourian, 1979: 11). Barale (1986) offers a down-to-earth definition: "Genitals are the given: what we do with them is a matter of creative invention; how we interpret what we do with them is what we call sexuality" (in Duggan, 1990: 95). Sometimes the term "sex" is used by researchers in place of gender to refer to embodiment or physical bodies, for example at some point in their lives most adults in industrialized nations will be asked to check a box on a form that asks them their sex, male or female. In the Euro-American gender schema (model of the world) **sex** typically refers to biological attributes including chromosomes, external genitals, gonads, internal reproductive structures, hormonal states, and secondary sexual characteristics, among others. **Gender** may be defined as the psychological, social, and cultural aspects of being a male or female. Gender is a cultural construction and system of meanings with multiple dimensions including gender identity, one's sense of self and awareness as a woman, man, boy, or girl, to greater or lesser degrees and/or as an additional or in-between gender (Bolin, 1996: 24). See Chapter 13 for further discussion of gender identity and gender roles.

Time and space

Definitions of human sexuality have varied across time and space. Human sexuality is symbolic behavior as much as it is reproductive behavior. Sex includes self-stimulation (masturbation) as well as copulation and other activities related to coitus. It also includes noncoitally oriented pleasuring as well as sex between partners of the same sex. Questions of where the boundaries are and what to include in the definition of sex are difficult. For example, Katchadourian asks if sexual fantasy can be included in the definition of sex? It is certainly erotic, "but is it 'behavior'" (1979: 11)? Others have attempted to avoid the problems of behavior and emotional arousal by using the term "sexual experience." When this array of terms is placed in the even wider context of the cross-cultural record, we are led to ask if there are indeed any sexual universals amidst such a wide range of human sexual expression.

For the purposes of this chapter, we have taken the broadest possible scope to explore the many meanings of sex including: species-wide behavior, biological, social scientific including behavioral, cognitive, and affective, and socio-cultural definitions and dimensions. Other attributes, such as the functions of sexuality in the cultural context, will be included. Contributing to the complexity of the definitional task is that sexual expression may be part of actual behavior or may be purely symbolic. Sexuality may also be expressed in terms of the metaphorical as is often found in rituals. For example, among the Ndembu as studied by Turner (1969: 10–43; Cohen and Eames, 1982: 250–251), the Isoma fertility ritual is rich with sexual symbolism. In one part of this ritual the infertile woman holds a white chicken which represents semen and good fortune in Ndembu cosmology.

Definitions of human sexuality do not remain stable over time, as is documented by the history of Euro-American views of sexuality in the field of sexual science. Scientific studies have shifted their interests from sex as reproduction to perspectives that focus on sexuality and its nonreproductive aspects, including larger issues such as gender variance (Jacobs and Roberts, 1989: 439–444). Medical views have fluctuated in tandem with changes in the wider culture. Thus, the well-known prudish and sexually repressive cultural atmosphere of "mainstream" (i.e., middle class) Victorianism in the period of mid-1800s to 1900 was reproduced in medical views so that masturbation was believed to cause mental illness (Johnson, Masters, and Kolodny, 1982: 11–12). The following quotation illustrates all too clearly the Victorian discourse on female sexuality. We quote from Ruth Smythers' (1989 [1894]) "Instruction and Advice for the Young Bride on the Conduct and Procedures of the Intimate and Personal Relationship of the Marriage State."

To the sensitive young woman who has had benefits of proper upbringing, the wedding day is ironically, both the happiest and most terrifying day of her life . . . On the negative side, there is the wedding night, during which the bride must pay the piper, so to speak, by facing for the first time the experience of sex. At this point, dear reader, let me concede one shocking truth. Some young women actually anticipate the wedding night with curiosity and pleasure! Beware of such an attitude. A selfish and sensual husband can easily take advantage of such a bride. One cardinal rule of marriage should never be forgotten: GIVE LITTLE, GIVE SELDOM, AND ABOVE ALL, GIVE GRUDGINGY . . . while sex is at best revolting and at worst rather painful, it has to be endured, and has been by women since the beginning of time, and is compensated for by the monogamous home and the children produced through it. (1989 [1894]: 5–7, emphasis author's)

This historical view represents a fundamental change over time in how sex is regarded for women. In the U.S. today the model of sex is one of "sex as pleasure" rather than sex as duty.

Despite this new model, there still exists a double standard in U.S. society wherein a woman's sexuality is bounded by a model of sexuality that emphasizes monogamous, committed heterosexual and potentially reproductive sex. Such changes in attitude influence how human sexuality is experienced and integrated within culture.

Species-wide behavior

Human sexuality, or more accurately the capacity for sexuality is a species-wide behavior. The term **species** is defined as "a population or group of populations that is capable of interbreeding, but that is reproductively isolated from other such populations" (Haviland, 1989: 66). Although all humans may mate with one another, it is characteristic of cultures to restrict sexual and reproductive activities between people. Sometimes the cultural meaning assigned to certain gene pools and/or physical attributes prohibits groups of humans from interbreeding with one another even though they are perfectly able to do so (Haviland, 1989: 66). Thus, all humans are capable of interbreeding and producing viable offspring, but cultural barriers may prevent people from marrying and reproducing.

BIOLOGICAL DEFINITIONS AND DIMENSIONS

Biological definitions include sex in reference to "the two divisions of organic beings identified as male and female and to the qualities that distinguish males and females" (Katchadourian, 1979: 9). This is frequently termed **biological sex**, yet this definition is problematic as well as ethnocentric. Relying on a model described by Money and Ehrhardt (1972: 4–15) and expanded upon in Bolin and Whelehan's undergraduate classes, we offer a multifaceted view of biological sex that challenges the simplicity of the notion of defining one's sex as either male and female. How, in fact, do we reach that determination? How do you know what sex you are? Our list of sex attributes includes: chromosomal sex, gonadal sex, hormonal (endocrine) sex, sex of internal reproductive structures in addition to the gonads, secondary sexual characteristics (including distribution of fatty tissues, hair growth, breast development), gender identity (self-perception as male or female), gender role, sex of assignment and rearing, and legal sex among others.

Obviously, there are many elements involved in defining one's sex. For example, male-to-female transsexual people/transgendered people who have undergone sex reassignment through surgery combine these definitions in unique ways. Postoperative male-to-female transsexual people/transgendered people have female genitals, a female hormonal mix with estrogen and progesterone dominant over testosterone, a legal sex as a female, but a sex of assignment at birth and rearing as male. They have a female gender identity but "male" secondary sexual characteristics until hormonal reassignment and alteration of hirsuteness through artificial means occur, and a history of a male gender role which is followed by a female one.

One can easily see how the biological can be mixed up with the cultural when the discussion turns to gender roles and legal sex. Yet, strictly biological determinants like hormones, secondary sexual characteristics, internal and external reproductive features are not so clear either. Biological sex exists on a continuum. There are a number of gender anomalies that illustrate this variety in biological sex (Fausto-Sterling, 2000; Masters, Johnson, and Kolodny, 1982: 504; Kessler, 2004).

In testicular feminizing syndrome, the male with **androgen-insensitivity syndrome** produces enough testosterone to make him into the "Incredible Hulk," but because of a genetic problem, "he" cannot absorb and process "his" testosterone. As a consequence, the fetus develops a blind vagina (it doesn't lead to a uterus) and female genitalia. At birth, the infant looks female but does not have the internal female reproductive organs and is usually identified as a girl. At puberty, "she" develops breasts but cannot menstruate and is infertile (Blackless, et al., 2000: 153–154; Money and Ehrhardt, 1972: 280).

To suggest to such a young woman at puberty that because her chromosomes and hormones are male that she is a man overlooks the fact that gender is a lived phenomenon (Kessler and McKenna, 1978: 76–77; Ward and Edelstein, 2006: 169–192). In U.S. society two choices exist: female or male. The androgen-insensitive male is reared as a female, and usually has a gender identity as a woman. In a socio-cultural sense, she is a woman although she may not be a physiological female. From a physiological perspective, she is an **intersexed** person because she has both male and female characteristics; xy chromosome structure, female genitals and undescended or partially descended testes (Intersex Society of North America).

Not only are there individuals who are biologically intersexed, but other societies may recognize more than two genders as well. In some cultures, gender may be an **achieved** (acquired) rather than an **ascribed** (assigned) status. The cross-cultural record reveals all these possibilities. Anthropologists have long reported on the existence of societies with more than two genders referred to as gender transformed statuses, alternative genders, supernumerary genders, gender variant persons, and **two spirits** among other terms[1] (e.g., Bolin, 1999: 27–30; Jacobs, 1994; Martin and Voorhies, 1975: 94). It now appears that a variety of kinds of behaviors and variations in gender expression have been lumped under these terms. For example, the two spirit has been referred to as a gender-transformed status, as an alternative gender, and/or as a cross-gender role. Nevertheless, this identity may generally be described as a position in society in which a person takes on some or all of the tasks, dress, and behaviors of the other gender. Rather than just two genders as in the Euro-American case, the Mohave recognized four genders: woman, *hwami* (female two spirit), man, and *alyha* (male two spirit). The Chuckchee reported seven genders, three female and four male (Jacobs and Roberts, 1989: 439–440; Martin and Voorhies, 1975: 96–99; 102–104). Jacobs and Roberts (1989: 439) have proposed that: "If one uses the criteria of linguistic markers alone, it suggests that people in most English-speaking countries also recognize four genders: woman, lesbian (or gay female), man, and gay male."

The other biological definition of sex focuses on the physiology of sexual arousal and coitus and on the reproductive biology of humans. This includes changes in the human cycle in both reproductive physiology as well as human sexual response. As Jacobs and Roberts (1989: 441) so eloquently point out: "[r]eproduction and sexuality are codependent variables in the human life cycle. But sex and sexuality are much more complex than linking them with reproduction."

Behavioral, cognitive, and affective definitions and dimensions

The social science perspectives broaden the study of human sexuality by looking beyond the mechanics of sexual behavior to other factors, most notably behavioral, cognitive, and affective factors, which influence sexual expression and perception. The behavioral definitions of human sexuality focus on behaviors and consequences that can be both observed and measured. When dealing with the cognitive dimensions of sexuality, yet another layer to sexuality is added by considering how we think about, judge, rationalize, attribute, and perceive sexual stimuli and behaviors. Finally, affective dimensions also are considered by social scientists studying sexuality. Our emotional or affective responses add many dimensions to our experiences by influencing how we interpret and view behavior. In this capacity, they can actually serve as motivators of behavior, influencing who and what we are willing to accept and approach.

The work of Kinsey and his colleagues represents one of the most well-known behaviorist studies of human sexuality: *Sexual Behavior in the Human Male* (1948) and *Sexual Behavior in the Human Female* (1953). The Kinsey reports focused on six sexual outlets leading to orgasm (masturbation, sex dreams, petting, coitus, homosexuality, and sex with animals). They were based on interviews with 5,300 males and 5,940 females. Kinsey was central in the creation of the scientific study of sex. He exemplified how such an emotionally charged subject could be studied with scientific rigor. The Kinsey reports opened a forum for the public discussion of human sexuality. Gagnon (1978: 93) believes that the public furor created by this work ushered in "a major increase in the publicly sexual character of society that occurred in the late 1960s and early 1970s." Others have argued, however, that since the 1980s our society has also experienced a backlash to these more liberal trends in sexual expression and education (Faludi, 1991; Kusz, 2001). Indeed, the Kinsey Institute for Research in Sex, Gender and Reproduction states: "the work is not done. And the stakes today are higher than ever—HIV/AIDS, sexual problems, abuse—the need for objective research and education has never been more urgent. Progress: Yes, Job Done: No" (Kinsey Institute for Research in Sex, Gender, and Reproduction, 2006).

The behaviorist approach to sexuality is concerned with the scientifically measurable, i.e., external states. Kinsey was critical of sex research done through the single case method or the method of ethnographic sexology. He advocated the sociological method of the survey of large populations with concern for accurate representation and the "statistical sense" without which one was "no scientist" (Gagnon, 1978: 93).

A behaviorist approach to sexuality provides important information about what behaviors are being displayed, by whom and with what frequency. But it does little to explain why those behaviors are occurring and why some behaviors are more likely to occur than others. Further, it neglects the role that our inner thoughts play in our behaviors. Why are we likely to engage in some behaviors than others? How do we perceive others' actions and what we believe is appropriate or inappropriate? What attracts us to some partners but not others?

A good example of the impact of cognitive factors on sexuality is sexual scripts (Gagnon and Simon, 1973). According to this theory, we, as individuals, conduct sexual encounters based on a script, just as if we were players in a theatrical production. In other words, our sexual encounters respond to a running script in our minds which dictates what behaviors are appropriate, when they are appropriate to display, and with whom it is appropriate to do them. These learned scripts are likely to influence many different aspects of our sexual lives. A recent study by Else-Quest, Hyde and DeLamater (2005) looked at the importance of the first sexual encounter and sexual scripts. They found that first sexual encounters that occurred outside of contexts generally accepted for sexual activity (i.e., prepubertal sexual experiences, forced sex with a blood relative, sex for pay, or sex while impaired by alcohol or drugs) were linked to negative consequences later in life such as more sexually transmitted diseases, sexual dysfunction, more sexual guilt, and lower life satisfaction. Based on these findings, they argue that those sexual encounters that violate accepted sexual scripts have long-term repercussions for sexual functioning.

One of the reasons that sexual scripts become important is the emotional responses that are a critical aspect of our sexual scripts. If shame or guilt becomes associated with sexual behavior it is not surprising that sexual difficulties might arise in the future. This relationship points to the importance of considering emotions or affect in the study of sexuality.

Affect can have a powerful impact on many different aspects of our sexuality. For example, in a number of societies, the transition into puberty is often marked with a wide range of emotions from joy to shame. Attitudes about certain groups, such as homophobia, are often accompanied by strong emotional reactions. Sexual encounters with partners are often colored by emotional responses such as trust, love, and liking. The potential impact of affect on what might be considered the "dark side of relationships," inflicting of aggressive behaviors on your partner, can be seen in a study conducted by Hammock (2003). This study investigated the ability of a number of variables to predict the use of physical and psychological aggression in intimate relationships. Physically aggressive behaviors were actions that either threatened or delivered physical harm (e.g., kicking, hitting, forcing sex, and choking). Psychologically aggressive tactics involved those that potentially harmed the self concept of the recipient (e.g., calling the recipient names, giving angry stares, isolating the recipient from friends and family, and humiliating or degrading the recipient). She found a number of variables reliably predicted the use of the participant's use of physical and psychologically harmful behaviors. These variables involved love, trust, and emotional commitment. Not surprisingly, those individuals who felt they could not trust their partner were more likely to use both physical and psychological aggression with that partner. On the other hand, those who reported high levels of love and commitment for their partners were more likely to use physical and psychological aggression. Though the last finding might seem surprising, an interesting explanation is given. We are not likely to bother using aggressive behaviors with our partners when the relationship is of little value to us – in other words, ones in which we have little emotional commitment. However, when we have high levels of emotional commitment, we might have a greater motive for controlling the partner or for retaliating against the partner for things the partner says or does. Certainly, this study suggests that emotional responses have interesting impacts on relationships and what we are willing to do in them.

Socio-cultural definitions and dimensions

As we have seen, biological definitions of human sexuality focus on anatomy and physiology, physical development, and changes in human sexual response throughout the life cycle with an emphasis on the reproductive. Biological definitions of human sexuality also include behavioral dimensions. The cognitive and affective dimensions involve our interpretations of sexual experience and behaviors. In contrast, socio-cultural definitions accent the role of customs in shaping human behavior and tend to take a relativistic stance. This position opposes the biological and behavioral definitions that look to physiology to explain alleged sex differences in human response. Socio-cultural definitions regard sexual behavior as culturally constituted and created (Gagnon, 1978: 95). Gender is a socio-cultural construct in which meanings are assigned to biology. The **sex-gender system** is defined by Rubin (1975) as: "the set of arrangements by which a society transforms biological sexuality into products of human activity" (in Vance, 1983: 372).

Socio-cultural studies have gradually evolved from an early interest in sex as reproduction (e.g., Martin and Voorhies' *Female of the Species,* 1975) to studies of sex as institutional (e.g., marriage systems) and finally to sexuality itself (Jacobs and Roberts, 1989: 439; Lyons and Lyons, 2004). This approach is amply represented from Chapter 7 through the Conclusions.

Sex, gender, masculinity, and femininity

In this section, we present a list of terms related to the concept and construct of gender. It is important to define gender early in our discussion of masculinity and femininity. Research conducted in the 1970s often intertwined and conflated the terms *sex* and *gender*, although by the early 1980s successful efforts were made at separation and redefinition carried through to the new millenium (Jacobs and Roberts, 1989: 439). Jacobs and Roberts (1989: 439) offer an excellent definition:

> **Gender** is the socio-cultural designation of bio-behavioral and psychosocial qualities of the sexes; for example, woman (female), man (male), other(s) [e.g., two spirit, see Chapter 13 for further discussion]. Notions of gender are culturally specific and depend on the ways in which cultures define and differentiate human (and other) potentials and possibilities.

Kessler and McKenna's (1978: 7–16) definitions also serve us well. Though it is conventional to define sex as the biological aspects of male or female, and to define gender as the "psychological, social, and cultural aspects of maleness and femaleness," Kessler and McKenna argue that even the concept of two biological sexes is a social construction (1978: 7).

For purposes of clarity, sex will be used in this context to refer to activities related to sexual pleasure, arousal, and intercourse whether recreational or for reproduction (Jacobs and Roberts, 1989: 440). Gender will refer more broadly to the cultural aspects of being male or female. Elsewhere, specific usages such as chromosomal, hormonal, or morphological sex will be presented, even though these biological characteristics are always interpreted through a cultural lens (cf. Kessler and McKenna, 1978: 7).

Through an understanding of the "attribution process," how people assign gender to others, insight can be gained into the social construction of femininity and masculinity. Euro-American femininity and masculinity are integrated in a gender scheme whose central tenants are that there are only two sexes, male and female, and that these are appropriately associated with the two social statuses of gender: men and women, boys and girls. "Whatever a woman does will somehow have the stamp of femininity on it, while whatever a man does will likewise bear the imprint of masculinity" (Devor, 1989: vii). Therefore, masculinity and femininity are associated with gender roles. The Euro-American **gender schema** is a shared belief system about sex and gender. It regards biological sex as the basis for gender status which is the basis for gender role. The actual process whereby people attribute gender to another actually occurs in the reverse to our gender schema; a person's display of masculinity or femininity (gender role) indicates gender which is followed by the presumption of appropriate genitalia which are not readily visible (Kessler and McKenna, 1978: 1–7, 112–141; Devor,

1989: 149). Without our portable gene scanners and x-ray vision, daily life consists of encounters in which the biological is clearly mediated by cultural expectation in the attribution process. We do not really see genitals and sex, but gender presentations of feminine and masculine beings.

In summary, masculinity and femininity may be defined as components of gender roles which include cultural expectations about behaviors and appearances associated with the status of man or woman in the industrial bi-polar model of the sexes. For the purposes of our discussion, the following definition for gender role will be used:

> Everything that a person says and does, to indicate to others or to the self the degree in which one is male or female or ambivalent. It includes but is not restricted to sexual arousal and response. Gender role is the public expression of gender identity, and gender identity is the private of experience of gender role . . . Gender identity . . . [is] . . . the sameness, unity, and persistence of one's individuality as male or female (or ambivalent), in greater or lesser degree, especially as it is experienced in self-awareness and behavior. (Money and Ehrhardt, 1972: 284)

Because of the attribution process, gender roles are often confused with sex and biology. Gender role stereotypes include ideas that differences in gender are the result of biology, for example, women are more nurturing, men are more aggressive, and women are emotional while men are rational. These differences are rather the result of learned behaviors. Stereotypes such as these are classified by sociologists as **expressive** and **instrumental gender roles**. Boys are socialized into instrumental roles that are associated with acting or achieving while girls are socialized into relationship-oriented or expressive roles (Renzetti and Curran, 2003: 167). That these roles are cultural and are not natural is amply demonstrated in the cross-cultural record in which a diversity of behaviors and expectations are recorded. Mead's study of the Arapesh, the Mundugumor, and the Tchambuli (they call themselves the Chambri) in *Sex and Temperament in Three Primitive Societies* (1963 [1935]) offers a classical account of gender role variation in counterpoint to our industrialized society's conceptions. Among the Mundugumor, both men and women were aggressive and non-emotional, while among the Arapesh, both sexes were cooperative and nurturant. The Tchambuli (Chambri) expressed the reverse of our Euro-American gender roles with cooperative caring men and assertive women as the behavioral norm.

Deborah Gewertz's research on the Chambri complicates Mead's perspective with a regional and historical approach. During Mead's research the Chambri had only recently returned to their home site after a twenty-year exile. Consequently the men were focused on refurbishing their ritual equipment and seemed to be highly involved in artistic and expressive endeavors.

The women appeared dominant to Mead because they had already established their economic system of barter. Nonetheless, Gewertz argues that Mead was essentially correct in her view that gender roles are flexible and responsive to changing environments (Gewertz, 1981; Ward and Edelstein, 2006: 60–61).

Biology and sex: political aspects

No definition of sexuality can be complete without viewing its political aspects. We conclude with the interface of politics of sexuality with biological, behavioral, and socio-cultural definitions of sex. In 1978 Burnham stated: "Whether the boundaries of women's place in society were erected with the bricks of theology or the cement of genetic determinism, the intention is that the barriers shall remain strong and sturdy" (Burnham, 1978: 51). Burnham's statement provides a good introduction for our discussion of the politics of biology and sex. Biological/sexual functions have been used to serve larger political purposes in societies and ours is no exception. For example, women's role in reproduction has been interpreted to justify conceptions of female inferiority which support ideologies of gender inequality.

Nineteenth-century physicians maintained the view that for medical reasons it was unhealthy for women to be educated. This was based on a medical ideology that the brain and the reproductive organs shared the same biological resources, so that development of one meant the other was deprived. Since women's role was defined as a reproductive one, feeding her brain through education was seen as jeopardizing her reproductive capabilities (Burnham, 1978: 51–52).

Other researchers have described the historical relations of sexuality to changes based on the expansion of industrial capitalism in developing and developed nations, thereby providing a political-economic interpretation (Ross and Rapp, 1983: 51–73). Ross and Rapp (1983: 51) note that "the personal is political" reflecting our point that what one may think of as private is also public in the sense that it is linked with broader institutions of the industrial and global political economy. These institutions are patriarchal and perpetuate beliefs about the differences between the sexes and their respective sexualities. Such ideologies are then supported by a sexology in which **androcentric** (male biased) views are legitimized as science, aided and abetted by biological reductionism.

Sanday's study of rape-prone societies clearly shows the relationship between male dominance and political power. Rape-prone societies were found to glorify strength, power, and violence *and* gave women no voice in the political sphere or in religious life. Women were regarded as being "owned" by men in such societies (Sanday, 2003; Benderly, 1987; 187). In this way, sexual behavior is defined as violent and as natural for men.

In opposition to the rape-prone societies are the rape-free societies which challenge the essentialist view of men as "naturally" aggressive. A society deemed rape-free was associated with resource stability, the absence of competition, and egalitarian social structures for men and women. Rather than a belief in a male supreme being, rape-free societies acknowledged a male and female deity or a "universal womb" (Sanday, 2003; Benderly, 1987: 187–188). These societies were identified by Sanday as those where rape did not occur.

Recent research suggests that as a result of the changes to the world's societies due to colonialism, industrialization, and globalization, there are very few societies remaining in which rape does not occur. An exception is Lepowsky's (1993) ethnography of the New Guinea people of the island of Vanatinai. This is an egalitarian decentralized matrilineal society which interrogates the notion that the male subordination of women is inevitable. Lepowsky notes "Physical violence again women—and men—is abhorred and occurs only rarely today [in Vanatinai]. I have never heard of a case of rape" (Lepowsky, 1993: 292).

To understand culture change and the impact of colonialism and globalization on sexuality, it is important to recognize the dynamic element of culture and the role of culture change in human life. Humans have never lived isolated lives, and culture contact between bands and tribes has probably existed since humans began to populate the world two million years ago. Wolf (1982: ix) argues: "Human populations construct their cultures in interaction with one another, and not in isolation."

The small-scale tribal world of autonomous decentralized, non-stratified societies as opposed to massively complex large-scale modern industrial states was the only world until 7,500 years ago (Bodley, 2005: 10–11, 165). According to Bodley "This was the beginning of a global cultural transformation in which very quickly a handful of ruling elites successfully constructed large, complex chiefdoms, kingdoms, city-states and empires in favorable locations worldwide" (2005: 165). By the 1600s, prior to the industrial revolution, a world commercial system was already developing as a precursor to modern global capitalism. From this time onward, commercial interests dominated extant political systems, spanning colonization, industrialization, and the expansion of modern nation states. A concomitant economic expansion resulted in the increasing division between wealthy developed nations and developing nations (Bodley, 2005: 341). This process is referred to as **globalization**, defined as "the ongoing spread of goods, people, information and capital around the world" (Ember, Ember and Peregrine, 2005: 545). Consequently, indigenous peoples have been drawn into a pervasive system of expanding global capitalism. Globalization has influenced the sex and gender systems of indigenous populations and developing nations in diverse ways. And women's status and sexual autonomy have been particularly affected in negative ways inspiring Ward and Edelstein (2006: 243) to remark that "women are the last and largest colony on earth... We are 'the Other.'" For further discussion of globalization and sex see Chapter 16.

Anthropologists refer to the influence of culture change on indigenous peoples as **syncretism**: the blending and mixing of indigenous cultural elements with those introduced by other societies; that is the "interplay of local, regional, national and international cultural forces" (Kottak, 2002: 504). This term highlights the indigenous response to the imposition of culture by external sources. It illustrates that indigenous peoples are creative and resistant in their response to efforts to assimilate and acculturate them and that globalization is not a uniformly flat and hegemonic process.

In conclusion, this chapter has presented terms and concepts necessary for understanding human sexuality from an anthropological perspective. We have elaborated the importance of culture in shaping our human sexuality, and have offered an examination of key concepts and points related to biological and psychological dimensions of sexuality.

SUMMARY

1   Psychology, sociology, and biology offer useful perspectives for the understanding of human sexuality. These viewpoints are incorporated to various degrees by anthropological approaches.
2   To understand the bio-cultural perspective, it is necessary to define our terms. These include concepts and constructs such as evolution, the culture concept, ethnocentrism, and cultural relativism.
3   Definitions of human sexuality have varied temporally and spatially.
4   Definitions of human sexuality include areas such as anatomy and physiology, the sexual life cycle, and human sexual response.
5   Sex has many components. These include behavioral, cognitive, affective, and symbolic dimensions.
6   Sex and gender are compared and contrasted.
7   Sex has been used to serve larger cultural ends in societies. We examine sex in the context of power and politics.

Thought-provoking questions

1   What is the relationship of the individual to culture and psychology? Provide an example of how sexuality represents this intersection.
2   How has the information in this chapter challenged you to think differently about your beliefs about what is "naturally" feminine or masculine?
3   Think of a specific behavior related to sexuality (e.g., sexual dysfunctions, attitudes about sexuality, the use of safer sex techniques) and identify potential behavioral, cognitive, and affective factors that might influence the behavior.

4   What have you learned in this chapter that you would choose to share with a partner or friend? Why did you choose this piece of information? How do you think it will influence your own thoughts and behaviors or those of the person you are sharing the information with?

SUGGESTED RESOURCES

Books

Altman, Dennis. 2002. *Global Sex*. Chicago: University of Chicago Press.
Lancaster, Roger N. 2003. *The Trouble with Nature: Sex in Science and Popular Culture*. Berkeley: University of California Press.
Lyons, Andrew P. and Harriet Lyons. 2004. *Irregular Connections: A History of Anthropology and Sexuality*. Lincoln: University of Nebraska Press.

Web sites

Alan Guttmacher Institute (www.guttmacher.org)
Association for Feminist Anthropology (http://sscl.berkeley.edu/~afaweb/index. html)
Gender Inn (http://www.uni-koeln.de/phil-fak/englisch/datenbank/e_index.htm)
Kinsey Institute for Research in Sex, Gender and Reproduction (www.indiana. edu/~kinsey)
New York/International Women's Anthropology Conference NYWAC/IWAC, 1972–2002 (http://homepages.nyu.edu/~crs2/index.html)

3 The evolutionary history of human sexuality

Wenda R. Trevathan, PhD

CHAPTER OVERVIEW

1 Presents an overview of nonhuman primate evolution and ancestral relations.
2 Discusses the consequences of human arboreal and terrestrial adaptations.
3 Focuses on the development of the grasping hand, stereoscopic vision, and grooming.
4 Considers the consequences of these adaptations for modern sexual behavior including the importance of touch, feeling, and vision as important components in sexual attraction.
5 Presents discussion of the importance of bipedalism, loss of estrus, the development of brain complexity, infant dependency and reliance on learning and examines the profound consequences this has had on hominid evolution and human sexuality as well as reproduction.
6 Explains the importance of the social group for human survival.
7 Introduces the concept of bonding in human and nonhuman primates.
8 Relates how the human brain is actively involved in human maturation, reproduction, and sexuality.
9 Addresses estrus and loss of estrus and its implications for human evolution.
10 Offers discussion of several controversial views on the role of orgasm for female evolution.

This book focuses on human behavior as it relates to sexuality. Human behavior is notably complex and requires us to look for explanations for certain behaviors at multiple levels. For example, if we want to understand why a person acts aggressively in a given circumstance, we must investigate the immediate environment and events that might have triggered an aggressive reaction. What in this individual's life history could help explain the reaction? What aspects of his or her cultural environment and socialization might explain the behavior? Let's say we are observing a nursery school classroom. We watch as a little girl approaches a little boy and tries to take a toy from him. He hits her. Why did he behave this way? Multiple explanations can be offered. He was provoked by her. Boys are socialized in this culture to act with aggression when their property is threatened. Or perhaps one could take an evolutionary view and argue that males have been selected to act aggressively and possessively under certain circumstances because those behaviors were adaptive in the past.

These multiple explanations can be roughly placed into three categories, or "levels of explanation." One, the **proximate level**, seeks causes in the immediate environment, both the external and internal environment. In the case here, the provocation by the girl can be seen as the most direct cause, the proximate cause. Physiological changes that the boy might have experienced as a result of the provocation (e.g., anxiety) may also be seen as proximate causes. The **ontogenetic** or **developmental level** seeks causes in external and internal experiences in the individual's lifetime. Learning, socialization, previous related experiences, all would be in this category. Finally, the evolutionary explanation can be considered the **ultimate level** of explanation. When a behavior is seen as being the result of natural selection, as having "adaptive significance," then it can be seen as the ultimate cause.

These levels of explanation are not mutually exclusive. No single level is necessarily more correct than the others. It is true that hypotheses about proximate causes can more easily be tested. For example, if a loud noise had immediately preceded the aggressive reaction of the nursery school boy, an observer might be unsure of which event, the noise or the threatening action of the girl, had provoked the reaction in the boy. This could be tested experimentally by having the loud noise occur without the provocation from the girl, and vice versa. Ontogenetic or developmental hypotheses can be indirectly tested by observing similar situations involving other members of the boy's family, other boys in the nursery school environment, boys in different social groups, and boys in different cultures. Evolutionary explanations are far more difficult, if not impossible, to test, and for this reason may be less satisfying. Those with an interest in the physiological basis of behavior will find more satisfaction in proximate levels of explanation. Those with an evolutionary interest will focus on ultimate causes. Again, this does not mean that one explanation is any better than another, but one may be more meaningful to an investigator than another.

Let's try some more examples. Why do male birds sing in the spring? Hormones (proximate), photoperiod (proximate), learning by observing other males (ontogenetic), to mark territory (ultimate), to attract a mate (ultimate). All of these answers are correct, on one level or another. Why does a male dog mount a female dog? She's in heat (proximate), to reproduce (ultimate). These examples help us see another way of looking at these multiple levels of explanation. The proximate can be considered the "cause" of the behavior, while the ultimate can be considered the "function" of the behavior. Here's another: Why do men and women differ in their sexual behaviors? Chromosome differences (proximate), differences

in brain structure (proximate), different hormones (proximate), socialization (ontogenetic), natural selection (ultimate). No one explanation is more
correct than another; they are complementary rather than exclusive. In this
chapter we will emphasize the evolutionary explanations, whereas other
chapters focus more on ontogenetic and proximate factors that help us
understand human sexual behavior.

To begin our discussion of the evolutionary history of human sexual
behavior, we need to have a basic understanding of evolution. As noted
previously, in most cases, evolutionary success is measured in terms of
reproductive success. In other words, biological, behavioral, and physical
features that enhance reproduction will usually be favored by natural selection over those that do not contribute to greater reproductive success. The
"winners" in the evolutionary race are those that have the most surviving offspring, not just those who live long and healthy lives. Thinking
of evolutionary success in this way enables us to reconsider many of the
"why" questions that arise when we think about aspects of human sexuality. Examples include, why do human females have sex even when they are
not likely to conceive, whereas other female primates have sex primarily or
exclusively when they are ovulating? Or why do most humans remain in
long-enduring pair bonds, whereas males and females in most mammalian
species come together briefly for mating and then live most of their lives
separately? Why are human infants so helpless at birth in comparison to
many other mammals, including most primates? We will see that at one
level, the answer to each one of these questions is because this behavior or
characteristic increased reproductive success in the past.

One of the ways in which we can try to understand how human sexuality evolved is to study our closest living relatives, the nonhuman primates
(see Figure 3.1 for the taxonomy that has been developed to show how
humans are related to other animal species). Examining the similarities
and differences in biology and behavior related to sexuality can help us

Kingdom: Animalia
Phylum: Chordata
Class: Mammalia
Infra class: Eutheria
Order: Primates
Suborder: Anthropoidea
Super family: Hominoidea
Family: Hominidae
Genus: *Homo*
Species: *sapiens*

Figure 3.1 The place of humans in the biological taxonomy of living organisms.
(*Source:* Jurmain, Kilgore and Trevathan, 2005, pp. 109 and 150.)

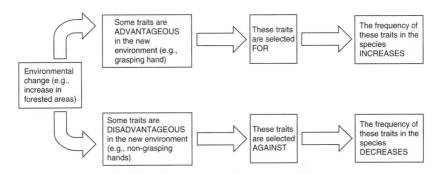

Figure 3.2 How natural selection works on traits. (*Source:* Wenda Trevathan, 2006.)

understand how they might have evolved through time and space. When we consider evolutionary changes, we understand that certain characteristics have adapted to specific environmental contingencies and, because they enhanced reproductive success, they survived in subsequent generations (see Figure 3.2). In this chapter, we are going to discuss aspects of our primate heritage that some researchers believe serve as models for early hominid[1] sexuality and that affect our modern human sexual behavior.

Nonhuman primate models are valuable in several ways. They help to show the continuities with other species of our order, and illustrate the high intelligence and sociability of primates. The models can serve as a reality marker to check our own biases and perspectives regarding dominance, division of labor, and sexuality. They provide evidence of the relationship of ecological variables such as food, shelter, and predators to social behavior and indicate the variety and flexibility of primate behavior and patterns of intra- and intergender and group cooperation and competition that may be evolutionarily deep-seated. Primate analogies may serve as models for reconstructing early hominid behavior. We need to be careful, however, not to take these analogies with our close primate relatives too far or they will defeat the purpose. We must remember that we have had our own line of evolution for five to eight million years and have adapted to almost every **econiche** on the planet. The development of our cerebral cortex allows for qualitatively different kinds of communications and social relations than other primates. These variables have worked to our advantage and disadvantage relative to the expression of our sexuality. Our complete dependence on language, sophisticated social systems, and complex technology make us very different animals from any others that live or have lived on our planet.

Because of their close immunological, genetic, and behavioral similarities to humans, the common chimpanzee *(Pan troglodytes)* and pygmy chimpanzee or bonobo *(Pan paniscus)* are frequently used as the most appropriate primate models for reconstructing the human past. We will follow that common practice by examining ways in which chimpanzee and human sexuality differ and are similar, and we will posit the evolutionary significance of the differences. But we need to start at the beginning. The fundamental aspects of our evolutionary history that affect our sexuality can be discussed under four topics:

1   adaptations first to arboreal and then to terrestrial environments, leading in humans to bipedalism,
2   increasing brain complexity, leading in humans to dependence on language, learning, and culture,
3   social organization, leading in humans to male-female pair bonds, sexual division of labor, and long infant and child dependence on family support,
4   sexual receptivity in females, leading in humans to the "loss of estrus" and sexuality unrelated to reproduction.

ARBOREAL AND TERRESTRIAL ADAPTATIONS

By the Eocene (54–38 million years ago), evidence of our first primate ancestors, the prosimians (sometimes referred to as strepsir-rhines), appeared. Profound changes were brought about by adapting to "life in the trees" also known as an **arboreal** niche. As a result of the arboreal adaptation, primates developed certain shared physical and behavioral features, primary among them the **grasping hand**, sensitive fingers and toes, as well as **stereoscopic vision**.[2] Hominid terrestrial adaptation is believed to have occurred around eight to five million years ago. This movement from the trees to the ground was affected in part by climatic changes as forests in Africa gave way to savannahs setting the scene for the development of bipedalism (walking on two legs). This freed the hands for carrying objects and manipulating them. It facilitated the primate trajectory of enhanced brain complexity, infant dependency, and reliance on learning, discussed later. It was not until about two million years ago that the brain enlarged significantly with the appearance of *Homo erectus*, an early human remarkably like modern people in appearance from the neck down.

The grasping hand, sensitive touching, and grooming

Primates have five digits on their hands and feet and most species are able to oppose the thumb and big toe to the other digits, enhancing the ability to grasp objects, including tree branches. When primate ancestors moved into an arboreal niche, the ability to grasp had obvious advantages so this trait was likely favorably selected and descendents of those early primates have grasping hands and feet (human feet are exceptions to this and reflect subsequent adaptation to bipedalism). Likewise, having sensitive pads on the fingers and toes was advantageous for moving in the trees and locating insects and ripe fruit, so today, touch is a very important sense for all primates. For humans the sense of touch is extremely important. In the course of hominid evolution, the loss of body hair probably enhanced touch as a means of assessing one's surroundings including the social milieu. It is linked with the unique development of primate forelimbs including the hands, precision gripping, tactile sensitivity, and manual motor skills.

Harlow and his colleagues demonstrated long ago that touch is more important to infant monkeys than food. Monkey infants who are deprived of touch do not develop normally physically or socially (Harlow, Harlow, and Hansen, 1963). Social touch, referred to as "grooming," is a distinguishing characteristic of primates that serves a number of functions including maintenance of social cohesion (Seyfarth, 1983), reduction of stress (de Waal, 1989; Goodall, 1986; Taylor et al., 2000), and hygiene. Given that our closest living relatives (monkeys and apes) spend 10–20 percent of the day involved in social grooming (Dunbar, 1996) and that human skin has a significant number of sensory receptors and nerve fibers (Greenspan and Bolanowski, 1996), we can infer that engaging in rewarding social touch was characteristic of human ancestors, and likely played an important role in sexual interaction. In human sexual activity, grooming is symbolically translated into stroking and patting and may also be found in a variety of cultural activities including cleansing of parasites, combing and arranging hair, and adorning one another's bodies with paints, feathers, and/or clothing. All of these involve the sensations of touch and sociality. Ford and Beach's (1951) *Patterns of Sexual Behavior,* a classic survey of the ethnographic literature on traditional peoples, reports that human grooming activities are frequently precursors to sexual relations and may be an integral part of foreplay in contemporary human cultures in which sex is treated in a positive manner. Whereas tactile contact between mother and infant and between sexual partners seems to be universally distributed in human cultures, other forms of social contact vary by gender, social class, and culture (Hall, 1966; Hall and Hall, 1990; McDaniel and Andersen, 1998; Montagu, 1978; Remland et al., 1995). In fact, touch between non-intimates or nonfamily members is often strictly regulated by cultural norms (see for example Hickson, Stacks and Moore, 2004).

While we have primate propensity for touch, rules, attitudes, and behaviors about touching and body space are culture-specific. For example, our culture has been described by some sexologists and sex therapists such as Domeena Renshaw, MD, as "touch deprived" (Renshaw, 1976). We have rather rigid rules about touching and body space and tend to confuse affection with sexual touching. Most dramatically, this can be illustrated by a middle class value on newborns, infants, and children "having their own room" and sleeping separately from their parents and siblings from birth. In contrast, in many traditional societies, women carry their infants with them while engaging in their daily activities and parents and children share a common sleeping space.

Vision and olfaction

In addition to the development of the grasping hand, our primate ancestors acquired highly developed visual cortices from their arboreal adaptation that remain with us today. Primate eyes are large, binocular, and stereoscopic and allow diurnal and color vision (Jurmain, Kilgore, and Trevathan, 2005). This represents a shift to vision from reliance on smell as a vehicle for information processing. Although smell (or **olfaction**) may still be important in sexual interaction (Pawlowski, 1999; Stoddard, 1990), visual cues provide much initial information about potential sexual partners for humans. Females in several primate species, including chimpanzees, have clear visual signals that they are in **estrus** (to be discussed later), that is, they are receptive to sexual advances from males. Their genital areas exhibit brightly hued purple swellings (see Figure 3.3) at the time of maximum likelihood of ovulation and this is when males are most interested in copulating with them.

Figure 3.3 East African baboon in estrus. (*Source:* Courtesy of shunya.net.)

(See color plates, between pp. 168–169)

Evolution of bipedalism

There is much debate among scholars of human evolution (known as paleoanthropologists) about the reasons that bipedalism evolved in our species, but, like most other evolutionary changes, there is little doubt that it was related to climate change. About seven million years ago, a drying trend in Africa resulted in a decrease in forested areas and an increase in woodlands and savannahs. At some point, human ancestors began spending more time in the savannahs and less time in the forests, although, like other terrestrial primates, they probably returned to the trees at night to sleep more safely. It was formerly hypothesized that movement into the savannahs preceded evolution of bipedalism, but recent evidence suggests that our ancestors became bipedal *before* they moved into the savannahs (Jurmain, Kilgore, and Trevathan, 2005). It is beyond the scope of this book to resolve the question of why humans became bipedal, but some hypotheses include that selection favored this form of locomotion because it enhanced the ability to see over tall grass, gather food, lower the costs of movement through greater energy efficiency, avoid predators, free the hands for carrying objects and babies, and for males to provision females and infants (Jurmain, Kilgore, and Trevathan, 2005). Suffice it to say that all of these behaviors are common in humans today because we are bipedal and this mode of locomotion is the hallmark of our species in the fossil record. In other words, if the fossil primate is bipedal, it is, by definition, hominid (Jurmain, Kilgore, and Trevathan, 2005). As we shall see, the subsequent evolution of the human brain is intimately linked with bipedalism, embellishing characteristics already developed in ancestral primates such as a large ratio of brain to body size. Bipedalism had a consequence for the evolution of the hand and manipulation of tools, the elaboration of the motor areas of the brain, as well as memory and thinking.

Bipedalism also had a profound impact on the evolution of human sexuality and reproduction. A number of skeletal and muscular changes accompanied upright posture. One of the major changes in anatomy that had an impact on hominid sexuality included a tilting forward of the pelvis; it became shortened and flared as well. The genitalia were moved forward and the female genitals became less exposed and more hidden than those of the male. Although we don't know if our human ancestors exhibited bright genital swelling when they were in estrus, these sexual swellings would have been difficult to see during bipedal walking and standing, so other ways of communicating sexual receptivity were developed. These were probably related to the expansion of communication skills in general, an essential component of culture.

With the shifting forward of the hominid female genitalia, face-to-face sex was a possibility and perhaps a probability. We are not necessarily referring here to the "missionary position" where males are on top, since this is not even the most preferred position cross-culturally. Face-to-face sex includes positions in which the female is on top of the male or side by side.

The position of the female genitalia in a more forward location certainly contributed to the human potential for a wide array of sexual positions.

Changes in the pelvis also affected childbirth by placing upper limits on the size of the birth canal (Trevathan, 1987). These limits, associated with increase in adult brain size in the last two million years of human evolution, have meant that the human infant is much less developed at birth than our closest primate relatives. In order for a species with such large heads to be born through a rather narrow birth passage, natural selection favored birth at an earlier stage of development before the brain had reached the size of most primate newborns. This meant that the human newborn was more helpless at birth and required much greater care from the parents, especially the mother. This also meant a longer period in which the infant was dependent on parental care, a period that became very important for learning.

EVOLUTION OF THE BRAIN

About two million years ago, the fossil record of humans shows evidence of increasing brain size. This is not to say that size alone indicates intelligence. We may assume that the small brains of the earliest hominids were also relatively complex ones. After all, chimpanzees are very intelligent creatures. The adaptive strategies utilized by the earliest hominids may have promoted a certain amount of cognitive complexity prior to the actual physical expansion of the brain. Generally, however, hominid trends indicate a correlation between increases in the size of the brain and complexity.

The early foraging strategies associated with an omnivorous diet (if it was smaller or less powerful than they were, they probably ate it) expedited the expansion of the brain complexity. In seeking food and carrying it someplace, the human capacity for evaluating circumstances and making decisions grew. To take something from one place to another requires brain power and the capacity for displacement—thinking about something that is not present in one's immediate environment. To make tools and baskets requires the articulation of cerebral centers with motor skills. The cognitive task of remembering locations of sites and sources for food, some of which were seasonal, also required a high level of cerebral functioning.

Throughout the course of hominid evolution, we can assume that humans continued a pattern of dependence on learning and hence culture as a primary means of survival. The size and complexity of the human brain reflect the increased reliance on learning as a means of adaptation. We adapt to our environment primarily through culture. Remember, culture is learned, shared, patterned behavior, including symbols and beliefs that are expressed between and within generations, individuals and groups. We need to interact with others of our own kind regularly in order to survive and be functional members of society. Like most primates, humans are known for their flexible behavioral patterns.

The development of a large and complex brain with elaborate centers that include memory, language, and symbolizing, to name just a few, is directly related to our sexuality. Human sexuality is experienced and mediated through a complex web of cerebral functioning that includes the capacity for elaborate fantasy, dreams, verbal and nonverbal thinking and images. Our human heritage as social beings facilitates how we communicate our sexuality, which is experienced as much in our "heads" as it is in our genitals. In addition, because we rely on learning for just about everything we do, sexual behavior, like other parts of our culture, is also learned. During our early lives, we learn how to experience our sexuality, including appropriate courtship behaviors, gender roles, and related norms and values. The biological capacity for sex is therefore intricately intertwined with a matrix of cultural constructions that shape our perceptions, experiences, and expressions of human sexuality.

EVOLUTION OF THE HUMAN FAMILY

As primates became bipedal, hands and arms could be used for carrying. With freed hands, early hominids could carry their babies and other objects. Based on contemporary gatherers and hunters, hominids probably used a strategy of carrying food back to some sort of base camp rather than just eating it on the spot, as most other primates do. Perhaps the females shared the food they collected with their infants and young children first and then with other kin and friendly unrelated males. The earliest stone tools appeared in association with evidence for an expanding brain. These were probably predated by tools and implements made of organic material that related to a food gathering strategy. Digging sticks and some sort of basket or net for carrying food items and babies could have been included. Unfortunately, we have no remains of these tools because they were made of organic materials that decompose rapidly.

Although most scenarios of human evolution put hunting by males as a central component, we posit that both males and females gathered plants and animal protein and used their expanding brains to hunt or chase small prey. Communal and group hunting by the Mbuti of the Ituri forest is well documented. There is ample evidence of women hunting small animals (Ehrenberg, 2005; Mascia-Lees and Black, 2000; O'Kelly and Carney, 1986: 12–21). Among the Agta of the Philippines, women hunt larger game including wild pigs and deer and participate in spear fishing as well (Estioko-Griffin, 1993: 225–232; Estioko-Griffin and Griffin, 2005: 141–150; Headland and Griffin, 2005). It is not necessary to propose that only men hunted unless the prey was some variety of large game.

But if we survey all known world cultures, we find that at least with large game hunting, the most common pattern is for men to be the hunters, even though women engage in smaller game or communal hunts.[3] Thus, we have a "why" question: "Why is big game hunted primarily by men?" The answer is related to the dangers inherent in hunting large animals and the impact of those dangers on **reproductive success**. Hunters can be wounded or killed in the hunt by either wayward spears in motion or the charges of a wounded animal. Also, big game hunting can involve exploring new frontiers—whose dangers, human or nonhuman, are unknown. Females who engaged in these relatively dangerous activities risked not only their own lives, but the lives of their fetuses, nursing infants, and dependent children. A related idea is that males are more expendable (it takes only one to contribute sperm) and therefore can "afford" to engage in more high-risk behaviors (Mukhopadhyay and Higgins, 1988). The costs of big game hunting to female reproductive success were usually greater than the potential benefits, whereas males, it is argued, stood to gain access to sexually receptive females via successful hunts and they were able to provide their mates and offspring with high quality animal protein. In most cases, the benefits of large game hunting to male reproductive success outweighed the costs.

Furthermore, both males and females have finite amounts of energy to expend and the costs of reproduction are much greater for females than for males (e.g., the costs of pregnancy and lactation are much higher than the costs of producing sperm). Thus, a female who puts her energy and efforts into bearing and raising healthy offspring will usually have more surviving offspring and, thus, greater reproductive success than one who puts her energy into hunting big game. An excellent example of this **division of labor** is seen in reports of hunting behaviors of the chimpanzees of the Gombe National Park in Tanzania (the community in which Jane Goodall conducted her famous studies). From 1982 to 1991, primatologists reported 195 kills of red colobus monkeys by seventeen members of the community (Stanford et al., 1994). Fifteen of the hunters were males and two were females, and, in fact, a female named Gigi was ranked ninth in the number of kills, ahead of seven and equal to one of the males. Doesn't this suggest that hunting by females may have been common in our ancestors? Perhaps, but the most interesting thing about Gigi is that she was apparently sterile and never had dependent young to care for. Thus, she was freed to engage in the relatively risky and energetically expensive endeavor of hunting without compromising her reproductive success any further than it was compromised already by her sterility. This suggests that females are mentally and physically quite capable of large animal hunting, but they rarely engage in the activity because of possible risks to their offspring. We would argue that similar conditions prevailed in our ancestors.

If ancestral women hunted small game and gathered other food resources, does this mean that they were much less dependent on men than men were on women for reproductive success in the past, and perhaps today, as well? Certainly males probably contributed by protecting the group; but is there any reason to believe that pair bonding beyond the period of sexual receptivity of the female was common in our ancestors? To explore this, we need to consider the helpless human infant that resulted from bipedalism and brain expansion. After impregnating a female, a male can either leave for another mating opportunity or can remain with the newly pregnant female and assist her in pregnancy and in raising the infant after it is born. If the male doesn't assist his mate in raising their children, her ability to have more than one dependent offspring at a time is severely constrained. If, however, the male stays and serves as caretaker for older children, she may be able to give birth every two to three rather than every four to five years, effectively doubling the number of children the pair can produce and successfully raise. Furthermore, if the male also provides some food resources to his family, in addition to those provided by the female, the entire family is more likely to survive, reproduce, and remain healthy. Infant mortality was probably much higher for the offspring of males who followed the "love 'em and leave 'em" strategy than for those who were provided paternal care. These are sometimes referred to as the "cad strategy" and the "dad strategy" (Cashdan, 1993), and the latter is believed to be related to higher reproductive success in ancestral and some contemporary human populations.

In some cases, having more than one "father" may be advantageous, however. A common response of female chimpanzees and langurs to infanticidal males is to "confuse paternity" by mating with several males during estrus (Hrdy, 1999). In some human cultures, this has been referred to as shared or "partible" paternity (Beckerman and Valentine, 2002), wherein more than one male assists in caring for children, particularly if it is possible that any of them could be the genetic father. In a few South American cultures where this concept exists (e.g., the Canela of Brazil), there is a belief that all men who have intercourse with a woman at the time she gets pregnant contribute to the makeup of the fetus. Ethnographic research among the Ache confirms that children with multiple fathers who provide them with care and resources are more likely to survive than children with single fathers; the optimum number of fathers appears to be two (Hurtado and Hill, 1996). As Helen Fisher (1992) has noted, adultery has probably always been an important reproductive strategy for women.

But do women in modern technologically advanced societies still need men to help with raising children? Despite recent reproductive technology, men still need women to impregnate, carry the fetus, give birth, and in many societies, breastfeed, to ensure the survival of the child. Now that we have technology to create babies, such as *in vitro* fertilization, chromosome selection, sperm banks and artificial insemination; technology for infant feeding, such as bottles and infant formula; and technology to secure our food and fight wars, there may well be a shift away from the need for women to act as primary child caretakers and from the two-parent family. How successful these new child-rearing strategies will be remains to be seen.

The development of lifelong social relationships or attachments is a hominid characteristic that reflects continuities from our nonhuman primate heritage (Hrdy, 1981; Hrdy, 1999; Jolly, 1985). We will review and illustrate the major forms of primate bonds or attachments as they relate to human sexuality. As stated, adult female-child bonds are probably one of the oldest, deepest, and most primal forms known. Female-child bonds are supported by female-female bonds which can be either cooperative or competitive. Cooperative female-female bonds are generally kin-based or take on kin terminology if *not* of biological (**consanquineal**) or marital (**affinal**) relations. These nonkin relations are called **fictive kin** and can be exemplified by relationships such as sorority "sisters" or by phrases such as "she is like a sister to me." Cooperative female-female bonds provide psycho-emotional support (Taylor et al., 2000), and socialize females into "female" behavior. Competitive female-female bonds in both the human and nonhuman primate worlds generally are adversarial over males. In humans this can be expressed by jealousy among co-wives in **polygynous** societies where men have more than one wife; or current U.S. culture wherein one female pursues another female's man, i.e., the "other" woman (Brown and Kerns, 1985; Fernea, 1965; Kilbride, 2005; Ward and Edelstein, 2006: 54–55).

Female-male bonds may also be cooperative or competitive. Cooperative female-male bonds tend to be nonsexual and take on familial characteristics—siblings or fictive sibling relations—"He is like a brother to me." They can provide a great deal of socio-emotional support, protection, and friendship. In **matrilineal** societies where descent is through the female line and a woman's brother often fills the social role of "father" to his sister's children, brothers and sisters have a lifelong supportive relationship that can supersede their marital relationships (Robbins, 2006: 172–173, and classic work of Kluckhohn and Leighton, 1962). Competitive male-female bonds often are sexual and revolve around issues of trust, intimacy, and sexual exclusivity. Concern over adult male-female relations is culturally widespread. In much of the world, adult male-female contacts outside the kin group are carefully circumscribed due to the belief that leaving unsupervised adult men and women together would "naturally" lead to sex (Faust, 1988; Fernea, 1965; Kilmartin, 2000: 269–270; Mernissi, 1975; Schlegel, 1977; Whelehan's field notes).

A whole "cottage industry" has developed around exploring factors that affect male-female mate choice in humans. Based on predictions derived from evolutionary theory, one idea is that men tend to be attracted to more youthful and attractive women because younger women have a greater number of years ahead of them to reproduce, whereas women tend to be attracted to men with more resources (who often, but not always, tend to be older) who can share those resources with her (their) children. Evolutionary psychologists have examined concepts of beauty to reveal that in many cases, the most attractive face or body shape is the most symmetrical (Singh, 1993; Thornhill and Gangestad, 1994). It appears that symmetry is related to health, meaning that the more symmetrical face or body is healthier and likely has the "best genes" (Hamilton and Zuk, 1982). In support of these predictions, David Buss (1989), who surveyed more than 10,000 people in thirty-three different countries, found that, consistently, women rated "good financial prospect" as more important in a mate than men did and that men rated "good looking" higher than women did. Of course, all we have to do is look around us and we will see many examples of mate choices that deviate from these predictions. Certainly there is great individual variation in what each of us finds attractive in our mates, but when we survey thousands of people, as evolutionary psychologists tend to do, we find that the predictions hold up more often than not.

Adult male-child bonds generally occur between males and those children the men believe to be their offspring. In **patrilineal** societies where descent passes through the male, and **bilineal** or **bilateral descent** societies where descent passes through both males and females but paternity is necessary for a child's place in the kinship system, knowing the biological father of the child is important. This knowledge is culturally secured by creating sexual double standards for males and females and placing female sexual behavior under restriction to ensure **paternity**, i.e., known fatherhood. Examples range from calling a female, in U.S. society, who has a number of sexual partners a "slut" or "whore" to "madonna-whore;" whereas in many agricultural societies where a woman is seen as virtuous as a sister and mother (i.e., nonsexual) and a whore as a wife where her sexuality is expected and obvious, to *"machismo/marianisma"* complexes of Latino cultures that emphasize male sexual prowess and female faithfulness among other characteristics.

Analogous to female-female bonds, male-male bonds can be both competitive and cooperative. Competitive male-male bonds in the human and nonhuman primate worlds center on dominance—status, power, position in a hierarchy—and sexual access to females. This is exemplified in human cultures by ongoing warfare found in **horticultural** societies (a form of farming discussed in Chapter 9). In these societies all resources—land, water, food, women—are in scarce supply. Ongoing warfare serves to forge political alliances and is a source of women. Wives are found among the warring factions and foster alliances between different groups. In U.S. society, male-male competition can be found in amateur and professional sports as well as for positions in the labor force. Competition for women is well known. In U.S. culture, males use their power, status, and economic success to attract women (Farrell, 1974, 1986; Goldberg, 1976, 1979, 1980; Kilmartin, 2000; Zilbergeld, 1978, 1992). Cooperative male bonds, exemplified by fraternities, men's groups, and men's houses in horticultural societies provide a sense of male solidarity and support, often to the exclusion and derogation of females (Buckley and Gottlieb, 1988; Murphy and Murphy, 1974; Robbins, 2006; Sanday, 1990).

FEMALE SEXUALITY

Anthropologists are often interested in finding characteristics that are unique for humans or at least clearly differentiate humans from other animals. Habitual bipedalism is a characteristic that is commonly cited as distinguishing humans from all other mammals, as is the dependence on language and culture. Additionally, aspects of sexuality, particularly female sexuality, are often presented as "uniquenesses" for humans. These include nonreproductive and nonovulatory sexual activity (sometimes referred to as "loss of estrus"), concealed ovulation, the common occurrence of orgasm in women, and, as previously discussed, pair bonding and paternal care. There is much debate about whether or not these characteristics are truly unique, but we can at least say that most are more common in humans than in any other primate species.

We begin with a discussion of the fact that human females engage in a great deal of sexual behavior that is unrelated to reproduction. As noted, most other mammalian females seek or allow copulation only when they are likely to conceive, i.e., when they are in estrus. At the time of maximal likelihood of conception, female mammals exhibit physical signs (e.g., the red swollen perineal area of baboons and chimpanzees; Figure 3.3), chemical signals known as **pheromones,** and behaviors indicative of willingness to be inseminated, so it is clear to potential partners (and probably to themselves) that they are capable of becoming pregnant. Beach (1976) proposed three terms to describe aspects of female sexual behavior: **receptivity** (willingness to be mated), **attractivity** (males are interested in mating with them,) and **proceptivity** (actively seeking a mating opportunity). For most primates, these three behaviors coincide at the time of ovulation and are rarely exhibited at other times. For humans, however, receptivity, attractivity, and proceptivity are largely independent of the ovarian cycle, although there is some evidence that women may be slightly more attractive to men when they are ovulating (Tarín and Gómez-Piquer, 2002) and female libido (proceptivity) may rise slightly at the time of ovulation (Burleson et al., 2002). Furthermore, women well past the time in which they can reproduce (i.e., post menopause) often show no sign of diminished interest in sex or diminished attractiveness, and indeed, their interest in sex may rise in the first few years after menopause when the likelihood of becoming pregnant is no longer a risk.

Concealed ovulation

Related to the loss of estrus is a phenomenon known as "concealed ovulation" meaning that most women and their partners are unaware when they ovulate, unless they are taking extraordinary measures to track their basal body temperature (BBT) or cervical mucus. When we consider how obvious it is when a female baboon or chimpanzee is in estrus, it is surprising that humans are so unaware of when they are likely to conceive. Thus, we have another "why" question to pursue from an evolutionary perspective. Not surprisingly, there are dozens of ideas for why human females lost estrus and concealed ovulation.

One scenario that has been around for a long time and fit former stereotypes about gender roles exemplifies exchange theory in which ancestral males traded meat for sex with females (Fisher, 1983; Symons, 1979). This has been observed in some chimpanzee groups (Goodall, 1986), but it is usually associated with females in estrus, that is those who are sexually receptive to the males. If females exhibit signs of sexual receptivity and are willing to engage in sexual activity at times other than when they are ovulating, they may receive more meat from the males. Eventually, according to this "meat for sex" scenario, sexual receptivity would become "decoupled" from ovulation and estrus behavior (sexual receptivity) would be "continuous." Females and their offspring would benefit from additional protein by this economic exchange for sex. But because males would be more likely to provide food for offspring that they have some confidence are theirs ("**paternity certainty**"), they would need to remain in proximity to the female they are provisioning to ensure that they are not **cuckolded**. Accordingly, marriage and the family developed from the situation of exchange (Symons, 1979).

Another scenario proposes that by concealing ovulation, an ancestral female could solicit sex from several males so that no one, not even the female herself, could be sure who the father of her offspring was (Hrdy, 1981). As noted, this confusion over paternity ("paternity uncertainty") enabled females to secure resources from a number of males, and, perhaps more importantly, minimized the likelihood of infanticide inflicted by males on young that they were certain were *not* their biological offspring. According to Symons (1979: 141), "By hiding ovulation, females may have minimized their husbands' abilities to monitor and to sequester them, and maximized their own abilities to be fertilized by males other than their husbands" (modified from Burley, 1979).

Yet another scenario for concealed ovulation relates it to population increase in the human species. In this view, ovulation was concealed not only from males, but from the females themselves, so that they were not able to control their fertility to the same extent that they could if ovulation were associated with obvious physical signs. Burley (1979) argues that the fear of childbirth would have led ancestral females to avoid copulation at times they were most likely to conceive so they would have had fewer offspring in their lifetimes. Females who were not aware of when they were ovulating could not exercise this degree of control over their fertility and would have had more offspring to pass along the characteristic of concealed ovulation so that today, it is true for all humans. This scenario invites a play on the paraphrase from the Bible: "Blessed are those who don't know when they are ovulating for their daughters shall inherit the earth."

The orgasm in evolutionary perspective

We would like to turn now specifically to the issue of the evolution of orgasm, and the significance of **orgasm** for reproductive success. The traditional theoretical stance is that it is not necessary for women to have an orgasm to become pregnant, but for males the contractions that expel the ejaculate into the vagina are usually associated with orgasm and seem more central (although not necessary) to the process of reproduction. The view that female orgasm is not necessary for reproductive success fuels a major controversy surrounding the role of the female orgasm in evolution. Furthermore, whereas orgasm in females may not be unique to humans, there is no evidence that it is routine or common in other primates. This leads to another obvious "why" question.

Two of the central figures in this debate were Elizabeth Sherfey and Donald Symons; today, the major players are Elizabeth Lloyd and David Barash. After analyzing evidence about female sexuality presented by Freud, as well as that from the nonhuman primate record, Sherfey, in her book *The Nature and Evolution of Female Sexuality* (1972), proposed that female nonhuman primates showed an "extraordinarily intense, aggressive sexual behavior and an inordinate orgasm capacity" that is inherent in human females but that is shaped and suppressed by culture (Sherfey, 1972, 52). At the time, this view was indeed a subversive one. It challenged western notions of a passive female sexuality, but Sherfey attempted to show that female orgasm was closely linked with reproductive success. For example, she hypothesized that pregnancy facilitated orgasmic response by enhancing the capacity for vaso-congestion and strengthening the uterus during orgasmic contractions.

Symons, in *The Evolution of Human Sexuality* (1979: 90–95), took issue with Sherfey and felt that the insatiability of females would actually be a deterrent to reproductive success. In his argument, an insatiable sexuality was more likely to detract from child rearing and subsistence activities. In Symon's scenarios, females who mated too promiscuously would actually decrease the likelihood of choice in selecting the father of their child through sheer volume of mates. According to Symon's "[t]he sexually insatiable woman is to be found primarily, if not exclusively, in the ideology of feminism, the hopes of boys and the fears of men" (1979: 92). For Symons, female orgasm is a by-product of the male orgasm.

Symons' perspective reflects western concepts of the passive female and overlooks the evidence of actual female sexual functioning, such as the capacity for multiple orgasms in women. Orgasm in human females is more probably an extension of the pleasurable sensations associated with coitus in primate females generally. Citing the role of oxytocin in both orgasm and nursing, Hrdy (1999) suggests that the pleasant feelings women experience with orgasm may be a heritage from the obvious selective value of pleasurable nursing of infants. Certainly it seems that the pleasure of orgasm is a powerful motivation for sexual behaviors. Without estrus marking visible fertility, increasing the sheer quantity of sex in humans is an ideal strategy for offsetting the ambiguity of concealed ovulation. That it feels good is a crucial element in the motivations of individuals, be they males or females. We learn how to have an orgasm; it feels good and we repeat the behavior. Consistent with our goal of examining behaviors through multiple levels of explanation, a pleasurable orgasm may be the proximate reward for engaging in sexual activity that occasionally leads to the ultimate goal of reproduction. Furthermore, recent research suggests that the pleasure a woman derives from partnered orgasm carries over into the following day by enhancing positive and decreasing negative mood (Burleson et al., in press). It seems reasonable to argue that overall good feelings relate to more positive relations with partners and offspring.

In a recent book, *The Case of the Female Orgasm* (2005), Lloyd reviews twenty-one theories that have been offered to explain its existence and argues that they all suffer from one of two biases: the **adaptationist** bias of seeing it as enhancing reproductive success and the **androcentric** bias of assuming that male and female sexuality are the same or similar. She attempts to remove the female orgasm from its effect on reproductive success and agrees with Symons that it is a by-product of selection for the male orgasm (similar to male nipples being a by-product of selection for female nipples) and has no "function" in itself. Further, she argues that focusing on the reproductive role of the female orgasm privileges heterosexuality and women as reproducers. David Barash (2005) has severely criticized Lloyd's book and is working on a book of his own offering support for the proposal that the female orgasm has direct benefits to reproductive success. Clearly, the debate and discussion of this most interesting phenomenon will not end soon.

HUMAN EVOLUTION: A SYNTHESIS

With the loss of estrus and the accompanying visible genital and chemical cueing came the capacity for sexual communication through other (nonverbal and verbal) means. Changes in human ovulation and sexuality are related to the increased reproductive success of humans. In this way we can clearly see the biological basis for the unique trajectory of human sexuality. It is rooted in principles of selection and adaptation, and the ultimate goal of successful reproduction. These evolutionary factors should not be confused with the immediate cultural factors influencing an individual's sexuality within specific cultural contexts, the proximate and ontogenetic factors. The reproductive capacity of human females exceeds that of our closest relatives. The human female has a longer reproductive life and a lower birth interval than the chimpanzee or gorilla and has the potential (without contraception and extensive breastfeeding) of producing twice as many offspring in her life.

In addition, reproductive success depends on the ability to care for offspring. An important part of our success as a species has been our ability not just to bear more young, but to raise them to reproductive age. Here success in individual terms is aided by survival and success of important social units such as the family and community ("It takes a village to raise a child," Hillary Clinton, 1996). We have argued that early hominid groups may have been matricentered or female centered and based on the original family unit of mother and infant, but increasing demands of raising more helpless infants led to the expansion of this social unit to include fathers, adult male kin, and unrelated friendly males.

It is not possible to place with certainty the exact time when early hominid females lost estrus, developed concealed ovulation, and when fathers began to contribute more than sperm to their offspring. These factors could well have been related to changes in human populations associated with *Homo erectus* around a million-and-one-half to perhaps even two million years ago. Naturally this has some implications that are of keen interest. Without estrus as a signal, humans have developed through culture an incredible array of ways of communicating sexual interest to one another—visually, verbally, and nonverbally. As we shall see as we focus on sex and reproduction through the life cycle, culture plays a significant role in shaping modern reproduction and sexuality.

SUMMARY

1   The grasping hand, stereoscopic vision, and grooming are adaptations related to primate arboreal and subsequent terrestrial environments.
2   These adaptations have consequences for modern sexual behavior including the importance of touch, feeling, and vision as important components in sexual attraction.
3   Bipedalism played a critical role in enhancing trajectories begun in association with adaptation to an arboreal niche. With bipedalism, probably, began trends for the loss of estrus and escalated reliance on communication and learning. Bipedalism and the consequent enlargement and development of complexity in the hominid brain were involved in the evolutionary tradeoff that selected for infant dependency.
4   Human reliance on learning is a significant aspect of our sexuality associated with the expansion of the neocortex.
5   For humans the social group is vital for survival.
6   As a continuation of nonhuman primate behavior, humans form a variety of socio-emotional ties with one another known as bonds; one of the most basic is adult female-child. Male-male, male-female, and female-female bonds can be both cooperative and competitive. Both social and biological fatherhood are important in most human societies.

7   The human brain is actively involved in human maturation, reproduction, and sexuality.

8   The loss of estrus for humans enhanced their reproductive success in comparison with other primates, in part through its effect on paternity.

9   There are several controversial views on the role of orgasm for female evolution. Orgasm is important as a reinforcing mechanism because it is pleasurable. This is critical in a species without estrus. Human females are unusual in being able to be sexually receptive throughout their cycle. With humans, because ovulation was concealed, sheer amount of copulation would enhance the chance for impregnation. Orgasm is important in facilitating this.

Thought-provoking questions

1   Some people have suggested that the "touch deprived" nature of contemporary American society may explain some inabilities to form healthy social bonds (e.g., parent-child, male-female). Do you agree? If you agree, what do you think can be done about it?

2   In what ways would a strong and healthy young woman with a nursing infant and a four-year-old child compromise her own reproductive success by engaging in hunting large game? Would the compromises be the same for her mate and father of her children to engage in this same type of hunting?

3   Why would males in dozens of societies rank female attractiveness higher than wealth and women rank the two qualities in reverse order? What do these preferences have to do with reproductive success?

SUGGESTED RESOURCES

Books

Buss, David M. 1994. *The Evolution of Desire: Strategies of Human Mating.* New York: Basic Books.

Ellison, Peter T. 2001. *On Fertile Ground: A Natural History of Human Reproduction.* Cambridge: Harvard University Press.

Hrdy, Sarah Blaffer. 1999. *Mother Nature: A History of Mothers, Infants, and Natural Selection.* New York: Pantheon Books.

Small, Meredith. 1998. *Our Babies, Ourselves. How Biology and Culture Shape the Way We Parent.* New York: Anchor Books.

Web sites

American Association of Physical Anthropologists (http://www.physanth.org/)
American Society of Primatologists (http://www.asp.org/)
Human Behavior and Evolution Society (http://www.hbes.com/)
Human Biology Association (http://www.humbio.org/)

4 Introduction to the hormonal basis of modern human sexuality

An evolutionary, interspecies perspective for our **hominid** sexuality has been presented in Chapter 3. This perspective establishes the roots for our bio-behavioral sexuality as modern humans by connecting us as a species to our primate heritage through time and space. This connection has been illustrated in discussions of the shift from **estrus** to a **menstrual cycle**, and the role of such intra-and inter-species behaviors as **bonding** and **orgasm**. Modern adult sexual and reproductive anatomy and physiology, which emphasize hormones, are introduced in this chapter and discussed in more depth in Chapters 5 and 6. This discussion of hormones also serves as an introduction to exploring male and female anatomy. Normative physiology and anatomy are assumed unless specifically stated otherwise.

A basic awareness of anatomy and physiology is important for the following reasons. First, our modern anatomy and physiology are panhuman, providing a baseline for understanding human sexuality as a bio-behavioral, psycho-cultural, and social phenomenon. Since we share anatomy and physiology as a species, we are able to engage in intra- and intergroup sexual and reproductive experiences. Second, while the biological aspects such as **gamete**—the egg or sperm—production are specieswide, their definition and interpretation are culture specific. Different cultures give different meanings to the reproductive and sexual processes. The behaviors, sentiments, and values attributed to our anatomy and its functions are culturally defined. For example, female breast development is a universal secondary sex characteristic. In current U.S. culture, it is an erotic symbol or sex signal. In many nonindustrialized societies, breasts are not eroticized but are seen as functional structures for nursing the young. This is obvious when one examines rules about breast coverage cross-culturally. In most places in the United States, it is illegal for a woman (but not a man) to bare her breasts in public due to the sexual connotations. In tropical areas cross-culturally, women frequently do not cover their breasts while their genitals, in contrast, are covered. Previous generations of adolescents in the United States have pored over *National Geographic* pictorials of bare-breasted, indigenous women. The ethnocentrism behind this phenomenon is another issue altogether.

On June 1, 1994, New York State passed legislation that allowed women to breastfeed their babies legally in public places such as malls, restaurants, and stores. Women may also appear bare-breasted on public beaches in New York. However, the legality of breastfeeding in public or appearing topless on public beaches if you are a woman is state specific. The suggested resources for students at the end of this chapter provide website addresses if you are interested in learning about the laws concerning these issues in your state.

We allow men to go topless in public due to an androcentric, heterosexist cultural perspective in which we do not see men's breasts, areolas, and nipples as erotic.

Another important reason for having an elementary understanding of anatomy and physiology is that many bio-behavioral aspects of our sexuality build on having a basic knowledge of our bodies. This includes such components of our sexuality as sexual response and birth control, as well as the life cycle phenomena of pregnancy and childbirth. In addition, it is pertinent to have at least a fundamental awareness of human anatomy and physiology in order to comprehend how recent technological innovations that affect sexuality and reproduction have impacted us as both individuals, members of a group, and as a species. Innovations such as penile implants, Viagra, and other erection-stimulating drugs, prostheses to alleviate some physiologically based erectile problems, *in vitro* fertilization (IVF), gamete/zygote/embryo transplants, gender selection, and sperm banks all have the potential to alter radically what has evolved as human sexuality (see Chapter 7).

DEFINITIONS OF AUXILIARY TERMS AND CONCEPTS

The following terms are essential to understanding sexual and reproductive functioning. You will find this list of terms useful for reference as you read about male and female anatomy and physiology. (See Figure 4.1.)

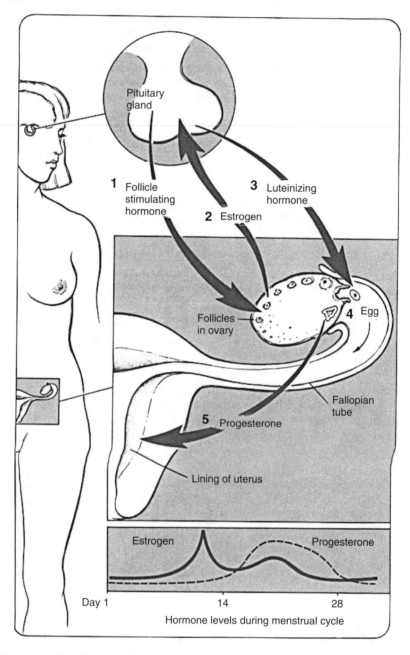

Figure 4.1 Female ovary. (*Source*: Dr. Susan Love, with Karen Lindsey. *Dr. Susan Love's Breast Book* by Susan Love. Reprinted by permission of DA CAPO PRESS, a member of Perseus Group.)

adrenal glands: Two small glands, located on top of each kidney. They are responsible for much of the other gender sex hormone production in males and females (testosterone in females; estrogen and progesterone in males).

analogous: Describing structures that share a similar function, such as the ovaries and testes in gamete (sperm and egg) production.

anatomy: Refers to a specific body part or structure.

androgens: The collective term given male sex hormones, of which testosterone plays a major role in sexual and reproductive development and functioning.

cerebral cortex (CC): The outer layer of the brain characteristic of humans and hominids, involved in perception, analytic and logical thought, and learning.

endocrine glands: These glands directly release hormones into the blood stream. Sex hormones are released by endocrine glands.

estrogen: The term given to a group of "female" sex hormones found in postpubertal males and females. It is largely responsible for primary and secondary sex characteristic development in girls.

gonadotropins: Sex hormones. The generic term given to those hormones involved in primary and secondary sex characteristic development and functioning.

gonads: Ovaries in the female, testes in the male. The gonads comprise one-third of the H-P-G axis. They are the primary source of estrogen and progesterone production in females, and testosterone in males.

homologous: Structures formed from similar embryonic tissue, such as the ovaries and testes or the clitoris and penis.

H-P-G axis: Hypothalamus-pituitary-gonad axis which monitors much of the biochemical aspects of human sexuality.

hormones: Substances released by the endocrine (ductless) glands that affect anatomical development and functioning.

hypothalamus: An evolutionarily old brain structure found in many species including humans, which monitors a variety of body functions.

physiology: The function of an organ or body structure.

pituitary (master gland): An organ in the brain which, as one of its functions, releases hormones necessary for sperm formation and egg development.

primary sex characteristics: Those structures in both the males and females related to the reproductive cycle (Frayser, 1985) and directly involved in sexual and reproductive functioning (e.g., testes and ovaries). Their role in sexual arousal, pleasure, and orgasm is an interaction of anatomical and socio-cultural influences, e.g., the penis is a sexual and reproductive structure. The uterus is a reproductive organ that can also be sexual for women who experience uterine contractions during orgasm.

progesterone: A "female sex hormone" found in postpubertal females and males. It is responsible for the development of certain primary sex characteristics in the female such as uterine tone and the maintenance of the endometrium (the uterine lining). In males, progesterone is involved in sperm motility, i.e., how fast the sperm move.

secondary sex characteristics: These structures in both the male and female are indirectly involved in sexual and reproductive functioning, but are frequently used as cultural markers of physiological sexual maturity and gender signals (e.g., pubic hair in boys and girls, female breast development, facial hair and beard growth in the male). These structures often correlate with the sexual cycle (Frayser, 1985), and can comprise visual cues of sexual attraction and arousal.

testosterone: Considered the "male sex hormone," it is found in postpubertal males and females. Testosterone is primarily responsible for the **libido** or innate sex drive in people, and primary and secondary sex characteristic development in the male.

Sexual/reproductive structure distinction

A given structure may serve **sexual** and/or **reproductive functions**. The **vagina** and **penis** are examples of organs which function both sexually and reproductively. **Sexual structures** are involved directly or indirectly in sexual response, without necessarily having to serve reproductively as well (e.g., **clitoris**). **Reproductive structures** are directly or indirectly involved in reproduction (e.g., the **vas deferens**).

Sexual and reproductive structures correlate with the **sexual** and **reproductive cycles** as proposed by Frayser (1985). These phenomena can be

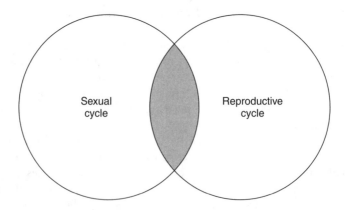

Figure 4.2 Venn diagram: sexual cycle/reproductive cycle. (*Source*: Anne Bolin with Elon University Department of Instructional and Campus Technologues.)

presented diagrammatically as shown in Figure 4.2. The sexual cycle relates to human sexual response, attractiveness, and sexual orientation. The reproductive cycle refers to puberty, fertility, conception, pregnancy, birth, lactation, and menopause. There is overlap in sexual and reproductive cycles and structures. For example, the penis and vagina are both sexual and reproductive structures; penile-vaginal (p-v) intercourse has both sexual and reproductive functions.

Much of our sexual and reproductive anatomy is analogous and homologous. On a hormonal, physiological, and anatomical level, men and women are more similar than different. For example, the gonadotropins, which are the male and female sex hormones, are found in both postpubertal men and women. Tables 4.1 and 4.2 respectively list analogous and homologous structures and hormones with their functions.

The following formula represents the biochemical basis of human sexuality:

CC + (H-P-G axis) = biochemistry of sexuality

CC = cerebral cortex
H = hypothalamus
P = pituitary
G = gonads

Table 4.1 Comparative anatomy

Male	Female	Homologous	Analogous	Function
Penis	Clitoris	X		Sexual pleasure in both. Transport of urine and ejaculate in the male.
Testes	Ovaries	X	X	Primary source of same sex gonadotropins. Responsible for production of sperm in male, maturation and release of eggs in female as well as primary source of estrogen and progesterone in the female.
Vas deferens	Fallopian tubes	X	X	Transport of sperm in male, of the egg in female. Site of fertilization (conception) in female.

Table 4.1 (Continued)

Male	Female	Homologous	Analogous	Function
Scrotum (scrotal sac)	Labia majora	X		Holds the testes and spermatic cord in the male. Covered with pubic hair and sexually sensitive in both male and female.
Penile skin (foreskin)	Labia minora, prepuce or clitoral hood at juncture with mons	X	X	Sexual pleasure. Covers glans of penis, clitoris in male and female.
Glans penis	Glans clitoris	X		Sexual pleasure in both. Site of urinary meatus in male.
Penile shaft	Clitoral shaft	X		Sexual pleasure in both. Contains internal reproductive/sexual structures in male.
Urethra	Urethra	X		Transports urine in both males and females. Transports ejaculate in male.
Cowper's gland	Bartholin's gland	X		Lubricates urethra and neutralizes urethral acidity in male. Function in female currently not well understood.

Although the cerebral cortex can dominate the functioning of the H-P-G axis (e.g., perceived unresolved stress can effect the menstrual cycle), for this discussion we are going to examine the H-P-G axis as it usually works. The H-P-G axis operates as a **negative feedback cycle**, similar to a thermostat, where fluctuations in one part of the axis induce hormone releases in other parts of the axis. Although the hypothalamus and pituitary monitor a number of body functions, we will focus on their role in sexual and reproductive processes (see Figures 4.3 and 4.4).

The hypothalamus, located in the parietal or side area of the brain, releases a hormone, **GnRH (gonadotropic releasing hormone)**, which triggers the functioning of the pituitary. In humans, the hypothalamus monitors the onset of **puberty** in both genders (puberty is also related to cultural, nutritional, and exercise practices as will be discussed in later chapters). The hypothalamus also controls the release of **pheromones**, i.e., sexual scent cues; the release of **follicular stimulating hormone (FSH)**, **luteinizing**

Table 4.2 Hormones involved in H-P-G axis functioning

Hormone	Comparative function: male	Primary release: male	Comparative function: female	Primary release: female	Source
Follicular stimulating hormone (FSH)	Stimulates spermatogenesis	Pituitary	Egg maturation, includes estradiol (an estrogen)	Pituitary	GnRH stimulation from hypothalamus
Luteinizing hormone (LH)—interstitial cell stimulating hormone (ICSH) in male	Maintains interstitial cells of testes	Pituitary	Stops egg maturation, releases mature egg from ovary, induces release of androgens at ovulation	Pituitary	GnRH stimulation from hypothalamus
Luteotropic hormone (LTH) (prolactin)	Unknown at present; may be involved in sperm and testosterone production	Pituitary	Uterine tone, stimulates lactation, promotes production of progesterone	Pituitary	GnRH stimulation from hypothalamus
Testosterone	Primary and secondary sex characteristics, libido	Testes	Libido, complement to female primary and secondary sex characteristics	Adrenal glands and ovaries	LH stimulation in pituitary
Estrogen	Skin tone, reduces osteoporosis risk, complement to primary and secondary sex characteristics	Adrenal glands	Primary and secondary sex characteristics, e.g., menstrual cycle	Ovaries	FSH stimulation in pituitary
Progesterone	Possibly anti-aggressor agent.	Adrenal glands	Primary sex characteristics	Ovaries	LH stimulation in pituitary

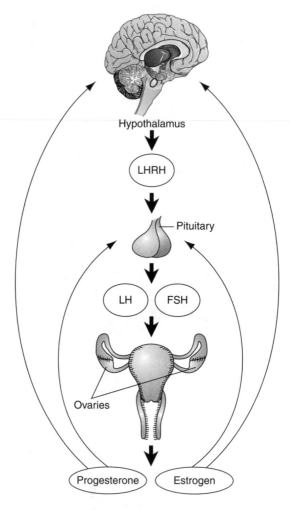

Figure 4.3 H-P-G axis graphics for female. (*Source*: Emanuele, Wizeman, and Emanuele, 1999.)

hormone (**LH**), and **luteotropic hormone** (**LTH**); and affects **erogenous zone sensitivity**, those parts of the body which produce sexual arousal when stimulated. It also is part of the limbic system of the brain which influences our emotions.

The pituitary or master gland monitors a number of body functions. Relative to male and female sexuality, the pituitary gland releases FSH (follicular stimulating hormone), LH (luteinizing hormone), and LTH (luteotropic hormone or **prolactin**), to stimulate the testes in males, and the ovaries in females. While males and females produce both their

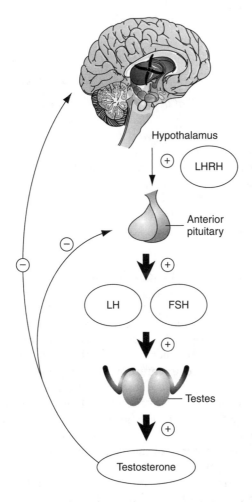

Figure 4.4 H-P-G axis graphics for male. (*Source*: Emanuele, Wizeman, and Emanuele, 1999.)

own and other gender gonadotropins, progesterone and estrogen are categorized as female sex hormones and testosterone is the male sex hormone.

In examining the functioning of the H-P-G axis specifically, concepts of **tonicity** and **cyclicity** are used. **Tonic**, which refers to male H-P-G axis functioning, is the ongoing nature of male hormone production and release. Ramey (1973) and others clearly document the cyclic nature of testosterone over a twenty-four-hour period by noting that testosterone levels in males generally are highest in the morning. These data do not, however, contradict the general belief that men, relative to women, experience tonic patterns of testosterone release. These male patterns are ongoing and continuous from puberty until death, although there is a gradual decrease in testosterone production in aging men.

Some researchers believe that in the course of one generation, United States men may produce as much as 50 percent less semen and sperm (ejaculate) than in 1950. Environmental pollutants are seen as the possible cause for this decrease (Glenmullen, 1993: 170). Environmental pollutants are also believed to affect the quality of both sperm and ejaculate (Aitken and Graves, 2002; Aitken, Koopman, and Lewis, 2004). Defects in sperm can effect fertility and/or increase the chances of fetal chromosomal abnormalities (Thacker, 2004).

In contrast, hormone release patterns in women are described as more cyclic, following a rhythmic flow which approximates a twenty-eight-day or lunar cycle. There is, however, variation in this pattern from individual to individual and within a woman's cycle. For example, very few women have menstrual cycles that are consistently the same length each month. This makes birth control options such as the **rhythm method, cervical mucous checks,** and **basal body temperature** monitoring less reliable than many other options. (See Chapter 12 for a discussion of contraception.) The female cycle is defined as a negative feedback loop, in which fluctuations in one part of the H-P-G axis influence hormone release in another part of the axis. For example, a drop in the pituitary-based FSH level in the follicular phase (described in Chapter 6) of the menstrual cycle triggers the release of **estradiol,** an estrogen, from the ovary.

When discussing the release of hormones in the H-P-G axis, particularly those released by the gonads (ovaries and testes), and the adrenals, we are referring to endocrine gland functioning. Endocrine glands are ductless, which means that hormones are released directly into the bloodstream and can be measured through tests on blood samples. Excess amounts of endocrine hormones are deposited in the urine. Therefore, excess amounts of androgens, male sex hormones, which are part of the steroids (a group of sex and other hormones) that some male and female athletes use to rapidly increase muscle size and strength, can be detected in the urine.

The hormones involved in H-P-G axis functioning that we will discuss include the pituitary hormones FSH, LH or **ICSH (interstitial cell stimulating hormone**), and LTH (prolactin), and the gonadotropins—androgens commonly referred to as male sex hormones, as well as estrogen and progesterone, frequently referred to as female sex hormones. (See Table 4.2.)

The hypothalamic hormone GnRH (gonadotropin releasing hormone) stimulates the frontal lobe of the pituitary to release FSH, LH or ICSH, and LTH in both males and females. FSH, follicular stimulating hormone, is released in the **follicular phase** of the menstrual cycle during which time immature eggs develop in their ovarian follicles or sacs. This is discussed in depth in Chapter 6. In men, FSH stimulates **spermatogenesis** or sperm formation in the **seminiferous tubules** of the **testicles**.

LH stands for luteinizing hormone. It is the same hormone as ICSH or interstitial cell stimulating hormone. LH functions in both the follicular and **luteal phases** of the menstrual cycle which will be discussed in depth in Chapter 6. In the follicular phase, LH serves to stop egg maturation and helps to release the mature egg from the ovary through triggering androsterone, a male sex hormone. In the luteal phase, LH stimulates the release of progesterone from the **follicle** or sac that released the mature egg.

In men, luteinizing hormone (LH) is also referred to as ICSH or interstitial cell stimulating hormone. ICSH maintains the cells of the testes which produce testosterone, the primary male sex hormone. These interstitial or **leydig cells** are necessary for testosterone production which is responsible for primary and secondary sex characteristic development in males as discussed in Chapter 5.

LTH or luteotropic hormone (prolactin) is another pituitary hormone involved in the H-P-G axis. It is involved in **lactation** (breastfeeding), in the maintenance of uterine tone, and in the production of progesterone. The function of luteotropic hormone in the human male is currently unknown.

This chapter is a brief overview of the hormonal basis of human sexuality. The specific hormones introduced here will be discussed in more detail in the next two chapters. Those chapters will integrate these hormones into male and female sexual reproductive anatomy and physiology.

When the limbic system, which is the center of our emotions and includes the hypothalamus, is added to the CC + H-P-G axis formula, we have a complete biochemical basis to human sexuality. These brain functions interact to comprise the cognitive, affective, and biochemical foundation of human sexuality. This basis is expressed through the physiological maturation and development process. It includes attainment of puberty, and the learned, culturally specific behaviors, values, norms, and beliefs we as a species believe and act on verbally, nonverbally and symbolically. The latter include each culture's shared definitions of masculinity and femininity, appropriate gender role behavior, speech, demeanor, and affect, as well as rules concerning what constitutes sexual, "normal," and reproductive behaviors. Hormones and behavior affect each other (this interaction will be illustrated in the next few chapters). The manifestations of hormones and of the physical characteristics they influence occur within a cultural context. The next three chapters discuss biological traits such as the onset of puberty, regular menstrual cycles, and the sexual and reproductive structures as they are expressed within the context of culture.

SUMMARY

1   The cerebral cortex plus the H-P-G axis comprise the biochemical and behavioral bases of our sexuality.

2   The hypothalamus, an evolutionarily old structure, and the pituitary gland make up the biochemical regulators of our sexuality.

3   The H-P-G axis comprises a negative feedback system which influences the onset of puberty, the release of gonadotropins, the release of pheromones, and erogenous zone sensitivity.

4   Many of our sexual and reproductive structures are both analogous and homologous. Men and women share a hormonal system. This means that bio-chemically, men and women are more similar than they are different.

5   The sexual and reproductive cycles are distinct but overlapping systems.

6   Male hormonal functioning is frequently described as tonic, female as cyclic.

7   The major sex hormones are androgens, specifically testosterone; estrogen, which refers to a group of hormones, and progesterone.

8   Culture and biology interact in the expression of our sexuality.

Thought-provoking questions

1   How do biology and culture affect each other?

2   If men and women share a hormonal system, what accounts for the differences between men and women?

SUGGESTED RESOURCES

Aitken, R. John, Peter Koopman, and Sheena E. M. Lewis. 2004. "Public Health: Environmental Pollution and Male Fertility." *Nature* 432: 48.

Web sites

B.E.A.C.H.E.S. Foundation (http://www.beachesfoundation.org) (Topless bathing legislation). Last accessed 1/20/06.
LaLeche League International (http://www.lalecheleague.org/bfinfo.html) (Breast-feeding legislation). Last accessed 2/9/06.

5 Modern human male anatomy and physiology

CHAPTER OVERVIEW

1 Applies the formula CC + (H-P-G axis) = biochemical behavioral aspect of human sexuality to males.
2 Discusses the role of FSH (follicular stimulating hormone) and LH (luteinizing hormone)/ICSH (interstitial cell stimulating hormone) as a tonic process in males.
3 Discusses the external and internal anatomy and physiology of the male sexual and reproductive systems.
4 Discusses male primary and secondary sex characteristics.
5 Introduces the concept of the libido and relates it to testosterone levels.
6 Discusses the effect of alcohol and marijuana use on testosterone levels.
7 Introduces HIV infection and AIDS in men.
8 Introduces male sexual response.

In this chapter (and in Chapter 6), physical normalcy is assumed unless specifically stated otherwise. A discussion of male anatomy incorporates the **CC + (H-P-G axis)** formula presented in the previous chapter.

Applying the CC + (H-P-G axis) formula to males involves a hormonal exploration of **FSH (follicular stimulating hormone)**, **LH (luteinizing hormone)/ICSH (interstitial cell stimulating hormone)**, which are the same hormones, and the **gonadotropins**, particularly the **androgens**. As introduced in Chapter 4, men tend to have a more continuous **(tonic)** release of H-P-G axis hormones in their bodies than do women, whose more rhythmic release is described as cyclic. Men's hormonal patterns continue from puberty until death. In men, the hypothalamic release of GnRH (gonadatropic releasing hormone) triggers pituitarian FSH and LH (ICSH) activity. FSH and LH activate testicular functioning and the production of androgens, male sex hormones. FSH aids in **spermatogenesis,** or sperm production, which occurs in the **seminiferous tubules** of the testicles. LH (ICSH) maintains and promotes the integrity of the **interstitial cells** of the testes, the major source of testosterone production. Testosterone, considered a "male" sex hormone, is the primary androgen and the focus of our discussion.

Testosterone is produced in the interstitial cells of the testicles in men. Another name for the interstitial cells is the **leydig cells**. In women, much of the testosterone is produced in the **adrenal glands** with some of it also produced in their ovaries. Testosterone is a crucial sexual cycle hormone in both genders and a reproductive cycle hormone in males. On a hormonal basis, testosterone is responsible for the **libido** or sex drive in both men and women. The amount of testosterone required to maintain the libido in men and women is referred to as the **threshold level**, and it exists in roughly the same amounts in both men and women. As long as this threshold level is maintained, the hormonal aspects of the libido are present in men and women. Men and women produce testosterone from **puberty** until death. Thus, both men and women can maintain a hormonal basis for the libido from sexual adulthood (i.e., puberty) through sexual and reproductive aging (e.g., postmenopause in women).

Testosterone, as a major sex hormone, is actively involved in the expression of primary and secondary male sex characteristics. For this to occur, men continuously produce, from puberty until death, about ten times as much testosterone on a tonic basis as do women (Greenberg, Bruess, and Mullen, 1993). Generally, the tonic release of free circulating testosterone in the male suppresses or binds the release of estrogen and progesterone, the "female" sex hormones, in the male. The primary sex characteristics are those directly related to sexual and reproductive functioning. In the male, they include the growth and development of the internal and external penis, the testes and scrotal sac, as well as the auxiliary reproductive structures such as the vas deferens, seminal vesicles, and epididymis.

SECONDARY SEX CHARACTERISTICS

The secondary sex characteristics are those features less directly involved in reproductive functioning, but generally highly involved in sexual functioning. Testosterone-induced male secondary sex characteristics include a number of features. It is important to remember that these are general patterns and a lot of normal individual variation exists within these patterns. These features are relativistic, not absolute, between genders. For example, as with the rest of the primate world, generally human males are taller, more muscular, and have more facial and body hair than do females. **Sex hormones** also interact with genetic and cultural variables which result in adult characteristics, e.g., height has a genetic, hormonal, and cultural basis. Genetic tendencies to be tall or short are reinforced by hormonal release that promotes bone growth and later closes the epiphyses, which are further influenced by such cultural practices as nutrition.

Secondary sex characteristics involve structures that often are culturally defined as visual sexual and gender cues and indicators of sexual adulthood. Since spermatogenesis is invisible compared to the visibility of menstruation, the appearance of secondary sex characteristics in the male can be used culturally to define sexual and reproductive adulthood in men. This illustrates how physiology can be culturally integrated and interpreted on a behavioral and attitudinal level. For example, the production of testosterone results in beard growth that can be used to define masculinity and manhood. In the United States, a boy's physical ability to produce facial hair is symbolically and behaviorally recognized as a sign of becoming a man. Shaving or plucking male facial hair is a cultural response to a secondary sex characteristic. It can serve as part of grooming and hygiene in the Euro-American, European, and Native American cultures.

Cross-culturally, there is a lot of variation within and between groups. Blonds tend to be the hairiest of people, while Africans, Asians, and Native Americans have less facial and body hair. Even within specific kin groups there are individual variations. The pattern and distribution of male facial hair, overall body hair, and pubic hair are a function of testosterone. Beard growth, and the male hairline shape, but not the amount of head hair,[1] are the functions of testosterone. Men tend to have a scallop-shaped hairline as contrasted to the women's which is more ovoid (see Figures 5.1 and 5.2).

In addition, the diamond-shaped pubic hair patterning in men as compared with the inverted triangle pattern in women is related to testosterone. As with women, men's pubic hair varies in color and amount with the individual and is subject to the aging process. Generally, it is curly, soft, and sensitive to sexual stimulation.

Although also a function of genetics and cultural practices regarding nutrition, exercise, and bone development, height and bone growth are related to testosterone. Generally, men are taller than women, with longer, heavier, and denser bones. This also allows them to have greater physical strength and speed than women.[2] The combination of testosterone and estrogen also puts men under seventy years old at a lower risk for **osteoporosis**, a degenerative bone disease common in older women.

The enlargement of the larynx that deepens the male voice is one of the nonreversible secondary sex characteristics. The enlargement of the larynx and changed voice are permanent, even if testosterone ceases to be produced. In male **castration** or **orchidectomy**, the testicles are removed. This happens, for example, as a treatment for some testicular cancer or as part of male-to-female transsexual surgery. Although other secondary sex characteristics are lost, the deeper voice remains. This has resulted in some male-to-female transsexuals who have deep voices taking voice lessons to soften and

Figure 5.1 Man's hairline.

(See color plates, between pp. 168–169)

raise their voices. In contrast, female-to-male transsexuals benefit from androgen therapy since their voices "naturally" deepen.

The male *castrati* who sang in choirs during the Middle Ages were castrated prior to puberty. Castration also meant that their overall bone size was smaller. Their chest bones were less well developed than non-*castrati*, which contributed to a higher voice. *Castrati* had smaller penises and did have active sex lives. Although testosterone is responsible for the sex drive (interest in sex) and reproductive male sex characteristics such as the production of **sperm** and **semen** (ejaculate), it is not responsible for erections or feelings of sexual pleasure per se. If this is confusing, remember that fetal and prepubertal boys are capable of erections. Prepubertal boys are also capable of **masturbation**, feeling sexual pleasure, and having an **orgasm**; they do not, however, ejaculate. *Castrati* tended to lead charmed lives. According to Henderson (1969), the fortunate few boys selected as *castrati* would have the choicest food, clothes, homes, and women at their disposal for the length of their careers. *Castrati* were not perceived with the same kind of horror that we perceive them in retrospect (Bullough, 1976; Davis, n.d.b, Rice, 1982).

Figure 5.2 Woman's hairline.

(See color plates, between pp. 168–169)

Eunuchs, also castrated and often after puberty, reflect feminized fat distribution. They were found in the harems in the Middle East and ancient China to prevent wives and concubines from having affairs with other men or from other men having access to these women. Their lack of testicles was culturally believed to sufficiently decrease their libido so that they would have no sexual interest in the women they were guarding. Depending on the situation, however, they may have formed deep personal and emotional attachments to the women they guarded.

Men generally also have more muscle mass,[3] are leaner, and have a lower body fat to overall body mass ratio than women. This contributes to men's overall greater physical strength. In current United States standards of aesthetic leanness for men, the range of body fat is from about 8 percent for athletes to about 19 percent for the "average" male ("Defining Overweight and Obesity," 2005). Males need a minimum of 4 to 6 percent body fat to reach puberty. Athletes in training, football players for example, may try to achieve a 4 to 6 percent body fat content during the playing season. They may be muscularly "bulky," but they are not soft-tissue fat.

Men tend to have upper body fat, i.e., their body fat is distributed around their waists and chests. Some physical aspects of men's comparative leanness and body fat distribution are that men tend to carry "spare tires," "love handles," or "pot bellies" of excess body fat around their midsections; they may be more prone to coronary heart disease; and they may float less easily than women. In general, both men and women have become fatter since the 1980s; both have greater amounts of subcutaneous body fat than previously ("Defining Overweight and Obesity," 2005).

For some types of prostate cancer, female sex hormones are given to slow or stop tumor growth. Depending on the type, amount, and duration of this form of chemotherapy and the individual man's hormonal system, he may develop some female secondary sex characteristics during treatment. This could include changes in body fat amount and distribution and breast enlargement.

Testosterone has an effect on men's skin. Men's skin tends to age more slowly, has fewer wrinkles, and is more prone to acne than women's. Men tend to have more severe acne than do women because testosterone can stimulate sebaceous (oil) gland secretions which contribute to acne. Skin smoothness and aging are also related to the estrogen levels that men retain from puberty until death, as well as cultural practices such as shaving, which removes dead skin cells.

Libidinous functioning or having an interest in sex has attributes of both primary and secondary sex characteristics. As stated previously, a comparable amount of testosterone known as the threshold level is required in both males and females in order to generate an interest in sex. Again, this baseline physiological level integrates with cultural values and beliefs about how, when, where, with whom, and how often the sex drive is expressed.

Estrogen and **progesterone** in men are primarily produced in the adrenal glands and generally are suppressed or bound by the testosterone. Unbound estrogen can produce secondary feminizing sex characteristics such as **gynecomastia** or breast development, loss of facial and body hair, or reduced sex drive.

Progesterone, which does not produce feminizing secondary sex characteristics in men, may be given in various forms to some convicted sex offenders. It is part of their rehabilitation and therapy, as it acts as an anti-libido hormone. It not only diminishes libido in both males and females, but may mitigate aggressive feelings as well. Silber (1981), a researcher in this area, has administered progestin-based drugs to some convicted sex offenders who have chronically elevated testosterone levels.

Silber (1981) investigated male sexuality and has developed a theory about certain kinds of sexual behavior related to hyper-testosterone levels. The normal level of free-circulating testosterone found in men allows for primary and secondary sex characteristic development and a sex drive. A few men, however, have chronically elevated levels of testosterone well outside the normal range. These chronically elevated levels of testosterone, coupled with strongly internalized and culturally supported values on aggression and violence as a means of expressing anger and frustration or resolving conflict, may be involved in some of the more dramatic sex crimes. Silber hormonally tested and interviewed a number of men convicted of sex crimes, which also involved extreme forms of violence (e.g., rape and body mutilation or dismemberment). In this sample, he found chronically elevated levels of testosterone, a psychological connection between thoughts of sexual violence and heightened arousal, and acceptance of physical violence as a means of expressing anger or frustration and resolving conflict. When these men in his prison sample were given progestin-based drugs, their testosterone levels lowered to within normal limits. The testosterone levels remained within normal limits as long as the progestin-based drug was taken. If the drug regimen stopped, the testosterone levels increased to their previously elevated levels. On the drug, the prisoners reported less of a connection between sexual arousal and violence (Silber, 1981).

This is fascinating and potentially powerful research which has controversial and potential social and legal implications. Although some Scandanavian countries physically castrate convicted male sex offenders, this is seen as cruel and unusual punishment in the United States. More likely, convicted male sex offenders in the United States will be given progestin-based drugs (Gis and Gooren, 1999; Grossman, Martis and Fichtner, 1966).

Drug usage can affect male sex hormones, particularly testosterone. Two commonly used drugs that affect testosterone levels are alcohol and marijuana. Extensive chronic alcohol and marijuana abuse can suppress testosterone levels below the threshold level. This can result in loss of libido and the appearance of feminizing secondary sex characteristics such as gynecomastia, or breast enlargement, increase in overall amount and redistribution of body fat, body hair loss, and beard softening. These effects are reversible if the alcohol or marijuana drug abuse stop. Some recent research suggests that chronic drug use or abuse by men can negatively affect both their fertility and the quality of their sperm as well as contribute to problems in fetal development (Daniels, 1997; Emanuele and Emanuele, 1998).

Steroids also affect secondary sex characteristics, particularly muscle size and the lean muscle mass to body fat ratio. Steroids contain androgens that can rapidly increase muscle mass. Their use for this purpose is illegal in most formal athletic situations. The 2004 Summer Olympic Games and the American Baseball Association have both had to address scandals involving steroid use by their players (Anon., 2005). Steroids are stored in the body for at least six weeks and excess amounts are secreted in the urine. This phenomenon explains the mandatory urine tests for steroids in competition-based athletes and for some employees. Steroids also can cause general metabolic problems. They are powerful and potentially dangerous drugs. If abused they may damage the kidneys, liver, and heart, or even result in the user's death. Injection of them through shared needles also puts the user at risk for hepatitis B, for HIV infection, the virus which causes AIDS, and for other infections.

PRIMARY SEX CHARACTERISTICS

Primary sex characteristics are those features in men and women that are directly involved in sexual and reproductive functioning. In men, they are hormonally controlled by the androgens or male sex hormones. Testosterone is the major gonadotropin involved in the growth and development of these characteristics.

The **penis**, which increases in size at puberty, is composed of internal and external structures. The external penis includes the **glans, shaft,** and **crura** or **root**, structures which are **homologous** to the female's **clitoris**. The glans of the penis, illustrated in Figures 5.3 and 5.4, is acorn-shaped and is formed by the internal **corpus spongiosum**. The corpus spongiosum also contains the **urethra**, which ends in the glans at the opening called the **urinary meatus**. The glans or head of the penis is hairless and is extremely sensitive to sexual stimulation. It is covered with penile skin called the **foreskin**.

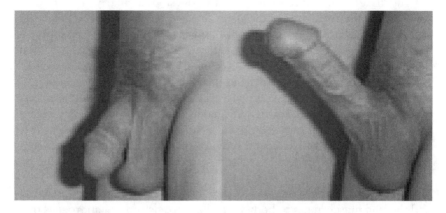

Figure 5.3 Circumcised penis. (*Source*: Wikipedia.)

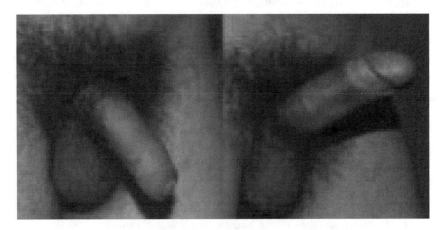

Figure 5.4 Uncircumcised penis. (*Source*: Wikipedia.)

In some cultures, including often in the United States since about 1850, males have their foreskins surgically removed in a procedure known as **circumcision**. Male circumcision is not universally practiced. Nonindustrialized societies that practice circumcision usually do it for social and symbolic reasons relating to status changes in males. Doctors in the United States originally performed circumcisions to reduce masturbation. Currently, about 65 percent of boy babies in this culture are circumcised, often without anesthesia, within two days of birth for social reasons, which have been given medical and hygienic explanations. These include reduction of body odor from accumulation of **smegma**, possible reduction for risk of HIV infection, increased sexual sensitivity, and to be "like the other boys." Since the early twenty-first century in the United States and elsewhere, circumcision has become a controversial practice whose medical rationale is certainly suspect ("Trends in Circumcisions Among Newborns," 2005). The controversies surrounding male circumcision in nonindustrialized societies to prevent heterosexual transmission of HIV will be discussed in Chapter 15. (See Figures 5.3 and 5.4.)

At the base of the glans penis where the head of the penis and the shaft meet, is the **frenum** or **frenulum**. This small structure is somewhat triangular in shape, sensitive to sexual stimulation, and is the place where the foreskin attaches to the glans. At either side of the frenulum are the preputial glands, which secrete smegma. Smegma is a waxy, lubricating substance that allows for smoother retraction of the foreskin over the glans. With circumcision, smegma no longer collects under the foreskin. In contrast to industrialized societies, some Islamic, Middle Eastern groups and Polynesians are meticulous about male genital cleanliness and see men in Europe and the United States as dirty by comparison (Bullough, 1976; Marshall and Suggs, 1971).

88   *Human sexuality*

The shaft is the body of the penis that is covered with relatively loose, hairless skin. The shaft contains the corpus spongiosum and **corpora cavernosa** or cavernous bodies. The shaft increases in size and firmness during arousal as the cavernous bodies engorge with blood to create an erection. The shaft is sensitive to sexual stimulation. Its size, erectile ability, connection with sexuality, and fertility are of great cultural interest in the United States and elsewhere. In this culture, penis size is of major concern to men regardless of their sexual orientation. In some other cultures, genital surgery on the shaft such as **subincision**, an incision on the underside of the penis, or **superincision**, an incision on the ventral (top) side, is performed to heighten men's sexuality, their masculinity, or as an indication of status change from boyhood to manhood. These procedures will be discussed in more detail in the chapter on adolescence (Chapter 10). The crura or root forms the base of the penis and can be felt externally as a ridge at the point where the penis attaches to the body at the lower abdomen.

The **scrotal sac** or **scrotum** is a multilayered pouch of loose skin located behind the penis that contains the **testicles, epididymis,** and **spermatic cords**. The scrotal sac generally is hairless and is sensitive to sexual stimulation. It is homologous to the **labia majora** in females.

From the base of the genitals to the anus is an area of skin in men and women called the **perineum;** in men the perineum extends from the scrotal sac to the anus. The perineum is soft, generally hairless and sensitive to sexual stimulation. Stimulation of the prostate gland through the perineum or anally can be highly erotic for many men (Ladas, Whipple, and Perry, 1982).

The testes or testicles, derived from the Latin *testare* (meaning to testify), are two spherical spongy bodies located in the scrotal sac. They are homologous and analogous to the female's ovaries. They are mobile in the scrotal sac. Testicles can be elevated or lowered in the scrotal sac in response to such factors as temperature, surprise, or fright. The ability of the testicles to move in the scrotum contributes to reproductive success. Retraction of the testicles in response to a threat may preserve them. Since sperm can only exist at temperatures of about 32°C, having sperm produced outside the body cavity helps to ensure their survival. In addition, retraction and extension of the testicles in response to external temperature maintains the proper temperature for sperm production and survival. Many men have experienced this when diving into a cold body of water and feeling their testicles retract toward their body. Most simply, the testicles, which may rest unevenly in the scrotum, are the site of spermatogenesis. The internal construction of a testicle is composed of tightly coiled tubes called seminiferous tubules, and a cellular arrangement resembling either a sponge or honeycomb. This cellular arrangement is referred to as the interstitial cells or leydig cells. They are the source of testosterone. The production of testosterone is influenced by the release of FSH and LH from the pituitary gland. LH acts directly on the leydig cells to maintain their integrity so that testosterone can be produced and secreted. FSH also acts on the formation of sperm in the seminiferous tubules. Testosterone release is continuous from puberty until death, as is sperm production, though both diminish in quantity as men age. Millions of sperm are produced in the seminiferous tubules each day from puberty until death. They are produced in an immature state and are matured outside the testicle, in contrast to the mature egg released by the ovary.

We do not have a particularly complimentary vocabulary for either male or female genitalia or reproductive structures. Here are examples of terms and phrases for male genitalia contributed from a human sexuality class:

Cock 'n balls	*Oranges 'n banana*	*Wanker*
Twig 'n berries	*Franks 'n bean*	*Goods*
Weenie	*Boner*	*Johnson*
Wink	*Pud*	*Boys*
Steel	*Package*	*Rod*
Family Jewels	*Skin Flute*	*Tube Stake*
Purple Hand	*Yogurt Slinger*	*Dick*

Testicular cancer is most commonly found in men in their twenties. As a means of early diagnosis of testicular cancer and as a means of maintaining a man's overall andrological health, regular testicular self-exams (TSEs) are encouraged. They need to be performed regularly and consistently, and are analogous to breast self-exams (BSEs) in women. TSEs are most effective after a warm shower, when the scrotal sac is relaxed and the testicles are descended. Visual examination to detect changes in color, size, shape, or to note the appearance of lumps or growths is done first. Then, the man is encouraged to gently palpate (feel) the testicles and spermatic cords, initially to familiarize himself with his own anatomy, and secondarily to feel for any unusual lumps or changes. Please note, for many men, one testicle rests lower in the scrotal sac than the other. This is an anatomically common occurrence. (See Figures 5.5, 5.6, and 5.7.)

From the seminiferous tubules, the newly produced immature sperm cross the testes to the epididymis. The epididymis are two, crescent-shaped, gray-ish structures which curve around the side of each testicle. They house the immature sperm for approximately seventy-two days until they are suffi-ciently mature to be released into the **vas deferens** (Daniels, 1997; Emanuele and Emanuele, 1998). It is important to remember that the manufacture and maturation process of sperm is continuous. Millions of sperm are produced and matured daily.

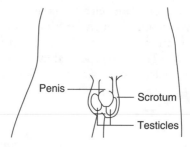

Figure 5.5 TSE: testicular self exam, 1. (*Source*: National Cancer Institute.)

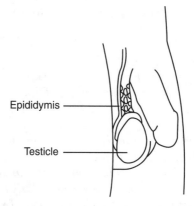

Figure 5.6 TSE: testicular self exam, 2. (*Source*: National Cancer Institute.)

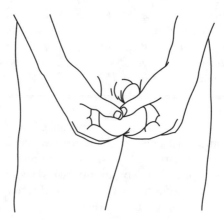

Figure 5.7 TSE: testicular self exam, 3. (*Source*: National Cancer Institute.)

The spermatic cords, located on the side of each testicle and extending to the pubis, contain several structures such as the **cremasteric muscle**, vas deferens, blood vessels, and nerves. The spermatic cord itself functions to raise and lower each testicle in the scrotal sac. The difference in the length of the spermatic cords is the reason that one testicle may hang lower in the scrotal sac than the other testicle. The elevation and lowering of the testicle in response to changes in temperature, fright, stress, or sexual arousal is a function of the cremasteric muscle. The actual response of the cremasteric muscle is called the **cremasteric reflex**. This reflex can be triggered spontaneously by running the side of one's thumb quickly along the inner thigh of an unsuspecting male. The testicles will spontaneously contract. Triggering this response is not recommended unless you know the male well.

Another structure located in each spermatic cord is the vas deferens. The vas deferens, analogous and homologous to the **fallopian tubes**, transport the mature sperm from the epididymis out of the pelvis to the **seminal vesicles** and **ejaculatory tracts** or **ducts**. Release of mature sperm by the epididymis into the vas deferens is continuous. However, during times of intense sexual arousal, an average of 200 to 400 million sperm are released into the vas deferens. The vas deferens begin as external structures in the spermatic cord and then proceed internally to loop around behind the bladder until they join with ejaculatory tract on each side of the man's body. The vas deferens are the site of a **vasectomy**, the most common form of voluntary male sterilization (see Chapter 12 for a description of this procedure).

After looping around behind the bladder, the vas deferens connect with the seminal vesicles. There are two of these structures as well, on each side of the man's body, adjacent to the bladder. The seminal vesicles produce the majority of semen.

After the vas deferens loop around the bladder joining the seminal vesicles, the vas deferens become the ejaculatory tract. The sperm carried by the vas deferens now becomes part of the ejaculate when the seminal vesicles release semen into the ejaculatory tract and the semen mixes with sperm to form **ejaculate**.

The tract contains ejaculate from the point where the vas deferens becomes the ejaculatory duct. By volume, ejaculate is about 98 percent semen and 2 percent sperm. Semen is a pearly-colored, sticky, viscous fluid that leaves a white stain on material such as clothing or bedding when dried. It will, however, wash out of clothing or bedding. Semen is essential to sperm for transport and survival. Semen is an alkaline or basic substance with a pH range from 7.5 to 9.5. Sperm needs an alkaline environment in order to survive (Guylaya et al., 2001).

Semen is composed of a number of ingredients including albumen, the same substance found in egg whites, which gives semen its slippery texture; it also has sugars—glucose and fructose; bases, which give it its salty taste; and proteins (Guylaya et al., 2001). Semen has several functions. Its composition nourishes the sperm. Semen also is a transport medium for the sperm, aids in sperm motility, and lubricates the urethra. The amount of ejaculate per expulsion averages about two teaspoons, although it may feel and appear to the male and his partner(s) to be a great deal more. Ejaculate contains about twenty to thirty-seven calories each expulsion. About twenty-three samples of ejaculate equal the calories in a piece of lemon meringue pie (*Menstuff*, 2005).

There is an infamous story about a prostitute who went to a doctor to be put on a diet. (Note: this true story occurred in the pre-AIDS days.) She followed the prescribed regimen carefully, but still did not lose weight. Frustrated, she returned to the doctor who told her to record everything she swallowed. Her special service to her clients was fellatio, oral sex, or giving head. She swallowed sufficient amounts of ejaculate in a day to prevent her from losing weight.

Currently, with the very real concern and problem with HIV transmission through semen and vaginal fluids, oral sex on either a man (fellatio), or women (cunnilingus), is only a safer sex activity when using a condom on the penis or vaginal dam barrier over the vulva, the external genitalia, of the female. The HIV virus is found in semen, not sperm (Padian, 1987; IXth International AIDS Conference, 1993; Griffin, 2005; *Menstuff*, 2005). On the risky sex continuum, HIV exists in sufficient quantities in semen to infect a partner through unprotected penile-anal, penile-vaginal, or oral sex (IXth International AIDS Conference, 1993; "Advancing HIV Prevention," 2003). Therefore, properly used latex barriers such as condoms and vaginal (dental) dams need to be consistently used to reduce the risk of infection (see also Chapter 15).

Semen, part of the ejaculate, an important substance in male sexuality and reproduction, also has socio-cultural dimensions. In many cultures it is recognized as a vital life substance. There are a variety of beliefs about its functions, quality, and quantity. Barker-Benfield (1975) has coined the term "**spermatic economy**" to connote the attitudes of some Mediterranean groups and the nineteenth-century British toward "semen" (sic), i.e., ejacu-late. In these cultures, ejaculate is seen to exist in finite supply and judicious caution against "spending," i.e., ejaculating "frequently," as with mas-turbation is advised. Until the present generation, among the Sambia, a patrilineal, horticultural group in New Guinea, prepubescent and adoles-cent boys ritually engaged in fellatio (oral sex) in order to build strength and physical reserves of ejaculate so that they do not run out of it in adult heterosexual relations (Herdt, 1982; Knauft, 2003). Among the Sambia, women are seen as sexually powerful and voracious. Ejaculatory contact with women is carefully regulated so as not to use up all of a man's vital life essence (see also Chapter 10).

We have mixed views on the wisdom of frequent ejaculation or "spend-ing" in our culture. One philosophy promotes a "use it or lose it" approach; the more orgasmic (ejaculatory) one is, the more one will continue to be

(Masters and Johnson, 1974). The other approach, exemplified by some college athletic coaches from the late-nineteenth century to the present, encouraged a "spermatic economy" perspective. Male athletes were advised not to engage in ejaculatory sex before an event so that they would "save" their strength and energy. Although many college coaches in the United States recognize this as a piece of folklore, and most do not pass it on as serious advice to their players (Gordon, 1988), athletes in a human sexuality class state that they are told by their coaches to avoid having "sex" before a game to avoid "being tired."

The ejaculatory tract is essentially an extension of the vas deferens. The ejaculatory tract transports the ejaculate (i.e., sperm and semen) to the urethra. The urethra is surrounded by the **prostate**, which produces the balance of the semen to deposit a full ejaculation in the urethra.

The prostate is a walnut-shaped, spongy organ that lies below the bladder. The urethra runs through it. The prostate can be felt through the perineum and by finger insertion into the rectum. Perineal and rectal stimulation of the prostate can produce intense levels of sexual arousal. The prostate produces semen that contributes to the ejaculate carried in the ejaculatory tract. The prostate is a common site of both minor irritation and major problems. In younger men, prostate trouble can be due to either localized or systemic infection or irritation and is known as **prostatitis**. This can generally be easily remedied through antibiotics. In older men, enlargement of the prostate due to either atrophy as part of the natural aging process or due to prostate cancer commonly occurs. Prostate cancer currently is most reliably diagnosed by a combination of a PSA blood test and digital rectal exam (Oesterling, 1991: 24). It occurs in a geometric proportion relative to age: in fifty-year-old men, there's a 40 percent chance of enlargement; in sixty-year-old men, a 50 percent chance and so forth. It's pretty much a given that the longer a man lives, the greater are the chances that he will have problems with his prostate. One of the more serious immediate concerns of an enlarged prostate, either due to irritation, atrophy, or cancer, is that the enlargement constricts the urethra.

Constriction of the urethra makes urination painful, difficult, or impossible. In fact, painful, slow, or incomplete urination is frequently a sign that prostate problems exist. Treatments include antibiotics, or in the case of enlargement or cancer, surgical removal of the prostate often happens. For benign, non-cancerous prostate enlargement, drug treatments, laser therapy, or a **TURP** is performed. TURP stands for **transurethral resection of the prostate**. A man does not ejaculate after a TURP, but should retain erectile and orgasmic ability. For prostate cancer, a number of treatments are available. These include more radical surgery, radiation, hormone therapy, chemotherapy, or "watchful waiting," depending on the location, size, and type of the tumor (Carroll and Nelson, 2004). An orchidectomy, or removal of the testicles, may be performed in some cases of prostatic cancer to avoid testosterone feeding the cancer.[4]

The male's urethra runs from the base of the bladder through the corpus spongiosum, the underside cylinder of the internal penis, ending in the urinary meatus at the glans of the penis. The male urethra has two functions. It transports urine from the bladder to outside the body, and it transports the ejaculate, which is deposited in the urethra during the emission phase of male ejaculation, from the ejaculatory tract and prostate to outside the body. Both urine and ejaculate leave the body through the urinary meatus.

As stated previously, sperm survive in an alkaline or basic environment. Urine is acidic and the urethra can be acidic from transporting urine. To counteract the acidity of the urethra so that sperm can survive, two phenomena occur. There is a sphincter or small closure between the bladder and urethra. This sphincter closes during arousal and ejaculation so that urine does not leak into the urethra and damage sperm. The common belief in the United States that one may swallow urine when swallowing ejaculate, "cum," during oral sex is therefore erroneous. Again, it is important to remember in this age of AIDS, that oral sex is risky without using a condom from beginning to end; with a condom oral sex becomes safer.

Some yogis, practitioners of Tantrism, a sensuous form of yoga, and Robert Noyes, the founder of the Oneida Community, a religious sect started in the nineteenth century near Oneida, New York, claim to be able to attain conscious control over the urinary sphincter. They use this discipline as a part of their birth control.[5] By concentrating intently during the emission phase of ejaculation when the ejaculate enters the urethra, they open the urethral sphincter and force the ejaculate into the bladder instead of out through the urinary meatus. This process is called retrograde ejaculation which also occurs as a side effect of a TURP, discussed previously. It may also occur as a side effect of taking some major tranquilizers or severe alcohol abuse. When the man urinates, the ejaculate is expelled, sometimes causing the urine to have a milky-white coloration.

To further counteract the acidity of the urethra, secretions from the **Cowper's glands** neutralize acid levels and lubricate the urethra for the passage of ejaculate. Cowper's glands and ducts are located just beneath the prostate on either side of the urethra. They are homologous to Bartholin's glands in the female. They release a clear, slippery fluid known as **preejaculatory fluid** or "precum" into the urethra. This fluid flows through the urinary meatus immediately prior to ejaculation and may be used to lubricate the glans and increase stimulation. This fluid may contain sperm, semen, or HIV if the man is infected. It is important, therefore, not to swallow precum, or to have it come in contact with either the women's genitals

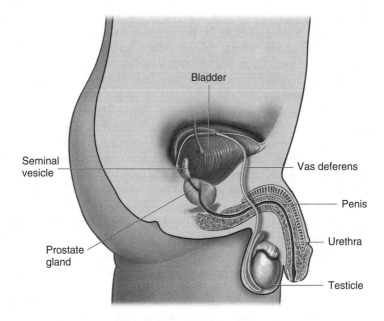

Figure 5.8 Scrotal wall. (*Source*: Medical Illustration Copyright © 2008 Nucleus Medical Art. All rights reserved. www.nucleusinc.com.)

or the anus of either gender in order to avoid possible HIV infection or conception in the case of heterosexual genital contact.

The internal penis is composed of three cylindrical or corpus bodies: two of which are the corpora cavernosa, Latin for cavernous bodies, and the corpus spongiosum, Latin for spongy body. (See Figure 5.8.)

The corpora cavernosa are the top two cylindrical bodies of the penis. They are composed of spongy tissue and a rich vascular or blood supply. During sexual arousal, it is primarily these two structures that engorge with blood to create an erection. In addition to neural responses, an erection is achieved and maintained vascularly as long as the blood flow into the corpora cavernosa occurs faster than the blood flow from it; this process is helped by sphincters which close to keep the blood in the cavernous bodies. Human males do not have a penis bone or other structure to maintain an erection. One drug known to have an effect on the vascular structure of the corpora cavernosa is nicotine. Nicotine constricts blood vessels. Since free-circulating blood is physiologically important in achieving and maintaining an erection, smokers and chewers may impair full erectile ability. People who have stopped smoking or chewing tobacco and whose bodies are nicotine-free report quicker, fuller, firmer erections (Buffum, 1982). Lack of nicotine allows the blood vessels of the penis to open more completely. Chapter 11 discusses other drugs that can affect erectile ability.

The third cavernous body of the internal penis is the corpus spongiosum. The corpus spongiosum forms the glans penis and is the structure through which the urethra runs ending in the urinary meatus at the tip of the glans. Men who have been subincised, i.e., who have had the underside of their penes slit open verticially as part of initiation (see Chapter 10), do not urinate through the urinary meatus in the glans. Urine is released farther back along the urethra.

Male internal and external genitalia comprise the sexual and reproductive structures. The male external genitalia, in contrast to the female's, are highly visible. Both internal and external structures operate dramatically during male sexual response. The distinctions between conscious and unconscious (out-of-awareness) responses and erection-ejaculation-orgasm are introduced here and will be discussed in more detail in Chapter 11.

Sexual response, in general, is an interaction of conscious and unconscious mechanisms. The conscious awareness involves the cerebral cortex, the limbic system (feelings), and to some extent the hypothalamus. It includes the perceived, learned triggers of arousal, and awareness of excitement or erogenous zone activity. The unconscious, out-of-awareness mechanisms involve the hypothalamus, the neural responses such as triggering the reflex arc on the spinal column, hormonal release (H-P-G axis functioning), and vascular responses. Of these two mechanisms, the conscious may dominate, defining pleasure, sensuality, sexuality, and the perception of the intensity of arousal and orgasm. In the male, this relates specifically to perceptions of erectile firmness, "staying power" (ability to maintain an erection), ejaculatory force, sensation, and amount. These are learned, culturally patterned responses. For example, male Tantrics in India exert conscious control over ejaculatory release. These learned responses can override physiological response and ability, as evidenced in the sensual-sexual arousability and pleasure experienced by people with spinal cord injuries.

Erection, ejaculation, and orgasm are physiologically distinct processes, although they may be perceived as being the same, particularly male orgasm and ejaculation. The fact that postpubertal males often achieve orgasm and the expulsion phase of ejaculation concurrently reinforces this belief and the sensation that orgasm and ejaculation are the same in males.

The voluntary control over erection is dramatically illustrated by the true story of Swami Rama. Swami Rama was debating with a group of United States graduate students about the voluntary aspects of erection. To illustrate the conscious control in erection, he had a graduate student fill a five-gallon bucket with water. Before his incredulous students, he spontaneously generated an erection without overt stimulation of his penis and proceeded to suspend the bucket of water from his erect penis! The man must have done thousands of kegels, an exercise which strengthens the muscles sur-rounding the crura. This is the most impressive case of the integration of conscious and unconscious mechanisms in erection that your authors are aware of.

SUMMARY

1   The CC + (H-P-G axis) discussed in Chapter 4 is applied to males.
2   FSH and LH are involved in the tonic process of spermatogenesis.
3   Androgens, particularly testosterone, are involved in male primary and secondary sex characteristic development. The role of estrogen and progesterone in men is presented.
4   Male internal and external sexual and reproductive anatomy and physiology is discussed relative to normal functioning, the libido, and effects of alcohol, nicotine, and marijuana use on male libido and sexual response.
5   It is possible for men to contract HIV infection and other STIs through unprotected penile-anal intercourse, unprotected penile-vaginal inter-course (particularly if the women is menstruating), and either unpro-tected fellatio (oral sex on a male), or unprotected cunnilingus (oral sex on a female), particularly if she is menstruating.
6   Cultural responses to male sexual and reproductive functioning include such practices as circumcision, subincision, and superincision, as well as cultural beliefs about sexuality.
7   Common problems of the prostate such as prostatitis and enlargement of the prostate can occur in men across the life cycle and increase as they age.
8   Erection, ejaculation, and orgasm are physiologically distinct processes.

Thought-provoking questions

1   How does the structure of culture influence how we think about male sexual and reproductive anatomy and physiology?
2   What are the cultural connotations given to slang terms for male genitalia?

SUGGESTED RESOURCES

Book

Joannides, Paul. 2004. *Guide to Getting It On.* 4th ed. Berkeley, CA: Publishers Group West.

Journal

International Journal of Men's Health. Men's Studies Press.

Web site

Menstuff (http://www.menstuff.org/frameindex.html). Last accessed 11/9/07.

6 Modern human female anatomy and physiology

The discussion of female anatomy and physiology parallels that for the
male. On a hormonal basis, the formula and systems are analogous for both
genders: the cerebral cortex (CC) + (H-P-G axis) is involved. On a relative
scale women's hormonal systems are described as **cyclic**. Over a period of
time, frequently measured in monthly or lunar cycles, a woman completes
one round of hormone release through the H-P-G axis. By comparison, the
male's relative tonicity means his pattern of hormone release occurs over
twenty-four hours.

To introduce the H-P-G axis in women is to discuss it as a **negative
feedback system**. The release of **LTH** (particularly during lactation), **FSH**
and **LH** from the anterior lobe of the pituitary is related to fluctuating
ovarian hormones (i.e., estrogen and progesterone). Analogous to the male
H-P-G axis, **gonadotropin releasing hormone (GnRH)** is released from

the hypothalamus which stimulates the production of pituitary hormones. **Follicular stimulating hormone** (FSH) helps eggs mature in the **ovary** during the follicular phase of the **menstrual cycle**. **Luteotropic hormone** (LTH) not only helps to maintain **uterine tone** and promotes progesterone production, but is directly involved in the lactation process. **Luteinizing hormone** (LH) which is synonymous with **interstitial cell stimulating hormone** (ICSH) in the male, helps to release the mature egg from the ovary, induces **androgens** at ovulation, and induces progesterone production and release in the **luteal phase** of the menstrual cycle. The cyclic release of these hormones in the female creates a system of balance and regularity. Contrary to popular lore in the United States, **female hormone patterning** is not "raging," "erratic," or "uncontrolled." It is interesting to note the level of cultural concern regarding women's hormone release vis-à-vis the relative lack of concern toward that of males. For example, Martin notes that even medical texts refer to **menstruation, menopause,** and female hormonal patterns in negative or injured terms—"degenerative, deteriorated, weakened, repaired." Analogous processes for spermatogenesis or other body functions are labeled more neutrally or even positively—"shedding of the stomach lining, phenomenon of spermatogenesis" (1987: 47–50). This will be discussed in more detail when the menstrual cycle and the bio-behavioral dimensions of **menstrual cramps, menstrual synchrony,** and **late luteal phase disorder (LLPD),** popularly known as **premenstrual syndrome (PMS),** are presented.

As with males, females produce their own gonadotropins (sex hormones), as well as those of the other gender (e.g., testosterone). In females, androgens, or the male sex hormones, are produced by both the adrenal glands and the ovaries (Emanuele, Wezeman, and Emanuele, 1999). Androgens, particularly testosterone, are produced from puberty until death in the female. Androgens are released at the end of the follicular phase of the menstrual cycle in order to help expel the mature egg from the ovary. The libido hormone, testosterone, is produced in roughly the same amounts in men and women to ensure the threshold level necessary for the **sex drive.** Women continue to produce testosterone postmenopausally. Thus, on a hormonal basis, women retain their libido and capacity for sexual response after menopause. The expression of postmenopausal women's sexuality varies cross-culturally. In the United States, it appears to be less dependent on hormones and more dependent on the responsibilities and stress women have in their lives and the quality of the relationships they have with their partners (Kaschak and Tiefer, 2001; Tiefer, 2004). Outside the United States, particularly in foraging and matricentered societies, for example, as well as in Thailand, postmenopausal women's sexuality tends to be accepted and the women are sexually active (Brown and Kerns, 1985; Im-em, et al., 2002).

Specific female sex hormones, **estrogen** (actually a group of hormones) and **progesterone,** are primary ovarian hormones produced from puberty until menopause. Their production and release follow an H-P-G axis pattern analogous to that of the male. FSH induces estrogen; LH induces progesterone. As with the male, the use of recreational drugs (such as alcohol, marijuana, cocaine) and some prescription drugs can affect this release pattern, influencing not only the libido and sexual response cycle, but the menstrual cycle as well (Buffum, 1982; Emanuele, Wezeman, and Emanuele, 1999; Gill, 2000).

Estrogen and progesterone are responsible for the development of primary and secondary sex characteristics. As with the male, these characteristics cover a wide spectrum of individual variation, are relative when comparing men and women, and are expressed through cultural variables of custom, nutrition, and health. Estrogen appears to be more operative than progesterone in the development of many of the female's secondary sex characteristics.

SECONDARY SEX CHARACTERISTICS

Secondary sex characteristics include hair patterning, skin quality, bone integrity, breast development, muscle mass, and the amount and distribution of body fat. Estrogen levels influence the ovoid shape of a female's hairline, axillary or underarm hair, and **pubic hair** growth, and the inverted triangle shape of her pubic hair. As with the male, pubic hair can be sexually sensitive to tactile stimulation or serve as a visual **sexual cue**. It is curly, soft, generally darker than other body hair, and tends to form an inverted triangle from the **pubis** down to the groin, or upper inner thigh area. The color, amount, and vagaries in distribution of pubic and axillary hair are individualized and tied to cultural and genetic factors. For example, women in some Arab societies pluck or shave their pubic hair as part of female hygiene practices. In many societies outside late twentieth-century United States culture, women do not shave their axillary and leg hair. In the United States, shaving or not shaving one's underarms and legs may be a political statement, a gesture of femininity and aesthetics, or a custom of hygiene.

Julia Roberts caused a stir in 1999 when she failed to shave her underarms before the film premiere of Mitchell's Notting Hill *as did Drew Barrymore who appeared at another public event with underarms unshaved ("Drew Barrymore's Hairy Armpit Shocker," 2005). That this simple act engendered media attention and comment reflects a cultural preoccupation with women's body hair.*

One of the functions of estrogen is to keep skin supple and soft, and promote collagen production, a substance which helps to maintain the integrity of skin cells. Estrogen and lower levels of testosterone also help to inhibit acne in women relative to men. Loss of estrogen in menopausal women, lack of facial hair, and not shaving promotes faster skin aging in women than men. In the United States, this is capitalized on by a highly profitable market in facial scrubs, emollients, and plastic surgery.

In general, women's bones are shorter, lighter, and less dense than men's. In part this is due to heredity and cultural factors related to diet and exercise, but it is also due to the ratio and release of estrogen relative to testosterone in a woman's body. The loss of estrogen at menopause also increases a woman's chances of broken and more slowly healing bones as she ages, as well as the risk of **osteoporosis**, a degenerative bone disease. While osteoporosis cannot be reversed or cured once it develops, it can be prevented and slowed. Prevention includes exercise (especially weight-bearing/resistance training), early life cycle attention to diet, with particular attention to sufficient calcium intake through food, not supplements; reduction in animal protein and in the amount of alcohol and nicotine ingested, and **hormone therapy/hormone replacement therapy** (**HT/HRT**). HRT, a controversial treatment due to its possible links with certain cancers, can be taken orally, as patches, gels, or vaginal inserts. Osteoporosis may be a culture-specific disease of middle-class industrialized women. It is not reported as often in China, Japan, or in certain Latin American peasant societies where diet and exercise may serve as preventative agents (Beyene, 1989; Ninghua et al., 2002). Interestingly, Japanese-American descendants of immigrant women to the United States do experience more North American menopausal symptoms, including osteoporosis and hot flashes (Lock, 1993).

Breast development, not breast size or firmness, is another estrogen-related secondary sex characteristic. Breast development includes the growth of the nipples, **areola** (the pigmented area surrounding the nipple), and the development of the milk ducts within the breasts. Lifting weights to increase upper body strength can strengthen the supporting pectoral muscles so that breasts sag less. Breast tissue is highly fatty. Over the past three generations, our culture has emphasized basing female attractiveness on breast size and shape. It is ironic that in a culture currently obsessed with female thinness, fatty (i.e., large breasts) are viewed so positively. In contrast, most nonindustrialized societies value women's breasts as a life-sustaining source of nourishment for the young rather than primarily as an erogenous zone. (See Figures 6.1a, b, c.)

Women's and men's bodies, not culturally manipulated through extreme dieting, use of steroids, or lifting weights, contrast markedly in relation to muscle mass and fat ratios relative to overall body mass. This difference is primarily attributed to the estrogen-testosterone hormone ratio. Women, overall, tend to have less muscle mass and more body fat than do men. Not only do they float in water more readily than men but they tend to have more endurance as well. This is exemplified in their roles as gatherers with kids in tow, and their ability to go through labor and childbirth—the supreme

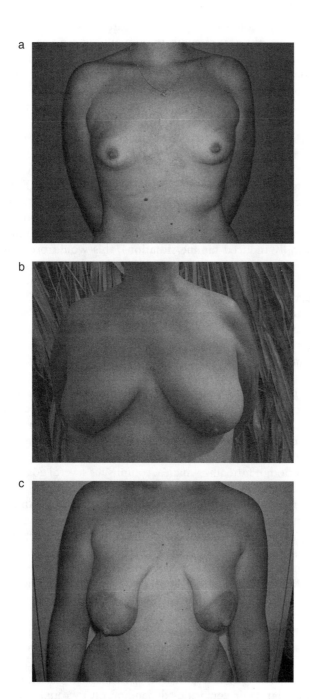

Figure 6.1 Range of female breast size and shapes. (*Source*: Provided by www.007b.com)

mobilization of prolonged energy expenditure. Women tend to be slower, lighter, have less physical strength than men, and tend to carry **body fat** lower, i.e., on their hips, buttocks, and thighs. Since fat is a metabolic insulator, it is one way of keeping reproductive pelvic organs (**uterus, fallopian tubes,** and **ovaries**) both warm and protected. It also means that women vis-à-vis men tend to be less prone to **coronary heart disease (CHD)**, which currently is correlated with upper body fat, more often associated with men.

From an evolutionary perspective, the higher fat/body mass ratio in women and its distribution pattern could be adaptive for a developing **fetus** and **neonate**. The fat insulates and protects the fetus. Pregnancy, birth, and breastfeeding require high energy expenditures. Given the reality of periodic food shortages and famines, which have occurred throughout hominid evolution, it is estimated that the fat reserves a woman carries could sustain her and a fetus/neonate for about eighteen months (Ember and Ember, 1990). In nonculturally induced famine situations, this would probably allow a group sufficient time to locate new food resources without seriously jeopardizing the survival of both a large number of their young and the females of reproductive age.

Females also need a minimum of 17 percent body fat in order to reach puberty, establish and maintain a regular menstrual cycle, including regular ovulation. According to the **Centers for Disease Control and Prevention (CDC)**, women who have less than 18.5 percent body fat are underfat/underweight ("Defining Overweight and Obesity," 2005). This also means that in many nonindustrialized societies, girls have greater muscle mass and aerobic fitness due to their mobility patterns. Because they eat less dietary fat, they may reach puberty later than girls do in industrialized societies where sedentism is more common and the diet is higher in fat and overall calories. In a few African societies for example, prepubescent girls undergo a period of fattening which accomplishes several goals. It increases their body fat to the point they achieve puberty and fattens them so they are culturally defined as attractive and eligible for marriage and pregnancy. The common occurrence in nonindustrialized societies of **adolescent sterility** may actually be a function of insufficient body fat for puberty and regular menstrual cycles to occur. See Chapter 10 for further discussion.

In the United States, current standards for a lean female are about 21 percent body fat; the average is about 24 percent ("Defining Overweight and Obesity," 2005). Given our current interest in female thinness, many younger women, in particular, diet and exercise themselves into fashionable leanness and irregular menstrual cycles. One clear sign of **anorexia nervosa**, a severe and dangerous eating disorder that primarily is found in middle-class adolescent females, is cessation of menstruation. Women athletes whose body fat is less than 17 percent also can experience menstrual and ovulatory irregularities depending on the quality of their diet. These irregularities are reversible upon increasing the body fat ratio beyond 17 percent. Our present standards of female beauty in essence would have women look like lean males with breasts, and reinforce a cultural pattern of potentially serious eating disorders for a sizable number of our population. It is also interesting that a female athlete's price for competitive leanness may be altered menstrual cycles. Similarly, extremely lean males who have less than 6 percent body fat may have reduced production of sperm (Wheeler et al., 1984).

These secondary sex characteristics can be culturally interpreted not only as indicators of sexual adulthood, but also as visual sexual cues exemplified by features such as breast development, appearance of pubic hair, or widening of the hips. In contrast to males where spermatogenesis is hidden, menstruation is a visible and clear marker that primary sex and reproductive characteristics have been achieved. The development of the primary sex characteristics is related to the H-P-G axis and release of estrogen and progesterone from the ovary.

PRIMARY SEX CHARACTERISTICS

Estrogen and progesterone overlap in their effects on the primary sex characteristics, which include the growth and development of the external genitalia and the internal reproductive structures. A female's external genitalia are referred to as the **vulva** (see Figure 6.2).

The **mons, mons pubis,** or **mons veneria** is a fatty pad of tissue covering the pubis. It is sensitive to sexual stimulation and is covered with the upper

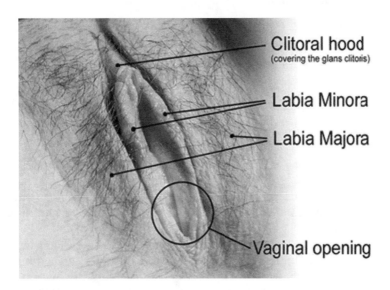

Figure 6.2 Female external genitalia. (*Source*: Wikipedia.)

(See color plates, between pp. 168–169)

part of the triangle of pubic hair. The **labia majora,** or outer lips, are homologous to the scrotum. They are fatty pads of tissue covered with pubic hair. Sensitive to sexual stimulation, they can engorge with blood during sexual arousal. They extend from the bottom part of the mons to the base of the exterior **vagina** or **introitus.** The **labia minora,** analogous and homologous to the foreskin and shaft skin of the penis are hairless, fatty pads of tissue which are surrounded by the labia majora. They form the **prepuce** or **clitoral hood** at their top and the base of the introitus at the bottom. Sensitive to sexual stimulation, they vary in size, shape, and degree of pendulousness with the individual. In some societies they are seen as symbols of beauty and erogenous zones. For example, the Mangaiians have more words to describe the aesthetics of the vulva and **clitoris** than do industrialized societies, where many of the terms carry negative connotations (Marshall and Suggs, 1971).

We are not particularly comfortable with or positive about women's genitalia in the United States. Many of the slang and colloquial terms for female genitalia have negative connotations. As they did for male genitalia in Chapter 5, the students in our human sexuality classes developed a list of terms for female genitalia, listed as follows. Compared to the list for the males, this list is more extensive and the terms are more negative than those for the male.

Terms for female genitalia:

Pussy	Beaver	Vertical smile	Taco (pink and brown)
Coochie	Cooter	Pootang	Roast Beef Curtains
Twat	Down South	Muffin	Sideways Sloppy Joe
Cunt	Biscuit	Bag	Promised Land
Vage	Monkey	Bush	Tuna Taco/Casserole
Box			

In other societies such as in the Sudan, the labia minora are ritually surgically removed in order to preserve a woman's modesty, virginity, and chastity. Currently, this female genital surgical procedure known as **excision** is generating tremendous controversy. It and other forms of female genital surgery will be discussed separately.

The **clitoral hood** or prepuce, formed by the juncture of the labia minora, loosely covers the clitoris. The prepuce is analogous and homologous to the foreskin, particularly where it covers the glans of the clitoris. **Smegma** also collects under the clitoral hood as it does under the foreskin and functions as a lubricant in both instances. The friction of the prepuce over the clitoris can produce intense sexual stimulation.

The clitoris, composed of a glans, shaft, crura or legs, and urethral sponge, is supported by a dense pelvic musculature and has more nerve endings in its glans than does the glans of the penis. Despite its depiction in a number of medical and physiology texts as a "small, pea-like structure, the clitoris is actually about four to six inches in length, most of which is located internally (Chalker, 2000). While homologous to the penis, it is not analogous to it (Freud aside!). The only known function of the clitoris is sexual pleasure. It is the only organ in the human body whose sole function is sexual pleasure. This characteristic functionally distinguishes it from the penis which has four functions: sexual pleasure, a transport mechanism for ejaculate, an organ of reproduction in penile-vaginal intercourse, and a transport mechanism for urine. (See Figures 6.3a and 6.3b.)

Long-standing, widespread, and ongoing controversies abound in Euro-American societies concerning the function of the clitoris. Within the twentieth century alone, there have been the Freudian clitoral versus vaginal model; Masters and Johnson's model with physiological centering of female sexual response in clitoral stimulation; the Singer model of sexual response, and the **G-spot model** of sexual response. See Chapter 11 for a more detailed discussion of female sexual response. The clitoris is a source of cultural interest and definition in nonindustrialized societies as well.

In both industrialized and nonindustrialized societies this interest has been expressed at times in various forms of clitoral surgery, including **circumcision** which removes the prepuce, and **clitoridectomy**, removal of

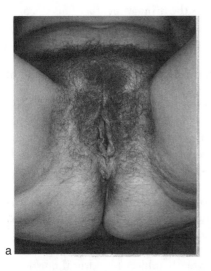 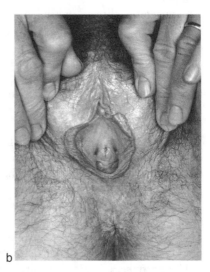

a b

Figure 6.3 Clitoris external structure (left) and exposed structure (right). (*Source:* Reprinted by permission of The Kinsey Institute for Research in Sex, Gender and Reproduction, Inc.)

the glans or shaft. In the United States, these surgeries began in the mid-nineteenth century to curb female masturbation and cure female insanity. The surgeries persisted into the 1930s. In the nineteenth century, women's sexual and reproductive structures were seen as the source of their behavior, affect, and attitudes. Female sexual and reproductive surgery was performed on women who did not conform to their culturally defined roles as good wives and mothers. Medical residents learned these procedures on slave women, lower-class women, and émigrées, and then performed them on middle-class women (Barker-Benfield, 1975; Ehrenreich and English, 1978; Martin, 1987). A gynecologist performed a variation of a clitoridectomy in the 1970s and 1980s by moving the clitoris closer to the introitus in order to "ease" vaginal orgasms for some women in the United States.

The twenty-first-century parallel to this practice is women who have their labia minora surgically sculpted to be "more symmetrical and less obvious."

Cultural-psychological and physiological studies of female sexual response in the United States consistently indicate that clitoral stimulation of some form is a necessary and important aspect of female arousal and orgasmic ability (Hite, 1976, 1987; Kinsey et al., 1953; Masters and Johnson, 1966, 1970, 1974). The clitoris is a physiological center of sexuality for many women.

Between the clitoris and the introitus is the **urinary meatus**. This opening is the end point of the urethra which transports urine from the bladder to outside the body in both men and women. **Urinary tract infections** (UTIs) and **cystitis** are two common problems which occur more frequently in women than men. This is due to women's shorter urethras and the kind of friction a woman experiences during **penile-vaginal intercourse** (p-v) which more readily leads to irritation of the female's urinary meatus and urethra than the male's.

The external vagina is below the urinary meatus. The introitus is the opening to the vagina. It is surrounded by a ring of muscle known as the **pubococcygeus muscle** which helps the introitus to open and contract. These are the same muscles surrounding the **crura**, or root of the penis. The introitus is the final passageway for a fetus and menstrual blood. It is also the entry point for penile-vaginal intercourse and for reproductive sex. The introitus as the external part of the vagina takes on culturally defined physical, sexual, psychological, and reproductive connotations.

The prepuce, clitoris, and introitus are all subject to cultural curiosity, definition, and interpretation in both industrialized and nonindustrialized societies. Industrialized societal interest has been discussed briefly. Nonindustrialized culture has been introduced. Circumcision, clitoridectomy, and infibulation are forms of genital surgery presently practiced in some nonindustrialized societies, most notably in Muslem sub-Saharan African groups. Infibulation entails extensive genital surgery.

Infibulation can include circumcision, excision of the clitoral glans, shaft, and labia minora, and closure of much of the introitus through excising and sealing the labia majora. These procedures have received a great deal of attention recently by varied groups including the media, United Nations, **World Health Organization (WHO)**, and researchers. Introduced here, the practices which follow are also discussed in Chapter 10. These indigenous procedures have been affected by **acculturation** or culture contact. They are sources of intense controversy concerning their sexual, reproductive, and psychological effects on the women, their partners, and the kin groups involved (Lightfoot-Klein, 1989, 1990; Ohm, 1980). Issues of **ethnocentrism, cultural relativism**, and **indigenous cultural integrity** are involved. For example, among the Gbaya, a horticultural group in central Africa, removal of the glans clitoris in pubescent girls is a *rite de passage* (**initiation ceremony**), a symbolic and real marker of her transition from girlhood to womanhood. The girls go through this ritual together as part of a larger social group. Gbaya interpret the clitoridectomy as making her less male and more female. She emerges from the ritual as a recognized adult. Pubescent boys, circumcised at a younger age, undergo a similar procedure in which their glans is nicked so they can participate in their female peers' ritual. Do we as members of industrialized societies have a right or obligation to interfere with these practices? How well do we socialize our adolescents into adulthood? What painful physical and psychological costs do we extract from our young? Are people being mutilated physically, socially, psychologically? Who makes this determination? These are extremely difficult, emotionally charged behaviors within cultures, let alone between cultures. Resolution of their controversial aspects will take a long time to achieve.

Another anatomical structure which generates much cultural interpretation and concern is the **hymen**. The hymen is most likely a vestigial organ with no currently known function. It is semi-permeable and partially or completely covers the introitus in many women. The nature of the hymen is of particular concern in patrilineal (descent through the male line), bilateral (descent through the male and female line), and patricentered (male-centered) descent groups where paternity must be known for offspring to have a legal, social, economic, and political place in the society.

The condition of the hymen is used to define a female's virginity and chastity. Virginity, a physiological state, is attributed to someone regardless of gender who has never had a penile-vaginal intercourse. Chastity is a socio-cultural condition in which an individual, regardless of gender, lives by the culturally appropriate sexual code of behavior, affect, and attitude as defined by the group. For example, a woman who is a "good wife and mother" by her culture's definitions and standards is no longer a virgin, but can still be chaste. How? By following her culture's rules concerning such behaviors as appropriate dress, speech (she "watches her language" in front of her children), or sexual behavior (she responds to her husband's advances, but does not initiate sex). In contrast, in the 1950s and early 1960s, in the United States a "girl" could be a virgin, but not chaste. These "girls," sometimes known as "cock teases," would do "everything" except p-v intercourse with boys or would arouse a boy ("get him hot") and then not "give" him an orgasm ("leave him hanging" or "not come through").

While chastity and virginity ideally are gender free, their cultural interpretation in bilateral and patrilineal descent groups usually results in a double standard of sexual behavior. Promoting nonchastity and nonvirginity for males demonstrates their potential fertility and actual virility, both necessary for reproductive success. In contrast, repressing female sexual behavior in these patricentered societies except under strict culturally controlled situations such as strictly enforced monogamous marriage accomplishes two goals. It achieves reproductive success since the woman does not have to be orgasmic or ejaculatory in order to conceive and give birth. Second, controlling her sexual behavior and severely limiting her sexual outlets and number of partners helps to make certain the paternity of the child. He is probably her one and only sexual partner. This double standard is culturally widespread and persists in the United States. For example, surveys of United States college students' sexual behavior over the past twenty years indicate women still are subject to greater disapproval than men for having multiple sexual partners, particularly when emotional attachment does not exist (Crawford and Popp, 2003; Reiss, 1986; Whelehan and Moynihan, 1984). In some Mediterranean societies, chastity and virginity are affirmed on a bride's wedding night when blood, either hers or from a vial of sheep's blood given to her as a gift by her female relatives, appears on the sheet after her first intercourse. During the Middle Ages *ius pramae noctis* or first night rite was a common ritual performed on brides on their wedding night. They were "deflowered" by the owner of the fief in order to establish proprietary rights over the serfs— men, women, and children, as well as the land (Bullough, 1976; Fernea, 1989). Currently, in some sub-Saharan African societies, virginity tests and certificates for females (but not males!) are issued as a means to reduce HIV infections.

Bartholin's glands are located on each side of the base of the introitus. These small glands generally are unnoticed unless they are infected, in which case they can swell painfully. Bartholin's glands secrete a clear fluid; their function is unknown presently. Bartholin's glands are homologous to Cowper's glands in the male (see Chapter 5).

The **perineum** is homologous in males and females and extends from the base of the introitus to the anus. Soft, generally hairless, and sensitive to sexual stimulation, the perineum stretches during vaginal childbirth to allow the baby to pass through the introitus. As with many other aspects of female sexual and reproductive anatomy, the perineum is subject to cultural scrutiny and controversy. The ability of the perineum to stretch during childbirth is culturally manipulated.

In most nonindustrialized societies women give birth semi-upright, which relaxes and stretches the perineum. In addition, many societies further stretch and soften the perineum through massage or the application of warm compresses or oils. These efforts reduce the chance of perineal tears during childbirth (Arms, 1975; Boston Women's Health Collective, 2005; Davis-Floyd, 2001; Janssen et al., 2002; Johanson et al., 2002; "Midwives and Modernization," 1981).

In the United States, a common way of stretching the perineum during childbirth is through an **episiotomy,** a surgical incision in the perineum. This is believed to reduce the possibility of perineal tears, a high probability given the **dorsal lithotomy position** (lying on one's back) used in over 90 percent of U.S. births (Arms, 1975; Davis-Floyd, 1992, 2001; Masters, Johnson, and Kolodony, 1982). Episiotomies are one of several current controversies in U.S. childbirth practices. These controversies will be dealt with in more depth in Chapter 8.

Internal sexual and reproductive structures include the vagina, uterus, fallopian tubes, and broad ligament. The internal vagina, a tubular, muscular organ, extends from the introitus, back about four to five inches in a curved manner, ending in a blind pouch or cul-de-sac known as the Pouch of Douglas. As a structure, the walls of the vagina rest on one another. Androcentrically (i.e., from a male perspective), the vagina is often described as a potential space. It is a passageway for menstrual blood, sperm, and the birthing fetus. Its expansion capacities are remarkable. From a state of collapsed walls to being able to accommodate a penis or a full-term baby indicates a high degree of flexibility. As a sexual structure, its orgasmic function is a source of cross-cultural interest, definition, and discussion (e.g., the *Kaama Sutra of Vatsayana* in Freud, 1920a; Garrison, 1983; Gregersen, 1983; Hite, 1976, 1981, 1987; Kinsey et al., 1953; Masters and Johnson, 1966). For many women in the United States, it is both a psychological center of sexuality and a sex organ (see Berman, Berman, and Bumiller, 2001; Hite, 1976, 1981, 1987). In addition to its sexual functions, it is a reproductive structure.

The vagina is a sexual and reproductive structure with a pH of about 4.5 to 5; making it slightly acidic. The acidity of the vagina and its natural flora keep it clean and healthy. It is the cleanest orifice in the human body. Regular, frequent douching is unnecessary and can upset the pH levels, irritating the mucosa, and leading to irritation and infections. Disruptions in the vagina's pH balance or flora can be caused by antibiotics, STDs, stress, or illness. A healthy vaginal mucosa premenopausally is pinkish, firm, springy, and moist. Vaginal lubrication or **exudate,** which occurs during sexual arousal, passes directly through the vaginal mucosa (lining). Healthy vaginal mucosa is maintained largely through estrogen, low stress, a balanced diet, and general hygiene.

Since a healthy vagina is slightly acidic, there is a possibility of incompatibility with a male sexual partner's semen, which is basic. In some instances this may cause fertility problems. Also, popular fads to alter the pH of the vagina to increase the chances of conceiving the desired sex are generally a waste of time, money, and effort, as they may damage sperm or irritate the vaginal mucosa.

The vaginal mucosa changes with menopause. The reduction in estrogen production can result in drying and thinning of the mucosa which can lead to painful intercourse. The irritated mucosa can be soothed through the use of water-based lubricants such as K-Y Jelly, Probe or Forplay, or through hormone replacement therapy/hormone therapy (HRT/HT), either as a topical ointment, or in pill or tablet form (Seaman and Seaman, 1977; Stewart and Spencer, 2002; Stewart et al., 1979). However, data from the nationwide Women's Health Initiative Study indicates that the risks of taking HRT may outweigh the benefits. There are alternative behaviors and herbal drugs that can ease the symptoms of menopause which women may want to consider either in addition to or instead of HRT (NIH, 2002). These include wearing layers of clothing, reducing the amount of hot liquids and caffeine drunk, and taking chasteberry or black cohosh to reduce the intensity and frequency of hot flashes. Water-based lubricants can alleviate vaginal dryness and make intercourse more comfortable.

Located on the anterior wall of the vagina, under the pubis and about one-third of the way in from the introitus, is the location of the alleged "G spot" or Grafenberg spot. "Alleged" is used because the very existence of the Grafenberg spot is challenged by some sexologists (e.g., Masters, Johnson, and Kolodny, 1985). MRIs do not show the existence of a G-spot during missionary position (man on top) p-v intercourse (Schultz et al., 1999).

Those researchers who accept the existence of a "G spot" state that it is a source of orgasmic potential and associate it with female ejaculatory ability (e.g., Kiefer, 2005; Ladas, Whipple, and Perry, 1982). Under penile penetration with the woman on top, or with direct deep finger pressure, the "G spot," an area of soft tissue, increases in size and produces a sense of sexual pleasure. Continued stimulation may result in orgasm as well as the ejaculation of fluid from **Skene's** or the **paraurethral glands** that are located on each side of the "G spot." The chemical composition of this fluid, sometimes referred to androcentrically as female ejaculate, is debated (Ladas, Whipple, and Perry, 1982; Mahoney, 1983). Since some researchers believe this fluid is similar in composition to prostatic fluid, skene's gland can be referred to as the "female prostate." This fluid is deposited into the urethra and expelled from there during "G spot" orgasmic response. The expulsion of this fluid from the urethra has led some women, their partners, some researchers, and physicians to believe that these women experience **urinary stress incontinence (USI)** or involuntary leakage of urine. Unless these individuals are into "water sports" (playing with urine which in the age of AIDS may be a risky behavior), this belief has created orgasmic problems for some of these women, distress for some of their partners and has led a few physicians to perform surgery on these women for USI (Ladas, Whipple, and Perry, 1982). The intensity of the controversy surrounding the entire "G spot" phenomenon as opposed to accepting it as a possible variation of sexual response is another indication of our continued discomfort with sexuality in general and women's sexuality specifically.

The broad ligament is a band of connective tissue across the woman's lower abdomen which supports the uterus, fallopian tubes, and ovaries. As a supportive structure, it is one reason why women have fewer abdominal and pelvic hernias than men.

The ovaries are homologues and analogues of the testes. Pearly gray and almond shaped, they are located in the lower pelvis, slightly lower and adjacent to the fallopian tubes. The ovaries are the female gonads, responsive to stimulation by the pituitarian hormones FSH and LH. They are the primary sources of estrogen and progesterone and are palpable under gentle stimulation during a pelvic exam. As an introduction, the ovaries contain the eggs, or **ova**, in tiny sacs called **follicles**. A woman is born with all the ova she will ever have. She matures and releases about 400 eggs during her reproductive life cycle. Egg development and number are in some ways a degenerative process in contrast to spermatogenesis. A female is born with about half the eggs she had as a fetus. Although several eggs start to mature with each menstrual cycle, usually only one achieves maturity and is released. The other ripening eggs during that cycle are reabsorbed by the ovary (Berek, Adashi and Hillard, 1996).

The ovaries serve hormonal, reproductive, sexual, and cultural functions. They produce the female gonadotropins, estrogen, and progesterone, and mature and release eggs in preparation for fertilization. By releasing estrogen and progesterone they help maintain uterine tone and functioning, and maintain a healthy vaginal mucosa, both of which play roles in reproductive and sexual response. Ovaries are given cultural significance related to femininity, maternal behavior, and appropriate gender role behavior. In fact, **oophrectomy**, removal of the ovaries or female castration, was commonly performed in the United States during the nineteenth century to "cure" female insanity or to enforce "gender appropriate behavior" (Barker-Benfield, 1975; Boston Women's Health Collective, 2005; Ehrenreich and English, 1978; Klee, 1988). This practice is another example of our culture's consistently negative attitudes toward female sexuality.

The fallopian tubes extend from the fundus of the uterus for about five to seven inches to the ovaries. They do not cover the ovaries. Hollow, with hairlike cilia projections along their inner walls, they are about the size of a broom straw or thin strand of spaghetti. Homologous and analogous to the vas deferens in males, they end as fibrillated or tendril-like organs. At ovulation, when an egg is released by the ovary, the adjacent fibrillated ends of the fallopian tube generally draw the egg into the tube. Fertilization usually occurs in the distal or far end of the tube called the **ampulla**, where the tube curves. The egg, regardless of whether it is fertilized, is moved down the tube by the cilia. It takes the egg several days to reach the uterus. If fertilized, it may implant in the corpus section of the uterus and begin to develop into an embryo, then a fetus. If unfertilized, the egg passes through the uterine cavity.

The fallopian tubes are the normal site of fertilization; the uterus is the normal site of implantation. Occasionally, however, a fertilized egg embeds outside the uterus. This is called an **ectopic pregnancy**. The most common site of an ectopic pregnancy is a fallopian tube. An ectopic pregnancy is a life-threatening medical situation. The embedded egg will grow in the tube until the tube bursts. Initially mimicking a uterine pregnancy (e.g., cessation of menstruation, possible breast tenderness, and nausea), an ectopic pregnancy can be diagnosed by a careful and thorough pelvic exam, pregnancy tests, or an ultrasound. Early diagnosis is important, as the tube will burst by the end of the first trimester. Treatment currently entails either drugs, resectioning of the affected tube after removal of the embedded embryo, or removal of the affected tube (Coste et al., 2004; Kamwendo et al., 2000; Lipscomb, Stovell, and Ling, 2000).

Although fallopian tube transplants in humans have been done (Schenker and Evron, 1983), as of yet, successful transplants of ectopic pregnancies to a uterine environment are not possible. Ectopic pregnancies occur in about 2 to 5 percent of pregnancies. The incidence of ectopic pregnancies is related to sexually transmitted infections such as gonorrhea and chlamydia which scar the fallopian tubes, and the growing occurrences of endometriosis and pelvic inflammatory disease (PID) that can result from these infections (Coste et al., 2004; "Current Trends Ectopic Pregnancy," 1995; Kamwendo et al., 2000).

The uterus or womb is composed of several parts and performs both sexual and reproductive functions. The uterus, a pear-shaped organ about the size of a large thumb, is located in the central lower pelvic area. It extends into the vagina. The uterus is a muscular organ which produces **prostglandins**. Prostglandins are hormones which perform a number of functions including contraction of the uterus. Prostglandins may be involved in the uterine contractions that occur during orgasm, those that occur during menstruation and cause menstrual cramps, and as a partial cause of uterine contractions during **labor**. As one of the strongest muscles in the human body, the uterus can be exercised and toned. Part of the tone of the uterus is due to the release of such hormones as LTH, progesterone, and prostglandins. Uterine tone is also maintained through orgasms, during which the uterus contracts (Answers.com, 2005; Sherfey, 1972). A healthy, toned uterus allows not only for greater chance of retaining an implanted embryo, but for its development and expulsion nine months later. Female orgasms then, not only feel good, but may help to contribute to reproductive success.

Among the Sambia and some groups in sub-Saharan Africa, regular intercourse with ejaculation and orgasm in the women is seen as helping the development of the fetus. During the Renaissance, in Italy, people believed that a child would be healthy, attractive, and intelligent if both partners had an orgasm during conception. "Folklore" may have more basis in science than is commonly believed in some situations (Herdt, 2006).

The uterus is composed of several layers, the **myometrium, parametrium,** and **endometrium**. The parts of the uterus to be discussed include the **fundus,** the **corpus,** the **cervix,** the **os,** and the endometrium. The fundus is the rounded top part of the uterus. As the uterus enlarges during pregnancy, the fundus can be felt externally through the lower abdomen as it rises above the pelvic bone. The corpus or body of the uterus is composed of several layers of which only the endometrium will be discussed. The fallopian tubes enter the uterus at the bottom of the fundus and beginning of the corpus. The corpus extends into the vagina from its lower section, the cervix.

The cervix extends into the vagina and can be felt by deep insertion of the fingers into the vagina, and can be seen by the use of a mirror and speculum. A speculum is the instrument used during a pelvic exam to separate the walls of the vagina. The cervix receives a lot of medical and lay attention. The cervix is the site of the **PAP smear (Papanicolaou smear)**. The PAP test is part of a gynecological exam. Cells are gently scraped from the cervix and analyzed to detect cervical normalcy and abnormalities, including cancer. Cervical cancer is one of the more common cancers to affect women. Regular PAP smears every one to three years help to ensure early detection and treatment (see Figure 6.4).

The cervix changes in color and texture depending on whether or not a woman is pregnant. In nonpregnant women, the cervix is pinkish and cartilaginous in texture, similar in texture to the tip of your nose. In response to hormones released during pregnancy, the cervix softens to a state more similar in texture to your lips, and changes color to a bluish-purplish hue. During sexual arousal and orgasm, the uterus, including the cervix, responds in various ways by retracting, contracting, and lowering into the vagina.

The cervix is the site of the os, an opening in the tip of the cervix generally about the size of a thin pencil lead. It also changes in color and shape depending on whether or not a woman is pregnant. A nonpregnant woman's os is pinkish and donut-hole shaped; a pregnant woman's os is purplish or bluish and more like a slit. This change in shape is irreversible after a woman

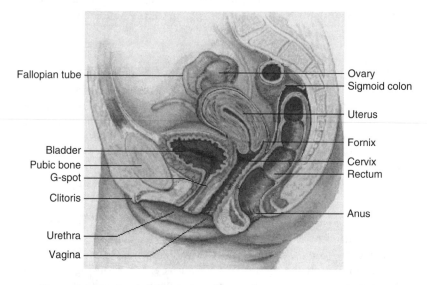

Fallopian tube

Ovary
Sigmoid colon

Uterus

Bladder
Pubic bone
G-spot

Fornix
Cervix
Rectum

Clitoris

Anus

Urethra

Vagina

Figure 6.4 Uterine development and musculature. (*Source*: Wikipedia.)

has a child. These changes in the cervix and os appear in the first trimester and are used as signs of pregnancy during a prenatal pelvic exam. The os is the passageway for **menses** (menstrual blood), the fetus, and sperm. During menstruation the os dilates slightly to allow the shedding endometrium to pass through. The os is the structure which dilates or opens during the first stage of labor to allow the baby to pass through.

Most of the month, the os is covered with a thickish, sticky substance called **cervical mucous**. Cervical mucous is a protective barrier to keep foreign objects such as sperm, douches, contraceptive foams, or bacteria out of the sterile uterine cavity. Just prior to and during ovulation, however, the cervical mucous thins and becomes more permeable in order to allow the sperm entry to the fallopian tubes where the egg may be fertilized. If the egg is fertilized and implants in the endometrium, another mucoid substance, the cervical plug forms over the os as a protective seal for the fetus against foreign substances entering the uterine cavity. The cervical plug usually is expelled during the first stage of labor and is used as a sign that labor is imminent or has begun.

The endometrium is the innermost lining of the uterus. In response to H-P-G axis hormones, estrogen builds up the endometrium, and progesterone maintains it in the uterus. The endometrium serves as the anchor for the embryo and fetus. The endometrium is a thick, cushiony layer of blood, tissue, and mucous which accumulates each month in preparation for a fertilized egg. The fertilized egg implants in the endometrium where it remains attached for nine months by the placenta as it develops into an embryo and fetus. The endometrium is shed as the menses or menstrual blood if fertilization and implantation do not occur.

There is a clinical condition called **endometriosis** which is primarily found among middle-class, college-educated, career women in the United States who are in their late twenties and thirties. Many of them are nulliparous (they have never borne a child). Endometriosis involves patches of endometrial tissue found on the ovaries, external uterus, or other pelvic and abdominal organs, and in the fallopian tubes. Endometriosis in the fallopian tubes can cause tubal blockage and scarring, interfering with conception. Although the exact cause of endometriosis is unknown, it is theorized that it may be due to a variety of factors including prenatal disposition, hormone fluctuations, and delayed pregnancy among some career women (Berek, Adashi, and Hillard, 1996; Stewart et al., 1979).

Symptoms of endometriosis include fertility and menstrual problems, pain during both intercourse, known as **dyspareunia**, and menstruation, known as **dysmenorrhea**. Definitive diagnosis of endometriosis is through **laparoscopy**, a surgical procedure that involves an incision in the abdomen where organs are viewed through a lighted tube or laparoscope. Treatment can be hormonal or surgical depending on the severity of the situation. In a number of cases fertility may be restored (Berek, Adashi, and Hillard, 1996; Wade and Cirese, 1991).

The uterus, composed of several structures, is a marvelous organ. Its capacity to change in size and function, depending on pregnancy, is phenomenal. As a reproductive and sexual organ, it is imbued with a range of cultural connotations and definitions. For example, the sexual function of the uterus is only recently being accepted and understood, making its already controversial ritual removal (hysterectomy) postmenopausally in the United States an even more debatable issue (Berman, Berman, and Bumiller, 2001; Boston Women's Health Collective, 2005; Klee, 1988). In general, in industrialized societies for the past several hundred years, women's mental health has been defined as a function of her reproductive organs (Barker-Benfield, 1975; Klee, 1988). Freud used a psychiatric classification known as hysteria from the Greek word for womb, another term for the uterus. According to Freud, hysteria is primarily an affliction of women, characterized by over-emotionality, denial, and depression (Freud, 1920a, 1920b).

In both industrialized and nonindustrialized societies the function of the uterus and ovaries are subject to cultural scrutiny. For example, in the Tiwi society, an Australian foraging group, the essence of sexuality is female. Female totems, religious, and animistic guardian spirits, which are inanimate symbolic structures that are given lifelike characteristics, play a role in conception. Although the Tiwi realize that heterosexual contact and penile-vaginal intercourse is necessary for conception, they need to explain why only certain incidences of p-v intercourse results in conception. Their causal explanation for heterosexual contact, which results in conception, is that a female totem breathes life into the woman's body. Part of Tiwi contraception then includes appeasement of the female totems to avoid pregnancy (Goodale, 1971). Cultural concern over this aspect of human behavior is matched by the degree of concern human groups have with another bio-behavioral phenomenon, menstruation. Key concepts related to menstruation (the shedding of the endometrium) are menarche, a girl's first menstruation or period, and the menstrual cycle.

MENSTRUAL CYCLE

The menstrual cycle, a primary sex characteristic, has both sexual and reproductive functions and is reproductively analogous to spermatogenesis discussed in Chapter 5. Both the menstrual cycle and spermatogenesis produce the **gametes**, the egg or ovum, and sperm, respectively, which are necessary for conception to occur. The menstrual cycle and spermatogenesis function in response to the H-P-G axis. Other similarities include the involvement of homologous structures such as the ovaries and testes, the fallopian tubes and vas deferens. The menstrual cycle and spermatogenesis are physiological processes culturally defined as signals of sexual and reproductive adulthood.

These are also sharp contrasts between the menstrual cycle and spermatogenesis. The menstrual cycle is just that, cyclic, roughly taking a lunar, twenty-eight-day month, to follow through a round of H-P-G axis hormone release. The menstrual cycle is rhythmic as opposed to the tonicity of spermatogenesis and male H-P-G axis functioning. The ovaries do not produce eggs as the testes produce sperm; rather, several immature eggs start developing each month in their follicles or sacs in the ovaries. Generally, only one egg reaches maturity and is released at one point in the cycle, **ovulation**, as opposed to the continuous, numerous—several-million-daily—production of sperm. The menstrual cycle is highly visible in the menstrual phase when the endometrium is shed through the os and out of the body vaginally. In contrast, spermatogenesis is unmarked. There are no clear primary markers of this process other than the irregularity of nocturnal emissions (i.e., wet dreams). Indicators of spermatogenesis often are culturally defined through secondary sex characteristics such as beard growth, voice changes, the growth spurt in height and limb length, or through the imposition of initiation ceremonies or *rites de passage*, rituals that socially take a person from one stage in the life cycle to another.

Another contrast between the menstrual cycle and spermatogenesis is the arbitrary, finite nature of the menstrual cycle. Menstruation begins at puberty, occurs roughly once a month for an average of four to seven days, and ends at menopause. It is bleeding without injury, illness, or provocation. In contrast, spermatogenesis is invisible. Sperm do not appear in other situations such as illness or injury as blood may, and spermatogenesis is continuous from puberty to death. The attributes of the menstrual cycle allow for a range of cultural interpretation and action.

The discussion of the physiology of the menstrual cycle is adapted from Speroff, Glass, and Kase (1978). The menstrual cycle is discussed in four phases: follicular, ovulation, luteal, and menstrual or menstruation. Born with all the eggs she'll ever have, about 700,000, a woman will mature and release a range of 200 to 400 eggs during her reproductive life cycle, barring illness, injury, pregnancy, or surgery on her reproductive organs (Berek, Adashi, and Hillard, 1996). Based on a lunar, twenty-eight-day calendar cycle, she will mature and release about thirteen eggs a year. These are averages for healthy industrialized women. In reality, there can be considerable variation relative to the length and regularity of the cycle and egg release, depending on variables such as nutrition, amount of body fat, stress, illness, or pregnancy.

The regular, relatively uninterrupted menstrual cycles that many twenty-first-century, middle-class, U.S. women experience is probably a recent, evolutionary anomaly. They are a function of bottle feeding, frequent use of external, chemical, or barrier contraceptives, and fewer pregnancies. The female hominid pattern, until recently, probably was one of fewer regular menstrual cycles, since much of a woman's life was spent lactating for several years, interspersed with pregnancies (Beyene, 1989).

The **follicular phase** is the longest and most irregular of the four phases of the menstrual cycle. Its length determines the overall length of the cycle and the regularity from one cycle to the next. The follicular phase ranges between eleven and sixteen days in length. Egg maturation occurs during the follicular phase. Based on hypothalamic release of GnRH, the pituitary releases FSH stimulating multiple egg maturation in the follicles of the ovary. About midpoint in the follicular phase, FSH starts to falter which induces the release of ovarian estrogen, specifically **estradiol**. Estradiol helps to stabilize the FSH level and induces the release of LH. At this point, the end of the follicular phase is approaching and LH performs several functions. It stops multiple egg maturation, and helps to release the most mature egg from the follicle, which is also aided by the release of androgens, specifically androstriol. During this time estrogen regulates the levels of FSH and LH, maintaining a delicate balance between them since a surge of FSH would stimulate egg maturation again and a drop in LH could impede the most mature egg's release from the ovary. For this reason, estrogen or estradiol is called the key regulating hormone in the menstrual cycle. At the end of the follicular phase, the egg is ready to be released, FSH is stabilized, LH and estrogen levels are high (see Figure 6.5).

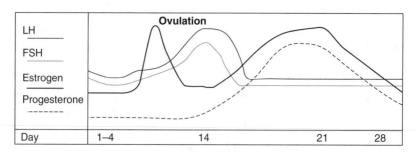

		Ovulation		
LH				
FSH				
Estrogen				
Progesterone				
Day	1–4	14	21	28

Figure 6.5 Menstrual cycle diagrammatically. (*Source*: Mary Emanuele.)

(See color plates, between pp. 168–169)

Data are inconsistent as to whether or not women experience an increased interest in genital, heterosexual contact at ovulation. From reports some women are "horniest" at ovulation, others are just prior to or during their periods, others are throughout their cycle, and some not at all (Hite, 1976; Masters and Johnson, 1966; Masters, Johnson and Kolodny, 1985). While biologically it would "make sense" to be most interested in sex during ovulation (consistently assumed to be p-v intercourse in much of the literature), human sexuality is a complicated interaction of biology and learned behavior, including perception and emotions. Human sexual behavior is culturally filtered and expressed, which can explain the variation in research findings.

Ovulation is the briefest phase of the cycle. It is the release of the egg from the follicle into the lower pelvis where it is generally drawn into its corresponding fallopian tube. Ovulation occurs at midcycle. Generally a woman ovulates once a month, but there can be variations due to stress, intense orgasms, or irregular follicular and ovulatory patterns (Speroff et al., 1978). Thus, since a woman can, though rarely does, ovulate more than once a month, it is untrue that she cannot get pregnant during her period— that she's totally "safe" then as some U.S. folk beliefs assert. In addition, some women's cycles are sufficiently irregular such that ovulation may occur during menstruation. A woman may be aware of ovulation through a cramping or pinching sensation in her lower abdomen from the ovary which just released its egg. This sensation is similar to a stitch in one's side after running. The cramping is called **mittelschmerz**. It occurs as the egg bursts through the surface of the ovary; a small amount of ovarian bleeding, which is absorbed by the body, may occur at that time as well.

The luteal phase is the third phase of the menstrual cycle. A lot of activity can potentially occur at this time. A woman with late luteal phase disorder (LLPD)/premenstrual syndrome (PMS) experiences this during the luteal phase. During the luteal phase the egg is either fertilized or not. Each case will be presented. The follicle that just released the egg is now called the **corpus luteum,** which is Latin for "yellow body." Upon stimulation by pituitarian LH, the corpus luteum secretes progesterone. Progesterone maintains the endometrium which was built up by estrogen in the uterine cavity. Progesterone is released throughout this phase until it receives a signal from the decomposing egg that fertilization has not occurred. LH levels are also elevated to stimulate progesterone release until a "no fertilization" message occurs. If the egg is not fertilized, it starts to break down. In turn, LH levels drop which triggers a drop in progesterone levels. At a certain point, the progesterone level is sufficiently low that the uterine lining, i.e., the endometrium, can not be maintained. It is then shed as the menses. Concurrently there are drops in FSH and estrogen. When estrogen and FSH are sufficiently low, the hypothalamus is triggered, releases GnRH, and the hormonal release pattern begins again.

If fertilization occurs in the luteal phase, another set of hormonal patterns occur. Estrogen and progesterone levels, maintained by FSH and LH, remain elevated to keep the endometrium in place. The fertilized egg begins producing its own hormones from the developing placenta, which at this stage is called the **chorion.** The chorion produces **human chorionic gonadotropin, HCG,** or "the pregnancy hormone." HCG is called the pregnancy hormone because it is the substance detected by standard at-home and clinical pregnancy tests. **HCG is produced until about the tenth to twelfth weeks** of gestation, at which time the placental steroids, another group of hormones, function to keep the placenta attached to the endometrium. Up to this point of embryonic development, HCG keeps the developing placenta attached to the endometrium. Excess levels of HCG are secreted in the mother's urine, with the highest levels of HCG secreted early in the morning. Thus, a woman uses a urine specimen for the pregnancy test.

The fourth phase of the menstrual cycle is menstruation or menses. On average, menstruation is the four to seven days when the endometrium is shed. Menses is composed of blood, tissue, and mucous. Menstrual blood amounts to about one-half cup of liquid, most of which is expelled in the first forty-eight hours of the woman's period. The entire menstrual cycle, as well as menstruation specifically, generates widespread cultural interest and reaction.

Negative attitudes and beliefs about menstruation and women's sexuality are common in horticultural societies that are **polygynous** (i.e., allow more than one wife), patrilineal (descent is through the male line), engage in endemic or ongoing warfare, and that have a high degree of segregation between the sexes. Men and women in these societies do not often interact and, therefore, do not know each other well. As adults, their marriages frequently occur as political strategies to settle disputes or form alliances against warring groups. In groups such as the Yanamamo and Mae Enga, men fight, bleed, and die for women who bleed spontaneously without apparent injury. In these societies, men must be careful of women's sexual behavior or the lineage will be damaged. These factors probably contribute to negative beliefs about menstruating women. In addition, in many of these societies women control the food supply and men are dependent upon them for food. The sum effect of these intense behaviors can result in strong antifemale ideology by men concerning women's sexual and reproductive functions (Buckley and Gottlieb, 1988; Herdt, 1981, 1987, and 2006).

In many of these societies, women are further segregated from their peers and men during menstruation by staying in a menstrual hut. Menstrual huts are frequently described in the anthropological literature as the *sine qua non* of female oppression and degradation. However, while in the menstrual hut, women spend time with other menstruating women, eat special (i.e., restricted) foods, and do not have to assume routine cooking, child care, food preparation, and other work responsibilities. Are menstrual huts oppression, a break from hard work, or an opportunity for women from different areas to socialize?

Menstrual taboos are by no means restricted to nonindustrialized societies. They are alive and functioning currently in industrialized societies, impacting women at work and at home (Olesen and Woods, 1986). In the author's human sexuality classes, students are asked to generate two lists. One list describes everything they have heard from peers, parents, media, books, and street talk about spermatogenesis and the other one is about the menstrual cycle. They are then asked to sort this list as to having neutral, negative, or positive connotations.

The menstrual cycle list can be extensive. Most of the phrases and terms are negative, a few are neutral, and even fewer are positive. This is sexually sophisticated, early twenty-first-century, post-"Sexual Revolution" U.S. culture! Readers might be interested in determining the value-laden connotations to these terms for themselves and their peers.

Spermatogenesis	Menstrual cycle
"cum"	that time of the month up
ready to have kids	on the rag
wet dreams	"bitchy"
being a man	moody, irritable
	irrational
	being a woman
	moon cycles
	dirty
	don't swim, bathe, shower or have sex

As stated at the beginning of this section, menstruation is a bio-behavioral phenomenon. Three specific examples of this include menstrual cramps, menstrual synchrony, and late luteal phase disorder (LLPD), more commonly known as premenstrual syndrome (PMS) and more specifically as LLPD/PMS. Data for these phenomena largely are derived from industrialized cultures. Prostglandins, released by the uterus, play a physiological role in menstrual cramps. Prostglandins cause uterine contractions. Depending on the amount of prostglandins released, and the strength, intensity, and frequency of the contractions, these contractions may be experienced as cramps. The woman's pain threshold and tolerance for this kind of sensation, in addition to her learned attitudes and behavior toward her body, menstruation, and expressions of pain, all contribute to the phenomenon of cramps. Exercise, orgasms, and aspirin are all reported to be helpful in alleviating cramps.[1] Cramps are no more "all in your head" than they are a complete function of "raging hormones," both of which are popularly held beliefs in the United States.

Menstrual synchrony is both documented and controversial. Menstrual synchrony is the eventual synchronization of menstrual cycles among women who live near one another and are in close contact. It may be an evolutionarily recent phenomenon with a number of determining variables that are not well understood (Mealey, 2004; Weller and Weller, 1998). Physiologically, menstrual synchrony may be a function of pheromone release. Pheromones, which were discussed earlier in this text, are **sexual scent signals** or **olfactory cues**. It is believed that pheromones may be the hormonal basis in evening out and regulating women's periods. Since menstrual synchrony only occurs among women who are both emotionally bonded and who are in frequent contact with each other (e.g., they live together and spend time with each other), this would allow for them to key into each other's pheromone patterns. The pattern is broken if either the emotional tie or contact is disrupted (McClintock, 1971). Menstrual synchrony could have potential for reproductive success if women have regular heterosexual genital sex partners. Regular ovulation and menstrual cycles coupled with continuous sexual receptivity among these women would increase the chances for conception. There is some evidence that women who have regular p-v sex with their partners have shorter and more regular menstrual cycles (Jarrett, 1984). How this works in polygynous societies would be an interesting study.

Late luteal phase disorder (LLPD) or premenstrual syndrome (PMS), the popular name for this phenomenon, currently is a controversial medical, social, and legal phenomenon in the United States and other industrialized cultures (Buckley and Gottlieb, 1988; Martin, 1987). Some physicians deny its existence (Masters, Johnson, and Kolodny, 1985), and others debate what it is. The American Psychiatric Association includes LLPD/PMS under the diagnosis of late luteal phase disorder (LLPD) in its new edition of the *Diagnostic and Statistical Manual (DSM IV)* (Berek, Adashi, and Hillard, 1996; Hamilton and Gallent, 1990; Lips, 1993: 217). There are clinics and physicians in the United States and other industrialized countries such as Canada and Great Britain that address LLPD/PMS. LLPD/PMS is a collection of symptoms that range in type, frequency, duration, and intensity. These symptoms occur during the luteal phase of the menstrual cycle and disappear when menstruation begins. LLPD/PMS may have a cumulative progression in its intensity, but it reportedly primarily affects women in their twenties and thirties. The cause continues to be investigated and debated. One current explanation is that LLPD/PMS is caused by fluctuating progesterone levels during this phase (Martin, 1987). It is estimated that the vast majority of women (numbers vary widely) experience at least the milder forms of LLPD/PMS at some point during their reproductive life cycles. Symptoms range from mild to extreme. Milder LLPD/PMS includes: headaches, irritability, water retention resulting in clothes or jewelry not fitting well, a feeling of lower body heaviness, lethargy, food cravings, particularly for salt and chocolate,[2] and weight gain that can range from two to fifteen pounds that is lost after menstruation. More severe symptoms tend to include emotional and behavioral ones: mood swings, depression, increase of drug intake—particularly alcohol—as well as nausea and migraines. In its extreme form, women state they experience uncontrollable fits of rage, violence, and depression, which may be acted out toward oneself or others in the form of suicide attempts, child abuse, and physical assault toward men they know (Martin, 1987; Tavris, 1992). These behaviors have legal and social consequences which will be discussed later.

Although LLPD/PMS clearly may be culture specific, it may also be further categorized as a folk illness in those industrialized cultures that report it. The controversy within the medical profession in these cultures concerns whether LLPD/PMS is an actual clinical entity or a vague collection of symptoms. Aside from this debate is the folk perception of LLPD/PMS. For example, a client of Patricia Whelehan's labeled every mood change she experienced as LLPD/PMS, regardless of when in her cycle these mood changes occurred. Increasingly on the college campus where one author teaches, many of the reasons given for "pigging out," being grouchy, or not working are attributed to LLPD/PMS by both men and women, regardless of the accuracy of the label.

Treatments for LLPD/PMS include lifestyle modifications and hormone therapy if necessary. A woman who believes she has LLPD/PMS needs to chart her symptoms over a period of several months to note whether a pattern emerges, and to try to control other factors such as stress at work or home. If a correlation appears between the symptoms and the luteal phase, and these symptoms do not appear at other times, a diagnosis of LLPD/PMS may be made.

Lifestyle modifications refer to nutrition, sleep, exercise, use of drugs, and reduction in stress. Interestingly, the lifestyle modifications currently recommended as "healthy living" simulate those of our hominid gathering and hunting behavior. These include a reduction in salt, saturated fat, refined sugar, caffeine, alcohol, red meats, and an increase in the consumption of complex carbohydrates, lean fish and poultry, grains, fruits, and vegetables. Sufficient sleep and aerobic exercise are encouraged as well as the reduction of the use of recreational drugs. Stress reduction techniques include biofeedback, meditation, guided imagery; anything that relaxes from within.

The extreme behaviors attributed to LLPD/PMS elicit legal and social responses. These behaviors include suicide attempts, child abuse, and murder. Over the past fifteen years, some women accused of child abuse and murder of men they knew have entered a plea of LLPD/PMS to courts in the United States, Canada, and Great Britain. This plea has been accepted, and in some cases, tried. In one case in Great Britain, the woman was acquitted on the grounds of LLPD/PMS. Culturally, this evokes a strong response from men, women, feminists, and nonfeminists in support of both sides of LLPD/PMS controversy. One set of arguments supports the reality of LLPD/PMS as a cause of violent behavior and wants judgment and treatments given with LLPD/PMS as a consideration. Another set of arguments believes the use of LLPD/PMS in legal cases supports the view of women as irrational beings, subject to raging hormones that control their behavior, and who are not hormonally fit or responsible beings. This side also believes that while intense depression and anger may be caused by LLPD/PMS, there are outlets for these feelings other than physical aggression toward oneself or others. By contrast, it is interesting that testosterone is not a defense entered by men for acts of violence, not even by the men Silber studied (see Chapter 5).

Rather than a clinical entity, LLPD/PMS may be a cultural construct that allows women to "rage" once a month. Our culture historically sees women as creatures of their hormones and denies them a legitimate way to express their anger or frustration. LLPD/PMS may be a culture-specific "illness" that permits women to show anger, frustration, or other culturally labeled negative emotions. LLPD/PMS also reinforces the belief that women are victims of their physiology, specifically their hormones (Tavris, 1992). It is linguistically and culturally interesting that in the United States, LLPD/PMS is considered a psychiatric disorder, not a medical or gynecologic problem (Berek, Adashi, and Hillard, 1996). Is LLPD/PMS another cultural double standard, a newly found physiological-behavioral phenomenon that we do not fully understand, or an interaction of the two (Martin, 1987)?

In the past two chapters, male and female adult sexual and reproductive anatomy and physiology have been presented. Their similarities are notable: they share a common hormonal system and functioning which varies by degree, amount, and patterning. Many of the structures are both homologous and analogous with each other. These similarities will be reinforced in the chapter on embryology and sexual differentiation *in utero*. In essence, on a biochemical basis, men and women are more similar than they are different.

Much of how and what we define, label, and respond to as sexual, male (masculine), or female (feminine) is probably as much a function of cultural patterning as it is biology (Rogers, 2001). Culturally, we learn to attribute positive and negative connotations to our bodies, behaviors, thoughts, and feelings relative to sexuality. As bio-cultural beings we are sexual creatures. To summarize this section, anatomy and physiology reflect:

- a species-wide bio-chemical commonality;
- a shared hormonal system as males and females;
- a number of structures that are analogous and homologous between males and females;
- the link between our sexual behavior and a biological foundation;
- the interaction of biology and learned behavior in the expression of our sexuality; and
- cultural meanings that are given to the biological basis of our sexuality.

REPRODUCTIVE TECHNOLOGY

Reproductive technology, developed since the mid 1970s, has had an impact on our physical evolution as hominids. Currently, **artificial insemination by husband (AI-H)**, or **donor (AI-D)**, *in vitro* fertilization (IVF), **chromosomal filtration** for gender selection, embryo transplants, **amniocentesis**, and **chorionic villi sampling (CVS)**, are all available as alternative means of direct heterosexual contact for reproduction.

Sperm banks for AI-D, -H are found in most major cities in the United States. Over 1,000,000 artificial inseminations are performed each year. A generation of artificially inseminated babies has reached adulthood, some of whom are trying to locate their biological fathers. Minimally, artificial insemination means that men are no longer directly needed for impregnation, only their healthy ejaculate is. AI-D is used by some lesbians who want to be both biological and sociological mothers without having p-v intercourse. A very simple process is involved. All one needs is a fresh, healthy ejaculate sample, a syringe, and an ovulating female.[3] What are the potential consequences of AI-D, -H for partnering, parenting, and for men? This is not a balanced situation. Men still need women to carry the fetus and to give birth. Surrogate mothers are not as accepted as are sperm banks and artificial insemination, although increasingly, women are egg donors for infertile couples (see Chapter 7).

In vitro fertilization, "test tube babies," is now rather common in industrialized societies for couples for whom the woman has irreparably damaged fallopian tubes (Nyboe, Gianaroli and Nygren, 2004; Reynolds et al., 2003; Wright et al., 2003). This procedure involves surgically extracting a mature egg from the woman's ovary, combining it with a fresh ejaculate sample from her husband, and then implanting the **conceptus** (the fertilized egg) into her uterus. Available since 1978, thousands of babies have been conceived and born by this method, and are apparently physically and developmentally healthy. As of 2002, the national average success rate for a live birth in the United States is 40.7 percent. The procedure is expensive—several thousand dollars per attempt (Andersen, Nyboe, and Nygren, 2004).

Chromosomal filtration of X and Y chromosomes to preselect a female or male fetus is gaining in success and popularity. Developed in the late 1970s to early 1980s by a reproductive embryologist in San Diego, this method reportedly has an 85 percent success rate for Y chromosome filtration. From a spun ejaculate sample, the lighter Y chromosomes filter to the top and the heavier X chromosomes settle to the bottom of the tube. Chromosomes and semen for the preferred sex are filtrated out and artificially inseminated into the woman. Given that there persists in our own and other societies a widespread cultural preference for sons, what are the implications of this procedure for future generations? What will happen with the "natural" gender ratio balance, if there ever was one, which was relatively untampered with except by cultural manipulations such as female infanticide (Benagiano and Bianchi, 1999; Malpani, 2002; "Toward Ending Violence," 2004)? We know that in both India and China currently, the preference for male children has changed the gender ratio balance sufficiently to be reflected in the adult population, affecting the number of women available as potential spouses (Malpani, 2002; "Toward Ending Violence," 2004).

Embryo transplants from one uterus to another are also being done. In this situation a woman is artificially inseminated with another woman's partner's ejaculate. The man's wife usually has blocked fallopian tubes or problems with implantation. After fertilization occurs in the "donor" woman, the conceptus or fertilized egg is carefully evacuated from her uterus after several days and implanted in the wife's uterus. In one case, the receiving parents were killed in a plane crash and the state of the floating embryo was of legal and social concern. In 1989, there was a court case in the United States in which a divorcing couple contested ownership of their fertilized eggs. The court decided in favor of the wife. She could have them implanted. Questions of paternity and future child support remain unanswered at this time. We do not have legal, social, cross-cultural, or evolutionary models or precedents which easily incorporate these phenomena into our sexual and reproductive behavior and belief systems. These technological options force us to rethink our attitudes about life, abortion, parenting, and "normalcy." The use of unused embryos for stem cell and other medical research comprises one of the current ethical debates in **assisted reproductive technology** (**ART**). (See Chapter 7.)

Amniocentesis and chorionic villi sampling, CVS, detect chromosomal normalcy, abnormalities, and gender in embryos and fetuses. By either withdrawing amniotic fluid from the amnion during the end of the first trimester (amniocentesis), or sampling chorionic tissue early in the first trimester (CVS), much chromosomal data can be obtained and used as a decision to continue or terminate a pregnancy. In either situation there is a small chance of spontaneous abortion (miscarriage). In the case of amniocentesis, a second trimester abortion would be performed, while with CVS, a first trimester abortion, if selected, would terminate the pregnancy.

Fetal reduction is one of the more recent reproductive choices. It is intended for use in a large multiple fetus pregnancy or where a twin or triplet is seriously chromosomally or developmentally impaired. Fetal reduction is highly controversial. Fetal reduction involves the induced abortion of the fetus which has serious problems to help increase the chances of survival of the other fetuses (Berek, Adashi, and Hillard, 1996; Kelly, 1990). The impact of these technologies could change our reproductive practices and future. There are clear implications for altered sex ratio balances, the number of adult men needed in a population, concepts of sexuality and sexual relations, definitions of gender and gender roles, as well as of parenting and families. These are not Orwellian (1950) or *Brave New World* (Huxley, 1946) fantasies, but realities of early twenty-first-century life. Sexual and reproductive choices and decision making now are qualitatively different than in previous generations or in other cultures including our own.

SUMMARY

1 Female sexual and reproductive anatomy and physiology are an expression of the CC + (H-P-G axis) formula.
2 Female hormonal functioning is generally described as cyclic, in contrast to the male's depiction as tonic.
3 The menstrual cycle is a function of a negative feedback interaction of the H-P-G axis.
4 Many of the primary and secondary female sex characteristics discussed are analogues and/or homologues of the male's.
5 Differences in male and female body fat and muscle mass are culturally interpreted. Female primary and secondary sex characteristics are often dramatically responded to culturally. Much cultural interest is shown toward female sexual and reproductive functioning. This can include controversial genital surgery such as circumcision, clitoridectomy, hysterectomy, and infibulation.
6 There are several models developed in industrialized societies to explain the variety of female sexual response.
7 Various diseases and cultural management of female sexual and reproductive structures affect a woman's fertility.
8 The menstrual cycle is a bio-behavioral phenomenon.

9 The menstrual cycle is culturally regulated and associated with taboos in many societies, including the United States.
10 Menstrual synchrony, menstrual cramps, and premenstrual syndrome (PMS) may be culture specific, industrialized phenomena.
11 Anatomically, physiologically, and hormonally, men and women are much more similar than they are different.
12 Numerous technologies such as AI-D, -H, *in vitro* fertilization and chromosomal filtration developed in industrialized societies over the past fifteen to twenty years have the potential to radically change human reproduction.

Thought-provoking questions

1 If virginity is defined as not having p-v intercourse, does that mean that self-identified, behaviorally consistent gays and lesbians are always virgins since they do not engage in this behavior?
2 Why do societies manipulate, pay more and different kinds of attention to female reproductive and sexual structures than they do male?
3 What kinds of immediate (proximal) and long-term (distal) evolutionary changes could occur from ART?

SUGGESTED RESOURCES

Books

Boston Women's Health Collective. 2005. *Our Bodies, Ourselves: A New Edition for a New Era*. New York: Touchstone Publishers, Ltd.
Chalker, Rebecca. 2000. *The Clitoral Truth: The Secret World at Your Fingertips*. New York: Seven Stories Press.
Diamant, Anita. 1997. *The Red Tent*. New York: St. Martin's Press. Federation of Feminist Women's Health Centers. 1995.
A New View of a Woman's Body. A Fully Illustrated Guide. Los Angeles: Feminist Health Press.

Web site

Museum of Menstruation (http://www.mum.org/)

7 Fertility, conception, and sexual differentiation

Fertility and infertility, conception, and the sexual differentiation of the embryo are the major topics covered in this chapter. As part of the discussion of sexual differentiation, three of the more common, random chromosomal errors are discussed. Some of the current biomedical theories that explain the causes of sexual orientation, transgender identity (TGs), and gender identity are based on data collected from intersexed and transgendered people, including transgendered women and men. Since these theories include embryologic arguments, they are introduced in this chapter as well. More complete coverage of transgender identity and community and of sexual orientations will be covered in Chapters 13 and 14.

FERTILITY AND INFERTILITY

Physiologically, fertility holds a different meaning for males and females. For males, it is the ability to impregnate a female with one's own sperm. For females, it is the ability to be impregnated, that is to ovulate, have patent or open, unblocked fallopian tubes, and carry a fetus to term. Currently in the United States, fertility is generally assumed unless proven otherwise.

People also are assumed to be the most fertile in their twenties. Without medical intervention, women's fertility declines after the age of thirty-five until they are no longer fertile one year postmenopausally. Men retain their fertility until they die, even though there is a reduction in the amount of semen and the quality of sperm produced per ejaculate as they age (Aitken and Graves, 2002; Guylaya et al., 2001; Thacker, 2004; Woolf quoted in Marino, 1993). Men also can produce chromosomal abnormalities as they age that contribute to either the ability to carry a fetus to term or to fetal problems (Aitken and Graves, 2002; Daniels, 1997). The heterosexual partnering pattern in the United States favors men who are older than their female partners. Since older women often are partnered with men who are older than they are, the male's age may then also increase the risk for chromosomal anomalies in their children (Aitken and Graves, 2002; Daniels, 1997).

By gender, criteria for fertility become more specific. Biomedically, female fertility is determined by age, regular ovulation, patent fallopian tubes, and cervical mucous. In addition, as women age, the chances of **Down's Syndrome**, a chromosomal abnormality, and other pregnancy-related problems including high blood pressure and gestational diabetes increase (Berek, Adashi and Hillard, 1996). Thus, women face a "biological clock" concerning fertility.

In addition to patent fallopian tubes, women need to ovulate regularly. A woman can only become pregnant when she ovulates. Ovulatory problems are one of the more frequent causes of female infertility (Boston Women's Health Collective, 1992, 2005; Speroff, Glass, and Kase, 1978; Stewart et al., 1979). A third criterion for female fertility is **tubal patency**. This means open, unblocked fallopian tubes that allow for the union of sperm and egg and the fertilized egg's passage to the uterus. Cervical mucous is another factor in female fertility. The texture, color, density, and amount of cervical mucous changes during ovulation to allow sperm to pass through the os, the opening in the cervix. See Chapter 6 for a more detailed discussion of this process. Female fertility ultimately entails the ability to be impregnated, carry a fetus to term, and give birth to it.

Male fertility is defined relative to **sperm count, sperm motility**, and **sperm form**. As stated in Chapter 5, men continuously produce millions of sperm daily from puberty until death. During the sexual arousal and ejaculatory process, somewhere between 200 and 400 million sperm are ejaculated each time. It is believed that the large number of sperm ejaculated help to move the other sperm along the way to the fallopian tubes. While it takes only one sperm to fertilize an egg, the pathway to fertilization is not a smooth one for the sperm. Only about 200 of the sperm actually survive to reach the fallopian tubes, a trip which takes several minutes after deposition in the vagina.

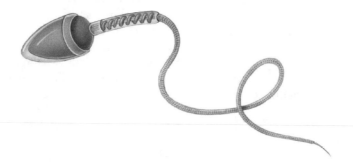

Figure 7.1 Sperm cell. (*Source*: Margaret Gerrity.)

As such, sperm motility or movement is a second important variable in male fertility. Semen aids in sperm motility (i.e., how fast and well the sperm move). Active, fast moving sperm have a greater chance of reaching the fallopian tube and being received by the egg than less active ones. A third component of male fertility is sperm form. In gross anatomic terms, sperm are composed of a head, midsection, and tail. (See Figure 7.1.) The head secretes an enzyme to dissolve the surface coating of the egg to make sperm envelopment by the egg possible. The midsection contains the chromosomal material and the tail aids in sperm motility. All three sections need to be present and functional for impregnation to occur.

Partner physiological compatibility is necessary for conception. Partner compatibility includes a harmonious pH balance between the woman's vagina and the man's semen, thinned watery cervical mucous, and active, numerous sperm which can pass through the os into the fallopian tubes. While fertility is assumed, its importance is not taken for granted. Fertility is important in all societies; it is probably one of the few universal concerns in human sexuality. This can be seen in art forms, myths, folklore, and people's value on fertility and kinship through time and space. Penis sheaths common among groups living in New Guinea, Michelangelo's sculpture of "David," and the Washington Monument in Washington, DC, are all examples of various cultures' appreciation of phallic forms. The Venus de Willendorf, a 25,000-year-old statuette of a woman with pendulous breasts, a rounded stomach, and large hips and thighs, is a commonly cited example of a female fertility symbol.

Beliefs about fertility and conception are widespread and culture specific. Though all human groups know that it requires penile-vaginal intercourse to conceive, various fertility enhancers are found cross-culturally. To enhance conception, potions are consumed, rituals are performed, seduction techniques are encouraged, and spirits are appeased. For example, the Mayan women of Mexico may consult a *curandera*, midwife, or traditional birth attendant (TBA) relative to fertility concerns (Faust, 1988). Among the

Brunei Malay, the *dukun*, a healer, may be consulted for advice as well as potions to ingest (Kimball and Craig, 1988). Among the Tiwi, which were discussed earlier, certain female totems are believed to be responsible for conception. They can be sought out or avoided depending on whether a woman wishes "to have life breathed into her body" or to avoid conception (Goodale, 1971). Among the Sambia, a horticultural group in New Guinea, fellatio (oral sex) performed on the husband is believed to "prepare a wife's body for childbearing by 'strengthening' her" (Herdt, 1993: 306). See Chapter 10 for a discussion of Sambian "growing a boy." Semen in this culture is thought of as a vital life essence which makes and keeps men strong and healthy while ensuring female fertility and embryonic development. Their sexual beliefs are representative of what Barker-Benfield (1975) refers to as the "spermatic economy." The spermatic economy is a belief system that is widespread cross-culturally, including the United States. It focuses on semen (i.e., ejaculate) as a precious, essential life substance that exists in finite supply and can be "used up" in a man's lifetime if he is not careful about where, how, and with whom he "spends" it (ejaculates). Sambian sexual beliefs existed in a culture in which **endemic** or **ongoing warfare** over scarce resources, including women, was common. Resources for food, shelter, and water exist in limited supply due to natural boundaries, sometimes referred to as **impacted habitats**. Women do most of the food procurement, processing, and distribution. They are frequently seen as the enemy since marriages are often political alliances amongst warring factions. Women can also be perceived by the men as sexually voracious and potential depletors of treasured ejaculate. The idea that men form the baby and women "grow it" is not that different than European thinking of several hundred years ago when the uterus was perceived as the receptacle of the homonucleus (little baby) "given" by the man.

Much of the effort to ensure and protect fertility, both within and outside the United States, rests with women. Until recently, the dominant fertility patterns among women were extended periods of lactation followed by pregnancy. Continuously uninterrupted menstrual cycles, varied by one or two live births and short or nonexistent periods of lactation are largely a middle-class, industrial, twentieth- and twenty-first-century phenomenon (Beyene, 1989; Frayser, 1985). Since fertility is critical to the continuation of any group, it is a topic which is taken seriously by most of the world's peoples. This includes means of enhancing conception, avoiding conception as discussed in Chapter 12, and means of dealing with infertility.

Infertility is seen as a tragedy societally and individually, regardless of an individual culture's positions about population pressures. Infertility, or the inability to conceive and bear a child, is a cause of societal and cultural concern. When it occurs, it is almost universally grounds for divorce and individual grief (Cohen and Eames, 1982; Ward and Edelstein,

2006: 82–83). There is much cross-cultural variation in response to infertility. However, a fairly widespread constant is that the woman assumes and is seen as being responsible for the fertility problem (Frayser, 1985). For example, among the herding Nuer in Africa, an infertile wife becomes a "husband" to another, assumably fertile woman. The female "husband" becomes the sociological father to her wife's offspring by a male. This practice allows the continuation of the infertile woman's patrilineage, the descent system where you trace your family through your male kin (Cohen and Eames, 1982). As with many other cultures, the Sambia believe it is only the woman who can be infertile. When infertility occurs in their culture, the Sambian male takes another wife, but does not divorce the allegedly infertile wife (Herdt, 1993).

In both industrialized and nonindustralized societies, infertility is managed by cultural means. Common solutions can include divorce and remarriage, polygyny, adopting a child, and fostering, the latter being primarily a nineteenth- to twentieth-century, industrialized alternative. "Aunting" and "uncling" also occur. In these situations, the infertile couple involve themselves intensively with the children in their extended kin group. This may include financial, social, psychological, and ritual activities, similar to what occurs in the unilineal descent groups in non-industrialized societies. Single-parent adoptions are also increasing for both men and women in industrialized societies. This extends to international adoptions for singles and couples. The economic and social flexibility that has occurred for some people in our culture since the latter part of the twentieth century makes this option more feasible. Some international babies are seen as easier to adopt—girls, for example, may be easier to adopt in societies that strongly value boys ("Towards Ending Violence Against Women in South Asia," 2004). Since most cultures have either bilateral or patrilineal descent, boy children perpetuate the lineage and are less likely to be put up for adoption. See Chapter 9 for definitions and discussion. Boy babies may also be preferred because they are seen as "brighter, stronger, and healthier" than girls (Whelehan's counseling file).

Overpopulation may be a global concern and an issue for mainstream groups. However, much of the nonindustrialized world as well as some ethnic groups in the United States such as the Amish, Hutterites, and African Americans may perceive these concerns and attempts to impose birth control on them as a threat of genocide by the larger society. Regardless of generalized concerns about population pressures, for the infertile couple who wants a biological child, it is a very remote, abstract argument. Given the universal value on fertility, the anguish an infertile couple experiences in not being able to conceive is understandable.

In some societies infertility is cause for divorce, grief, and loss of status, particularly for the female. Many societies actively try to treat infertility indigenously either through biomedicine, potions, behavioral changes, consultation with specialists, or gender selection (Becker, 1990; Faust, 1988; Kimball and Craig, 1988; Malpani, 2002; Marmor, 1988).

Since much of the biomedical work on infertility has occurred in industrialized societies in the last decades of this century, the focus of this discussion will be on the industrialized countries. In the United States, fertility problems have stabilized with about 10–15 percent of the couples who are trying to conceive and bear a child unable to do so (Berek, Adashi, and Hillard, 1996: 915; Hatcher et al., 1986; Ragone, 1994; Stewart et al., 1979). In the United States, a couple is defined as infertile after they have been trying for a year to have a child without success (Berek, Adashi, and Hillard, 1996: 915; Ragone, 1994; Stewart et al., 1979).

Physiologically, infertility may rest with the man, the woman, or the couple. Although the statistics on causal attribution vary, roughly 35 to 40 percent of the time the problem is with the male; 35 to 40 percent of the time the problem is with the female; and the remaining percentage is either couple incompatibility, behavioral, or unknown (Berek, Adashi, and Hillard, 1996: 915; Hatcher et al., 1986; Ragone, 1994; Stewart et al., 1979). Physiological causes for both male and female infertility relate to the established criteria for fertility.

Male infertility can be due to low sperm count, motility problems, or deformed sperm. STIs (sexually transmitted infections), abusive-addictive drug usage, and congenital problems can cause infertility in males (Aitken Koopman, and Lewis, 2004; Kenkel, Claus, and Eberhard, 2001; Thacker, 2004; Thomas, 2000). Relative to numbers, a subfertile or infertile male is one whose sperm count is below 20 to 40 million sperm per ejaculate (Berek, Adashi, and Hillard, 1996: 920; Kelly, 1988; Stewart et al., 1979). This is the most common cause of infertility in men.

Sperm motility is another factor in infertility. As stated, sperm need to move quickly and continuously in order to reach a fallopian tube and be able to fertilize an egg. Slow-moving, sluggish sperm probably will not survive the trip or be taken in by the egg. Problems with sperm motility are the second most common cause of male infertility in the United States. Finally, a man may produce misshaped sperm, or sperm missing one or more of its necessary parts. A semen analysis, which notes sperm count, size, shape, and motility, is a key diagnostic tool in a male fertility workup.

Female infertility can be caused by endogenous hormonal imbalance, illnesses, or stress, as well as by STDs, endometriosis, pelvic inflammatory disease (PID), and drug abuse or addiction. The most common form of female infertility is due to problems with ovulation. The second most common problem is some form of tubal blockage, followed by a combination of the two. Diagnostic tests for female fertility problems are usually more complicated, extensive, invasive, and costly than for males. These tests include hormonal assays, measurements of tubal patency, and studies of cervical mucous.

The causes of couple or male-female infertility may be behavioral or physiological. Behavioral problems include either too frequent ejaculatory-penile vaginal intercourse that depletes the sperm supply,[1] too infrequent ejaculatory intercourse, or ejaculatory intercourse at times when the woman is not ovulating. Physiological problems include pH imbalances between the woman's vagina and the man's semen, incompatibility between the cervical mucous and sperm, often referred to clinically as "hostile",[2] and occasionally, an allergic reaction by the woman to her partner's sperm (Aitken and Graves, 2002; Guylaya et al., 2001; Stewart et al., 1979).

Fertility may be decreased in "spermatic economies." Infrequent p-v intercourse reduces the chances of conception. Among some groups such as the Sambia, Mae Enga, and other horticultural groups in Melanesia, specifically New Guinea, p-v intercourse occurs relatively infrequently, resulting in a low birth rate. As discussed, women in these societies are also seen as sexually voracious, powerful, and dangerous—eager to "swallow" a man's precious and limited life essence (Gregersen, 1983; Herdt, 1982, 1993; Williams, 1986).

Currently, there are a wide range of treatments having variable degrees of success available to infertile couples in the United States. Male infertility problems may be treated by isolating and concentrating his viable sperm and then artificially inseminating his partner with them (AI-H), by artificial insemination donor (AI-D), or combining donor-husband sperm in artificial insemination. Generally, vitamin or drug therapies do not alleviate the condition. If the vas deferens is blocked, or a varicocele, a varicose vein of the scrotal sac, exists, surgery may be helpful.

AI-H may be more successful if the man makes love with his partner using a condom to catch the ejaculate, rather than masturbating into a specimen jar in a doctor's bathroom. The greater eroticism of partner lovemaking is believed to cause a more forceful ejaculation of younger, fresher, healthier sperm (McCarthy, 1990; Medical Aspects of Human Sexuality, 1991: 16).

For females, treatments may be hormonal, surgical, or both depending on the situation. Ovulation problems often are treated hormonally. Tubal blockage problems generally are treated surgically to remove the source of the obstruction. These treatments are revolutionary, dramatic, and can be controversial. Some of the more controversial treatments such as *in vitro* fertilization (IVF), embryo transplants, and embryo-sperm (gamete) implantation in the fallopian tube were discussed relative to their socio-cultural implications in the previous chapter (Peris, 2005). Even AI-D is controversial, since some adult AI-D babies have searched for their biological fathers (Francoeur, 1989).[3]

Legal and social questions arise in our culture as to whether AI-D donor files should be open to AI-D children, and as to whose rights take precedent—the donor's right to anonymity or the child's right to know biological paternity. It is noted that AI-D donors are medically and genetically screened prior to being accepted as participants, that phenotype and sociocultural matching occurs between the donor and child's family, and that the donor's medical and social history data are available to the AI-D child's family.

Couples' treatments range the behavioral-physiological spectrum. For those infertility problems caused by intercourse-related behaviors, education about ovulation, the timing of fertilization, and sperm supply can help to alleviate the situation. While this may appear to be a relatively "simple" solution, sensitivity to the couple's psycho-emotional state is important. Making love by the calendar in order to conceive a child can produce anxiety, tension, **spectatoring**, i.e., observing how well you are doing, and can be less than a spontaneous, passionate, sensuous experience for both people. Couple infertility due to sperm-cervical mucous pH incompatibility may be treated with drugs, with AI-H as a by-pass mechanism, or with the use of condoms for a while to see if the problem may self-correct (Stewart et al., 1979; Wright et al., 2003).

American lay and folk remedies for infertile couples abound. They include increasing the frequency of p-v intercourse and ejaculation, which can actually decrease the sperm count; using different positions in intercourse; or ingesting vitamins or aphrodisiacs, which enhance neither fertility nor virility. There is anecdotal reporting of two generations' duration of "infertile" couples who conceive a biological child after adopting a baby.

The inconsistent use of safer sex and the increase in sexually transmitted infections (STIs) since the late twentieth century have resulted in a rise in fertility problems that are occurring at a younger age ("Current Trends Ectopic Pregnancy," 1995; Coste et al., 2004; Kamwendo et al., 2000; Lipscomb et al., 2000). The financial expense and psychological and emotional costs are great for those affected by infertility. It is interesting that even with all the sophisticated technology to treat problems and knowledge about infertility that we have in this country, the responsibility for a fertility problem is still largely seen as the woman's. In a study of middle-class, professional couples in the San Francisco Bay Area it was found that regardless of the physiological "cause" of the problem, the woman was expected to somehow "fix it." If the physiological problem was not the male's, he offered support to his partner, but did not assume responsibility for its resolution (Becker, 1990). This is not that far from the generalized industrial and nonindustrial response of seeing the woman as responsible for fertility. About half of the infertile couples in the United States can be successfully treated so that conception and a live birth can occur (Boston Women's Health Collective, 1992: 500; Reynolds et al., 2003; Wright et al., 2003).

CONCEPTION

As the preceding discussion indicates, fertility is a necessary condition for conception. Biomedically, conception is the union of the sperm and egg, which is dependent upon regular spermatogenesis and ovulation. Conception is not the same as **viability**, or the ability to create and bear offspring. Viability necessitates implantation of the fertilized egg into the endometrium and the development and birth of a full-term fetus (Allgeier and Allgeier, 1991; Reynolds et al., 2003). In terms of reproductive success, there is a great deal of waste. Relative to an individual who may or may not wish to impregnate or be pregnant, conception and viability may be akin to playing roulette.

Conception is regulated and interpreted through culture. In most cultures, there are explanations given as to why and when intercourse results in conception (Frayser, 1985; Gregersen, 1983). It is a myth in industrialized societies that nonindustrialized groups do not know that heterosexual genital contact is necessary for conception. That members of these societies do not openly discuss this, particularly with researchers from industrialized societies, is not surprising. Specifics of sexual behavior and conception, particularly across gender lines (most researchers until recently have been and are male), are not topics of everyday conversation. Explanations for conception are embedded in people's views of sexuality, reproduction, and male-female relations. For example, the Tiwi, whom we discussed previously, believe that the essence of sexuality is female. Male totems, animistic spirit beings, are important in their patrilineal kinship system; one's spiritual totems are inherited matrilineally through females.

A woman conceives through a given act of intercourse when her spirit totem breathes life into her body (Goodale, 1971). Given that much of the embryonic process is still unknown from an industrialized, technological perspective (e.g., Muecke, 1979; Sizonenko, 2003; Wilson, 1979) and that new knowledge about sexuality continually unfolds, a measure of humility is needed in understanding these explanations. It was only a generation ago (when your authors were children) that we were often told that the "stork brought babies," or that they were picked from the "cabbage patch." Conception occurred by a "seed being implanted in a woman's tummy," — leading a number of girls to swallow watermelon seeds. Students in one human sexuality class reported they "knew people who believed if you had 'sex' standing up, you wouldn't get pregnant because it 'would all fall out.'" These were (are?) common U.S. folk beliefs about conception and birth.

Due to current and future **assisted reproductive technology** (ART), heterosexual genital contact is no longer necessary for fertilization to occur. The full impact of these industrialized developments on conception in both industrialized and nonindustrialized societies remains to be seen (Benagiano and Bianchi, 1999; Malpani, 2002; Todosijeviæ, Ljubinković, and Arančić, 2003). Some potential consequences of these developments have been presented in Chapters 5 and 6.

From an industrialized bio-behavioral perspective, there are several aspects of prenatal sexual differentiation and postnatal phenotypic expression that culturally define sexual physiological "normalcy." Although there are a variety of ways to biologically define one's sex, as discussed in Chapter 2, from a biomedical perspective, four criteria need to be met. Prenatally, the establishment of genetic or chromosomal sex and appropriate differentiation *in utero* need to occur. Postnatally, appropriate gender identity, or the knowledge that you are male or female, and gender role development and puberty (i.e., sexual adulthood) need to occur.

Genetic or **chromosomal sex** is determined at conception. Genetic or chromosomal sex is the arrangement of either the XX pairing for a girl, or the XY pairing for a boy. Although a range of chromosomal X and Y combinations is possible and may occur, only XX or XY are genetically normal. Based on genetic sex, sexual differentiation or gonadal sex develops in the fetus (Muecke, 1979; "Syndromes of Abnormal Sex Differentiation," 2005; Sizonenko, 2003; Wilson, 1979). Gonadal sex gives rise to **phenotypic sex**, or, the external and internal physical characteristics that allow a culture to label a child a boy or girl. These characteristics include, but are not limited to, such structures as the penis, testicles, vas deferens, or prostate in the boy, and the clitoris, ovaries, fallopian tubes, or vagina in a girl. At birth, a child is labeled as a boy or girl based on visual inspection of the genitalia; the child's sense of itself as a boy or girl is referred to as **gender identity.** It is believed that children know their gender identity by the time they are eighteen to twenty-four months old (Money and Ehrhard, 1972). Based on gender identity, **gender role** develops. Gender role, sometimes referred to as **script** or **scripting** (Gagnon, 1979), is the internalization and acting out of culturally defined male or female behavior, affect, and attitudes. The ideal, at least in United States culture, is to have genetic, gonadal, and phenotypic sex, gender identity, and gender role synchronized so that one looks, acts, thinks, and feels like a culturally defined boy or girl, man or woman.

The process of sexual differentiation *in utero* and attainment of gender identity and gender role has received a great deal of attention from the Middle Ages through Freud to the present (e.g., Bullough, 1976; Freud, 1929 [1929]; Gagnon, 1979). Sexual differentiation, the most physiological aspect in this continuum, has also received a great deal of scrutiny (Jost, 1961; Muecke, 1979; Sherfey, 1972; Sizonenko, 2003; "Syndromes of Abnormal Sex Differentiation," 2005; Wilson, 1979). These theories range from postulations that as humans we are all embryologically female in our composition (Sherfey, 1972 based on Jost, 1961), to a very complex inter-pretation of the hormonal-anatomical differentiation process ("Exploring the Biological Contributions to Human Health," 2001; Wilson, 1979).

A simplified interpretation of sexual differentiation follows based on more than thirty years of research (Institute of Medicine, 2001; Muecke, 1979; Sizonenko, 2003; Wilson, 1979).

Genetic or chromosomal sex is determined at conception by the pairing of either XX or XY chromosomes for a girl or boy respectively. As part of embryonic development regardless of genetic sex, the following schema occurs:

- The embryo is sexually undifferentiated for the first six weeks of life. Phenotypic sex cannot be determined by visual observation.
- Both male and female embryos contain both the **Mullerian ducts**, which will develop some female sexual and reproductive structures, and **Wolffian ducts**, which will develop some male sexual and reproductive structures.
- The Wolffian ducts develop part of the urinary tract system in both males and females, specifically the ureters, the collecting tubules of the kidneys, and part of the bladder.
- The presence of Wolffian ducts is a necessary condition for Mullerian duct development in the female ("Exploring the Biological Contributions to Human Health," 2001b; Muecke, 1979; Sizonenko, 2003).

In the male, the following process occurs. At about six weeks of embryonic development, the male begins to sexually differentiate. Several hormones are released by the embryo to expedite this process. They are testosterone, the **H-Y antigen**,[4] both of which facilitate male anatomic development, and **Mullerian Inhibiting Substance** (MIS) which closes the Mullerian ducts and causes them to atrophy ("Exploring the Biological Contributions to Human Health," 2001; Sizonenko, 2003; Wilson, 1979). Based on the hor-mone release and the XY chromosomal arrangement, the penis, testes, and scrotum develop. The Wolffian ducts develop into the **rete testes**, a rudi-mentary structure, the epididymis and vas deferens. During the course of fetal development and with the help of testosterone, the other accessory organs appear (e.g., prostate, seminal vesicles). The testicles descend into the scrotal sac during the third trimester. If all goes well, approximately nine calendar months after conception an infant is born, is given the gender identity of boy, and his formal gender role socialization begins.

A girl's differentiation process begins later, around ten to twelve weeks of fetal development.[5] Although estrogen may be involved in later pren-atal development, its role, if any, in the differentiation process is not as clear as is testosterone in the male's ("Exploring the Biological Contribu-tions to Human Health," 2001; Hyde, 1994; Wilson, 1979). The Wolffian ducts spontaneously close in the female. A **Wolffian Inhibiting Substance,** analogous to MIS, does not exist. The genital tubercle, homologous and analogous with the males, develops into the clitoris. The Mullerian ducts develop into the uterus, fallopian tubes, broad ligament, and upper third of the vagina with the other accessory organs (e.g., labia minora) following. The presence of an X chromosome in both males and females, the need for MIS and testosterone release in the male and lack of comparable hormone release in the female, the live birth of an X or XO "female" and not of a Y or YO male, all lead some researchers (e.g., Sherfey, 1972) to take a strong stand that human embryos are innately female.

OVERVIEW OF INTERSEXED INDIVIDUALS

As stated, only XX or XY arrangements are considered to be normative genetic sex in this culture. There are, however, a number of other X and Y combinations that can occur. Three of the most common are Turner's Syndrome, Klinefelter's Syndrome, and the XYY Syndrome. **Turner's Syndrome,** represented by an X or XO combination, occurs in about 1/4000 live births (Fausto-Sterling, 2000; Mange and Mange, 1980; Stine, 1977). **Klinefelter's Syndrome,** represented chromosomally as XXY, occurs in about 1/500 to 1/1000 live births. The XYY Syndrome, formerly known as the **"Supermale Syndrome,"** occurs in about 1/1000 live births (Fausto-Sterling, 2000; Mange and Mange, 1980). See Table 7.1 for a description of these and additional forms of intersexuality.

Probably about only 2 percent of the Turner's Syndrome individuals live to be born (Mange and Mange, 1980). Turner's Syndrome individuals often have a number of severe physiological problems and frequently die in their twenties. They are sterile, have incomplete or rudimentary ovaries, uterus, and fallopian tubes, a blind vagina that may be corrected surgically, immature postpubertal external genitalia, are often short, and have webbed neck or fingers (Money and Ehrhardt, 1972). Webbing is a fold of skin between the neck and shoulder or digits. Turner's Syndrome individuals may have cognitive development problems (Mange and Mange, 1980; Stine, 1977).

Although they have some female phenotypic sex characteristics, they do not meet the criteria of normative genetic and physiological development presented earlier in this chapter. Turner's Syndrome individuals chromosomally represent the single X chromosome that some writers have used to postulate the innate femaleness of the human embryo. Single X chromosome individuals are not physically normative females either. This position is believed by your authors to be a feminist bias, since an X or XO female is not a physiologically normative female. This politicization of the embryo (i.e., that males are "incomplete" since they need hormonal release during differentiation to become a phenotypic male and without it would develop female characteristics) may be a backlash reaction by some feminist researchers.

The backlash could be a reaction against Freudian interpretations of the clitoris as a "half-formed" penis and the vaginal orgasm myth (1959 [1929]), as well as a general industrialized tendency to present male culture as total culture in which women are defined in terms of their relationships to men. Perhaps bias needs to be recognized more openly whenever it is found to avoid politicizing the differentiation process.

Klinefelter's Syndrome (XXY) individuals have an essentially male phenotype. They are sterile and tend to have underdeveloped primary and secondary sex characteristics. Atrophied testicles[6] produce low levels of testosterone, frequently resulting in gynecomastia, or breast enlargement, low libido, problems with erectile ability, and more fat than muscle mass per overall body composition. In essence, both male and female secondary sex characteristics appear. Some XXY individual's psychologic development has been labeled schizophrenic, which may be more perceived than real (Money and Ehrhardt, 1972; Mange and Mange, 1980).

The XYY Syndrome receives attention because of the alleged aggressive and physically violent tendencies of these individuals. According to some theorists (Allgeier and Allgeier, 1991), the extra Y chromosome produces men who are not only taller and more muscular than XY males, but who also have a greater propensity for acting out violently. Many of these studies are methodologically flawed (Allgeier and Allgeier, 1991). About 50 percent of the XYY males are sterile. See Table 7.1. for a description of behavioral characteristics.

All three of these syndromes (Turner's, Klinefelter's, and XYY) are believed to occur randomly. Since both Turner's and Klinefelter's Syndrome individuals are sterile, they are self-limiting. They do not reproduce. Fertile XYY males do not appear to be more likely to produce XYY sons than XY males. Causes of these chromosomal variations are unknown (Mange and Mange, 1980).

Our society relies heavily on genetic, hormonal, and phenotypic sex characteristics to assign gender identity and gender role. Some nonindustrialized societies offer an interesting contrast to ours regarding how they define gender identity and gender role. Among the Sambia in New Guinea and in those cultures that recognize "two spirit" or third gender individuals (e.g., the *nadle* among the Navajo, *hijras* in India, *mahu* in Hawaii, and *xanith* in Oman), maleness and femaleness are not defined entirely by phenotype (Herdt, 1982; Williams, 1986; Wikan, 2000).

The essence of being male or female is important as a defining characteristic and is culturally valuable. It can include substances such as semen or menstrual blood as well as spiritual, aesthetic, kinesics, or occupational attributes. Therefore, cross-culturally a man can be phenotypically and genetically male, but be labeled female or something else (i.e., "not man" or "near man") by his affect, demeanor, or special talents as exemplified above. Similarly, a phenotypic and genotypic female may succeed in being a warrior woman (Williams, 1986). With the Sambia, oral intercourse among

Table 7.1 Summary of anomalies of prenatal differentiation

Name	Cause	Basic clinical features	Frequencies
Congenital Adrenal Hyperplasia (CAH)	Genetically inherited malfunction of one or more of six enzymes involved in making steroid hormones	In XX children, can cause mild to severe masculinization of genitalia at birth or later; if untreated, can cause masculinization at puberty and early puberty. Some forms drastically disrupt salt metabolism and are lifethreatening if not treated with cortisone.	One in 13,000
Androgen Insensitivity Syndrome (AIS)	Genetically inherited change in the cell surface receptor for testosterone	XY children born with highly feminized genitalia. The body is "blind" to the presence of testosterone, since cells cannot capture it and use it to move development in a male direction. At puberty these children develop breasts and a feminine body shape.	One in 60,000
Turner's Syndrome	Females lacking a second X chromosome (XO)	A form of gonadal dysgenesis in females. Ovaries do not develop; stature is short; lack of secondary sex characteristics; treatment includes estrogen and growth hormone.	One in 4,000 births
Klinefelter's Syndrome	Males with an extra X chromosome (XXY)	A form of gonadal dysgenesis causing infertility; after puberty there is often breast enlargement; treatments include testosterone therapy.	One in 500 to one in 1,000

Table 7.1 (Continued)

Name	Cause	Basic clinical features	Frequencies
Ovotestes (formerly called true hermaphrodites)	Usually XX chromosome, more rarely XY or mosaic. Some evidence of family history Cause in XX unknown, possible gene translocation from Y	More commonly born with both testicular and ovarian tissue; combination of ovaries and testes. Sometimes has a male side and female side; or grow together in one organ. Appearance of external genitals varies considerably in terms of intermediate states.	One in 100,000 births
XYY Syndrome (formerly called Supermale Syndrome)	The extra Y is not an inherited condition but due to an error in cell division in the fertilizing sperm or in developing embryo	This condition was called SuperMale Syndrome because some early flawed studies found a high number of prison inmates with XYY; they were also thought to be overly aggressive. Subsequent research has disproved this stereotype. XYY males typically have no distinctive characteristics although they may be slightly taller than average and about 50% have learning disabilities although mild.	Frequency: one in 1000. However this number is conservative, since many men with XYY are unidentified

Source: Adapted from: Fausto-Sterling, 2000: 52–53; Blackless, et al., 2000: 151–166; Dreger, 1998: 24–35; Intersex Society of North America: ISNA "How Common is Intersex?" (www.isna.org/faq/frequency); Levay and Valente, 2002: 130–133. "XYY Syndrome"; Families.com (http://encyclopedias.families.com/xyy-syndrome-1221-1223-gecd); Gotz et al, 1999: 953–962.

Note: Total number of people whose bodies differ from the normative male or female is one in 1,500–2000 (ISNA: "How Common is Intersex?"). Fausto-Sterling reckons 1.7 percent of all births are intersexed people (2000: 51).

adolescent males is seen as a way of preserving and recirculating semen—a vital, life-sustaining fluid believed to exist in finite quantities. Male-male fellatio during adolescence builds up male energy *(jergunda)*. Accumulating *jergunda* allows him to fulfill his sexual obligations as a husband and semen-nurturer to his unborn children. By definition, then, p-v intercourse is a potential drain of this energy and therefore must be carefully controlled (Herdt, 1982). These male gender role expectations are valued and fulfilling them grants status and respect to men.

TRANSGENDERED PEOPLE

Gender dysphoria and a trans. people gender dysphoria

Gender dysphoria[7] is a clinical term that refers to distress felt by those who are uncomfortable identifying with or behaving according to their culturally assigned and defined gender (Harry Benjamin International Gender Dysphoria Association, 2001; Money and Weideking, 1980). This clinical perspective is codified in the various versions of the *Diagnostic and Statistical Manual of Mental Disorders* (currently DSM-IV-TR, refers to Text Revision, 2000). The **Diagnostic and Statistical Manual of Mental Disorders** is published by the American Psychiatric Assoication and is the handbook used most often in diagnosing mental disorders in the United States (i.e., "DSM-IV"). In 1980, the diagnosis of "Transsexualism" was introduced in the DSM-III, and:

> In 1994, the DSM-IV committee replaced the diagnosis of Transsexualism with Gender Identity Disorder (GID). Depending on their age, those with strong and persistent cross-gender identification and a persistent discomfort with their sex or a sense of inappropriateness in the gender role of that sex were to be diagnosed as Gender Identity Disorder of Childhood (302.6), Adolescence, or Adulthood (302.85). For those who did not meet these criteria, Gender Identity Disorder Not Otherwise Specified (GIDNOS) (302.6) was to be used. This category included a variety of individuals, including those who desired only castration or penectomy without a desire to develop breasts, those who wished hormone therapy and mastectomy without genital reconstruction, those with a congenital intersex condition, those with transient stress-related cross-dressing, and those with considerable ambivalence about giving up their gender status. (The Harry Benjamin International Gender Dysphoria Association, 2001: 3–4)

As this review of DSM diagnostic terminology illustrates, social categories are not stable over time and may change. This is true not only of the classification categories used by the American Psychiatric Association, but social categories found in various sectors of society and in society at large as well.

Of concern here are the evolving meanings and social categories associated with people who self-identify as members of a transgendered—sometimes referred to as the "T"—community, "transpeople," "transfolks". "Social labels are also useful to individuals because they provide actual or perceived psychosocial connections, legal, and often economic protection, and political or civic validation. "It is important to distinguish between self-constructed labels and those that others impose on groups" (Kottak and Kozaitis, 1999: 164). Thus "what's in a name?" is very important to individuals, especially to sexual or gendered minorities, since it is related to concerns of power and voice. This issue is relevant for transpeople since DSM-IV classification is required for those who desire to pursue hormonal or various surgical alterations. The Harry Benjamin International Gender Dysphoria Association's *Standards of Care for Gender Identity Disorders* (also referred to as HBIGDA *Standards of Care*) is an international organization for professionals with the goal of establishing parameters and clinical guidelines for treatment of persons with Gender Identity Disorder thus linking professional standards of care with the DSM-IV. In 2006 HBIGDA changed their name to World Professional Association for Transgender Health (WPATH).

In 1952 George Jorgenson rocked the world with his sex change surgery in Denmark. Although not the first "sex change" surgery it was certainly the most publicized. In the United States, the first sex change surgery occurred in 1966 at the Johns Hopkins Gender Identity Clinic (Bullough and Bullough, 1998: 15, 20). The 1960s spawned an era that may be characterized as the flourishing of the postoperative transsexual. During the 1970s and 1980s more than forty North American gender clinics were offering programs leading to surgical reassignment (Bolin, 1998a, 1998b: 68). Coinciding with this was a proliferation of grass-roots self-help organizations catering to the needs of transsexuals and cross-dressers.

Prior to the early 1990s, transgendered people were in their infancy as activist organizers, focusing on self-help and education (Bolin, 1996: 470). They stratified their own using social identities of "**transsexual**" and "**transvestite**" (specifically heterosexual transvestite), separating themselves from sectors of the lesbian and gay communities that also involved people wearing the apparel of the other gender such as self-identified "drag queens" and "drag kings." During this era, pursuit of hormonal therapy and surgery was the *sine qua non* of transsexual status. The social identity of transsexual evolved to refer to people who believed themselves trapped in the wrong body and who psychically identified with the other gender. At that time if one wasn't absolutely committed to surgery, then one was de facto a transvestite. Those who claimed transvestite status were people who may cross-dress intermittently and/or for extended periods of time. It included, but was not limited to, those who felt compelled to cross-dress and those who are aroused by cross-dressing. Over time the term transvestite with its clinical and fetishistic implications came to be replaced by the term cross-dresser, regarded as a much more acceptable and less negatively charged social identity by community members and one that has gained widespread usage since the 1980s (Bolin, 1996a, 1998a, 1998b). However, **transvestic fetishism** remains as a DSM-IV-TR (302.3) classification as a paraphilia, the psychiatric term for problematic sexual desire or behavior (LeVay and Valente, 2002: 454). It refers to a heterosexual male, who for at least six months, experiences "recurrent, intense sexually arousing fantasies, sexual urges or behaviors involving cross-dressing" (DSM-IV-TR, 302.3). There are many in the trans community who find this classification objectionable (see below for discussion).

In the early 1990s, another term arose to describe gender variance. The social identity of **transgender** originated in the community of people who self-identify as transsexuals, cross-dressers, and those outside and between these kinds of gender variant options. Transgender supplants the dichotomy of transsexual and cross-dresser with a concept of continuity. It also reflects a growing acceptance of nonsurgical options and the recognition that there is a great deal of diversity in gender variant identities not represented by the clinical and community categories of cross-dresser and transsexual (Bolin, 2000: 27–30). In an article that is destined to become a political classic in transgender activism, Boswell defines transgender as a middle ground: "a viable option between cross-dresser and transsexual person" (1991: 29).

The transgender community is a reflection of the expanding political concerns of involved individuals who want a voice in treatment, in defining themselves and in offering activities, support groups, and other events to further their interest and needs as a growing community that gained momentum throughout the 1980s. Thus, the social construction of identities has become the cultural property of a community with a political and activist agenda for transpeople's rights. With "transactivism" and its message of valuing and respect for gender variance have come new possibilities for gendered identities. This is expressed through the cultural creation of a transgendered community that embraces a continuum of gendered possibilities from the cross-dresser who dresses for pleasure, to those who may "alter their anatomy with hormones or surgery but... purposefully retain many of the characteristics of their gender to which they were originally assigned. Many lead part-time lives in both genders, most cultivate an androgynous appearance" (Denny, 1991: 6). Others choose to live as nonoperative transsexuals. There is currently a wealth of possibilities and ways to self identify. Some transsexuals who are postoperative desire to disappear into society as women and denounce their "trans status" while other postoperative transsexuals proudly claim to be transsexual men or transmen (female-to-male or female2male), or transsexual women (male-to-female or male2female), recognizing that their current gender is informed by a past life as a sojourner in the other gender. Throughout the 1990s, the transgender social identity became even more expansive and the boundaries between cross-dressers and transsexuals became even more blurred representing the dual identity politics of consolidation and disruption of gendered identities (Bolin, 1996a: 460–482, Bolin, 2000: 27–30; Broad, 2000: 255).

According to Dallas Denny, a leader and social activist in the transgender social movement,

> ...people began to color outside the lines, experimenting with physical presentations and gender identities for which there were no terms, or for which new terms had to be created: genderfuck, gender transient, stone butch, she-male, drag king, Supermodel. Eventually...[transgender] came to stand for the entire community of persons with trans-gressive gender identity and behaviors—cross dressers (gay, straight and bisexual), transgenderists, and transsexuals (gay, straight, and bisexual.) There has been some opposition to this usage...but trans-gender has entered the common parlance and is the term most widely used to describe the transgender community. (Denny, 1995: 9)

Given this flourishing and revisioning of trans identities along with the concomitant growth of transactivism of the past twenty years, it is not surprising that the DSM-IV-TR classification for Gender Identity Dis-order (GID) and Transvestic Fetishism has been challenged by individuals and organizations in the transgender movement. For those in support of GID reform, the debate is centered on the inclusion of GID and Trans-vestic Fetishism as psychosexual disorders in the DSM-IV-TR. (Gender Identity Reform Advocates, 2000). Gender Identity Disorder Reform act-ivists argue that inclusion of these categories may be used to support and validate intolerance of gender diversity in the community, workplace and courts even resulting in the loss of civil liberties. In addition, the DSM-IV classification scheme is regarded as a deficit model, one that implies trans-gender impairment and "fails to consider the incidence of functional, well adjusted transgendered peoples and couples in society" (Wilson, 2000: 34). According to (Wilson, 2000: 37):

> American psychiatric perceptions of transgendered people are remark-ably parallel to those for gay and lesbian peoples before the declas-sification of homosexuality as a mental disorder in 1973...Revising these diagnostic categories will not eliminate transgender stigma but may reduce its legitimacy, just as DSM reform did for homophobia in the 1970s. (Wilson, 2000)

> GID is a contentious issue even in the transgender community. Those opposed to GID reform fear that access to the surgery will become much more limited because the DSM-IV is so tightly linked to the HBIGDA Standards of Care.

In this regard, Gender Identity Reform Advocates, an organization dedic-ated to advocating reform of the psychiatric classification of transgender identity as a mental disorder argue:

The transgender community and civil rights advocates have long been polarized by fear that access to SRS (sex reassignment surgery) procedures would be lost if the GID classification were revised. In truth, however, transsexuals are poorly served by a diagnosis that stigmatizes them unconditionally as mentally deficient and at the same time fails to establish the medical necessity of procedures proven to relieve their distress. (GID Disorder Reform Advocates)

The question of **etiology** (exploring the causes or origins) of gender identity disorder as a clinical category is therefore a complicated one enmeshed in the politics of identity. This is particularly relevant since the search for causes is invariably framed as a medical-clinical discourse with policy, insurance, and economic implications. In fact, the DSM-IV-TR acknowledges that there is currently no diagnostic test to identify gender identity disorder (Bower, 2001: 4). Although the cause of gender identity disorder is currently unknown, various researchers have offered theories to explain its occurrence. The literature on etiology spans the diversity of identities in the transgender community, but emphasis is placed on the self-identified and surgically oriented or postsurgical transsexual including both male-to female and female-to-male transsexuals depending on the particular study. We are sensitive to community preferences for the use of the term transgender and we have added it where appropriate. However, since the review of the research that follows emphasizes clinical literature, and transgender is not a clinical term, we have necessarily reproduced the authors' clinical terminology (usually transsexual) in order to more accurately represent their research theories and findings.

Since biomedical explanations for transsexual identity explore prenatal and biochemical causes for its existence and expression, they are discussed here along with psychodynamic explanations as well. There is a small cadre of clinically oriented researchers who offer alternative explanations, including those that link transgenderism to sexual orientation. These include Person and Ovesey (1977) who argued that there are two kinds of transsexuals: the primary transsexual who is neither predominantly homosexual nor heterosexual, and the secondary transsexual is an effeminate homosexual whose transsexual identity is evoked in response to stress. Note that these researchers and those that follow refer to the transsexual's sexual desire based on sex of birth, or preoperative genitals. A more respectful discussion and one that does not co-opt the voice of the transgendered people is an emic perspective that makes reference to the transsexual person's gender identity rather than their genitals. For example, a male-to-female transsexual, that is a transsexual woman, attracted to women may very likely regard herself as lesbian rather than heterosexual.

Blanchard (1989, 1991, 1993) and his supporters Bailey (2003) and Lawrence (1998) have followed this paradigm of transsexual/transgendered

sexual orientation bipolarity, including the use of gender of birth in reference to sexual desire. According to Blanchard autogynephilic transsexuals
(male-to-female) are sexually attracted to women, and are aroused by the
thought of themselves in a woman's body. He regards this form of transsexual identity as a paraphilia of tranvestic fetishism in its most exaggerated
form. In contrast, the classic transsexual in this scheme is a male-to-female
who is attracted to men and wants to be a woman so she can have relationships with men. Neither of these approaches includes female-to-male
transsexuals. It should be noted that this approach has been met with a great
deal of controversy and critique among the transgendered community.

The problem with these approaches is that they regard gender identity as derivative of sexual desire, consider these as essential and eternal
characteristics, and they ignore the myriad ways identity and desire are
derivative of cultural context and hence variable. Such approaches ignore
the diversity of sexual desire in transsexual people who span and transcend
our Euro-American categories of heterosexual, bisexual and homosexual.
Bolin, for example, found a high degree of bisexuality in her transsexual
research distinct from fetishistic autogynephilic tendencies (1988a: 62).
Transpeople, like nontranspeople, are a diverse population with diverse
desires. In fact, transpeople may actually have more numerous possibilities
for desire because terms for sexual attraction are defined by gender of the
actor and subject of desire. The gender identity of woman as lived by male-
to-female transsexuals, other transgendered persons and nontrans women is
not necessarily framed or limited by an attraction to men. Transwomen may
be attracted to nontrans men, women, or to transgendered people as well.
For transpeople, sexual orientation as a critical characteristic for gender
identity is not a salient feature. As one preoperative transwomen states:
"When you're transsexual every sex is the opposite sex" (Bolin, 1998: 91–
92). Trangendered people reiterate what the cross-cultural record reveals:
sexual orientation and identity are not coherent and stable categories. In this
regard Blackwood notes: "Europeans and Americans tend to think that individuals have fixed sexual identities and orientations. The sexual practices
and identities of the United States and Europe often bear little resemblance
to sexual relationships and practices in other cultures" (2005a: 268).

Anthropological and cross-cultural explanations and examples of gender
non-conformity and transgendered identities are usually referred to as
gender variance and are discussed in Chapter 12 in greater depth. This
research articulates the relationships between broader gender systems, the
social construction of identity and sexuality.

Etiology of transsexualism: prenatal and socialization explanations

Etiology or seeking the causes of transsexual identity is a prominent and
a prolific area of clinically orientated research activity. This question is

addressed not just in the clinical areas as might be suspected, but is also discussed by anthropologists and sociologists as well. Though paying respect to the diversity of clinical approaches, it is perhaps not unfounded to suggest that these perspectives tend to focus on the individual factors affecting the development of a gender identity at variance with morphological sex. Such a perspective tends to follow a disease model and may be construed as part of a Euro-American process of the medicalization of gender variance. Researchers emphasizing etiology are working from a medical model that stresses psychoanalytic, social learning, or cognitive developmental theory and/or biogenic variables. According to Ekins (1998: 184) these approaches emphasize a concern for patients' well-being over challenging their own presuppositions about sex and gender-role stereotyping that embeds the classification in the DSM-IV-TR of GID and Fettishtics Transvestism. "In particular, the focus on doctor-patient encounters precludes systematic exploration of the social worlds of cross-dressers and sex-changers outside the clinic and consulting room" (Ekins, 1998: 183).

In contrast, as will be discussed more fully in Chapter 12, anthropologists have tended to look at larger domains stressing systems of interaction including the gender and sexual system, gender relations, socialization, kinship, warfare, and political and economic variables related to gender inequality (Besnier, 1996; Burton and Whiting, 1961 among many; Munroe, Whiting, and Hally, 1969; Nanda, 2000; Wikan, 1977, 2000). Rather than viewing the individual as gender dysphoric as described in the clinical literature, the anthropological model seeks to understand how gender variance links up with other cultural institutions including the belief system around gender. Therefore, etiology is considered by anthropologists in terms of social constructs as is gender.

The etiology of clinically defined transsexual identity is of interest because it throws light on the broader subject of how gender identity is established not only in transgendered populations whose identity is in conflict with their morphological sex, but also for the population at large for whom gender identity is not problematic. In addition, it provides insight into understanding the cultural construction of gender in our society, and how gender is integrated within systems of gender relations such as inequality between the sexes.

Clinical transsexualism is of interest to embryology because it has been framed in the clinical literature as part of a nature/nurture or essentialist/constructionist debate. Money (1986) was among the first and subsequent numerous others to question this polarized argument as simplistic and unrealistic, emphasizing the interaction of biology and culture, a position that even those with a social constructionist approach do not find offensive. Today many theorists align themselves on the relative degree that they feel culture or biology influences gender identity and expression. It is the clinical studies that we shall draw on here in our discussion of fetal development, as these illustrate historic and current debates in these fields.

Socialization variables

Over thirty years ago, Money and Ehrhardt (1972) and Stoller (1968) regarded socialization variables as taking precedence over prenatal sex hormones in the formation of cross-gender identity, although these researchers acknowledged that there may be some unknown biological (hormonal metabolic) factor in the prenatal environment that may play a role. Stoller's model points to maternal overprotection and paternal distance—either emotional or geographical—in transsexual etiology. According to Stoller, the child fails to identify with the father and becomes effeminate. Other researchers sharing this view support the notion of a non-normative socialization, father absence or prenatal dynamics such as a mother's wish for a daughter (Cohen-Kettenis and Gooren, 1999: 317). However, subsequent studies of these hypotheses were not supported (Zucker and Bradley, 1995). Green (1974a, 1974b) supports the view that transsexuals share effeminate childhoods and then are subsequently channeled into transsexualism as their options for normative gender identity development have become closed off. Some support from the literature is found that parental influences may be a contributing factor (Cohen-Kettenis and Arrindell, 1990; Garden and Rothery, 1992), but not necessarily a sufficient condition for gender identity disorder (in Cohen-Kettenis and Gooren, 1999: 318).

Prenatal biogenic causes

The "parent" of the study of transsexualism, Dr. Harry Benjamin (1966), favored biogenic variables, even in those cases where socialization may have clearly been a factor. Researchers have focused their energies on several biogenic variables including chromosomal, hormonal, and brain dimorphisms. Hengstschlager et al.'s research with thirty male-to-female and thirty-one female-to-male transsexuals found that "genetic aberrations detectable on the chromosome level are not significantly associated with transsexualism" (2003: 639–640).

Eicher (1981) and others have suggested that the H-Y antigen may be atypical in transsexual people. In preliminary research Eicher found in his research population of forty male-to-female and thirty-one female-to-male transsexuals, that 84 percent were at variance with the norm. According to Ohno (1979), "H-Y antigen is a cell surface component present in all male tissues and absent in genetic females," although this association is regarded controversially as to whether it is a predictor of one's sex. But Pfafflin (1981), who studied transsexuals with a control group of nontranssexuals, found that the nontranssexuals were atypical for H-Y antigen in about 50 percent of the cases. This finding questions Ohno's thesis that H-Y antigen is a predictor of sex to begin with, therefore having little influence on gender dysphoric individuals. Since this research, H-Y antigen has been found to be produced by the Y gene locus. The literature debates whether it is involved in spermatogenesis (Jenkins, 1990) or in facilitating the development of the embryonic gonad into testes (*The American Heritage Dictionary* editors).

Studies have also investigated hormonal atypicality. Others taking this position include Starka, Sipova, and Hynie (1975) whose findings of lowered levels of testosterone in seventeen male-to-female transsexuals, three transvestites, and four homosexuals have *not* been replicated and must be regarded as "atypical." The phenomenon of transsexualism is in fact noted for its normal hormonal profile in individuals whose identity is variant.

Other research has linked gender differentiation of the human brain with how transsexual persons process hormones. The implication is that hormonal atypicality may influence male and female differentiation of the brain (Cohen-Kettenis and Gooren, 1999). It has been argued that the brain undergoes differentiation into male or female as a result of prenatal hormones (Swaab, 2004: 302). Although both male and female fetuses are exposed to high levels of estrogen prenatally, only males are exposed to high androgen levels that are ten times higher in males than females at thirty-four to forty-one weeks of gestation (Swaab, 2004: 302). However, there is disagreement about what actual brain dimorphisms, if any, result. Although some research has suggested that male and female brains are differentiated in the size and shape in the area of the corpus collosum, Fausto-Sterling offers a compelling reexamination of the problems with this research. Indeed only a few researchers have found sex differences in the corpus collosum area, and studies of fetuses and children found no difference; thus, if there is a difference it occurs with age (Fausto-Sterling, 2000: 131). Other researchers such as Manfredi-Romanini (1994: 783–787 in Cohen-Kettenis and Gooren, 1999: 318) and Swaab (2004: 303) argue that male and female brain differentiation may be due genetic factors, independent of hormonal mechanisms.

Seyler et al. (1978) found female-to-male transsexuals' hormonal responses to DES (diethylstilbestrol) were intermediate, falling between the "normal" female and male pattern. Migeon, Rivarola, and Forest (1969) administered estrogens to male-to-female transsexuals and to control groups of nontranssexual males and females and concluded that the transsexual hormonal response to estrogen was atypical to both control groups. Though some prenatal hormonal disturbance suggests itself, Seyler and colleagues also offer the possibility of a psychological factor since it is well documented that psychological states may be as causal as the effect of hormones. Lish et al. (1992) and Money and Mathews (1982) have not found a correlation between children exposed *in utero* to estrogens and transsexualism. Devor (1989) notes that cases in which females have been exposed to androgens *in utero* have not increased the incidence of transsexualism in those populations. Cross-sex identity (transsexualism) was not found in men or women exposed to progestins (which may have antiandrogenic or androgenic qualities) *in utero*. Nor was it found in CAH girls (prenatal exposure to relatively high levels of androgens) who were consistently assigned and reared as girls or in cases of prenatal exposure to estrogenic drugs, such as diethylstilbestrol (DES) (Collaer and Hines, 1995, Lish et al., 1995 among others in Cohen-Kettenis and Gooren, 1999: 318–319). This line of evidence presents a strong argument against the hormonal basis of gender identity variance.

One other line of research emphasizing biogenic variables has been pursued in regard to the etiology of gender dysphoria. This research has been based on male and female differences in the size of the hypothalamus brain cell nuclei, specifically that of the "central subdivision of bed nucleus of the stria terminalis (BSTc)" (Cohen-Kettenis and Gooren, 2000: 319). Zhou and colleagues (1995) examined the brains of homosexual men, heterosexual men and women, and six male-to-female transsexuals. They found that male BSTc were larger in males than females and that the male-to-female transsexuals BSTc were within the size range for females, but was only 52 percent of the volume of the BSTc in heterosexual men and 46 percent of homosexual men (Zhou et al., 1995: 68; Breedlove, 1996). Sexual orientation was irrelevant in the findings (Zhou et al., 1995: 68). The authors inferred a hormonal link, since nontranssexuals who had taken estrogens for medical reasons did not have smaller BSTc (Cohen-Kittenis and Gooren, 1999: 319) nor did menopausal women or heterosexual men castrated to treat prostate cancer have atypical BSTc for their gender (Zhou et al., 1995: 70; Breedlove, 1996). However, since this research is in its infancy, it is not known when BSTc differences appear in individuals, and further evidence may support possible long-term exposure to specific hormones as influencing this variable. The transsexuals in the study had received long-term treatment with estrogens. Currently we do not know what other factors are responsible for this difference in BSTc in men or women, or in transsexual women reported by Zhou and colleagues (Breedlove, 1996). This research has not been replicated on transmen.

The etiology of the industrialized transsexual identity remains as undetermined. Although there is strong support among some researchers for atypical socialization variables (Cohen-Kettenis and Arrindell, 1990; Green, 1974a and 1974b; Garden and Rothery, 1992; Money and Ehrhardt, 1972; Stoller, 1968), other research indicates the potential for a fetal hormonal atypicality (Benjamin, 1966; Eicher et al., 1981; Seyler et al., 1978; Swaab, 2004: 302) or other biogenic factor (Zhou et al., 1995). Still other research finds no support for either socialization or biogenic variables. Bower argues: "Despite intensive biological and psychological research, the aetiology of gender identity disorders remains an enigma. It may well be an interaction of genetic, hormonal and subtle psychodynamic factors awaiting elucidation" (2001: 8).

A bio-cultural approach holds promise for understanding gender identity and gender dysphoria. Bio-cultural perspectives are prevalent in the literature on gender identity and point to the interaction of both biological and environmental variables and the nature of this interaction. This is why they are called **interactionist** or integrationist **approaches** (Archer and Lloyd, 2002). In fact, Breedlove notes, "that for over thirty years neuroscientists have provided demonstrations that...experience can alter the structure of the brain" (1996: 6). Devor's research on female-to-male transpeople offers such an approach to understanding gender dysphoria. She presents an interactionist/integrationist approach to the development of gender identity in which the environment may be seen to potentiate prenatal influences either by inhibiting their development or by enhancing it. According to Devor (1989: 22):

External environmental experiences set into motion a momentum which may be in continuation of pre-natal influences, or in contradiction to them. In either case, social factors may be capable of overriding most, if not all, prenatal influences. Social influences may actually reset the direction which future development of a hormonal system will take. They may act to suppress or enhance biological predispositions. If social forces continue to exert pressure over long periods of time, a chronic situation can develop which may crystallize into relatively stable physical configurations that reflect the direction of social pressures. In this way, hormonal abnormalities might be seen to be the result of chronic social abnormalities ... [O]ne might interpret the gross hormonal differences between socially normal men and women as being a result, rather than a cause of the chronic social pressures which males and females undergo in the process of becoming socially normal men and women.

She concludes that the brain and its interacting endocrine system "learn" behaviors just as humans acquire behavior through cognitive processes. Thus: "Not only is the human mind in dynamic interaction with its environment...so too is the human body changing, learning and growing through its experience within its environment" (Devor, 1989: 22). The transgender identity is discussed further in regard to cross-cultural evidence in Chapter 13.

Reproductive technologies may offer transsexuals unique opportunities for roles as parents that are unavailable to other human beings, laws and policies notwithstanding. Male-to-female transsexual/transgender women may have their sperm stored so that if they develop a relationship with a woman, they may be able to take advantage of IVF technologies and have children. In such a situation, they may find themselves in the rare position of being a father (contributing sperm) as well as being a social mother to a child. Heterosexual female-to-male transsexual/transgender persons may have donor sperm (donor insemination) fertilize his eggs (ovarian cryopre-servation) and place the fertilized egg in the uterus of his wife, thereby also assuming the role of a mother (egg donor) and social father co-terminously (Psychology of Gender Identity and Transgenderism, Baetens, Camus, and Devroey, 2003).

HOMOSEXUALITY

In some ways the numerous attempts to define the causes of homosexuality, or the sexual and romantic attraction to same-sex partners, are even more controversial than trying to explain biologically the causes of a transgender identity. Having to explain these identities and orientations clearly illustrates the assumption and bias that we are born heterosexual and hence sexually and emotionally attracted to people of the other gender. The continuum of sexual orientations and accompanying lifestyles will be discussed in Chapter 14; the biological explanations for homosexuality are introduced here.

Given that we spend little time in this culture explaining the causes and desire to be heterosexual, the amount of energy invested in explaining homosexuality is a clear indication of our cultural discomfort with the topic, the narrowness of our range of culturally acceptable sexual orientations and behaviors, and our continuing value on sex for reproduction.[8] At the same time, there is an increasing academic and popular-press research interest which supports a prenatal disposition to one's sexual orientation, regardless of preference (Bailey and Pillard, 1991; Goldstein, 1990; Hamer and Copeland, 1994; LeVay, 1991).

Theories that explain the causes of homosexuality include psychoanalytic (Freud, 1975 [1922], 1959 [1929]), learning-environmental (e.g. Green, 1978; Storms, 1980), and biological (e.g., Gladue, Green, and Hellman, 1984; Goodman, 1983; Hamer and Copeland, 1994; LeVay, 1991; Meyer-Bahlburg, 1977 and 1979). Many of these theories assume some level of "unnaturalness" about homosexuality, and tend to be more explanatory of male (gay) than female (lesbian) homosexuality. With the exception of Meyer-Bahlburg (1979), they are basically nontestable, and are strongly focused on explaining how and why. The biological theories, by definition, tend to downplay socio-cultural variables that influence behavior. The theories also tend to be post-hoc explanations, particularly the biological ones; they don't clearly differentiate between sexual orientation and behavior, and they tend to ignore the cross-cultural record which illustrates our sexual flexibility.

Biological theories tend to focus on prenatal determinates and/or postnatal hormonal patterns. In general, it is accepted that relative to genetic, gonadal, and phenotypic sex, homosexuals are gender concordant for these traits. Generally, it is increasingly more accepted that their gender role is compatible with their gender and biological identities (Crooks and Baur, 1987; Kelly, 1988).

Prenatal theories focus on hormonal release patterns during the differentiation process, particularly for males. The release of prenatal hormones into brain receptors is such that a predisposition toward homosexuality may be established, but not enough to disrupt the development of phenotypic sex characteristics (Bailey and Pillard, 1991; Gladue, Green, and Hellman, 1984; Goodman, 1983; Goldstein, 1990; Hamer and Copeland, 1994; LeVay, 1991). Postnatally, there is investigation not only as to the absolute levels of testosterone and estrogen in gays and lesbians, but also as to the timing and sequencing of these hormones and LH release (Gladue, Green, and Hellman, 1984; Meyer-Bahlburg, 1977, 1979). In general, both the pre- and postnatal hormonal evidence is inconsistent and inconclusive. Most frequently, hormonal studies on homosexuals indicate that their hormone levels are within the range of those who are heterosexual or straight. It would be very difficult to posit a cause-effect relationship between hormone fluctuation or variation, sexual orientation and sexual behavior (Gladue, Green, and Hellman, 1984; Meyer-Bahlburg, 1977 and 1979).

The weaknesses of many biologically based theories include a homophobic bias, their researcher-admitted inconsistency, the post hoc nature of the explanations, their androcentric or male-oriented bias, and nonrecognition of homosexuality as an intra- and interspecies-wide behavior. They often ignore the cross-cultural record where evidence supports sexual flexibility or adaptability (Bullough, 1976; Gregerson, 1983; Herdt, 1982; Kahn, 2001; Ruan, 1988; Ruan and Bullough, 1992a; Williams, 1986). We know very little about the cause of sexual orientation in general. The controversial nature of many of the biologically derived theories about the cause of homosexuality may be used to feed the belief that homosexuality is deviant, or unnatural. Biological theories may be used to support a disease model. We face threats to our civil liberties regarding abortion choice, certain forms of birth control, and lifestyle options as well as ongoing ignorance and stigma about HIV/AIDS. In some ways, the alleged Sexual Revolution of the 1960s did not fulfill its aim of sexual choice and acceptance. Attitudes toward homosexuality are one example of this. It is extremely important that we maintain a relativistic stance and regard homosexuality and bisexuality as evidence of our human variability.

SUMMARY

1   Fertility, infertility, and conception are bio-behavioral phenomena.
2   There are a number of technological procedures in industrialized cultures to deal with infertility problems.

3 There are a number of theories used to explain sexual differentiation *in utero*. Some theories used to explain transgender identity and homosexuality rely on interpretations of the differentiation process.

4 Genetic or chromosomal sex, hormonal, or gonadal sex, phenotypic sex, gender identity, and gender role are cultural terms used to explain the prenatal differentiation process and postnatal development of identity and roles in the United States.

5 Turner's Syndrome, Klinefelter's Syndrome, and the Supermale Syndrome are variations of XX or XY chromosomal arrangements.

6 Gender dysphoria is a sense of discomfort with one's gender identity.

7 The etiology of gender dysphoria is still unknown. The current theories of etiology are controversial and not particularly compelling.

8 Of all the known sexual orientations, heterosexuality is the only one our culture believes does not need causal explanation. Increasingly, it is believed that predeterminants for one's sexual orientation may occur prenatally.

Thought-provoking questions

1 How are phenomena such as fertility, conception, and gender culturally influenced and expressed?

2 What are the controversies around ART and what are the potential changes in human reproduction as a result of ART?

SUGGESTED RESOURCES

Web sites

Gender Education and Advocacy (http://www.gender.org/). Last accessed 6/7/06.
Gender Identity Reform Advocates (http://www.transgender.org/gidr/index.html). Last accessed 11/09/07.
International Foundation for Gender Education (http://www.ifge.org/). Last accessed 6/6/06).
ISNA Intersex Society of North America (http:// www.isna.org). Last accessed 11/09/07.
Peris, Anna. 2005. "ART: ZIFT, GIFT, ICSI." Fertilititext. http://www.ferilititext.org. Last accessed 11/09/07.
Sizionenko, P. C. 2003. "Human Sexual Differentiation." Geneva Foundation for Medical Education and Research. http://www.gfmer.ch/Books/Reproductive_health/Human_sexual_differentiation.html. Last accessed 6/6/06.

8 Pregnancy and childbirth as a bio-cultural experience

CHAPTER OVERVIEW

1   Examines pregnancy and childbirth as biological, psychological, and cultural phenomena.
2   Views pregnancy and childbirth as a physiologically normal, healthy process in which complications may occur.
3   Examines childbirth as the means to culturally create and extend kinship.
4   Examines male participation in the female experience of pregnancy and childbirth.
5   Examines cultural responses to pregnancy, childbirth, and the postpartum period.
6   Explains the stages of labor.
7   Explains the noninterventionist/interventionist birth continuum and places U.S. culture's birth practices along the continuum.
8   Discusses postpartum depression biologically, psychologically, and culturally.

This chapter examines **pregnancy** and **childbirth** as biological, psychological, and cultural phenomena, comprised of an integration of physical, socio-cultural, and psycho-emotional variables. While focusing on physiologically normal pregnancy and birth as a part of the hominid life cycle, the chapter emphasizes how reproduction is culturally managed. It focuses on pregnancy, birth, **lactation (breastfeeding)**, and the postpartum period as essentially physiologically normal processes. The chapter discusses pregnancy relative to fetal development, and the impact that health and lifestyle have on the overall experience.

Pregnancy and birth are key life cycle status changes. With the birth of a child, a kin group is not only begun (**the family of orientation**), but is extended (**the family of procreation**). The birth of a child forms a union between extended kin groups that can include **blood (consanguineal)** and **marital (affinal) ties**. See Chapter 9 for a further discussion of kinship. It frequently transforms the social status of both the biological parents (the genetic contributors) and the social parents, those people involved in raising the child. Raphael refers to this social transformation as **matrescence** and **patrescence** (Mead and Newton, 1967; Newton, 1981; Raphael, 1988). The individuals involved such as the mother, the child, possibly the father, and the group are affected by the pregnancy and birth process. The cultural management of pregnancy and childbirth is discussed from industrialized and nonindustrialized societal perspectives.

The anatomical and hormonal changes in a woman's body are matched by cultural concern over her pregnancy and the birth process. Many societies recognize pregnancy as a unique state, placing the woman and by extension, the fetus, under special rules of behavior extending to diet, exercise, normal routine, social and sexual interaction, and cultural/institutional participation.

THE FETUS

The humanness of the fetus is culturally defined. Currently, industrialized countries' interpretations of when the fetus becomes human are controversial, and are the topics of intense debate relative to abortion and certain forms of birth control. For example, since the 1980s, conservative religious groups in the United States believe that human life begins at conception and take strong positions about assisted reproductive technology (ART), stem-cell research, and **EC** (**emergency contraception**). In colonial days, a fetus was not defined as alive until the onset of quickening, or fetal movement, usually detected in the fourth month during the second trimester of pregnancy (Bullough, 1976).

Late twentieth-century biomedical explanations trace fetal development by trimesters (see Figure 8.1). Much of the organ and system development occurs during the first trimester. In these first three months when neural, brain, muscular, and organ development is forming and sexual differentiation begins, the fetus is seen as extremely vulnerable to external factors such as drugs, pollutants, toxins, or X-rays. For this reason, early confirmation of pregnancy and modification of diet, drug use, sleep, and exercise are seen by health care providers in industrialized societies as very important to healthy fetal development. The second trimester, months four to six, involves elaboration of skeletal, muscular, and system development. It frequently is an end to the nausea experienced by some women in industrialized societies, and to the breast tenderness caused by high levels of progesterone secreted by the mother. The third trimester, months seven to nine, is generally a period of major weight gain in the fetus and ongoing maturation of systems in preparation for postnatal life. The testicles descend into the scrotal sac during the third trimester. Hearing, however, is the only system totally mature at birth.

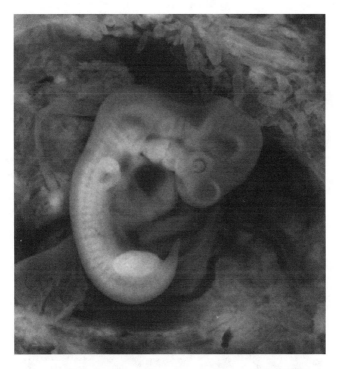

Figure 8.1 Human embryo at seventh week of pregnancy. (*Source*: By Eurhman, Wikipedia.)

THE PREGNANT FEMALE

Women's bodies during these three trimesters undergo radical changes. There are surges and elevated levels of estrogen and progesterone in her body that may initially contribute to morning sickness or nausea. Morning sickness is not a universal phenomenon. It is not reported as often in nonindustrialized societies as it is in the United States. This may be due to the higher complex carbohydrate diet in nonindustrialized societies than in the industrialized countries. Some recommendations to the pregnant woman experiencing morning sickness are to eat whatever she can swallow and keep in her stomach, regardless of its nutritional component. Some food ingested is better than none or food which is rejected (Erick, 1994).

The woman's breasts increase in size by several pounds as the milk ducts, stimulated by pituitary hormones such as LTH, prepare for lactation. Her uterus increases in size to accommodate the fetus, **amnion**, or bag of waters, **placenta**, and **umbilical cord**. Weight gain, slight separation of the pubis, slight lowering of the red blood cell count, and slightly elevated

Figure 8.2 Pregnant woman near the end of her term. (*Source*: Wikipedia.)

blood pressure are all normal physiological developments in pregnancy. (See Figure 8.2.)

Labor and birth

The birth process itself is a normal physiological event in which problems may develop for the fetus, mother, or both. It is estimated that in an otherwise healthy pregnant woman, about 92–95 percent of the births are normal (Arms, 1975; Boston Women's Health Collective, 1976, 1984, 1992, 2005; Davis-Floyd, 2001; Reibel, 2004). This approach is a radical departure from the accepted view in the United States. Currently, we in the United States, structure pregnancy and childbirth as a physiologically dangerous, pathological state that is medically "managed" (Davis-Floyd,

1989/1990, 1992, 2001; Johanson, Newburn, and MacFarlane, 2002; Mitford, 1992; Reibel, 2004; Williams, et al., 1985; Williams, 1989).

Although the exact causes for the onset of labor are unknown, it is probably a function of the interaction of fetal maturity and **oxytocin**, a labor-stimulating pituitary hormone. Labor is generally depicted as a three- or four-stage process depending on the medical text used. Prior to or early in the first stage of labor, "**show**" (i.e., the mucous plug) is usually expelled. Show is a bloody mucoid substance that covers the os (cervix) during fetal development.

The first stage of labor is characterized by several events. The os fully dilates or opens during this stage and generally takes several hours. A fully dilated os is ten centimeters or five fingers in breadth. In the United States, digital or finger vaginal exams are regularly performed during this period to assess the state of dilation. The cervix effaces during the first stage of labor as well. **Effacement**, measured from 0 to 100 percent, is the gradual softening of the cervix. A "softer" cervix allows for greater ease in the passage of the fetus through the os. The bag of waters or amniotic sac may break during this or subsequent stages of labor or the baby may be born with the amnion intact, called the **caul**. If the water does not break for a woman in labor in the United States, the amnion is usually ruptured by a medical attendant.

Transition, the second stage of labor, occurs when the cervix is fully dilated. Transition is the passage of the baby's head through the dilated os and may take several minutes to several hours. The third stage of labor is the actual birth of the baby through the introitus. (See Figures 8.3 and 8.4.) The perineum stretches to accommodate the baby.

Stretching the perineum is culturally managed and an example of the bio-cultural nature of sex and reproduction. In most societies outside the United States, the perineum is stretched through massage, application of warm compresses, or an upright birth position which allows the baby to pass through the introitus at an angle which fits the mother's body (Fisher, Bowman, and Thomas, 2003; Janssen et al., 2002; Jordan, 1983, 1993; "Midwives and Modernization," 1981; Michaelson, 1988b). In the United States for the past several generations, in anywhere from one-third to three-fourths of the births, the perineum is stretched surgically with an **episiotomy**, an incision in the perineum. This procedure is controversial. Proponents in favor of episiotomies say they reduce perineal tearing. Opponents to episiotomies state that tearing rarely occurs if upright birthing positions and massage are used (Arms, 1975; Boston Women's Health Collective, 1984, 1992; Davis-Floyd, 2001; Jordan, 1983, 1993; Michaelson, 1988b). In a recent article in the *Journal of the American Medical Association*, researchers recommended against routine episiotomies, stating that they offered no benefit, increasing both pain and the chances of tearing (Hartmann et al., 2005). In response to opposition to overly medicalized birth, innovations such as water births, more flexibility in birthing positions,

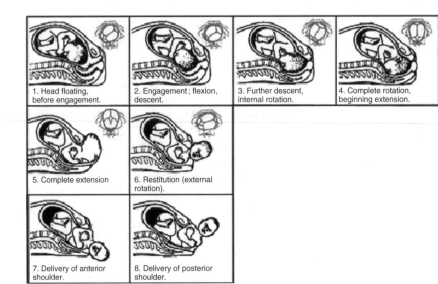

1. Head floating, before engagement.	2. Engagement; flexion, descent.	3. Further descent, internal rotation.	4. Complete rotation, beginning extension.
5. Complete extension	6. Restitution (external rotation).		
7. Delivery of anterior shoulder.	8. Delivery of posterior shoulder.		

Figure 8.3 Major stages in the birth process. (*Source*: Kelly, *Sexuality Today: The Human Perspective*, © Copyright 1998, The McGraw-Hill Companies, Inc. All rights reserved. Reprinted with permission of the McGraw-Hill Companies.)

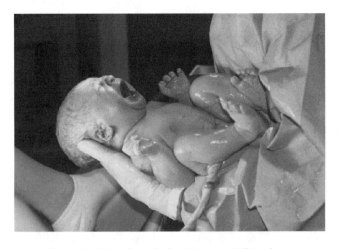

Figure 8.4 Newborn baby. (*Source*: Wikipedia.)

and birthing chairs (originally developed for birthing women in Europe in the 1500s), have been introduced into maternity suites in some "progressive" United States hospitals as the newest, most female-centered aspect of high-tech childbirth.

The fourth stage of labor consists of the expulsion of the placenta. During this period, the umbilical cord is cut. In most societies the baby is cleaned to remove blood and the **vernix,** the waxy, protective coating, which covers the baby *in utero.* In most societies, the baby and the mother have some contact at this time. This is the first stage of infant-mother bonding. Again, this is a controversial belief in the United States, where babies and mothers in hospitals frequently are separated shortly after birth for up to several hours, ostensibly to give the mother rest (Boston Women's Health Collective, 1992, 2005; Mitford, 1992).

After the expulsion of the placenta, the uterus starts a six-week process of **involution,** or return, to its nonpregnant size and shape. Involution is also culturally managed by massage in some nonindustrialized societies (Fuller and Jordan, 1981; Jordan, 1983, 1993), and through the use of drugs in the United States (Davis-Floyd, 2001; Jordan, 1983, 1993; Michaelson, 1988b). In many societies, women are encouraged to nurse immediately after birth in order to stimulate milk production and to help the uterus to involute. In general, the United States still sees pregnancy as a biomedical condition that needs to be medically controlled. Other societies see it as a normal state in which problems may or may not occur (Davis-Floyd, 2001; Jordan, 1983, 1993; "Midwives and Modernization," 1981; Michaelson, 1988b; Williams, Pritchard, MacDonald, and Gant, 1985).

Cultures treat the placenta differently. We dispose of it. In other cultures, it is buried in a tree or underground, the umbilical cord may be worn around the neck as an amulet until it dries and falls off, or the placenta may be eaten.

Although recognizing and attending to the physiological aspects of labor and birth, many nonindustrialized societies see birth as a significant social event. Birth unites women and reinforces their bio-social sameness (Frayser, 1985; "Midwives and Modernization," 1981). Birth attendants often are known and respected women in the cultures in which they practice. They assist, support, and are with the parturient woman before, during, and after childbirth (Boston's Women's Health Collective, 1992, 2005; "Midwives and Modernization,"1981; Mitford, 1992). Birth also creates the family of procreation for the parents and family of orientation for the child.

BIRTHING MODELS

There are two general models developed as the cultural response to pregnancy: the **interventionist** and **noninterventionist**. These models exist on a continuum, since all cultures intervene in the pregnancies and births of their members. Those societies toward the noninterventionist end tend to view pregnancy and birth as a natural phenomenon and emphasize the socio-psychological dimensions over the physiological. In these societies, the well-being of the mother and fetus is a primary concern with the expectation that the woman needs support. The physical birth process, while long and "laborious," is generally believed to occur on its own timetable. This model is characteristic of many societies outside the United States and the United States prior to the late nineteenth century (Davis-Floyd, 2001; Fisher, Bowman, and Thomas, 2003; "Midwives and Modernization," 1981).

The interventionist model is characteristic of current U.S. society, even with the range of birthing alternatives available such as birthing centers, family-centered childbirth, water births, and the increased use of midwives and *doulas*. Adopted from the Greeks, *doulas* are women who provide support for pregnant women throughout the pregnancy and early postpartum period. Almost 95 percent of the births in the United States occur in hospitals. Birth is primarily viewed as a biomedical phenomenon with a "maxi-min" mind-set (Davis-Floyd, 1988, 2001; Janssen et al., 2002; Reibel, 2004). The interventionist view perceives childbirth as inherently dangerous and prepares for the crisis situation as a general rule. Thus, there is much medical and technological intervention in normal as well as complicated births (Davis-Floyd, 1992, 2001; Reibel, 2004). This includes routine use of internal and external fetal monitors to chart the fetal heartbeat, episiotomies, use of IVs and drugs in the vast majority of births (Davis-Floyd 2001; Jordan, 1983, 1993; Michaelson, 1988b; Reibel, 2004; Sargent and Stark, 1989; Williams, 1989). It also reflects a rising Caesarean rate of 29.1 percent of the hospital births in this country in 2004 ("Births: Premliminary Data for 2003," 2004; Martin et al., 2005; "Pregnancy and Childbirth," 2005; Sargent and Stark, 1989).

Cultures address pregnancy through the postpartum (post-birth) period in a variety of ways. These include the role of the *couvade* , birth attendants, birth practices, and breastfeeding customs. The *couvade* is a culturally created bio-behavioral phenomenon in which the father can simulate the pregnancy and birth of the woman who is bearing his child. Fathers may participate in the rituals and ceremonies accompanying the birth. **Birth attendants** are those people who take care of the woman during her labor, the birth of the baby, and immediately after. Who these people are varies widely. Outside the United States, they usually are female; they usually are known to the pregnant woman; and they may be **midwives**, women who are trained in pre- and postnatal care and indigenous birthing practices. These women attend to the socio-psychological and physical needs of the woman and her baby before, during, and after birth (Faust, 1988; "Midwives and Modernization," 1981; "Quality of Midwifery Care Given Throughout the World," 2000; Raphael, 1988; Semenic, Callister, and Feldman, 2004).

The following passage is a description of a birth in a Mayan community in Latin America. It provides an interesting contrast to our biomedical approach.

"Notes from a Field Log: Doña Bernarda at Work"

Michele Godziehen-Shedlin, an anthropologist who works in Central America, wrote up her observations of a birth to a sixteen-year-old girl. Her rich description focuses on the support and presence of female attendants and the girl's husband during the labor and birth process. The midwife, Doña Bernarda, incorporates indigenous and biomedical methods in assisting the girl and also works with a medical doctor. The emphasis on birth as a normative part of a woman's life experience is paramount in this description. The ritual aspects of this transition for the mother and baby are an integral part of the birth.

Doña Bernarda examined her, massaged her; she was lying down. First, four of the five women helped her – two aunts held her, with Doña Bernarda at her feet and me holding her hand. She was made to squat, first supported by an aunt, later by an older man, and finally by her husband. She (Doña Bernarda) never stopped, her hand under the black Indian skirt (*chinquete*), her words and sounds constantly reassuring the tired, frightened girl (Godziehen-Shedlin, 1981: 13–15)

Birth practices are changing cross-culturally. A recent study in Holland, a society known for a high incidence of home births, indicated that a midwife's attitude, the pregnant women's positive values towards home births, and their critical attitude towards hospital births were factors involved in the decision to give birth at home (Wiegers et al., 2000).

Cecilia Von Hollen, an anthropologist, studies maternal and child health care in Tamil India. In her book, she discusses how working and lower class women engage the services of both midwives and biomedical practitioners during their pregnancies and births (2003).

Since the mid-nineteenth century in the United States, the entire birth process has been increasingly medicalized, removed from the home and familiar settings, and has become a mostly male-physician specialty.[1] Hospitalization for childbirth usually means the woman is in an unfamiliar, socially sterile, medical environment, attended by a series of strangers. Although women may have a number of friends or family with them during labor and birth in the United States currently, the physiological aspects of pregnancy are emphasized over the socio-psychological. Women are delivered in the United States; they do not give birth. In nonindustrialized societies, the locus of control rests with the pregnant woman; in the United States, control rests with her medical birth attendants (Davis-Floyd, 1992, 2001; Martin, 1987). In many nonindustrialized societies, birth attendants are integrated into the fabric of the woman's life; in the United States, they are distinct, discrete entities who act on her. (See Figure 8.5.)

Examples of birth attendant-parturient woman relationships from Greece, Latin America, and Egypt illustrate the importance of this role. The following examples illustrate the shared characteristics of the birth attendants. These older, experienced females may be involved in nonobstetric health care as well. The birth attendants are known to the pregnant woman and are part of her social support system. They provide her with care, advice, and guidance from pregnancy through the postpartum period.

In Greece, this woman is called the *doula*. She is particularly helpful in establishing a breastfeeding pattern and assisting the postpartum woman. She gives advice, helps with the daily routine, and provides socio-emotional support in teaching the new mother how to breastfeed. She temporarily becomes part of the new extended kin household (Raphael, 1988).

Figure 8.5 A mother and her newborn baby. (*Source*: Wikipedia.)

Figure 3.3 East African baboon in estrus. (*Source:* Courtesy of shunya.net.)

Figure 5.1 Man's hairline.

Figure 5.2 Woman's hairline.

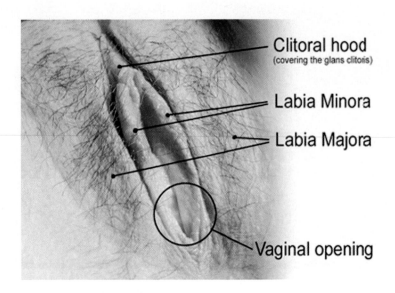

Figure 6.2 Female external genitalia. (*Source*: Wikipedia.)

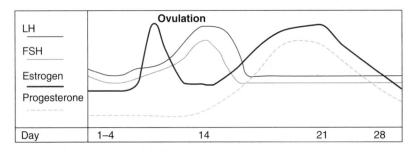

Figure 6.5 Menstrual cycle diagrammatically. (*Source*: Mary Emanuele.)

Figure 10.1 Earth paint. Apache girl's puberty ceremony. Whiteriver Arizona. (*Source*: Stephen Trimble, Photographer, DRKPHOTO.com.)

Figure 10.2 Maasai people: the warrior jumping dance. Young Maasai moran – warrior – youth leap into the air from a standing position in order to demonstrate their strength and agility. (*Source*: Martin Harvey, Photographer, DRKPHOTO.com.)

Figure 16.1 Globalization in Japan. (*Source*: Courtesy of *Art Explosion 600,000 Images*, Nova Development Corporation.)

Night view of Tokyo skyline.

In Latin America, midwives are often called *doña,* a title of respect (Faust, 1988; Godziehen-Shedlin, 1981; Sukkary, 1981). These women take seriously the overall health of their patients or clients, and frequently care for both their gynecologic and obstetric needs. These midwives monitor diet, social activity, and if government-trained, may record maternal blood pressure, fetal heart rate, and other physical signs during pregnancy (Faust, 1988). In much of Indian Latin America, pre- and postpartum massage and binding, in which the woman's abdomen is tightly wrapped, are part of prenatal and perinatal care. This necessitates the midwife's presence and her support of the pregnant woman (Fuller and Jordan, 1981).

Egyptian midwives or *dayas,* also provide known, continuous pre- and postnatal care. They stay with the new mother for seven days after birth, taking care of both her and the baby. As with the *doula, dayas* become part of the extended kin household, more like a family member than an outsider (Sukkary, 1981).

Fathers have various degrees of involvement in the pregnancy. In some societies, the sociological role of the prebirth father is highly ritualized through the *couvade.* He may "experience" morning sickness and labor, and undergo comparable forms of food, activity, sexual taboos, and modifications of his daily routine that the mother of his child incurs. The father may take to his hammock and experience simulated labor contractions during his partner's birthing process. The *couvade* is a cultural means of acknowledging and enjoining men to participate actively in the pregnancy and birth phenomenon (Kottak, 1991; Raphael, 1988).

For most of the twentieth century in the United States, fathers were not allowed to participate actively in pregnancy and birth. They were forbidden to be with women during labor and birth. They were seen as economic contributors, but not as interested, involved participants during the pregnancy. Since the mid to late-1960s, childbirth advocates have actively encouraged greater participation by fathers, extended kin, and friends. This has resulted in the involvement of a greater number of fathers and others in women's pregnancy, birth, and postpartum care (Leavitt, 2003; Raphael, 1988). The father-involved childbirth movement in the United States may serve some of the same functions as the *couvade.*

In the United States, some heterosexual couples talk about "our pregnancy," and men wear a strap-on "pregnant-stomach" to simulate later stages of pregnancy.

Confinement refers to the period spanning the pre- through postpartum (birth) phase. Most societies, including the United States, modify the pregnant, birthing, and postpartum woman's behavior in various ways.

Dietary and sexual habits are often changed. Pregnant women experience restrictions of their daily routine relative to work, sleep, and social activities here and in other societies (Daniels, 1997; Frayser, 1985). For example, we caution women to limit their intake of all forms of drugs during pregnancy, especially caffeine, nicotine, alcohol, and recreational drugs. We encourage a "balanced diet" rich in grains, calcium, fruit, and vegetables. Among the Maya in the Yucatan, women are encouraged to eat chicken and soups (Jordan, 1983, 1993). Our postpartum sex taboos usually end within six weeks; among the Ju/wasi of the Kalahari Desert in South Africa, they last several years (Frayser, 1985).

The actual birth of a child in the United States falls to the interventionist end of the continuum. Most women want and receive drugs for pain, have an episiotomy, and undergo a "prep," a surgical preparation procedure that may involve shaving the pubic hair, and receiving an enema, in order to "clean out" the intestines. Most women are hooked up to IVs and fetal monitors, either external or internal (Davis-Floyd, 1992, 2001; Janssen et al., 2002; Johanson, Newburn, and MacFarlane, 2002). Rarely does a woman wear her own clothes; jewelry may be removed and she wears a hospital gown (Michaelson, 1988b).

Ironically, the medical interventions in pregnancy and childbirth in the United States do not make them safer. We have the highest rate of infant and maternal mortality rates in the industrialized world (Chaya and Dusenberry, 2004; UNIFEM, 2005). There are a number of explanations for this. One, we have more girls under fifteen years of age giving birth than in other industrialized societies. Younger adolescents have immature reproductive tracts, tend to smoke more, and have poorer nutrition than older adolescents and adults. These behaviors can result in more complicated pregnancies and births. Two, we have differential access to health care in this country; poorer people get less health care and it is of poorer quality than found among middle-class, insured people. Three, reproductive technology allows women to become pregnant who wouldn't otherwise, and older women (those in their forties getting pregnant for the first time) who are pregnant have more complications. Fourth, our interventionist approach to almost all births, not just those with complications, results in more procedures such as C-sections that increase the risk of complications.

Outside the United States, pain may be relieved with herbal remedies or talked through. Childbirth pain is seen as normal and tolerable, part of a process to get the baby born (Godziehen-Shedlin, 1981; Jordan, 1983, 1993; Newton, 1981). Traditionally, episiotomies were unknown. The perineum stretches through the upright birthing position, spontaneous rupture of the bag of waters, massage, and hot compresses (Jordan, 1983, 1993). "Preps" are unknown and the woman's own clothing is usually worn. Babies and mothers are kept together after birth; babies usually are nursed immediately and whenever they cry. It is interesting that the counterpart of high-technology childbirth in the United States, "family-centered childbirth," advocates procedures and behaviors that are common and widespread practices in cultures outside the United States. These include recent "advances" such as birthing rooms and birthing chairs, having women move around during labor, or having a childbirth coach present to help the woman.[2] Most recently, they include shorter hospital stays. Postpartum infant-mother contact, a given in societies outside the United States, is beginning to be reestablished here through the practice of "rooming in", where for most of a twenty-four-hour period, the newborn and mother share a room.

POSTPARTUM

The **postpartum** period, a bio-social event, extends from the birth of the baby until the woman resumes her full prepregnancy roles and new status in the society as a mother and adult. This may take several weeks as in the United States, or longer in other societies such as the Ju/wasi where postpartum sexual taboos last two to three years (Frayser, 1985; Murdock et al., 1964). Biologically, the woman's body returns to a nonpregnant state: the uterus involutes, and her menstrual cycle resumes, irregularly at first depending on whether she nurses. Nursing is common outside the United States and engaged in sporadically and for shorter periods of time in the United States. Nursing may inhibit ovulation when it lasts for greater than eighteen months, when it occurs regularly and without interruption, and when it is correlated with relatively low body fat in the lactating female (Ember and Ember, 1990; Frayser, 1985). Breastfeeding then serves as a means of birth control under these conditions. For most U.S. women, nursing is not a reliable means of birth control for several reasons. First, most U.S. women do not breastfeed long enough for the hormonal suppression of ovulation to occur on a regular basis. Second, most U.S. women do not nurse regularly enough and they give "supplemental" feedings – bottles of juice, formula, or solids, and thus interrupt the rhythm that is established by frequent, regular nursing. Third, most U.S. women's body fat is too high to suppress the H-P-G axis regulation of ovulation. To reiterate, nursing as a means of birth control is not recommended for most women in the United States.

Breastfeeding itself is nutritionally complete for younger infants, and helps to protect them from disease by supplying them with their mother's antibodies. HIV-infected breast milk can be passed from the lactating woman to the nursing infant. There is international debate and controversy regarding whether women with either unknown HIV status or who are HIV infected should breastfeed (Altman, 1998) (see Chapter 15).

Postpartum depression, well documented in the United States, and less so in other industrialized and traditional societies, is both physiological and cultural. The elevated levels of estrogen and progesterone during pregnancy drop dramatically after birth. In addition to this internal hormone withdrawal, many women in the United States do not have extended kin and nonkin social networks and models for child rearing and social support. They are expected to read about child rearing and turn to the experts, health care, and social service people for help with parenting. Frequently, they do not know what they are doing and are alone at home. They may be isolated from other adults and have one or more infants, toddlers, and other young children to care for. The response to this situation may be "postpartum depression" (Boston Women's Health Collective, 1992 and 2005; Fisher, Bowman, and Thomas, 2003; Semenic, Callister, and Feldman, 2004).

In nonindustrialized societies, an individual exists as part of the larger social group, generally the extended family. A postpartum woman is part of that group as a continuous aspect of her life. Her midwife, as discussed, may also join this group briefly in the first few days or weeks after birth. Although the confinement period may extend through part of this time, it also offers benefits: rest from the daily routine, regular food, and relaxation from overall social and familial obligations. At the same time, mother-infant bonding occurs.

The relative separation of woman and baby from hour-to-hour social obligation may also provide some immunity from infection for the baby.

The pregnancy through postpartum continuum is an example of a physiologically widespread phenomenon that receives cultural attention wherever it occurs. The variability and forms of interpretation are culture specific. They range from highly technological to highly psycho-sociological.

SUMMARY

1   Pregnancy and childbirth are bio-cultural phenomena. Cultures intervene in the management of pregnancy and birth in a variety of ways.

2   While this chapter treats pregnancy and birth as a physiologically normal process, the dominant view in the United States culture for over 150 years has been that they are dangerous processes requiring medical management and intervention.

3   Birth creates and extends kin groups.

4   Pregnancy generally is discussed in terms of trimesters relative to fetal development and changes in the woman's body.

5   Cultures involve the father of the child in the woman's pregnancy and birth in a variety of ways.

6   Labor and birth are a four-stage process which is managed culturally with a wide range of interventions.

7   The postpartum period is culturally defined and involves biological and social dimensions.

Thought-provoking questions

1   What are some of the cultural values in the United States that support the notion of pregnancy and childbirth as dangerous phenomena that need to be medically controlled and managed?
2   What can we learn from cross-cultural childbirth practices and what can industrialized societies contribute to childbirth practices cross-culturally?

SUGGESTED RESOURCES

Book

Jordan, Brigitte. 1992. *Birth in Four Cultures: A Cross-Cultural Investigation of Childbirth in Yucatan, Holland, Sweden and the United States.* 4th ed. Long Grove: Waveland Press.

Web site

La Leche League USA (http://www.lllusa.org). Last accessed 11/09/07.

9 Early childhood sexuality

CHAPTER OVERVIEW

1 Introduces definitions of childhood and parenting.
2 Outlines the various functions of the family.
3 Discusses kin groups and family forms including the nuclear and extended family.
4 Presents the importance of residence patterns and their relationship to descent patterns.
5 Provides an overview of kinship and its various forms and structure.
6 Reviews the major theories of the incest taboo, including issues of universality and the interrelationship of kinship structures with the incest taboo.
7 Discusses incest in the United States.
8 Traces historically the changing perspectives of children's sexuality in industrialized societies.
9 Introduces major theories of childhood sexuality including the psychoanalytic views of Freud and Horney as well as those of pediatrician Dr. Spock.
10 Presents evidence of the development of children's early capacity for sexual responses as well as masturbation and child-child sexual experimentation in the United States.
11 Presents an overview of nonindustrialized society's childhood sexuality to emphasize its diversity and the cultural shaping of children's development.

DEFINITIONS

Early childhood sexuality is a highly charged issue which is made more complex by news stories of child molestation, incest, and the violation of a child's innocence. To comprehend fully the issue of childhood sexuality, researchers focus on the way culture interprets childhood as a specific time with a beginning and end with its own social and physiological changes. This necessitates that one must first understand the bio-cultural aspects of childhood from a physiological view, as well as the role that one's culture assigns to the physical body, in particular the genitals. An understanding of childhood relates to cultural conceptions of parenting, cultural notions of the family as well as kinship and descent.

It is important to remember that one of the unique aspects of human evolution is cooperation. Individuals who are not necessarily biologically related have, in our evolutionary past and under various cultural conditions, made a valuable contribution to survival of the group through parenting and nurturing the young. It is part of our deep human capacity to bond. Many children today have godparents who act in the place of the family in medical emergencies, death, or other situations necessitating help. In the South, the "courtesy aunt/ uncle" is a family friend who acts as the parents if the necessity arises. This may include nothing more than picking up a child from playschool, but it is a bond that is forged through time and respect ("Fictive Kin," 2006; Kottak, 2004). Godparenting is also referred to as *compadrazgo* in Latin American cultures. The godparents may agree to raise the child catholic if the parents are unable to, or if they die.

It has been posited by physical anthropologists that one of several factors accounting for female hominids' long postmenopausal life span is their contribution to survival of infants and children through care giving. Human females are unique in their long postreproductive lives. What information is available from our closest relatives confirms that reproduction and the life span converge in nonhuman primates. It is only in human females that longevity far exceeds the period of reproductive fertility. As grandmothers and socio-partners, we can imagine the enormous contribution of human females to the survival of the group in evolutionary terms. Hominid females, in the past and today, act as role models, caregivers of the young, parent substitutes, providers of the vast reservoir of knowledge in regard to the socialization of the young, and as educators of new parents. Like most human behavior, human parenting is a biologically adaptive behavior that interacts with the socio-cultural dimension. This is also true of kin groups in which biological relations are culturally shaped.

It is easy to forget, given the truncated nuclear families found in industrialized societies, that kin and family are the core units of culture. Children are born into a kin group in which descent is reckoned. For the majority of the world's cultures, descent is **unilineal** (Holmes and Schneider, 1987: 387). This refers to tracing descent through only one side of the family, either the mother or the father, unlike Euro-Americans who reckon descent through both the mother and father (note indigenous groups in North and South America were largely unilineal in descent). Kin groups and descent are important for our discussion because they relate to the social positioning and cultural meaning of children in a society, to issues of parenting and parenting roles, to rules of incest, marriage and reproduction boundaries, and why paternity certainty is important under some conditions and not others.

The industrialized worldview of parenting often emphasizes its connection to biological paternity or "paternity certainty." This is in reference to the biological principle that an individual is usually aware of whom his/her mother is, but without the use of technology to determine genetic heritage, the biological father is not readily apparent. Even in a minority of cases such as adoption, this quest is documented by people's desire to find their "biological parents," often at great cost and expense. We suggest, however, that family is socially constructed through the meaning we give to biology.

In understanding how family is a bio-cultural phenomena, let us explore briefly the cultural emphasis on the importance of paternity certainty and the conditions that are correlated with its emphasis (see Chapter 3). These variables include male-centered descent rules (tracing descent through the father's side of the family) and/or residence patterns. Concern with paternity certainty is also associated with certain kinds of subsistence strategies, specifically those found in horticultural societies that are under resource pressure and in agricultural societies. These kinds of societies also are associated with male-centered descent systems (patrilineal systems discussed in a later section). Thus certain kinds of horticulture (farming characterized by slash and burn techniques and fallow periods between plantings) are associated with male-oriented descent patterns. And agricultural societies (farming using irrigation, the plough; plough animals and fertilizer) generally are associated with this pattern. Finally, concern with paternity certainty is found in societies in which males hold privileged positions, such as the majority of agricultural societies, some horticultural societies and industrialized nations generally. It is hypothesized and supported by a good deal of evidence that these conditions are correlated and historically related to one another (Brettell and Sargent, 2005: 135–141 among numerous others; Martin and Voorhies, 1975).

For example, male-centered descent systems wherein individuals trace their ancestry through the father's kin play a role in the sex and gender system of a society. In some types of horticultural and generally in agricultural societies, the male line of descent establishes the continuation of the family property and business. Thus in the Sudan, according to the legal system dominated by Islamic law, women cannot inherit property. Nor are they positioned to support themselves due to lack of educational and employment opportunities as well as cultural customs related to the separation of the genders and ideologies of gender and work. This places them in a position where they must marry, or risk becoming a social and economic liability to their families (Gruenbaum, 2005: 481–494). Women must be virgins or they bring shame on their family. Virginity is therefore a mechanism that functions to support the certainty of paternity and is linked to ideas of kinship and the family (Gruenbaum, 2005). Descent and kinship rules around inheritance can have profound consequences on the lives of people, especially in regard to women and their status. Concern over biological paternity is clearly not a random cultural concern, but must be understood in relationship to the broader cultural context, especially kinship rules.

Kinship is important for ordering human social relations and creating groups and boundaries. Throughout the course of evolution and in most nontechnologically complex societies, the family is the primary unit for production and consumption. Kin groups are formed through marriages and reproduction. Marriages should not be confused with mating which is defined in terms of **premarital** and **extramarital sex**. A definition of marriage then can be stated as follows: Marriage is the "socially approved relationship between a socially recognized male (the husband) and a socially recognized female (the wife) such that the children born to the wife are accepted as the offspring of both husband and wife" (Kottak, 2004: G. 8). Note that these spouses need not always belong to the other sex nor are they necessarily limited to a single spouse at a time (Bolin, 1996b; Blackwood, 2005a; Kottak, 2004: 281). Marriage partners will share economic, reproductive, and sexual obligations. The functions of marriage are numerous and relate to these obligations. Marriage provides a setting that facilitates infant survival as well as a stable setting for children's socialization. Group survival is enhanced by extending social relations and providing sexual outlets and economic advantages to the participants (Ferraro, 2004: 195; Holmes and Schneider, 1987: 388). As will be discussed, all groups have **incest taboos** which prohibit sex and marriage with various kin and hence structure kin groups.

Just as there are socio-cultural rules regarding whom one may have sex with in the family (incest rules), there are also marriage rules. There are two forms of marriage rules: exogamy and endogamy. **Exogamy** prohibits marriage within one's own group. The definition of group will vary from that of a particular group of kin, to village, or groups of villages (Ember, Ember and Peregrine, 2005: 360). According to **alliance theory**, exogamy creates economic and political relationships between groups, some of which might otherwise be in conflict, and/or forges broader social networks and economic ties providing greater integration. For example, the Indian village of Rani Kera with a 150 households was linked to 400 other nearby villages through the practice of village exogamy (Ember, Ember, and Peregrine, 2005: 361). **Endogamy** is marriage that must take place within the group. This may include groups of relatives, the tribe, or even a caste or class. Hindu castes, although illegal but still practiced, endorse caste endogamy, marrying within the same caste, but not below in order to avoid the risk of ritual pollution (Ferraro, 2004: 201) Endogamy does not refer to marriage within nuclear families, but may include marriages between cousins or other related individuals. **Descent theory** regards endogamy as a vehicle for families to contribute to cohesion and solidarity by keeping wealth, power, and prestige within the group (Cohen and Eames, 1982: 121–122; Kottak, 2002: 406–407).

Families are primarily of two types, the **nuclear family** and the **extended family**. Nuclear families consist of the parents and their progeny. While blended families, single-parent-headed households, and extended families exist in the United States, the nuclear family is regarded as the cultural ideal represented in a variety of discourses including the media and political rhetoric. Other forms of marriage are also prevalent such as the **blended family**, which represents children from previous marriages, single female- or male-headed households, extended families, and childless couples. Extended families include consanguineal (blood) and affinal (marriage) relatives in addition to the nuclear ones. In nonindustrialized societies, the extended family usually includes relatives from either the male or female lineage and is the most common family form (Ember, Ember, and Peregrine, 2005: 366–368).

Family forms represent adaptations to different livelihoods. For example, the nuclear family is adaptive in situations which require mobility such as in gathering and hunting societies and among complex urban industrial peoples. Nuclear families are associated with **independent households** in which the new couple may practice a form of residence pattern called **neolocality**, where the couple lives apart from their parents in their own home and/or in a different area. Where the couple resides is very important for understanding marriage patterns, household composition, and descent. In many societies, the newly married couple practices a form of **joint household residence**, living with or very near one of the married partner's parents. In **patrilocal residence** forms, the couple lives with or near the husband's family, and in **matrilocal residence**, with or near the wife's family. Matrilocality and patrilocality are the residence rules which lead to the formation of joint households. Using ethnographic samples tabulated from Murdock's *Ethnographic Atlas* (before the massive changes brought about by the 1960s and the subsequent expansion of commercial capitalism), 69 percent of the world's societies practiced patrilocality, 13 percent of the societies practiced matrilocality and neolocality is practiced in 5 percent. The remaining practice other alternatives. These may include **avunculocality** (4 percent of the societies) in which the couple lives with the groom's mother's brother, or **bilocality** (9 percent) in which the couple may pick which residence rule they wish to follow. A rare form of residence is **duolocality** in which the married couple live apart from one another so that only blood relatives constitute the household. This is referred to as a consanguineal family or blood-related family in contrast to affinal relatives which connotes relatives by marriage. Residence patterns are important since they influence, although do not necessarily determine, the kind of descent system by fostering interaction among certain categories of kin. For example, patrilocality and patrilineality are closely correlated as are matrilocality and matrilineality (Ferraro,

2004: 215). These ideal types of residence patterns are subject to disruptions brought about by various events such as natural disasters, epidemics, and economic changes such as globalization that influence where newlyweds will live.

Anthropologists have proposed that independent households are found in simple societies like gatherers and hunters and complex industrial societies, while the joint household occurs in **intermediate societies** with domesticated food economies like pastoralists and horticulturalists. In the case of intermediate societies, Winch and Blumberg argue that the domesticated food economy provides sufficient resources for joint households who can benefit from the additional household labor as well as the group cohesion. These are not societies in which farm technology is available. Conversely, the independent household in urban industrial societies may be evidence of the capacity of individual households to support themselves, as well as for the necessary mobility required in these kinds of economies. They are similar to gatherers and hunters who also require mobility (in Cohen and Eames, 1982: 137; Ferraro, 2004: 217).

There are several types of marriage represented in the cross-cultural spectrum. These include single **mateships** which are composed of two spouses. According to Ford and Beach's (1951) classic study using ethnographic samples, 16 percent of the world's societies required this form, while in 84 percent of them, men can practice **polygyny** if they can arrange it. A recent statistic suggests that 75 percent of the world's societies prefer polygyny; although only a few of the men in these societies are actually able to practice this highly priced endeavor—it takes a multitude of wealth to sustain multiple wives (Broude, 1994; Ponzetti, 2003; Saxton, 1993). Polygyny refers to multiple wives while the generic term for multiple spouses is **polygamy**. However, in 49 percent of the polygynous societies single mateships are actually the rule, since a man must have a certain amount of economic wherewithal to acquire additional wives. As is illustrated by the Tiwi of Australia, once a man has demonstrated that he is a good prospective husband in terms of his status and economic condition, having several wives enhances his economic standing considerably (Hart and Pilling, 1960). In 14 percent of the polygynous societies, the only acceptable additional wife is her sister. This is known as **sororal polygyny**.

Another form of marriage is polyandry in which a woman may have more than one husband. Although the percentage is small, less than one percent, this pattern has been common in Tibet, India, and Sri Lanka and has also been reported historically among the Marquesans of the Pacific (Levine, 1988; Suggs, 1966). However, polyandry is currently no longer practiced in some areas and is under pressure to change in others (Ember, Ember and Peregrine, 2005: 365; Cohen and Eames, 1982: 126–127). It is believed that less than a dozen such cultures are currently in existence, and the cause for this marriage pattern is unknown. The most common polyandry is known as **fraternal polyandry**, which occurs when the multiple husbands of one woman are brothers. Possible advantages stemming from polyandry include keeping scarce resources, such as land, within the patrilocal family (Ponzetti, 2003: 1096). Fraternal polyandry occurs in Nepal and India where brothers may marry one woman and live patrilocally. All the brothers are recognized as the wife's husbands, and all take on the parenting role of father to her children. The wife has equal sexual access to all the brothers. In fraternal polyandrous societies, sororal polygyny may also be practiced (Schultz and Lavenda, 2001: 476–477).

Associated polyandry occurs among the Sinhalese of Sri Lanka (Levine and Sangree, 1980), and is reported in the Pacific and among indigenous peoples of North and South America (Schultz and Lavenda, 2001: 407–408). Associated polyandry refers to a marriage in which a woman may have multiple husbands, but these husbands are unrelated. The Nayar represent one of the most famous anthropological reports of this kind of polyandry. The Nayar woman engages in a **ritual marriage** to a man from a linked lineage. After three days of seclusion where sex might occur if the wife is old enough, the couple parts and they go their separate ways with no further obligations or relations. The woman is then free to marry and have sexual relations with men of her own choosing as long as they are of the same caste or higher (endogamy). The only restriction is that these husbands cannot be brothers. This system is referred to as one of **visiting husbands**. The men and women in these relationships have more than one spouse. The households are consanguineal ones in that a woman lives with her children, her sisters, and her sisters' children. The marriages are valuable for their alliance functions, not economic ones. Men take on financial responsibility for their sisters and sisters' children (Kottak, 2004: 257; Schultz and Lavenda, 1990: 301–302).

Like polygynous marriages, polyandrous ones reflect adaptations to subsistence conditions. In Tibetan fraternal polyandry, polyandrous marriages help maintain family landholding units against possible subdivision through individual inheritance and partition of lands. The ecological conditions are such that households must pursue both agriculture as well as animal husbandry in order to survive. In such a situation a division of labor among co-husbands is advantageous (Goldstein, 1987: 39–48; Ponzetti, 2003: 1096).

Other forms of marriage exist but are not widespread. These include a form of **group marriage** practiced by the Oneida utopian Christian community in New York. All members regarded one another as spouses. As a result of local hostility, this system was discontinued in 1879 (Gregersen, 1994: 310). Out of a study of over 100 of these "multilateral marriages," only 7 percent exceeded five years (Constantine and Constantine, 1973; Ponzetti, 2003: 1096). Other forms include **woman marriage** as among the Nuer in which two women are married. One woman takes on the role of a social male and arranges for "her" wife to become pregnant by "another" man. The woman-husband then becomes the social father of the child (Blackwood, 1984a: 56–63; Brockman, 2004: 688; Cohen and Eames, 1982: 128–129). The **levirate** and **sororate** represent marriage systems related to the death of spouses. In the levirate the wife will marry her dead husband's brother. Seventy percent of a sample of 159 societies reported on in Murdock's (1965) classic cross-cultural correlational study of traditional societies preferred this form, while 60 percent preferred the sororate in which a man marries his dead wife's sister. One explanation of these practices suggests that remarriage between relatives is important for maintaining the stability of the familial group which may be threatened by the death of the parent. Alliance theory argues that these marriage forms maintain alliances originally established by the dead sibling (Scupin, 2003: 75–76).

Marriage creates kinship relationships between individuals and groups. We shall begin our discussion of kinship by focusing on **descent groups**. Descent groups are characterized by a permanent set of relations that are not changed by residence or death. These groups are formed through various principles of descent and represent ways in which human groups organize themselves. **Descent** is defined as "the cultural principle based on culturally recognized parent-child connections that define the social categories to which people belong" (Schultz and Lavenda, 1990: 261). Descent groups comprise people who recognize shared ancestry. It is the primary way people are organized in nonindustrial and prestate societies. Though nuclear families are defined by common residence and are therefore impermanent, the descent group is permanent (Ferraro, 2004: 228). Two principles of descent occur worldwide. In order to illustrate the forms of descent and kin relations, anthropologists use a kinship diagram. (See Figure 9.1.)

Although marriage seems to be a staple in the lives of many Americans, some social groups have attempted to operate sans matrimony. Some examples of these institutions include communes, religious orders, and/or warrior castes. The most well-known people in the United States practicing this tradition are the Shakers. Since the 1700s, Shakers have coveted religion over sexual unions, and have practiced communal living as well as celibacy. In the 1840s, the Shaker movement reached its peak with more than 6,000 members, spanning from Florida to Maine in over twenty-five communities. Since they practice celibacy, the Shakers relied on the recruitment of new members as their strategy for growth. After the Civil War, membership in the Shaker community began to decline seriously. Today, only a small community of believers remains in Sabbathday Lake, Maine (Foster, 1991; Ponzetti, 2003; Robbins, 2006: 145–148).

Anthropologists use kinship diagrams to illustrate relationships among relatives. The basic symbols employed are:

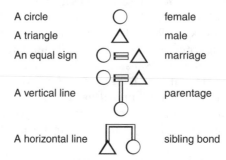

A circle	○	female
A triangle	△	male
An equal sign	○▱△	marriage
A vertical line		parentage
A horizontal line		sibling bond

Each relationship to an individual is often described from the perspective of one person labeled EGO as in the following diagram

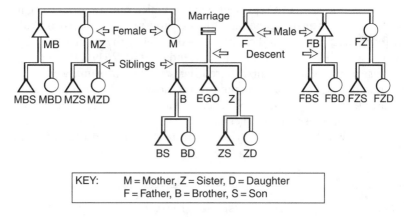

KEY: M = Mother, Z = Sister, D = Daughter
       F = Father, B = Brother, S = Son

Figure 9.1 Kinship diagram. (*Source*: Brian Schwimmer. Kinship and social organization, an interactive tutorial. www.umanitoba.ca/faculties/arts/ anthropology/tutor/fundamentals/fund2.html.Accessed April 12, 2007). (*Note*: Letters and sequences of letters are used to designate relationships to Ego, such as a mother, father, mother's brother, mother's sister. Each relationship is described by a sequence of primary components, which are strung together to indicate actual biological relationships.)

Descent systems are either unilineal, tracing one's ancestors through one side of the family and not the other, or are **nonunilineal**. Nonunilineal descent is also referred to as **bilateral** or **cognatic** descent and is based on the principle of tracing descent through both parents equally (Ferraro, 2004: 235–236). Approximately 40 percent of the world's societies are nonunilineal. These include bilateral, ambilineal and bilineal descent. The U.S. descent system is called the bilateral kindred.

A **bilateral kindred** is a group that forms around a particular individual. It includes all people who are linked to that individual through the kin of both sexes. These are the people Euro-Americans conventionally call **relatives**. Relatives form a group only because of their connection to the central person or persons, known in anthropological kinship terminology as **ego** (Ferraro, 2004: 236). An example of this can be found in the U.S. tradition. The Daughters of the American Revolution trace their kinship through maternal and paternal lines to a particular person who was a "patriot" during the Revolutionary War. Bilateral descent is shown in Figure 9.2.

The principle of **ambilineal descent** forms groups known as the **ramage**. In ambilineal systems, descent is traced from a founding ancestor through either the male or the female line or both. **Bilineal** or **(double) descent** is similar to ambilineal descent in that descent is traced through both the patrilineage and matrilineage, but each controls different areas of activity and property. The Yako of Nigeria are a good example of this. Nonmovable property such as houses, farms, and groves of trees are inherited through patrilineal descent. Movable property such as cattle and home furnishings are inherited through the matrilineage (Ferraro, 2004: 235). In contrast,

Bilateral systems involve the inclusion of all of an individual's relatives within a given range. They are usually Ego focused and are formed by tracing relationships from both parents throughout an ever widening network of kinship called a **kindred**.

Bilateral kinship network (kindred)

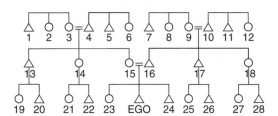

Figure 9.2 Bilateral descent and kindred. (*Source*: Brian Schwimmer. Kinship and social organization, an interactive tutorial. www.umanitoba.ca/faculties/arts/anthropology/tutor/fundamentals/bilat.html. Accessed April 12, 2007). (*Note*: The kindred of EGO includes his sister (#23), his brother (#24), his parents (#15, #16), his mother's sister (aunt, #14), his mother's brother (uncle, #13), his father's sister (aunt, #18), his father's brother (uncle, #17), his mother's parents (#3 and #4) and their siblings (#1, #2, #5, #6), his father's parents (#9 and #10) and their siblings (#7, #8, #11, #12). Also included are his cousins (#19, #20, #21, #22, #25, #26, #27, #28. The kindred depicted is extended to the range of first cousins. Larger kindreds, such as those of second, third, or fourth cousin ranges, are usual. In contemporary American society the range of a kindred varies from person to person. Kindreds assume greater or less importance in different societies. In medieval Europe people were bound to give support in feuds to any relative within a kindred that extended to fourth cousins.)

the unilineal principle of descent traces kin membership through either the mother's or the father's line exclusively.

Matrilineal descent traces membership through the female line only, while patrilineal descent traces group membership through the male line only. In these systems, an individual will trace ancestry through either their matrilineage or patrilineage. Unlike the **clan**, the lineage has demonstrated descent in that members can trace their kinship and exact relationships to one another and a founding ancestor. In contrast, stipulated descent occurs among people who claim to be related to a common ancestor, but

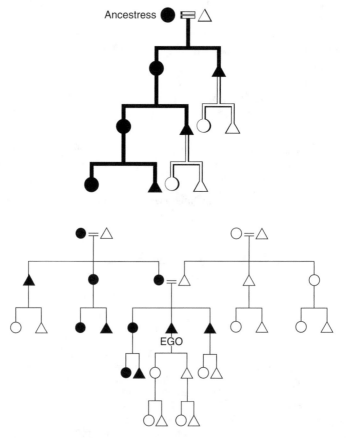

Matrilineal descent is established by tracing descent exclusively through females from a founding female ancestor. The individuals indicated in black constitute the matrilineal descendants of a common ancestress. Both men and women are included in the matrilineage formed but only female links are utilized to include successive generations.

Figure 9.3 Matrilineal and patrilineal systems of descent. *(Source:* Brian Schwimmer. Kinship and social organization, an interactive tutorial. www.umanitoba.ca/faculties/arts/anthropology/tutor/fundamentals/ matri01.html.)

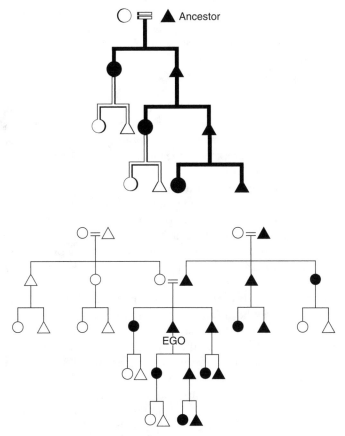

Patrilineal descent is established by tracing descent exclusively through males from a founding male ancestor. The individuals indicated in black constitute the patrilineal descendants of a common ancestor. Both men and women are included in the patrilineage formed but only male links are utilized to include successive generations.

Figure 9.3 (Continued)

are unable to document the exact relationship because the ancestor is either hypothetical or very remote. Stipulated descent is associated with clans.

The Mosuo (also known as Moso, Nari, among other terms) ethnic group of southwest China illustrates a society in which family is based on the principle of matrilineal descent. The Mosuo are unique among China's ethnic groups who typically are patrilineal. Among the Mosuo, descent is traced and property inherited exclusively through women. Fathers have a peripheral role in the lives of their children, in fact the word "father" does not exist in the Mosuo language nor are in-laws recognized as a category. Sons typically reside with their mothers. This kinship system creates a family that consists of mothers, daughters/sisters, and sons/brothers. The Mosuo are indeed a society in which women are in charge. This matrilineal system provides women with a great deal of power, including selecting their lovers and claiming position as the head of a household, the *dabu* (Mackie, 2005: 1–3; Yuan and Mitchell, 2000: 58–65).

Mosuo women and men practice a very loose system of relationships referred to as "walking marriage." Although they are similar to the precolonial Nayar in terms of matrilineal descent and visiting "husbands," the Mosuo are unique in their absence of any formal marriage practices at all. The Mosuo system differs from the definition of marriage in that it is not contractual, obligatory, or exclusive (Shih, 2001: 381). The Mosuo participate in a system of visiting relationships between lovers. In the Mosuo language it is called *sisi* which translated means walking back and forth. The *sisi* arrangement is also referred to as *zou hun* (walking marriage) or *azhu huny* (friend marriage). In the *sisi* relationship men visit their lover at night but must return to their mother's home before breakfast where they reside and have responsibility. At around age twelve, Mosuo women are given a right of passage ceremony and after puberty they can begin to receive male visitors. Children born of these relationships live with the matrilineage. As is typical of matrilineages, brothers have an important role to play in the lives of their sister's children both economically and socially. It is the matrilineal household that takes full economic and social responsibility for children born to daughters and sisters. Although fathers may be close to their offspring, they have no social or economic obligations to their children and these relationships can be ended at any time by the mother.

This form of household and relationships is preferred by the Mosuo who note that one of the benefits of this system is there is no dowry or economic relationship involved at all. According to Mosuo community members, this means the relationships are based solely on love without any strings attached. When couples are no longer happy, they can very easily terminate the relationship. The Mosuo maintain that with friend marriage there is very little conflict and fighting, since couples can so easily terminate their relationships. This family structure provides a large extended family to share the work, one not found in neighboring neolocal households where the couple is responsible for all the work (Mackie, 2005; Yuan and Mitchell, 2000: 58–65).

With the Cultural Revolution in China (1966–1976) the Mosuo were pressured to change their way of life. They accommodated the Chinese demand that they formally marry, with couples living matrilocally. However, at the end of the Cultural Revolution, they returned to their friend marriage system. Although still practiced today, the Mosou have recently become part of the Chinese tourist industry, which has stimulated their economy and allowed more people to be educated. In addition, as young women begin to marry outsiders, as media and the Internet become more widespread and available, there will undoubtedly be changes in this traditional pattern of kinship and marriage (Mackie, 2005: 1–3; Yuan and Mitchell, 2000: 58–65).

The Kapauko Papuans of the central highlands of western New Guinea provide an example of a patrilineal society. The male members of a patrilineage can trace their decent through males to a common ancestor. These men typically represent the male population of a village or several adjoining villages. They live together or nearby because of a residence rule that requires patrilocality; that is, upon marriage they must remain in the village/household of their father (see above discussion). When a son marries he brings his wife to live in his village, in or near his father's home, while daughters must leave their natal villages. The members of a patrilineage are discouraged from hostility towards one another, since they are regarded as relatives and affectionate and friendly relations are encouraged. The Kapauku also belong to larger patrilineal decent groups called clans and phratries. As members of a patriclan they believe themselves to all be related through their father's lineage although the specifics of this relationship are not necessarily known. The **patrician**, unlike the lineage does not share a common village/residence. Kapauku cannot marry within the clan and must practice clan exogamy.

The Kapauku are also related patrilineally through a phratry which is composed of two or more clans. The two clans of the Kapauku phratry believe themselves to be related through a myth in which the original phratry, which consisted of one clan, was bifurcated when conflict between two brothers occurred. In the myth, the younger brother was ousted from the original clan and founded a new one, thus creating a relationship between the two clans of the phratry. Although members of the same clan cannot intermarry, members of the same phratry may intermarry if they practice clan exogamy, that is the married partners are from two different clans (Ember, Ember and Peregrine, 2005: 381).

Clans are groups whose membership is based on the principle of unilineal descent. Clans are defined as a descent group who are affiliated through the belief that they have a common ancestor, even if that ancestor cannot be directly traced. The ancestor may be a person or a mythical being. Consequently, clans have greater size and generational depth than the lineage. While the lineage is the smallest unit of unilineal descent and may be a part or a segment of a clan, even larger groups may occur. People of Scottish ancestry in the American South perpetuate ancient traditions of Scottish clan affiliation through the annual Scottish Highland Games and Gatherings. Although by the early 1700s the power of the Scottish clans had diminished, a Scottish revival reinvigorated clan identity through the association of clans, surnames, and tartan patterns. These games reproduce the blending of a traditional Southern emphasis on kin with Scottish clan social identity (Ray, 2003: 252–256). When a society is divided into two large kin groups, this is referred to as a **moiety system**. **Phratries** are unilineal descent groups made up of more than two clans. Phratries are rather rare in the ethnographic and ethnohistorical literature (Ferraro, 2004: 234). Having discussed marriage and family forms, the organization of human groups based on marriage and children, and affinal and consanguineal relationships, we now turn to the subject of sexuality and kin.

INCEST TABOOS

Childhood sexuality, like adult sexual expression, is managed by culture. One of the ways in which it is managed is through proscriptions against incest. The incest taboo is cited as an example of a cultural universal, although there are exceptions to the taboo. The incest taboo is defined as a "[u]niversal prohibition against marrying or mating with a close relative" (Kottak, 2002: 700). The incest taboo refers to those family members that we in the United States call the **immediate family**. In virtually every society, sex is prohibited between an individual and her/his siblings, parents, and children. These people are termed "primary relatives." Anthropologists continue to debate the origin of the incest taboo, since it is such a widely shared institution. As a consequence of this debate a number of theories have emerged. We shall review several of the more prominent perspectives. These perspectives span a long time frame and cross disciplines including biological, psychological, anthropological, and integrative approaches. Meigs and Barlow argue that "[t]he incest taboo is to anthropology what Shakespeare is to English literature—"fundamental and classic" (2002: 38). The study of the incest taboo emphasizes prohibitions rather than the consequences of actual incest taboo violations (Patterson, 2005). In those societies where sex was allowed within families such as the ancient Egyptians, Hawaiians, and Incans, it was restricted to nobility who were considered gods and above human laws (Ember, Ember and Peregrine, 2005).

Psychoanalytic theories represent one kind of explanation about incest. Perhaps the most famous psychoanalytic view of the incest taboo is Sigmund Freud's theory of the Oedipus complex. The Oedipal complex has had an important impact on early- to mid-twentieth-century anthropological reflection on the subject, particularly in the anthropological school of thought known as culture and personality. This subfield regarded personality as causal in shaping culture's more expressive aspects such as art, religion, and mythology. Not all anthropologists agreed with Freud's formulation. In fact, the anthropologist Bronislaw Malinowski in 1927 challenged the view that the incest taboo was a result of the existence of the Oedipus complex.

Freud's theory of the Oedipus complex was derived from his work with specifically western European clients. The Oedipus complex is represented as one stage in the psychosexual development of a child. The first phase a child experiences lasts from birth through one year of age and is the **oral stage** in which the infant's interests center on the mouth as a source of pleasure. Freud regarded pleasure seeking in the human as a given, that is instinctual. The **anal stage** occurred at approximately two years of age. It is the period in which the child achieves control of his/her bladder and anal sphincter and finds pleasure in this sensation. However, toilet training can cause conflicts as the child's wishes may be controlled by external pressures such as toilet training practices. The Oedipal phase, or **phallic stage**, is characterized by love, hate, envy, and guilt, and occurs from about three to five years old. This is followed by a period of latency, from about six to twelve years of age, when the sexuality of the Oedipal phase is repressed. At puberty interest in sexuality is reasserted. **Libido,** or the desire for sex which Freud considered panhuman and natural, underwent various expressions and repressions through these developmental stages. Freud felt these stages were embedded in our human biology and were universal. Freud's theory of development is linked to his view that sexuality is both a conscious and unconscious force throughout the life course. This was an astonishing view in light of his Victorian milieu.

The **Victorian era** is named for the reign of Queen Victoria who ruled from 1837–1901. The Romantic period, which began around the 1800s, fed the Victorian era. The Romantic era celebrated nature and the unspoiled. These notions filtered into the Victorian period. At this time the concept of the **noble savage** flourished, derived from anthropological reports of "exotic natives" communing with nature in its unspoiled and pristine state. Middle-class English children, too, were seen as having a nobility derived from purity. They were viewed as yet unspoiled by civilization. As the industrial revolution gained momentum, children "became the last symbols of purity in a world which was seen as increasingly ugly" (Sommerville, 1990: 198). Children were glorified during the Victorian era. In short, they were next to the angels in virtue. While middle-class adult Victorians had to suppress their impulses in an era where sexuality and sexual symbolism were not publicly expressed, children represented innocence of desire. They were in a state of natural privilege associated with "childhood goodness" (Sommerville, 1990: 204). Sommerville (1990: 209) has suggested that this view of children did not extend to the United States during this same time period. Middle-class United States perspectives of children demanded competence and performance in contrast to British views of children who "symbolize[d] the innocence which a severely repressed society felt it had lost."

Sigmund Freud's work on childhood sexuality followed closely on the heels of the Victorian period. In 1905 Freud published his *Three Essays on the Theory of Sexuality*. Freud felt that human sexual energy, which he called libido, was present at birth and that through the course of children's development; this energy became focused in different body zones during the different stages of psycho-sexual maturation. This embodied a very different interpretation of the child from the Victorian notions of innocence. For Freud, the infant was charged with an undifferentiated sexual energy; that is, he or she could find sexual pleasure in the entire body in the erotogenic zones. This is what Freud meant when he referred to the infant as "polymorphously perverse." Libido is an energy rewarded by the "aim" of pleasure. The **erotogenic zones** were areas of the body through which libido could be discharged. Freud emphasized these in his stages of childhood. The oral stage of development focused on the mouth area as the first zone for pleasure. This is the pleasure the child derives from sucking and nursing. The second zone emphasized the anus and was termed the anal stage of development. This was the period where the child has learned to control her or his bowels and finds pleasure in the process of evacuation. The third or phallic stage actually refers to the phase when children, between three or four years of age, explore their genital areas and find self-stimulation to be pleasurable. This stage which accented the genitals also included the Oedipus complex which occurs around the ages of five or six. For boys, as will be discussed shortly, the Oedipus complex is resolved out of fear of the father and identification with him. The little girl conversely desires her father and resents her mother (Appignanesi, 1979: 76–88; Gleitman, 1987: 352–353; Lindsey, 2005: 26–27). The **latency stage** follows the Oedipal phase. This was the period from about six years old to puberty when children, according to Freud, lost interest in sex. This phase initiated the end of the four stages of infantile sexuality. It should be remembered that sexual interests were seen as repressed, but not eliminated from the psyches of children (Appignanesi, 1979: 92; Westheimer and Lopater, 2005: 424–425).

The Oedipal phase is the cornerstone of Freud's theory of psychosexual development. Freud named this after Oedipus, the tragic hero in a mythical story of a man who married his mother unknowingly and, upon finding this out, blinded himself as punishment. According to Freud, the young boy covets his mother and regards his father as a rival for his mother's affections. In contrast, the young female desires her father and regards her mother as a competitor. Her complex is called the **Electra complex.** In the Electra complex, the little girl subconsciously desires sex with her father which comes about as a consequence of penis envy and a concomitant sense of inadequacy. These wishes of both boys and girls cause the child to feel fear and guilt toward the same-sex parent. The Oedipus and Electra complexes are resolved through renunciation of the love object and identification with the same-sex parent (Gleitman, 1987: 351; Lindsey, 2005: 26). The gender bias in Freud's theory was clearly expressed when he wrote: "It does little harm to a woman if she remains in her feminine Oedipus attitude... She will in that case choose her husband for his paternal characteristics and will be ready to recognize his authority" (in Sayers, 1986: 101).

To account for the Oedipus complex as universal, Freud turned to an evolutionary explanation. From Freud's perspective, the almost worldwide appearance of the incest taboo could be viewed as a mechanism to prohibit that which we desire. But from where did this taboo and desire arise? Freud addressed this in *Totem and Tabu* (1950 [1913]). At some early and unspecified point in time, there existed a "primal horde" in which a father kept a harem of women, but expelled his male children. The expelled brothers colluded and murdered their father and ate him so they could have sexual access to their sisters and mothers. However, after their dastardly deed, they felt a great deal of remorse. Out of respect for their slain father's wishes, they renounced their mothers and sisters. This was the beginning of the incest taboo which prohibits sex and marriage between immediate blood relatives. Freud cited evidence cross-culturally of the **ritual totemic meal** which he interpreted as a symbolic re-enactment of this original crime. To Freud, the **totem animal** represents the father who is ritually eaten in commemoration of this event. According to Freud, the consequences of this primal scene have been transmitted to all of us through the collective unconscious, presumably somehow inherited (Freud, 1950 [1913]: 34; in Bock, 1988: 32–36; Lyons and Lyons, 2004: 107).

In response to Freud, Malinowski argued that the Oedipus complex was not a cultural universal, but was relative to the particular family structures found in a given culture. Since Freud's theory was based on middle-class western European values with family constellations in which the father was the dominant figure, Malinowski tested this theory in a situation in which the family constellation was quite different, that of the Trobriand Islanders. He addressed this in his book *Sex and Repression in Savage Society* (1961 [1927]). He reasoned that different family structures would likely lead to different kinds of conscious and unconscious conflicts in individuals (Brown, 1991: 32). As we have seen, the Oedipus complex proposes that a young male child will desire his mother and want to get rid of his father. As the child matures, this complex is then outgrown.

But the Trobriand Islanders had a very different family structure. They were a matrilineal society in which kinship was traced through the mother. In fact, the Trobrianders believed that the procreator of a child was a dead kinswoman of the mother. Although the mother was the primary authority figure, she had a warm relationship with her children. In contrast to the European system in which the father was the authority figure, the mother's brother among the Trobriand Islanders assumed the role of disciplinarian. He was also the person from whom the child would inherit. In contrast, the father (like the Trobriand mother) had a warm and affectionate relationship with his children.

In the Trobriand Islands, it was the mother's brother who earned the boy's hostility; and it was his sister, not his mother, whom the boy desired. Trobriand children were subjected to a rigorous brother/sister incest avoidance rule (taboo) at puberty (Bock, 1988; Brown, 1991). Unfortunately, the comparable complex for women—the Electra complex—has been relatively unexplored. The Electra complex "received much less attention from Freud and almost none from Malinowski . . ." (Brown, 1991: 32). This is typical of the "unmarking" and silence around women that occurs in patriarchal societies and which is reflected in scientific theorizing. Despite this shortcoming,

Malinowski's finding became "the cornerstone for the thesis propounded by relativists of all persuasions"—anthropological and nonanthropological, Freudian as well as anti-Freudian—that...the Oedipus complex...is a product of Western institutions and, more particularly, of the Western "patriarchal" family structure. (Brown, 1991: 33)

Malinowski's theory was a functionalist interpretation of the incest taboo that focused on its role in the maintenance of society. For Malinowski, the incest taboo was necessary to maintain order because, without it, confusion in positions and family statuses would occur.

Other anthropological thinking on the subject includes those theorists who suggest a biological explanation, proposing that some sort of genetic avoidance mechanism exists against inbreeding. Arguments are mustered on both sides of this debate. One side argues that deleterious genes have greater opportunity for expression in incestuous unions; the opposing side counters that genetic cleansing can in fact occur through this very process leaving the familial line healthier in the long run. We know evolution works upon genetic variation and that variation is a very effective mechanism for coping with environmental changes. Breeding outside of the immediate family provides the genetic variation upon which natural selection can act. Shepher (1983) has reviewed the literature on the consequences of incestuous inbreeding in human populations and has found that 42 percent of the offspring were nonviable (in Brown, 1991: 123–124). "If the figures Shepher cites are even approximately correct, mechanisms to avoid the cost of incest between close kin are quite expectable" (Brown, 1991: 123).

Primatologists and evolutionary psychologists have recently argued that incest avoidance is evolutionarily old behavior (Meigs and Barlow, 2002: 40). The primate data suggests this. There is evidence that both male monkeys and female apes emigrate from their natal groups thereby decreasing the potential for incestuous matings (in Walter, 1990: 441). Those that oppose the biological explanations and promote more culturological perspectives cite the evidence of preferred marriage and incest regulations associated with parallel and cross-cousin marriage in unilineal societies. The distinction between these sets of first cousins is not one made by Euro-Americans. A **parallel cousin** is the child of ego's mother's sister or father's brother. A **cross-cousin** is the child of ego's mother's brother or father's sister (see Figure 9.4) (Kottak, 2002: 402).

In societies which prefer cross-cousin marriage, parallel cousins are regarded as belonging to ego's descent group and are seen as similar to one's siblings. They may even be referred to by the terminology for brother and/or sister. Because cross-cousins are not regarded as consanguineal relatives, incest prohibitions apply only in the case of parallel cousins (Kottak, 2002: 402). While most societies prohibit marriage with parallel cousins,

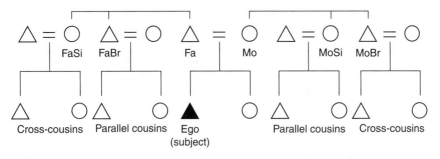

Figure 9.4 Parallel and cross-cousin kinship. (*Source:* Wikipedia.)

marriage with cross-cousins is the preferred form cross-culturally (Ember, Ember and Peregrine, 2005: 362). About 30 percent of the world's societies have a system where cross cousins are the preferred marriage partners (Cohen and Eames, 1982: 125; Kottak, 2002: 402). There are some societies, for example, among Middle Eastern groups, that prefer parallel cousin marriage (Ferraro, 2004: 204).

At this point, the issue of exogamy is relevant. The incest taboo is defined by avoidance of sex between primary family members; rules of exogamy refer directly to marriage (Spradley and McCurdy, 1987: 91). When the incest taboo is expanded to include groups of people outside the family of origin, this is called exogamy. Whole groups of people may be excluded as potential partners if they fall into certain relationships with "ego," the person from whom one is tracing relationships. The groups may be lineages, clans, moieties, or tribes. To clarify the issue, rules of exogamy refer to marriage, but the incest taboo may be expanded to cover a much wider range of prohibited individuals than just biological parents and siblings. Marriage prohibitions can include people who are not consanguineal relatives. Thus, exogamy may include incest prohibitions, but may also extend much further to include prohibitions against marrying a particular kin or groupings of kin, or sanctions to marry outside a village(s) (Ember, Ember and Peregrine, 2005: 360). The incest taboo propels the practice of exogamy by requiring people to find marriage partners outside their own groups (Kottak, 2002: 406). This is often discussed anthropologically as the extension of the incest taboo.

As we discussed earlier, sex and marriage with cross-cousins may be accepted or even preferred in unilineal descent societies, but sex with parallel cousins may be considered incestuous. Another cultural pattern illustrating that cultures vary in how they define which relatives are forbidden occurs among the strictly patrilineal Lakher of Southeast Asia. In this society ego may marry his mother's daughter by a different father (his half-sister). In this case of strict patrilineal rule, mothers are regarded more as an in-law than not a relative, since a mother is not part of the same descent group as her children. By virtue of this same principle, ego couldn't marry his father's daughter (half-sister) from a second marriage because they are part of the same patrilineal descent group (Kottak, 2002: 403).

Some anthropologists believe the incest taboo arose as a vehicle for establishing alliances outside the family. In fact, Edward Tylor's adage "marry out or die out" is one explanation for the origin of the taboo. According to Tylor, the "hatreds and fears" associated with closed families forced people to extend alliances to other families and therefore to build societies (Patterson, 2005; Shapiro, 1958: 278; Scupin, 2003: 75). This explanation is typical of the functionalist approach in anthropology which maintains that institutions exist to fulfill needs. Other notable anthropologists, such as Leslie White, George Peter Murdock, and Levi-Strauss have explained the incest taboo along these same lines with various refinements and additions, yet maintaining the theme of alliance building. Such hypotheses have been critiqued as explaining rules for marrying outside one's group, but not necessarily incest taboos, a subtle but important distinction (Scupin, 2003: 75).

In 1922, Edward Westermarck offered an explanation for the incest taboo which argued that the taboo reflects an absence of sexual desire expressed in people's intrinsic "horror" of incest. Incest rules, therefore, exist for those who have gone "awry" or deviated (Brown, 1991: 119). Westermarck felt that the lack of erotic desire that people raised in proximity feel toward one another was an evolved sentiment ingrained in the psyche through biology. This theory is often summarized as "proximity breeds contempt."

The **Westermarck effect** has garnered substantial support particularly as it relates to sibling incest. Spiro (1965) and Fox's (1962) analysis of Israeli kibbutzim marriage, and Wolf's study of marriage in China (1966, 1968, 1970) provide provocative evidence for this theory. Spiro found that children who were raised together as cohorts on kibbutzim as part of social planning to reduce the role of the nuclear family, practiced sex and marriage avoidance of one another as adults (in Brown, 1991: 120). Fox interpreted this as support of the Westermarck effect. He concluded that in societies in which children are raised with close physical intimacy, they will not have sexual desires for one another; and the incest taboo will be more like an afterthought since siblings will not desire one another anyway. However, societies where siblings are raised in the absence of physical intimacy are more likely to have strict taboos since desire will need curbing. Fox's hypothesis integrates a Freudian thrust not incorporated by Westermarck (Brown, 1991: 120). Shepher's 1971 and 1983 research on kibbutizm marriages supports the finding of lessened sexual attraction to partners raised in proximity. In a study of 211 kibbutzim, there were only 14 marriages of peers out of 2,769 married couples (Meigs and Barlow, 2002: 39; Scupin, 2003).

Arthur Wolf's investigation of marriage in China has intriguing implications for the Westermarck effect. Wolf studied two forms of marriage practiced in a Chinese village in Taiwan (1966, 1968, 1970). The minor form of marriage was one in which a girl was adopted into her future husband's family at an early age and raised as a member of the family. In the major form, marriage took place in adulthood without any previous familial association between the partners. Wolf (1970) suggested that wife adoption would lead to a sexual aversion in the couple who was reared together. In comparing major and minor forms of marriage, he found that in the minor form there were 30 percent fewer offspring, the divorce rate was 24.2 percent and extramarital relationships were found in 33.1 percent of the marriages. In contrast, major marriages had a 1.2 percent divorce rate and 11.3 percent rate of extramarital sex (Wolf, 1970: 503–515). This evidence strongly supports the contention that familiarity leads to disinterest and even aversion.

This is by no means an exhaustive review of anthropological theories of the origin of the incest taboo, but only highlights some of the more prominent ones. The more recent theories on incest and its taboo integrate the work of some of these earlier theorists. For example, bio-social approaches argue that close attachment of father and daughters reduces the likelihood of incest occurring later as a result of some biological process activated through the social process of active father involvement in childrearing (Meigs and Barlow, 2002: 42; Parker and Parker, 1986; Roscoe, 1994). Barlow and Meigs (2002) argue that a fruitful direction for research lies in the psychoanalytic direction. They suggest exploring the possible relationship reported in the anthropological literature between trance/dance behaviors that are linked with spiritualist ecstatic religious experiences and the disassociative experiences of incest survivors.

The incest taboo may be explained by a convergence of several theoretical positions discussed in this chapter.[1] The incest taboo

- establishes alliances and extends peaceful relations beyond the group;
- facilitates social networks and trade;
- promotes genetic mixture; and
- preserves family roles, guarding against socially destructive conflict (Kottak, 2002: 406; Meigs and Barlow, 2002: 40).

These theories are not necessarily mutually exclusive, but could be regarded as interactive. For example "cultural learning and genetic transmission are not mutually exclusive alternatives and may interact to produce incest avoidance in ways that are complex and flexible" (Meigs and Barlow, 2002: 40). We would add that the Westermarck effect of childhood proximity leading to lack of desire could be added to this list as a vehicle of psychological conditioning. Thus, the incest taboo is a consequence of what people would not want to do anyway under certain conditions. Walter argues that in societies where children are exposed to prohibitions that prevent the familiarity of the Westermarck effect, then desire for the forbidden could arise. In such a case, the incest taboo would operate as a mechanism to prevent incest (1990: 440).

Despite the universality of the incest taboo, the particular form, focus, meaning, and response to it is extremely variable cross-culturally This diversity is especially apparent in the case of exogamy, in which the incest taboo is extended. In spite of the near universality of the incest taboo, incest does occur. We have discussed the special situations of exceptions for elites. We want to turn now to incest in the United States which is primarily nonconsensual and involves victimization. This is because children and adolescents are not in a position vis-á-vis their parents and older siblings to give informed consent.

It is difficult to get an accurate estimate of the incidence of incest. One of the problems with assessing the incest statistics is that these are clouded by the "false memory" controversy. Over the last twenty years a recovered memory movement in psychotherapy has flourished. Therapists report that victims of incest/child abuse experienced amnesia about these events and only through therapy was this sexual abuse "recovered" and discovered. Detractors argue that therapists were leading or suggesting this to their clients, and that there is little evidence that actual incest or sexual abuse occurred (Patterson, 2005, note 1; Tyroler, 1996).

One report suggested that 250,000 children are victims of incest, with half of these cases involving fathers and stepfathers (Kelly, 1990 [citing Russel, 1983]). Another suggests that as many as one in twenty women may be victims of father-daughter incest (Scupin, 2003: 77). Depending on the report and the time period of the study, statistics for incest range from four percent in Gebhard's (1965) study to 27 percent in Hunt's (1974) survey (in Francoeur, 2004c: 613) and 15 percent in the work of Becker and Coleman (1988, in King et al., 1991: 380). Recent figures by the Bureau of Justice note that 27 percent of all child sexual assaults were by a family member ("Sexual Assault of Young Children," 2000). Almost thirty percent of the father-daughter incest cases in United States include an alcoholic father (Berger, 1993). It must be remembered that although a stepfather or stepmother is not a biological parent, but a social parent, the severity in terms of trauma may be the same for the victim. The victim has had a trusted parental figure violate her or him.

The survivors of incest suffer a host of psychological problems and maladjustments throughout the life course as a result of their experiences. These include sexual acting out, sexual dysfunctions as adults, low self-esteem, self-blame, and self-destructive behaviors. They may experience psychological problems not unlike the Vietnam veterans who suffered post-traumatic stress syndrome. In addition, Newman and Peterson report that women experience anger that is specific, towards mothers and fathers (1996: 463–474).

Anthropologist Mark T. Erickson has been exploring the incidence of incest using a model based on evolutionary psychology and medicine (1999). He suggests that within contemporary societies, as the family unit becomes more fragile with weaker kinship attachments, incest is likely to occur more frequently. In the cases of incest that do occur between father and daughter, the father is usually a person who has been sexually abused himself and has not developed close kinship and familial attachments with his children. An extreme lack of nurturance and mutual bonding between family members increases the likelihood of incest arising within families. Erickson's finding suggests that the incest avoidance biological processes can be stunted and distorted, leading to tragic results in contemporary societies (Scupin, 2003: 77).

Incest should not be confused with children's curiosity about their own genitalia and that of their siblings that occurs around two to three years of age. Incest as reported between a brother and sister is five times more likely than between a father and daughter in the United States (Westheimer, 2000: 154; Westheimer and Lopater, 2005). According to recent statistics, 13 percent of all college-aged students had experienced some type of sexual activity with a brother or sister. Four percent of these cases involved full coitus, while most reports involved looking at and touching sibling genitals (Westheimer, 2000: 154; Westheimer and Lopater, 2005). In one study by Finkelhor (1980), 15 percent of the women and 10 percent of the men in a college population reported this behavior with 75 percent brother-sister exploration and 25 percent same-sex behavior. But even in such a benign sibling context, there is still the possibility for coercion and possible incestuous sexual abuse. Twenty-five percent of this population, mostly women, were uncomfortable because force was used (in Francoeur, 1991a: 111). Incest survivors are invariably the less powerful person in such interactions. Generally, the survivor is not in a consensual position because of differences in authority or because of actual or threatened physical force.

The double standard of the industrialized society's gender system is reflected in the incest statistics in the United States. Boys' sexual abuse tends to be perpetrated by a stranger, while girls'is much more likely to be by a relative (Baker and King, 2004: 1235). According to Stark (1984), 85 percent of the incest victims are female with "only 20 percent of the sexual abuse of boys and 5 percent of the sexual abuse of girls perpetrated by adult females" (in

Kelly, 1990: 356). Recent figures suggest that between 20 percent to 30 percent of girls are abused by a relative with 4 percent involving father-daughter incest, but only about 10 percent of boys are abused by a relative (Baker and King, 2004: 1234; Herman and Hirschman, 1981). Of those children sexually abused, the Bureau of Justice Statistics (2000) reports that nearly one-third of all male sexual assaults were by family members, whereas only 25.7 percent of female assaults were by a relative. Remember that sexual assaults on females far exceed those on men. Stepfathers are more likely than biological fathers to engage in incest (Baker and King, 2004: 1235).

Statistically speaking, family members were more likely to abuse younger children with about half the incest victims under age six ("Sexual Assault on Young Children," 2000). A 1994 national survey revealed that 12 percent of men and 17 percent of women reported that they had been sexually touched by an older person when they were children. The offender was reported as typically being a family friend or relative as opposed to a stranger (Laumann et al., 1994).

Children who are survivors of incest are in a disadvantaged position in relationship to the abuser. One common response is "accommodation" in that they may feel they have no other alternative. They may be conflicted by the love and trust they feel for the biological or social parent. Or they may not want to cause family problems by telling; very often they have been manipulated or threatened with consequences if they do tell. Thus, the accommodation strategy is one of serious denial. Researchers note that some survivors have no direct memory of the incest as adults. Only through psychotherapy do they become aware of the memories so long denied and hidden.

One aspect of father or stepfather incest is the purported acceptance of the situation by the mother. In such cases, the mother is reported to default in her role as spouse, and the daughter or stepdaughter takes the mother's role in relation to her father or stepfather. In such situations, the young female is doubly injured in terms of betrayal of trust, both by her father/stepfather and by her mother who tacitly allows the relationship. The mother, not usually overtly, may permit it to go on because it is part of the family denial system. However, this is a very controversial theory and some researchers such as Chandler (1982), Ward (1985) and Myer (1985) deny that the mother has any role at all (in Francoeur, 1991: 615; in Kelly, 1994: 356). Certainly, the degree of the mother's tacit involvement varies depending on the family dynamics.

The father's role as perpetrator is more clearly identified. In fact, the sexually abusive father or stepfather follows a pattern in which gender inequality is an important factor. The father is typically hypermasculine in his disregard and respect for women and children. We may view him as oversubscribing to his gender role. Another contributing cultural factor, which may also play a part, includes the perpetrator's valuing (sexual attraction to) women for their youthfulness. Finkelhor (1984) has identified four cultural and psychological factors that converge to place children at risk for sexual abuse by fathers or stepfathers. These factors are embedded in a patriarchal system of masculinity and include the following ideologies and values:

• In sexual relations men must dominate.
• Most emotional needs are regarded by men as sexual ones.
• There is an inability of men to identify with the needs of children.
• There is a belief in patriarchal privilege and prerogative and the special rights of the father/stepfather within the family (see Phelan, 1986: 531–539).

Flores and Mattos' (1998) study in Brazil identified several predisposing factors for incest that bear further scrutiny in other settings. These are identified as "problems of family structure, extreme poverty, mother's incapacitating illness, mental illness of the aggressor, extreme violence in the family structure, social interaction difficulties, multiple victims, incest recurrence in the family, and mental retardation in the victim" (in Westheimer and Lopater, 2005: 741).

Discussions of adult-child sexual contact, whether incestuous or nonincestuous, are highly charged with emotion in the United States. Given our cultural mores and values, much adult-child sexual contact very probably will have negative consequences for the child. However, the universality of the negative consequences of adult-child sex for children in the United States is questioned by some researchers (Nelson, 1989a and 1989b).

In an intensely debated article, Nelson posits that it is important to learn if *every* incestuous sexual experience is always negative for the child (in Maltz, 1989). Nelson offers several conditions that may mitigate the deleterious consequences for the child. These include:

• an emotionally bonded nonsexual relationship between the individuals;
• sexual contact which occurs between people relatively close in age;
• an egalitarian relationship between the parties (1989).

Given these three variables, an incestuous relationship may *not* always result in long-term emotional scarring and damage for the child.

Pat Whelehan has dealt with a small number of adult male and female incest "survivors" over the past three years. Some of these individuals did experience extreme emotional damage with long-lasting negative consequences relative to their self-esteem and romantic relationships with others. Three of these individuals came through the experience intact. The difference is that the three individuals who viewed their incest/adult-child sexual experience positively were males who were not coerced and who had a positive nonsexual relationship with their older sexual partners. (They "checked in" with the author because they wondered if "something was wrong with them" because they felt "okay" about their experiences and who they are currently as sexual adults.) The other survivors fit the model of incest "survivor." They are women who were coerced and had hostile or nonbonded sexual relations with males who were not only older, but in a position of authority over them. They experienced much emotional and psychological trauma from their earlier sexual contact (Whelehan's counseling files).

Although it is difficult to remain objective about this issue given our culture's view on adult-child and incestuous sexuality, it is important to do so in order to help those individuals who have been traumatized to regain a positive sense of self and sexuality. We need to know when such contact may or may not be harmful and then consider the individual's unique experience across this continuum.

THEORIES OF CHILDHOOD SEXUALITY

Freud's theories of childhood sexuality present a conflict model of development. Each stage has its unique set of conflicts centered around the erotogenic zones. Neo-Freudians such as Karen Horney (1885–1952) and Erich Fromm (1900–1980) among others challenged the Freudian view that erotogenic zones and stages of development are the key to understanding human behavior. Rather than focusing on the zones, some neo-Freudians felt that the relationships people had with one another were primary. This represents a shift from biology, libidinal energy and erotogenic zones to social relations in understanding childhood development (Gleitman, 1987: 355–356).

Horney took issue with Freud on several specific points in his theory of childhood sexuality. She contested Freud's position that children did not recognize gender differences at birth by asserting that children knew "intuitively" the differences because each gender had sensations of being penetrated and penetrating. Horney brings a less male biased view to the psychoanalytic scenario of child development. She argues that both genders envy one another's genitalia. This is in contrast to the Freudian perspective which proposed that women have penis envy, but men have no comparable womb envy. Later in her career, she challenged the Freudian notion of the Oedipus complex. She regarded the Oedipus complex as situationally derived from a particular kind of family dynamics where emotional dependency of the child was combined with self-centered and unresponsive parents (Sayers, 1986: 40).

Dr. Spock's Baby and Child Care book has had a tremendous impact on childrearing worldwide, spanning over fifty years and continuing past Dr. Benjamin Spock's death in 1998. His book has sold over 50 million copies (making it second in sales only to the Bible) and has been published in thirty-nine languages (Spock and Needlman, 2004; The Doctor Spock Company, 2004). Since 1945, Spock's book has been revised to accommodate changes in gender roles and family structure in the United States. As he neared his eightieth birthday, Spock added a co-author in anticipation of the need for a successor to carry on the tradition (1985). The most recent edition of *Dr. Spock's Baby and Childcare,* the eighth edition, is updated and revised by Robert Needlman, MD, the vice president of Development and Behavioral Pediatrics at The Dr. Spock Company. Dr. Spock passed away March 15, 1998, at the age of ninety-four. Spock's model of childhood development, like Freud's whom he admired, was also based on stages of development, for example, he notes that "[b]oys become romantic toward their mothers, girls toward their fathers" (Spock and Needlman, 2004: 165). For Spock, these feelings about wanting to marry the other gender parent happen as between the ages of three and six years old. He regarded such feelings are important for preparing the child for adult sexual attraction and relations: stating "[w]e realize now that there is a childish kind of sexual feeling at this period which is an essential part of normal development" (1985: 447). Later, he notes "these strong romantic attachments help children to grow spiritually and to acquire wholesome feelings toward the opposite sex that will later guide them into good marriages" (Spock and Needlman, 2004: 166). Again like Freud, Spock perceived that this attraction brought up sentiments of rivalry, jealousy, and fear toward the same-sex parent. For Spock, the resolution follows as a natural process. "Nature expects that children by 6 or 7 will become quite discouraged about the possibility of having the parent all to themselves" (Spock and Needlman, 2004: 167). This marks the end of this phase of attachment which will be "repressed and outgrown" and which is succeeded by an interest in other activities such as athletics, education, and same-sex peer involvement (Spock and Rothenberg, 1985: 437; Spock and Needlman, 2004: 177). Spock is rather Freudian in that he regards these interests as caused by the sublimation of sex that takes place from ages six until about twelve years of age.

Spock advises parents not to give in to their children's feelings of rivalry by refraining from overt affection with one another. It is important for children to be confronted with the fact that they cannot ever marry the parent. Spock's account is obviously influenced by Freudian theory of the Oedipus complex (1985: 437; Spock and Needlman, 2004: 167–168). However, Spock's representation of Freud is much less sexually oriented around the pleasure principle. For example, Spock regards the interest in sex that occurs between two-and-one-half and three-and-one-half years of age as part of a much broader pattern associated with the "why" stage of curiosity (1985: 451; Spock and Needlman, 2004: 169, 174–175). He regards this as part of children's natural curiosity about why the genders are different and where babies come from.

CULTURAL RELATIVISM AND CHILDHOOD
SEXUAL BEHAVIOR

The messages many U.S children get from their parents are that sex is bad and should be delayed until marriage and that love must precede sex. This is part of a cultural "ideal of childhood sexual innocence . . . that children and adolescents need legal protection from all sexual contact and, in some cases, from sexual information and contraception as well" (Konker, 1992: 147; Weiss, 2004c: 1181). In addition, this message is frequently gender biased. The double standard for male and female sexuality is patently apparent to the young child although it may not be to the parents (Darling and Hicks, 1982; Francoeur, 1991: 107; Francoeur and Noonan, 2004). Notably, young boys cause their parents less concern when they express an early interest in sex and romance than do young girls who may be thought of as "precocious" (Kelly, 1990: 166). This is evidence of the double standard applied at a very early age; a little boy's sexuality is far more acceptable than a little girl's in the United States.

Evidence from a variety of sources verifies the childhood capacity for sexual response. In males, *in utero* penile erections have been reported as early as seventeen weeks. Orgasm in boys occurs as young as five months old although ejaculation is not possible until puberty (King, 2005; Kinsey, Pomeroy, and Martin, 1948: 177). Orgasm is reported in girls as young as seven months old (Calderone, 1985; Bakwin, 1974). The human physiological sexual response function is clearly in place early in infancy. This should not be confused with the meaning we give to that response in terms of adult sexuality. The child is merely exploring her/his body and responding to pleasurable sensations. Childhood capacity for sexual response and pleasure is part of our biological heritage. It is experienced very differently from adult sexuality.

Although the classic work of Ford and Beach (1951) classified U.S. society at the time as a sex-negative culture, a more contemporary view might regard it as sex ambiguous, rather than purely negative, since elements of the positive coexist with the negative. Sex-negative aspects are evident in attitudes toward childhood masturbation. Yet the evidence shows

> [that children] [w]hen left alone . . . spontaneously explore their bodies, their genitals and experience their developing sexual nature. Sex play and exploration are major factors in a child's development. Even when discouraged or prohibited by adults . . . children manage to explore their bodies and their sex organs. (Francoeur, 1991a: 107)

Sexual curiosity is a normal part of childhood growth and development. It is expressed in play activities and seems to be a component of learning one's sexual identity and who one is as a member of a gender category vis-à-vis body awareness (Spock and Needlman, 2004: 446–459; Weiss, 2004c: 1181).

Goldman (1982) in a comparative study of children in Austria, Sweden, England, and the United States found that U.S. children were less knowledgeable about sexuality than the others. This may reflect generalized trends in North American socialization practices wherein most parents respond negatively to children's explorations of their genitals. Children's curiosity about sex continues, but becomes less overt in reaction of parents' negative reaction to sexual exploration (King, 2005: 299–301; Weiss, 2004c: 1184). It may even become worse in the future if widespread fear about AIDS negatively impacts sexual practices, or if parents respond to fears about incest by not expressing affection to their children.

In the industrialized society, children experience several stages in their sexual development. From about two or three years of age, children express interest in their own genitalia and engage in various kinds of sex play with other children. The doctor-nurse game is a common one whose sexual connotation is acknowledged. Masturbation is prevalent among three- to six-year-olds (Konker, 1992: 148). According to Kinsey, Pomeroy and Martin (1948, 1953), by five years of age 10 percent of boys and 13 percent of girls will have experienced some kind of sex play. Current research supports the age of five or six as when children develop an erotic interest in the same or the other gender. This age is confirmed by cross-cultural data where children may imitate copulatory behaviors of adults in societies where sleeping arrangements allow children to observe adult sexual relations (Weiss, 2005: 1183).

Although Freud argued for a period of sexual latency between the ages of six and twelve, Weiss (2005c: 1183–1185) argues that research has countered this with ample evidence of sex play during middle childhood. For example, Borneman's (1983) research on childhood sexuality along with that of Goldman and Goldman (1982) has seriously challenged this view. These researchers report a capacity for sexual response from infancy throughout the life course. In preparation for the adolescent period, children develop affectionate relationships with special friends during childhood. In industrialized societies, where there exists a well-defined concept of romantic love and heterosexuality, children also express romantic interests. Ninety percent of the children aged nine to eleven years in one study reported having a boyfriend or girlfriend (Broderick, 1972). Although this is the period cited by Freud as one of latency and lack of interest in sexual partners, children continue to be increasingly interested in sex as they approach puberty. U.S. sexual norms shape an inverse relationship between public expression and sex.

Children between the ages of six and eleven during the alleged latency period are anything but disinterested in sex. Research has confirmed that during this period children are actively involved in heterosocial interaction and love relationships. Indeed it is not premature to argue that with globalization and an increasingly mediated society, an industrialized trend for decreasing age norms for behaviors such as having a boyfriend or girlfriend, being in love and dating will occur. Specific frequencies of childhood sociosexual responses are difficult to ascertain because the specific research studies have major limitations preventing generalization, i.e. they include small samples selected from specific groups, and are based on volunteers recalling experiences from a decade earlier (Weiss, 2004c: 1183–1185).

In addition, as children become increasingly interested in sex, their public expression of that interest in terms of self-exploration, play with others, and questioning is generally suppressed, further inhibiting estimating frequencies of socio-sexual play. While sexual interest increases, sexual expression decreases. The same may be said of same-gender sexual exploration and romantic attachments. Generalized homophobia is presented at an early age and compounds broader sex-negative trends which children in the United States are exposed to relatively early.

It must be pointed out that there is a great deal of variation in parenting perspectives regarding sexuality from the extremely punitive to the permissive in our pluralistic society. Children also learn sexual mores from peers and the media as well. The consequences of these childhood experiences can have a profound impact on sexuality later in life. Sex therapist Dagmar O'Connor fears that concern over AIDS will give children the notion that "sex will kill" and this will enhance an existing industrialized society's trajectory of fear of sexual feelings (Jackson, 1990: 184).

Noted sexologists (the late) John Money and Gertrude Williams challenge deeply embedded industrialized values when they state "a childhood sexual experience, such as being the partner of a relative or an older person, need not necessarily affect the child adversely." They continue unfortunately in the U.S., "no matter how benign, any adult-child interaction that may be constructed as even remotely sexual qualifies, *a priori*, as traumatic and abusive." According to Konker (1992: 148) the evidence is unconvincing that adult and child sexual contact is inherently deleterious. The research indicates that children's short-term and long-term reactions to adult-child sexual contact are heterogeneous, from negative and traumatic to highly positive (Weiss, 2004c: 1183). Money cited the recent social trends toward sexual conservatism as potentially harmful ("Attacking the Last Taboo," 1990: 72). For example, funding has been curtailed for research on sexually troubled children as a consequence of such concerns (Jackson, 1990: 186). A fear exists that the response to child abuse may have gone too far. Adults may become uncomfortable expressing affection to children and children may consequently be denied affection and touch, which is so important in their development and capacity for bonding.

It is with this *caveat* that we explore childhood sexuality cross-culturally. Evidence from the more restrictive societies such as ours will be contrasted with more liberal approaches to childhood sex. This research is situated during the ethnographic present to suggest broad trends in human sexuality prior to the massive changes wrought by globalization. The classification of societies as restrictive, semi-restrictive and permissive by Ford and Beach (1951) represents a continuum of sexual mores among traditional societies. This is not to suggest that restrictive and permissive societies are "pure" types without variation as we mentioned previously. Undoubtedly within this classification scheme, there are necessarily mixed and contrasting cultural elements in regard to sexual expression. However, Ford and Beach's approach is nonetheless a useful tool for comparison and contrast in spite of its limitations in recognizing overlapping diversity. Some of our examples will include incidences of adult-child sexual interaction. It must be remembered that relativism is essential as well as an awareness that such interactions cannot be viewed from an adult, industrialized perspective. These examples must be regarded as contextually framed.

We will turn to Ford and Beach (1951: 178–192) to begin our review of the cross-cultural correlational approach to childhood sexuality (see Chapter 1 for discussion). Ford and Beach's study of human sexuality employed the Human Relations Area Files and relied on a sample of 190 societies, although the sample size fluctuated in relation to available information for particular questions and hypotheses. The United States along with fourteen other societies, among them the Ashanti, Dahomeans, Kwoma, Murngin, Manus, and Trukese, are labeled as restrictive societies in that children are denied any form of sexual expression at all. How children are sanctioned varies from reprimands around masturbation to more extreme measures. For example, among the Kwoma of New Guinea, a woman has the right to hit a boy's penis with a stick if she catches him with an erection. Ford and Beach note that sex-negative cultures such as these maintain a similar attitude about sex education by keeping sexual information away from children. As we shall see in our discussion of adolescence, a society that is restrictive in terms of childhood sexual exploration may not be so restrictive for adolescents, or may have a double standard for females and males. Regardless, punishment and discipline does not stop children from exploring their bodies. For example, Trukese children will play at having intercourse although they will be punished with a whipping if caught. Other groups in which children's sexual expression occurs despite negative sanctioning include Haitians, Manus, and Kwoma (Ford and Beach, 1951: 180–187).

Semirestrictive societies are defined by Ford and Beach as those in which there may be formal sanctions against sexual behavior, but these are not enforced or regarded with great concern. The Alorese have a formal restriction against children's sexual expression, but unless it is blatant, the adults will overlook it in the case of older children (Ford and Beach, 1951: 187–188).

Permissive societies are those in which there is a liberal attitude about children's sexuality. These societies are also permissive about issues of sexual education. Included among these are: Copper Eskimo, Easter Islanders, Hopi, Ifugao, Marquesans, Samoans, Lesu, Tikopia, Wogeo, and Yapese. The Ponapeans, for example, give a full and detailed sexuality education to four- and five-year-olds. In societies in which children have access to covert observations of adult sexuality because of the sleeping arrangements, this may serve as a form of sex education. We are not suggesting that adults engage in sex publicly and in full view of their children. One of the components of human sexuality, apart from certain ritual situations, is its privacy. However, where families share a room as among the Pukapukans, children will take advantage of the opportunity to observe and to learn about sex, despite their parents' efforts at discretion (Ford and Beach, 1951: 188–192).

Among the nonrestrictive societies are those in which adult-child sexual interaction occurs. These are societies in which adults may stimulate the genitalia of children and include the Hopi, Siriono, the Kazak, and the Alorese (Ford and Beach, 1951: 188). It must be remembered that this kind of stimulation on the part of the adult cannot be understood from the perspective of industrialized society's adult sexuality. Such adult-to-child behavior occurs for a variety of reasons. It may be done to calm the child down or give it pleasure, not unlike the way in which an infant or child stimulates herself/himself. It may also be considered part of the maturation and development of a child's sexual functioning. There is a great deal of heterogeneity in such practices and the Lepcha of India provide an excellent example of a society that condones childhood sexual expression. Because the Lepcha believe sexual intercourse is important for stimulating maturation, eleven- and twelve-year-old girls engage in full coitus. According to Ford and Beach, "Older men occasionally copulate with girls as young as eight years of age. Instead of being regarded as a criminal offense, such behavior is considered amusing by the Lepcha" (1951: 191). Other cases of adult-child sexual interaction include finger defloration of female infants among some Indonesian societies, "first" Australians, and Hindu Indian groups. The Tontonac of Mexico invite a priest to deflower the infant girl about a month after her birth, followed by the mother's defloration of her six years later. Among the Kubeo, an old man would deflower the eight-year-old girl by stretching the vagina until three fingers could be inserted (Gregersen, 1994: 291). In fact, child-adult sexual contact is institutionalized as part of initiation rituals in at least twenty countries (Konker, 1992: 148).

Such cultures are also permissive toward auto-stimulation or self-pleasuring as well, i.e., masturbation. Societies which are tolerant of self-stimulation include the Pukapukans and the Nama Hottentot in which public self-masturbation by children is considered acceptable behavior. Other societies are indulgent of children's early efforts to imitate adult copulation. Trobriand children even engage in oral and manual genital practices with no parental objections. As children approach puberty different restrictions or proscriptions may be placed upon them (Ford and Beach, 1951: 190–192). We shall discuss these later childhood experiences in greater depth in our discussion of adolescent sexuality in Chapter 10.

The subject of cross-cultural childhood sexuality requires cultural relativism and sensitivity. It is all too easy to allow our own ethnocentric attitudes about sex to color our understanding of the cross-cultural record. Kelly (1990: 223) has coined the term **erotocentricity** to define the process whereby we allow our own culture's sexual attitudes, values, and mores to bias our understanding of sexuality in other cultures. Judith Levine cautions against views of childhood sex as pathological or high-risk behavior and argues that children should be educated with the view that most sexual expression is normal and healthy (in Weiss, 2004c: 1186). This will continue to be important as we discuss adolescent and adult issues in sexuality. Relativism is vital not just in respect to the cross-cultural record, but in regard to the variety of sexual experiences and expressions found in complex industrialized societies.

SUMMARY

1 Childhood and parenting are discussed.
2 The functions of marriage and the family are presented.
3 The subject of kinship is introduced along with kin terms, including residence and descent.
4 Some of the major theories of incest are offered along with the consequences of incest.
5 Theories of childhood sexuality are reviewed including the psychoanalytic perspective and Dr. Spock's perspective on childhood sexuality.
6 Attention is given to childhood sexual expression in the United States and cross-culturally.

Thought-provoking questions

1 How could cultural definitions of incest shape the way individuals actually experience and interpret sexual encounters with a culturally defined family member?
2 As a child, do you recall participating in childhood sex play? If so, what type of parental response did this invoke? Do you recall what messages you received from society about this behavior? Did your behavior continue, or did it become covert due to negative responses from parents, and/or society?
3 If you were given the opportunity to practice one of the other forms of marriage discussed in this chapter, which one would you prefer and why?

SUGGESTED RESOURCES

Books

Francoeur, Robert T. and Raymond J. Noonan. 2004. *The Continuum Complete International Encyclopedia of Sexuality.* New York, NY: Continuum.

(For detailed information on childhood sexuality within specific societies see section 4 "Autoerotic Behaviors and Patterns" part A. Children and adolescents, section 5 "Interpersonal Heterosexual Behaviors" part A. Children, section 6 "Homoerotic, Homosexual, and Bisexual Behaviors" part A. Children and adolescence, and section 8 "Significant Unconventional Sexual Behaviors" part A. Coercive sex, Child sexual abuse, incest, and pedophilia.)

Namu, Yang Erche and Christine Mathieu. 2003. *Leaving Mother Lake: A Girlhood at the Edge of the World.* Boston: Little, Brown and Company.

Web sites

Bureau of Justice Statistics, 2000. "Sexual Assault of Young Children as Reported to Law Enforcement: Victim, Incident, and Offender Characteristics." Department of Justice Programs. Electronic document. http://www.ojp.usdoj.gov/bjs/abstract/saycrle.htm Last accessed 11/17/07.

Janssen, D. F. 2002–2005. "Growing Up Sexually." Magnus Hirschfeld Archive for Sexology, Berlin, Germany. http://www2.rz.hu-berlin.de/sexology/GESUND/ARCHIV/GUS/GUS_MAIN_INDEX.HTM

10 Puberty and adolescence

CHAPTER OVERVIEW

1 Defines and contrasts puberty and adolescence.
2 Discusses rites of passage as initiation ceremonies that facilitate the transition to adulthood.
3 Presents the three phases of rites of passage.
4 Presents female genital cutting as a controversial issue in rites of passage.
5 Uses the Sambia as a case study of rites of passage in which older boys orally inseminate younger boys.
6 Outlines adolescent sexual behavior in nonindustrial as well as industrial societies.
7 Addresses the issue of adolescent sterility.
8 Reviews the topic of sex education in the United States.
9 Compares and contrasts adolescence in the United States with nonindustrial transitions to adulthood.

PUBERTY AND ADOLESCENCE: A BIO-CULTURAL PHENOMENON

In the dominant, Anglo culture of the United States, remembering that the United States is a plural society of culturally and ethnically diverse peoples, adolescence or "the teen years" are considered a tumultuous time when young people are trying to find their identities and places in both their culture and adult society. The U.S. and other industrialized nations regard adolescence as a distinct phase in the life course noted for its youthful turmoil and rebellious behaviors (Mead, 1961 [1928]). In fact, it is this industrialized culture-based view of adolescence as a life crisis that inspired researchers such as Margaret Mead in the now classic *Coming of Age in Samoa* (1961, [1928]) to explore the cross-cultural record to search for the alleged causes of teenage trauma. Mead's contribution to the study of adolescence has been discussed in Chapter 1 and will be again later in this chapter; recall her argument that the "storm and stress" of adolescence is shaped by culture rather than due to raging hormones.

It should come as no surprise to learn that the ethnographic spectrum challenges such a narrow view of this period in young people's lives. Adolescence is not universally regarded as a stressful period, nor is it considered by all societies as a distinct phase in the life course. For purposes of linguistic convenience, we shall use the term "adolescence" to refer to the teenage years, bearing in mind that it is not a cultural universal. Though people in the United States and other industrialized nations generally utilize a life course scheme that includes five phases: infancy, childhood, adolescence, youth, and adulthood, other societies have far different views of how the life course may be segmented. For example, indigenous peoples, according to Oswalt (1986: 99): "usually recognized few formal age groups, and by the time children were eight years old, they were working for or with same sex adults." In traditional Aboriginal Australia, girls were promised to husbands before they were born and married before menarche (in Ward, 2005: 72). Although nonindustrial peoples do not elaborate the adolescent stage as do we, most of the world recognizes that the period of sexual maturation is one in which readiness for adulthood occurs. With such a time-oriented culture as our own, we often think of age in absolute terms, such as adolescence occurring with the teenage years; yet it must be remembered that age is a relative concept that is best understood as membership in a social category (Suggs and Miracle, 1993: 78).

Before continuing, it is appropriate here for us to define our terms since adolescence is often confused with puberty. **Puberty** is generally defined biologically. It is the period in life when secondary sexual characteristics develop and a person becomes capable of reproduction (Kelly, 1990: 512; Offir, 1982: 521; Ward and Edelstein, 2006). Puberty usually takes from two to four years. In girls, the ages for the onset of puberty are approximately nine to sixteen, and in boys, from twelve or thirteen to fifteen or sixteen (Ford and Beach, 1951: 170–171; Goldenring, 2005). A detailed discussion of the physiology of puberty has been described in Chapters 5 and 6. In females, **menarche** occurs at the same time as the hips widen and about a year or two subsequent to the development of breasts. Girls in the United States on the average reach menarche around twelve years old, although the age at which this occurs is affected by diet and nutrition (Spock and Needlman, 2004: 192–215). The cross-cultural evidence suggests that females in nonindustrial societies are generally not fertile following menarche (Ford and Beach, 1951: 172; Schlegel and Barry, 1991). An increased interest in sex as a result of the physiological changes that happen with puberty is also reported (Byer and Shainberg, 1991: 375). However, it must be reiterated that interest in sex is extremely variable in individuals and is influenced by culture (Kelly, 1990: 167; King, 2005: 306; Spock and Needlman, 2004: 446–464). How one experiences the biological baseline of puberty is shaped by social structure, subsistence technologies, stratification, kinship and descent, cultural values such as conservative or liberal attitudes of parents, religious orientations, and a number of other factors (Schlegel and Barry, 1991).

Menarche is one of the more obvious indicators of puberty. The onset of **menstruation** has followed a historical trend of occurring at an increasingly younger age. General changes in growth and development over the generations are referred to as a "secular trend." In industrialized countries, menarche is now reached two years earlier than it was in 1900 and four years earlier than in 1840 (Moore et al., 1980: 138–139; see also Keizer-Schrama, de Muinch, and Mul, 2001: 289). In nonindustrialized countries, the pattern for menarche occurs at a younger age in urban areas than rural ones (Keizer-Schrama, de Muinch, and Mul, 2001). Economic variables are also important. In higher economic strata menarche begins earlier than in lower classes of the same population (Eveleth and Tanner, 1976; Moore et al., 1980: 140). Better nutrition and overall body fat seem to be partly accountable for this change, and better health care, and the aforementioned improvement in socioeconomic status along with genetic influences also contribute to this phenomenon (in Moore et al., 1980: 140; Keizer-Schrama, de Muinch, and Mul, 2001: 290). More recent research by Herman-Giddens et al. (1997) argues that features associated with puberty such as breast development and pubic hair growth have occurred earlier, but that the average age for U.S. Caucasian girls' menstruation has remained stable since the 1950s. Anderson and Must (2005: 753–760) confirm this noting that the average age at menarche in the United States declined by only 2.3 months between 1988–1994 and 1999–2002; by race/ethnicity declines were even smaller. A similar trend was noted for British girls ("Girls Maturing Slightly Earlier," 2001). Reasons cited for the earlier development of secondary sexual characteristics are the increase in obesity, and exposure to environmental estrogens and other chemicals (Lydon, 2006). Hauspie, Vercauteren, and Susanne (1996) suggest that this leveling off of age of menarche may be due to reversing of socioeconomic factors and/or due to genetic limits.

Although puberty is identified by a series of physical changes, **adolescence** is a cultural construct defined as a "period of emotional, social and physical transition from childhood to adulthood" (Goldenring, 2005; Kelly, 1990: 505). For Anglo-Americans, adolescence is the time of life that spans puberty and ends with adulthood. Spock and Needlman (2004) classify adolescence into three phases: early adolescence from age twelve to fourteen; middle adolescence from age fifteen to seventeen; and late adolescence from eighteen to twenty-one. Each phase is characterized by its own unique psychological tasks. Thus, early adolescence is a period focused on rapidly changing bodies and feelings, middle adolescence emphasizes coming to terms with sexuality and romantic feelings and the process of emotional separation from parents, while late adolescence is focused on finding a career and developing longer-lasting emotional relationships (Spock and Needlman, 2004: 203–211). It is important to recognize, however, that adolescence is a social category and is not limited to just the teenage years. This period of psychosocial maturation may even extend into the late twenties in some societies such as the United States and Ireland (Francoeur, 1991a: 41). Spock argues that late adolescence may be extended even further into the early thirties for students who enter graduate school straight from college and who may continue to be supported by their parents. Thus, independent living may not occur until relatively late prolonging late adolescence (Spock and Needlman, 2004: 210).

If adolescence is recognized as a distinct life stage in a society, how and when it begins, as well as what it means, differ a great deal throughout the ethnographic spectrum. In an industrialized society, adolescence as a separate period in the life course has varied historically as well. Adolescence did not appear in European culture until the nineteenth century. And it was not until the 1800s that adolescence also came to be regarded as a time of conflict, especially among upper-class youths. Prior to that time, youth was regarded as a period of preparation for adulthood that covered a long time span with gradually increasing responsibilities. There were various symbolic markers for the transformation of youth into adulthood. This was related to the economic situation in which working-class children at age ten or twelve years old entered occupations, as apprentices for example, in the case of boys, or perhaps as domestic servants in the case of girls. These decisions were made by their parents (Sommerville, 1990: 211–212).

> Having entered upon their calling, children were playing parts in the adult world and had a recognized status there, even though they were not yet considered adults. Rights and responsibilities came gradually, with a number of milestones on the way to maturity. In some respects they were still considered children for years afterward. But the adult world was not a foreign and unknown territory to them. (Sommerville, 1990: 213)

Other options varied by class for girls and boys. Upper- and middle-class boys were also involved with training for their profession by the latter part of their teenage years. During this period, the age of marriage was around fifteen years old, and puberty did not happen until much later—around eighteen or twenty years old (Francoeur, 1991a and 1991b).

The Industrial Revolution changed the nature of work and, consequently, the apprenticeship as a mechanism to integrate youth into society was lost. As the population grew so did employment opportunities for the middle and upper classes. Male aristocrats sought positions in the military and government which, in turn, had to be expanded to accommodate their need for employment. At the same time, education for the upper and middle classes also kept youngsters in the home under their parents' guidance. The results of these trends were the creation of adolescence as a separate phase in industrialized youths' lives characterized by their separation from the world of work and adults (Sommerville, 1990: 216). Along with this trend, the age of puberty also gradually dropped from the late teens and early twenties to what it is today (Aries, 1962). This historical overview points to the importance of cultural molding and varying context of adolescence as a life stage. Therefore, when researchers such as DeLameter and Friedrich (2005) define preadolescence as the years from eight to twelve and adolescence as spanning ages thirteen through nineteen, this must be placed within the current context of early twenty-first-century middle-class U.S. perspectives, remembering that adolescence is a social construction.

Turning to the cross-cultural data, we find that the most elemental ways that peoples categorize and define themselves are based on two criteria: age and gender. Adolescence is an example of an **age grade**. Age grades are a social classification of people whose ages lie within a culturally distinguished age range. As individuals progress through different age grades they acquire different rights and obligations as their status changes (Cohen and Eames, 1982: 411; Scupin, 2003: 158). In many societies one's age grade is a significant part of one's life and place in society. This is particularly true in nonstratified societies in which other ways of identifying and categorizing individuals such as on the basis of power, wealth, and status are absent.

The magnitude of age grading in people's lives is related to **age sets**. An age set is "[a] non-kin association in which individuals of the same age group interact throughout their lives" (Oswalt, 1986: 432). This means a group of people of the same gender and similar age will move together though the various life stages of a particular society together. For example, among the Shavante of Mato Grasso area of Brazil, boys of seven to twelve years of age are inducted into the bachelor hut together where they begin a right of passage wherein they learn hunting, weapons making, and ceremonial skills, ultimately culminating in adulthood and elder status. At the end of five years, the boys enter the age stage of young men together where more learning occurs. After another five years, the boys marry (in a group age set ceremony) their wives who have been selected for them by their parents. After this ceremony they may sit on the village council and are regarded as young warriors. The final stage for the age set is a progressive one occurring at five-year intervals as each age set matures with the eldest age set consisting of the senior men with the most authority. Although Shavante women also have age sets, their participation is much more limited and doesn't include the initiation ceremonies, life in bachelor huts, or elaborate ceremonials. In fact their age set doesn't really function as a same-sex association for women as it does for the men. This may be because the Shavante society is gender stratified to a certain degree; for example women are not allowed to sit on the council where community business is transacted. Such a set of initiations and stages of increasing authority of Shavante men provides them the opportunity to strengthen and validate cultural conceptions of masculine superiority and privilege in societies in which women have less prestige and power (Ember, Ember and Peregrine, 2005: 393–394). One of the consequences of initiation ceremonies is to foster age sets among initiates.

The residents of Salem (old Salem today), of the Protestant Moravian faith that came to the colonies from the present-day Germany, believed in a system whereby people of a similar social status lived and worshipped together, representing an historical example of U.S. age-grading system. The community was divided into choirs, a Greek word for "group," according to age, sex, and marital status: married people, single sisters, single brothers, widows, widowers, and children. Each choir had its own meetings for religious instruction, its own festal days, and tasks for which it was responsible. Some choirs lived together: there were dormitory-style houses for single brothers and single sisters which children joined at the age of fourteen and where they remained until marriage. Colored ribbons in females' caps also indicated an age grade as well; a red ribbon for little girls, pink for unmarried women, blue for those who are married, and white for widows (Old Salem, The First Moravian Church, "An Old Salem Christmas").

PUBERTY RITUALS: INITIATION CEREMONIES AS RITES OF PASSAGE

In many societies there occurs a "[c]eremonial recognition of a major change in social status, one that will permanently alter a person's relationship with members of the greater community" (Oswalt, 1986: 437; also Nanda and Warms, 2004: 329). Such ceremonies are called **rites of passage** or a **passage ceremony**. Not every society marks the transition from childhood to adulthood with elaborate ceremonies. The United States is an example of a society that does not do this.

It has been proposed that this absence of rites of passage rituals is the cause of much trauma in Anglo status transitions (Shapiro, 1979: 283), although the converse may be argued as well. Rituals may actually increase stress and anxiety. For example, Plains Indian boys/youths participated in a vision quest to find their guardian spirit through altered states of consciousness promoted by isolation, fasting, and ingestinging hallucinogenic drugs (Kottak, 2004: 350–351). Rites of passage often include initiation ceremonies in which a child undergoes a transition and transformation to the new status of adult. In 1909, Arnold Van Gennep originated the rites of passage model (*rites de passage*) as a tripartite scheme and explained the functions of these ceremonies. According to Van Gennep (1960: 3):

> Transitions from group to group and from one social situation to the next are looked on as implicit in the very fact of existence, as that a man's [and a woman's] life comes to be made up of a succession of stages with similar ends and beginnings: birth, social puberty, marriage, fatherhood and motherhood, advancement to higher class, occupational

specialization, and death. For every one of these events there are ceremonies whose essential purpose is to enable the individual to pass from one defined position to another which is equally well defined.

Rites of passage have three distinct phases: separation, transition, and incorporation (Van Gennep, 1960: 12). In **separation**, an individual is removed from his/her previous world or place in society. **Transition** or **liminality** involves "threshold" rites that prepare an individual "for his or her reunion with society." This is the phase in which the initiates undergo training for their anticipated status. As part of this, they are likely to experience some sort of ordeal or testing. **Incorporation** rites integrate the initiates back into their society/social group. This includes a return to the community after the initiate has been socially and perhaps even spatially removed. It is the public recognition of the person's new status in society (Van Gennep, 1960: 21, 46, 67). (See Figures 10.1 and 10.2.)

In the case of the pubescent, rites of passage function to ease the journey from the status of child to that of adult. According to Chapple and Coon (1942), changes of status are disturbing for personal and social relations within the group. Initiation ceremonies, like other rites of passage, help ease and facilitate the transition to adulthood. They do this for the novice who must experience an identity shift as he/she takes on a new position, as well as for the broader social group who must now accept the youth as an adult.

Figure 10.1 Earth paint. Apache girl's puberty ceremony. Whiteriver Arizona. (*Source*: Stephen Trimble, Photographer, DRKPHOTO.com.)

(See color plates, between pp. 168–169)

Figure 10.2 Maasai people: the warrior jumping dance. Young Maasai moran – warrior – youth leap into the air from a standing position in order to demonstrate their strength and agility. (*Source*: Martin Harvey, Photographer, DRKPHOTO.com.)

(See color plates, between pp. 168–169)

Initiation rites are often stressful and include rigorous tests, hazing, isolation from previous associates, and/or painful ordeals. These attributes provide symbolic referents for learning about what the new status as adults includes. Adolescent rites of passage provide an opportunity to practice and gain knowledge about adulthood. Chapple and Coon (1942: 484–485) maintain that these ceremonies restore equilibrium to the individual as well as the community. In addition, the dramatic, painful, and stressful elements may help prepare the youth for the "stresses" of adulthood as well as function to enhance group solidarity (Oswalt, 1986: 106). The rites of transition are particularly important as a period in which the novice is liminal, or "betwixt and between statuses," according to Victor Turner (1969). By occupying this liminal status, the pubescent individual will be in a unique position to unlearn her/his position as a child and take on new responsibilities as an adult.

In summary, many societies provide rites of passage for adolescents to help facilitate the transformation from the status of child to that of adult. As we have seen, the transition to a new position in society may be marked by new sets of rights and obligations as well as relations with people, including kin and nonkin. It may include new expectations and changes in the individual's identity as well. In preparation for this transformation, rights of passage participants undergo a journey through three characteristic phases: separation, transition or liminality, and integration. The phases of transition facilitate new learning and the development of identity components necessary for the new status. Ritual activities demarcate and actually facilitate the transformation of the individual's identity. They impress upon the novice the importance of the new status and what it means to be an adult man or woman (or perhaps some other option) in that society. By being separated socially and/or even geographically from their families, novitiates are given an opportunity to develop themselves as future adults. In addition, their families and others who have previously related to them as children may now regard them in their new status as they are reintegrated into society as adults. In such a way it is clear to the neo-adult what their position and place in society will be.

There are, however, gender differences in rites of passage that may be related to variation in socialization. Chodorow (1974, 1989, 1995) has argued that female and male socialization may be contrasted in terms of continuity and discontinuity. She believes that this is based on the universality of women as caregivers of children, that is, the majority of children experience an intimate relationship with a female, usually their mothers, during their early years. However, there is a gender difference in the mother-child relationship. Male socialization is discontinuous, in that boys must eventually experience a separation from the domestic worlds of their mothers, while girls do not. Young females learn to identify with their mothers and other women as associational role models and need not learn a new role as they mature. In contrast, boys' association with women during childhood prevents them from making an easy transition into masculine role identification (Chodorow, 1974, 1989, 1995). Boys' initial role model is a cross-sex one in contrast to the associational one of little girls. This model has been critiqued as ethnocentric because it is based on notions of the traditional nuclear family in which father is the breadwinner and mother works in the home. Although it may apply to some white middle-class Euro-American families, it does not necessarily apply to all, for example African American and Mexican-American families. Despite these shortcomings, Chodorow's work remains as a major contribution in feminist psychoanalytic identification theory and psychological anthropology, and has continued to promote debate (Renzetti and Curran, 2003).

Theories about why initiation ceremonies are often much more elaborate and at times more severe for males than females, although female ceremonies are more prevalent, may be related to Chodorow's thesis. There are a number of ideas on this subject. Burton and Whiting's (1961) cross-sex identity hypothesis suggests that young men in polygynous and patrilineal households are more likely, for a variety of reasons, to acquire a cross-sex feminine gender identity. In order to switch their cross-sex identification with their mothers to that of men, a severe initiation ceremony is mandated. It is designed to impress upon the boys that the world of men is more important and valued than that of women. According to this theory, severe practices such as circumcision or genital surgeries are guaranteed to catch the young man's attention and to reverse the feminine cross-sex identity. An important facet of these ceremonies is a mockery or "put down" of women which contributes to masculine self-definition as "*not* feminine." This argument has been criticized because the alleged cross-sex identity is not demonstrated or verified by the researchers but only speculated upon. Other less psychodynamically focused theories include Young's socio-cultural interpretation of initiation ceremonies.

Young's (1965) research emphasized that the functions of rites of passage varied by gender; male initiation ceremonies were designed to incorporate men into the entire community, while female initiations integrated women into domestic groups. Young postulated that this was related to the differential roles and tasks that each sex was assigned in society: women were assigned domestic roles, and men public roles. For Young, male solidarity was an important feature overlooked by the psychoanalytic approaches of researchers such as Burton and Whiting (Bock, 1988: 117). Solidarity was also a salient feature for the female household as well. Young explained that female initiations were less elaborate because the domestic sphere is more private and less extensive as opposed to the public world of males (1965: 106). The domestic arena is also a continuous and familiar one in that females are born into it and exposed to information about their role as they are growing up. This was suggested in Chodorow's (1974, 1989, 1995) approach as well.

Female initiation ceremonies will often ritually mark menarche, when a girl begins to menstruate. The time frame in a girl's life between menarche and full adulthood is referred to as **maidenhood**. Maidenhood, a period in girl's life where she is prepared for adulthood, is coterminously a phase when there is also great deal of cultural interest in her behavior. Maidenhood is a social construction (not a biological period) and the length of time it encompasses varies (Ward and Edelstein, 2006: 72).

Menarche is an event that is regarded as a very important in many cultures, signaling a girl's sexual and/or reproductive maturity (Ward and Edelstein, 2006: 273). How a society responds to menarche is related to the broader cultural context such as attitudes toward women in general, women's positioning in society vis-à-vis men, forms of social organization, and beliefs about menstrual blood. For example, New Guinea highland groups are well known for their view of menstrual blood as polluting. **Menarche rituals** are as varied as there are cultures. In some groups, like the Gussii, a clitoridectomy, removal of the clitoris, may be part of the ceremony acknowledging menarche (see discussion of female genital cutting). In other societies such as the Tlingit, a girl was confined for at least a year with a series of proscriptions around her behavior (she must not gaze at the sky or must scratch an itch only with a stone)

(Oswalt, 1986: 108–109). Among Andaman Islanders, according to Service (1978: 60–61):

> Once menarche is attained, a girl in this society is secluded in a hut for several days. Her behavior is closely regulated by prescriptions concerning bathing, posture, speaking, eating, and sleeping. Their personal name used during childhood is replaced by one taken from a plant in bloom during the ceremony and is retained until the next rite of passage (marriage). A boy reaching puberty does not experience physical isolation but is singled out by the occasion of an all-night dance held in his honor. Scarification of his back and chest further emphasizes his coming change in status. Dietary restrictions are enforced for a period of a year or more at the end of which time the boy is given a new name.

The meanings of menstrual blood vary from "power" to "pollution" and may be related to specific menstrual taboos. Menstrual taboos are cultural rules defining contact with menstruating women. According to Ward and Edelstein (2006: 71), "[t]here is no cross-cultural evidence that menstruation is everywhere considered unclean, that women uniformly feel shame or pain, or that menstrual blood repulses men." They argue that if early anthropologists and others would have labeled the seclusion of women in menstrual "sanctuaries" rather than "huts" we would have a very different prism for regarding this practice. Currently it is difficult to evaluate whether menstrual seclusion practices suppressed women or invigorated them with rest and recreation in a woman-only domain (Ward and Edelstein, 2006).

Schlegel and Barry's (1980: 696–715) classic study of 186 societies found that societies that emphasized female initiation ceremonies were more likely to be gatherers and hunters. They suggested this was because reproduction is important for foraging groups whose population density is low. Such ceremonies among foragers emphasize the importance of the life-giving attributes of women. In contrast, initiation rites in small-scale plant cultivators (like nonintensive horticulturalists) emphasize equally both girls and boys. However, when rigid separation of the sexes is enforced during the rites of passage, this accents the cultural importance of gender differentiation in such societies (Schlegel and Barry, 1980: 712). In fact, this characteristic is not uncommon in puberty rites in general. Despite variance in social organization, a general feature of female initiations is that they are centered on fertility while male's initiations are focused on responsibility. In horticultural societies with both male and female initiation ceremonies, same-sex bonding is an important function of the initiation ceremonies where homosocial relations (same-sex) are an integral part of such cultures (Schlegel and Barry, 1980: 712). Before turning our attention to an extreme form of ritualized masculinity in which boy-insemination rituals flourish among the Sambia (Herdt, 1981, 1984a, 1984b, 1987, 2006, among others), we will turn our attention to the topic of female genital cutting to highlight issues in rites of passage for women.

FEMALE GENITAL CUTTING

As discussed in Chapter 6 female genital surgery/cutting including circumcision, removal of the prepuce and clitoridectomy, the removal of the glans or shaft, has been practiced in both industrialized and nonindustrialized societies. These practices may be included as rites of passage or alternatively, as in the United States as late as the 1930s, as "cures" for female masturbation, "nymphomania," and/or insanity. Embedded in practices of female genital cutting are cultural beliefs that link women's sexual behavior to their sexual/reproductive structures.

Female genital cutting in nonindustrialized societies is categorized as falling into four types according to the World Health Organization (Gruenbaum, 2005). **Clitoridectomy (Type I)** is defined as partial or complete removal of the clitoris. This is known by Muslims and others as "*sunna* circumcision" or "*sunna* purification." The practice of **circumcision**, in which the clitoral hood is completely removed, is very rare although partial removal is common. In **excision (Type II)**, the cutting includes removal of the prepuce, the entire clitoris, and partial or total removal of the labia minora. An even more extreme form of genital cutting is **infibulation** (**Type III**) also referred to as "pharaonic circumcision" in which part or all of the external genitalia are excised. This may include the prepuce, clitoris, labia minora and all or part of the labia majora; in some forms the labia majora are left intact. The edges of the remaining tissues are infibulated; that is, held or sewn together with stitches or thorns. As a consequence, the vulva has a smooth appearance with a small hole for urination and menstrual blood. In order to give birth a midwife must make an incision for passage of the baby. After childbirth, the midwife then must reinfibulate the mother. The World Health Organization classifies as **Type IV** the practices that include various modifications of the female genital area but not removal of tissues. These include "pricking, piercing, incision, stretching of the clitoris or labia, cauterization, cuts or scrapes of the genitalia, or the use of harmful substances inserted into the vagina" ("Female Genital Mutilation," 2000; Gruenbaum, 2005: 483). For example, men's desire and valuing of "dry" sex in some East African countries has prompted women to insert harmful astringent agents into vagina to "dry" it out prior to intercourse (Gruenbaum, 2005; Walley, 2006). This classification is not meant to suggest that female genital surgeries are a unitary phenomenon. The particular form of cutting/surgery varies by socio-cultural context and historically.

Female genital cutting encompasses many forms both in industrialized and nonindustrialized countries. Traditionally and historically female genital surgeries span various religions including Islam, Christianity, Falasha

Judaism, and various indigenous beliefs and ethnicities from Indonesia to the Middle East and Africa. It is prevalent in the Middle East and Islamic Africa including North African and sub-Saharan countries (Gruenbaum, 2005; Walley, 2006). However, because of the immigration of peoples (to the United States/other industrialized countries) who practice female genital cutting, it has become an issue that Euro-American and other industrialized countries have had to address. Female genital cutting was first brought to the attention of the popular media in the early 1990s in France in several legal cases in which a circumciser and parents were charged with child abuse, and in subsequent cases of women seeking asylum in the United States in order to avoid genital surgeries in their home countries (Walley, 2006). The age for cutting varies cross-culturally and may include infants and or teens of fourteen to fifteen or even older for example the Maasai. It is most commonly performed on girls four/five and eight/nine years old (Badri, 2000; Gruenbaum, 2005). What does this controversial practice mean? Certainly this depends on the cultural context and the stance of the observer and/or participant. For example, as we saw in Chapter 6 among the Gbaya, a horticultural group in central Africa, removal of the glans clitoris in pubescent girls is a rite of passage, a symbolic and real marker of her transition from girlhood to womanhood.

Before discussing both emic and etic explanations, we must be attentive to issues of cultural relativism and respect. As we stated earlier in this chapter, we have been sensitive to the politics of naming (identity politics) and have made reference to female genital cutting, surgeries, and operations instead of the terminology "female genital mutilation." Walley (2006) argues against using the terminology of "circumcision" since it underplays the impact on sexual functioning; that is, the loss of feeling in genital tissues and resonates with male circumcision which has not been regarded as "mutilating" (also Gruenbaum, 2005: 482). In fact, Walley notes, even the act of naming itself is controversial. Using terminology such as female cutting, surgeries, or operations (such as we do in this chapter) implies a culturally relativistic stance while "mutilation" denotes "moral outrage" (2006: 335). We have followed Gruenbaum's (2005) use of the terminology female genital cutting, and/or surgery/operations, rather than female genital mutilation as is commonly used by the World Health Organization, the popular media and among various scholars including some schools of Euro-American feminism. Gruenbaum (2005: 481) makes a cogent argument against using the terminology of female genital mutilation:

[S]ince "mutilation" connotes intentional harm, its use is tantamount to accusing the women who do it of harmful intent. Some people, even those who favor stopping the practices, have been deeply offended by the term FGM, arguing that it is not women's intent to mutilate their daughters but to give them proper, socially expected treatment. Their intent is simply to "circumcise" or "purify." The words commonly used for female genital cutting in Arabic-speaking countries, *tahur* or *tahra,* means "purification," that is, the achievement of cleanliness through a ritual activity.

The politics of naming are closely articulated with the consequences of these practices for girls and women and penetrate Euro-American and other industrialized national discourses about human rights and cultural relativism. The psychological, reproductive, sexual, and health consequences of this surgery on women, their families and partners are part of heated debates (Lightfoot-Klein, 1989, 1990). As we stated earlier, female genital cutting is a highly charged issue that is influenced by acculturation, immigration, emigration, and globalization. Issues of ethnocentrism, cultural relativism, and **indigenous cultural integrity** are involved.

Over 100 million girls and women are believed to have undergone some form of genital cutting with estimates of 3 million a year according to UNICEF and the World Health Organization (Klapper, 2006; Walley, 2006). There are well-established negative health consequences of female genital cutting including: infertility, shock, hemorrhage, septicemia, retention of menstrual blood and urine *(hematocolpos)* resulting in urinary tract infections and chronic pelvic infections, and serious complications in childbirth. Sexual functioning may be interfered with resulting in painful intercourse and loss of sexual response. In the situation of infibulation, first intercourse may not only be painful but virtually impossible (Gruenbaum, 2005; Klapper, 2006; Kopelman, 2002). Lightfoot-Klein (1989) and Gruenbaum offer some opposing evidence regarding sexual functioning, arguing that many women maintain their capacity for sexual responsiveness and are orgasmic even with infibulation. This may be related to the degree and type of cutting, expertise of the midwife, barber, "surgeon," as well as the nature of the relationship with the partner (Gruenbaum, 2005: 483).

In a 2006 study published by the World Health Organization in the *Lancet,* it was reported that women who have who undergone Type III surgical cutting (infibulation) have a 70 percent greater chance of hemorrhage after childbirth and neonatal death rates are 15 to 55 percent higher than in uncut women ("Female Genital Mutilation," 2000; Klapper, 2006; "New Study Shows Female Genital Mutilation Exposes Women and Babies to Significant Risk at Childbirth," 2006; WHO Study Group on Female Genital Mutilation, 2006).

Joy Phumaphi, Assistant Director-General, Family and Community Health, World Health Organization, argues that: "'FGM' is a practice steeped in culture and tradition but it should not be allowed to carry on. We must support communities in their efforts to abandon the practice and to improve care for those who have undergone FGM. We must also steadfastly resist the medicalization of FGM. WHO is totally opposed to FGM being carried out by medical personnel." ("New Study Shows Female Genital Mutilation Exposes Women and Babies to Significant Risk at Childbirth," 2006)

Note the use of terminology of "FGM" in this statement. The emic and etic explanations for this practice sometimes converge and sometimes don't. Female genital surgeries cross diverse religions and therefore are not etically the result of religious dictums, although people who support or denounce the practice may offer religious reference. For example, the Qur'an does not require it, but various interpretations of Islam and the Prophet Mohammed may be cited as justification for acceptance or rejection of the practice (Gruenbaum, 2005). The emic reasons given for female genital cutting can be summarized as falling into five categories:

1   meets a religious requirement.
2   preserves group identity, i.e. custom and tradition.
3   helps to maintain cleanliness and health.
4   preserves virginity and family honor and prevents immorality.
5   furthers marriage goals including greater sexual pleasure for men (Kopelman, 2002: 50–52; Ward and Edelstein, 2006).

This said, understanding the practice of genital surgery requires a context which can complicate a discussion of the practice. For some, such as the Maasai of Kenya, it is a rite of passage and occurs usually at marriage when a girl is excised. After she is healed she is allowed to join her husband as a woman, no longer a girl. Yet for others, genital surgery may be resisted as part of ethnic identity or adopted as part of acculturation for an immigrant group such as among the Zabarma and Hausa minorities in the Sudan (Gruenbaum, 2005). For some peoples, the genital cutting is part of an aesthetic for smoothness that is regarded as part of an ideology of beauty held by both men and women (Gruenbaum, 2006; Ward and Edelstein, 2006). It is also articulated with beliefs that female genital cutting enhances male sexual response (Gruenbaum, 2006; Ward and Edelstein, 2006).

From an etic perspective, Boddy refers to such practices as well as the concomitant rules for women's modesty and chastity as the "**overdetermination of women's selfhood**" (1989: 252). These are rules of conduct that are more restrictive for women than for men. Such rules and the practice of genital cutting are associated with patricentric and patriarchal societies in which males are dominant. This is not to say that women may not have power in the domestic sphere, but that men hold the power in the formal spheres of society including the public, economic, and the political arenas. Genital surgery is therefore embedded in women's subordination and ideologies that support that subordination. These may include notions that women are "essentially" sexually voracious and the genital cutting "tames" those tendencies along with the belief that women are unclean and hence are purified by the practice (Badri, 2000; Gruenbaum, 2005; Kopelman, 2002: 52).

These are extremely difficult, emotionally charged behaviors not only within cultures, but across cultures as well. Resolution will take a long time to achieve because female genital surgery is a complicated issue. Reference to female genital cutting as mutilation and torture are culturally insensitive ways to approach this issue. The international reaction of industrialized nations to "eliminate" the practice is not always welcomed. There is a growing response of African and other international/indigenous women who wish to eliminate genital surgeries or who wish to introduce less invasive and more symbolic forms of the surgery (Mutisya, 2002; Ward and Edelstein, 2006). Such approaches recognize how complex this issue is and include respecting the symbolic aspect of genital surgery as a rite of passage signaling a young woman's readiness for marriage (Gruenbaum, 2005; Mutisya, 2002; Ward and Edelstein, 2006). As we have seen there are agencies such as the World Health Organization that are completely against the practice and/or individuals, such as Alice Walker in her film *Warrior Marks,* who asserts an unequivocal anticultural relativistic stance toward this issue (Ward and Edelstein, 2006). However, as Ellen Gruenbaum cautions: "[T]he first step in changing anything is to understand what it means to the people who do it. With more insight, we can better understand why people have resisted widespread change and why some are now pursuing change" (2005: 488). Those wishing to introduce change in this practice such as grassroots and local women leaders as well as their supporters argue that increasing women's educational and economic opportunities is an important part of the solution for change. In addition, young men must also take a stance that resists the practice by not marrying women who are genitally cut (Gruenbaum, 2005).

Others have suggested surrogate rites of passage that don't involve cutting (e.g., a Kenyan rural group created "Circumcision through Words," an alternative rite for girls that involves seclusion and learning women's specialized knowledge [Reaves in Gruenbaum, 2005]). More controversial and illegal in many industrialized nations, are alternatives that involve medical professionals in the nicking/pricking of the clitoris (Mutisya, 2002). This is clearly a difficult subject traversing human rights, justice, fairness, respect for difference, emic and etic approaches, and avoidance of harm among others (Salmon, 2006).

Lest we take a position of moral superiority as industrialized women and men, it is important to understand how our own societies intervene in girls' and women's bodies through diet, exercise regimes, and other techniques that make women beautiful and sexually desirable, such as shaving the pubic area, bikini waxing, labial piercing, and plastic surgeries including breast implants and "vaginal rejuvenation surgeries." Vaginal rejuvenation surgery, also referred to as vaginaplasty includes specific procedures to tighten a "loose vagina" and to reduce the appearance of enlarged labia. These have been marketed as enhancing sexual satisfaction and beautifying the appearance of the genitals (CosmeticSurgery.com, 2006; Navarro, 2004: 8; "Vaginal Rejuvenation Surgery," 2003).

MALE INSEMINATION RITES: THE SAMBIA

Gilbert Herdt's study, *The Sambia: Ritual, Sexuality, and Change in Papua New Guinea* (2006, first edition, 1987), describes the rites of passage of the Sambia male children/adolescents as they pursue adulthood. What makes the Sambia of particular interest is that their initiation into manhood involves an extended period of masculine insemination rites in which older boys orally inseminate younger boys. All males among the Sambia will have experienced the roles of **inseminatee/fellator** and **inseminator/fellatee** with other men during the course of their initiation and journey into manhood (see also Herdt, 1981, 1984a and 1984b, 1988). Herdt notes that boy inseminating rites were once practiced among fifty or sixty traditional (precontact) cultures in Melanesia (2006). According to Herdt this ritual is part of "culture specific initiation rites, secret male cults, and small-scale patrilineal societies involved in rampant warfare among men and sexual antagonism between men and women" (Herdt, 2006: xvi). Herdt's research began in 1974 and spanned more than thirty years and involved over twelve research trips. Since beginning his research, the Sambia have undergone tremendous change including the ending of warfare (six years before Herdt's arrival), the increasing influence of Christianity through missionization, the growing impact of the wage labor economy, and a concomitant escalation in women's status (Herdt, 2006). Although the following discussion situates the Sambia in the ethnographic present of 1974, Herdt (2006: 154) comments on some of the more recent and dramatic changes that have occurred:

A sexual revolution has overtaken the Sambia. In the past decade or so, they have undergone huge life-changing, culture-breaking, and culture-making alterations in their sexuality—greater than anything we have experienced in our civilization in such a short period of time—and much greater than the so-called sexual revolution of the 1960s in the United States. To go from absolute gender segregation and arranged marriages, with universal ritual initiation that controlled sexual and gender development and imposed the radical practice of boy-insemination, to abandoning initiation, seeing adolescent boys and girls kiss and hold hands in public, arranging their own marriages, and building square houses with one bed for the newlyweds, as the Sambia have done, is revolutionary.

The Sambia are a highland Papua, New Guinea, group characterized by warfare and male privilege. As is typical in groups like this, there is great disparity in the status of men and women, with men being privileged and dominant. At a prepubescent age boys will leave their mothers and live in all-male clubhouses, where for the next seven years they will fellate the older males (teenagers and men in their early twenties) who share the clubhouse with them. It is only by swallowing the ejaculate of the older boys that a young boy can hope to grow into manhood. Manhood is defined by semen, which is regarded as a very powerful substance. Boys are believed to be born without semen; so it is important that a boy consume as much as possible in order to have an ample supply. The obvious way to get this is by fellatio, or oral insemination. Semen has a power known as *jerungdu* (Herdt, 1987: 101; Herdt, 2006: 57). *Jerungdu* is defined as "the principle of male strength, virility, and manliness associated with semen and warrior prowess in Sambia culture" (Herdt, 2006: 167).

Like sexuality in general, there are rules and practices regulating homo-erotic behavior. When a young man reaches about twenty-five years old, he is married. However, he must remain attentive to preserving his supply of sacred fluids, lest his spouse, who is regarded as potentially dangerous and polluting, sap him of his strength and use up his semen during inter-course. Societies like the Sambia are noted for female pollution avoidance rituals, which dramatize women's social inequality to men. Female pollution avoidance rituals may restrict menstruating women by confining them to a special structure (a menstrual house). These rituals are based on beliefs that females are impure. Avoidance of women and concepts of female impurity associated with the female menstrual cycle contribute to status inequalit-ies and disparities between the sexes (Herdt, 1987, 2006). Such rituals do not occur in societies in which women share power with men, but tend to be found in patrilineal societies and societies in which women have lower prestige (Zelman, 1977: 714–733). Note that this does not necessarily con-tradict Ward and Edelstein's perspective that such seclusion may indeed be a sanctuary for women and while it may be personally empowering, such practices according to cross-cultural research, do reproduce the relations of inequality and apparently do not augment women's overall status. The critical variable in whether seclusion is oppressive or enhancing to women may be the patrilineal kinship system. Clearly more research is needed on this subject.

The purpose of initiation among the Sambia is to make men out of boys. Little boys inhabit the world of women and are dangerously contaminated by it. As a result of this, they are regarded as not quite masculine. Mas-culinity is not something that is seen as "naturally" occurring for Sambian boys and men; *jerungdu* must be acquired as the source of masculinity. Con-sequently males have two major barriers in becoming masculine: in addition to the feminization of young boys that is believed to occur through their close ties with their mothers, there is also the problem that males cannot manufacture their own semen. To make matters worse they can lose *jerungdu* through ejaculation. The Sambia ritualized insemination initiation resolves this dilemma of manhood. Fellatio is the means of acquiring an initial supply of semen. The proof of the power of the initiation among the Sambia is that young boys provide evidence that it works by becoming bigger, physically strong, and assertive. In the end, the pre-initiated and feminized boy (polluted by contact with his mother) has been remade into a fierce warrior (Herdt, 1987, 2006). Through the course of initiation the boys have learned the cultural values associated with masculinity and with it the secrets of manhood hidden from Sambian women. For example, heterosexual coitus is particularly dangerous for men since through it they can lose their power. Once the initiates are past the stage of ingesting semen through fellatio, they must learn secret lore on how to replenish their *jerungdu* by drinking a white tree sap that can restore their power (Herdt, 1987, 2006).

The Sambia are a provocative example to contrast with our own industrialized society's concepts of manhood and sexuality. During most of the initiation cycle the initiate is not permitted any heterosexual activity. In the early stages, the boys act as the fellators and ingestors of semen which contains the power to make them grow into manhood. The initiates are prohibited from masturbation or anal sex as well. In other words, they have no sexual outlets other than wet dreams. However, from about fifteen years of age through eighteen, the boys enter the third stage of initiation when they become bachelors and inserters rather than fellators. Their ability in the "inseminator" role proves:

> that they are strong and have *jerungdu,* because their bodies are sexually mature and have semen to "feed" to younger boys. They feel more masculine than at any previous time in their lives. So the bachelors go through a phase of intense sexual activity, a period of vigorous homoerotic activity and contacts, having one relationship after another with boys. Their sexual behavior is primarily promiscuous, for the initiates are concerned mostly with taking in semen, while the bachelors mainly desire sexual release through domination of younger boys ... Eventually Sambia adolescent boys become more interested in females. (Herdt, 1987: 162; Herdt, 2006: 115)

The purpose of the boy insemination is to acquire semen so that the youths may ultimately marry and achieve fatherhood. Around the age of seventeen, the bachelors enter the fourth stage of initiation in which they are permitted interaction with women. From the beginning of the initiation until the fourth stage, they have not been in contact with women. In their late teens and early twenties, the initiates go through a fifth stage of bisexuality as married men which is followed by a sixth stage of adulthood in which heterosexuality is practiced (Herdt, 1987, 2006). This stage is associated with the birth of the man's first child. Thus, the birth of a child is the marker for full adulthood.

ADOLESCENT SEXUAL BEHAVIOR: NONINDUSTRIALIZED COUNTRIES

The Sambia initiation ceremony provides an excellent example for beginning our discussion of adolescent sexuality in nonindustrialized countries and among indigenous peoples. As we have seen, the Sambian male's first experiences involving the genitalia are as fellators from about age seven through age fourteen. At fifteen years old, they then move into a new stage (the third stage in their initiation) where they can experience sexual outlets for the first time (other than wet dreams). Prior to this they were prevented from doing so. In this phase they become the bachelor recipients of fellatio. The inseminator phase is a very pleasurable one for the bachelors. From about the ages of fifteen to eighteen, the third stage in the initiation, there is no opportunity of interaction with females, although it is a period of vigorous sexual activity for the bachelor inseminators. This is a phase in which males experience "profound homoerotic pleasures" (Herdt and Stoller, 1989: 33; Herdt, 2006: 115). The inseminator role moves with them as they take on a new status as newlyweds in the fourth stage of their initiation (they do not cohabit with their wives), but continue their behavior as inseminators with boys. It is not until the men enter the fifth stage of initiation in their late teens and after their wives have experienced menarche that they are allowed to have genital sex with their wives (Herdt, 2006: 60, 119).

This case clearly points to the difference between sexual behavior and sexual orientation. The Sambia initiation ceremony is an important vehicle for sex education facilitating the young man's transition to a heterosexual lifestyle. The bachelor inseminator, whose primary sexual experience is homoerotic, is gradually shifted into the status of newlywed which allows him to make the transition in sexuality by going through a bisexual phase. According to Herdt: "[t]he customary first sexual intercourse between spouses is fellatio" usually taking place in the late teens or early twenties (Herdt, 1987: 164; Herdt, 2006: 117). Culturally-shaped sexual practices help ease the male into his change of lifestyle from bachelor inseminator to that of newlywed and married man. The newlywed bride is given sexuality instruction during her menarche initiation (at around the same time as the men's fifth stage initiation). She is given direction on how to dress in such a way that she resembles the young initiates in appearance for her first sexual encounter with her husband. The bride covers her breasts and wears a noseplug similar to that of the young males that are the fellators. "The bride's similarity to the boys in appearance and the fellatio she performs on her husband, thus helps to provide an erotic bridge between the homoerotic and heterosexual lifestyles" (Herdt, 1987: 165; Herdt, 2006: 118). Herdt's research on the Sambia challenges clinical theories that early homosexual experiences invariably lead to later adult homosexual behavior (Schlegel and Barry, 1991: 109). In addition, Herdt's work interrogates the very concept of homosexuality as a Euro-American culture-bound social identity contextualized in time and space; hence his use of the term boy-inseminating rites in the second edition of his book rather than "institutionalized homosexuality" (Herdt, 2006: xv).

The Sambia are a fascinating example of nonindustrialized sexuality as it is experienced in adolescence and into young adulthood. Male-female relations are part of a well-reported phenomenon of sex antagonism in this particular area of New Guinea. Women are regarded as potentially dangerous because of their ability to pollute and deplete men of their semen. Wives were acquired by politically motivated and arranged marriages. Because they came from outside the group (exogamy), they can never be completely trusted. While the arranged marriages may help create alliances, they are also potentially disruptive because at any time the bride's family might become enemies. Warfare plays an integral part in Sambia homoerotic as well as heterosexual behaviors (Herdt and Stoller, 1989: 32). Keep in mind that our concepts of homoerotic, bisexual, and heterosexual are in the context of our industrialized experience. The Sambia do not have categories analogous to ours. Their heterosexual, homoerotic, and bisexual behavior is obviously vastly different from the industrialized one and cannot be translated into our industrialized clinical and homophobic perspective (Francoeur and Noonan, 2004: 814; Herdt and Stoller, 1989: 31–34; Herdt, 2006: xv, xxii; Olive-Miller, 2004).

Turning now to our more general topic of pubescent and adolescent sexuality cross-culturally, we need to point out that young men and women may experience sexuality at different ages. For example, among the Tiwi, adolescent women have sex with postadolescent men, not men of their own ages (Hart, Pilling, and Goodale, 1988). Age of marriage is an important variable to consider since sex may occur in the context of premarital, marital, and/or extramarital sexual behavior. In countries in which individuals marry late, such as Singapore where women marry at 24.4 years old, the premarital sex period may extend into the twenties. Many of the studies of premarital sex in industrializing nations target students as the research population so the ages may span both teens as well as the early twenties. Conversely, marital sex may also include the pubescent age groups since in many societies people who marry in their teens may be regarded as adults. Marriage in most traditional societies ends adolescence as a cultural stage (Schlegel and Barry, 1991: 109). In 74 percent of forty societies, males marry at eighteen years or older and in 69 percent of forty-five societies females marry at seventeen or younger. Cross-culturally, the modal age of male marriage is eighteen to twenty-one years old and for females it is twelve to fifteen years old. Men tend to be older than their wives at first marriage, and hence experience premarital rules for a longer period of time. However, it is important to remember that males generally have greater access to a double standard that allows them more premarital sexual freedom (Frayser, 1985: 208; Lewin, 2006: 10; Ward and Edelstein, 2006).

The meaning premarital sex has for industrialized countries is not necessarily convergent with that in other societies. The cross-cultural research may also have embedded ethnocentric assumptions. For example, data from the *Human Relations Area Files* biases the definition of premarital sex by focusing on heterosexual penile-vaginal intercourse. The degree to which premarital sex among youths is approved of, disapproved of, and even condemned will vary cross-culturally as well. Despite the diversity, all cultures have rules regarding sexual relations with appropriate partners. A variety of factors interact and are related to these rules surrounding premarital sex. Societal approval of premarital sex is related to the type of social organization, population density, subsistence and resource patterns, all of which are directly related to the status of women (Ember, Ember and Peregrine, 2005; Manderson, Bennett, and Sheldrake, 1999; Martin and Voorhies, 1975). However, sexual attitudes and behaviors are not static, and vary over time and within populations by ethnicity, generation, and class as a result of culture contact, or culture change brought on by colonialism, missionization, escalating capitalism, and globalization (Herdt, 1999; Mascia-Lees and Black, 2000). Relevant also to this discussion is the role of adolescent sterility and cultural attitudes toward children conceived outside marriage. Sexuality and its cultural regulation are related to gender statuses and are rooted within specific social-structural systems, cultural and temporal context as well as articulated with symbols and meanings (Manderson, Bennett and Sheldrake, 1999).

Although the HIV/AIDS epidemic has amplified anthropological interest in how youths experience their sexuality from the subjective to the ethnographic and the international (Herdt, 1999), Ford and Beach's (1951), classic work in the codification of cultures as restrictive and permissive based on a massive review of 190 different societies continues to provide us with a useful approach in describing adolescent sexuality. Their cross-cultural perspective has been refined and continues to be an important source for understanding how and why adolescent sexuality is structured. Most notable in this genre is the work of Schlegel and Barry (1991) discussed later in this chapter. Again, this model of ideal types represents what in actuality is a continuum. Ford and Beach recorded fourteen very restrictive societies in which children are prevented from sexual expression and acquiring sexual knowledge. However, sex with the onset of puberty is allowed for girls in ten restrictive societies, and for boys in one; the Haitians. "For the most part these peoples seem particularly concerned with the prepubescent girl, believing that intercourse before menarche may be injurious to her" (Ford and Beach, 1951: 18). In the majority of the African societies studied by Ford and Beach, boys were prevented from having sex before their initiation ceremonies. In some societies rules against sex after puberty may remain restricted or may actually be intensified. To restrict premarital sex among young people, societies will:

- separate the sexes;
- chaperone females; and/or
- negatively sanction premarital sex (Ford and Beach, 1951: 182).

Of these measures the first is the most successful, while the third has not proven to be a deterrent to the highly motivated youngster (Ford and Beach, 1951: 183–184). One of the means restrictive societies use to ensure control of youngsters' sexuality is by placing a value on female virginity. Some may even have tests of this virginity through demonstrations of bloodied cloth or defloration ceremonies (Ford and Beach, 1951: 186, also Delaney, 1991).

Virginity testing has been initiated among the KwaZulu-Natal in South Africa as a way to prevent HIV. Virginity testing of girls from six years old to marriageable age is supported by mothers and grandmothers to prevent and curb "sexual licentiousness." External genital exams and inspections are publicly performed by village women who use the same latex glove for each exam, and who then grade the girls on their degree of virginity. Girls who "pass" are cheered and given a certificate; girls who "fail" are publicly shamed. Anthropologist Suzanne LeClerc-Madlala notes that this practice, while not traditional to the group in its present form, upholds deeply held patriarchal views about women's worth and sexuality among the Zulu. LeClerc-Madlala discusses the potential health risks, false sense of security that derive from passing the exam, the double standards about sex, and the culturally-structured beliefs about female sexuality that exist among this group. Boys are not tested since "they wouldn't come anyway," and "are like animals; they can't control themselves" (LeClerc-Madlala, 2001: 457). These practices can foster the spread of HIV since they reinforce larger view about disease, blame, and women as vectors of transmission" (Whelehan, in press).

In semirestrictive societies, there may be formal proscriptions directed at teenage premarital sex, but these are not regarded as serious offenses. Prohibitions against premarital sex for females specifically occur in twelve societies, for older children in two, while sanctions against both sexes are found in thirty-four societies (Ford and Beach, 1951: 187). Forty-three societies are classified as permissive in which there are no gender-specific restrictions on premarital sexual expression; the only restrictions regarding sexuality are those around incest, which would be expected (Ford and

Beach, 1951: 190). Of these forty-three societies, there are three permissive societies that allow coitus for adolescent boys only, the Crow, Siriono, and Tongans; one society that allows premarital permissiveness for girls only, the Thonga (Africa); and one that limits permissiveness to the commoner class, the Nauruans. According to Ford and Beach (1951: 190): "[b]y the time of puberty in most of these [permissive] societies expressions of sexuality on the part of older children consist predominantly of the accepted adult form of heterosexual intercourse, the pattern which they will continue to follow throughout their sexually active years of life" (Ford and Beach, 1951: 190).

Though Ford and Beach documented the variation in adolescent sexuality, other anthropologists have been interested in explanations, asking questions such as how social structure influences premarital sex norms. Schlegel and Barry's *Adolescence: An Anthropological Inquiry* (1991) continues to be a valuable compass in this regard. A summary of some of their findings and review of the research is presented to illustrate how socio-cultural features pattern sexual behavior (Schlegel and Barry, 1991: 109–121).

- For both sexes, adolescent permissiveness is related to the absence of a double standard.
- Adultery for women and men is frequent in societies that are permissive for adolescent sexuality.
- Premarital sexual permissiveness for females is associated with simpler subsistence technologies, absence of stratification, smaller communities, matrilineal descent, matrilocal residence, absence of belief in high gods, absence of bride's wealth, high female economic contribution, little or no property exchange at marriage, and ascribed rather than achieved status, an evaluation of girls' position as equal or higher than boys'.

GENERAL TRENDS IN NONINDUSTRIALIZED AND INDUSTRIALIZED COUNTRIES

As mentioned earlier, concern for AIDS has resulted in an increase in research on the subject of sex, including sexual behavior among youths in countries such as Thailand, the Philippines, Taiwan, Hong Kong, Sri Lanka, Japan, Malaysia, Micronesia, and Melanesia (Bennett and Sheldrake, 1999; Manderson, Bennett, and Sheldrake, 1999; Sittitrai, 1990: 173–190). These countries have experienced a growth in the transmission of AIDS from other areas through immigration and tourism (see Chapter 15). Unfortunately, our industrialized heteroerotic bias has focused primarily on male populations and heterosexual behavior (Sittitrai, 1990: 177).

However, contemporary research is countering this bias. A study by Singh et al. (2000: 1–19) reports on the timing of first intercourse from fourteen countries, including developing nations in sub-Saharan Africa, Asia, Latin America, and the Caribbean as well as from two developed countries, Great Britain and the United States. Teenage sexual activity reveals disparate trends,

- In most countries one-third or more of teenaged women have had intercourse.
- In four countries, Ghana, Mali, Jamaica, and Great Britain, three in five women are sexually experienced.
- Between approximately one-half and three-quarters of adolescent males in seven countries have ever had intercourse.
- One-third or fewer of the teenaged men in Ghana, Zimbabwe, the Philippines, and Thailand have ever had intercourse.
- In most countries teenage sexual intercourse occurs outside marriage for men but within marriage for women. For more specific information on percentages of fifteen- to nineteen-year-olds and their first intercourse experience, visit the Guttmacher Institute's Web site at http://www.guttmacher.org/.

In many developing nations young women in their teenage years are married; very often this is a result of arranged marriages (Cohen, 2004: 1). Though marriage is valued and brings social rewards in virtually all societies, teen marriages are known to be unstable. Rates vary considerably internationally; this practice is most prevalent in western Africa such as in Cameroon and Mali, although it is also pronounced in several other countries including Bangladesh, Mozambique, Nicaragua, and Uganda. More than half of today's twenty- to twenty-four-year-old women married before turning eighteen. These young women are not in a position to negotiate sex and contraceptives or HIV/STI prevention strategies with their husbands who may be older and have more power in the relationship. Consequently they are more at risk for sexual violence, and their health and their child's may be compromised by early pregnancy (Cohen, 2004; Mathur, Greene, and Malhotra, 2003). According to Mathur, Greene, and Malhotra in the 2003 *International Center for Research on Women Report* "Too Young to Wed: The Lives, Rights and Health of Young Married Girls" the practice of marrying girls at or near puberty occurs for two reasons: (1) to maximize fertility in cultures with high mortality rates, and (2) to cement kinship alliances for social, political or economic ends. See Figures 10.3 and 10.4.

Mathur, Greene, and Malhotra (2003) suggest that incorporating data from both figures provides a more accurate view of teenage marriage, and attention to the diversity within the various regions must also be taken into consideration. Early marriage for women is an important issue for policymakers in developing nations since such practices reinforce women's

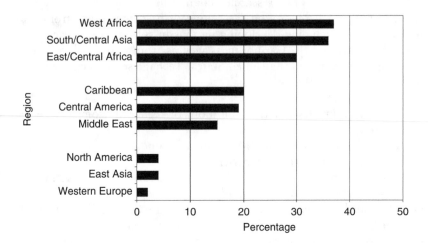

Figure 10.3 Percentage of girls aged 15–19 who are married. (*Source*: Population Reference Bureau 2000; Mathur, Greene, and Malhotra, 2003.)

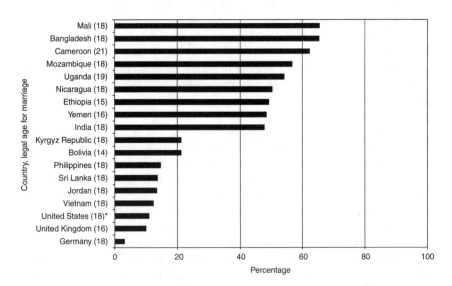

Figure 10.4 Percentage of women aged 20–24 married before age 18.* (*Source*: Based on DHS data since 1990; UN, 1989; Cornell University, 2003; *Too Young to Wed,* by Mathur, Greene, and Malhotra, 2003, International Center for Research on Women.) (*Note*: U.S. legal age at marriage may vary by state.)

lower status by preventing them from pursuing educational and occupational training that will help economically empower them (Cohen, 2004; Mathur, Greene and Malhotra, 2003).

There are some studies available on adolescent sexuality that include homosexual and/or bisexual behaviors and experiences. Most of the cross-cultural and international studies of adolescent homosexuality/bisexuality do not focus on the specifics of homoerotic sex practices and meanings among youth, but emphasize self-reports of sexual attraction and interest and/or statistics on same-sex encounters. For example, a study of adolescents in nine Caribbean countries spearheaded by the Pan American Health Organization and the WHO Collaborating Centre in Adolescent Health at the University of Minnesota represents one of the few comprehensive studies of youth health including sexual health in the Caribbean. This study asked adolescents about same-sex attraction (WHO Collaborating Centre on Adolescent Health, 2000). However, social norms make discussion of same-sex behavior/bisexuality difficult for young people. This study details the following findings:

- 4.5 percent percent of females under eighteen and 5.5 percent of males under eighteen acknowledge same-sex attraction only.
- 5 percent of girls under eighteen and 2.3 percent of males under eighteen reported equal attraction to both sexes.
- 44.7 percent of the girls and 56.8 percent of boys report other sex attraction with the remainder either uncertain, or not understanding the question.

Same-sex attraction is apparently reported anecdotally as becoming more prevalent in Caribbean adolescent social circles. Sexual tourism is also a factor in perceived escalation of same-sex behaviors as well. However, these were anecdotal reports; actual data on same-sex experiences were not provided in this research (WHO Collaborating Centre on Adolescent Health, 2000: 16–17). In this regard Herdt (1999) has argued that much work remains to be done in the study of the intersection of the individual and culture in homoerotic and bisexual experiences.

The *Continuum Complete International Encyclopedia of Sexuality* (Francoeur and Noonan, 2004) offers a stunning collection of sexual data from fifty-eight countries, spanning both industrialized and nonindustrialized nations including information on heterosexual adolescent sexual behavior, as well as specific discussion of homoerotic, homosexual/lesbian, and bisexual behavior. Unfortunately, information on adolescent homosexuality/bisexuality is not available from all the countries surveyed, for example Turkey (Aydun and Gulcut, 2004: 1065) and Nepal (Schroeder, 2004: 719). The data may also be very general, depending on the country. In the Czech Republic for example, it is noted that 10 percent of the men and 5 percent of the women in the heterosexual population had reported same-sex experiences in childhood and early adolescence (Zverina, 2004: 323), while for Nigeria, the authors comment that the incidence of same-sex sexual behavior for adolescence is very low (Esiet, 2004: 765). With enhanced international interest in HIV, STIs and adolescent sexual health, and the importance of cultural sensitivity in sexual health education, we can anticipate more specific information on adolescent homoerotic, homo-sexual and bisexual experience and the meanings given to the experience in nonindustrialized and industrializing nations.

However, a Japanese study offers unique insight into the specific erotic experiences of adolescents and provides a useful model for the kinds of research needed. Sittitrai (1990) reported 7 percent of the male and 4 percent of the female research population experienced some male or female homo-sexual behavior such as kissing, petting, and/or mutual masturbation. These researchers did note that the age of the first same-sex experience was fifteen to seventeen years old with partners usually older (Sittitrai, 1990: 178).

These kinds of targeted data are essential for understanding adolescent sexuality, particularly as it relates to STI and HIV transmission. A great deal of research remains to be done in this area. Schlegel and Barry (1991) have made a substantial contribution in this regard and remain a valuable resource for their comparative data on same-sex and bisexual sexuality. Using the cross-cultural correlational approach, they compared homosexual behavior among pubescent boys and girls in twenty-four societies. They found "[i]n virtually all cases, if homosexual relations are tolerated or per-mitted for one sex they are for the other as well." In addition, their research indicates that cross-culturally, homosexuality in adolescence tends to be transient and "appears to be a substitute for heterosexual intercourse when intercourse is prohibited or access to girls is problematic" (Schlegel and Barry, 1991: 126).

Enhancing our understanding of adolescent sexuality is an interna-tional and domestic health and sexual health issue. According to a recent report, sub-Saharan youth are particularly at risk HIV/AIDS. Nearly ten million women and men aged fifteen through twenty-four are infected with the virus and about one in fourteen young adults are living with HIV/AIDs (Bankole et al., 2004). See Chapter 15 for further discussion of HIV/AIDS.

ADOLESCENT SEXUALITY: A FOCUS ON INDUSTRIALIZED COUNTRIES

In dominant U.S. Anglo society, adolescence is commonly considered a period of anxiety. It has been linked with a capitalist ideology of com-petition and gender stratification as well as that peculiarly industrialized view of personhood as one of autonomy and independence. Industrialized adolescents may well wonder if they measure up. Both males and females at this time experience concerns over adequacy; males are worried about their penis size and females are worried about the size of their breasts. This is tied to their newly developing sense of self as sexual beings. While there is no relationship between breast or penis size and one's capacity for sexual functioning, these myths prevail.

We would like to point out that the data on industrialized adolescent sexuality are biased toward the white middle class and do not typically include variation by class and ethnicity. In addition, we are citing general patterns and trends, not stereotyping or assuming that these features are true for everyone. Generally, adolescent males or females are socialized differently in regard to human sexuality and their respective roles in the process. Both sexes may encounter increased sexual interest as a result of the physiological changes accompanying puberty. Sexuality is an integral component in the dual gender system of socialization. Males learn that they are the initiators of sex, that this is a reward that they will, in all likelihood, have to work for in some way. Because they are the initiators, they also face the risks of sexual rejection.

Females learn that they are the keepers of a desired resource, sex. They are not the direct sexual initiators, although frequently they are the initiators of courtship through nonverbal actions and displays (Kilmartin, 2007; Perper, 1985). Adolescent sexuality is related to broader conceptions of gender ideologies. Young females are taught that once a male begins the process of sexual arousal there may be no stopping him. So adolescent girls are warned not to tease a boy and get him sexually excited. In addition, sexual experiences for adolescent females are connected to intimacy needs, relationships, and love. Adolescent female sexuality is not centered on orgasm or the genitalia in contrast to adolescent boys' sexuality with its genital focus and emphasis on physical gratification (Hyde, 1985: 290; Westheimer and Lopater, 2005). Simon and Gagnon (1973) refer to this as a **relational ideology** in comparison to a **recreational ideology** (in DeLameter, 1989: 46). Reiss has referred to this as permissiveness with affection, that is, premarital sex is acceptable if the couples have a bonded interpersonal relationship (Reiss, 1980). This is embedded in a **sexual double standard** that incorporates gendered assumptions about the relative sexual experience and expertise of women in comparison to men as well as expectations about experience and its meanings, i.e. women are more culturally circumscribed in their sexuality than men.

The sexual double standard refers to an ideology that encourages boys to experience their sexuality, i.e., allows boys to sow their wild oats, while girls are socially sanctioned for the same behavior (Renzetti and Curran, 2003: 171). There is compelling evidence that the double standard still exists (Hyde and Jafee, 2000), although it has begun declining and/or shifting toward an affectional model since the 1970s (Weiss, 2004: 1187; Westheimer and Lopater, 2005). Sexuality is a developmental process in industrialized society; over time, female sexuality develops a more genital component and coterminously male sexuality may mature into a "more complex, diffuse sensuous experience" much like that of the adolescent female (Hyde, 1985: 290; also Kimmel, 2000: 241). In this manner, as people age in industrialized society, their sexuality becomes more alike than different.

Adolescent sexuality in the industrialized society includes masturbation as a component, as it does cross-culturally. A male's first ejaculation is usually experienced during masturbation. Kinsey, Pomeroy, and Martin's (1948) research reported that in 5 percent of the cases with male masturbation during homosexual/homosocial activity, and in 12 percent of the population as a wet dream. Generally, the rate of female masturbation is somewhat lower than males as is their sexual activity in general, both homosexual and heterosexual (Kinsey, 1953). Fifty-eight percent of adolescent boys and 39 percent of adolescent girls reported masturbating at least once in more recent research (Sorensen, 1973). In a study by Gagnon, Simon, and Berger (1970) of high school students, 77 percent of the males and 17 percent of the females self-reported masturbating twice a week or more. More contemporary studies have shown distinct temporal changes with an increase in self-reported masturbation rates. Statistics range from three-quarters of both genders to 80 percent of female adolescents and ninety percent of male adolescents, with frequencies ranging from once a week to daily (Francoeur and Noonan, 2004: 1170; King, 2005). According to Robert T. Francoeur, there are a number of weaknesses and challenges in current autoerotic behavior research conducted in the United States. These include: the absence of recent data on noncollege men and women; the prevalence of small sample sizes; very limited or no data on African Americans or other ethnic groups; and lack of funding for research (Francoeur and Noonan, 2004: 1178).

It is difficult to acquire reliable information about masturbation rates in the United States and other industrialized nations. Adolescent sexual experimentation also includes the custom of making out, enhanced by the car culture of the 1950s and 1960s. Making out usually refers to kissing, but it also may escalate into petting. Petting includes everything up to and short of vaginal intercourse, including oral and manual practices. Through petting, adolescents learn to negotiate cultural rules against vaginal intercourse by discovering alternatives that lead to orgasm. For example, in a study by Newcomer and Udry (1985), 25 percent of the males and 15 percent of the females in a population who had no previous experience with heterosexual coitus engaged in oral-genital practices. Another survey conducted in 2003 by Hollander shows that out of 580 ninth graders in two California high schools, 20 percent of the students were reported as having experienced oral sex whereas 14 percent reported having engaged in penile-vaginal intercourse (Hollander, 2005). The alarming part of this study was that 13 to 14 percent of the students were unaware that chlamydia and HIV were contractible from oral sex. Thirty-eight percent felt that the chances of chlamydia and HIV infection through oral sex were lower than those associated with vaginal sex; and only 50 to 53 percent perceived that chlamydia and HIV could be transmitted through vaginal sex (Hollander, 2005). Another discovery is that these ninth graders acknowledged lower percentages of relationship deterioration, development of bad reputations, getting into trouble, and feelings of guilt associated with oral sex (36 to 63 percent) than with penile-vaginal intercourse (42 to 71 percent) (Hollander, 2005). This suggests that oral sex is now becoming more socially acceptable among U.S. teens. A 2002 study reports that 55 percent of males and 54 percent of females aged fifteen to nineteen years old had engaged in oral sex with someone of the other sex ("Healthy Youth Sexual Risk Behaviors 2006," 2006; Mosher, Chandra and Jones, 2003).

Adolescents also engage in homosexual and heterosexual intercourse. Kinsey and colleagues' statistics, although dated (1948 and 1953), are revealing considering the time frame. Sixty percent of the males and 33 percent of the females reported at least one homosexual or lesbian experience by fifteen years old. These data again support the highly flexible nature of our sexuality and the distinction between behavior and orientation. Studies in industrialized nations reveal that teen sexual activity has fluctuated depending on the time period and the industrialized nation under consideration. Two periods of increases in U.S. premarital sex have been identified; the "Roaring Twenties" from 1918–1930 whose sexual revolution corresponds with women born after 1900 having premarital sex with their fiancés; and 1965–1980, a second sexual revolution with generalized increases in premarital sex (Weiss, 2004a: 1187). Subsequent reports in the eighties substantiate a continuation of this trend. For example, a study of women aged fifteen to forty-four years old (n = 8000) by the Alan Guttmacher Institute found that female teen sexual activity, especially in Caucasian middle and upper classes, was on the increase in the 1980s. They cite the following findings (in "Teen Sexual Activity Rises," 1991: 25) for this period in the United States:

- The percentage of girls aged fifteen to nineteen who reported engaging in sexual activities increased from 47.1 percent in 1982 to 52.25 in 1988.
- The percentage of sexually active girls in the fifteen- to seventeen-year-old age bracket rose from 32.6 percent to 38.4 percent in the same period.
- In 1986, 58 percent of sexually active teenage girls reported having had two or more sex partners.
- In 1982, 48 percent of the sexually active girls aged fifteen to nineteen reported that contraceptives were used in their first sexual intercourse.
- In 1988, 65 percent of the girls fifteen to nineteen reported that contraceptives, mostly condoms, were used in their first sexual intercourse (Alan Guttmacher Institute).

In the 1990s through the present, research indicates that 38 percent of fifteen-year-old girls and 45 percent of fifteen-year-old boys have had sexual intercourse, and 17 percent of seventh and eighth graders have experienced sexual intercourse *(Life's First Great Crossroad,* 2000). Recent statistics on adolescent sexual behavior from the United States Centers for Disease Control and Prevention report that in 2005, 47 percent of high school students have experienced sexual intercourse, and 14 percent of high school students had four or more sex partners during their life ("Healthy Youth Sexual Risk Behaviors 2006," 2006; "Youth Risk Behavior Surveillance— United States, 2005," 2006). Other research points to the average age of **sexarche** or first intercourse as sixteen-and-a-half-years old with the suggestion that American teens are delaying the age of first intercourse (Francoeur and Noonan, 2004: 1188). Black and Hispanic adolescents are significantly more likely to have had intercourse than whites *(Life's First Great Crossroad,* 2000: 16). (See the following discussion of statistics on ethnicity and sex/reproduction/contraception.) Recent research has found that 11 percent of males and females aged fifteen to nineteen years old had engaged in anal sex with someone of the opposite sex; and 3 percent of males aged fifteen to nineteen years old had had anal sex with a male ("Healthy Youth Sexual Risk Behaviors 2006," 2006; Mosher, Chandra and Jones, 2003).

The National Youth Risk Behavior Survey 1991–2005 ("Trends in the Prevalence of Sexual Behaviors") provides additional patterns for ninth through twelfth grade students in private and public schools. This survey is conducted every two years and augments the trends noted. The National Youth Risk Behavior Survey 1991–2005 includes evidence of changes in the following behaviors: decrease in ever had sexual intercourse, decrease in those who have had four or more partners, decrease in those sexually active three months before the survey, an increase in condom use, no change in number of women using birth control pills (other delivery systems not reported). Alcohol or drug use before sexual intercourse increased from 1991–2001 and decreased slightly from 2001 to 2005. AIDS/ HIV education increased from 1991–1997, but decreased from 1997–2005, suggesting an alarming trend. See Figure 10.5.

Countervailing trends for adolescents to make pledges and promises for chastity until marriage are occurring through religious organizations which emphasize abstinence-only sexuality education. These efforts gained funding under the Bush Administration, despite cautions by national and internationally recognized bodies of sex educators including the American Association of Sexuality Educators, Counselors and Therapists; Sexuality Information and Education Council of the United States, and The International Planned Parenthood Federation. How the George W. Bush administration's policy of support for abstinence-only sex education will impact adolescent sexuality over time remains to be determined. However, comparative statistics from other industrialized nations can provide evidence of the influence of trends in sex education (see discussion). Reiss's

1991	1993	1995	1997	1999	2001	2003	2005	Changes from 1991 – 2005	Change from 2003 – 2005
Ever had sexual intercourse									
54.1 (±3.5)3	53.0 (±2.7)	53.1 (±4.5)	48.4 (±3.1)	49.9 (±3.7)	45.6 (±2.3)	46.7 (±2.6)	46.8 (±3.3)	Decreased, 1991 – 2005	No change
Had sexual intercourse with ≥ 4 persons during their life									
18.7 (±2.1)	18.7 (±2.0)	17.8 (±2.7)	16.0 (±1.4)	16.2 (±2.6)	14.2 (±1.2)	14.4 (±1.6)	14.3 (±1.5)	Decreased, 1991 – 2005	No change
Were currently sexually active (Had sexual intercourse with ≥ 1 person during the 3 months preceding the survey.)									
37.5 (±3.1)	37.5 (±2.1)	37.9 (±3.5)	34.8 (±2.2)	36.3 (±3.5)	33.4 (±2.0)	34.3 (±2.1)	33.9 (±2.5)	Decreased, 1991 – 2005	No change
Condom use during last sexual intercourse (Among currently sexually active students.)									
46.2 (±3.3)	52.8 (±2.7)	54.4 (±3.5)	56.8 (±1.6)	58.0 (±4.2)	57.9 (±2.2)	63.0 (±2.5)	62.8 (±2.1)	Increased, 1991 – 2005	No change
Birth control pill use before last sexual intercourse (To prevent pregnancy, among currently sexually active students.)									
20.8 (±2.3)	18.4 (±2.1)	17.4 (±2.2)	16.6 (±2.0)	16.2 (±2.6)	18.2 (±1.7)	17.0 (±2.3)	17.6 (±2.6)	No change, 1991 – 2005	No change
Alcohol or drug use before last sexual intercourse (Among currently sexually active students.)									
21.6 (±2.9)	21.3 (±2.0)	24.8 (±2.8)	24.7 (±1.8)	24.8 (±3.0)	25.6 (±1.7)	25.4 (±2.3)	23.3 (±2.2)	Increased, 1991 – 2001 No change, 2001 – 2005	No change
Ever taught in school about AIDS or HIV infection									
83.3 (±2.8)	86.1 (±2.4)	86.3 (±5.9)	91.5 (±1.1)	90.6 (±1.4)	89.0 (±1.3)	87.9 (±1.9)	87.9 (±1.9)	Increased, 1991 – 1997 Decreased, 1997 – 2005	No change

Figure 10.5 National Youth Risk Behavior Survey 1991–2005, "Trends in the Prevalence of Sexual Behaviors." (*Source*: Department of Health and Human Services, National Center for Chronic Disease Prevention and Health Promotion, Centers for Disease Control and Prevention.) (*Note*: Based on linear and quadratic trend analyses using a logistic regression model controlling for sex, race/ethnicity, and grade; based on t-test analyses.)

"**autonomy theory**" (1967) has relevance for understanding historical and cultural patterns and changes in adolescent sexual expression. Autonomy theory argues that sexual permissiveness will increase in cultural contexts in which adolescents have courtship and dating autonomy. Where systems of control such as parents, religious institutions, and schools inhibit the autonomy and independence of adolescents, premarital sexual permissiveness will be reduced. The trend for increasing autonomy has been occurring in the United States and other industrialized nations (Francoeur and Noonan, 2004; Reiss, 1967).

The evidence suggests that comprehensive sex education (which includes AIDS education, discussion of various STI/HIV and pregnancy prevention options in addition to abstinence) must be having some impact because

58 percent of the fifteen- to nineteen-year-old males used a condom during their first intercourse (Sonenstein, Pleck, and Ku, 1989). According to data from the National Survey of Adolescent Males (NSAM), between 1988 and 1995, the rate of condom use at last intercourse among fifteen- to nineteen-year-old males increased from 56 percent to 69 percent (Murphy and Boggess, 1998); although data from the Centers for Disease Control and Prevention indicates that in 2005, 34 percent of currently sexually active high school students did not use a condom during last sexual intercourse ("Youth Risk Behavior Surveillance-United States, 2005," 2005).

It is possible to become pregnant during first intercourse and it is also possible to contract HIV as well. We cannot assume that U.S. adolescents are using contraceptives regularly. The rate of contraceptive use with first sex has increased substantially among adolescents. For females (ages fifteen to nineteen) in 2002, 75 percent used some form of contraception at first intercourse, while 82 percent of males (ages fifteen to nineteen) did so. Despite this positive trend, teens are inconsistent in contraceptive use. For example, only 28 percent of females and 47 percent of males reported use of a condom every time they had penile-vaginal sex in the previous twelve months (Franzetta et al., 2006). Using contraception is difficult for adolescents since it is loaded with symbolic meaning about oneself as a sexual being. By using contraception adolescents must acknowledge that they are engaging in preplanned sex. This may lead to conflicting feelings regarding values and sense of self as a "moral" being. With adolescence in industrialized society comes a number of questions for the individual concerning sexuality and contraception.

ADOLESCENT STERILITY/FERTILITY

The decision to engage in sex is not without risks. AIDS and other STDs are endemic in this culture as are the consequences of an unwanted pregnancy. Teen pregnancy is a particular problem in the United States. Why is the United States' adolescent pregnancy rate higher than in other countries? What factors influence teen pregnancy from a socio-cultural perspective? One possible contributing factor is a phenomenon known as **adolescent sterility**. This is presented in greater depth in our discussion of birth control in Chapter 12. Adolescent sterility or subfertility refers to a period between the age of menarche and reproductive maturity, which occurs at about twenty-three years old. Despite the onset of puberty, intercourse is less likely to result in pregnancy than in a reproductively mature woman (Ford and Beach, 1951: 172–173). In a number of societies, adolescent females are permitted premarital sex, yet pregnancies are unlikely to result (Ford and Beach, 1951). Adolescent sterility occurs in societies that Ford and Beach (1951: 190) list as permissive, that is, there are no sexual restrictions on adolescent sexual activity short of incest regulations. The list of permissive societies is too long to reproduce here, but examples include the Ainu, Aymara, Trobriand Islanders, and Yapese among numerous others. Ford and Beach (1951) list forty-nine societies, although adolescent sterility does not necessarily correlate with this entire list.

Adolescent sterility allows teenagers and youths to experience their sexuality as well as learn and grow as individuals. It provides for an extended period of practice and discovery about oneself as a sexual being without the burden and the additional concern and responsibility of parenthood. Sexual experimentation in these societies allows for a far easier transition to marital sex than in societies which prohibit exploration during adolescence, and then expect that the couple will be able to reverse their attitudes about sex after marriage (Ford and Beach, 1951: 195). Adolescent subfertility in combination with permissive cultural attitudes also provides for an important period of learning without the status changes that accompany childbirth. In most societies, childbirth provides men and women special status; sometimes it may confer adulthood while in others adulthood may occur prior to parenthood. Regardless, having a child is viewed as an important status marker.

As we suggest in Chapter 12, adolescent sterility does not seem operative in U.S. populations. Based on the "critical fat hypothesis" (Frisch, 1978), it is believed that ovulation occurs only when certain relative levels of body fat have been reached. This is directly related to the requirements for successful reproduction and lactation. Lancaster (1985: 18) attributes the loss of adolescent sterility among teenage girls in contemporary societies to: "[s]edentism combined with high levels of caloric intake [that] lead to early deposition of body fat in young girls . . ."; this " 'fools' the body into early biological maturation long before cognitive and social maturity are reached" (Lancaster, 1985: 18).

Without adolescent sterility as a damper on fertility in combination with adolescent sexuality without contraception, the result is a very high adolescent pregnancy rate in the United States. In the 1980s, for every 1,000 females, 110 aged fifteen through nineteen became pregnant (Henshaw et al., 1989). Teen pregnancy rates peaked in 1990, but since then, U.S. teenagers have shown a decrease in these rates by twenty-two percent. More recent data show an average of only 83.6 pregnancies per 1,000 women aged fifteen to nineteen in 2000 with a decreased rate of 2 percent from 1999 ("U.S. Teenage Pregnancy Statistics," 2004). This differentially impacts adolescent African American females where adolescent pregnancy is twice as high as for Caucasian females in this age group. If we compare Caucasian female pregnancy rates with those of African American teens, the former shows a rate of 71.4 per 1,000 girls while African American women show a rate of 153.3 per 1,000 ("U. S. Teenage Pregnancy Statistics," 2004). See discussion regarding abstinence-only sex education and comprehensive sex education in industrialized nations.

Interestingly, in comparison with thirty-seven other countries, the United States pregnancy rate is "higher than that of almost any other developed country. While U.S. adolescents are no more sexually active than young people in other industrialized countries, they are much more likely to become pregnant" (Byer and Shainberg, 1991: 386; also Darroch et al., 2001). According to a recent article found in the Guttmacher archives, teenagers in the United States are still more likely to have sexual intercourse before age fifteen and have shorter and more sporadic sexual relationships than teenagers in Canada, France, Great Britain, and Sweden. As a result, they are more likely to have more than one partner in a given year (2002). Figure 10.6 illustrates the trends in birth, abortion, and pregnancy rates of fifteen- to nineteen-year-olds by specific developed countries. For further information, consult the Guttmacher Institute, The Centers for Disease Control and Prevention, the Population Resource Center, The Henry Kaiser Family Foundation, and the Population Council.

Unfortunately, the statistics for the United States, and the other countries for that matter, do not distinguish differences among ethnic groups and other minorities. Nevertheless, these differences between the United

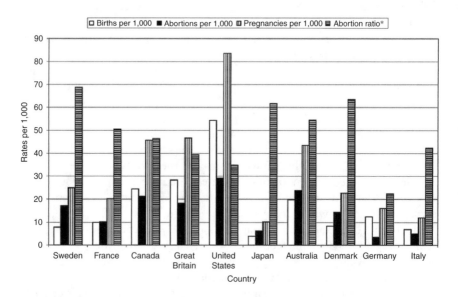

Figure 10.6 Birth, abortion, and pregnancy rates in selected industrialized countries ages 15–19 by country. (*Source*: Compiled from information provided by Alan Guttmacher Institute, Centers for Disease Control and Prevention, Population Resource Center, The Henry Kaiser Family Foundation, and Population Council. *Data from 2000–2003.)

States and other industrialized nations have been largely attributed to the absence of:

• national comprehensive sex education programming;
• readily available birth control; and
• a sex-positive attitude in this culture in contrast to other industrialized societies.

If we in the United States are to reduce pregnancy and STI rates effectively, we must desensitize the issue of condom use and remove taboos associated with this method (Sinding, 2005). It is also important that we not only provide condoms, but make available information on how to use condoms correctly in a culturally sensitive manner to enhance their effectiveness (Sinding, 2005). In summary, lessons from industrialized countries with low levels of teenage pregnancy/birth and STIs correlate social acceptance of adolescent sexual relations with comprehensive sexuality education that emphasizes the avoidance of STIs/HIV and pregnancy prevention, and provides easy access to contraceptive and reproductive health sources ("Teenagers' Sexual and Reproductive Health," 2004).

What is the price of adolescent pregnancy and childbirth?

• Teen mothers are more likely to drop out of school than their peers and are significantly less likely to earn a high school degree (only one-third go on to earn a degree) or to earn a college degree (only 1.5 percent earn a college degree by age thirty).
• Teen motherhood costs the United States 7 billion dollars annually in public assistance, child health care, foster care, etc.
• The children of teen mothers are often more inclined to have health problems which are a result of birth weight and premature births. Low birth weights lead to problems in childhood development and extended health risks (Weiss, 2000, 2006).

In addition, other problems prevail among teenage mothers. Adding to their economic vulnerability is an increased likelihood of a repeat birth to teenaged mothers; more than one in five give birth each year ("Repeat Births to Teenagers Carry High Individual and Societal Costs," 2000; "Risks and Disadvantages are Raised for Teenage Mothers," 2001). Children of teenaged mothers are at a higher risk of having educational difficulties and disabilities that are related to their mother's socioeconomic positioning (Weiss, 2006; "Young Mothers Disadvantage, Not Their Age Itself," 2001).

SEX EDUCATION IN THE UNITED STATES

Directly related to the problem of teenage pregnancy is the issue of sex education in the United States. Sex education in the United States can be contrasted with traditional nontechnologically complex societies. As we discussed previously, families whose sleeping quarters are shared provide an opportunity for children to become aware of the sexual activities of their parents and/or siblings. Sex in these situations is undertaken with discretion, and we know of no culture in which children and youths are allowed to watch openly. For example, among the Mangaians, a sex-positive Polynesian culture in which premarital sex is the norm, parents do not discuss sex with their young children. But because Mangaians live in one-room houses, the opportunity for discrete observation does occur. However, the specifics and details of sex and reproduction are learned outside the home, not unlike in the United States (Marshall, 1971: 109).

Without rites of passage to help them make the transition to adult status and also to provide avenues for learning about sexuality, where do industrialized adolescents learn about sexuality? Research suggests that it isn't from parents, but rather from peers. This is not to suggest that parents have no influence on their children's sexual behavior. In fact, during the childhood and the "tween years" (ages nine to thirteen), parents are the most important influence on children's lives regarding their values, attitudes, and beliefs. However, a national survey by the Kaiser Foundation of fifteen- to seventeen-year-olds regarding parent-teen communication found:

- Many teens wait until after they have had sex to talk to their parents about sex; that is, if they ever do. One in four teen girls and nearly one in two teen boys who have had sexual intercourse say their parents don't know about it.
- Among parents in the know, many are finding out about their teens' sex lives later than they might like to, or at least too late to have an influence on the choices their children make, or to encourage them to protect themselves.
- Of all the teens surveyed—including both those who have had sex as well as those who have not—half have never had a conversation with a parent about how to know when you are ready to have sex.
- Even fewer have talked with a parent about how to bring up topics like birth control, condoms or sexually transmitted disease (STD) testing with someone they are dating.
- Most teens aren't talking about their sexual health with a doctor either. Less than a third report having talked with a health care provider about HIV/AIDS, other STDs, or condoms ("Sex Smarts: A Public Information Partnership," 2002).

Communication between parents and children is an essential ingredient in adolescent sexual behavior; open communication with parents has been shown to influence the timing of first intercourse and whether protection against STI and pregnancy occurs ("Sex Smarts: A Public Information Partnership, 2002). A study of 1,000 parents of thirteen- to seventeen-year-olds found that there are gender, ethnic, and socioeconomic variables related to teen-parent communication (Swain, Ackerman, and Ackerman, 2006: 753.e9):

• Low income, minority parents reported more discussion with their teens about the negative consequences of sex and where to obtain birth control than high income, white parents.
• Politically conservative, religious parents reported more discussion with their teens about the negative consequences of sex than their liberal and nonreligious counterparts.
• In general, nonreligious parents reported more discussion about where to obtain birth control than religious parents.
• Parents were less likely to talk with males, younger teens, and teens not believed to be romantically involved.

Salience of gender in parent and teen discussions (see last bulleted point) has been recorded by other researchers as well. Diiorio, Kelly, and Hockenberry-Eaton (1999: 181–189) found that adolescents of both genders talked about sex more with their mothers than their fathers; they were more inclined to talk about sex with their mothers than their peers, but more likely to discuss sex with their peers than their fathers.

The mass media should not be underestimated as a source of sex education (Kunkel et al., 2003, 2005). In fact, media, specifically television viewing, takes precedence over the peer group according to some researchers (Kunkel et al., 2003, 2005). In fact, Brown, Halpern and L'Engle (2005) refer to the media as the "sexual super peer." Research indicates that children and adolescents watch on the average three hours of television a day. Television can have both a positive as well as negative outcome on young people's sexual decision making, including use of safer sex and pregnancy prevention strategies. Donnerstein and Smith (2001) and Gunter (2002) regard television as an important vehicle for sexual socialization of adolescents influencing knowledge, values, beliefs, attitudes and behavior (in Kunkel et al., 2005). Although television programming, which may offer sexuality education information (e.g., STI/HIV information, safer sex and pregnancy prevention has increased since 1998), it has subsequently leveled off since 2002. Unfortunately, the vast majority of content does not include attention to these issues (Kunkel et al., 2005).

Other significant sources of information on sexuality and influences on adolescent sexuality besides parents and the mass media include schools, political policy, and religious institutions (Halpern et al., 2000). Virginity pledges are abundant in church programming, although not all churches support abstinence-only approaches. For example, a survey of African American churches found church leaders were open to including sexuality as a topic for their health education programs, including information on contraceptive education (Coyne-Beasley and Schoenbach, 2000). The "virginity pledge" approach was begun by the Southern Baptist Church with their "True Love Waits" program. Virginity pledges burgeoned in the mid-1990s especially among evangelical Christian organizations. However, research has found that teens making a private pledge to wait until they are more mature to have sex is more effective in reducing the likelihood that they will engage in sexual intercourse and oral sex. This is contrasted with those who made formal pledges such as a virginity pledge, which had no effect on teens' sexual behavior (Bersamin et al., 2005: 428).

In contrast to this research, which showed no effect on teenage sex, Hannah Brückner of Yale University and Peter Bearman of Columbia University conducted a study of virginity pledging teens and reported virginity-pledging teens were actually more likely to engage in riskier sexual behavior; they were less likely to use condoms, and more likely to engage in oral and anal sex. In addition, intercourse was only delayed (but not prevented) by twelve to eighteen months among the virginity pledgers and they were less likely to know their STI status (Brückner and Bearman, 2005; 271–278; Wind, 2005). The Bush government redefined what was meant by abstinence in their program for Community Based Abstinence Education out of concern that virginity-pledging teens might indeed be engaging in oral and anal sex as methods of fulfilling abstinence vows. Abstinence vis-à-vis Community Based Abstinence Education was defined as "no sexual activity until marriage with sexual activity defined as any genital contact or sexual stimulation." Indeed, critics maintained that this definition could even be extended to include kissing (Dailard, 2006; Verrilli, 2006).

The public and private school systems in the United States that offer sex education curriculums are also an important institution in teen sexuality education. Nationwide, schools are not uniform in terms of content and coverage. Socioeconomic variables influence teen sexual expression and can impact the influence of variables such as religion, the schools, and the mass media. According to the Centers for Disease Control and Prevention (2000) low family income, high unemployment, and high crime rates are associated with adolescent risky sexual behavior and unprotected sex (in LeVay and Valente, 2002: 384).

Concerns over sex education gained prominence in the 1960s as a result of SIECUS (The Sex Information and Education Council of the United States) and AASECT (the American Association of Sex Educators, Counselors and Therapists). Research indicates that the question of sex education is not "if" such programs should occur but rather "what kind of approach." Surveys indicate that that the majority of Americans favor more **comprehensive** sexuality education; that is, education that includes information on a variety of options, over abstinence-only education ("Facts in Brief: Sexuality Education: Sex and Pregnancy Among Teenagers," 2002). Keep in mind that comprehensive sexuality education programs in schools are still fairly rare. Eighty-six percent of the public school districts that have a policy to teach sexuality education mandate that programs must promote abstinence only. Abstinence as the only option occurs in 35 percent of the programs for sex education. Such programs either completely prohibit discussion of contraception or limit discussion to focus on the ineffectiveness of contraceptive techniques. The remaining 51 percent demand abstinence must be taught as the preferred option but permit discussion of the effectiveness of contraception. And only 14 percent of those schools with policies for sexuality education include a comprehensive approach that includes abstinence as one of several options. There is regional variation in sexuality education with half the districts in the south promoting abstinence-only education, compared with 20 percent of the school districts in the Northeast ("Facts in Brief: Sexuality Education: Sex and Pregnancy among Teenagers," 2002).

Sex education programs vary a great deal in their success rates. Though a number of stances may be taken, we have an excellent example of what doesn't work. This has historical precedence: the "Reaganesque" "Just Say No" approach of the 1980s. This slogan was the result of a 1981 effort to reduce teenage pregnancies without advocating birth control through the Adolescent Family Life Act (ALFA), a congressional act that funded programs promoting premarital abstinence. One study even found that "participants [in one ALFA project] engaged in more sexual activity than controls" (Troiano, 1990: 101). This approach has continued with subsequent Republican and conservative perspectives on sexuality education. For example, there are three federal programs that funded restrictive abstinence-only under the Bush government:

- Section 510 pf the Social Security Act,
- the Adolescent Family Life Act (incorporates a teenage pregnancy prevention component),
- the Special Projects of Regional and National Significance program (SPRANS).

Since scare tactics have proven ineffectual, sex education curriculums whose goals are to reduce adolescent pregnancy (and STI/HIV) through the use of contraception can be very successful. Such programs must take a multidimensional and comprehensive approach (Troiano, 1990: 101). By that, we mean that not only should the mechanics of reproduction be addressed, but the psychological and social aspects as well, including lesbian, gay, bisexual, and transgender issues. Concern over the threat of AIDS has recently given a new impetus to sex education. Other societal trends are also reflected in new approaches to sex education development. For example, sexuality is in a historical niche where it is now regarded as an important and very natural component of one's life. This view is also related to trends in which sex and procreation were separated resulting in a greater emphasis on sex for pleasure. These patterns are in their incipient stages and are just beginning to be felt in sex education which is still suffering from conservative paradigms of fear and abstinence only.

The evidence in regard to abstinence models is intriguing. Apparently sex education programs do not impact the likelihood of sexual activity one way or another, but rather may actually increase the likelihood of contraception and hence affect pregnancy and STI transmission including HIV infection (Kirby, 1984; in Kelly, 1990; Kirby, 2001: 337–340). This is expressed in the contrast between European sex education programs and those in the United States. European programs take for granted that adolescents are having sex and their approach consequently focuses on the issues of how to combat STIs/HIV and pregnancy (Francoeur, 1991a: 125; Boonstra, 2002): "Americans are mainly concerned with keeping teenagers from being sexually active and enjoying it" (Francoeur, 1991a: 125); and U.S. adults are less accepting than their European counterparts about teens having sex. European adults and their sexuality education programs carry a message that sex is a natural part of committed relationships and that teenagers have a responsibility to practice safer sex strategies and prevention of pregnancy (Boonstra, 2002).

Extensive yet ineffective programming is abundant in the United States. This has arisen from the explicit assumption that teens do not posses enough information on sexuality in general and its consequences (Francoeur and Noonan, 2004: 1192). The truth, however, is that teenagers are receiving plenty of sexual information from peers and the media, yet our prevalent abstinence-only approaches are severely ineffective in their assumption that teens will discontinue sex as a recreational activity (Koch, 2004: 1174–1175). Additionally, the use of contraceptives, particularly the "pill," by sexually active teenage women is lower in the United States than in other developed countries. This contributes to the high pregnancy rates in the United States as compared with other countries (Tew and Wind, 2002). Until very recently, all fifty states had taken advantage of federally sanctioned abstinence-only sex education funding available for use in high schools. Several states, however, including Maine, Pennsylvania, and California, turned down this federal subsidy for sex education specifically because it did not include a comprehensive approach (Kehrl, 2005).

COMPARISON AND CONTRAST: PREPARATION FOR AND TRANSITION TO ADULTHOOD

Adolescence is a culturally constituted phase associated with puberty. As we have discussed, whether a culture even acknowledges a period of adolescence differs, as does the length of time allocated to such a stage. Therefore, adulthood and the age at which we are perceived to reach it also differs considerably. Despite the variability of how and when children reach adulthood, cultures provide mechanisms for the change of status. As we have seen, this occurs through rites of passage.

As we introduced earlier, Mead's study of Samoan girls' adolescence challenged our own industrialized conceptions of adolescence as a period of strife due to the pubescent surge of hormones. Mead's study refuted this view in a controversial analysis that argued that Samoan girls experienced a harmonious adolescence. Mead was as interested in U.S. adolescence as she was in Samoan adolescence and has provided some clues about the industrialized adolescent experience at the time. Some of her ideas still ring true since the publication of her book, *Coming of Age in Samoa*, in 1928, although parts of her conclusions are dated. For example, her frustration hypothesis with its obvious Freudian dimension is regarded as a questionable explanation. Mead's interpretation of why adolescence was such a torturous time for U.S. youths rested on the idea that urges for sex were frustrated and suppressed by norms against teenage sex. This thesis ignored other dimensions of adolescence as a period of growth. In the United States, these norms were associated with the age of marriage which at the time was ideally delayed until after graduation from high school. Mead felt that teenage sexual norms that allowed making out and petting just flamed a libidinal inferno that must ultimately be repressed. Teens expressed their frustration with this through rebellion and revolt (Davis, n.d.: 3). In Mead's view, U.S. culture emerged as a repressive one and Samoan culture was regarded as permissive because these sexual urges in teenagers were not frustrated.

Like Mead, Spock regarded as the U.S. expert on childrearing, has also accepted rebelliousness as a given for adolescents. In this regard he stated: "It isn't often realized that the rebelliousness of adolescents is mainly an expression of rebelliousness with parents, particularly the rivalry of son with father and girls with mother..." (with Rothenberg, 1985: 503). In contrast to Mead, Spock and Needlman (2004) recognized rebelliousness as a powerful and positive force leading to the establishment of autonomy in the individual and ultimately to creative change in society. While the question of U.S. adolescent strife is interesting, there is a danger in perspectives such as Mead's and Spock's when applied to a complex society such as ours. Dona Davis' (n.d.: 4) comment relates equally as well to Spock, although it addresses Margaret Mead:

> This...comparison of types...not only stereotyped sexual behaviors in non-Western societies, it stereotyped adolescent sexual behavior in our society. Researchers ignored the social complexities of sexual styles among adolescents as well as the many and various ways in which young people negotiate the rules of their culture to achieve sexual satisfaction (Davis, n.d.: 4).

Although there is a widespread belief that adolescence is a period of turmoil for U.S. teens, we must be careful not to overgeneralize. Bear in mind the importance of ethnicity and socioeconomic status as factors affecting how adolescence is experienced and expressed. This is not to say that we cannot describe some of the patterns among U.S. adolescents, but that we must remember these trends usually represent the white middle class, and by so doing gloss over the variety of expressions of U.S. adolescence among different ethnic groups and classes.

Let us contrast what we have learned about rites of passage (discussed earlier in this chapter) with the experience of the U.S. teenager. Again, we are not referring to the various indigenous and ethnic peoples in the United States that may have very rich rites of passage. For example, many Native American peoples maintain their traditional rites of passage for young females and males including the vision quest, and the Jewish bar/bat mitzvahs also provide critical recognition of life-passage changes as do many other immigrant and ethnic groups. As the industrialized child undergoes puberty with its accompanying physical signs, are there any rituals or rites of passage that publicly recognize these changes on a cultural level? Although individual parents may celebrate their daughter's first menstruation when that occurs, very often it is treated with secrecy and embarrassment. With the growth of male body hair and deepening of the voice, a father may acknowledge this with "You're a man now, son!" But what does that mean? The meaning is not spelled out, neither are the markers of adulthood evident. Where are the ritual referents to know when adolescence is over and adulthood starts? How does an adolescent know when this is going to happen?

In the United States, generally the transition to adulthood is a diffused one unmarked ritually. We live in a ritually poor society. Though the symbolic aspects of adulthood are few, there are several societal markers that give an individual the legal status of adult as opposed to that of minor. This is known as reaching the **age of majority** and includes issues such as: the age at which one is considered a consenting adult, the age at which an individual may be married, and the age one may be tried in court as an adult. These vary state by state. Other events that may contribute to adult status include economic independence, marriage, and the birth of a child. But none is sufficient in and of itself as a clearly defined event that identifies the individual as an adult. In short, adulthood, for many U.S. people occurs in an unintegrated way, in contrast to U.S. ethnic groups and nonindustrialized societies in which distinct symbolic referents for adulthood are expressed ritually or ceremonially. The industrialized adolescent finds herself/himself no longer a child, but certainly not an adult. They are betwixt and between youth and adulthood in a society that provides very little in the way of well-defined status markers. In fact, they often receive conflicting messages from society about their transitioning through the stages from childhood to adulthood.

Initiation ceremonies are well known for their ritual ordeals, yet the novices know that at the end of these tests they will be unequivocally declared adults. In contrast, U.S. adolescents generally have no tests or tasks that once accomplished will identify them unequivocally as women and men. Without rituals of transition to guide the adolescent on a journey into adulthood, social adaptation and transition to adulthood may breed areas of conflict and tension (Shapiro, 1979: 283). One of these is in the area of sexuality. In fact, Miller and Simon (1980: 153) have described adolescent sexuality as "behavior in search of meaning."

The U.S. teenager is kept in a liminal status of no longer a child but not yet an adult despite their biological maturity. In our society, adulthood is associated with sexual rights and until that time teenagers do not "own" their own bodies—they do not have the freedom to experience their sexuality until they are adults. This is supported as well by the legal system. Thus, U.S. teenagers may be fully functioning sexual beings, but they are not regarded as having rights to that sexuality. In this regard they are still children. Their sexual desires are not regarded as legitimate as adult ones.

This situation stems from a variety of sources, including an industrialized sex-negative or sex-ambiguous worldview, a dogma that confounds sex with romantic love, definitions of adulthood, and conflicting attitudes about contraception and abortion. Though adolescent sexuality is a complex issue, one dominant perspective regards teenagers as too immature psychologically to handle the sexual experience, although we have seen this is not the case in many societies that are not sexually restrictive or in European industrialized societies. We must, however, pay attention to the cultural context of the adolescent experience in the United States. The industrialized view of sex is that it is not to be taken casually (Clement, 1990: 58; Herdt, 2004). There is, however a double standard that allows males more leeway in this regard than females (Reiss, 1967). This standard is one which stems from the equation of love and marriage, and expands to also include premarital couples. As a result sex is problematic for many U.S. adolescents.

We must also remember that the world is getting smaller through globalization, migration, emigration, and the Internet. It is all the more important to emphasize the cultural factors in the construction of adolescence including ethnicity, class, and other social and economic variables as these intersect with the gender and sexual system of young people approaching adulthood. Teenage pregnancy and the concomitant reduction in life changes, STIs and AIDS are all-important issues in adolescent sexuality. U.S. ambivalence about teenage sexuality, in contrast with other industrialized nations, leaves U.S. youths undereducated regarding sexuality and hence unprepared for making informed decisions about the many challenges to their health and life chances as we have discussed. Early pregnancy and childbirth, inequities in power for adolescent girls in making decisions affecting their sexual health, STIs, AIDS, and the exacerbation of these problems because of poverty are incredible challenges facing us today.

SUMMARY

1   Puberty is a physiological phenomenon, while adolescence is a cultural one that may or may not be coterminous with puberty.
2   Rites of passage are introduced as rituals that facilitate the transition from childhood to adulthood.
3   Rites of passage have three phases and distinct functions in nonindustrial societies.
4   Theories of rites of passage are addressed. Female ceremonies are more common, but male ceremonies are more elaborate and severe.
5   Female genital cutting is discussed including prevalence, practices, and controversial issues.
6   The Sambia are discussed as an example of a rite of passage in which homoerotic behavior occurs in boy-inseminating rites in male rites of passage.
7   Nonindustrialized sexual behavior among adolescents is presented in nonindustrial as well as third world countries.
8   Industrialized, particularly U.S. teenage, sexuality is reviewed.
9   The role of adolescent sterility and its relationship to sexual practices is described.
10   Sex education in the United States is analyzed.
11   The transition to adulthood in the United States is contrasted with the transition in societies that have rites of passage.

Thought-provoking questions

1   Where do you stand on female genital cutting? Why do you think there has not been a similar concern around male circumcision? Do you think there is a relationship between female genital cutting and male circumcision in the countries where it is practiced?
2   Compare and contrast high school and college graduation as a rite of passage for U.S. youths. How would you describe the changes of status after each graduation? Are they similar or different? What other rites of passage are found in industrialized nations? Do not limit your discussion to the white middle class but bring in diversity in your discussion.
3   What are your feelings about abstinence-only sex education? Have you, would you, or have you known anyone who has taken a virginity pledge? What is your/their experience? Do think collegiate men and women have different perspectives on the issue of virginity pledges and abstinence-only perspectives?

SUGGESTED RESOURCES

Books

Carpenter, Laura. 2005. *Virginity Lost: An Intimate Portrait of First Sexual Experiences.* New York: New York University Press.

Chang, Heewon. 1992. *Adolescent Life and Ethos: An Ethnography of a US High School.* Washington: The Falmer Press.

Gruenbaum, Ellen. 2001. *The Female Circumcision Controversy: An Anthropological Perspective.* Philadelphia: University of Pennsylvania Press.

Mernissi, Fatima. 1994. *Dreams of Trespass: Tales of a Harem Girlhood.* Reading: Addison-Wesley.

Web sites

Boonstra, Heather. 2002. "Teen Pregnancy: Trends and Lessons Learned." *The Guttmacher Report on Public Policy*, February, 5(1): 1–6. www.guttmacher.or/pubs/tgr/05/1/gr050107.html.

Darroch, Jacqueline, Jennifer J. Frost, Susheela Singh, and Study Team. 2001. "Teenage Sexual and Reproductive Behavior in Developed Countries: Can More Progress Be Made?" Occasional Report Number 3. The Alan Guttmacher Institute, November, 1–120. http://www.guttmacher.org. Last accessed 11/09/07.

"Sex Smarts: A Public Information Partnership." 2002. Henry J. Kaiser Family Foundation and *Seventeen Magazine*. http://www.kff.org/entpartnerships/upload/Teens-and-Sexual-Health-Communication-Summary-of-Findings.pdf.

11 Topics in adult sexuality
Human sexual response

CHAPTER OVERVIEW

1 Discusses the importance of culture in shaping beliefs and practices; introduces erotocentricty.
2 Focuses on the ethnographic and cross-cultural record and human sexual response, including Mangaian and Tantric perspectives.
3 Presents classic and contemporary industrialized theories of sexuality.
4 Outlines major topics in problems of desire and sexual response.
5 Emphasizes the importance of context and culture in understanding concerns with sexuality, including industrialized approaches.
6 Examines nonindustrialized and indigenous emic perspectives regarding issues in sexual functioning.

EXPERIENCING SEXUALITY AND HUMAN SEXUAL
RESPONSE (HSR)

How we experience and express our human sexuality is a physiological response that occurs within the larger context of culture. Like other behaviors, human sexuality varies cross-culturally and is influenced by:

- our adaptation to the environment (how people survive).
- social organization including family and kin group.
- the structure and complexity of the political and economic systems including rank, class and power.
- sacred and religious systems.
- gender stratification and the position of women in society.
- gender ideologies and expectations, including status, roles and gender relations.

These are just some of the cultural influences shaping human sexuality.[1]
   Anthropologists and others have recently turned their attention to scrutinizing even further the "variations in meanings and narratives between

individuals, across cultures, moving research, education and policy closer to the voices and experiences of local cultures and their moral worlds" (Herdt, 2004: 48). How humans experience their sexuality in terms of desire, arousal, and expression is a biological, psychological, and cultural phenomenon. The biology/physiology of sexuality is encountered through the lens of culture which informs our psycho-emotive worlds. According to Herdt (1999: 101), there is also a great deal of individual variation among us in our **sexual subjectivity**, that is, how we experience and express sexuality, including individual attributes like personalities, histories, and sense of self. Each of us brings subjectivity into our interpretation of our society's sexual system, to include both internal meanings as well as those derived from the wider social system. An interest in how individual variation intersects with the cultural in understanding sexuality is part of a broader revolution in anthropology that has challenged notions of homogeneity and stability (Herdt, 1999; Manderson, Bennett, and Sheldrake, 1999; Suggs and Miracle, 1999). Culture must therefore be understood as dynamic, containing elements of contradiction and negotiation as well as historicity and must be inclusive of individuals and events (Bolin and Granskog, 2003).

By presenting human sexuality in its widest possible scope, incorporating biological, psychological, and cultural perspectives, with attention to the subjectivity and agency of individuals within their cultural matrix, our intent is to avoid Euro-American erotocentricity—that is, using our own values in judging the erotic lives and sexual cultures of other people.

The sexual values of the industrialized world are not the only standard for sex, nor are these always the best or "right way." Nonindustrialized societies and indigenous cultures are not exotic, strange, bad, or wrong—in short, "other." Approaching sexuality through cultural relativism will facilitate an appreciation of other cultures and lead us to a critical analysis of our own industrial worldviews. Industrial society did not create sex, nor are its citizens the only ones with theories of human sexual response. Ethnocentrism operates like blinders, shaping our view of what is normal and abnormal and good and bad. Ethnocentrism prohibits us from accepting variation for what it is, the expression of our biological, psychological, and cultural diversity.

THE CROSS-CULTURAL SPECTRUM: INDIGENOUS AND NONINDUSTRIALIZED SEXUALITY

The ethnographic record is filled with sexual behaviors both familiar and foreign to the denizens of industrial society. Cross-cultural evidence highlights not only the vast spectrum of sexuality, but its equally dramatic variation in meaning, metaphor, and symbol. The **social construction** of sexuality (**cultural constructionism**), that is, how societies produce and create sexual meanings, behaviors and subjectivities, is not only important in fostering cultural awareness, but is crucial in formulating strategies to deal with global social problems such as HIV/AIDS and other STIs, unplanned pregnancies, and women's reproductive rights. Vance and Pollis assert that cultural constructionism:

> [has] suggested that sexuality was not a biological given determined by organs and acts but a profoundly social product in which bodily sensations were linked to sexual acts, identities and meanings in ways that were fluid and changeable over place and time. (1990: 2)

The importance of culture in the patterning sexuality has been the cornerstone of anthropological research on this subject. (For anthropological research emphasizing evolutionary and more biologically framed approaches to sex see Chapter 3.) The now classic ethnographic studies that emphasized or included data on sexual practices such as the work of Malinowski (1961 [1927]), Benedict (1934), and Mead (1961 [1928]), among numerous others, provided the fodder for the HRAF files and ethnology, furthering the comparative study of cultures (discussed in Chapter 1). The HRAF allowed for cross-cultural comparisons for hypothesis testing, identifying trends, patterns, and themes in sexual behaviors. As noted earlier, Ford and Beach (1951) offered the first and most provocative work on sexuality at the time, providing a compendium of information on the details and specifics of sexual practices and beliefs. The ethnographic and the comparative perspectives represent two approaches that are still current in the cross-cultural study of sexuality. However, as definitions of sexuality have changed over time, so has the discipline of anthropology and the interests of anthropologists.[2]

Herdt (1999: 102–103) and others have commented on the changes that have occurred in anthropological research since the early days of ethnography: "anthropologists from the 30s to the 70s, largely ignored erotics and sexuality, the body, the emotions of the individual actor, and the passions pertaining to them (e.g., Lewin and Lelap, 1996). Sexual excitement and orgasm were completely unstudied until recently. Differences in meanings of social practices, such as the difference between the genders and their experience of sexual relations, were largely ignored in the paradigm (Vance, 1991). Even more fundamental is the thesis that nonindustrialized communities differ substantially in sexual and social desires; hence, different individuals within the same social strata or class or age group might feel contrasting or even aberrant desires compared with their peers or contemporaries in the society (Herdt and Stoller, 1990). Consequently, it is not so curious that the cross-cultural study of sexuality advanced so little until the recent work of a small number of heterosexual scholars, followed by feminist and gay and lesbian scholars after the 1970s (Gagnon and Parker, 1995).

Until relatively recently the ethnographic research has also been far richer on the subject of heterosexual erotic preferences rather than homoerotic and bisexual behaviors with a few exceptions, such as the earlier work of Westermark (1956 [1906]), Stewart (1960), Ford and Beach (1951), to name a few. Over the past thirty-five years this situation has been in the process of being remedied through the work of anthropologists such as Gilbert Herdt, Walter Williams, Evelyn Blackwood, Ester Newton, Kath Weston, and Richard Parker among numerous others (Manderson, Bennet, and Sheldrake, 1999). Chapter 14 addresses sexual orientation in greater depth. The recent anthropological approaches offer nuanced explorations of emic constructions of sex.

Carrillo's (2002) The Night is Young: Sexuality in Mexico in the Time of AIDS *is instructive. Mexican gender relations are patriarchal, supported by a masculine paradigm of machismo. Gender norms expect women's subordination and submissiveness. This power differential can impact sexual risk taking and pregnancy prevention as well. According to Carrillo, in contrast to men, "good" women are expected to be sexually inexperienced. For a woman to ask a man to use a condom implies that she is a "loose" woman; consequently women are reluctant to ask men to use condoms. Machismo also extends into the relationships of men who have sex with other men. The active and penetrating partner is not regarded as gay, only the passive and receptive partner is considered* maricon *(queer), a stigmatized identity in Mexico. The system of* machismo *also creates inequities in power between male sex partners, with the man who is penetrated regarded as passive/subordinate. Like women, the* maricon *partner is reluctant to negotiate condom use for fear of losing or antagonizing his partner. Both women and men who are penetrated fear asking for a condom because it carries a message of infidelity or mistrust.*

Included among the sexual behaviors reported for heterosexuals, regardless of marital status, are: vaginal, anal, and **interfemoral intercourse** (the penis is placed between the partner's thighs), **cunnilingus** (oral stimulation of the vulva), **fellatio** (oral stimulation of the penis), **masturbation** (sexual self-stimulation), and **mutual masturbation** (stimulating one's partner's genitals usually manually) (Davis and Whitten, 1987: 73; Herdt, 2006). Cross-culturally, erotic practices between men who have sex with men include oral and anal sexual practices, mutual masturbation, interfemoral intercourse; and for women who have sex with women this also includes oral, manual stimulation, "dry humping," and the use of an artificial penis made of various materials. The traditional ethnographic information on what women actually do in terms of behavior and pleasure is scant (Blackwood, 1984b, 1986, 1998; Ford and Beach, 1951; Gregersen, 1983, 1994; Herdt, 1988 and 2006). The meanings of the same-gender sexual behaviors varies widely. For example as the Sambia illustrate, although oral insemination occurs as a right of passage among young men, it is not equivalent to industrialized "homosexual" behavior/ identity; nor is the Lesotho "mummy-baby" ritualized friendship of an older and younger women a lesbian one, although it incorporates erotic elements (Blackwood, 2005a and 2005b). The terms homosexual/lesbian/bisexual/queer are loaded with Euro-American sentiment. Given the evidence of third and more genders in many societies, the exportation of industrialized transgender and "GLBTQ" identities through globalization and the variety of extant emic interpretations of sexuality, the appropriateness of the term "homosexual" just because two bodies have the same genitals must be seriously questioned (Lancaster, 2003; Nanda, 2000).

What is regarded as erotic in one culture may not be in another. There is tremendous heterogeneity in virtually every aspect of sexual arousal encompassing what is regarded as foreplay, whether it is emphasized in the sexual repertoires, the sexual positions that are preferred, and what positions are considered "natural" and unnatural, as well as the embodiment of erotics. For example, in some societies, breasts are not erotic but the source of food for an infant. Although the missionary position with the man on top is the most common position for Euro-Americans, this too is not universal. Other positions for heterosexual intercourse include the Oceanic position, which involves the man squatting between the thighs of his partner with her legs straddling his thighs; another position preferred in some African and Native American societies is lying side by side, face-to face (Gregersen, 1994). Gregersen (1994: 62–70) summarizes a number of additional positions described in the ethnographic record. These include:

- man lying, woman squatting, face-to-face, woman on top.
- rear entry.
- man sitting, woman squatting, face-to-face, woman on top.
- standing (worldwide this position is usually associated with brief encounters with "illicit" partners).

Colonization, missionization, globalization, and the Internet have influenced the conceptions of the erogenous as well. For example, kissing is not universally recognized as erotic behavior. While kissing is widespread in industrialized countries, the Middle East, and among Hindu groups, for others such as those in Japanese and Chinese societies, kissing was not in the sexual repertoire until contact with industrialized society (Ford and Beach, 1951; Gregersen, 1994; Tiefer, 2004). Cross-culturally, in the **smell** or **olfactory kiss**, the nose is placed on the partner's face as one inhales; nose rubbing may be a variant of this kind of kiss reported among Inuit and others (Gregersen, 1994).

The Mangaians, a Cook Island society, offer a classic example of the complexities of a society that generally valued sexuality in a very positive way. Marshall, who initially conducted his research in the 1950s, argued that underpinning this positive ethos is evidence of some cultural ambivalence. Two examples of this patterned ambivalence were:

- a cultural emphasis on the genitalia and intercourse was contrasted with rigid rules of modesty for adults.
- rich oral traditions with explicit stories of intercourse were juxtaposed by sexual norms that sanction parents and children from talking about sex with each other.

One of the many ways Mangaian society culturally elaborated sexuality is through attention to the genitalia. An emphasis on pleasure was bolstered with considerable sexual knowledge about the genitals, expressed in an elaborate taxonomy of terms for the size, shape and consistency of the genitals. The linguistic elaboration incorporated a lexicon for classification of the clitoris that included degree of sharpness or bluntness as well as terms for specific areas on the penis unclassified in the lexicon of English speakers.

Prior to marriage, youths were encouraged to have as many partners as possible, similar to Mead's controversial claims regarding the sex lives of Samoan adolescent girls. Marshall (1971) reports that Mangaian youths in their teens and twenties may have had intercourse as many as eighteen to twenty times a week. Although coitus was emphasized over foreplay, the latter incorporated manual and lingual caressing of each other's nipples, cunnilingus and fellatio as well as "dirty talk" by the male to make his partner hotter. Despite this variety, the foreplay was typically only about five minutes long. Mangaian attitudes toward sex centralized the activity of penile-vaginal intercourse, emphasizing lots of pelvic action for both women and men, and valuing the ability of a man to prolong the in-and-out of coitus. Mangaian erotics accentuated the woman's sexual satisfaction and valorized a man's responsibility in facilitating multiple orgasms in his partner. The Mangaian masculine ideal was for his partner to have two or three orgasms to his one. Intimacy and affection were considered a possible but not an invariable prerequisite for sex, as in the Euro-American relational view of sex for women.

The Mangaians are not unique in their development of a positive and elaborate approach to sex. While Mangaians' sex education during the period of Marshall's research occurred through oral conventions as is typical of many nonliterate indigenous societies prior to colonization, missionization, and globalization, other societies with writing traditions may accent texts for sex education. For example, India has a very old and complex tradition of sexology exemplified in texts such as *The Kaama Sutra* (*The Precepts of*

Pleasure by Vaatsyaayana), written between 200–400 AD (Gregersen, 1983: 32). Please note that there are several spellings of this text. Through Euro-American eyes, the *Kaama Sutra* appears to be in the genre of a sex manual or text. However, there are some very important distinctions between texts such as the *Kaama Sutra* and industrialized sex manuals. Although the *Kaama Sutra* includes chapters on sexual positions and pleasure, it also incorporates discussions on issues in human relations, ethics, and living a sacred life. In Euro-American sexology, sex manuals have been secularized by a scientific approach; we look to science for the "truth," and we separate the sacred and the profane. By contrast, in India, the *Kaama Sutra* was considered a testimonial of the gods (Gregersen, 1994).

The book described 529 possible positions for intercourse, categorized women by depth of the vagina and men by penis size, as well as offered some helpful hints on how to enlarge the penis. While the number of positions may seem high, many consist of only minor variations in position (Gregersen, 1994: 62). The *Kaama Sutra* was a widely accepted text representing various themes in Hindu ideology. Hinduism generally incorporates a positive approach to sexual expression that is framed by Hindu ideologies that blend the sacred and the profane, uniting the spiritual with the erotic in ways that are anomalous to Judeo-Christianity. For example, the themes of righteousness and spirituality (the sacred) are merged with the profane elements of prosperity and pleasure (Bodley, 2005; Francoeur, 1991c; Gregersen, 1994). Sexual love and pleasure are one of the ways to achieve spiritual knowledge (Francoeur, 1992c; Garrison, 1983). Since the Vaatsyaayana writing, Hinduism has incorporated some sex-negative attitudes as a result of influences from Islam and the colonial/postcolonial encounter. Globalization and the Internet, however, are influencing younger people's attitudes in more sex positive directions.

Hinduism is a complex and heterogeneous religion with many sects, diverse and historical trajectories, and consequently, a panoply of views of sexuality evolving over the course of 3,500 years (Bodley, 2005). Several sects within Hinduism have specifically regarded sexuality as a means to reaching spiritual union with the higher powers of the universe. We shall focus on one of those sects, **Tantra**. Tantric traditions existed prior to the advent of Hinduism in India. As Hinduism developed and spread, Tantric philosophies were adopted into branches of Hinduism as well as Buddhism (Francoeur, 1991; Parrinder, 1996; Urban, 2003). Tantric schools that are associated with Buddhism have developed their own unique direction; our discussion focuses specifically on Hindu Tantrism (Devi, 1977; Francoeur, 1992; Gregersen, 1994). Despite a flourishing of Indian Tantrism during the eleventh and twelfth centuries, it remained a somewhat marginalized sect because of conflict with wider Hindu beliefs against eating meat, having sex with a woman who was menstruating, and the violation of caste prescriptions in certain Tantric sex rituals (Devi, 1977). Despite this history, it is still practiced in parts of India today (White, 2003).

In Tantric doctrines sexual expression is regarded as a religious experience and a vehicle to achieve transcendence. *Maithuna*, or the sexual union, is a way to approximate merging with the sacred. This contrasts sharply with the mind-body dualism of Christianity that views chastity/celibacy as the ultimate sacred experience, while sex is relegated to the profane. Sex is tolerated in some of the more fundamentalist Christian sects provided it is heterosexual marital intercourse for procreation. While there are Hindu doctrines that also value celibacy as a virtue, these occur for different reasons than in Judeo-Christianity; for example they emphasize concerns over ritual pollution and the belief that because semen is a source of male health, it must be controlled. These doctrines supporting celibacy are generally inconsistent with various Hindu versions of Tantrism.

Tantrism follows the teachings of books called *Tantras*. The oldest Tantra is part of the Hindu sacred text known as the *Vedas*. In the Tantric worldview, sex is much more than a physical experience; it includes the process where men and women can achieve a sense of common humanity or "communitas" (Turner, 1969). Through sexual union, a woman and a man can transcend their masculinity and femininity to recognize the qualities of the other gender in themselves and thereby gain access to her or his spirit being. In this way:

A doctrine of primal androgyny also pervades the Tantric approach: a male seeks out a female and the female a male, because they do not know that the opposite sex is lodged within their own being. To realize this fully is important for the future life. (Gregersen, 1983: 222).

The power of the universe is expressed through two oppositional forces: the static inertia of the female and the dynamic inertia of the male. Spiritual power is created through the union of these opposite cosmic forces. This creates a primal energy that can lead to spiritual perfection resulting in a sacred unity called *prana* (Garrison, 1983: 7).

In contrast to industrialized concepts of heterosexual sexual expression as having only two phases, foreplay and intercourse, the Tantric texts view sex as occurring in multiple phases. These include (Devi, 1977):

- having one's thoughts dwell on sex.
- spending time with the other sex.
- flirting.
- intimate conversation.
- desire for coitus.
- firm determination.
- physical copulation.

These phases illustrate the central principle of Tantrism as a form of sacred "worship [that] is through the flesh, with body and mind" (Devi, 1977: 16). Consequently coitus is regarded as a vehicle for creating a sexual energy that leads to religious ecstasy.

This is nowhere as apparent as in the Bengali Panchattattva *sex ritual. This ritual exemplifies the path to oneness that is achieved through the mystical elements of coitus. Participants in the Rite of the Five Essences, a Tantric love ritual, use the five forbidden Ms (wine or madya, meat or mansa, fish or matsya, parched grain or mudra, and sexual union or maithuna) in a kind of holy communion. This love ritual begins with embellishing the immediate physical environment with flowers, incense, music, and candlelight. The couple bathes and massages each other with fragrant oil. After alternate-nostril breathing and meditation designed to invigorate the vital energies of the kundalini, the couple chants a Mantra and imagines themselves as the embodiment of Shiva and Shakti, the supreme couple. With the woman on his right, the man kisses and caresses her whole body, from feet to head and back to her toes followed by the woman reciprocating with caresses and kisses all over his body. Finally, after the woman moves to the left of the male, the couple moves through a series of coital positions until each experiences the "transcendental power of love." Usually, the male refrains from orgasm in order to retain the vital life energies of his semen (Francoeur, 1991c: 6–7).*

Tantric philosophies of sexuality differ considerably from prominent perspectives in Christianity. St. Augustine of Hippo is credited with infusing Christianity with negative sentiments about sexuality. In his interpretation, the Garden of Eden is the locus of original sin. Because Adam and Eve defied the authority of the creator god by discovering sex, that sin was passed on to all of humankind. Although sex was regarded as necessary for procreation, sexual desire and arousal were thought to be sinful. The story of Adam and Eve provides the framework for establishing a rationale for regulating sexual behavior, gender relations, and marriage. As opposed to the Tantric perspective of sex as sacred, in Christianity celibacy became the exalted state because the original sin of sex meant a fall from grace. In industrialized worldviews, heavily influenced by Judeo-Christianity, sex is located in the body, distinct from spirit and mind (Tiefer, 2004: 24). According to Francoeur (1992: 7): "Christianity, for the most part, has not been able to integrate sexuality into a holistic philosophy or see sexual relations, pleasure, and passion as avenues for spiritual meaning and growth."[3]

The traditional practitioners of Tantrism in nonindustrialized societies are very diverse; some incorporate more conservative approaches to sexual rituals. However, in the United States and Europe, a modern or neo-Tantric tradition proliferates in a truncated form which may emphasize the sexual-spiritual connection or take a sexual therapy/self-help approach emphasizing Tantric techniques to improve performance and pleasure (Kuriansky, 2005; Urban, 2003).

THEORIES OF SEXOLOGY IN INDUSTRIALIZED SOCIETY

Twentieth and twenty-first century industrial theories of human sexual response (HSR) have been modified as a consequence of socio-cultural change, especially in regard to gender roles. In this section we shall focus on some, but certainly not all, of the sexologists who have influenced the study of human sexuality. The history of Euro-American sexology testifies to the shifting definitions of human sexual response over the course of time. While we will emphasize research spanning the last century and the current one, many of these perspectives were influenced by earlier thinking on the subject of human sexuality.

Freudian theory dominated sexology until Kinsey and his colleagues ushered in a new era of scientific sexology devoted to challenging myths about sexuality by collecting data on sexual practices in the United States. One of the major changes in the discipline of sexology has been in how women's sexuality was regarded. The Freudian view emphasized women's sexuality as a passive expression in contrast to men's sexuality which was interpreted as essentially important, active, assertive, and domin-ant. Freud's account of the gendering of sexuality was interrogated first by Kinsey, Pomeroy, and Martin (1948: 1053) and followed by other researchers such as Masters and Johnson (1966), Singer and Singer (1972), Kaplan (1974, 1979), and Perry and Whipple (1981) whose research affirmed women's capacity for sexual arousal and pleasure. As a con-sequence, these researchers transformed the discipline of sexology from one that had emphasized gender differences in human sexual response as a result of Freud's legacy, to one that argued that women's and men's sexual responses were more alike than disparate. Although the assumption of gender concordance in human sexual response continues as a major theme in contemporary sex research, it has been challenged by researchers who underscore the importance of culture, history, and context in how women and men subjectively experience their sexuality (Castro, 2001; Gagnon, 1977, 2004; Herdt, 2004; Kaschak and Tiefer, 2001; Parker, 2000; Tiefer, 2004 among numerous others). Although sexual behaviors among U.S. women and men have been converging over time and becoming more similar, such as rates for teenage intercourse, premarital intercourse, and number of partners, the debate has centered on the issue of sexual response (Laumann et al., 1994). The essentialist paradigm argues for a "unisex" model of human sexual response while the constructionist paradigm asserts that although women's and men's sexual behavior and responses may appear similar, their sexual experiences including sexual interest, desire and arousal are divergent because of their gendered positions and relations in society. Ethnocentric biases and assumptions about heterosexuality; monogamy, serial or lifelong; and the potential for reproductive success clearly circumscribe these approaches, eliding the voices from diverse sexual cultures.

The 1960s marked an era of massive social unrest and discontent. The second Sexual Revolution (the first occurring in the 1920s with a sharp increase in premarital sex for women) was officially under way by the mid-1960s. The media credited youth with engagement in a socio-sexual transformation, although some scholars questioned whether a Sexual Revolution had occurred at all, since:

> Put briefly, men changed their sexual behavior very little in the decades from the fifties to the eighties. They "fooled around," got married, and often fooled around some more, much as their fathers and perhaps their grandfathers had before them. Women, however, have gone from a pattern of virginity before marriage and monogamy thereafter to a pattern that much more resembles men's ... (Ehrenreich, Hess, and Jacobs 1986: 2)

Nevertheless, trends for democratizing sexuality were preceded by the women's movement by two or three years, implicating the influence of feminist trends for gender role parity in sexuality (Ehrenreich, Hess, and Jacobs 1986). By the late 1960s, issues of "sexual freedom" were integrated with second wave feminist concerns for women's equality and expressed in arguments advocating women's sexual and reproductive rights. Central to second wave feminist thinking was the perspective of sexual politics—that inequality between women and men was not just a public social problem, but a private one as well. This could be located in the intimate and sexual relations between women and men, where inequities even pervaded the bedroom. The rumblings of the Women's Movement contributed to a separation of sex from marriage and reproduction, enhanced by the widespread availability of the oral contraceptive pill that was developed in the 1950s and granted FDA approval in 1959. The 1960s and 1970s were punctuated by the "hippie" counterculture, whose ideology of "free love" and normalizing of premarital sex infiltrated the youth culture of wider U.S. society. By the end of the 1970s, researchers found few gender differences in premarital sex and as D'Emilio and Freedman argue, "American society seemed to have reached a new accommodation with the erotic" (1988: 300; Ehrenreich, Hess, and Jacobs, 1986: 40).

Since the 1980s and continuing into the new millennium, the United States has witnessed a tremendous backlash to the gains women have made regarding their reproductive rights to control their fertility (Faludi, 1991; Herdt, 2004; Kimmel, 2000). This backlash was extended more widely under the George W. Bush administration through the reduction in federal funds for sex research and in the promotion of "abstinence-only" approaches to sex education domestically and internationally. We encourage the reader to be alert to changes in policy over time and with different administrations and to pursue reputable government and scholarly sources for updates subsequent to the publication of this textbook.

The meaning of sex was also reformulated as a consequence of the social upheavals heralded by the 1960s. Masters and Johnson (1966) demonstrated that women's sexuality was more extensive than previously thought, so that sex came to include more than just penile-vaginal intercourse for heterosexual coitus. The importance of the clitoris in female sexual response was one factor in this new view. The definition of sexuality was expanded to include additional behaviors such as cunnilingus which was only whispered about in the 1950s. Populist currents for the democratization of sex were felt as Freudian theory began to lose some of its foothold and popular sex books appeared. Sex experts sprang up everywhere during the 1960s and 1970s including: J's *The Sensuous Woman* (1969), Comfort's *The Joy of Sex* (1972), Friday's *My Secret Garden* (1974), and Hite's *The Hite Report* (1976).

With these books, a more humanistic trend evolved that offered sexual advice as the changing meanings of female sexuality were being felt in the bedroom (Ehrenreich, Hess, and Jacobs, 1986). These popular accounts were not scientific and were not based on the principles of sound research methodologies, but, in all fairness, this was not their purpose. Rather they represented a trajectory in the "democratization" of sex, which was a popular genre that would coexist with current proclivities for scientific and empirical research initiated by Kinsey and coupled with newly emerging medical and scientific perspectives of the 1960s such as that of Masters and Johnson (1966).

Sexological research is not only a product of history and culture (i.e., reproduces culture); it also contributes to the wider **sexual culture** of our times and place (produces culture) defined as the "intrinsic or internal meaning, as well as extrinsic or environmental sources of sexual behavior" (Herdt, 1999: 100). Though the media plays an ever-increasing role in sexuality nationally and globally, the scientific literature is also part of the diverse ways that sex is framed and "spun" (Gagnon, 2004). In the following sections we review the contributions of selected researchers in the field of sexology. By no means is this meant to be an exhaustive review;

rather it highlights several of the most prominent theorists and their significant influences on sexology in the twentieth century and the new millennium.

Freud

Freud had a tremendous impact on sexological thinking up through the 1950s. As discussed in Chapters 2 and 9, Freud's theory of psychosexual development emphasized phases in childhood and adolescence and the importance of the Oedipus complex. For Freud sexuality was the cornerstone of his psychoanalytic approach, i.e., adult sexuality is determined by childhood psychosexual development. Freud regarded male sexuality as the norm against which he judged women's sexuality as more timid and passive, as well as inherently more problematic. In his 1905 book, *Three Essays on the Theory of Sexuality,* he identified two types of female orgasms. The clitoral orgasm was regarded by Freud as an immature one centered on the erogenous zone of the clitoris, and related to girls experiences with masturbation. In contrast, the vaginal orgasm was considered the mature form of orgasm, associated with reproduction. This shift from clitoral to vaginal orgasm occurred after puberty as the vagina became the central foci of women's sexuality. In Freud's view, women who experienced sexual pleasure in ways other than through penile penetration were immature and fixated in an earlier phase of development (Bullough, 1994; Byer and Shainberg, 1991: 186; Freud, 1975 [1922]).

Critiques of the Freudian approach are numerous, but the most often cited charges address the issue that the psychoanalytic approach is not subject to scientific methods of verification since Freud's theories emerged from his practice, and he offered no systematic data *per se.* He only treated 130 patients, none of whom were children. In addition, his perspective on women's sexuality has been denounced as androcentric (Westheimer and Lopater, 2005).

Kinsey

In 1948 Alfred Kinsey (see Figure 11.1) and his colleagues published the Kinsey Reports on male sexuality *(Sexual Behavior in the Human Male)* followed by 1953's *Sexual Behavior in the Human Female.* Their work had a profound impact on the scientific community as well as on U.S. conceptions of sexuality. Although Kinsey and his collaborators' contributions are many, we shall highlight a few of the most significant findings about American sexuality. In contrast to Freud's psychoanalytic perspective that stressed the differences between female and male sexuality, Kinsey concluded male and female sexuality were much more alike (Ehrenreich, Hess, and Jacobs, 1986), which is a surprising view of sexuality given that their research occurred in the context of the post-WWII baby boom. Thus, their position, that there were few differences in male and female orgasm and

Figure 11.1 Portrait of Alfred C. Kinsey by William Dellenback. (*Source*: Reproduced by permission of The Kinsey Institute for Research in Sex, Gender, and Reproduction, Inc.)

human sexual response, contradicted not only the legacy of Freud but the popular gender culture of the times that was in the midst of celebrating gender difference as essentialistic.

The Kinsey approach to human sexuality was a dedicated to scientific rigor that emphasized the behavioral, although critics have argued that it left the affective and experiential component of sex unrecognized. Despite background training as a zoologist, Kinsey emphasized a sociological approach to measurement, analyzing data using gender, age, education, marital status as variables in understanding sex as a "natural" and essential drive (Giami, 2005). Kinsey's passion and mission were devoted to ending sexual ignorance by using the scientific method to collect data on people's sexual experiences that could subsequently be quantified into behavioral terms. *Sexual Behavior in the Human Male* was based on 12,000 case histories and *Sexual Behavior in the Human Female* was based on 8,000. Although detractors have focused on Kinsey and his colleagues' lack of attention to sexual meanings and culture, this was not indeed the objective of their research. Kinsey was a dedicated proponent of sexuality education, hoping to end sexual ignorance and mythology; he brought to the United States a much needed culturally relativistic approach to sexual behavior (Lyons and Lyons, 2004).

In 2004, the film Kinsey, *written and directed by Bill Condon, spanned Kinsey's life. Liam Neeson starred as Alfred Kinsey and Laura Linney as Clara, his spouse. The movie provides insight into the sexual climate of his times.*

Betty Friedan, an early feminist and author of *The Feminine Mystique* (1963) (Ehrenreich, Hess, and Jacobs, 1986: 43), criticized the Kinsey reports for presenting sexuality "as a status-seeking game in which the goal was the greatest number of 'outlets,' [or] orgasms." Ehrenreich and colleagues (1986) suggest that Kinsey's dedication to an evidence-based scientific sexology that could be quantified had a profound influence on America's conceptions of sexuality by shifting the focus to the number of orgasms. He has been accused of bias in his statistics due the number of male prisoners in the first book and for reliance on volunteers in both volumes (Lyons and Lyons, 2004).

Despite these critiques of his/and his colleagues' work, Kinsey made a huge contribution to creating the emergent discipline of sexology and influenced society at large by confronting traditional attitudes toward sexuality (Bullough, 1994, 2004). Kinsey and his colleagues offered a new sexual paradigm for mainstream U.S. culture that normalized and familiarized homosexuality, masturbation, premarital sex for men and women, heterosexual coitus, and extramarital affairs by making them topics of conversation in popular culture (Bullough, 2004; Giami, 2005). Kinsey may be credited with establishing the survey as a method for understanding U.S. sexual practices that has continued today, albeit with more rigor. See the discussion of Laumann and colleagues' research, which follows.

The Kinsey Institute at the University of Indiana persists today as Kinsey's legacy. This institute continues to promote and fund sexuality research, creating new opportunities for interdisciplinary sex research and education as well as housing a massive archive of print, film and video, fine art, artifacts, and photography.

Masters and Johnson

William H. Masters and Virginia E. Johnson continued Kinsey's efforts to develop a scientific sexology. Their research emphasized an innovative approach to the collection of data on human sexual responses during sexual stimulation. This was achieved through controlled observations in a laboratory that integrated various medical technologies to measure physiological indicators of human sexual response (Masters and Johnson, 1966). Masters and Johnson's research was initiated in 1954 and resulted in the publication of the now famous *Human Sexual Response* (1966).

Recognized as much for their research methods as their findings, Masters and Johnson incorporated married and unmarried participants in their study; women ranged in age from eighteen to seventy-eight (n = 382) and males' ages were from twenty-one to eighty-nine (n = 312) (Masters and Johnson, 1966: 12–13). Though offering significant contributions to sexology, their research subjects were overrepresented by those with formal education and biased in regard to class, economic privilege, and race/ethnicity. Of the non-Caucasian research population, only eleven family units were African American (Masters and Johnson, 1966: 12–15), nor was the homosexual data they collected presented in their final research (1966).

The research setting (a laboratory) allowed for direct observation and measurement of physiological changes and responses during a variety of sexual activities including manual and mechanical manipulation and intercourse in different positions (Masters and Johnson, 1966: 21). Their clinical and high-tech methods included artificial coital equipment (artificial penises) equipped to measure female sexual response, as well as various kinds of monitors to measure genital and other physiological responses. The clinical procedure was enhanced by in-depth interviews.

Masters and Johnson documented and established four phases in the human sexual response cycle (HSR): excitement, plateau, orgasm, and the resolution phase (Masters and Johnson, 1966: 4). Over the eleven years of their study they observed over 10,000 sexual acts of married and unmarried people from ages eighteen to eighty-nine. As a result of their extensive research, they concluded that males and females had the same physiological responses in the HSR cycle, although women had more varieties of sexual orgasms than men and could be multi-orgasmic (Bullough, 1994).Variations in this four-stage model included some gender differences. Male response cycles varied among individuals primarily along the dimension of duration of response, while females differed by duration and intensity.

The excitement phase is characterized by **vasocongestion** defined as engorgement of the blood vessels in the pelvic region and increased muscle tension. In women, lubrication of the vagina occurs in association with the swelling of erectile tissues including: clitoris, labia, vaginal opening, and in men this is associated with penile swelling.

The plateau stage precedes orgasm and varies in duration. In males, full erection and engorgement of the testes are reached. In females, the vagina expands and lengthens as the uterus gradually elevates. The **orgasmic platform** is reached during this stage in which the vaginal opening is reduced in size because of engorgement of the surrounding erectile tissues (Bullough, 1994; Byer and Shainberg, 1991: 182; King, 2005).

Orgasm marks the third stage. The female orgasm is characterized by three to twelve contractions at 0.8 second intervals (Francoeur, 1991a: 182; Hyde, 1985: 278). While the female orgasm lasts for thirteen to fifty-one seconds, the male orgasm lasts from ten to thirty seconds (in Francoeur, 1991a: 182) and is usually, but not inevitably, associated with ejaculation. As noted, orgasm was found to vary among women, with some capable of multiple orgasms and others not. These occurred sequentially during the orgasm stage without the woman returning to plateau levels (McAnulty and Burnett, 2003). Orgasm and ejaculation are physiologically distinct. It is possible for men to experience orgasm without ejaculation before puberty, in old age and in some cases of erectile disorders.

The final phase of human sexual response is that of **resolution**. This is the process where blood is released from the engorged areas, muscle tension is relaxed, and the body returns to its previous state. For the female, this process may last up to half an hour if orgasm occurred, or an hour if only the plateau stage was reached (Masters and Johnson, 1966).

During resolution men experience a refractory period where sexual stimulation will not produce another erection. It has been argued that the refractory period is what prevents men from having multiple orgasms. Reports of multiple orgasms in men are still controversial and undoubtedly clouded by definitional interpretation. Self-reports of multiple orgasms in Kinsey, Pomeroy, and Martin (1948) are defined as occurring during one sexual encounter. In the Kinsey data, 15 percent to 20 percent of the teenage boys reported multiple orgasms with only 3 percent of the subjects claiming this ability after the age of sixty. Masters and Johnson maintain that once ejaculation has occurred it is not possible for a man to experience orgasm without a refractory period. However, there is some suggestive evidence around this issue. For example, Dunn and Trost (1989) have reported on multiple orgasms in twenty-one men who experienced a variety of orgasms; some had one or more dry orgasms before ejaculation and others experienced these after ejaculation. Men's reports of multiple orgasms may be part of the incredible variation in how humans experience sexuality. Multiple orgasms in men illustrates the tremendous difference in the individual experience in human sexual response (King, 2005).

Masters and Johnson discredited the dominant Freudian view that there were two kinds of orgasms possible for women: the clitoral and vaginal. In the Freudian view, a woman was doomed to vaginal frigidity if she could not make the transition from the childish/immature clitoral orgasm to the mature vaginal one. Masters and Johnson argued that there was no purely vaginal organism and that the clitoris was central in the female orgasm whether from indirect stimulation during coitus or through direct stimulation. Ehrenreich, Hess, and Jacobs (1986) points out that this was not really news since earlier research demonstrating this had been available "for decades," although the psychiatric doctrine had been tenacious in sticking to the Freudian view.

In addition, Masters and Johnson also verified women's capacity for multiple orgasms and challenged the myth that women's orgasms were like men's in requiring a refractory period prior to a subsequent orgasm(s). As early as 1953, Kinsey et al. had reported that 14 percent of the female population in the United States was capable of multiple orgasms. Masters and Johnson found that women's multiple orgasms were no different than their single ones.

Masters and Johnson's detractors criticized their research for the same reason as Kinsey's; that is, they had "reduce[d] human sexuality to physical responses, though, of course, only physical responses are accessible to quantitative measurement" (Ehrenreich, Hess, and Jacobs, 1986: 66). This model of human sexuality has been denounced for its androcentric bias with its focus on penetration and orgasm as well as being one-dimensional in scope (Basson, 2005; Francoeur, 1993: 72; Tiefer, 2004). In addition, Masters and Johnson's research methods have been critiqued for sampling bias in the research population; it was preselected for coital and masturbatory experience as well as higher SES (socioeconomic status). Tiefer (2004: 43–61) has further criticized Masters and Johnson's human sexual response cycle, regarding it as reductionistic in its unwavering universal stages; offering a view of human sexual response as confined and fragmented into physiological parts; and emphasizing sexuality as a primarily genital experience as opposed to a whole body response. Although Masters and Johnson's research asserts that women and men have similar physiological responses, it ignores the wider socio-cultural context of gender relations, e.g., the relational and recreational models of sex that are still pervasive in U.S. society and the influence of the experiential component of sexuality. (See discussion on Tiefer, and the section "Problems in sexual response.")

Masters and Johnson are also known for their study of problems in human sexual functioning. In 1970 they published Human Sexual Inadequacy. *Their therapeutic approach was distinctive; they treated couples rather than the individuals; utilized a behaviorist model rather than a psychoanalytic one; and boasted high success rates through short-term psychotherapy.*

Singer and Singer

In 1972, Singer and Singer offered another model of female sexuality that included three kinds of orgasms: the **vulval orgasm** (that described by Masters and Johnson), the **uterine orgasm,** and the **blended orgasm.** The blended orgasm combined the vulval and the uterine types. Singer and Singer's evidence involved the possibility of women experiencing orgasm without "vulval contractions" or, in Masters and Johnson's terminology, contractions of the orgasmic platform (Singer and Singer, 1972: 256). Their research seriously challenged Masters and Johnson's clinical research on women's orgasms by suggesting a greater range of variation. Although they concurred with Masters and Johnson that women's vulval orgasms are a result of either direct or indirect clitoral stimulation, they described another type of orgasm that they labeled the uterine orgasm. According to Singer and Singer (1972: 259–260) "the 'uterine orgasm' does not involve any contractions of the orgasmic platform ... this kind of orgasm occurs in coitus alone, and it largely depends upon the pleasurable effects of uterine displacement. Subjectively the orgasm is felt to be deep, i.e., dependent on repeated penile-cervix contact." This orgasm is characterized by interrupted breathing with the orgasm and the expulsion of breath occurring simultaneously (Singer and Singer, 1972: 260).

The blended orgasm combines characteristics of both the vulval and the uterine orgasm. It incorporates contractions of the orgasmic platform, but is experienced as deeper than a vulval orgasm and more akin to the uterine in that breathing is interrupted (Singer and Singer, 1972: 260). The same critique of Masters and Johnson has been applied to this research. While Singer and Singer expanded Masters and Johnson's perspective on women's orgasms, similarly their research suggests a "biological uniformity" that underrates the complexity of how meanings and symbols, culture and context can influence the individual's experience of sexuality (Tiefer, 2004).

Kaplan

Helen Singer Kaplan wrote extensively on the subject of human sexuality (1974, 1979, 1983, 1989) and was known for her modification of Masters and Johnson's four-stage human sexual response cycle. Kaplan (1979) remodeled the human sexual response cycle into three phases. She added **"desire"** as a precursor stage to arousal defining it as the specific "sensations' that lead to an interest in having sex. The addition of "desire" has earned her the most acclaim in contributing to an understanding of human sexual response. She categorized the second phase in human sexual response as the **"arousal" phase** in which she collapsed Master's and Johnson's excitement and plateau phases, followed by orgasm. For Kaplan sexual desire was considered an appetite or drive motivating sexual behavior. Other researchers more recently have emphasized the socio-cultural and relational parameters of desire (DeLameter and Sill, 2005). The stage of desire has been integrated into the human sexual response cycle in the *Diagnostic and Statistical Manual of Mental Disorders*, a compendium of the Euro-American nosology of mental distress and is regarded as one of the categories of sexual disorders. (See section "Problems in sexual response" for further discussion.)

Unlike Kinsey and Masters and Johnson, Kaplan proposed that female and male sexuality were distinctive. Subscribing to theories of the biological basis of sex differences, Kaplan believed that these different sexualities are due to testosterone which she argued accounted for a much stronger sexual drive in males than in females. In contrast to men, the female sex drive was shaped to a greater degree by lived experience in Kaplan's view. Kaplan felt that clitoral stimulation was essential to female orgasm and that vaginal intercourse alone would not necessarily result in an orgasm without additional clitoral stimulation (King, 2005). According to Klein (1981: 73–75, 77, 92) Kaplan also regarded humans as monogamous pair bonders, although she left open the possibility that it may be serial. While offering a more complex view of human sexual response, this model has been subject to the same appraisal as that of Masters and Johnson—that of reducing human sexual response to physiological indicators at the expense of the personal, cultural, and contextual. Though contributing to knowledge of the physiology of sexuality, the HSR cycle as conceived by Masters and Johnson, Singer and Singer, and Kaplan does not consider the tremendous variety in individuals' sexual arousal (McAnulty and Burnette, 2003; Tiefer, 2004). Kaplan also made an important contribution to sexology through her earlier work on sexual dysfunction. In *The New Sex Therapy: Active Treatment of Sexual Dysfunction* (1974), she synthesized Masters and Johnson's behaviorist approach to sexual dysfunction with psychoanalysis. Unlike Masters and Johnson's therapeutic model based on symptoms, Kaplan's integrated concern for interpersonal interaction with an emphasis on the unconscious (Ficher and Eisenstein, 1984: 143; Kaplan, 1979 and 1974).

Whipple and Perry—the "G Spot" controversy

The **Grafenberg** or **G spot** is located approximately one or two inches inside the opening of the vagina on the anterior wall about halfway between the outer labia and the cervix. It is named after Dr. Ernst Grafenberg (1950) who first located and described the dime-sized spot in a 1950 report. In their book *The G-Spot and Other Recent Discoveries about Human Sexuality* (1982), Ladas, Whipple, and Perry proposed that the G spot is an area of sensitive tissues that when stimulated may lead to orgasm. This research initiated a controversy regarding whether the G spot actually exists as a distinctive physiological area and if it does whether or not it is universal among females. Subsequent research has indicated that the G spot may not be universal to all females, but present in only about 10 percent or less of the population (Alzate and Londono, 1984; Masters, Johnson and Kolodny, 1985). However, The Federation of Feminist Women's Health Centers (*A New View of a Woman's Body*, 1995: 39, 162) names and describes this area as the **urethral sponge**, a sheath of erectile tissue around the urethra which becomes engorged during sexual excitement and protects the urethra during sexual activity. Others have found this area to be responsive to stimulation as well including the work of Zaviacic and colleagues in Czechoslovakia (1987 and 1988). Although the evidence is currently inconclusive from the clinical vantage (Whipple, 2006), it is testified to in women's self-reports, discourses and narratives.

The G-spot is important for another reason since Ladas and colleagues contended that it is involved in one of three possible kinds of orgasms in the female human sexual response cycle. Ladas, Whipple, and Perry proposed that there are three kinds of female orgasms: **tenting, A-frame** and **blended**. The tenting orgasm occurs with clitoral stimulation. This is like the orgasmic platform of Masters and Johnson. The vaginal entrance restricts and "tenting" occurs when "the inner portion of the vagina often balloons as a result of the lifting up of the uterus inside the abdomen" (1982: 144–145). The A-frame orgasm is quite distinctive in occurring as a consequence of stimulation of the Grafenberg spot. This type of orgasm includes no orgasmic platform, rather "the vaginal musculature relaxes and the entrance opens" (Ladas, Whipple, and Perry, 1982: 144). The tenting is absent so that "the uterus seems to be pushed down and the upper portion of the vagina compresses" (Ladas, Whipple, and Perry, 1982: 145). The third type is classified as the blended orgasm. This response involves the pubococcygeal muscle as in the tenting orgasm and is also similar to the A-frame orgasm triggered by stimulation of the G spot, but the focus is on the muscle response in the uterus (Ladas, Whipple, and Perry, 1982: 150). In 1999, Whipple and Komisaruk point to yet another kind of orgasm resulting from stimulation of the cervix. At this juncture, we can consider G spot orgasm as one of the many diverse ways women experience sexual arousal and response.

The G spot research is interesting for another reason. Perry and Whipple (1981) have proposed that during orgasm ten to twenty percent of women have the capacity to ejaculate a substance similar to seminal fluid. They have argued that female ejaculation is most often associated with the G spot stimulation. This assertion has been contested by researchers such as Goldberg et al. (1983) and Belzer, Whipple, and Moger (1984). In an analysis of female ejaculate, Belzer, Whipple, and Percy (1982) found the same enzyme present as produced by the male prostate, only the chemical structure varied. However, Goldberg et al. (1983) found no difference between female ejaculate and urine. Ladas, Whipple and Percy (1982) have suggested that that as many as 40 percent of women have experienced an ejaculatory substance from time to time. Subsequent research and self-reports of women confirm that indeed it is not a question of whether some women emit a fluid during orgasm, but rather what is the nature of the fluid. For some it may be due to incontinence, but for others the origin continues to be debated (Federation of Feminist Women's Health Centers, 1991; King, 2005; Whipple, 2006).

Deborah Sundahl, co-publisher of the women's erotic magazine for lesbians On Our Backs *(initially 1984) has made several videos/DVDs on the G spot and female ejaculation: These are:* How to Female Ejaculate: Find your G-spot with Deborah Sundahl *(2002); and* How to Female Ejaculate for Couples *(2003) as well as published a book on the subject:* Female Ejaculation and the G-Spot *(2003a).*

Laumann and the National Health and Social Life Survey

Edward O. Laumann is the principal investigator in a massive undertaking by the National Health and Social Life Survey, a survey of American adult sexual behavior (the University of Chicago, NORC: A National Organization for Research). The results of this survey have been reported on by Laumann and his colleagues in numerous publications. These include three books: *The Social Organization of Sexuality: Sexual Practices in the United States* (1994) by Edward O. Laumann, John H. Gagnon, Robert T. Michael, and Stuart Michaels; *Sex In America: A Definitive Survey* (1994) by Robert T. Michael, John H. Gagnon, Edward O. Laumann, and Gina Kolata; and *Sex, Love and Health in America: Private Choice and Public Policies* (2000) Edward O. Laumann and Robert T. Michael.

In a 1992 random sample, Laumann and his colleagues interviewed 3,432 English-speaking adults between the ages of eighteen and fifty-nine. They had a high participation rate, with 79 percent of the population selected choosing to respond. Their methods included face-to-face interviews, a self-administered questionnaire and focus groups. Like earlier surveys, Laumann's research covered numerous topics related to U.S. sexual practices including frequency, partners, masturbation, and STIs and offered statistical analysis of the findings. Their approach emphasized that changes in sexual activity throughout the life cycle occurred in response to major life course events and the vicissitudes in one's social environment ("The National Health and Social Life Survey Summary," n.d.). A few of the findings from National Health and Social Life Survey are:

- Age of first of sexual intercourse is better predicted by personal variables such as age at puberty than ethnicity or socioeconomic status.
- Males generally find fellatio more appealing than females do.
- Caucasian women and men prefer cunnilingus more than other ethnic groups.
- For both genders, sexual satisfaction increases with emotional commitment and relationship exclusivity.
- Problems with sex affect younger women and older men more than other age-gender groups (Michalski, 2002: 156).

In contrast to other sexological research such as Kinsey's that emphasized the individual, Laumann and his colleagues accented the sexual dyad (couple) as the center of analysis and focused on the importance of sexual interaction (Bullough, 2004; "The National Health and Social Life Survey Summary," n.d.). "The National Health and Social Life Survey" has been regarded by many as the "the most comprehensive nationally representative survey to date, as in-depth as the Kinsey surveys, but with scientifically sound sampling techniques" (King, 2005: 19). The shortcomings of this impressive and comprehensive effort are that the survey only included English speakers. In addition, the researchers conceded that their data based on self-reports are always limited since the degree to which they correspond to actual behavior is unknown.

Tiefer: a constructionist view of sexuality

Leonore Tiefer has been writing and publishing since the late 1970s on the subject of human sexuality from a social constructionist position. Originally trained as a biologically oriented psychologist, she returned to graduate school to respecialize in clinical sexological psychology. According to Tiefer, "In the 1970's, writings from the Women's Movement convinced me that the primary influences on women's sexuality are cultural norms internalized by women, reinforced by institutions and enacted in significant relationships" (2004: xiii). She has also made this argument regarding male sexuality as well, maintaining that ideologies of masculinity and sexuality are unstable and change over time (Tiefer, 2004: 1986). Along with various colleagues, Tiefer has challenged the biomedical orientation of Kinsey and his successors such as Masters and Johnson, whose model of human sexuality frames sex as a purely physiological response. In contrast, Tiefer defines and locates sexuality in the "personal, relational, and cultural, rather than physical terms" (Tiefer, 2004: 23). In her book, *Sex Is Not a Natural Act and Other Essays* and in numerous other publications, Tiefer argues that our understandings of human sexology in Western industrialized society are dominated by a biological model driven by the quest for an ever more scientific sexology. This results in an approach that fragments sexuality into particular body parts. In Tiefer's view, the scientific imperative with its biocentric approach to understanding human sexuality has shortchanged us into regarding sex as a biological drive/instinct, causing us to miss the importance of culture in shaping our desires. Tiefer has challenged the very notion of biological drive as a cultural universal. In this regard she states:

So, if sex is not a natural act, a biological given, a human universal, what is it? I would say it's a concept, first of all—a concept with shifting but deeply felt definitions. Conceptualizing sex is a way of corralling and discussing certain human potentials for consciousness, behavior and expression that are available to be developed by social forces, that is, available to be produced, changed, modified, organized, and defined. Like Jell-O, sexuality has no shape without a container, in this case a socio-historical container of meaning and regulation. (Tiefer, 2004: 3)

Her work on sex from an "antinaturalist"/constructionist perspective has coalesced with like-minded colleagues into a campaign named and dedicated to "A New View of Women's Sexual Problems." This approach has challenged the medicalization of women's sexuality that reduces "sex" to orgasms and offers an alternative perspective ("Female Sexual Dysfunction: A New Medical Myth: Current Campaign Activities," 2006; Kaschak and Tiefer, 2001; Tiefer, Brick and Kaplan, 2003). "A New View of Women's Sexual Problems" is discussed further in the section "Problems in sexual response."

Understanding ourselves as sexual, potentially sexual or nonsexual beings in the early twenty-first century requires attention to understanding U.S. cultural assumptions and ideologies surrounding sexuality, including diverse influences and disparate and competing discourses such as the media, politics, science, etc. From a Euro-American perspective, vaginal-penile intercourse is naturalized as the "definitive heterosexual act." Yet, such a view is embedded in assumptions that sex is an instinctual drive because of the human "need" to procreate (Gavey, McPhillips and Braun, 1999). In this regard, Parker notes that a dominant viewpoint in much sex research, but not all, is that culture "inhibit(s) us from encountering some kind of enduring truth—a 'cultureless' model" of sex (2000: 308). This biocentric perspective represents the confluence of Euro-American scientific beliefs as well as popular and media discourses (Lancaster, 2003).

As we continue our discussion of various themes in human sexual response, the importance of socio-cultural factors in the social construction of sexuality is emphasized. This viewpoint is an integral part of anthropological perspectives on human sexuality that highlight variation and diversity through time and across cultures. The biological and physiological basis of human sexuality is interpreted by individuals through a cultural and historical lens, intersected by personal and relational experiences. Human sexual desire and pleasure are biological, psychological, and cultural phenomena that change through time.

Because so much of this discussion has focused on the clinical sexological aspects of human orgasm, the "nuts and bolts" of orgasm have been emphasized by researchers at the expense of the playful, liminal, and wondrous. College students from one Human Sexuality course offer descriptions of orgasm experiences as well as their ideas of what constitutes good sex.

Orgasm experience

It's great! It's the one time when every nerve in your body seems alive.

It was not until two years ago that I experienced orgasm on a regular basis. The first one happened while I was fully clothed and "dry humping." I was so excited that I started laughing hysterically. The guy thought he did something weird. It is an intense sensation that I can feel in my eyelashes!

It felt real good. It's one of the best feelings in the world. Sometimes it makes me get up and scream or if I can maybe knock down a wall or something.

It feels as though someone is tickling me with a feather. I can feel myself about to explode at times. You feel it coming on, the mind gets blank and the stomach feels light and then, let's just say good. After sex I feel really close with my girlfriend.

I usually need my partner to stimulate me with his fingers or tongue in order for me to orgasm. I have never had a multiple orgasm and I am trying to achieve orgasm just from sex.

While you're having sex it's as if you never want to stop, as it keeps feeling better until finally . . . Complete satisfaction. Once the orgasm has been reached there is a feeling as if I am at peace with myself.

Hard thing to remember after it has happened. At first it builds up and then it just feels like you let

Conditions for "good sex"

Partner that is responsive and likes to have fun with it. Not always serious.

Atmosphere can be anywhere because sex is fun everywhere. I prefer being alone with my boyfriend at home or in the park. Anywhere we feel close and intimate or just horny!! The craziest place was on the top floor of a parking garage!

Being sexually attractive, the mood I'm in or the atmosphere as long as strangers are not around. If friends are around, it doesn't matter.

Television on with lights dimmed. Start by cuddling and kissing.

I must be alone in the bedroom with my girlfriend. I usually have the radio on. We usually have the lights out but a night-light on.

My condition for good sex is a partner I am highly attracted to and feel comfortable with—yet not too comfortable to be totally used to. I like hours of foreplay leading up to sex and I like sex to be in the heat of summer or on a really cold day.

Spontaneous mood with a partner who really enjoys having sex with you. Some kind of rainstorm loose—not physically, but more emotionally. I usually scream very loud, it seems uncontrollable. I cannot just orgasm, I need a partner to try to make me and give effort.

happening outside with loud slow music would definitely add to the atmosphere.

A very tense, contractive explosion! My body freezes and then melts in a matter or seconds.

If it felt good, it usually was good—I like it loud and wild!

Feels like your body is tensing and feels like you're losing sensation of things around you.

The right frame of mind!

Tensing and relaxing—Great stuff.

Love. Great sex, in my opinion is practiced and not reached the first time, so I feel I must love my partner and appreciate their view and ideas of what is good sex.

No real particular conditions. Afternoon is always fun. Must both be in the mood. Romantic exciting mood is good too. Spontaneous.

OVERVIEW OF U.S. SEXUAL ATTITUDES

The United States has been categorized as a restrictive and sex-negative society (Ford and Beach, 1951). This is largely because of a history that has idealized **heteronormative** cultural rules (the idea that everyone is heterosexual), thus reflecting a Judeo-Christian legacy that sanctioned premarital sex and emphasized sex for procreation. However, the nineteenth century ushered in new meanings of the family establishing the companionate marriage, one that accentuated modern notions of love and the importance of sharing and intimacy, diverging from earlier views of marriage that focused on reproduction and reciprocal roles of men and women. By the early twentieth century, sexual pleasure and desire came to be seen as core features in how love and marriage were defined in the United States. This spawned two competing ideologies dominating the twentieth and twenty-first centuries: "[o]ne viewing sex as legitimate only in marriage, but as a necessary component of marital happiness, and the other viewing sex as a valid and important experience in its own right" (Weiss, 2004b: 1136). It has been argued that the huge changes that have occurred in United States sexual practices over the past century are a result of these countervailing and competing perspectives about sexuality and its role in society (D'Emilio and Freedman, 1988). Therefore, rather than viewing the United States as a sex-negative society, we can say it is generally a sex-ambivalent one (remembering that we are a plural society, with much variation). Conflicting themes and messages are expressed in an increasing influence of the media which in turn reflects and reproduces these contrasting ideologies. These debates continued with the second Sexual Revolution in the 1960s and 1970s. Changes in sexual attitudes resonated in bumper stickers, which read, "make love not babies." Trends for the separation of sex and reproduction were fueled by the Women's Movement and the widespread availability of the birth control pill. This has resulted in the increasing importance on sex for self-expression and pleasure, with the debate framed in terms of marital versus nonmarital sex (Tiefer, 2004).

Ambivalence toward sex is echoed in various institutions and cultural discourses (ways of constructing what we think of as truth including, the media, medicine, religion, etc.). The double standard, while loosening up dramatically in the 1970s, has not changed much qualitatively from the 1950s; it has been revamped into the "conditional double standard, in which males are allowed more freedom than females to engage in premarital sex, but females are permitted to be sexually active as long as they are in affectionate relationships (Sprecher, McKinney, and Orbuch, 1987: 24). An assortment of beliefs and practices related to sexuality throughout the life course and in different contexts testifies to this ambivalence.

All media use sex—rock videos, soap operas, weekly prime-time television, magazines, and advertising. Under the George W. Bush administration and its supporters, a nationwide campaign was developed to try to convince young people to remain celibate until marriage through abstinence-only education and virginity pledges. Sexual monogamy has been proclaimed as the antidote to AIDS; sexual abstinence is touted over sexual education both domestically and internationally.

PROBLEMS IN SEXUAL RESPONSE: DIAGNOSIS AND DISAGREEMENTS

In discussing sexual difficulties in the United States, a biological, psychological, and cultural lens is necessary to visualize this issue further. As discussed, oppositional and ambivalent messages about sexuality in the United States have a historical and current reference to the expression and definition of sexual problems. Bear in mind that the United States is a society spanning diverse classes and ethnicities, so our discussion here will necessarily emphasize broad trends. Sexual problems must be understood as developing in biological, psychological, and cultural context including biological factors such as general health, activity level, and medications; psychological factors such as the individual's experience, the partner relationship; and cultural factors spanning a wide range of influences such as societal ambivalence, inequities in gender relations, differences in sexual knowledge and access to sexuality education, economic influences, and various dimensions of embodiment including ideals of beauty, among others. This perspective is typically anthropological, and includes attention to issues such as sexual norms and the **medicalization** of sexual problems into notions of health, illness, and normalcy—that is, classification into dysfunctions and disorders. According to Riesmann (1983: 4) "The term medicalization refers to two interrelated processes. First, certain behaviors or conditions are given medical meaning—that is, defined in term of health and illness. Second, medical practice becomes a vehicle for eliminating or controlling problematic experiences that are defined as deviant" (in Tiefer, 2004: 23). This perspective is reiterated in Leonore Tiefer and her colleagues' "campaign" known as "A New View of Women's Sexual Problems" (Kaschak and Tiefer, 2001) and a "New View of Men's Sexual Problems" (Tiefer, 2006a).

In the United States sexual problems are discussed in a variety of arenas from popular culture to the clinical sector. Because identifying the sources of sexual problems spans biological, psychological, and socio-cultural perspectives, research reflects this rich array of interests. Research on this subject involves the medical professions, including urologists, gynecologists, and endocrinologists and psychiatrists, the mental health sectors, such as psychologists, mental health professionals and therapists, and social scientists from many disciplines. Since sexology and concerns over sexual well-being are such a heterogeneous field with an extensive literature, we shall focus a critical eye on the perspective taken in the American Psychiatric Association's *Diagnostic and Statistical Manual of Mental Disorders* (DSM). This publication offers a U.S./industrialized classification of sexual dysfunctions. Since the 1970s and escalating in the following thirty-five years, trends showed an increase in medicalization of sexual dysfunctions. This has been occurring domestically and internationally and is associated with expansion of pharmaceuticals and capitalism generally. The *nosology* (classification of disease) of sexual dysfunction has changed over time and is reflected in various versions of the DSM. The most current version is the DSM-IV-TR (revised in 2000). The DSM sexual dysfunction nosology incorporates the linear model of human sexual response developed by Masters and Johnson, but altered by the addition of Kaplan's stage of desire to the model (Tiefer, 2004). Currently DSM-IV-TR sexual disorders include but are not limited to:

- Sexual Desire Disorders: Aversion and Hypoactive.
- Sexual Arousal Disorders: Female Sexual Arousal Disorder and Male Erectile Disorder.

- Orgasmic Disorders: Female, Male and Premature Ejaculation.
- Sexual Pain Disorders: Dyspareunia (genital pain in women and men) and Vaginismus (involuntary muscle spasm in women interfering with intercourse) (DSM-IV-TR, 1997–2006).

This DSM classification is premised on the assumption that the human response cycle is primarily the same across the genders. Women and men share the same sexual disorders of desire, arousal, orgasm and pain with some disorders specific to each gender: for example, male erectile disorder and vaginismus. The experiencing of subjective distress and/or interpersonal problems is also included in the DSM-IV-TR as one of the criteria in each of the sexual disorders. The DSM-IV-TR classification affirms a perspective that sexual dysfunctions are largely psychogenic in origin, although sexual disorders are embodied in very real physiological problems in sexual functioning. Sexual dysfunctions in the DSM-IV-TR also include those caused by general medical conditions such as: female and male hypoactive sexual desire disorder; male erectile disorder; female and male dyspareunia or other female or male sexual dysfunction; and substance-induced sexual problems in functioning.

According to some studies, diverse sexual problems are widespread in the United States. For example, in studies from the 1980s of 100 happily married couples, 40 percent of the men reported erectile or ejaculatory dysfunction with 63 percent of the women referencing arousal or orgasmic dysfunction, and 50 percent of the men and 77 percent of the women complained of loss of sexual interest or an inability to relax (Goldberg, 1985: 147). More recent research by Laumann, Paik, and Rosen (1999) using the National Health and Social Life Survey has found figures as high as 40 percent of women and 30 percent of men surveyed recounted problems with sexual functioning.

Disorders of desire

The sexual disorders of desire include aversion and hypoactive forms that affect both men and women are generally described as a disinterest in sexual gratification. Aversion is defined in the DSM-IV-TR as a "[p]ersistent or recurrent extreme aversion to, and avoidance of, all (or almost all) genital sexual contact with a sexual partner." And hypoactive disorder is defined as "[p]ersistently or recurrently deficient (or absent) sexual fantasies and desire for sexual activity. The judgment of deficiency or absence is made by the clinician, taking into account factors that affect sexual functioning, such as age and the context of the person's life."

Hyposexual desire disorder was first identified in 1970 (King, 2005). In the 1980s, Harold Lief, a therapist, suggested that hyposexual desire occurred in "20 percent of all adult Americans" (in Leo, 1984: 83). More recent research for males by Laumann, Paik, and Rosen (1999) reports that

16 percent of men under sixty reported low sexual desire; Rosen's (2000) figures suggest a range of zero to 15 percent and Simons and Carey's (2001) data suggest it is even lower in the zero–3 percent range. Mueleman and Van Lankveld (2004) regard hyposexual desire disorder as a particularly difficult problem to diagnose and treat in men, due to its biological and psychological causes. However, a review of literature by Basson (2005) found that as many as 30–35 percent of women ages eighteen to seventy have had problems with sexual desire in the previous year. Research on difficulties in desire has been attributed to biological influences such as low levels of testosterone in both men and women and to the role of dopamine. It must be pointed out, however, that reports of treatments with testosterone and dopaminergic drugs improved arousal and intensity of orgasm, but desire was not increased. In guidelines issued by the Endocrine Society, Wierman et al. (2006: 17) note that "[a]lthough there is evidence for short-term efficacy of testosterone in selected populations [of women], such as surgically menopausal women, we recommend against the generalized use of testosterone by women because the indications are inadequate and evidence of safety in long-term studies is lacking." Davis et al. (2005: 96) have concluded that "[t]he measurement of serum testosterone, free testosterone, or DHEAS in individuals presenting with low sexual function is not informative and levels of these hormones should not be used for the purpose of diagnosing androgen insufficiency." In addition, psychological factors alone or in combination with biological factors also influence both men and women's desire. For example, depression and the use of antidepressants can inhibit sexual desire, as can low self-esteem, anxiety, and past negative experiences with sex (Bancroft, Loftus and Long, 2003; Basson, 2005). Like other sexual problems, disorders of desire for both women and men may increase with age. We shall discuss this aspect in Chapter 12.

In addition to aversion and hypoactive desire disorders, the media gave a lot of attention to another desire disorder in the 1980s: "hypersexual" response, known popularly as sexual addiction. This "problem" is not included in the DSM, although it is included in the World Health Organization's International Classification of Diseases (International Statistical Classification 10, 1992; King, 2005). It has been estimated that as many as 6 percent of U.S. people are hypersexual, using sex in the same way as substance abusers. These individuals' sexual behavior may place them at risk for sexually transmitted infections. Whether hypersexuality is a sexual disorder is debated by therapists and social scientists alike. Sociologists like Martin P. Levine and Richard Troiden (1988: 347–363) warn that the creation of hypersexuality as a disease category will enable the convergence of medicine and politics, two very powerful institutions, in defining what is "normal" sexual behavior. Other mental health professionals believe that people with hypersexual disorder want and need help with this serious psy-chological disorder. This nexus of medicine and politics can be used not only to define what is normal, but to control people through their sexu-ality, for example political efforts to prevent gay and lesbian marriage/or unions.

Various theories have arisen specifically to address disorders of desire including biological, psychological, and cultural explanations (we shall address sexual dysfunctions more generally after discussing various discord-ances in the current DSM-IV-TR). Some sexologists attribute hyposexual desire disorder to fallout from the 1960s Sexual Revolution. Caplan and Tripp regard sexual taboos as basic to sexual excitement, consequently as the last sexual taboos were broken during the 1960s and 1970s, so was the excitement associated with the forbidden lost (Lee, 1985: 83). Irvine (1990a) offers a socio-cultural analysis that regards hyposexual desire as "the medicalization of a simple non-pathological product of sexual bore-dom or indifference, due to the widespread problem of flagging sexual interest in marriage" (in Davis, n.d.: 13). Others have argued for a more multidimensional view of sexual desire and of dysfunction (Bancroft, Loftus and Long, 2003; Kaschak and Tiefer, 2001; Hicks, 2005; Tiefer, 2004, 2006a) that does not privilege biological explanations or imply normative cultural expectations in the evaluation and treatment of sexual problems. In this regard, Basson (2005: 1327) has asserted:

> Clinical and empirical studies, mainly of North American and European adult women . . . have clarified sexual response cycles that are different from the linear progression of discreet phases . . . Women describe over-lapping phases of sexual response in a variable sequence that blends the responses of mind and body. That women have many reasons for initiating or agreeing to sex with their partners is an important find-ing. Women's sexual motivation is far more complex than simply the presence or absence of sexual desire (defined as thinking or fantasizing about sex and yearning for sex between actual sexual encounters).

Arousal disorders

In the DSM-IV-TR female arousal disorder is defined as the "[p]ersistent or recurrent inability to attain, or to maintain until completion of the sexual activity, an adequate lubrication-swelling response of sexual excitement" (1997–2006). Estimates in the United States population of female arousal disorder range from 6 to 16 percent; with statistics increasing with age in women. Laumann, the principle investigator in "The Global Study of Sexual Attitudes and Behaviors Survey," funded by Pfizer (the creators of sildenifil/Viagra), collected data from 27,000 women and men aged forty to eighty from twenty-nine countries. This research has identified an increasing incidence of men's sexual difficulties as they age including arousal problems. Problems with lubrication are distinguished as the main age-related sexual issue for women who are not more likely to have other age-related sexual dysfunctions. However, these findings from "The Global Study of Sexual Attitudes and Behaviors Survey" are problematic in that arousal disorders were defined using a strictly physiological response without including the subjective element of the response, for example, does the woman report feeling aroused (Bancroft, Loftus, and Long, 2003; Basson, 2005).

Male erectile disorder is defined as the "[p]ersistent or recurrent inability to attain, or to maintain until completion of the sexual activity, an adequate erection" (DSM-IV-TR, 1997–2006). Prevalence of this disorder includes statistics that 2 percent of men under forty, 10 percent of men aged thirty to forty-nine and 18 percent of men fifty to fifty-nine attested to erectile problems in the previous year; other figures for erectile disorder indicate that 10 percent of men aged fifty-five years old had experienced this problem (Dunn et al., 2002; Laumann, Paik, and Rosen, 1999; Simons and Carey, 2001). The term impotence has been widely used in popular culture to describe a man's inability to obtain an erection. The concept of male potency does not have a counterpart in terminology for women and is an obvious example of the dual and sexist symbolization of male sexuality (Richardson, 1988: 129).

Erectile problems can occur for a variety of reasons. Most men have at some time experienced the inability to have an erection due to "excessive fatigue, heavy drinking, and/or over anxiousness about sexual performance—all of which are characteristically associated with masculine activities" (Richardson, 1988: 129). Some, but not a complete list of, additional factors identified as causing or contributing to erectile disorder include: prescription medications (especially those for high blood pressure), diseases like atherosclerosis and diabetes, damage to nerve fibers due to surgery or trauma, and low testosterone levels (Johannides, 2004).

Before the advent of the "sexopharmaceutical revolution" in the 1990s, research on men's erectile problems emphasized psychogenic and sociocultural factors, although harbingers of medicalization had begun earlier in the 1970s followed by an initial expansion in the 1980s as the fields of urology and pharmacology carved out a treatment niche. Industrialized masculinity in the late twentieth and early twenty-first centuries continued to emphasize a penis-centered model of performance and orgasm. The loss or decline of erectile and orgasmic functioning is a serious threat to masculine identity shaped by an ideology of phallocentrism—the ideal of producing erections at will and as well as having staying power or sexual stamina (Kilmartin, 2007). Performance not pleasure is emphasized in this industrial ideal of masculinity.

A psycho-cultural perspective toward male erectile problems was developed out of the convergence of men's studies and various social scientific approaches. Generally speaking, before 1970, young men's erectile problems were attributed to psychological causes (related to the stresses of masculinity and other contextual factors), and erectile disorders in midlife and older men were considered part of the aging process, not necessarily a disorder. After 1970, however a shift in emphasis occurred and male dysfunction came to be socio-culturally defined incrementally over the last 35 years as a biomedical phenomenon (Tiefer et al., 2006a). At one time Masters and Johnson stated that as much as 80 percent of erectile disorders were due to psychological factors; currently it is estimated by doctors that perhaps 80 percent have a physical basis (King, 2005).

Viagra was born (approved by the FDA) March 27, 1998. With its invention and that of its cohorts, it has become a major player in the ideologies of "normative" masculine sexuality. Treatments for erectile disorders were revolutionized by Pfizer, the creators of sildenafil (Viagra), whose clinical studies found sildenafil produced erections in 70 percent of a test population of men with erectile problems (Ault, 1988: 1037; Handy, 1998: 54). Other additional treatments for erectile dysfunction currently available include psychological therapy, hormone replacement therapy, vacuum devices, urethral suppositories, penile injections, vascular surgery, and penile implants (King, 2005; "Putting the Pill (for Men) in Perspective," 1998: 4; Tiefer, 2006). All testify to the lengths that men will go in the quest for phallic performance and living up to an industrialized (and sometimes nonindustrialized) ideal of masculinity. New oral medications for increasing blood flow to the penis are on the horizon. In the "New View of Men's Sexual Problems," Tiefer (2006a) offer a multidimensional approach to masculine sexual difficulties, one that underscores the integration of bio-psychogenic and cultural variables, including context and the nature of the partner relationship. Tiefer (2004: 233) asserts:

> Erectile dysfunction, a condition in the man's genitalia, has become the only acknowledged focus of interest, focus of evaluation, and focus of treatment. This represents a substantial narrowing from sex therapy—erasing the partner, erasing subjective meaning, and ironically, perpetuating the obsession with penile hardness which many sex experts have argued is itself a primary cause of sexual unhappiness.

Orgasmic disorders

Orgasmic disorders include both female and male, as well as premature ejaculation in men. Female Orgasmic Disorder is defined by the DSM-IV-TR (1997–2006) as the:

> [p]ersistent or recurrent delay in, or absence of, orgasm following a normal sexual excitement phase. Women exhibit wide variability in the

type or intensity of stimulation that triggers orgasm. The diagnosis of Female Orgasmic Disorder should be based on the clinician's judgment that the woman's orgasmic capacity is less than would be reasonable for her age, sexual experience, and the adequacy of sexual stimulation she receives.

This disorder includes several variations. **Primary orgasmic dysfunction** is associated with women who have never had an orgasm. **Secondary orgasmic dysfunction** occurs in women that have been orgasmic but are no longer. **Situational orgasmic dysfunction** occurs under certain contexts but not others (*DSM-IV-TR*, 1997–2006; King, 2005; Masters and Johnson, 1970). It has been estimated that 10 to 15 percent of women have never experienced an orgasm (Althof and Schreiner-Engel, 2000). Causes have been ascribed to biogenic factors. Low levels of testosterone have also been debated as playing a role (Basson, 2005). Kaplan and Owett (1993: 3–24) initially identified the "female androgen deficiency syndrome" substantiating an earlier Waxenberg et al. study in 1959, asserting that the loss of androgens in women can lead to loss of sexual desire, decrease in orgasms, and loss of orgasmic ability. Androgen deficiency syndrome was found to occur among women who had undergone chemotherapy or oophorectomies (removal of the ovaries), and testosterone replacement therapy was the prescribed treatment. However, as our discussion of hyposexual desire disorders noted, guidelines by the Endocrine Society (Wierman et al., 2006) have challenged the efficacy and safety of testosterone treatments (also Davis et al., 2005).

With the invention of sildenafil (Viagra), the pharmaceutical search for a female Viagra has been vigorous. However, women's sexual response has proven far too complicated to be "fixed" with a pink Viagra. FDA approval for a women's Viagra has not occurred although it is prescribed off label for women (Tiefer, 2006a). Medicalized perspectives on women's orgasmic problems neglect the importance of a variety of other factors including sexual knowledge, the relationship with the partner, personal history, stress, emotional well-being, etc.

Male orgasmic disorder is defined as the "[p]ersistent or recurrent delay in, or absence of, orgasm following a normal sexual excitement phase during sexual activity that the clinician, taking into account the person's age, judges to be adequate in focus, intensity, and duration" (DSM-IV-TR, 1997–2006). Prevalence rates are recorded as low as 1 to 3 percent to as high as 7 to 9 percent of men (Laumann, Paik, and Rosen, 1999; Simons and Cary, 2001). Research suggests that this problem is primarily of psychocultural origin associated with the pressure for performance.

Another orgasm disorder for men is premature ejaculation. This is defined in the DSM-IV-TR as "[p]ersistent or recurrent ejaculation with minimal sexual stimulation before, on, or shortly after penetration and before the person wishes it. The clinician must take into account factors that affect duration of the excitement phase, such as age, novelty of the sexual partner or situation, and recent frequency of sexual activity." Research indicates that this may occur in 15 to 30 percent of the male population (Dunn et al., 2002; Laumann, Paik, and Rosen, 1999). Premature ejaculation is a problem of control and is the most prevalent sexual dysfunction reported for men up until age fifty-nine. It may be due to biological factors, but this is rarer; it is more likely related to performance anxiety and other psychocultural factors. Debates as to rates of occurrence include figures from 15 to 30 percent of men experiencing premature ejaculation, with disagreement on how it is defined (King, 2005).

Sexual pain disorder

Sexual pain disorder includes dyspareunia for both men and women and vaginismus for women. Dyspareunia is defined as "[r]ecurrent or persistent genital pain associated with sexual intercourse in either a male or a female, before during and after intercourse" (*DSM-IV-TR*, 1999-2006). One study ascertained that 16 percent of women between the ages of eighteen to sixty-five experience chronic burning vulvar pain lasting longer than three months, and 8 percent experienced pain at the time of the survey. The overall incidence of women eighteen to sixty-five who can't have intercourse due to pain is 10 percent according to Basson (2005). Vaginismus is defined in the DSM-IV-TR as the "[r]ecurrent or persistent involuntary spasm of the musculature of the outer third of the vagina that interferes with sexual intercourse, but it is also associated with unexplained recurrent or persistent involuntary contraction of the perineal muscles around the outer third of the vagina associated with penetration with any object" (1997–2006). Etiology is usually attributed to psychological and/or biological factors. Treatments include psychotherapy, antidepressants, topical and injected steroids, and estrogen among other interventions (National Vulvodynia Association (NVA) Research Update Newsletter, 2005). The National Vulvodynia Association is a patient advocacy group dedicated to improving the sexual lives of women who have vaginal pain.

Sexual difficulties in cultural context

According to Goldberg (1985), our cultural conditioning undoubtedly creates a situation in which "sex is at cross-purposes." The gendering process of sexual socialization creates mismatches between the genders. Men are socialized through a recreational model of sexuality to experience sex as conquest with the goal orientation of orgasm. Women are socialized in a relational model to experience sex as intimacy and as a process of achieving closeness. Gender role mismatches also occur. As the initiator, the male carries the entire responsibility for making sex fulfilling and, consequently may experience guilt and resentment over this role. In tandem, the female, in her role as reactor, may come to feel anger over being sexually controlled. Goldberg suggests other cultural oppositions occur as a result of divergent gender role expectations including cultural assumptions of male "promiscuity"/desire for multiple partners countered by female desire for monogamy, and in the role dichotomy of male as animal—female as Madonna. In addition, the expression-repression mismatch is one in which males learn to regard sex as a "preoccupation" and females see "sex...[as]...something that may be enjoyed under special conditions of commitment and intimacy but, at the same time, something a woman feels she can do without if the circumstances are not right" (Goldberg, 1985: 147).

Although these trends may be exaggerated and not representative of the heterogeneity nor of ethnic diversity in sexual attitudes of the twenty-first century, there is still some truth to these as cultural ideals for many middle-class Anglo Americans. Much sexual dysfunction is due to the anxiety, guilt, and repression spawned by inequalities between the genders and the disparities in gender status and role, i.e., gender stratification. Paradoxically, while the Sexual Revolution and the new age of sex research may have tempered some of these problems caused by gender status and role inequities, a host of new fears associated with performance anxieties have arisen.

A critical constructionist perspective integrates not only the cultural context in which sexual dysfunctions occur but the numerous ways in which the medical and mental health sectors define, label, categorize, diagnose, and treat sexual dysfunctions; for example, the terms for describing human sexuality such as "dysfunction" and "dyspareunia" focus on difficulties and pain. Medical terms emphasize a disease model and concentrate on the dysphoric aspects of sex rather than the euphoric. The clinical approach to diagnostic categories for sexual disorders has been critiqued as ethnocentric, classicist, and sexist by an ample body of socio-cultural literature (Bancroft, Loftus, and Long, 2003; Davis, n.d.: 1; Tiefer, 2004, 2006a and 2006b).

Although the condition is all too real for the individual suffering from these problems, this should not blind us to recognizing that there are cultural biases in approaching sexual dysfunctions (Davis, n.d.: 1–28). For the disorders associated with timing, such as too soon or perhaps too late, cultural beliefs shape the tempo of sexual arousal and these can vary by gender, ethnic group, class, and cross-culturally. For example, some heterosexual males may regard delayed ejaculation as more of a problem than their partners do. A woman's orgasm difficulties may be related to a lack of understanding of sexual functioning, beliefs that sex is dirty or bad, or that sex is immoral. Both men and women may have sexual problems caused by the partner's lack of knowledge and sexual expertise.

A new view of women's and men's sexual problems

In 2003, Lenore Tiefer and a working group of colleagues launched a campaign entitled *A New View of Women's Sexual Problems* that offered an alternative standpoint. This campaign took issue with the increasing medicalization of women's sexuality, such as the pharmaceutical quest for a female Viagra, the encroachment of the medicalization of menopause, as well as the system of classification of women's sexual disorders in the DSM. This campaign resulted in publications, conferences, and a web site (FSD-Alert; Kaschak and Tiefer, 2001). *A New View of Women's Sexual Problems* regards the medical classification scheme in the *Diagnostic and Statistical Manual of Mental Disorders* as a "fundamental barrier to understanding women's sexuality" ("Female Sexual Dysfunction: A New Medical Myth," 2006; "The Manifesto," 2002). The DSM was criticized on several grounds in *A New View of Women's Sexual Problems.*

- It assumes there is a universal, normal sexual response; i.e. drive.
- It defines human sexuality response primarily in terms of physiological function.
- It assumes that human sexual response occurs in a linear cycle.
- It ignores the differences among women.
- It disregards the importance of the relationship in sexual functioning.
- It assumes that women and men are alike by disregarding the socio-cultural parameters of sexuality (Hicks, 2005; Tiefer, 2004).

A burgeoning body of research supports this critique and perspective. Compelling evidence attests that women's sexual responses do not follow the linear DSM model, but are rather "overlapping" and heterogeneous, blending mind and body, influenced by socio-cultural context and relationship satisfaction in a bio-psycho-social matrix (Bancroft, Loftus, and Long, 2003; Basson, 2005: 1327; Mah and Binik, 2005).

In 2006, "The 'New View' Approach to Men's Sexual Problems" created by Lenore Tiefer (2006a) reflected similar concerns regarding men's sexual problems; that is, men's sexuality is reduced to erections, with a similar critique of the DSM resulting in a "New View Classification of Sexual Problems (Affecting both Women and Men)" (Tiefer, 2006a: 12). "A New View of Sexual Problems" self-consciously uses the terminology sexual "problems," not sexual "dysfunctions" or "disorders" and denies that there is linear sexual response cycle. It argues that women and men "may be dissatisfied with any emotional, physical, or relational aspects of the sexual experience" (Tiefer, 2006a: 12). The causes of this dissatisfaction may range from social, relational, personal, or physical. These four aspects are interrelated dimensions of people's sex lives and are presented in order of "likely prevalence" and in order of suggested interventions as well. These are identified as:

- sexual problems due to socio-cultural, political, or economic factors.
- sexual problems due to partner and relationship.
- sexual problems due to psychological factors.
- sexual problems due to physiological or medical factors (Tiefer, 2006a: 12–13. For a detailed view see "The 'New View' Approach to Men's Sexual Problems").

The causes of sexual dysfunction may be analyzed from the societal/cultural level to that of the individual. When discussing the psycho-somatic aspects of sexual dysfunction that are associated with anxiety, the cultural perspective must be included so that the effects of cultural pattern-ing may be considered. In addition, there are physiological factors that can affect sexual functioning including disease (cancer, bladder disorders, dia-betes, structural damage) and response to drugs (diuretics, adrenal steroids) (Kaplan, 1979). Davis (n.d.: 1–35) has reviewed and critiqued the Sexual Disorders in the *Diagnostic and Statistical Manual of Mental Disorders IV*, and has proposed that in order to maintain and understand the role of cul-ture in shaping diagnosis in our industrialized society, we need to move beyond "categorizing and classifying sexual behavior to an emphasis on questioning and analyzing the constructions of the categories themselves, as culture-bound" (Davis, n.d.: 11). This is particularly important in seek-ing to understand sexual dysfunction in other ethnic groups or cultures because the industrialized clinical theories of sexual dysfunction ignore the role of culture and ethnicity. This perspective combined with "A 'New View' of Sexual Problems" provides a template for understanding the complex-ities in human sexual response as biological, psychological, and cultural phenomenon.

This chapter has covered much territory, including discussion of human sexual response, theories of sexuality in industrialized societies and industri-alizing societies, the influence of globalization and the cross-cultural record including diverse points in time. We have explored sexual problems in sexual response from a biological, psychological, and cultural perspective, including attention to global issues with an emphasis on the importance of cultural context. This chapter represents a snapshot in time current with publication. Because sex research, scholarship, data and statistical evidence are dynamic just like people and the cultural worlds they inhabit, readers are encouraged to explore recent research in human sexuality in all its facets including evidence spanning the local to the global.

SUMMARY

1 Sex is defined as a biological, psychological, and cultural phenomenon with attention to the importance of culture in shaping its meaning and expression.

2   Cross-cultural evidence is introduced including Mangaian and Tantric models of sexuality; these are contrasted with industrialized models.
3   Industrialized models of sexuality are introduced in a critical and historical framework.
4   Prominent researchers of sexology are discussed including: Freud, Kinsey, Masters and Johnson, Kaplan, Singer and Singer, Whipple and Perry, Laumann and colleagues, Tiefer and colleagues.
5   Problems in sexual response are addressed including sexual dysfunction and sex therapy. These are placed in a biological, psychological, and cultural framework.
6   The clinical perspective of sexual dysfunction is compared to the "New View of Women's and Men's Sexual Problems."

Thought-provoking questions

1   How do college students define "hooking up"? Describe how sexuality is negotiated by women and men in the encounter? What expectations do you think are involved?
2   What is your response to the "New View of Women's and Men's Sexual Problems"?

SUGGESTED RESOURCES

Books

Gagnon, John H. 2004. *An Interpretation of Desire: Essays in the Study of Sexuality.* Chicago: University of Chicago Press.
Tiefer, Leonore. 2004. *Sex Is Not a Natural Act.* Boulder: Westview Press.

Article

Noonan, Raymond J. 2001. "Web Resources for Sex Researchers: The State of the Art, Now and in the Future." *The Journal of Sex Research* 38 (4): 348–351.

Web sites

"Female Sexual Dysfunction: A New Medical Myth: Current Campaign Activities." www.fsd-alert.org. Last accessed 12/12/06.
The Kinsey Institute for Sex, Gender, and Reproduction. See sections: Research Program, Current Research Projects, Research Publications, Selections from the "Kinsey Reports"s 1948–1953 and Kinsey Institute Data and Codebooks. http://www.kinseyinstitute.org/research/surveylinks.html. Last accessed 12/12/06.
Shiva Shakti Mandalam. This is a comprehensive Tantric resource site on the Internet: http://www.religiousworlds.com/mandalam/index.html. Last accessed 12/12/06.

12 Topics in adult sexuality
Birth control

CHAPTER OVERVIEW

1 Defines key terms and concepts related to birth control including contraception, population, fertility, mortality, migration, theoretical effectiveness rate, actual effectiveness rate, and woman years.
2 Compares and contrasts population trends between industrialized and nonindustrialized nations.
3 Examines industrialized, nonindustrialized and indigenous approaches to birth control.
4 Explains various birth control and contraceptive methods.
5 Discusses prevalence and availability of various kinds of contraceptive techniques globally with reference to policy and unmet needs in industrializing nations.
6 Provides an overview of abortion trends and practices in the United States including the historical and political context.
7 Explores abortion trends in industrializing/nonindustrialized nations.
8 Summarizes preindustrial and traditional methods of birth control in cross-cultural and historical context.

BIRTH CONTROL: PRACTICES AND PREVALENCE IN INDUSTRIALIZED AND NONINDUSTRIALIZED NATIONS

Dramatic changes have occurred in terms of overall population in the world. The time it took for the earth's population to reach the first billion spanned from *Homo sapiens* around 150,000 years ago to 1850. By 1930, it took only eighty years to reach the second billion; in the course of another thirty years, the third billion. Circa 1976, the world's population reached four billion (Gordon and Snyder, 1986: 155). By 2005, the world population climbed to 6.5 billion people. This represents a gain of 76 million people annually and 380 million more than in 2000. By 2050, it is estimated that population will reach 9.1 billion people (*World Population Prospectus*, 2004). Because sex research, scholarship, and statistical evidence are generated continuously, readers are encouraged to update the data we present.

Before venturing into our discussion of birth control in the United States or globally, it is important to define our terminology. **Birth control** refers to any method whereby births are prevented and includes any method for controlling fertility (including contraceptive methods) through birth spacing, late marriage, long postpartum sex taboos, herbs, abortions, etc. **Contraception** refers to methods that interfere with the fertilization of an ovum by sperm and include barrier, hormonal, and surgical means. Therefore, abortion is considered a method of birth control, but not a contraceptive method, since it terminates an established pregnancy. In popular usage and some of the literature these terms (birth control and contraception) are often used interchangeably although sometimes inaccurately. **Population control** is an abstract concept used to discuss major demographic trends that includes births, deaths, and migrations. **Fertility** is a measure of the rate at which people are born. **Mortality** is a measure of the rate of deaths. **Migration** is defined as the "movement of people into or out of a geographical area" (Eshleman, Cashion, and Basirico, 1988: 591). Until approximately 200 years ago, high death rates with high birth rates maintained worldwide population stability. In 1850, a major demographic transition occurred in which birth rates continued at high levels while death rates decreased. Death rates declined because of improved diet and advances in preventative medicine and treatment as well as improvement in public health measures such as clean drinking water and safer disposal of waste (Bates and Fratkin, 2003; Gordon, 1978: 513). These trends created a period of explosive population growth. However, gradually, family planning and birth control methods began to have an impact, and the rapid growth was moderated (Eshleman, Cashion, and Basirico, 1988: 595).

Although industrialized nations followed this pattern, the transition may not yet be completed in nonindustrialized countries (Gordon and Snyder, 1986: 155; Wells, 1978: 517–518; *World Population Prospectus,* 2004). For example, although the world's population continues to increase overall, this is almost exclusively a result of population growth in the industrializing nations. Fertility is below replacement levels in the most industrialized nations (1.56 children per woman), while it is still high in the least industrialized countries (five children per woman). Mortality remains low and continues to decline in industrialized nations; in other countries such as those with transitional economies it has either leveled off or is increasing due to poverty. This is also true for those industrializing nations affected by HIV/AIDS whose mortality has increased (*World Population Prospectus,* 2004). A United Nations report has summarized the differences in population trends between industrialized and nonindustrialized nations:

- Currently, 95 percent of all population growth occurs in the developing world and 5 percent occurs in the developed world.
- By 2050, it is predicted that the population of the more developed countries as a whole would be declining slowly by about 1 million

persons a year and that of the developing world would be adding 35 million annually, 22 million of whom would be attributed to the least developed countries.

- Fertility is predicted to continue at a low and declining rate of growth in industrialized nations remaining at about 1.2 billion estimated for 2005–2050.
- The population of the least developed fifty countries is projected to more than double, going from 0.8 billion in 2005 to 1.7 billion in 2050.
- Predictions of overall worldwide fertility declines are contingent on access to family planning, especially in developed countries (*World Population Prospectus,* 2004: xiv–xvii).

If we assume fertility as the norm, the relative chances of conception in a year of unprotected intercourse are 85 to 90 percent (King, 2005; King, Camp, and Downey, 1991: 130). This is important information for a sexually active heterosexual couple trying to evaluate the effectiveness of contraceptive methods over the course of a year. Two strategies for assessing contraceptive effectiveness are used. The **theoretical effectiveness rate** refers to the percentage of couples who would conceive using a particular technique correctly and systematically. The **actual effectiveness rate** is lower than the theoretical effectiveness rate since not all couples use birth control methods properly or consistently. The effectiveness of a technique is reported in terms of the number of failures per 100 couples in a year of use called a **woman year**, since women are the people who are impregnated. Over time the chances for pregnancy increases with any technique. For example, a technique with a 5 percent failure rate the first year will increase to between 23 and 40 percent over the course of ten years (King, 2005; Fu et al., 1999).

The problem of unwanted pregnancy is far more complex than just an issue of access to contraceptives and birth control. Although the middle and upper classes in the United States, dominated by whites, may be more aware of birth control methods through the availability of sex education information (remembering the constraints of national and state policy), this is not necessarily true for the lower socioeconomic classes, including various ethnic groups, and immigrant populations. In addition, the cultural context for birth control and family planning programs must consider age and generation, status, gender, religion, economics, cultural pluralism, and other factors including the impact of globalization. Sexuality education programs may not be sensitive to the cultural variation in the domestic arena and globally. For example, Mohammadi et al. (2006) found that despite religious codes that prohibit sex before marriage, 28 percent of their sample of 1,385 Tehran males aged fifteen to eighteen had engaged in sexual activity, but were not knowledgeable about contraceptives or STI/HIV transmission. These patterns of sexual behavior were associated with the use of the internet, drugs, cigarettes, and alcohol as well as work experience and living apart from their families. Another example from Vietnam is also illustrative of cultural influences on sexuality and contraceptive choices. The industrial emphasis on individuality and autonomy in sexual decision making would not be a culturally appropriate model for Vietnam. For Vietnamese, birth control in the 1980s through the early 1990s was used only by married couples with the input and approval of the couples' parents. For the Vietnamese then, contraception was a family concern, not an individual choice. Consequently, class and cultural bias occur in terms of access to information, availability of birth control methods, and societal and economic support (Taylor and Ward, 1991: 129).

Other factors must also be considered in understanding how people choose contraceptive techniques. For example, there are distinct age and gender differences in choices of contraceptives among men and women in the United States. The Alan Guttmacher Institute (2002) reports the following:

- Although two-thirds of men and women rely on condoms for their first experience, this declines with age.
- Only 16 percent of women and men aged thirty-five to thirty-nine had used a condom in the past month.
- As people age, regardless of marriage status, there is an increased dependence on women's birth control methods, e.g., 45 percent of men and 44 percent of women use women's methods by their late twenties.
- By their late thirties, 15–20 percent of women and men rely on vasectomy.
- The majority of sexually active people still favors female contraceptive methods: 31 percent of women and 24 percent of men use female sterilization, 14 percent of women and 21 percent of men use other female methods ("Facts in Brief: Sexual and Reproductive Health: Women and Men," October 2002).

Researchers in Brazil have found that women who had three or more children were more likely to choose sterilization as a method of birth control and were less knowledgeable about other methods of birth control. Having children was also found to be initiated earlier among Brazilian women with more than three children and they also had a lower income than women with fewer children (Leone and Hinde, 2005; Tamkins, 2004). These findings may help explain Brazil's high sterilization rate for women; 50 percent of women aged thirty-five and older had been sterilized according to 1966 data offering historical depth to this practice. Subsequently sterilization has continued as a popular method and may account for the declining fertility of Brazil recorded for the second half of the 1970s. Currently researchers suggest that education about contraception should be provided for adolescent women since this is the age they are making reproductive choices and need to be informed about effective reversible methods (Leone and Hinde, 2005; Tamkins, 2004).

In a classic piece of research Luker (1975) has suggested a gendered theory of "contraceptive risk taking." What happens, according to this theory, is that a woman engages in a cost and benefit analysis of using contraception so that if the costs of contraception outweigh the perceived risk of pregnancy, then unprotected intercourse is likely to occur. The costs to women of using contraceptives are social in that their reputations are at risk in terms of self-concept and peer approval. The double standard, although modified, still prevails and affects the contraception decisions of females. A public "coming out" as sexually active may be expressed by purchasing over-the-counter contraceptives at a drug store or making an appointment to see a physician. This necessarily has emotional and psychological consequences for the individual and relations with peers and family. As students, do you think the double standard for women's use of contraceptives is still in effect among your peers?

Motives in choice of contraception and methods used vary. Some forms of contraception, such as condoms, reduce spontaneity. This may be perceived by women as a potential problem in their relationships with men. They may fear the possibility of being rejected or abandoned by their partners should they ask them to use contraception, or in some contexts they may even be at risk for violence. Issues of women's power to mediate the use of condoms, for example, are important in understanding women's risk for STI/HIV, pregnancy and physical harm. Moore's (2006) study of how sex is negotiated by Brazilian women has implicated the importance of gendered ideologies. In order to be regarded as "girls to marry," rather than "girls to date," women were expected to be sexually ignorant and passive. Yet, women were also under pressure to give in to demands for sex. There is a pervasive belief among the Brazilian women that there are extremely negative consequences to saying no to sex with a man. Moore (2006: n.p.) concluded that the sexual system is a coercive one because "women engage in unwanted sexual intercourse because they believe their partner will otherwise abuse or abandon them even if no threat is made..."

There are also young women for whom pregnancy is regarded as a positive event, a quick ticket to adulthood and status for those who have not reckoned with the economic realities of childrearing as a single parent or as a young couple. It is important to consider the cultural meaning of pregnancy and sex, as well as its socio-cultural matrix including socioeconomic factors, male-female relations, power inequities, and ethnic issues when evaluating contraceptive use.

Table 12.1 Contraceptive methods by world region, percentage of population, and type

Region	Any contraceptive method	Two most prevalent methods
Europe	68%	Pill (18%) Condom/IUD (12%) Withdrawal (11%)
Latin America and the Caribbean	82%	Female sterilization (31%) Pill (14%)
North American (Canada and the United States	76%	Female sterilization (25%) Pill (16%)
Australia/New Zealand	75%	Female sterilization (25%) Pill (23%)
Oceania (Melanesia, Micronesia, Polynesia)	27%	Female sterilization (8%) Injectable implant (7%)
Africa	27%	Pill (7%) Injectable implant (5%)
Asia	63%	Female sterilization (25%) IUD (17%)

(Source: Data compiled from information from "World Contraceptive Use 2005," United Nations Department of Economic and Social Affairs Population Division, 2005.)

A wide array of modern contraceptive options is available in the world today. See Table 12.1. This table illustrates the prevalence of various kinds of contraceptive techniques found in nonindustrialized and industrialized societies.

These methods include: abstinence, "natural" methods referred as rhythm methods, barrier contraceptives, spermicides, hormonal contraceptives, intrauterine devices, and surgical methods ("Birth Control," 2006; "Birth Control Guide," 2003). However, birth control is not a recent invention or one limited to modern nation states. Women and men throughout history and around the world have developed ways to control births and population, some more effective than others. Cross-culturally and historically these have included *coitus interruptus*, prolonged abstinence, various approaches to safe periods in a woman's cycle (rhythm methods), extended breast feeding (lactational amenorrhea method), oral contraceptive recipes, douching, blocking the eye of the cervix, use of oral abortificants, abortion and infanticide among others (Riddle, 1992 and 1997; Ward and Edelstein, 2006). See the discussion under "Traditional methods of birth control in cross-cultural context."

Birth control methods described for industrialized society are often referred to as "modern" methods by national and international agencies; although we know some are not so modern at all. Table 12.2 "Birth control methods guide," excerpted from the "Birth Control Guide of the Food

Table 12.2 Birth control methods guide

Type	Side effects and health risks	Protection from STIs	Failure rate (births per 100 women)*	Convenience	Cost and availability
Male condoms FDA approval: Latex: before approval required Polyurethane: 1989, cleared; 1995, marketed	May develop an allergic reaction especially to people with latex. If man or partner is allergic to latex use polyurethane condom.	Best protection against STDs except for abstinence. Very effective in preventing HIV when used consistently and correctly.	11[1,2]	Placed in position before intercourse and worn during intercourse then immediately discarded.	No doctor's visit. Free or low cost from health department or drug store.
Female condoms FDA approval: 1993	Irritation or may develop allergic reaction to material (usually not serious).	Protection from STDs and HIV transmission; not as safe as a male latex condom.	21	Used immediately before and worn during intercourse.	No doctor's visit. Cost is $3 to $5 each.
Diaphragm with spermicide FDA approval: before approval required.	Occasional reaction to spermicide; urinary tract infection; risk of toxic shock syndrome (rare).	No protection known at this time from STDs or HIV.	17[2,3,5]	Placed in position immediately before and worn during intercourse. Remains in position 6 hours after intercourse. May need to be refitted after abortion or weight loss/gain. May become dislodged in certain positions.	Must visit the doctor for prescription. Diaphragm itself costs around $35. Doctor must re-check yearly.

Table 12.2 (Continued)

Type	Side effects and health risks	Protection from STIs	Failure rate (births per 100 women)*	Convenience	Cost and availability
Lea's Shield with spermicide FDA approval: 2002	Made of silicone, the risk of allergic reaction is slim. May increase chance of toxic shock syndrome, bladder and vaginal infections.	Some protection against STDs like gonorrhea and chlamydia but none against herpes, HPV, or HIV. Recommended that men use condoms in association with this method.	15	Used immediately before and worn during intercourse. Does not need to be sized by a physician. After use should be washed.	Must visit the doctor for a prescription. Lea's Shield itself usually costs around $65.
Cervical cap with spermicide FDA approval: Prentiff Cap, 1988 Fern Cap, 2003	May experience some irritation or an allergic reaction. Pap smears may be abnormal and suffer erosion of the cervix. Risk of toxic shock syndrome (extremely rare).	While the spermicide kills the sperm, there is no evidence that it protects against STDs or HIV.	17 or 23 (depending on make of device)[2,4,5]	While it may be applied up to 48 hours before intercourse, it is difficult to insert. Sizing can be a problem for some women. May be dislodged if positions change.	Must visit the doctor for prescription. Cost of the device around $45.

Method / FDA approval	Side effects		Convenience / use	Cost / doctor's visit
Sponge with spermicide FDA approval: 1983 (not currently on the market).	May cause irritation to the vagina and occasional dryness to the area. Could lead to toxic shock syndrome and abnormal Pap smears.	While the spermicide kills the sperm, there is no evidence that it protects against STDs or HIV. Frequent use of spermicides alone or in combination with other barrier methods may cause skin irritation in the lining of the vagina and may increase the risk of STI infection.	14 to 28[4,5]	Difficult for some women to remove after use. Can remain in place for 48 hours without needing additional spermicide.	No doctor's visit required. Where available, cost would be around $3. Not currently on the market in the United States.
Spermicide alone FDA approval: Before approval required. Since November 2002, only one active ingredient has been allowed.	May cause allergic reactions and genital irritation or rash. May develop urinary tract infection. Skin rash.	While the spermicide kills the sperm, there is no evidence it protects against STDs or HIV. Spermicide may irritate vaginal tissue and can increase the risk for HIV.	20 to 50	Time differential for applying depending on type chosen. Can be used as part of sex play. Can be messy.	No doctor's visit required. Cost varies based on type used—usually $5 to $10.
Oral contraceptives (combined pill) FDA approval: First in 1960; most recent, 2003.	May cause dizziness and nausea. Women may experience changes in menstruation and possible weight gain. In extreme cases, other health risks include high blood pressure, chance of blood clots, strokes, and heart attacks.	None	1 to 2	Very convenient but must be taken on a daily schedule without fail. If the chewable tablet is used, 8 ounces of liquid must be drunk immediately after the pill is taken.	Must visit the doctor for prescription. Cost varies from $9.50 to $30 depending on the manufacturer.

Table 12.2 (Continued)

Type	Side effects and health risks	Protection from STIs	Failure rate (births per 100 women)*	Convenience	Cost and availability
Oral contraceptives (progestin-only, minipill) FDA approval: 1973	May lead to women experiencing irregular bleeding, breast tenderness, and weight gain. In extreme cases, may also experience an ectopic pregnancy.	None	2	Very convenient but must be taken on a daily schedule without fail.	Must visit the doctor for a prescription. Cost varies from $9.50 to $30 depending on the manufacturer.
Oral contraceptives (91-day regimen—Seasonale) FDA approval: 2003	May cause dizziness and nausea. Women may experience changes in menstruation and possible weight gain. In extreme cases, other health risks include high blood pressure, chance of blood clots, strokes, and heart attacks. May experience some bleeding and spotting between periods.	None	1 to 2	Very convenient but must be taken on daily schedule. Since a woman will experience fewer periods, pregnancy should be considered if a scheduled period is missed.	Must visit the doctor for a prescription. Cost varies from $9.50 to $30 depending on the manufacturer.
Patch (Ortho Evra) FDA approval: 2003	Women may experience bleeding between periods and breast tenderness. Mood changes can occur and some experience nausea and headaches. In extreme cases, may increase risks of heart attack, strokes and blood clots in women over the age of 35.	None	1 to 2 (weight could be a factor)	Patch is worn for a three-week period and not worn during the fourth week. It is recommended that medicine and herbs be checked as some make the patch ineffective. Patch must be used as directed to be effective.	Must visit the doctor for a prescription. The patch costs between $30 to $40 a month.

Method	Side Effects		Effectiveness	Description	Cost/Notes
Vaginal contraceptive ring (NuvaRing) FDA approval: 2001	Vaginal discharge and irritation. Breast discomfort, headaches, nausea are common. In extreme cases, women may experience blood clots in the legs. Increased risk of heart attacks and strokes and in extreme cases liver tumors.	None	1 to 2	Inserted into the vagina, it remains in place for three weeks and then removed for one. If the ring is expelled from the body, another birth control method must be used for 7 days until ring has been re-established in the body for 6 days.	Must visit the doctor for a prescription. The NuvaRing costs between $30 to $35.
Post-coital contraceptive (Preven and Plan B) FDA approval: 1998–1999	Nausea, vomiting, headaches, dizziness, lower abdominal pain are common side effects which stop within a day or two. Some experience unexpected bleeding from the hormones	None	80% reduction of risk in pregnancy for single act.	Use must be within 72 hours of unprotected sex. Cannot be taken before sex. Some prescription drugs hinder its effectiveness.	As of November 2006, Plan B does not need a prescription and can be bought over the counter by men and women over the age of 18. Preven costs between $30 and $45. Some pharmacists have refused to sell the drug.
Injection (Depo-Provera) FDA approved: 1992	Headaches, depression, dizziness, weight gain are common side effects. Side effects may include breast tenderness, nervousness, nausea. Irregular menstrual bleeding, possible bone loss, and ectopic pregnancy are more severe risks.	None	Less than 1	Extremely effective. One injection every three months and there is no daily regime. There are few hormonal side effects. Women cannot discontinue its use for three months after injection.	Must visit the doctor for an injection. Cost is less than $50 per injection.

Table 12.2 (Continued)

Type	Side effects and health risks	Protection from STIs	Failure rate (births per 100 women)*	Convenience	Cost and availability
Injection *Lunelle) FDA approval: 2000	Women can experience changes in their menstrual cycle, vaginal bleeding, weight gain, headaches, and breast tenderness. In extreme cases, the drug can lead to blood clots, heart attacks, strokes, gallbladder disease, or liver tumors.	None	Less than 1	Extremely effective. One injection every month. A woman can attempt a pregnancy after being off the injections for three months.	Must visit the doctor for the injection. The injection itself costs around $30.
Implant (Norplant) FDA approval: 1990 No longer avilable except for those presently using device.	Women may experience headaches, dizziness, nausea, acne, weight gain, breast tenderness, and nervousness. Also, enlargement of the ovaries and irregular menstrual bleeding. Blood clots, ectopic pregnancies, and infection are not rare.	None	Less than 1	While an outpatient surgical procedure, the device is effective for up to five years. No pills or hormone effects are seen. If the woman decides to get pregnant, the device must be removed through outpatient surgery.	No longer available. Must visit the doctor to arrange the procedure. Cost may be as high as $750 for the insertion of the capsule. Estimate of average monthly cost is $12.50.
IUD (intrauterine device) FDA approval: "Some IUDs were sold before premarket approval was required in 1976. Those products are no longer on the market" (FDA, 12/2003).	The main side effect is cramping and heavy menstrual discharge. While no proof, some fear it could lead to pelvic inflammatory disease. Perforation may occur upon insertion to the wall of the uterus and infertility.	None	Less than 1	After insertion by physician, the device may be used from one to ten years. The device does not change menstrual cycle. It can introduce bacteria into the uterus and may be ejected or become incorrectly positioned.	Doctor must insert the device. In addition to cost of doctor's visit, the device runs around $200 to $400 for insertion.

Method					
Rhythm method/basal body temperature method (periodic abstinence) FDA approval: NA	None	None	20	Women must know their body functions including period regularity and body temperature. If judged inaccurately, pregnancy could result.	Health care providers can usually supply information to be used for determining the periods when pregnancy is most likely.
Transabdominal surgical sterilization—female (Falope Ring, Hulka Clip, Filshie Clip). FDA approval: "Sold before premarket approval was required (1976)" (FDA, 12/2003).	Surgical complications are a possibility along with pain, bleeding and the chance of infection. Slight risk of ectopic pregnancy.	None	Less than 1	One-time procedure that requires an abdominal incision. The woman's fallopian tubes are blocked, thus pregnancy is prevented.	Doctor's visit and surgery. Cost could run $1300 upward.
Sterilization implant—female (Essure System)	Pain can be experienced after insertion of tube through minor surgery. "Considered permanent as reversal is typically unsuccessful (FDA 12/03)."	None	Less than 1	Device is inserted by minor surgery into the vagina by catheter. Scar tissue forms in fallopian tubes preventing conception. Another birth control method must be used for three months or until confirmation of placement.	Doctor's visit and surgery. Cost would run $1300 upward.

Table 12.2 (Continued)

Type	Side effects and health risks	Protection from STIs	Failure rate (births per 100 women)*	Convenience	Cost and availability
Surgical sterilization—male	Men can experience pain, bleeding and some infection from the surgery. "Considered permanent as reversal is typically unsuccessful." (FDA 12/03).	None	Less than 1	One-time surgical procedure	Doctor's visit and surgery. Cost would run $850 upward.

(Source: From the "Birth Control Guide" (2003), Westheimer and Lopater's *Human Sexuality* (2002), Epigee Women's Health, Planned Parenthood, "Answers to Frequently Asked Questions About…How to Get Emergency Contraception" (2007), "Objections, Confusion Among Pharmacists Threaten Access to Emergency Contraception" (2007), and American Pregnancy Association.)

Notes:
* These statistics do not note the distinction between theoretical effectiveness rate and actual effectiveness rate. In selecting a method of birth control, these distinctions should be explored.
1 Projected from six-month study and adjusted for use of emergency contraception.
2 If spermicides are used with barrier methods, be sure that the spermicide is compatible with the condom or diaphragm (won't cause it to weaken or break). Oilbased lubricants (such as petroleum jelly or baby oil) will cause latex to weaken and should not be used with these methods.
3 Spermicides used alone, with barrier devices, or with condoms can cause irritation to the skin lining the vagina, especially when the spermicide is used frequently. There is a possibility that spermicide might increase the risk of acquiring some sexually transmitted diseases because of disruption of the vaginal skin. Spermicide has not been proven to be effective against bacteria and viruses in people. Therefore, there is no reason to use spermicide during pregnancy.
4 Medications for vaginal yeast infections may decrease effectiveness of spermicides.
5 Less effective for women who have had a baby because the birth process stretches the vagina and cervix, making it more difficult to achieve a proper fit.

and Drug Administration" (2003) and other sources, offers a summary of birth control options available in the United States as well as generally worldwide, although access and hence prevalence rates differ domestically and internationally. This table also includes failure rates, risks, protection from STIs/HIV, convenience and availability, possible medical problems, and contraceptive benefits.

In nonindustrialized societies availability of the methods described in Table 12.2 is expanding as a result of international family planning programs, government programs, NGOs and other organizational efforts. However, "traditional" methods for birth control are still utilized in nonindustrialized societies among ethnic, indigenous, and migrant populations and may coexist, and/or be culturally fused with more traditional methods. For the sake of convenience and simplicity we use the term "**traditional**" to refer to indigenous, ethnic, and cultural practices prior to and coexistent with industrialized methods of birth control.

There are significant differences in the availability of industrialized methods of birth control between rich and poor countries (Potts, 2003: 93). According to Planned Parenthood's "The Unmet Need for Family Planning" (2006):

- 350 million couples throughout the world lack access to a full range of family planning services.
- 150 million married women around the world actively want to use family planning but lack access to the contraceptives, information and services that would make that possible.
- The number of couples in their reproductive years increases by 20 million couples every year, creating a growing demand for family planning.
- The world's one billion youths are just now entering their reproductive years, with another 2 billion to follow in future generations.

The United Nations reported on world contraceptive use in 2001 and 2005 and has identified some distinct differences between industrialized and nonindustrialized nations (note many agencies, organizations, and scholars use the term "developed" and "developing nations"). Refer to Table 12.1. This information was collected on contraceptive use by women between the ages of fifteen and forty-nine who are married or in consensual unions. Selected trends from this research found:

- Sixty-two percent of married/in-union women of reproductive age in the world are using contraceptive methods.
- In more industrialized nations that figure is approximately 70 percent; the pill is most prevalent (16 percent) with the condom as second most common (14 percent).

- In less industrialized nations that statistic is 60 percent; female sterilization is most prevalent (22 percent) with the IUD as second most common (15 percent). ("World Contraceptive Use 2001", 2002; "World
  Contraceptive Use 2005," 2005).

There are encouraging trends over the past ten years through to the twenty-
first century indicating a rise in contraception use overall in industrializing
countries, increasing by at least one percentage point in 68 percent of the
countries. For example:

> In Africa contraceptive usage among married/consensual union women
> increased from around 15 percent to 25 percent in 2001; in Asia, from
> 52 to 66 per cent; Latin America and the Caribbean, from 57 to 69
> per cent...[However] high levels of unmet need for family planning
> remain in the developing countries, despite the recent rapid growth in
> the use of contraception. ("World Contraceptive Use 2001," 2002)

Figure 12.1, "Unmet need for contraception in industrializing nations,"
testifies to the urgency of continuing to address the unmet need for contraception despite substantial increases with the exception of sub-Saharan
Africa (Sonefield, 2006). Also refer to Table 12.3, "Health and economic
indicators in countries with a high unmet need for family planning"

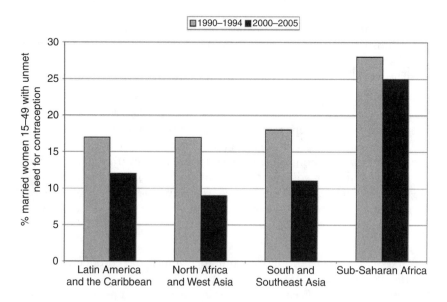

Figure 12.1 Unmet need for contraception in industrializing nations. (*Source*:
   Excerpted from Guttmacher Policy Review, 2006; Sonefield, 2006.)

Table 12.3 Health and economic indicators in countries with a high unmet need for family planning

Country	Gross national income per capita 2003 (US$)	Value of donated reproductive health supplies per capita (US$)	Maternal deaths per 100,000 live births in 2000	Adult HIV prevalence rate (%)	Unmet need for family planning (%)
Nepal	$1,420	$13.05	740	0.5	27.8
Mali	$960	$9.82	1,200	1.9	28.5
Burkina Faso	$1,180	$6.09	1,000	4.2	28.2
Malawi	$600	$5.89	1,800	14.2	29.7
Cambodia	$2,060	$0.80	450	2.6	29.7
Pakistan	$2,060	$1.11	500	0.1	32.0
Togo	$1,500	$16.07	570	4.1	32.3
Uganda	$1,440	$12.79	880	4.1	34.6
Ethiopia	$710	$5.82	850	4.4	35.2
Rwanda	$1,290	$3.36	1,400	5.1	35.6

(Source: Excerpted from Leahy, 2006, Population Action International.)

(Leahy, 2006), which indicate the many methods used globally for family planning.

The Alan Guttmacher Institute has summarized some important trends regarding contraceptive prevalence among 62 million women of child-bearing age in the United States ("Facts in Brief: Contraceptive Use," 2005). Preferred birth control methods reflect an individual's stage in the life course, ethnic differences, and cultural milieu. Some of the important findings excerpted from this research on United States birth control are:

- The pill and female sterilization remain the most prevalent methods since 1982.
- The pill is most preferred in younger women, never-married, and college-educated women.
- Sterilization is most common among women over thirty-five, married, or previously married, and those without a college education.
- Sterilization is the leading method among black and Hispanic women, while the pill is the leading method for white women.
- Fifty percent of all women aged forty to forty-four who practice contraception have been sterilized, and another 18 percent have a partner who has had a vasectomy.
- Women in their teens and twenties are more likely to rely on the three-month injectable method than are older women.
- Women aged twenty-five to twenty-nine are more likely than women in other age groups to rely on the implant, one-month injectable or patch.

- Hispanic and black women are less likely to rely on their partner's vasectomy or the pill, and more likely to rely on the three-month injectable or no method.
- Poor and low-income women are more than twice as likely as higher-income women to use the three-month injectable.
- 7.3 million women use barrier contraceptives, such as the male condom.
- Condom use is most prevalent among teenagers, twenty to twenty-four-year-olds, childless women, and never-married women ("Facts in Brief: Contraceptive Use," 2005).

In summary, availability and prevalence differs worldwide between more industrialized nations and less industrialized nations. Differing prevalence and popularity is due to many factors: age, ethnicity, class, education, women's status and gender inequity, economic, political, religious and other cultural features that impact practices at the local, regional, national, and global levels.

Globalization can have a significant impact on birth control practices. For example, although we have addressed problems with the U.S. abstinence-only-until-marriage approaches to birth control (favored by George W. Bush since 1995 as governor of Texas and subsequently championed in his presidential role) in Chapter 10, this policy also has important implications for the international arena as well ("State Profiles," 2004). The United States federal government provides funding for international family planning efforts as well as HIV/AIDS prevention and treatment. Although access to contraception and abortion are hotly debated issues in some social sectors nationally and internationally, the costs of unintended pregnancies and births have been proven to contribute to increased poverty, starvation, and death. This particularly has consequences for women who are the childbearers and caretakers (King, 2005; Ward and Edelstein, 2006).

In the United States, the George W. Bush administration favored funding abstinence-only education at the expense of a comprehensive sexuality education program that includes information on available birth control options. President Bush has described abstinence as "the surest way, and the only completely effective way, to prevent unintended pregnancies and sexually transmitted diseases" (quoted in Dailard, 2003: 4). As discussed, the critique of the abstinence-only initiative has been immediate and widespread including numerous professional, medical, social, religious, and grass-roots organizations such SIECUS, The Society for Adolescent Medicine, the American College Health Association among numerous others. Representative Henry A. Waxman has issued a report critiquing abstinence-only education from a human rights as well as ethical prospective (Dailard, 2003; Waxman, 2006).

At the international level, the Bush administration had several policies that relate to contraceptive use that have also drawn debate. For example, the Bush administration's **PEPFAR** (President's Emergency Plan for HIV/AIDS Relief) since 2000 has doubled funds going to international campaigns that promote abstinence-only and fidelity strategies. This limits funds for the promotion of condom usage in preventing HIV/AIDS. Most important, this has repercussions for women as partners and wives; it has implications regarding women's reproductive rights and family planning choices as well (see Chapter 15).

As we have discussed, there remains a large unmet need for contraception internationally and people's very lives are at stake with unintended pregnancy resulting in maternal mortality and health problems, poverty, and starvation. Contraceptives help prevent at least 187 million pregnancies every year. The largest contributor to funding for contraceptives in industrializing nations is from the United States through USAID (Cohen, 2006). This is why the Bush administration's proposed cutting of funding for USAID's family planning program for 2007 was regarded with such apprehension. The global gag rule, according to Cohen (2006): "is an obstacle that impedes the availability of contraceptives at least in certain parts of the world..." Sixteen developing countries in Africa, Asia, and the Middle East had lost their USAID supply of contraceptives as of 2002. The gag rule can be blamed for the loss of contraceptive supplies to leading NGOs in twelve other countries (see discussion on abortion). The global gag rule (reinstated in 2001 under Bush administration) is in reference to U.S. policy that denies any family planning assistance to international agencies that include information on abortion (except in cases of rape, incest, or life-threatening circumstances) or who support the legalization of abortion in their respective countries.

Contraceptive methods described

We will briefly describe the most well-known methods of contraception in the United States. Please see Table 12.2, "Birth control methods guide," as it offers a summary of birth control options available in the United States as well as in other industrialized/industrializing countries, although prevalence rates differ as described earlier. This chart is excerpted from the "Birth Control Guide" (2003). For specific information on each country see Table 12.1. Where available, we include international data for the method under discussion. In addition, keep in mind that new contraceptive choices and government regulation are dynamic phenomena, thus new methods may become available while this book is in the production and publication process.

Some of these methods of birth control are more effective than others. For example, **abstinence** is effective in avoiding pregnancy provided one's discipline and determination are not challenged. **Withdrawal** *(coitus interruptus)* where the male pulls out prior to ejaculation and douching are very ineffective methods. Yet, 8 percent of the women in the more industrialized world practice this method and over 2 percent in the less industrialized nations. The following statistics indicate the prevalence of *coitus interruptus* among married/consensual union women practicing contraception by country/region: Africa (1 percent), Asia (2 percent), Europe (11 percent), Latin America and Caribbean (4 percent), North America (2.1 percent), Australia and New Zealand (2 percent) and Oceania (Melanesia, Micronesia and Polynesia) (less than 1 percent) (figures are rounded to nearest percentage point, data from "World Contraceptive Use 2005," 2005).

Fertility awareness methods (FAMs) are based on keeping track of the woman's menstrual cycle to predict safe and unsafe days for coitus; during unsafe days either abstinence or other methods should be used for sexually active people. Worldwide data from married/consensual union women indicate the percentage using the rhythm method by country and region is: Africa (4 percent), Asia (2 percent), Europe (6 percent), Latin America and Caribbean (5 percent), North America (2.1 percent), Australia and New Zealand (2 percent) and Oceania (Melanesia, Micronesia and Polynesia) (3 percent) (figures are rounded to nearest percentage point, data from "World Contraceptive Use 2005," 2005).

FAMs include: the **calendrical method**, the **basal body temperature** method, the **Billings method** (cervical mucous or ovulation method), along with general efforts by women to keep records of their menstrual cycle. These **rhythm methods** are based on identifying when a woman ovulates. There is a twenty-four-hour fertility window that occurs immediately after ovulation in which the woman's egg can be fertilized. The calendar method is based on a formula in which 18 is subtracted from a woman's shortest cycle and 11 from her longest cycle observed over a minimum of eight cycles (day one is the start of menstruation). This figure will represent the days that unprotected sex should be avoided. Typical-use failure rates with this method are reported from 25 percent to as high as 45 percent depending on the study (King, 2005: 148).

In the basal method, a woman takes her temperature daily upon rising and charts when her temperature rises slightly over the course of her cycle. Within twenty-four to seventy-two hours after ovulation, a woman's temperature rises by a few tenths of a degree. With this method, no intercourse should occur from the end of menstruation until two to four days after her temperature rises. According to King (2005), this method is a serious challenge to one's will power since it involves what can be perceived as a long period of abstinence, as does the rhythm method. In addition, this technique requires a certain amount of expertise in recognizing small temperature increases that may be due to causes other than ovulation, such as illness. It has a typical-use failure rate of 75 percent. The Billings method is based on the evaluation of vaginal mucous to determine when ovulation takes place. Usually cloudy mucous becomes clear, slippery, and stretchy one to two days prior to ovulation and then returns to its cloudy form. Its typical-use failure rate has been reported as high as 80 percent. The Billings method may be combined with the basal metabolic method to enhance the effectiveness of either technique ("Birth Control," 2006; King, 2005).

Barrier methods include: the male and female condom, the diaphragm, cervical cap, and Leas' Shield. Barrier methods prevent pregnancy by placing a barrier between the egg and sperm so that the sperm cannot reach the egg to fertilize it.

The **male condom** is made of a variety of substances including latex rubber, lamb intestine, polyurethane, or synthetic elastomers. The polyurethane condoms are half the thickness of rubber condoms and offer enhanced sensitivity and a more natural feel (King, 2005). The condom works by covering the penis and containing ejaculated sperm. The male condom and the female condom are effective against sexually transmitted infections, including HIV ("Birth Control," 2006; "Birth Control Guide," 2003; Centers for Disease Control and Prevention, 2006). There are many advantages to the condom. Besides its effectiveness in reduction of sexually transmitted infections and pregnancy prevention, the male condom is easily available and may help with premature ejaculation. The condom is the most frequently used method in some industrialized nations including Japan, England, and some Northern European countries (King, 2005). Worldwide data from married/consensual union women indicates the percentage using condoms with their partners by country/region is: Africa (2 percent), Asia (4 percent), Europe (12 percent), Latin America and Caribbean (5 percent), North America (13 percent), Australia and New Zealand (6 percent) and Oceania (Melanesia, Micronesia and Polynesia) (less than 1 percent) (figures are rounded to nearest percentage point, data from "World Contraceptive Use 2005," 2005.)

The polyurethane **female condom, FC1**, was introduced by the Female Health Company as a barrier method in the 1990s ("HIV Prevention Strategy Highlights Women," 1994: 26; Klugman, 1993: 70; "The Female Condom FC2," 2005). It offers women a method of pregnancy prevention with a 95 percent success rate if used correctly and facilitates the prevention and transmission of HIV/AIDS and other STIs. Unfortunately this product was expensive to manufacture, seriously limiting its adoption in the international sector. It is made of a seven-inch polyurethane bag held in place by two flexible rings. One ring holds the condom against the cervix and the outer ring holds it in place outside the vagina, partially covering the labia. It can be inserted up to eight hours before intercourse. More recently, the Female Health Company has developed **FC2**, a new version made of synthetic latex that is much cheaper to produce. According to the World Health Organization, the lower cost may lead to wider acceptance in international programs in preventing pregnancy and STI/HIV transmission ("The Female Condom FC2," 2005).

The female condom has certain advantages including offering women the possibility of more control over STI/HIV and pregnancy, although the issue of power inequities between men and women in the negotiation of sex is still not resolved by this method. Its advantages are that it does offer women an alternative with a partner resistant to condom usage and FC1 may be worn by women with latex allergies. Users report that it feels more "natural" than sex with male condoms and it may stimulate the clitoris providing women more pleasure. Both the male and female condom may be put on or inserted as part of sex play ("Birth Control," 2006; "The Female Condom FC2," 2005; "World Contraceptive Use 2005," 2005).

The **diaphragm**, a thin dome-shaped barrier that prevents sperm from entering the cervix, is used with a spermicidal gel or cream. The diaphragm fits snugly over the cervix and holds the spermicide in place. As a method of birth control, the diaphragm is 86 to 94 percent effective. The disadvantages of the diaphragm are that it does not protect against STIs/HIV. It may be inserted up to two hours before intercourse (the effectiveness period of spermicide) and additional spermicide must be inserted vaginally if more than two hours has passed since insertion. It should not be removed for six to eight hours after intercourse and additional spermicide must be used with every act of intercourse. Its advantages are a high effectiveness in pregnancy prevention, ease of use, comfort and it does not affect the menstrual cycle. A diaphragm does require a fitting by a health care professional. In the event of pregnancy and/or weight change a refitting may be required. It has been found to cause allergic reactions and may increase bladder infections ("Birth Control Comparisons," 2006).

Additional barrier methods include the **cervical cap**, a much smaller barrier than the diaphragm, also requiring the use of spermicide. Learning to insert it may require practice and some technique, but it may be used for up to forty-eight hours without reapplying spermicide. Another barrier method, the **sponge**, is 90 percent effective when combined with a spermicide and can be inserted up to twenty-four hours before penile-vaginal intercourse ("Birth Control," 2006). However, the FDA notes that the sponge is not currently marketed in the United States due to concerns over an increased risk of toxic shock syndrome. **Lea's Shield** was approved by the FDA in 2002. It is a dome-shaped rubber disk with a valve and a loop that is held in place by the vaginal wall. It covers the upper vagina and cervix so that sperm cannot reach the uterus. Spermicide is applied before insertion, but it provides no protection against STIs/HIV. It can be inserted prior to intercourse and must be left in place for at least eight hours ("Birth Control," 2006; the "Birth Control Guide," 2003).

The barrier methods are designed to be used with spermicide. Since the 1950s, spermicides using nonoxynol-9, an agent that kills sperm, have been available. Spermicide comes in various forms including foam, cream, jelly, film, suppository, or tablet. Nonoxynol-9 does not provide protection against STIs, including HIV/AIDS. It may actually increase the likelihood of STI/HIV infection by irritating and causing lesions and exfoliation of the cellular lining in the vagina and anus. Therefore, the World Health Organization and Centers for Disease Control and Prevention recommend nonoxynol-9, preferably used with a barrier method, for women who are at low risk for HIV transmission, but it is not recommended for women at higher risk such as those who have vaginal intercourse several times a day. Because nonoxynol-9 can damage the lining of the rectum it should not be used as a lubricant for anal intercourse (Johnson and Friedman, 2002). Worldwide data from married/consensual union women practicing contraception aggregate the various vaginal barrier methods such as diaphragm, cervical cap, sponge and spermicidal methods. The percentage using vaginal barrier methods by country/region are: Africa (0 percent), Asia (less than 1 percent), Europe (1 percent), Latin America and Caribbean (less than 1 percent), North America (0 percent), Australia and New Zealand (0 percent) and Oceania (Melanesia, Micronesia and Polynesia) (0 percent) (figures are rounded to nearest percentage point, data from "World Contraceptive Use 2005," 2005).

Hormonal methods offer several options for women. The **oral contraceptive pill** (OCP) traditionally combines estrogen and progesterone to trick the body into thinking it is pregnant and prevents the egg's release. There are a variety of kinds of OCPs on the market from the combination pill, those that include both estrogen and progestin, to the mini pill. The **mini pill** contains only progesterone which inhibits the development of the uterine lining. In 2003, the U.S. Food and Drug Administration approved a new prescription drug called Ovcon 35, the first chewable (spearmint-flavored) oral contraceptive tablet for women. Ovcon 35 contains a progestin (norethindrone) and an estrogen (ethinyl estradiol) found in other OCPs that are already marketed. Another recent OCP is Seasonale, approved by the FDA in 2003. This oral contraceptive pill containing estrogen and progestin is taken in three-month cycles of twelve weeks followed by one week of inactive pills. Women taking this OCP have their periods every thirteenth week of the pill cycle. Consumers are attracted to having more control over their cycles as well as providing contraceptive protection, although no protection against HIV/STIs is provided. Other options include a class of synthetic progesterone that includes norgestimate and desogestril, approved by the FDA in 1993. These are similar to other OCPs, but with reduced side effects of weight gain, breast tenderness, acne, spotting, and nausea (Austin, 1993: 57). Currently, there are conflicting reports as to whether OCPs increase the risk of breast or cervical cancer. However, there is an increased risk of blood clots, and cardiovascular health problems (heart attack and stroke) are reported in women who smoke cigarettes and take OCPs, particularly if they are over the age of thirty-five ("Birth Control Comparisons," 2006; "Legislative Update," 2003).

Worldwide data from married/consensual union women indicate the percentage taking "the pill" by country/region is: Africa (7 percent), Asia (less than 5 percent) Europe (18 percent), Latin America and Caribbean (14 percent), North America (16 percent), Australia and New Zealand (23 percent) and Oceania (Melanesia, Micronesia and Polynesia) (5 percent) (figures are rounded to nearest percentage point, data from "World Contraceptive Use 2005," 2005).

Emergency contraception comes in several forms of OCPs. These include an OCP referred to as "the morning-after pill" in its early days, but recently conceived as post-coital contraceptive or **emergency contraception (EC)**. Typical protocol for EC consists of two doses of an **oral combination contraceptive** pill that contains a synthetic estrogen (ethinyl estradiol) and levonorgestrel. If taken within seventy-two hours of intercourse, there is a 75 percent effectiveness rate in preventing pregnancy (King, 2005; Klugman, 1993: 59). It has no effect on an established pregnancy and operates to prevent ovulation, fertilization and possibly implantation of a fertilized egg ("Get in the Know: 20 Questions About Pregnancy, Contraception and Abortion," 2006; King, 2005).

Plan B offers another hormonal option for emergency contraception. Plan B is a progestin-only pill taken in two doses twelve hours apart or the two doses may be taken at the same time. It is more effective than the combination pill offering 99.5 percent effectiveness within twenty-four hours of intercourse and 85 percent effectiveness if taken within three days ("Birth Control," 2006; "Birth Control Guide," 2003; King, 2005). On August 24, 2006, the FDA approved over-the-counter sale of Plan B to women eighteen years of age and older. According to Planned Parenthood (2006), particular birth control pills may be used in the same way and for the same end; the dosage varies by brand/type of pill. A third method of emergency contraception is implantation of an IUD. It is 99 percent effective if inserted within five days of unprotected sex ("Emergency Contraception: How to Take," 2006).

The National Women's Health Network states: "There is no scientific or medical reason for the eighteen and older age restriction that the FDA has imposed on obtaining non-prescription Plan B. Studies show that increased access to EC does not cause teen promiscuity or other health risk behaviors. And top FDA officials have privately acknowledged that the age restriction is a political concession to conservative activists who have been fighting to keep barriers to contraception access in place" ("Plan B: One Step Forward, Two Steps Back," 2006).

Other methods of delivery of hormonal contraception include **the patch** (Ortho Evra), approved in 2001. The patch contains estrogen and progestin that is applied once a week for three weeks to the upper body, lower abdomen, or buttocks. During the fourth week it is removed and menstruation occurs. Implants under the skin are another way to deliver hormonal birth control. **Norplant** is a three-inch-long delivery system that is placed under the skin of the arm. Easily implanted, but more difficult to remove, Norplant releases progestin and provides protection against pregnancy for five years at a 99 percent efficiency rate. However in 2002, as a result of lawsuits due to problems in removal and side effects, the makers of Norplant announced they were halting manufacture of their product and women should find other options after the five-year expiration ("FDA Approves Long-Term, Implantable Birth Control," 2006; Findlay, 1991: 126; Klugman, 1993: 70; Sivin et al., 1983).

Similar to Norplant are several other types of implants that deliver hormones. **Implanon** recently became available in the United States in 2006. Implanon is a small rod about 1.5 inches long that is injected under the skin (requiring a local anesthetic) of the upper arm. It is 99 percent effective and provides protection for up to three years through the delivery of a progestin that prevents ovulation, thickening the cervical mucous to interfere with fertilization by the sperm and altering the lining of the uterus to prevent implantation ("Birth Control," 2006). Implanon has been sold in over thirty countries since 1998 ("FDA Approves Long-Term, Implantable Birth Control," 2006). Jadelle, a two-rod levonorgestrel contraceptive implant was FDA-approved in 1996, but has not been sold in the United States. It may provide protection for up to five years and is currently available in developing and developed nations ("Jadelle Implants: General Information," 2005).

In 1992, the FDA approved the hormonal method, **Depo-Provera**. An injectable synthetic progesterone, Depo-Provera prevents the release of ova and interferes with the implantation of the egg in the uterus lining. One injection works for three months with a 99 percent effectiveness rate. A new formulation of Depo-Provera was approved by the U.S. FDA in 2005, "Depo-SubQ Provera 104." This is delivered by subcutaneous injection four times a year (every twelve to fourteen weeks). Lunelle, a once- a-month shot, is no longer available in the United States ("Birth Control Guide," 2003).

Worldwide data from married/union women practicing contraception indicates the percentage using injectable or implant hormone methods by country/region are: Africa (5 percent), Asia (3 percent), Europe (less than 1 percent), Latin America and Caribbean (4 percent), North America (2 percent), Australia and New Zealand (less than 1 percent) and Oceania (Melanesia, Micronesia and Polynesia) (7 percent) (figures rounded to nearest percentage point, data from "World Contraceptive Use 2005," 2005).

Introduced in 2001, the **vaginal contraceptive ring** (NuvaRing), a flexible ring that releases estrogen and progestin, is worn for three weeks and removed for one week. The downside of this method is that if the ring has been expelled for more than three hours, another method of birth control must be used.

The **intrauterine device** (IUD), a small metal or plastic device placed in the uterus, was popular in the 1960s and 1970s in the United States. Unfortunately, subsequent medical follow-up revealed negative side effects and health risks. These included an association between some IUDs and Pelvic Inflammatory Disease as well as other health problems including infertility. One consequence of this research was that the Dalkon Shield was taken off the market. Despite this, the IUD remains the most predominant reversible method of birth control practiced in the world today ("IUD," 2006). IUDs prevent sperm from uniting with an egg and/or may alter the lining of the uterus to prevent implantation. Several kinds of IUDs are currently available. IUDs are small plastic inserts made with either copper or progesterone. ParaGard is a copper IUD that may be left in place for up to twelve years, and Mirena is a progesterone hormone IUD that may be left in place for five years. As previously mentioned, according to Planned Parenthood Federation of America, ParaGard may also be used as emergency contraception and is 99.9 percent effective if inserted within five days of unprotected sex ("Emergency Contraception: How to Take," 2006). Worldwide data from married/consensual union women indicates the percentage using an IUD by country/region is: Africa (5 percent), Asia (17 percent), Europe (12 percent), Latin America and Caribbean (5 percent), North America (13 percent), Australia and New Zealand (6 percent) and Oceania (Melanesia, Micronesia and Polynesia) (less than 1 percent) (figures rounded to nearest percentage point, data from "World Contraceptive Use 2005," 2005).

In the early 1990s, the World Health Organization studied testosterone enanthate (TE) injections as a form of hormonal contraception in 271 men in seven countries. The weekly injections had few side effects and a success rate of 99.2 percent which made it more effective than OCPs (97 percent), IUDs (94 percent), and condoms (88 percent). After four months of weekly testosterone injections, a man's level of sperm was reduced enough to have a contraceptive effect. This was reversible after six-and-a-half months ("Men's Shots Used as Contraceptive," 1990; Prendergast, 1990). A 2006 review of clinical trials by Peter Liu and associates (2006) verifies that testosterone hormone treatment can temporarily stop sperm production. Dr. Peter Liu and his research team analyzed thirty trials conducted from 1990–2005 that included more than 1,500 men, and confirmed the findings of the earlier WHO study of testosterone that this method appears to be effective, reversible (sperm levels returned to normal within about three to five months after stopping the treatment) and could be available in five to ten years with few side effects ("A Contraceptive Pill for Men," 2006; "Male Contraceptive Reversible," 2006). The Population Council is researching MENT, a synthetic steroid similar to testosterone that holds promise as a method to suppress sperm production without enlarging the prostate (Kumar et al., 2006).

Other approaches to lower sperm counts couple testosterone and progestin. Because progestin reduces testosterone production and hence sperm production, researchers have administered low doses of testosterone in conjunction with various kinds of progestins. Trials using oral progestin or progestin implants, combined with various types of testosterone injections and/or a patch were analyzed with the preliminary finding that the progestin implant plus testosterone injection was the most effective approach in suppressing sperm production (Anderson et al., 2002; Christensen, 2000; Gonzalo et al., 2002).

Other methods to control births include surgical procedures for sterilization. The **vasectomy** interferes with sperm ejaculation by surgically cutting or cauterizing the vas deferens through a procedure that involves small incisions in the scrotum under local anesthetic. This typically takes about twenty minutes in the doctor's office. The no-scalpel technique is an alternative method invented and widely used in China and subsequently in the United States since 1985. It involves puncturing the skin with a special instrument, followed by severing or blocking vas deferens. The benefits of this method are that only one cut is made without the need for stitches and recovery is faster than in the conventional method ("No-Scalpel Vasectomy," 2006). In 2003, Vasclip was introduced in the United States. This technique uses a very small plastic clamp (the size of a grain of rice) that is snapped onto the vas deferens to block sperm through a micro-surgical procedure. Vasclip is less painful than the traditional vasectomy and reversing the procedure is also easier. Ejaculation still occurs with the various vasectomy techniques since the majority of fluid comes from the prostate and seminal vesicles. Although doctors are improving their success rates in reversing vasectomies, with some reporting up to a 50 percent success rate, vasectomy should be regarded as a nonreversible and permanent method of sterilization. Success rates depend on a number of variables including the type of vasectomy and length of time passed ("Birth Control Guide," 2003; King, 2005; Kirby, Utz and Parks, 2006).

Sterilization methods for women include **tubal ligation**, a surgical procedure that involves cutting, cauterizing, banding, or tying the fallopian tubes. This may be accomplished with a very small incision either through the abdomen or through the navel. This technique known as a laparoscopy includes insertion of a scope/tube through the navel to view and perform the tubal ligation. The unfertilized egg is subsequently absorbed by the body. The failure rate is less than one in 100 pregnancies (Birth Control Guide, 2003). The **Essure method** was approved by the U.S. Food and Drug Administration in 2002. In this technique, a tiny insert shaped like a spring is placed in each tube which irritates the tubal lining causing it to form scar tissue and resulting in the obstruction of the fallopian tubes and passage of the egg. In contrast to tubal ligation, the Essure method is a nonsurgical procedure done through the vagina. The down time is low and the woman can return to work/regular routines within twenty-four hours. Currently success in reversing female sterilization is still limited ("Birth Control Guide," 2003; Ubeda, Labastida, and Dexeus, 2004).

Worldwide data from married/union women and men practicing birth control indicate the percentage using female sterilization by country/region is: Africa (less than 2 percent), Asia (25 percent), Europe (4 percent), Latin America and Caribbean (31 percent), North America (25 percent), Australia and New Zealand (25 percent) and Oceania (Melanesia, Micronesia and Polynesia) (8 percent). The percentage using male sterilization by country/region is: Africa (less than 1 percent), Asia (4 percent), Europe (3 percent), Latin America and Caribbean (2 percent), North America (13 percent), Australia and New Zealand (12 percent) and Oceania (Melanesia, Micronesia and Polynesia) (less than 1 percent) (figures are rounded to nearest percentage point, data from "World Contraceptive Use 2005," 2005). The gender differences in sterilization are in some cases very dramatic and are anchored in gendered cultures, ideologies of reproductive responsibility, and power inequities.

ABORTION

Contemporary methods of abortion include surgical abortions and medical abortions. Generally, medical problems arising from abortions are few if conducted by trained professionals in hygienic environments; less than 1 percent of all abortions in United States incur complications. The risk of death due to abortion is less than one-tenth as large as the risk of childbirth; roughly less than 0.6 per 100,000 procedures. Furthermore, abortions do not increase a woman's future health risk for other pregnancies and there is no increased incidence of infertility, miscarriages, tubal, or cervical pregnancies or breast cancer ("Abortion," 2006; Waxman, 2004). In countries where abortions are illegal, 68,000 women a year die from complications, and many more have their health compromised by unsafe conditions ("Unsafe Abortion: Global and Regional Estimates of the Incidence of Unsafe Abortion and Associated Mortality in 2000," 2004).

The majority of abortions, about 90 percent, occur during the first trimester, with 56 percent prior to the eighth week ("Abortion," 2006; "Get in the Know: 20 Questions About Pregnancy, Contraception and Abortion," 2006; "Who Gets Abortions" 1990: G1). The vacuum aspiration method is the most common first trimester technique. This method involves the insertion of a tube into the cervix. The tube is attached to a hand-held device or a suction machine that withdraws the endometrial tissues from the uterus. In the **manual vacuum aspiration method** (**MVA**), the tissues from the uterus are gently suctioned through a hand-held device. This method may be used as early as three weeks and up to approximately seven weeks after the last menstrual period. Between six and twelve weeks, the **machine suction** procedure is preferred. For these first trimester pregnancies later than six weeks, local anesthetic and dilation of the cervix is performed along with suction. Dilation of the cervix may include insertion of an absorbent material the evening before which enhances the stretching of the cervix. As with the dilation and evacuation (D and E) procedure (discussed as follows), medication and/or the use of dilation rods may also be incorporated. In addition to either the MVA or machine suction, the use of a curette to further evacuate the uterine walls may also be used if suction alone was not enough (referred to as dilation and curettage or D and C); although this approach is seldom used during the first trimester but somewhat later (weeks twelve to fifteen). The benefit of the vacuum aspiration method is that it takes only ten minutes and is done on an outpatient basis under a local anesthetic requiring only a few hours of recuperation in a clinic ("Abortion," 2006; Goldberg et al., 2004; Hyde, 1985: 266).

Second trimester abortion rates drop dramatically with only 10 percent occurring during this period with the most prevalent method that of **dilation and evacuation (D and E)** ("Abortion," 2006). Dilation and evacuation combines the vacuum aspiration method with elements of dilation and curettage (D and C). D and E may include the insertion of an absorbent material that dilates the cervix. The dilation material is usually inserted the night before the procedure is performed to facilitate the absorbent material in gradually stretching open the cervix. Medications used either alone or in conjunction with dilators (rodlike devices) may also be incorporated. During the D and E, the patient is sedated or given IV medication as well as numbed locally; the dilator material is removed followed by evacuation of the uterus using suction and medical instruments (such as the curette) to clean the uterine walls further. The procedure takes between ten and twenty minutes. Dilation and evacuation is the preferred method for second trimester abortions (weeks thirteen to twenty-four) and even third trimester abortions because of the safety, efficacy, and time efficiency involved in this procedure. Only about 1 percent of late-term abortions occur after the twentieth week with less than one-tenth of one percent occurring at the twenty-fourth week and then only if the mother's health is at risk ("Abortion," 2006; Westheimer and Lopater, 2005).

Another but infrequently used option for late-term pregnancy termination is the **induction method**. This method is seldom used and only when there is a severe medical problem in the mother or fetus during the latter part of the second trimester or into the third trimester. Medications are injected into the amniotic sac and the vagina to cause contractions and the expulsion of the nonliving embryonic tissues; these medications include prostglandin, saline and/or other substances ("Abortion," 2006; "Planned Parenthood," 2006).

Hormonal methods of abortion, also referred to as **medication abortions,** are another choice for women but currently are limited to the first trimester of pregnancy. One type of medication uses the drug **mifepristone** as an abortificant. It is known more popularly in the United States as RU 486. This method is effective in the first two months of pregnancy and is 95 to 97 percent successful if used with misoprostol, a prostglandin. This protocol was tested on 2,000 women in the United States in the fall of

1994 (American Health, 1994: 8). Mifepristone works by inducing men-struation and preventing implantation in women who suspect fertilization by interfering with the production of progesterone and causing the lining of the uterus to slough. A second medication, **misoprostol**, is taken three days following mifepristone causing the cervix to soften and the uterus to contract thereby prompting a miscarriage in the early stages of gestation ("Abortion," 2006; Dowie, 1991: 137–140; Hall, 1989: 44; "Historical Information on Mifepristone," 2006; King, 2005; Klugman, 1993: 59).

Mifepristone was originally produced by a French company and accepted for use in 1988. It was not approved in the United States until 2000 amidst substantial controversy. It is authorized by the Federal Food and Drug Administration to terminate pregnancy up to forty-nine days after the last menstrual cycle. Other countries have adopted it although not without con-troversy; the United Kingdom and Sweden approved it in 1991, Germany in 1992 and other European countries by 1999. Currently it is available in twenty-nine countries and it has been proven safe with few adverse reac-tions and complications. However, some research indicates it has more side effects than a surgical abortion, although 90 percent of the women in one study stated they would opt for it again (Jones and Henshaw, 2002; "RU 486 Non-Surgical/Medical Abortion," 2006). In France it is used in about one-third of the abortions. Figures for the United States indicate it is increas-ingly used, from 5 percent of the abortions in 2001 to 24 percent in 2004 ("Get in the Know: Medication Abortion, 2006). Anti-abortion advoc-ates are against the legal use of mifepristone ("Historical Information on Mifepristone,"2006). Mifepristone is relatively fast acting and producing a medical abortion within a week in 92 percent of the cases with 95 percent to 97 percent effective within two weeks. The side effects include cramping, bleeding, and clotting ("Abortion," 2006; "Abortion Information," 2006).

Methotrexate is another drug commonly used in the United States that produces the same effect as mifepristone; it is followed by misoprostol about five days later. Methotrexate is an injection that inhibits reproduct-ive growth and can be used up to the ninth week of gestation. It is FDA approved but is used off label as an abortificant and is effective 90 to 97 percent of the time ("Abortion," 2006; Westheimer and Lopater, 2005). With methotrexate/misoprostol, approximately 75 percent of the abortions are completed within a week, but in 15–20 percent of the women it can take up to four weeks ("Abortion," 2006; "Abortion Information," 2006).

In the United States abortion is a hotly debated issue framed in diverse terms such as choice, life, personhood, and reproductive rights reflecting heterogeneous scholarly, religious, political, biological, and philosophical perspectives. The cultural meaning surrounding birth control methods such as abortion have varied considerably through time and across cultures. Worldwide and throughout history women everywhere have always been interested in having some control over their reproductive lives, whether it was to ensure and manage fertility, space births, or control the number of births and offspring. A cultural constructionist perspective will allow us to better understand this current controversy. Cross-culturally and historically there is considerable variation regarding when a blastocyst, embryo, fetus, neonate, or infant has been socially recognized as human and achieved personhood (Morgan, 1996). The anti-abortion camps in the United States have focused on creating "fetal personhood" and hence fetal rights, i.e., to life. Those sectors that support a woman's right to choose whether to terminate a pregnancy focus on women's reproductive rights, and their sexual and reproductive autonomy. Cross-culturally the possible approaches to defining humanity and personhood are much further reaching than the perspectives currently taken in the United States (Morgan, 1996). Notions of abortions and fetal personhood are related to wider socio-cultural patterns including the status of women, social stratification, gender ideologies, beliefs about the life cycle and bodies, mythology, the sacred world and other features of social life including the family and kinship (Morgan, 1996; Ward and Edelstein, 2006).

For an example of how abortion is embedded in the socio-cultural matrix, we need look no further than our own history. Before the nineteenth century, it was a woman's decision regarding termination of a pregnancy that was made up to the time of the **quickening**, when she first felt fetal movements, at about four months of pregnancy. Abortificants (drugs for abortions) were widely advertised and available; reflecting the pre-nineteenth-century belief that life began when the child moved, not at conception (Crandon, 1986: 471). "In 1800 there was not, so far as is known, a single statute in the United States concerning abortion" ("Abortion in American History," 1990: 8). However, over the next 100 years abortion became illegal in every state, with the only exception allowed if the woman's life was endangered. This may be partially attributed to the efforts of the newly formed American Medical Association's desire to legitimize and co-opt the maternal/female body as territory that had previously been under the control of women and midwives. According to the medical view, only physicians were sufficiently informed to know when abortions were necessary and justified (Crandon, 1986: 471). Until the 1960s, women were excluded from equal entry into medical schools, thereby ensuring that females had no voice in this issue until *Roe v. Wade* ("Abortion in American History," 1990: 8).

The controversy surrounding abortion in the United States is represented by two dominant perspectives: Pro Choice and Pro Life. The Right-to-Life (Pro-Life) position argues that the blastocyst/embryo/ fetus is a human life from the moment of conception and has the right to life regardless of the health risk, societal bias, and personal cost to the woman. The Pro-Choice position believes that the woman has the right to autonomy over her reproduction and that women's reproductive rights should prevail. In 1973 in the landmark case of *Roe v. Wade,* the Supreme Court, ruled 7 to 2 that a woman could decide (with her physician) to terminate a pregnancy in the first trimester and that the state could not interfere with that right. The judgment also allowed for second trimester abortions (Renzetti and Curran, 2003). Ironically, the *Roe v. Wade* decision set a standard for future government interest in the rights of the fetus during the third trimester (Lacayo, 1990: 23). Although *Roe v. Wade* has been held up by the Supreme Court in various challenges, antichoice supporters have been successful in putting limits on access to abortion for some women, especially teenage, poor, and rural women at the state level. For example, In July 1989, the Supreme Court ruled in favor of *Webster v. Reproductive Health Services*. A Missouri law allowed states to deny Medicaid funds for abortions as well as facilities for abortion and required doctors to test for fetal viability at twenty weeks (potential of fetus to survive outside the women's body). The decision paved the way for states to pass laws limiting and restricting abortions in a variety of other ways (Carlson, 1990: 16; *March E-News*, 2006; Renzetti and Curran, 2003).

The election of President Bill Clinton and a Democratic pro-choice platform subsequently resulted in greater government support of the *Roe v. Wade* decision in recent years. However, Clinton's successor, George W. Bush, voiced his opposition to abortion and has passed legislation to undermine *Roe v. Wade* in several ways. This included the global gag rule that denies funding to any international agencies that provide information on abortion or abortion services. This presidential mandate was first implemented by Ronald Reagan (1984), endorsed by George Bush (I), subsequently overturned by Clinton (1993), and then reinstated by the George W. Bush administration in 2001 on the anniversary of *Roe v. Wade*.

Other legislation has followed whose goal is to undermine *Roe v. Wade* and to create a culture supporting fetal personhood over the reproductive rights of the woman. This legislation is backed by far-right fundamentalist Christian leaders, their followers, and conservative legislators who seek the support of this constituency. Antichoice legislation in some states has sought to limit women's access to abortion by requiring counseling, waiting periods prior to abortion, parental permission, and parental notification before abortion can be performed. These laws are regarded as part of a political strategy to lay the groundwork for restricting women's reproductive freedom and eventually overturning *Roe v. Wade*. While these tactics do limit the number of abortions in a given state, the abortion rates of adjacent states increase ("An Overview of Abortion in the United States," 2003). In 2003, George W. Bush proposed the "Partial Birth Abortion Ban" to outlaw procedures as early as twelve to fifteen weeks of pregnancy. Federal judges ruled the law unconstitutional (Harrison, 2004).

In March 2006, South Dakota passed a law that made abortion illegal except in cases where the mother's life is in jeopardy. It was one of the most restrictive anti-abortion bans nationally; it did not allow abortion in cases of rape or incest, and charged doctors who performed abortions with a felony (Gibbs, 2006). The passage of this law was tantamount to a full frontal attack on *Roe v. Wade.* It was followed with support from other states considering similar bans; for example by March 2006, at least twelve other states were considering similar bans (Boonstra et al., 2006). However, in the 2006 midterm elections, voters clearly critiqued the undermining of *Roe v. Wade,* most notably in rejecting the South Dakota virtual ban on all abortions. Although women's reproductive rights were endorsed in the 2006 midterm elections, the reproductive freedom of women in the United States and elsewhere for that matter is far from established. Continued vigilance is required to maintain and affirm women's reproductive rights. For information on state policies on abortion, see Table 12.4, "Laws and abortion policies by state" (excerpted from "State Policies in Brief: An

Table 12.4 Laws and abortion policies by state** as of April, 2007

Law or policy	State
Parental notification required with minors	Colorado, Delaware*†, Florida, Georgia, Iowa, Kansas, Maryland*, Minnesota‡, Nebraska, South Dakota, West Virginia*
Parental consent required with minors	Alabama, Arizona, Arkansas, Idaho, Indiana, Kentucky, Louisiana, Massachusetts, Michigan, Mississippi^, Missouri, North Carolina, North Dakota^, Ohio, Pennsylvania, Rhode Island, South Carolina`, Tennessee, Wisconsin*, Wyoming
Mandatory counseling	Alabama, Alaska, Arkansas, California, Connecticut, Delaware, Georgia, Idaho, Indiana, Kansas, Kentucky, Louisiana, Maine, Michigan, Minnesota, Mississippi, Missouri, Nebraska, Nevada, North Dakota, Ohio, Oklahoma, Pennsylvania, Rhode Island, South Carolina, South Dakota, Tennessee, Texas, Utah, Virginia, West Virginia, Wisconsin
Mandatory wait	Alabama, Arkansas, Georgia, Idaho, Indiana, Kansas, Kentucky, Louisiana, Michigan, Minnesota, Mississippi, Missouri, Nebraska, North Dakota, Ohio, Oklahoma, Pennsylvania, South Carolina, South Dakota, Texas, Utah, Virginia, West Virginia, Wisconsin
Physician-only restriction: certain qualified health professionals restricted from performing abortions	Alabama, Alaska, Arizona, Arkansas, California, Colorado, Connecticut, Delaware, District of Columbia, Florida, Georgia, Hawaii, Idaho, Illinois, Indiana, Iowa, Kentucky, Louisiana, Maryland, Massachusetts, Michigan, Minnesota, Mississippi, Missouri, Nebraska, Nevada, New Jersey, New Mexico, New York, North Carolina, Ohio, Oklahoma, Pennsylvania, Rhode Island, South Carolina, Tennessee, Utah, Virginia, Washington, Wisconsin, Wyoming

Table 12.4 (Continued)

Law or policy	State
Refusal: certain individuals or entities can refuse to provide reproductive health services, information, or referrals	Alaska, Arizona, Arkansas, California, Colorado, Connecticut, Delaware, District of Columbia, Florida, Georgia, Hawaii, Idaho, Illinois, Indiana, Iowa, Kansas, Kentucky, Louisiana, Maine, Maryland, Massachusetts, Michigan, Minnesota, Mississippi, Missouri, Montana, Nebraska, Nevada, New Jersey, New Mexico, New York, North Carolina, Ohio, Oklahoma, Oregon, Pennsylvania, Rhode Island, South Carolina, Tennessee, Utah, Virginia, Washington, West Virginia, Wisconsin, Wyoming
Freedom of Choice Act in state law	California, Connecticut, Hawaii, Idaho, Maine, Maryland, Minnesota, Nevada, Washington
State funding of abortion under Medicaid in cases of life endangerment, rape, and incest	Alabama, Arkansas, Colorado, Delaware, District of Columbia, Florida, Georgia, Idaho, Indiana, Iowa, Kansas, Kentucky, Louisiana, Maine, Michigan, Mississippi, Missouri, Nebraska, Nevada, New Hampshire, North Carolina, North Dakota, Ohio, Oklahoma, Pennsylvania, Rhode Island, South Carolina, Tennessee, Texas, Utah, Virginia, Wisconsin, Wyoming

(Source: Information excerpted from: ProChoice America, http://www.prochoice america.org/choice-action-center/in_your_state/who-decides/state-profiles/, and the National Conference of State Legislatures, http://www.ncsl.org/programs/health/aborlaws.htm.)

Notes:
* Specified health professionals able to waive parental involvement if judge is involved.
** Supreme Court on April 18, 2007, by a 5 to 4 ruling upheld the ban on partial birth abortion. The impact this will have on the states are still to be determined.
† Minor laws in Delaware apply to women under 16, and minor laws in South Carolina apply to women under 17.
‡ Both parents must be involved.

Overview of Abortion Laws," 2006: 1–3). For the most recent information summarizing state policies on abortion, see the Alan Guttmacher Institute web site at www.guttmacher.org/sections/abortion.php.

Efforts to undermine *Roe v. Wade* have galvanized the pro-choice supporters and activists favoring women's reproductive rights. Not only was this represented in the 2006 midterm elections and in three states voting for legislation to protect abortion rights, but it is represented in numerous policy statements by diverse professional organizations, nonprofit organizations, family planning agencies, religious organizations, and various citizen groups. According to a Pew Research Center for the People and the Press Survey in 2003 of United States adults, approximately 66 percent support finding a middle ground on the abortion issue. This position, according to

Scott Keeter, Pew Director of Survey Research, reflects recognition by the survey participants that abortion is a very divisive issue in the United States ("Pragmatic Americans Liberal and Conservative on Social Issues: Most Want Middle Ground on Abortion," 2006). Results of this survey include some of the following statistics.

- 31 percent endorsed the view that abortion should be generally available.
- 20 percent felt abortion should be available but under stricter limits than it is now.
- 35 percent support banning abortion with the exceptions of rape, incest, and risk of maternal death.
- 11 percent thought abortion should be banned ("Pragmatic Americans Liberal and Conservative on Social Issues: Most Want Middle Ground on Abortion," 2006).

In fact, according to Renzetti and Curran: "Public opinion polls show that most Americans personally dislike abortion and feel that it should be discouraged. However, the majority also feels that regardless of one's personal views, the decision to have an abortion should be left up to the pregnant woman and her doctor" (2003: 177; also Harrison, 2004). Considerable research substantiates that most Americans do not want *Roe v. Wade* overturned ("Abortion and Birth Control Polling Report," 2006; Gibbs, 2006).

Abortion: trends and practices in the United States and industrialized nations

To discuss abortion and other birth control methods in the United States, internationally, and cross-culturally (emphasizing indigenous populations) requires that we maintain a culturally relativistic stance. Though abortion is certainly not the most desired practice in family planning, for some women it may be their only opportunity to have control over their reproduction. According to the Alan Guttmacher Institute, globally about 46 million women have abortions each year, with 20 million of them surreptitious, illegal, and conducted under unsafe conditions. More than three quarters of all abortions occur in the industrializing nations. In the United States, about 6 million women become pregnant annually, with about half of all the United States pregnancies unintended (about 3 million) and about half of the unintended pregnancies end in abortion ("Facts in Brief: Sexual and Reproductive Health: Women and Men," 2002; Finer and Henshaw, 2006). As we discussed in Chapter 10, U.S. teenagers have the highest pregnancy, childbearing, and abortion rates among the industrialized nations. The reason for this is that they use contraceptives less than do teens in other industrialized nations. Socioeconomic status (class) are variables associated with abortion that must be considered. Despite the decline in abortions in the United States generally, abortion has increased among poor women. Ethnicity is also a factor in abortions: black women are twice as likely as women from other ethnic groups to have an abortion, and Hispanic and Asian women rates are higher than the average also (Boonstra et al., 2006; "Get in the Know: 20 Questions About Pregnancy, Contraception and Abortion," 2006; "Teenagers' Sexual and Reproductive Health: Developed Countries,"2004). See Table 12.5, "Reported legal abortions obtained at

Table 12.5 Reported legal abortions obtained at ≤8 weeks of gestation, by known weeks of gestation, age group, race, and ethnicity of women who obtained abortion—selected areas of United States, 2003

Characteristic	Weeks of gestation						Total	
	6		7		8		No.	(%)*
	No.	(%)	No.	(%)	No.	(%)		
Age group (yrs)								
<15	570	14.8	463	12.0	509	13.2	1,542	40.0
15–19	21,193	20.2	16,293	15.6	15,556	14.8	53,042	50.6
20–24	54,820	25.7	37,734	17.7	33,174	15.6	125,728	59.0
25–29	42,379	29.5	27,292	19.1	22,256	15.5	92,028	61.1
30–34	28,050	20.8	18,515	19.7	14,760	15.7	62,225	66.2
35–39	16,224	30.8	10,345	19.7	8,450	16.1	35,019	64.6
≥40	6,522	32.9	3,855	19.4	3,106	15.7	12,483	62.0
Total†	170,658	27.0	114,583	18.1	97,821	15.5	243,067	60.6
Race								
White	89,629	20.6	52,277	18.2	44,127	15.0	107,123	62.0
Black	44,598	22.7	35,499	18.1	31,176	15.9	111,273	56.7
Other	12,445	32.9	7,294	19.2	5,404	14.5	25,222	66.6
Total‡	145,672	27.8	96,170	18.2	90,797	15.3	323,639	61.4
Ethnicity								
Hispanic	24,025	28.8	14,548	17.5	12,664	15.2	51,237	61.5
Non-Hispanic	96,601	26.1	65,451	18.0	56,874	15.4	219,936	59.5
Total§	120,626	26.6	81,009	17.9	49,538	15.6	271,172	59.5

(Source: Lilo Strauss et al., "Abortion Surveillance—United States, 2003," MMWR: Surveillance Summaries, November 24, 2006. CDC.)

Note:

*Percentages were calculated using total number of abortions obtained at all known weeks of gestation. Percentages might not add to the percentage obtained at ≤8 weeks of gestation because fewer states are included in certain variables. Also, percentages might not add to the total percentage because of rounding.

†Data from 40 states and New York City.

‡Data from 30 states and New York City, excludes nine states (Maine, Nevada, New Mexico, New York [Upstate], Rhode Island, South Dakota, Utah, Washington, and Wyoming) where race was reported as unknown for >15% of women.

§Data from 26 states and New York City, excludes nine states (Maine, Montana, Nevada, New Mexico, North Carolina, Oklahoma, Rhode Island, Virginia, and Washington) where ethnicity was reported as unknown for >15% of women.

< 8 weeks of gestation, by known weeks of gestation, age group, race, and ethnicity of women who obtained abortions" (CDC, 2006).

How do women feel about having an abortion? Research has found that the majority of women feel a huge sense of relief, and are not, in fact, traumatized by the experience. Although many may experience ambivalence, sadness, and guilt in their decision making, research indicates that fewer than 10 percent of women experience psychological problems afterward and these women were likely to have emotional problems prior to the abortion ("Abortion," 2006; "Abortion Information," 2006; Hyde, 1985: 266; Westheimer and Lopater, 2005). There is no scientific evidence that having an abortion leads to psychological/emotional disorders. In fact, Gilligen (1982) argues:

By studying abortion decisions and their consequences, we may come to see the whole process of making a decision to have an abortion (or to have the baby and give it up for adoption, or to keep the baby) as fostering psychological development and growth, at least if handled well. Women may emerge from the process being more mature and having better-developed moral sensitivities. (cited in Hyde, 1985: 268)

Abortion rates are higher in countries where it is illegal. See Table 12.6. Ward and Edelstein propose that women "will do anything" to have control over fertility and childbearing—even pursue an illegal abortion (2006). That they will pursue abortions under unsafe and illegal conditions testifies to the anguish women feel in having an unintended pregnancy.

Table 12.6 Examples of trends in international abortion

Liberal access	Very restricted or prohibited	Increased restrictions since 1995	Liberalized since 1995
Belgium	Afghanistan	El Salvador	Albania
Cambodia	Bangladesh	Hungary	Australia
Canada	Bhutan	Poland	Benin
China	Brazil	The Russian Federation	Burkina Faso
Cuba	Brunei	United States*	Cambodia
Denmark	Central Africa		Chad
France	Republic		Colombia*
Germany	Chile		Ethiopia
Greece	Colombia*		France
Hungary	El Salvador		Guinea
The Netherlands	Guatemala		Mali
Norway	Indonesia		Mexico*
Portugal	Ireland		Nepal
Sweden	Iran		South Africa
Switzerland	Iraq		Switzerland

Table 12.6 (Continued)

Liberal access	Very restricted or prohibited	Increased restrictions since 1995	Liberalized since 1995
Ukraine	Mexico*		
United States*	Nigeria		
Vietnam	Sudan		
	Tanzania		
	Uganda		
	Venezuela		

(Source: Boonstra et al., 2006, "Abortion in the United States Today;" Schlangen, "Global Illegal Abortion: Where There Is No 'Roe'," Planned Parenthood; "The World's Abortion Laws," Center for Reproductive Rights.)

Note:
* Although abortion law reform may expand or reduce access to abortion, this may not impact the classification of the country's status as liberal or restricted.

Getting accurate statistics on abortions, both legal and illegal, is not an easy task. Where abortions are legal and where there are few restrictions, accurate data can be collected. However, where it is illegal or restrictive, data must be collected by other methods than government reports and accuracy is therefore somewhat questionable (Henshaw, Singh, and Haas, 1999).

Abortion: a focus on industrial nations

The lowest abortion rates occur in western European countries where abortion is legal, covered by national health insurance, and where unintended pregnancy rates are low. Four developed countries with complete data have rates below 10 per 1,000: Belgium, Germany, the Netherlands, and Switzerland (Henshaw, Singh, and Haas, 1999). Countries in which abortion is legal tend to be industrial nations; where it is illegal, the countries tend to be industrializing/nonindustrialized nations.

- In fifty-four countries (61 percent of the world population) abortions are legal.
- In ninety-seven countries (39 percent of the world population) abortions are illegal.
- Generally, women age fifteen to seventeen in industrialized nations are more likely to get an abortion than to give birth.
- East Central Europe has the highest abortion rate in Europe with 65 percent of the pregnancies ending in abortion.
- In the former Soviet Union, and those of the former Yugoslavia, abortion has been legal since the 1950s.

- In countries where abortion was illegal, such as Romania and Albania, there are high death rates for women due to unsafe conditions.
- The number of abortions in developed nations falls from thirty-nine to twenty abortions per 1,000 women when Eastern Europe is not included in the statistics on abortion. (Boonstra et al., 2006; Compiled from Henshaw, Singh, and Hass 1999; "Get in the Know: 20 Questions About Pregnancy, Contraception and Abortion," 2006; "Teenagers' Sexual and Reproductive Health: Developed Countries, 2004.)

Aside from Eastern Europe, Ireland is also a special case in our discussion of illegal abortion in industrialized nations. Ireland bans abortion except when the mother's life is endangered. Abortion was first made illegal in 1861 and in 1983 a constitutional amendment was passed granting the fetus the right to life, which remains in effect. The consequences of this are that between 1980 and 2004 at least 117,673 (Irish) women traveled to Great Britain to have abortions, with estimates of approximately 6,000 a year. Recent findings suggest that Irish women may be traveling to other European Union countries where abortions are less expensive than in England, although statistics on this are not currently available ("Abortion Law in Ireland: A Brief History," 2006; "Irish Abortion Statistics," 2006; "Submissions of the Irish Family Planning Association to the UN Committee on the Elimination of Discrimination Against Women," 2005).

Several trends emerge from this discussion of abortion. High rates of abortion are found in countries where women lack information and access to controlling reproduction; in many countries, women lack the personal and political power to implement family planning strategies as well. Low abortion rates, such as occur in the Netherlands, are correlated with widespread accessibility to comprehensive sexuality education. Although it is important for the world's women to have the option of abortion as one strategy to limit unintended pregnancies and provide them with autonomy over their reproductive choices, it would be preferable for women to have affordable and effective birth control rather than the more medically intrusive abortion.

A focus on industrializing/nonindustrialized nations

One report argues that the availability of family planning services in industrializing nations can reduce abortions by 75 percent. According to Sonefield (2006: n.p.): "beyond their medical impact, family planning programs also have far-reaching social, economic and psychological benefits for women, families and nations." However, abortion remains an important option for women who find themselves with an undesired pregnancy regardless of their motives for termination. Many of the women who seek abortions in countries where it is illegal are married with children that they cannot support. The irony of the Bush Administration's gag rule is that this policy actually inhibits education and dispersal of contraceptives that can, in fact, reduce the numbers of abortions (Cohen, 2006). Without the availability of contraceptive information and the option of a legal abortion, women with undesired pregnancies are compelled to seek out the illegal and unsafe methods. Unsafe abortions are the major cause of maternal death in the industrializing/nonindustrial nations where it is illegal. Research reveals:

• Lack of access to family planning results in some 76 million unintended pregnancies every year in the developing world alone.
• 19 million abortions are carried out annually in unsanitary and unsafe conditions.
• 68,000 deaths are attributed to illegal unsafe and unhygienic abortions.
• One in 10 pregnancies will end in an unsafe abortion.
• Asia, Africa, and Latin America account for the highest numbers of women seeking unsafe abortions (Grimes et al., 2006; Henshaw, Singh, and Haas, 1999; UNFPA State of the World, 2005; *Unsafe Abortion: Global and Regional Estimates of the Incidence of Unsafe Abortion and Associated Mortality in 2000*, 2004).

Grimes et al. (2006) refer to the international scope of unsafe abortion as "the preventable pandemic" which can be mitigated by legal, safe and accessible abortion. They attribute "[t]he underlying causes of this global pandemic [to] apathy and disdain for women; they suffer and die because they are not valued" (2006: 1).

Many industrializing countries have access to modern methods of amniocentesis and sonograms to detect fetus abnormalities, but in China, India, Bangladesh, Parkistan, and Indonesia, these technologies are used to select male fetuses and abort the female fetuses ("Asia: Discarding Daughters," 1990: 40; Ward and Edelstein, 2006). According to Ward and Edelstein (2006: 231): these are the "disappeared and endangered daughters" represented in countries where gender inequity leads to excess mortality and asymmetrical gender ratios in births. For example, in South Korea, "male births outnumber female births by 14 percent, in contrast to a worldwide average of 5 percent" (Burton, 1990: 36). Such an imbalance can have far-reaching consequences in terms of adult marriage patterns. China's policy of one child per couple, encouraged by severe financial sanctioning, has resulted in the continued practice of female infanticide and amniocentesis to identify and then abort female fetuses. In a society that historically favored males, females were considered an economic liability (Burton, 1990: 36; Ward and Edelstein, 2006).

TRADITIONAL METHODS OF BIRTH CONTROL
IN CROSS-CULTURAL CONTEXT

We shall now shift our emphasis to indigenous and cross-cultural methods for birth control. As discussed earlier, it is important to remember that for many in nonindustrialized nations, traditional methods also co-exist with modern methods. This is also true of industrialized nations with indigenous and immigrant populations. The importance of culture in shaping the practices and meanings of birth control is illustrated by Marvin Harris (1989: 210) when he asserts:

> Sex does not guarantee conception; conception does not lead relentlessly to birth; and birth does not compel the mother to nurse and protect the newborn. Cultures have evolved learned techniques and practices that can prevent each step in this process from occurring.

In our discussion of the cross-cultural context for birth control, we will emphasize ethnographic research both classic and contemporary. This spans a wide time frame including research on indigenous societies prior to contact with colonizing countries, post contact, and contemporary indigenous and ethnic communities within a global context, at various points in time. Methods of birth control have a long history and tremendous variety since people have been interfering with reproduction prior to the invention of twentieth/twenty-first-century methods like the pill; although methods like IUDs certainly have their antecedents. Earlier we discussed birth control in developing nations. Here we focus on preindustrial and indigenous peoples. It is important that we approach this subject with the lens of cultural relativism because some of the methods used to control fertility and births, manage birth spacing and population include methods that challenge industrial ideologies, beliefs and values, such as infanticide and abortion.

In this regard, the terminology "traditional methods" needs explication. Various industrialized national and international organizations such as the United Nations and researchers who study fertility, birth and population control define traditional methods as "non-technological and less effective than more recently invented methods such as the oral contraceptive pill" (Hirsch and Nathanson, 2001: 413). This dichotomy represents an etic approach and not one necessarily used emically (Hirsch and Nathanson, 2001). Moreover the notion that some of the traditional methods are "ineffective" has been challenged by research on various contraceptive herbs, as well as the predecessors to modern methods such as IUDs and abortificants. With this caveat in mind, we use the term "traditional" method for convenience and to emphasize preindustrial practices to avoid impregnation, control birth spacing, births and offspring. However, this does not mean that women have not engaged in practices that were not only ineffective, for example Plains Indians wore a contraceptive charm known as a "snake-girdle" made of beaded leather over the navel (Gregersen, 1983: 291), but some were also dangerous as well. In this regard, Ward and Edelstein (2006: 77) note: "It is clear from all the ethnographic and historic accounts we have that human desire for controlling the life stream is universal; it transcends time and space." Much of the knowledge and practices for controlling fertility, number of births and birth spacing is women's secret and sacred knowledge, shared by networks of women and passed on through generations. The lengths women will go to to control their fertility have been and are extraordinary; prior to *Roe v. Wade,* U.S. women exposed themselves to infection and even death in order to have illegal abortions, as many do today in countries where abortion is illegal. As noted earlier, Ward and Edelstein (2006: 81) refer to this as the "women will do anything" principle in order to have control of their reproductive lives.

Worldwide traditional methods are still practiced in industrialized, industrializing and nonindustrialized countries. The United Nations defines traditional methods as including prolonged abstinence, breast feeding (lactational amenorrhea), douching, and various other folk methods. The data aggregated by country/region for use of traditional methods are as follows: Africa (2 percent), Asia (less than 1 percent), Europe (less than 1 percent), Latin America and Caribbean (less than 1 percent), North America (1 percent), Australia and New Zealand (less than 1 percent) and Oceania (Melanesia, Micronesia and Polynesia) (3 percent) (figures rounded to nearest percentage point, data from "World Contraceptive Use 2005," 2005).

However, indigenous and preindustrial methods include a far wider array than that defined by the United Nations as "traditional" or "folk" methods. For example, *coitus interruptus* is the predominant method found cross-culturally (Gregerson, 1994; Harris, 1989), but it is not defined by the U.N. as an indigenous or folk method since it is also used by modern industrialized and industrializing people, including U.S. teenagers. (See earlier discussion for worldwide statistics on this usage in more industrialized and less industrialized countries.) As noted earlier this method's effectiveness is limited, with twenty-five out of a hundred women using this technique conceiving within a year (King, 2005). Cross-cultural examples illustrate how cultural meanings define and permeate this practice. For example, in East Bay, a Southwest Pacific people studied by William Davenport, abstinence from marital coitus was the preferred method for controlling birth spacing, while *coitus interruptus* was the technique used in extramarital relationships (Davenport, 1977).

The cross-cultural and historical records reveal numerous other ethnotheories and practices. Various indigenous peoples use techniques to expel the semen after intercourse with ejaculation; for example the Kavirondo and Zande rely on body movement such as standing and shaking after intercourse (Gregersen, 1994: 83, 290–291). This is not unlike the sexual folklore among some college students that standing up immediately after sex reduces the chance of conception. Other approaches have emphasized the avoidance of intercourse and timing of intercourse through the use of postpartum sex taboos that last from two to five years. Alternatives to intercourse with ejaculation have included mutual masturbation and "outercourse" methods that avoid vaginal penetration (Ward and Edelstein, 2006).

Historical and cross-cultural research reports an abundance of contraceptive and abortificant recipes of herbs, medicines, and potions used by the ancient Greeks, Romans, Egyptians and other preindustrial and indigenous peoples, past and present (Kroeber, 1953: 248; Riddle, Estes, and Russell, 1994: 29–35; Schneider, 1968: 365; Ward and Edelstein, 2006). For example, the demand for Silphium, a plant in the parsley family, which was widely used by the Greeks as a contraceptive and abortificant from the seventh century BC to the fourth century AD, contributed to its extinction. The ancient and cross-cultural record reveals a variety of herbs that inhibited conception and terminated pregnancy including Queen Anne's Lace, pennyroyal, willow, date palm, pomegranate, and acacia gum. The effectiveness of the chemical properties of these herbs in affecting fertility has been clinically demonstrated (Riddle, Estes, and Russell, 1994: 29–35). According to Ward and Edelstein (2006: 78):

> Recipes over the last seven thousand years recommend a wide variety of oily, astringent, acidic, gummy or fibrous substances, alone or in combination. The bark and nuts of many kinds of trees provide tannic acid, an astringent vegetable compound that is a remarkably effective spermicide. Vinegar or ascetic acid, yogurt, honey, salt, butter and buttermilk are also reported from China, India or the Middle East. The [women] of history made tampons or contraceptive suppositories out of lint, cotton, wool, silk, seaweed, or other common household fibers and absorbent substances. Any household spermicide could be used with a tampon or as a douche for washing out the vagina. These were relatively effective and easily available.

Modern sponges, barrier methods, and IUDs have their antecedents as well. Women have placed various barriers against the cervix including beeswax, lard, and tissues made of bamboo. IUDs were made of buttons, stone, and gems placed in a woman's uterus. Sponges soaked in spermicides such as lemon juice and then placed against the cervix are one of the oldest and most effective methods. As mentioned earlier, a diverse array of oral abortificants, recipes for contraception and sterility were part of women's culture (Ward and Edelstein, 2006).

In addition to these methods, women's desire to control their reproduction included other approaches and interventions such as abortion and infanticide. In a cross-cultural study of preindustrial societies, George

Devereux found that 464 groups practiced abortion (1967: 92–152). A variety of techniques was used for abortion. Oral recipes for abortificants and emmenagogues challenge industrial emic and etic distinctions between encouraging a menstrual cycle to occur and an abortion. An emmenagogue is a recipe that causes menstruation and in the process it may include the termination of an early pregnancy by inducing a miscarriage (Ward and Edelstein, 2006: 271). In this regard, Ward and Edelstein assert: "Historic and ethnographic accounts make no sharp distinction between contraception and abortion" (2006: 79). Cultures may openly condone or condemn such forms of managing reproduction. Women are placed in conflicted situations in those societies that simultaneously prevent contraception and abortion.

Infanticide in which a neonate is allowed to die or is purposely killed has primarily occurred in situations where survival of parents or the group is at stake as in cases with overpopulation, or in times of scarce resources such as famine. It also is found in indigenous cultures with strong gender preferences for males (see Chagnon, 1983; Divale and Harris, 1976; Harris, 1993; Yanomamo discussed in greater depth). Morgan's (1996) research has found that it is also distinctly tied to cultural notions of humanness and personhood. For example on Truk, abnormal or deformed newborns were not defined as human but rather as ghosts; they were burned or thrown into the sea. To the Trukese a ghost was not a human and was not a person, therefore it could not be actually killed. In such societies, neonates are not presumed to be born human, but must be conferred with humanity based on certain physical characteristics as in Truk. Once humanity is designated then cultural ideologies of personhood can come into play. For many societies, personhood is a process and an attribute that is acquired and socially recognized. In the United States personhood is not just ascribed at birth, but has become part of a political and religious philosophy that is accorded to fertilized eggs, blastocysts, embryos, and fetuses (Morgan, 1996).

Preindustrial and indigenous women have employed a number of techniques to engage in the control of births and reproduction. As discussed earlier in this chapter, attitudes, beliefs, and birth control practices including abortion are related to subsistence, economic, political, social, historical, and religious factors among others. These are also linked to the gender system including women's status and power. We shall discuss several examples highlighting the interrelationship of culture including ideologies, features of social organization, and culture change to methods used for controlling reproduction. For example, how people make a living and methods of fertility/birth control are interrelated. With plant cultivation, horticulture, and agriculture, population growth has occurred over the last 10,000 years. This has resulted in an escalating system of sedentism, surplus, complexity of social organization (ranking and hierarchy), centralization of authority, unequal access to prestige, power and resources and the loss of status for women. These features are related to issues of birth spacing, beliefs about family size, the value of children to the household economy, and gender preferences for children. There is a complex relationship between culture and the social system that impacts birth control beliefs and practices. We shall offer three case studies illustrating the bio-cultural basis for understanding the complex relationship of culture, reproduction, population and social organization. Three case studies: the Ju/wasi, the Yapese, and the Yanomamo are used to illustrate these intersections.

Ju/wasi

Foragers (gatherers and hunters) are excellent examples of how culture shapes biology in relation to population. One widely accepted anthropological theory correlates sedentism, that is, permanent residence due to plant cultivation with population expansion. This line of reasoning is supported by data from the ethnographic spectrum and includes evidence from the Ju/wasi (formerly known as !Kung, or San, also known as Ju/'hoansi) peoples of the Kalahari Desert (Robbins, 2006). The settlement of Ju/wasi into permanent villages has provided evidence of the effects of sedentism on a previously foraging population and, together with other lines of evidence, contributes to understanding the impact of sedentism on populations prehistorically/historically, offering insight into environmental adaptation and demographics (Bates and Fratkin, 2003).

The Ju/wasi, like tropical foragers in general, are known for small populations. A number of interacting factors are believed to contribute to this situation. Foragers have diets low in fat and high in protein, and, consequently, they have less body fat than food cultivators. The critical fat theory (Frisch, 1978: 22–30) argues that fertility can be reduced in several ways by the low body fat levels; most notably through adolescent sterility (introduced in Chapter 10) and through the practice of extended lactation without supplemental food sources. In order to ovulate, women need a certain amount of body fat, minimally estimated at 15 percent. Body fat levels are influenced by extended lactation which requires a great deal of caloric energy, and this combined with a foraging lifestyle, keeps fertility and reproduction low among gatherers and hunters. In contrast plant cultivators, especially agriculturalists, can generate a large surplus of calories. Sedentism along with the increased calories encourages higher body fat levels in women, counteracts trends for adolescent sterility seen among foragers and results in increased fertility and reproduction, i.e., population expansion associated with food producers especially agriculturalists.

The critical level of fat storage necessary for menstruation and ovulation to occur is about 150,000 stored calories of energy, enough "to permit a woman to lactate for 1 year or more without having to increase her pre-pregnancy caloric intake" (Lancaster, 1985: 18). A period of subfertility for several years after *menarche* exists among some foragers, but this declines in settled populations. According to Lancaster (1985: 18): "Sedentism com-bined with high levels of caloric intake leads to early deposition of body fat in young girls and 'fools' the body into early biological maturation long before cognitive and social maturity are reached."

Foragers typically have other cultural practices that contribute to smaller populations. One method is birth spacing (Ember, Ember, and Pereg-rine, 2005). Foragers who may roam over vast territory cannot afford to nurse and carry more than one child who has not yet achieved the ability to walk competently. The Ju/wasi for example, have solved this dilemma by spacing children about four years apart. Several cultural practices contribute to Ju/wasi birth spacing. One of these is a long postpartum sex taboo that requires abstinence from coitus for a min-imum of a year. Foragers are well-known for long postpartum sex taboos for women as a way to space and indirectly control births. A correla-tion exists between societies that have long postpartum sex taboos and those with low fertility rates (Ember, Ember, and Peregrine, 2005; Nag, 1962: 79).

Foragers with low body fat ratios can interrupt ovulation by prolonged nursing, which in turn contributes to keeping body fat levels low. "It is now well established that the longer a mother nurses her baby without supplementary foods, the longer the mother is unlikely to start ovulating again" (Ember, Ember, and Peregrine, 2005: 168). Ju/wasi mothers nurse for two or three years without the additional sources of food available to settled agriculturalists and industrialists such as milk from domesticated animals or harvested grain. Lactating females, in populations where body fat is low, are less likely to become pregnant because ovulation is depressed (Ember, Ember, and Peregrine, 2005; Kottak, 1991: 203).

Two other techniques that are used by foragers to control births are infanticide and abortion. Hunters and gatherers practice abortion and are known for their knowledge of pharmacology in which animal and plant poisons are used to cause the fetus to miscarry (Gregersen, 1983: 291). Procedures include the use of herbal treatments and toxic sub-stances from animals, vigorously hitting or manipulating the stomach through massage or squeezing, and having someone jump on the abdo-men (Devereux, 1955; Gregersen, 1983: 290–291; Riddle et al., 1994: 29–35; Sarvis and Rodman, 1974; Ward and Edelstein, 2006). In addi-tion, Devereux (1955) and Sarvis and Rodman (1974) report attempts to abort the fetus through strenuous activity or through the use of devices or substances that are inserted into the uterus. These techniques may cause harm to the mother and are dangerous, but show the lengths that women will go to for control of their reproductive lives (Ward and Edelstein, 2006).

Yapese

In regard to methods of abortion, David M. Schneider's (1968: 383–406) report and analysis of abortion on Yap, a Caroline Island in Micronesia, is a classic ethnographic example of how beliefs, political economy, gender relations, and demographics intersect. Yap is an island that once supported 50,000 people. Yet, by 1945, the population had fallen dramatically to only 2,500. The culture was one that was geared to a much larger population; consequently, the population decline affected socio-political organization in that there were no longer enough people to fill positions and perform necessary political functions and services. This resulted in a generalized Yapese concern and desire for more children. In spite of this, women continued the practice of self-abortions. Self-induced abortions on Yap have, in fact, exacerbated the depopulation problem since these also tended to occur "during the maximum years of fecundity" (Schneider, 1968: 384). However, abortion may not have been the sole cause of the continued depopulation of Yap as gonorrhea or possibly some other diseases have undoubtedly contributed to the low fertility rate.

Given this situation, it is not surprising that self-induced abortion on Yap was negatively sanctioned and kept secret, especially from the men. Because abortions were objected to on moral grounds, Yapese women were under pressure to remain secretive, lest they become known as aborters which could jeopardize their marriages or chances for marriage since men want and desire children. To understand the perpetuation of abortion practices by women in spite of depopulation, it is necessary to engage in a holistic analysis of Yapese culture; that is, one that considers all aspects of Yapese life. There were three methods of self-induced abortions on Yap. According to Schneider (1968: 385):

One [method] consists in a series of magical manipulations with little apparent efficacy.... The other two techniques are empirically more effective. One of these is drinking boiled concentrated sea water. Women described the effect as a general feeling of illness accompanied by vomiting and severe cramps.

The other technique consists in introducing a thin rolled plug of hibiscus leaves (which expand when moist) into the mouth of the cervix and then injuring and scratching the mouth of the cervix with a bit of stick, stone, iron, fingernail, or other sharp object until blood is drawn. Women informants generally agreed that injuring the area about the mouth of the cervix was necessary in addition to inserting the plug...

The latter method can lead to infection and associated reproductive problems, although medical reports suggest that the resulting infection is mild and not life threatening.

Historically, Yapese population decline may be traced back to a period when population had peaked. What is remarkable about this situation is that, despite the serious depopulation that followed, Yap culture in its traditional form has continued as an adaptation to a dense population; this is an example of culture lag. Abortion was a part of this earlier adaptation and represented an effective solution to an overpopulation problem at the time. The persistence of abortion in the face of decline in population however, must be understood in the context of the totality of the culture, including gender relations and expectations.

Abortion was tied directly to gender role expectations for Yapese women over the life course.

> Women up to the age of thirty do not want children because they would no longer be free to fall in and out of love, to attract lovers, to have and break off affairs at will, to practice the elaborate games of love and sociability that appeal to young Yap men and women. They do not want to be tied to a child and to a husband when they are in the best position to gain and enjoy the rewards of being unattached.... On Yap the standard and available means of avoiding children is to induce abortion when pregnancy occurs. (Schneider, 1968: 393)

After the age of thirty, however, women's attitudes began to change and the desire for children was accelerated. This coincides with the transition from youth to adult status. In summary, abortion persisted on Yap in spite of population decline because the period of youth was regarded as a time when women have access to the rewards and pleasures of love affairs in a system in which they will never achieve the prestige positions and rankings available to men.

Infanticide cross-culturally also illustrates the complexity and necessity for a holistic perspective in understanding birth control. This should not be construed to mean that infanticide has not been practiced in industrialized societies as a method of regulating unwanted births. It has! Historically, Europeans favored indirect methods of infanticide such as overlaying (where a mother "accidentally" suffocated her child by rolling over on it when in bed); wet nurses whose reputations for infant care literally guaranteed that the child would die; or foundling homes such as those in France between 1824–1833 where 336,297 children were abandoned. "Between 80 percent and 90 percent of the children in these institutions died during their first year of life" (Harris, 1989: 214).

Infanticide as a method to control birth is found in a variety of forms around the globe. It includes the indirect methods just discussed that are favored by the Europeans and others such as the northeast Brazilians (Scheper-Hughes, 1987: 535–545), or may include conscious systematic neglect, starvation, and/or environmental exposure as more direct approaches. In many contexts and for many reasons both personal and cultural (for example poverty, the desire to limit family size, and gender preferences among others), surreptitious infanticide may be the only solution for the mother with an unwanted pregnancy (Harris, 1989: 211). Reports of direct infanticide in nontechnologically complex societies suggest that between 53 to 76 percent of these societies allow for the practice of this method. In such situations, the cultural conception of being a person, a member of the family and the group is not given to newborns (Harris, 1989: 212, 214).

Yanomamo

Marvin Harris's (1974, 1993) reanalysis of Napoleon Chagnon's study of the Yanomamo of Venezuela and Brazil is a classic work that illustrates how infanticide relates to warfare and a male supremacy complex among tribal cultivators. The Yanomamo represent a case study supporting a broader theory by Divale and Harris (1976) whose cross-cultural correlational study of the HRAF files proposes that warfare is the most common way for tribal cultivators to regulate populations. This happens in an indirect way through the practice of female infanticide, rather than directly by male deaths due to war. The thesis behind their argument is that in order for population size to be controlled, the limiting factor must be females and not males. The idea behind this is that one male can impregnate a number of females; therefore, societies can afford to lose adult males without affecting their population. Warfare and conflict encourage a strong preference for male children because they can be raised into strong and aggressive warriors (Robbins, 2006).

At the time of Chagnon's original research, the Yanomamo were a tribal society of 15,000 living in 125 villages (Chagnon, 1983). They were originally riverine Indians whose ancestors were pushed into a forest adaptation due to population pressure and colonization. These Yanomamo became skilled hunters and engaged in shifting cultivation in the forest. About 400 years ago they began cultivating plantains and as a result of this semi-sedentary existence combined with additional calories supplied by the plantains, they experienced a rapid population growth spurt. Eighty-five percent of the Yanomamo diet was from the plantains and the bananas that they cultivated. This feature is a central part of Harris's (1993; and Divale and Harris, 1976) argument. Increased calories and sedentism offset natural mechanisms for birth spacing and low population that we have seen operating in gatherers and hunters such as the Ju/wasi. Plant cultivation, which provides more carbohydrates and higher caloric intake than foraging, allows for earlier puberty, increased conception, and generally a longer childbearing period.

According to Harris's (1993) argument, shifting cultivation did not meet Yanomamo needs for protein. As they became semi-settled cultivators, their high carbohydrate diet and increased population led them to put increasing pressure on the local game resources for protein. Anthropologist Brian Ferguson's (2001) study of Yanomamo warfare adds some nuances to Harris's theory although they are generally on the same page in terms of the Yanomamo preferences for males and the development of a male supremacy complex and its role in female infanticide. Ferguson (2001) argues that the real impetus for the Yanomamo warfare and aggression was the availability of Euro-American manufactured goods in the 1950s and 1960s. For Ferguson, this is what led to the creation of permanent settlements as Yanomamo founded anchor villages near trading outposts. The establishment of these more permanent villages is what Ferguson believes led to the depletion of game.

Both Harris and Ferguson agree that the development of a male supremacy complex occurred in order to help create fiercer hunters and warriors in response to the dwindling game. In addition, the growing populations who settled in villages came into conflict over protein as a scarce resource which also contributed to and escalated warfare. According to Ferguson, fierce aggressive males were needed to protect and acquire manufactured goods as well. This complex of warfare, hunting, and competition for manufactured goods placed a premium on males, rather than females. In the history of the world, it is rare for women to participate in warfare since this would make poor evolutionary sense. The premium on males ultimately led to female infanticide as a method for parents to select for sons over daughters. The Yanomamo preferred that the firstborn was a son and practiced infanticide if a girl was the firstborn. Because Yanomamo females did not fight, hunt, and bring home the protein, they were valued less than males. Female infanticide contributed to a population inequity in the ratio of male to females; there were 449 males to 391 females in seven villages studied by Chagnon (1983). This gender inequity perpetuated fighting and raiding to acquire women from other villages which, in turn escalated the warfare even further. The Yanomamo practiced polygyny so that the best fighters and hunters could acquire several wives through the lure of protein, rank, and prestige. Twenty-five percent of the men were polygynous. This added fuel to the fire by creating an even greater shortage of women. In this situation warfare operated as a way to disperse populations and relocate them in the environment in order to temporarily relieve population pressure on resources. Among tribal cultivators, warfare and the female infanticide it engendered served as the primary mechanism to limit population (Harris, 1974; Kottak, 1991; Robbins, 2006).

As we have illustrated in this discussion of birth control in cross-cultural context, sexual practices as well as fertility control are intricately tied to the broader cultural system and articulate clearly with a number of cultural variables as well as ecological ones relating to demography, types of subsistence, and adaptations. This chapter has covered much territory related to birth control and contraception. Contemporary birth control methods in industrialized nations and nonindustrialized nations were discussed as well as methods used throughout the ethnographic spectrum, illustrating the importance of a culturally relativistic stance in understanding sex and reproduction.

SUMMARY

1 Definitions for concepts related to birth control are offered including: contraception, population control, fertility, mortality, theoretical effectiveness and actual effectiveness rate and woman years.
2 Differences in population trends among industrialized and nonindustrialized nations are discussed.
3 Currently available methods of birth control in the United States are presented.
4 Comparison of the prevalence, availability and policy implications for contraceptives in industrialized and nonindustrialized/industrializing nations are provided.
5 The abortion controversy is discussed in the United States, other industrialized nations, and nonindustrialized/industrializing nations.
6 Birth control is placed in cultural context: selected examples of indigenous contraceptive and birth control practices are provided.
7 Preindustrial examples of birth control include: *coitus interruptus,* lactation, abortion, and female infanticide emphasizing the Ju/wasi, Yapese, and Yanomamo.

Thought-provoking questions

1 Why is the birth control method of extended breastfeeding/lactational amenorrhea not a reliable method for U.S. women? Can you explain this?
2 How do college students define "hooking up"? Describe how sexuality is negotiated by women and men in the encounter. What expectations do you think are involved?
3 What are your perspectives on the issue of abortion? Where did your views on this issue come from? Is there any way that the Pro-Choice and Anti-Choice perspectives can be reconciled?

SUGGESTED RESOURCES

Books

Carpenter, Laura M. 2005. *Virginity Lost: An Intimate Portrait of First Sexual Experiences*. New York: New York University Press.
Riddle, John M. 1997. *Eve's Herbs: A History of Contraception and Abortion in the West*. Cambridge: Harvard University Press.

Russell, Andrew, Elisa J. Sobo, and Mary S. Thompson, eds. 2000. *Contraception Across Cultures: Technologies, Choices. Constraints.* New York: Berg Press.

Sobo, Elisa Janine and Sandra Bell. 2001. *Celibacy, Culture and Society: The Anthropology of Sexual Abstinence.* Madison: University of Wisconsin Press.

Web sites

Planned Parenthood of America. (http://www.plannedparenthood.org/). Last accessed 12/18/06.

Waxman, Henry A. "United States House of Committee on Government Reform Minority Staff Special Investigations Prepared for Henry Waxman: The Content of Federally Funded Abstinence-Only Education Programs." http://www.democrats.reform.house.gov.

Waxman, Henry A. "Letter to Michael O. Leavitt, Secretary of health and Human Services." February 16, 2006. http://www.democrats.reform.house.gov.

13 Topics in adult sexuality
Life course issues related to gender identity, gender roles, and aging

CHAPTER OVERVIEW

1   Examines gender role relative to concepts of psychological masculinity and femininity.
2   Incorporates an anthropological discussion of gender variance including the transgender community in the United States/other industrialized societies and cross-cultural gender variance
3   Discusses concepts of androgyny, scripts, bonding, and intimacy.
4   Applies concerns about intimacy to the late twentieth and early twenty-first centuries in the United States.
5   Discusses the biological, psychological, and cultural aspects of sexual aging in the United States and cross-culturally.

Although concepts of **gender identity** (knowing that you are male, female, or intersex) (Williams, 1986) and **gender role** (adopting culturally defined male and female behavior) are probably widespread cross-culturally, their expression is highly culture specific. Chapters 1 and 2 discuss the symbolism of maleness and femaleness and the diversity of gender role behavior among cultures (e.g., Margaret Mead's classic work is one body of recently challenged research on this topic: Mead, 1949, 1961 [1928], 1963 [1935]). We also know from the literature that culture change can impact gender roles cross-culturally (Lurie, 1973; Radin, 1926; Sharp, 1981). However, the extensive amount of energy vested in examining and trying to understand gender role behavior through the life cycle in the late twentieth and early twenty-first centuries is largely a function of middle-class industrialized and, specifically, U.S. culture.

In this chapter, some of the current issues in male-female relationships, sexual aging, and gender roles in mainstream United States culture, as well as subcultures within the larger society, are addressed. As part of the "**Sexual Revolution**" of the 1960s, a tremendous amount of time, energy, and attention was directed toward defining and elaborating concepts of gender role and gender identity, masculinity and femininity.

The 1960s and 1970s alleged Sexual Revolution served as a sexual, social, economic, and political statement against the perceived negative aspects of traditional gender role behaviors and expectations. In its most extreme form, anything defined as "traditional" was seen as negative. Some question arose as to whether a sexual revolution occurred (radical or root change, qualitative, wide-scale, behavioral and attitudinal changes) (Ehrenreich, Hess, and Jacobs, 1986; Elshtain, 1989; Farrell, 1986; Goldberg, 1979, 1984), or whether a reform movement occurred (a rebellion in which behaviors became more overt and widespread, and attitudes remained relatively constant) (cf. Hendrick and Hendrick, 1987; McCabe, 1987). Since the 1960s, sexual behaviors have become more visible, open, and discussed in the culture. (Note the advent of the *Oprah* and *Dr. Phil* television shows discussing sex issues and the portrayal of sex on television in sitcoms and dramas.) For example, the United States has the highest teenage pregnancy rate of all industrialized countries, including Japan (Cohen, 2006; Wattleton, 1990; *World Health Statistics Annual,* 1988; see Chapter 10 for discussion.) The Sexual Revolution introduced the concepts of **liberated** and **androgynous gender role** behaviors and expectations. Androgyny advocates for situation-appropriate behaviors, not gender-stereotyped behaviors. But whether there are qualitatively "new behaviors" and whether attitudes about sexual behavior have qualitatively changed is arguable. For example, a double standard of heterosexual nonmarital sexual behavior persists, even though more nonmarried people openly admit to being sexually active (Kelly, 1988; Masters, Johnson, and Kolodny, 1985).

Thus, gender identity may be the perception of oneself as a man or a woman or another gender. In a biomedical, industrialized mode it rests on phenotypic sex (i.e., the presence of male or female primary and secondary sex characteristics) as well as an early, deeply ingrained sense of "I am a boy or girl, man or woman." Gender identity is labeled at birth. Gender role, which is learned based on the gender identity, is the internalization of culturally recognized attitudes, behaviors, beliefs, and values that complement one's gender identity and includes both verbal and nonverbal behavior, and relates to concepts of masculinity and femininity.

Masculinity and **femininity** are patterned, learned, verbal and nonverbal signs, symbols, and behaviors that reinforce socially defined concepts of gender. Culturally specific, they include speech and dress patterns, activities and affect, worldviews, and body language. The boundaries between innate and learned aspects of gender role/identity and masculinity and femininity are controversial and unresolved as the debates on various theories on left- and right-brain dominance illustrate (Rogers, 2001). See also Chapter 7 for discussion of this issue, especially the intersex and transgender section.

GENDER VARIANCE: THE TRANSGENDER IDENTITY
AND CROSS-CULTURAL GENDER DIVERSITY

The cultural specificity of gender identity categories such as maleness and femaleness, masculinity and femininity, status and role variance are most dramatically represented by gender variance and diversity in the United States and cross-culturally. The ethnographic record provides a rich history of societies whose gender schema offers social identities that exist beyond the United States and industrial binarism of woman and man, girl and boy, female and male. These positions include third or more genders, liminal genders (those between male and female), intergenders, people who are "not men" and "not women" and more (Nanda, 2000).

Anthropologists have referred to this spectrum of genders using a variety of terms such as supernumery genders, third sexes and third genders, gender transformed statuses and alternative genders, among others, and have generally agreed at this point to use the term "gender variance" or "gender diversity" (Bolin, 1996b, 1998 [1996], 2000; Davies, 2007; Martin and Voorhies, 1975; Williams, 1986). In some nonindustrialized countries, the sex/gender system has created a place for gender variant peoples through the social construction of multiple genders; in some these are legitimized and valued and in others not (Nanda, 2000). The United States/industrial transgender social identity[1] and the gender variance found cross-culturally illustrates both the culture-bound (i.e., unique to a given culture) dimensions and cross-cultural continuities of defining one's gender within the context of society. These topics are expanded in this section.

The cultural lens and United States gender variance: anthropological perspectives

The anthropological literature on gender variance suggests the importance of the cultural overlay in understanding gender diversity. Taking a traditional anthropological perspective, gender variance is situated in specific cultural contexts and historical moments. For example as we discussed in Chapter 7, a relativistic perspective toward U.S. gender variance challenged the notion that the transgender identity is a "syndrome," regarding it rather as rooted in the gender system whose rigidity may have potentiated its development.

In contrast to the clinical perspective of the DSM-IV-TR, an anthropological perspective on U.S. transgender identity emphasizes the cultural construction of gender and its learned parameters. For example, in Bolin's initial research with transgendered people in early 1980s (*In Search of Eve: Transsexual Rites of Passage*, 1988a), the central question of "how can men become women in a system where gender is regarded as an ascribed characteristic?" is part of understanding the industrialized gender ideology about masculinity and femininity referred to as a gender schema (or belief system about how males and females are distinguished).

A socio-cultural understanding of the U.S. industrialized sex/gender system is necessary to understand gender variance. Following the now classic theoretical model suggested by Kessler and McKenna (1978), the Euro-American sex/gender schema is a social construction that pretends to be biological (Tiefer, 2004). In this way, culture impersonates nature and creates a set of beliefs about what is natural or biological about gender. For purposes of clarification when referring to sex, we mean those biological attributes related to reproduction, while gender refers to those characteristics that are psychological and cultural: men and women, girls and boys, masculinity and femininity, femaleness and maleness. Central to the industrialized cultural gender schema is the notion that there are only two genders. This is regarded as inevitable; it is an "incorrigible proposition" about what is constant and unchangeable in reality (Kessler and McKenna, 1978). Gender is regarded as not only binary or dichotomous but also as oppositional in industrialized societies. The schema posits only two options: male and female with nothing in between or outside of this dichotomy. As we shall explore shortly, this is a rather rigid and polarized view of gender and one not necessarily universal and shared by everyone.

As discussed in Chapter 7 the transgendered identity is itself a recent creation that was not recognized as an identity option in the early 1980s when Bolin first encountered North American gender variance among transgendered people, emphasizing transgendered women, emically self-identified at the time as "male-to-female transsexual" people who were affiliated through a support group she called the "Berdache Society" (Bolin, 1988a).[2] This should not be construed to mean that one's sense of gender identity as woman, man, transwoman, transman, transgendered person, is not deeply experienced and an intrinsic part of self and being. Gender is not just performed but felt (Cromwell, 1999).

To refresh some of the points made in Chapter 7, remembering that in the early 1980s among Bolin's research collaborators, there were only two social identity options available: surgically oriented "male-to-female transsexuals" and male cross-dressers who called themselves "transvestites," but who were not self-identified as gay. "Male-to-female transsexuals" defined themselves by a bottom-line criterion of desire for hormonal reassignment and surgery. If one was not absolutely committed to having the surgery, then one was *de facto* a "TV" ("transvestite") (Bolin, 1996a: 451–452). Transsexual women distinguished "transvestites" as putatively heterosexual men who had the urge to cross-dress but were not "really" women. Emically, cross-dressers were not defined as having a gender identity conflict, but were regarded as people who cross-dressed for other reasons, including relief from male role strain or perhaps a compulsion to cross-dress. However, this view had changed dramatically by the 1990s with these distinctions coming to be regarded as more of a continuum, blended and more blurred than was ever imagined earlier (Bolin, 1996a, 1998 [1996], 2000). A similar framework for transmen may also be argued. While the surgery for female-to-male transgendered people has not been as successful, the pursuit of hormones, mastectomy, and modifications of genitals also framed the transman experience (see Cromwell, 1999; Devor, 1997; Green, 2004).

Prior to the emergence of the transgendered identity by the 1990s, gender identities across a broad spectrum were shuffled into only two categories: male-to-female transsexual and female-to-male transsexual and male cross-dresser. Female cross-dressing was not regarded as an emic category at the time within the transpeople community. Though there were numerous transfolks whose gender identity would have placed them in intermediary gender positions, they tried to find the best fit among the two gender-variant social identities available at the time. For self-identified transsexual women, hormonal and surgical resolution was the only hope for a non-stigmatized life and sense of "normalcy." The quest for surgery became a mark of authenticity reflecting the feminine gender identity of male-to-female transsexual people. The social organization of identities among those in the Berdache Society was a bipolar system, with "transsexuals" hoping to disappear into society as "women" leaving their trans past behind, while cross-dressers remained as stigmatized men. Male-to-female transsexuals regarded these identities as qualitatively discrete, but many cross-dressers did not agree. For them it was a distinction of degree rather than kind. However, the transsexual dichotomization came to dominate the Berdache Society in various subtle and clearly visible ways, resulting in an emic stratification system that reproduced the dominant indus-trialized bio-centric gender schema (Bolin, 1988a, 1988b, 1998 [1996], 2000).

By the early 1990s the polarization of transpeople and cross-dressers was challenged from within and began to be replaced by a concept of continuity and multiplicity of social identities collectively referred to as the trans-gender identity. The label "transvestite" with its loaded psychiatric and stigmatizing valence was replaced with the more neutral "cross-dresser." The transgender identity grew out of expanding political concerns of indi-viduals who wanted a voice in treatment, in defining themselves and in offering support and services for a growing community. The pantheon of personal identities that had previously been shuffled into two options (trans-sexual and emic "transvestite"/cross-dresser) was the raw material for the cultural creation of the transgender identity. The growth of the transgender community with an agenda of valuing and respect has advanced the possib-ility of a permanent and nonsurgical transgender social identity rather than a temporary one as in its early days, an "out" cross-dressing, and a pride in one's past social history as gender variant people (Bolin, 1998 [1996], 2000). In this regard, "Lydia," a middle-aged postoperative transsexual, argued that:

> transsexualism has two closets...That's where people go after their transitions to deny their pasts and their transsexualism. In the past, there was little choice but to go into the closet at the end of the rainbow, for public identity as a transsexual person meant media attention, ridicule, loss of employment and employability, and even physical danger. As times have changed, it has become possible to have a public identity as transsexual and still have a reasonably normal life. (Bolin, 1996a: 493)

Dallas Denny (1992: 10), one of the early transgender freedom fighters, asserts: "Even those who have chosen to alter their bodies with hormones and surgery like myself, maintain a proud transgender identity rather than attempting to assimilate into mainstream culture" (Bolin, 2000: 28).

Bolin's research (1988a) argued that rather than being born with a "cross-sex identity," some individuals develop an identity as women through group interactions, social networks, and experience in a feminine gender role. The Berdache Society created its own rites de passage and Bolin found that these rites of passage fostered the development of their identities as women. Part of the process whereby self-identified transsexuals (emic) learned to present themselves successfully as women in order to "pass" was through the management of gender cues and the embodied cultural meanings of physical, verbal, and nonverbal expressions. Learning to "pass" in the early 1980s, was important in the development of one's gender identity as a woman. According to Devor (1989: 140), "gender status is learned by displaying the culturally defined insignia of the gender category with which one identifies."

Male-to-female transsexuals were aware of the "cultural reality" of gender. In the everyday process of living one's gender, gender is attributed on the basis of gender cues or insignias that are visible, not hidden from view such as the genitalia. Transgender theory incorporated two seeming contradictions. First, gender is a socially constructed phenomenon that transsexuals learn; Bolin maintains that it is escalated through a rite of passage. Second, while gender is learned it is based on an ideology that privileges the biology of genital differences. Therefore, subscribing to this logic, transsexuals must have surgery because sex/gender, male/female, man/woman is dictated by genitals. While endorsing this view, transsexuals paradoxically acknowledged that in the course of their physical feminization produced by female hormone therapy and learning the art of passing, they become, in fact, women with penises for a while (cf. Bolin, 1987a: 50–52, 1988a: 73–105, 1988b, 1996a). Their personal experience testified that genitalia are not, in fact, the ultimate determinant of gender. Rather they had learned their new gender as women through their rites of passage, not unlike how "genetic" women learn theirs. Moreover, they recognized that gender identity, the component transsexuals regard as the core criteria of gender, is independent of genitalia and gender roles, for their gender identities were not congruent with their male bodies.

Clearly the transgendered identity is not a docile one. It creates rebellious bodies—hybrid and intersexed ones that create disarray and challenge not only medicalization, but threaten central tenants in the Euro-American gender schema as biological attributes, gender identity, role concomitants, and gender of erotic interest are rearranged and recombined in new ways by those in the gender variant community. For example, another collaborator in Bolin's later research stated:

> I currently maintain a full-time androgynous persona, eliciting as many "ma'ams" as I do "sir" responses. My goal is to be free to present myself as a full female all the time, while still expressing a healthy degree of androgyny. Living as a woman gives me a much fuller range of expression than as a man. In time, I may feel more comfortable confronting the world with the unabashed ambiguity of total androgyny. (Bolin, 1996a: 455)

Since the gender revolution of the 1960s, elements of the Euro-American gender schema have been assaulted from diverse sectors and various fronts to challenge the biological implications of gender roles (e.g., notions about femininity and masculinity, such as women are "naturally" more emotional and men more aggressive), but in the United States we have not gone so far as to challenge the system of gender as dichotomous and to remake it into a sex/gender system that defines gender as continuous (cf. the classic work of Kessler and McKenna, 1978). However, as we have discussed, the transgender community have taken on this task with enthusiasm (as has the gay, lesbian, and "Q" communities of "queer" and "questioning").

In summary, we have suggested, U.S. transgender identity is a social creation subject to change and the subjectivity of individuals, who may reproduce but also resist and challenge dominant ideologies. In the next section we will focus on cross-cultural gender variance. At this juncture it is important to note that industrialized ideologies of gender have variously collided and fused with indigenous gender statuses including gender diverse ones. Through colonization, nationalization, and globalization, indigenous gender variance has undergone extreme transformation in industrialized and nonindustrialized nations. Nanda (2000: 6) summarizes this cogently:

> Culture contact is an important source of change in sex/gender ideologies and identities. Throughout the contemporary world and, and since the first European encounters with non-European cultures, ideologies of sex/gender diversity have been influenced, changed, and, as in the pre-contact Philippines and American Indian societies, practically destroyed. This diffusion of Euro-American culture continues today through tourism (including international sex tourism), the global media, and the spread of academic and scientific discourse. [Worldwide] Euro-American sex/gender identities such as "gay" and "lesbian," have been incorporated into traditional sex/gender ideologies, though often in ways that change their original meanings. The widespread incorporation of Western ideas means that in most societies today several sex/gender systems—indigenous and foreign—operate simultaneously, with gender variant individuals moving between and among them as they try to construct their lives in meaningful and positive ways.

"The many faces and voices of transgendered people" offers photographs and personal statements by transgendered people in an effort to provide a sense of individuality, agency, and personhood to what has been a somewhat abstract and historical rendering of transgendered people's lives. We are grateful to all those who have contributed stories and photographs for your courage and your desire to contribute to transgender education.

THE MANY FACES AND VOICES OF TRANSGENDERED PEOPLE

Dallas Denny's photos show the same individual at twenty-three and forty-two years of age. Differences in appearance are due to age, electrolysis, and the long-term use of estrogens (female hormones). Dallas Denny, MA, has had sex reassignment surgery, but, this of course, is not apparent from the photographs. Dallas is a leading authority and prolific author on transgender issues. Dallas was the editor of *Transgender Tapestry* magazine, director of the transgender conference Fantasia Fair, and has written many books and articles on gender identity. The founder of AEGIS, the American Educational Gender Information Service, she served for eight years as the executive director. The National Transgender Archive was founded by Dallas and has become one of the world's largest catalogued collection of material about gender identity. For twenty years she was licensed to practice psychology in Tennessee, and currently serves as secretary to gender.org (Gender Education and Advocacy), an online organization focused on "the needs, issues and concerns of gender variant peoples." She is now a resident of Georgia.

Age twenty-three

Age forty-two

Biology is not destiny. The technology for changing my body was available, and I took advantage of it in the same way that other Americans use technology to improve their vision or repair physical defects.

I didn't ask to be transgendered. The feelings that my body and social role were not as they should be were always there, and they made it very difficult for me to function in society as a man. There was nothing about being male that was of value to me.

I made the decision to change my body only after careful thought. It was a moral choice based on my gender identity, and not my sexual orientation. I don't ask people to understand or to approve of my decision, nor do I apologize for who I am. I'm proud to be transgendered.

When I appeared to be a male, people who knew that I thought and felt as a woman weren't able to relate to me on any level as a female. Neither did they believe that I could have a viable future as a woman. Now people have difficulty bringing themselves to believe that I could ever have been a man. But only the outside has changed. I'm the same person. I always was.

Dallas Denny

LuLu Ford Manus

I consider myself to be a transsexual woman. After struggling to live as a man for fifty years, I reached a point where living a life of denial was no longer an option. Thanks to a supportive partner, hormone therapy and an accepting community, I am able to present and live as a woman. I am fortunate to be able to "pass," but "passing" is not my primary goal; it helps me to avoid troubling situations.

Reaching self-acceptance has been an immensely empowering experience. Transitioning shattered so many preconceptions I had about people. I found people reacted favorably to me and often said, "You just need to be happy."

I work as a Trans Community Co-coordinator with the Diversity Center of Santa Cruz. As a social worker, I know that life is challenging for trans people. We can be marginalized in so many ways. Mainstream culture is still quite unaware of us and we often suffer from discriminatory practices with very little legal recourse. I think we are on the cutting edge of civil rights, although we are few in numbers, people are gaining awareness. Young people are beginning to realize there is life beyond binary social constructs.

As my mom once said, "A transsexual is just someone who has an overwhelming conviction that their brain functions as the other gender." To me, being transsexual is just as natural as being anything else. There is really nothing wrong with me. I am just "wired" a little differently, the way God created me.

LuLu Ford Manus

Gypsey Elaine Teague

Gypsey Elaine Teague is the Branch Head of the Gunnin Architecture Library and Clemson University's only transgender faculty member. She holds graduate degrees in business administration, landscape architecture, regional and city planning, and library and information sciences. Currently she is pursuing a PhD in rhetoric, communication, and information design at Clemson University.

Miss Teague has written three novels, the first, *The Life and Deaths of Carter Falls,* was an American Library Association Stonewall Award nominee for 2004, and she is the editor of *The New Goddess: Transgender*

Women in the Twenty-First Century. She presents and publishes in a number of venues to include peer-reviewed journals, serials, and Popular Culture Conferences, where she is the Chair of Gender for the SW/Texas Regional District.

Although never thinking of herself as transgendered until recently, she transitioned to postoperative status when a prognosis for testicular cancer mandated a regimen of hormones. During the treatment it was discovered that Miss Teague's mother was prescribed DES (diethylstilbestrol) during the pregnancy. It is believed that the latency of the DES in the brain reacting with the estrogen regimen triggered a mental transition from male to female, similar to other cases of DES male prostate cancer survivors. To that effect Gypsey realized she was no longer male, neither mentally nor, thanks to the hormones, physically, something she now appreciates.

Currently Gypsey is working with the National Institute of Health and other health organizations on the tipping point of subconscious self-identity in transgenders and whether DES accelerates the process. She may be reached at the Gunnin Architecture Library at Clemson or on her web site at: http://claire_daniels.tripod.com.

Curt

Curt is a thirty-six-year-old pre-op, prehormone transman identifying as gay male. He is the parent of five children, not fully understanding his gender identity dysphoria until he was expecting his fourth child. Although surgical measures were taken, a fifth child was born fifteen months later. Curt no longer has vaginal sex. He lives outside of metro Atlanta, and is hopeful that someday his circumstances/finances will allow for his physical transition. Curt is a seasoned writer of gay erotica, poetry, and surreal fiction, and paints also. He is out to about half of his friends, all but one of his children, and his SO's family as well. His partner has had difficulty in dealing with the whole gender issue, but at this time things do seem to be smoothing out. Curt was seeing therapist Rebecca Wood, PhD, up until the arrival of his latest child, and found her guidance and knowledge very helpful. He hopes to resume his sessions with her in the New Year. He has been aware of his gender identity issue since he was five, but always believed that if he acted like a female long enough, it would "go away," and he'd eventually "be normal." Today, he knows that it won't go away, and that he is normal.

Rachel Laverne

Born: January 16, 1939

[I] first cross-dressed at age four and felt at peace with my female self.

[I] Continued to wear mother's clothes and makeup when left alone until about seven. As I reached puberty my breasts became tender and grew. I was scared and delighted all at once. Sex was unimportant to me, but I started and enjoyed wearing my first and second wife's clothes secretly. I thought I was the only person in the world that had these feelings and was ashamed, but delighted when dressed. I bought clothes and built a substantial wardrobe. I purged many times, only to rebuild my wardrobe.

At age forty I resigned myself to the fact that I was not going to cure myself. At age forty-seven I found a transgender support group in San Francisco. After a second divorce, I got my own place and lived as Rachel full time, except for work. I saw a counselor and became comfortable with myself. I saw a psychiatrist who considered me transsexual and [I] went on HRT, developing breasts. Recent new unrelated medication is now enlarging them even more as a side effect.

[I] married my third wife who knew from the beginning and is relatively comfortable with it. I hate to see my male face in the mirror. I love to view the reflection of my en femme persona. When completely dressed, skirt and blouse, dress, suit...I feel complete. I dress conservatively.

Rachel Laverne

Pieta Georgina Schofield

I don't like to describe myself as transsexual although maybe I am. I first started feeling I didn't fit in the male-equals-masculine, female-equals-feminine duality before the age of four. I know this as I can remember secretly smuggling my sister's clothes from her room in a house we moved from before my fourth birthday. These are my earliest memories and they tell me two things: I have been gender dysphoric all my life and the fact I was being secretive means even then I knew it was not socially acceptable to be gender dysphoric. I have lived now as both male and female and I think I understand what it is I need. Gender is the most fundamental aspect of human interaction, before race and religion, we subconsciously assess someone as potential mate or rival, and gender is the most crucial element that colours all our remaining interactions. What I need is for others to treat me as they instinctively treat females. That is how I feel comfortable interacting with others. I am not sure if this means I want to be female, but perhaps I would have been much happier if I had been born female. Maybe my deep desire for a female body is a side effect of this emotional need.

I thought I could fight millions of years of evolution and get others to see me as male but treat me as female. I have realised now my only realistic option is to try to con them into thinking I am female. So I have transitioned to living fully as female, female on my passport, my driving license etc., but this still leaves all kinds of contradictions in my life. With no fixed gender identity I long ago gave up trying to classify my sexuality except as monogamous with a female partner. Along the way in my life I have acquired a family, who it seems can only see me as him, husband or daddy. So now I live and work as female, but I am also still husband and daddy, albeit an unusual husband and daddy. How far my physical transition will go I don't know. I have been diagnosed with Factor V Lieden, a genetic mutation that dramatically increases my risk of embolism and thrombosis if I take estrogen, which is widely recognised as the effective treatment for transsexuals. Not being able to take estrogen means the medical profession is also somewhat reluctant to offer me GRS and hence remove my main source of testosterone. This means I am now in gender limbo, living as female with a functional male body, and living as a female husband and daddy.

Living in stealth as female is hard without the feminizing effects of estrogen and genital reconstruction but impossible, with a family who call me daddy, to explain. This means my need for people to treat me instinctively as female is rarely satisfied. The best I can usually hope for is to be treated as transsexual, which really isn't the same thing. I think many people struggle with the concept of transsexuality as sex and gender are so biologically fundamental and the transsexual is seen as the ultimate confidence trickster, which does not endear us to the buying public. However in our defense, we don't choose to be transsexual, and the confidence trick we try to pull on others is nothing to the one we have to pull on ourselves every waking second of our lives. However the alternative is too grim to contemplate. My endocrinologist told me embolism aggravated by estrogen treatment was the second biggest killer of transsexuals, but it is given because the number one killer of the transgendered is suicide. So although transition may not be ideal, it seems to be the best option I have.

Pieta Georgina Schofield

Dalelynn L. Sims

I am responding to this request as we believe that there are many parallels that the intersex community share with the LGBTI community. All too often those letters stop at LGBT and we are working for inclusion of the I. While there are those that would argue that those of us that are intersex are unique and should not be grouped with the others in the gender community, I have learned from experience and my work with others that there are too many parallel issues to stand alone. Additionally having overcome many obstacles in changing my sex has allowed me a unique perspective into our community. Having understood my own uniqueness for all too long I began my quest for peace many years back, and today, thanks be to the Creator, many friends, family and caregivers I know in my heart that I have found more than that which was sought. I have truly been blessed.

Today I have a loving spouse and a beautiful daughter. We also share our lives with many other family members as most live close to us. We also support others in the community through our web sites, A Kindred Spirit (AKS) and Organization for Intersex International (OII), which is only possible because of our expert translator Curtis. We have seen many successes including correcting the birth record policy in Florida. This not only impacted those of us that are intersex, but the trans members of the community as well. We continue to promote the advancement and diffusion of knowledge and understanding of gender by educational seminars at medical and legal colleges, conferences and providing literature explaining just how unique humanity and each individual is. Once society understands the flaw in believing *Homo sapiens* is absolutely dimorphic with the respect to sex chromosome composition, gonadal structure, hormone levels, and the structure of the internal genital duct systems and external genitalia then they will understand that there is not a single, universally correct developmental pathway and outcome. Not my words, but those of the *American Journal of Human Biology.* With as many as 12 million Americans that have one condition or syndrome labeled as intersex and more and more reasons for this endocrine disruption surfacing daily in nature, society will soon have to face the facts that the physical gender variation found in nature does not magically become a mental issue when seen in humanity. While I believe that we are getting there as we see more and more doctors letting intersex children decide if and when surgery is necessary, we still have a long way to go. I hope this project helps in the endeavor.

Dalelynn L. Sims is a researcher, instructor, and analyst for a government contractor. Retired from the army with multiple trips overseas including two to southwest Asia, the last just completed November 2005. Prior adjunct lecturer for three colleges. Dalelynn has a degree in Christian Religious Studies. She has served on the board of other originations, e.g., Bodies Like Ours, and continues to educate society about gender.

See http://www.kindredspiritlakeside.homestead.com/ and http://www.intersexualite.org/ for more information.

Dalelynn L. Sims

Part kitty cat, part butterfly, all girl. As with the felines with whom she identifies, **Ms. Cohn** (Robb) has led multiple lives. In one, she was an Eagle Boy Scout, in another licensed photographer for the Grateful Dead, and, in yet another, aspiring historian of religions studying with Dr. Carrasco,

Ms. Robert Kelly Madison Cohn

himself a student of the renowned Dr. Mircea Eliade. Yet throughout these multiple existences, Robbi lived as though in a cocoon, created partly by her and partly by society. The metamorphosis, which turned this caterpillar into a butterfly, did not happen until she approached her fiftieth year. That cocoon, comprised of denial, fear, misunderstandings, self-loathing, and confusion, shielded her from her true self which remained dormant, submerged beneath the surface, waiting for events to actualize them. Thus, the little boy, born Robert Cohn, learned she was transgender and embarked upon a new and wonderful path. Today, she has returned to the academic world, this time working toward a paralegal technology degree. Her goal is to work within the legal community toward a greater acceptance in society for those whose lives are not governed by the conformity considered acceptable in this patriarchal dominated world. She believes all individuals should be judged by their actions, not by their race, religion, sexual orientation or gender presentation and that life's manifest diversity should be embraced as reflected in the lives of each and every individual.

Miqqi Alicia Gilbert

Miqqi Alicia Gilbert, PhD, aka Michael A. Gilbert, is a Professor of Philosophy at York University, Toronto, Canada. She has published two novels as well as a popular book on argument, now going into a third edition. More recently she has been publishing scholarly articles in the areas of argumentation theory and gender theory in scholarly journals. Miqqi Alicia was born in 1945 in the Flatbush section of Brooklyn, New York, and moved permanently to Canada in 1968. She began cross-dressing at about age twelve, and has never stopped. She went through all the usual guilt and shame with its concomitant purges and "relapses." After the death of her common-law wife in 1985 Miqqi Alicia finally came to terms with who and what she is, and determined to stop pretending and live her life.

After "leaking out" to friends and family for several years, Miqqi Alicia decided in 1995 to address York University's Task Force on Homophobia and Heterosexism on issues of transgenderism. Following that she presented a paper at the first International congress on Cross-dressing, Gender and Sexuality in Northridge, California. In 1998, an article about her and several other academics appeared in the *Chronicle of Higher Education,* and was subsequently picked up and published by *The Globe & Mail* in Toronto, making her Canada's most famous cross-dresser.

Miqqi Alicia has developed the concept of the "committed cross-dresser," (CD) as a CD who accepts herself/himself, and uses cross-dressing to grow personally and explore gender differences. Since then she has presented numerous papers, workshops, and talks across the United States and Canada. Her best-known essays include "Beyond Appearances," "The Transgendered Philosopher," and "The Feminist Crossdresser." She is a long-time member of the Fantasia Fair organizing committee, book review editor and regular columnist for *Transgender Tapestry,* the magazine of the IFGE (the International Foundation for Gender Education), and a recipient, in 2007, of an IFGE Trinity Award. Her web site, with many of her writings, is at www.yorku.ca/gilbert/tg.

Micheline Anne Montreuil

Micheline Anne Montreuil is certainly the most well-known transgender lawyer, professor, writer, and hostess in Canada. Her battles over her name and her position have been fought against the government of Canada, the government of Quebec, and the big enterprises and have been highlighted in the news. She continues to seek for her rights to live peacefully as a transgender person. Graduated in law, industrial relations, management and education, and a candidate at the next federal election for the New Democratic Party, she is the living proof that nothing is impossible.

Jesse G.

My name is **Jesse G.** I was lucky enough that this is my real name, or rather, a shortened form of it. I'm not afraid to use my real name in this bio, as I have nothing to hide, or be ashamed of. In fact, I kind of consider myself one of the lucky ones. I have never really experienced much homophobia, or transphobia for that matter. Shocking in a way, as I live in a pretty small Ontario town. I just assumed that having worked in this community, I was well liked and respected enough that no one has ever really pointed their fingers at me. I'm surrounded by a great group of friends, and a somewhat supporting family. My mother is French Catholic, and while she is quite hard on me sometimes about my masculine features, she loves me and would rather accept me than have me not be in her life.

I have always known that I was different. I remember at the age of six or seven, that I wasn't a lesbian. Sure genetically I was female, but I never felt "female." I never really felt either way. I knew that I was attracted to girls only, but that I wasn't gay. Queer, yes, but not a lesbian. I had somewhat conformed to society as a little person, until around the time of the fifth grade. I had started cutting my hair short, and wearing boys' clothing much to the disappointment of both parents. They did try to feminize me, but I stood my ground, and stuck to what I was feeling on the inside—for what I could get away with anyways. It was during my puberty years, even when I was developing my breasts and getting my period, that I was also developing hair growth. Not just on my legs and armpits, like most other girls, but on my face, chest, and stomach as well. Shocked as I was at the time, it also secretly thrilled me too. I did, however, try to hide it by waxing and shaving (painfully), way into my young twenties. As comfortable as I was with it,

I knew society would have other ideas about it. I was always asked, are you a boy or a girl, something which I grew really tired of, and while most strangers mistook me for a boy, my voice always seemed to give me away. That, and people once they analyzed my face, would stare down at my chest and body for any other telltale signs of "what" I was. I guess I hid it because I was afraid of their reaction to their own embarrassment.

I lived most of my young adulthood as a lesbian, even though I always felt differently. I despise the use of labels, but found out that some people need these labels in order for them to make sense of things. Visually, and sexually, even though people assumed me a lesbian, I acted quite like a young man. Marriage had even entered my life. I was married at the ripe old age of twenty-six to a woman. A self-identified lesbian herself. I fell hard in love with her, but fell short in the fact that I couldn't give her the "woman" she needed and wanted. While she liked my masculinity, she still wanted me to be a woman for her. I couldn't let her touch my breasts, as the feel of them repulsed me, nor would I let her do other things to me, that made me feel like a girl. This wasn't fair for either of us, and needless to say, despite other reasons as well, we are no longer together, and are preparing for our divorce. I don't regret anything that has happened, just more lessons for me to learn in this life.

I guess it's been only the past year-and-a-half that I have been living as a transman. I've always let people use whatever pronouns they wish to describe me, as "she" and "he" have been used interchangeably. Neither one offends or bothers me, and sometimes I find it interesting how some people actually see me. Although I am more masculine in everything that I do, some people still just see me as being quite androgynous. Almost like a Ken doll...no gender parts. I do find myself being more and more comfortable in my own skin and appearance every day. I let my facial hair grow in sometimes for a week at a time and am not ashamed that I can actually grow a full beard. Naturally. While I'm not on any hormone treatments, I sometimes wonder if I really need to. I am not intersexed, but I was lucky enough to be quite a hairy person. (I didn't quite realize just how lucky, until my trans friends were jealous at my facial and body hair.) When I was in my early teens, I did end up going to an endocrinologist here in town, and he just deemed that I had a chemical imbalance where my testosterone levels were higher than my estrogen levels. Sure it could have been corrected through medication, but I was scared that I wouldn't feel like me any more, so I refused. I mean, my body functioned normally, everything in its rightful place and all that, so I felt like I shouldn't mess with what was given to me. I felt masculine, I looked masculine, and I grew hair. Secretly as a teen, I was happy about it. Despite looking like a girl underneath my clothes, outwardly I liked how I was feeling on the inside.

I would never consider having "bottom" surgery, unless a miracle could be performed and it would look and act like the real thing, but I would however love, and hope to have my breasts removed. That is about the only part of my body that truly embarrasses me to no end. Until the day I can afford it, as I am definitely ready mentally, I am reduced to having to bind myself (painfully). I do however look forward to the day where I have the freedom of not having these two things (breasts) that drive me crazy. The one part of me that I hide, and shy away from.

I have come quite a long way in my short life, and I guess the toughest part that I have had to face was just turning thirty. If that has been the worst part, then I'm not so bad off in life. As the years progress, I have become more and more of who "Jesse" really is. I have no idea what is in store for the rest of my future, or how society will react to the person that I am, but as long as I myself am comfortable, smart, and happy, I know that I will be all right in this life!

Jesse G.

Cross-cultural gender variance

As we have seen, U.S. transgender identity is embedded in the wider Euro-American gender schema, sometimes reproducing but also challenging beliefs and assumptions about embodiment as a male or female through the creation of hybrid bodies and identities. The Euro-American gender schema assumes that there is coalescence between physical characteristics such as genitals, gender status, gender identity and social identity. However, not only does the transgendered community challenge these views, but the ethnographic spectrum presents a much more complicated picture than the view that anatomy necessarily leads to a gendered destiny. Nanda (2000: 2) argues: "Many cultures do not make the distinction between the natural and the cultural or between sex and gender, for many cultures, anatomical sex is not the dominant factor in constructing gender roles and gender identity." For example, occupation or the kind of work one does may be a more important attribute of gender than are genitalia, once the initial assignment at birth is made on the basis of visual inspection. For some Native American groups it was possible for a physiological female to become a social male by taking on the occupation of men (Besnier, 1996; Bolin, 1996b; Nanda, 2000; Whitehead, 1981).

Further complicating the picture of gender identity is sexual expression/behavior with people of the same sex/gender. Homosexual behavior does not carry the same meaning cross-culturally (as discussed in Chapter 14 and the section on homosexuality that follows). Until recently in the United states the LGBTQ communities were bifurcated around sexual orientation and gender identity, with transgendered people forming a community based on issues of identity, not sexual interest. Weiss (2007) has argued that these divisions are being eroded, specifically that the borderlands between butch lesbian identity and FTM (female-to-male transgender) are being broken down by the younger generation. These social identities are beginning to converge as a result of changes in both communities, as youth cultures blur and erase the borders between lesbian and FTM identities. In this regard, Weiss (2007: 219) suggests:

> In 1998, Dr. Jacob Hale wrote about a "borderland" between butch lesbian identity and FTM masculinity, suggesting a "demilitarized zone." While the intervening years have brought no "demilitarized zone," the border may not have a long future. Converging trends in identity among the younger generation in their teens and twenties suggest this, such as changing meanings of "lesbian" and "FTM," blending of sexuality and gender, and understanding these as personal, rather than identity, differences. The socio-historical circumstances that gave power to anti-trans feminist attitudes and trans rejection of lesbian identity are disappearing. This is not to say that we are "post-lesbian" or "post-transsexual" but the tension between identities, the need to distinguish clearly between them, and the arguments about who is "really" lesbian or "really" FTM may be of supreme unimportance to the next generation. Time will tell.

However, other societies have gender schemas that incorporate gendered homosexuality. In this situation the insertee or recipient of anal intercourse takes on characteristics and behaviors associated with the feminine gender role and feminine social identity. Unlike the United States gender schema, in Brazil, one's position as a recipient of homosexual anal intercourse defines one as gender variant; the inserter is not considered homosexual or gender variant (Nanda, 2000; Kulick, 1998). In some nonindustrialized countries, the sex/gender system has created a place for various gender variant peoples through the social construction of multiple genders, outside, inside and in between. Although gender variance is legitimized and valued in some nonindustrialized/industrializing societies, in others it is not. There is a tremendous amount of diversity in the way gender variant peoples and cultures define, experience and practice gender variant identities, statuses and roles; for some peoples such as Plains Native Americans and some Hindus, it may be part of a sacred or religious experience and for others it is secular (Nanda, 1999, 2000). For example, Thayer's (1980) analysis argues that gender variance among Northern Plains Indians represents an interstitial positioning of gender between the secular and the sacred (in Bolin, 1987a, 1987b) and in contrast Besnier (1996) notes that Polynesian gender variance has no historical or current association with the religious.

From its early days through today, anthropologists have been documenting and analyzing this panoply of genders; for example Bogoras reported on the Chuckchee "softman" in 1907. The cross-cultural study of gender variance reveals the limitations of our own Euro-American perspective of gender. Scholars and researchers are not immune to the power of the industrial gender schema to frame their analysis of the expression and meaning of gender variance, even when trying not to. Consequently it is far preferable in a discussion of cross-cultural gender variance to use the indigenous or local name for the gender variant identity, for example *alyha* for the Mohave male gender variant status and *mahu* for the Polynesian "liminal" gender. It may be acceptable to use the generic "two spirit" as a generic reference to Native American male and female gender diversity (Lang, 1998). One major caveat relates to our modern terminology that differentiates gender status/identity from gender role and gender of erotic/sexual interest. The anthropological literature offers distinctions between these four insignias of gender in interpreting, for example, whether a woman who behaves like a man is a cross-gendered or gender transformed status, or whether such behavior is just part of gender role variability for women (Bolin, 1996b, 2004b; Lang, 1998).

This is a subtle distinction that may be more evident through example than explanation. Among the Northern Piegan, a highly sex-disparate culture studied by Lewis (1941), women could assume attributes associated with masculinity through participation in economic venues. Among the Piegan, to acquire wealth and display generosity had even higher prestige than war. Women who pursued this career were known as *manly hearts*. The *manly hearts* were assertive women characterized by aggression, independence, boldness, and sexuality, all traits associated with Piegan masculinity (Lewis, 1941: 181f). But to be a *manly heart* also required that one be wealthy and married. In this regard they were highly valued as spouses because of their economic contributions. The *manly hearts* gender was not a transformed status, although they "acted like men." Manly hearted women cursed like men, excelled in men's and women's work, and generally behaved in ways associated with the masculine role but, were essentially gendered as feminine in that they did not use their skills to escape the gender constraints of being a wife and mother. The Piegan *manly hearts* role inscribed the privileging of masculinity for both males and females, while women's pursuits were valued in women only (Lang, 1998: 305–306).

We must keep in mind that the distinction between gender statuses and gender role may not be an emic one. A related point in the consideration of gender diversity is that when gender varies, then industrial paradigms that gender and sexual orientations are oppositional are dismantled rather rapidly. When gender is destabilized then so is sexual orientation. Gender variance also disrupts Euro-American notions of sexual orientation. U.S. polarization of homosexual and heterosexual does not translate well into the ethnographic record as we saw in the case of Latin America wherein only the receptor in anal sex is regarded as homosexual (Kulick, 1998). This polarization has also been under cultural assault in the United States in the new millennium by youth cultural "Q" (queering and questioning), the "down-low" and the recognition of a category of "men who have sex with men."

A final point in the cross-cultural study of gender variance is that the ethnographic record is decidedly thin on female supernumerary/transformed statuses and female same-sex relations as well. In spite of the considerable contributions of a cadre of women anthropologists including the valiant efforts of Evelyn Blackwood who has dedicated her research to this subject area since 1984—including Blackwood and Wieringa (1999), Blackwood (1999), Elliston (1999), Lang (1998), and Whitehead (1981) among others—the study of female gender variance and same-gender sexual behaviors is still in its infancy and much work remains to be done. The classic anthropological literature on additional/transformed genders is biased heavily toward examples of presumed genetic/genital males and male gender variance is reported among many more societies than for females (Lang, 1998). Unfortunately, since we offer discussion of the classic ethnographic literature, our examples will necessarily reflect this emphasis in the literature. However, women also occupied these positions. Whether female two-spirit genders and other expressions are similar to male gender variance is unclear (Lang, 1998). It may be argued convincingly that, because gender statuses are structured differently for women and men globally, gender variant statuses for women may not be expected to be mirror images of men's gender variance. In fact, Nanda (2000: 7) asserts: "[F]emale gender diversity has its own cultural dynamic and is not simply a derivative, a parallel, or the reverse of male gender diversity" (Nanda, 2000: 7). The bias in the literature has been speculated upon and may be explained as follows:

- There is a general cultural valuing and privileging of males among many but not all cultural groups.
- There may have been observer bias of male researchers (who dominated the field in its early days).
- Male researchers lacked access to females.
- Female gender variance is simply less obvious to the observer.
- It may be related as well to more rigid boundaries around the male status so that transgression leads to additional genders. The female role is more accommodating of diversity so that women may have more freedom to cross over roles without transforming their gender as in contemporary North America (Bolin, 2004b; Lang, 1998: 261–267; Nanda, 2000).

A final caution: although many cultures have gender variant positions for men and women to transgress their gender by acting like or being identified with the other gender, these must be understood within the context of the specific culture at a specific point in time, since social identities are dynamic, situational, and contextual (Nanda, 2000: 4). Towle and Morgan (2006) offer a cautionary voice to the use of the term "third gender" warning that in spite of the acceptance of diversity implied by this term, it paradoxically signifies an industrialized classification and appropriation of indigenous gender variance, obscures the heterogeneity and complexity of gendered social identities. As a consequence, we have relegated the term "third gender" to those examples in which the author uses the term.

Although cross-dressing may be part of gender variance, very transient cross-dressing for ceremonial purposes is not defined as gender variance. Transient cross-dressing is found in many cultures and on many occasions. It is frequently associated with ritual events such as among the Iatmul men of New Guinea who mockingly dress as elderly matrons (Bateson, 1958); among the Dani when women don the garb of young warriors to celebrate; and in the United States in the "powder puff football" of an earlier era, with men and women reversing the gendered division of players and cheerleaders. Rituals that include gender reversals occur in numerous other groups as well as in Brazilian Carnaval.

The spectrum of gender variance cross-culturally is a wide one and includes a number of examples in which some of the gendered behaviors usually associated with one gender/sex are adopted by those of another in part or in whole; these are broadly conceived to include demeanor, dress, activities, and occupations; and may or may not converge with sexual expression. One of the ways that cultures recognized and institutionalized gender variance is through codification in the indigenous lexicon that recognized the status of individuals who were in some ways divergent from the cultural gender paradigm in terms of anatomy, gender status and/or behavior.[3]

Classic ethnographic reports on gender variant identities suggest it was once widespread among indigenous peoples prior to colonization. Westermarck (1956) offered the first ethnological overview in 1906. Stewart (1960: 19) recorded its presence among Native Americans for Kroeber's *Culture Element Distributions* (1937–1943), Devereux (1937) among the Mohave, Hoebel (1949) and Lewis (1941) reported it for Plains Indians; Hill noted it among the Navajo (1935) and Pima (1938), Bogoras for Chuckchee (1904–1909), Evans-Pritchard for the Azande (1970), among others. And more recent accounts covering precolonial and colonial gender variance among Native Americans (including men and women) include, for example, Lang (1998), Williams (1986), and Roscoe (1991, 1998) for the Zuni. Anthropological literature on gender variance in light of the influence of globalization is also growing; examples of this work include Davies (2007), Towle and Morgan (2002), Matzner (2001), Sinnott (2004), Blackwood (1999, 2005a), among others.

Although the current trends in anthropological approaches to understanding gender variance are very context specific emphasizing local culture and gender ideologies, other approaches have used the cross-cultural correlational method to test hypotheses generated by the ethnographic accounts. This earlier research has focused on identifying the relationship between gender variance and gender roles. For example, Hoebel (1949) proposed that the male gender variance (two spirits) represented male protest in societies in which the extant warfare complex demanded excessive male aggression. However, Goldberg's test of this hypothesis found no correlation between warfare and two-spirit traditions. Downie and Hally (1961) and Munroe, Whiting and Hally (1969) correlated male gender variant identities with societies that had low sex role disparity (differences) rather than high as previously suggested in Hoebel's research. They hypothesized that societies that had low gender role disparity would be more likely to have gender variance because it would make it easier for the "predisposed" to change genders, arguing that these societies would be more tolerant of gender variance.

Williams' (1986) historical and ethnographic research argued that the Native American two-spirit traditions were an additional gender mixed status rather than just role variation for men (Callender and Kochems, 1983). Williams' analysis proposed that the two spirit must be understood in light of Native American spiritual systems wherein one's spirit is the most important aspect of sex/gender in contrast to the industrialized gender schema with its genital focus. Williams cited the enhanced status of the two spirit among Native American groups whose gender relations included a high valuation of women. He suggests that "[b]ecause women are valued, androgyny is allowed, but if women are devalued, are regarded as polluting, female characteristics in males will be denied" (Williams, 1986: 268–269).

Levy's (1973) research on the Tahitian *mahu* (gender variant status for men) has also argued that gender variance is related to the gender paradigm and gender role disparity, as has the earlier research discussed above by Downie and Hally (1961), Munroe, Whiting and Hally (1969), and Williams (1986). Levy's interpretation of Tahitian gender variance, unlike previous researchers, maintained that the *mahu,* as a third gender, was vital in making gender difference apparent. Tahitian society is one in which gendered behavior is not clearly polarized; therefore the *mahu* identity served as a way to culturally elaborate the differences between men and women. Besnier (1996) has taken issue with Levy's interpretation of the *mahu,* proposing that the *mahu* is not a third gender, but rather a gender liminal position embedded in Polynesian views of personhood. Moreover, Besnier (1996: 307) contends: "the *mahu* blurs gender categories rather than affirms them...[in a society where]...gender boundaries are anything but blurred." Matzner's (2001) research on O'ahu transgendered people (male bodied) incorporates narratives to reveal the complexities of the current overlay and fusion of the colonial experience, immigration and globalized transgender identity with the *mahu* of Old Hawaii.

Wikan's (1977, 2000) study of Omani *xanith* (a male gender variant position) relates this third gender to socioeconomics, gender relations, roles, and sexuality. A man could become a *xanith* temporarily to earn income through sex work with heterosexual men. According to Wikan, the *xanith* gender was an important social position that functioned to preserve female honor by providing an inexpensive sexual outlet for heterosexual male desire. This was a flexible and an intermittent gender; a *xanith* could resume his position as a man, including marriage and family, without negative repercussions.

Anthropological research has and continues to demonstrate that gender variance can take many forms in addition to what we have discussed. One line of research has reported on intersexed individuals among a number of cultures (see Chapter 7). Intersexuality provides society the opportunity for cultural creativity in response to genital variation from the anatomical norm. As discussed in Chapter 7, an intersexed person may be identified at birth (but not invariably) by the appearance of the genitals. Societies have responded in diverse ways to the presence of people with intersexed genitals; for example, the traditional (precolonial) Navajo culture provides an example of a society in which an intersex status was a highly valued one (Bolin, 1996b, 2004b; Hill, 1935, Lang, 1998).

The Navajo recognized three physical sexes: hermaphrodites, males, and females, and at least three or more gender statuses: men (boys), women (girls), and *nadle*. There were three categories of *nadles*: real *nadle* and *nadle* pretenders who may be genital men (males) and women (females). The *nadle* were ascribed their position on the basis of ambiguous genitals; or in the case of the *nadle* pretenders, they displayed interests ascribed to the other gender. Therefore, either genital or psychic/behavioral ambiguity qualified one for the status. The *nadle* assumed occupational tasks and behaviors associated with both men (with the exception of hunting and warfare) and women. But they also had special status not shared by other Navajo; they were in fact regarded as extraordinary people associated with prosperity. In the words of one Navajo: "They know everything. They can do the work of a man and a woman. I think when all the *nadle* are gone, that it will be the end of the Navajo" (Navajo consultant to Hill, 1935: 275). *Nadle* sex partners included women or men but not other *nadle* or *nadle* pretenders. Women could therefore select as sexual partners men, *nadle,* or *nadle* pretenders, and men could choose as partners women, *nadle,* or *nadle* pretenders. However, homosexuality, defined as intercourse between partners of the same gender, was not accepted among the Navajo. This serves to illustrate problems of interpretation cross-culturally. If the *nadle* was a third gender status or something other, then the term homosexual is inapplicable to *nadle* partnerships. Such relationships cannot be classified within our industrialized schema based on heterosexuality, homosexuality, or bisexuality (Bolin, 2004b).

Another example of gender variance associated with, but not limited to, genital ambiguity bears mentioning and that is Serena Nanda's study of the *hijras* of India (1999, 2000). The *hijras* are a recognized third gender, who are usually born as men (although some may be born intersexed) and become transformed through a ritualized surgical emasculation in which the genitals (penis and testicle) are removed. *Hijra* translates as "eunuch" or "intersex" and emphasizes sexual impotence; defined as having no desire for women; making them "not men" (Nanda, 2000: 29). After the surgery, they adopt the demeanor, behavior, and clothing of women, but they are still "not women" because Hindu womanhood implies marriage and children. Although *hijras* are like women in taking feminine names, using female kinship terms for each other, and wearing women's dress, they also violate norms of feminine behavior by public dancing, use of aggressive speech, verbal insults and exaggerated expressions of dress and demeanor.

Central to understanding the *hijra* are the religous elements of the position. These "neither man nor woman" worship Bahuchara Mata, a Hindu Mother Goddess associated with transgendered people. The surgical emasculation comes at the bequest of their goddess. Only through the surgery, a form of rebirth religiously, can the *hijras* enact the procreative power of the Mother Goddess. These procreative powers are enabled through the *hijras'* performance at life cycle events including marriages and in rituals after the birth of a child. They perform songs, dances, and blessings for fertility in the name of their goddess and receive traditional payments of money, sweets and cloth.

Hijra gender variance suggests a flexible gender category. The ideal for *hijras* is that of the life of an ascetic in which sexual desire is renounced. Through the renunciation of sexuality and reproduction, sexual desire is transformed into sacred power. But as a variant third gender, the *hijra* community attracts different kinds of persons, most of whom join voluntarily as teenagers or adults. It appears to be a magnet for those with a wide range of cross-gender characteristics arising from diverse motives. The *hijra* gender accommodates different personalities, gender identities, and sexual needs, including persons who have sex with men (sometimes for money) or the ideal of an ascetic sexless life without losing its cultural meaning. It is embedded in Hinduism which celebrates the coexistence of unresolved oppositions in the acknowledgment of multiple genders existing among both gods and humans. Thus, the person who does not marry and cannot have children is not excluded from a place in Hindu society but can become a *hijra* (Nanda, 1999, 2000; Nanda and Warms, 2007).

Not only is gender variance associated with ideologies of gender, fertility, and the spiritual system, but it may also occur in a nexus of gender and marriage such as in the woman marriage still practiced today among some peoples (Brockman, 2004). It has been recorded for thirty Bantu societies, including a dozen Kenyan ethnic groups (O'Brien, 1977). **Woman marriage** is a predominantly African institution where one woman marries another and becomes a female-husband. There are a number of types of woman marriage, but debates occur over the kinds of sexual practices associated with this form of marriage and/or whether a woman-husband is a third gender, a transformed gender or an expression of gender role variance. For example, the Igbo of Nigeria do not limit male gender roles to just male bodied people, but allow females to fill male gender roles without sacrificing their position as women. This suggests that gender status is not necessarily linked to particular bodies (Amadiume, 1987). Among some groups, women may marry women for economic independence, but will not necessarily be regarded as social men (O'Brien, 1977). Oboler's (1980) work among the Nandi notes that female-husbands do take on men's roles and tasks such as cultivating and herding. However, Blackwood (1986) maintains that woman marriage was not a cross-gender institution, although reports suggest a great deal of diversity in this marital form. Blackwood (1986) also maintains that same-sex behavior may have been part of this type of marriage, while the majority of researchers consider woman-marriage a nonsexual institution. Evans-Pritchard's (1951) early research on woman marriage among the Nuer maintained that it occurred in situations where a female was infertile. The infertile woman would take a wife, hence becoming a cultural man. "She" would also arrange for a progenitor for the wife so that "she" could become a father. Evans-Pritchard's (1951) interpretation of woman-woman marriage was that it functioned as a kin recruitment strategy thereby optimizing the potential loss of kin through an infertile woman (Evans-Pritchard, 1951; more recently Blackwood, 2004).

The meaning of what it is to be a woman-husband in this institution is not resolved, nor is it clear whether lesbian relations occurred within these relationships (Blackwood, 1999, 2004). Indeed, if the woman-husband is regarded as a man, then the term lesbian is ethnocentric. Blackwood proposes that woman-marriage presents a "model of relations between women within the gender system" rather than a gender crossing role (1986).

Summary: gender variance

In summary, what can we learn from this panorama of gender variance and how can it inform Euro-American/industrialized gender schema? We propose that:

- Gender variance reveals our Euro-American dichotomous gender classification system as just one of many paradigms.
- We can learn from these tribal voices that man and woman, male and female are not universal categories for gender, that there may be more than two as testified by the intersex genders, *hijra* and the two-spirit traditions.

- Gender variance is very complex, incorporating a great deal of diversity within gendered categories, contesting notions of bipolarity, and suggesting liminality and diversity beyond that offered by the notion of third genders, e.g., status and role variation.
- Gender identities may be achieved and shed within one's lifetime.
- Categories such as homosexuality and heterosexuality are exploded when gender is destabilized.
- The ethnographic record has indeed revealed a fluidity and flexibility in sexual behaviors and choice of sexual partners that suggest an independence of identity and sexuality.
- Intersex genders indicate that identities are not clearly or directly tied to a detectable biological baseline/hormonal environment but are interpreted through the cultural paradigm.
- Cross-gendered roles suggest the embeddedness of concepts such as masculinity and femininity in culture (Bolin, 2004b).

This cross-cultural overview of gender variance demonstrates the differences between the anthropological and the clinical approaches to this subject (discussed in Chapter 7). Both anthropologists and clinicians are concerned with understanding gender variance but it is encountered from two very different perspectives. Though the clinical is distinguished by its search for biological and psychological factors, the socio-cultural perspective is interested in the cultural construction of gender and how gender variance is anchored in broader systems of gender ideologies and relations within the cultural context, emphasizes the importance of cultural meanings, including gender subjectivity in the experience and socio-cultural expressions of gender variance within the totality of a gender system (e.g., Blackwood, 2005a; Herdt, 1999).

CROSS-CULTURAL GENDER ROLES: A SYNOPSIS

Transgenderism/transsexualism and the alternative gender roles cross-culturally such as the *xanith*, *mahu*, and manly-hearted women are examples of the cultural variety and response to gender identity. Our fascination with gender identity extends to various beliefs concerning gender statuses and roles, changing gender role behaviors, and how to manage male-female relations in the twenty-first century. These beliefs will be examined relative to changes in gender roles and gender relationships both in the United States and cross-culturally. The effects of culture change on gender roles and sexuality are introduced in this chapter and expanded upon in Chapters 14, 15, and 16 where we explore sexual orientations, HIV/AIDS, and globalization, respectively.

Traditional gender roles refer to those preferred behaviors and expectations that are clearly gender specific and are associated with male and female middle-class behavior from the late 1800s to the mid-1960s. These include affective and behavioral characteristics based on gender which tend to emphasize female passive-aggressiveness, overt displays of emotion other than anger, as well as those emphasizing nurturance, intuition, gentleness, and softness. Male behavior is sharply contrasted: aggression, emotional constriction other than expressions of anger, rational-logical interpretation, decisiveness, hardness. In fact, a now classic study, Broverman et al., (1970) clearly relates culturally defined gender role appropriate behavior with definitions of adulthood and mental health in this society. Basically a mentally healthy adult is a phenotypic male who expresses appropriate gender-role behavior. Culturally, appropriate female gender role behavior and expectations generally are considered less healthy. It is a clear statement that what was (is) valued in this culture is male behavior and female behavior is viewed ambivalently at best. For example, motherhood is both exalted and seen as innate, natural, not something which is learned, defined, and expressed as the role is experienced through the child's life.

Androgyny is a Greek word combining the words for male, *andros* and female, *gyny*. It refers to a state of being in which an individual behaves, thinks, and emotes in response to the situation, regardless of gender-defined characteristics. As a situation-specific response, it synthesizes culturally defined categories of male and female behavior such as femininity and masculinity. For example, fear is a common human reaction to a threatening or dangerous situation. Traditional males in the United States would show no fear; females would express fear. An androgynous individual would express fear as the appropriate response to the situation regardless of gender. Androgyny extends from behavioral-affective situations to include modes of dress, speech, and demeanor in popular U.S. culture (e.g., gender-neutral clothes or colors). Culturally, androgynous behavior and affect are still **androcentric** or male oriented and easier to achieve for females than for males. For example, while both men and women now wear earrings, this was a difficult and not totally resolved barrier for men to cross. Men's earrings tend to be less ornate, smaller and simpler than women's, and currently may be worn in either or both ears. In contrast, women can freely shop in men's clothing departments and be considered stylish. There is little fear or chance of reprisal or discrimination toward women who do this.

The application of androgyny can be seen in popular culture. The "New Age Sensitive Kind of Guys" of the 1990s were appreciated (in theory, at least) as more emotionally open and expressive. "Metrosexuals"—heterosexual men living in urban environments who pay a lot of attention to grooming, clothing, and other outward forms of appearance—are regarded positively. Popular music stars such as Elton John and Marilyn Manson gender bend, i.e., they push traditional gender role boundaries for men.

The concept of androgyny may be very culture specific, even within industrialized societies. Some cross-cultural examples may help to illustrate this. Within other societies which have roots in European traditions such as Latin America, there is a very clear recognition and acceptance of men's culture and women's culture.

Among Latinos, men and women know who they are and accept, sometimes with anger and resentment, that men and women are different. They behave very differently in each other's presence, particularly in public, than they do when they are with their own gender. These changes can be subtle—a shift in facial expression or body posture, or more overt—such as changes in the volume, inflection, or tone of voice, vocabulary used or the topics considered appropriate for discussion in a mixed group. Through affinal ties, one of your authors, Patricia Whelehan, belongs to an extended Peruvian kinship system which encompasses three continents and islands in the Caribbean. These households are middle class and female centered. However, the presence of a male, particularly an older one, shifts attention away from the females to his needs.

Females, for example, create their own space in several ways when men appear. There are clear distinctions in space between *en casa* (home) and *al fuera* (outside, the public/work world). Home is women's space. Women attend to the man's desire for food and drink in order to "take care of him and get him out of the way." Women can move to another area of the house or engage in a "female activity" such as cooking, being with other female family members, or going shopping with them. Although this behavior takes them out of the house, it also serves to assert their space (Whelehan, n.d.).

An even clearer example is found in Muslim societies in the Middle East. *Purdah* is the veiling and seclusion of women. It is perceived by many in industrialized societies as an extreme situation of female submission to and oppression by men. However, in the classic book, *Guests of the Sheik*, Fernea discusses the gradual changes in her perception of *purdah*, and her eventual acceptance of it for herself and the women with whom she lived. Veiling, which is done in public and in the presence of unrelated males, provides women with a sense of privacy, space, and protection. Women are not veiled in their own space at home, which is considered one of the most important sectors of Muslim society. At home, they make decisions that are integral to daily life and the welfare of the family. Veiling separates them from a male world which they do not necessarily want to join, nor which they necessarily define as superior to their own. They know that their work and effort maintains the kin group, a key survival unit in society. To them, androgyny is a very strange concept to societies with clearly defined men's and women's cultures (Fernea, 1965).

INTIMACY

The concepts of psychological masculinity and femininity have been widely discussed in the United States since the 1970s by writers such as Hite (1976, 1981, 1987), Cassell (1984), Farrell (1974, 1986, 1993), Zilbergeld (1978, 1992, 1999), Goldberg (1976, 1980, 1984), and Tanner (1995, 2001). Relative to relationships, this research generally explores what men and women need and want from each other and in their romantic and love relationships. In essence, this research states that men and women have very similar needs and wants in relationships. However, their means of expressing and getting their needs met are different, and are not necessarily well communicated to or well understood by the other gender. For example, both men and women state they want emotional bonding and depth in their relationships and that trust, being able to be one's self, and honesty are important. They also state they value these needs over genital sexuality, per se. However, according to the work by the researchers cited above, culturally defined ways of communicating and meeting these needs and perceptions of the other gender may either impede or enhance need fulfillment. In general, men and women attitudinally and culturally still fulfill their **scripts**, those socially defined roles of masculinity and femininity (Gagnon, 1973; Gagnon and Parker, 1995). People's deep sense of who and what they are, regardless of their overt behavior, rests on fairly well-ingrained pre-1960s ideas of masculinity and femininity. This is expressed in women when they value relationships, communication, and being physically attractive over sexuality per se and when they assume primary responsibility for the relationship (Cassell, 1984; Hite, 1976, 1981, 1987; Tanner, 1995). Men express this by using sex as an example of emotional caring by defining the quality of a relationship sexually rather than through verbal or affective means, or choosing partners primarily on physical characteristics (Farrell, 1974, 1986; Fisher, 2004; Goldberg, 1976, 1980; Hite, 1981; Zilbergeld, 1978, 1992).

The result is that while needs for closeness, trust, and bonding exist, the means people use to express and meet these needs may not achieve this purpose. In addition, pre-1960s rules about male-female interaction have changed. New ones have not been culturally recognized and accepted socially on a wide scale. While some individuals have achieved relationship satisfaction, there is much confusion, anxiety, and miscommunication on a cultural level about male-female relationships (Tanner, 1995, 2001). There is also a wider variety of relationships more openly and visibly present in this society today (Blumstein and Schwartz, 1983; Lippa, 2006; McWhirter and Mattison, 1984).

One aspect of this phenomenon is the relatively recent focus on **intimacy**. Intimacy, a late-twentieth-century, middle-class term, essentially is a relabeling of the anthropological concept of bonding, a primate and human primate behavior (see Chapter 3). As human primates, we need to interact with others of our own kind and establish close social and emotional or affective ties with each other. Development of intimacy or bonding rests on biobehavorial interaction (Fisher, 2004; Perper, 1985). Intimacy develops in stages that include verbal and nonverbal cueing, kinesics, and interaction (Perper, 1985). Perper, an anthropologist and biologist, suggests that the most elementary steps toward intimacy may rest in forms of cueing that are universal. Intimacy draws on our social evolution as primates in relation to our need for continuous social interaction and recognition from members of our own kind, species, and group. Paths to intimacy are culture specific and culturally defined. For example, in many nonindustrialized societies, adult social intimacy is found with members of one's own gender through men's and women's groups, initiation ceremonies, voluntary associations, or extended kin group participation (Frayser, 1985; Gregersen, 1983; Murphy and Murphy, 1974; Turnbull, 1961, 1972; Ward, 2005).

In the United States, intimacy is an elusive goal. There are a variety of books, talk shows, and self-help groups to help us achieve intimacy (e.g., Goldberg, 1976, 1980, 1984; Hite, 1987). Both men and women in this culture express a strong desire for intimacy in their social relationships and interactions with one another but seem to have a difficult time achieving it (Farrell, 1986, 1993; Hite, 1987; Kaschak and Tiefer, 2001; Lippa, 2006; McGill, 1987; Tiefer, 2004). In part, this is due to the changes in socio-sexual rules and the lack of new, culturewide rules to guide male-female interaction. Clear, well-defined roles for male and female behavior and affect no longer exist in this society. At the same time **culture lag** exists. Culture lag occurs when behavior changes faster than the belief systems that support it. There is a lag or gap between how people behave and the consonant belief system that underlies the behavior. So, people behave one way and may hold beliefs or values that do not fit comfortably with the behavior. This may be exemplified by the number of people in counseling for sexual and relationship problems, and the discrepancy between people's sexual behavior and the comfort level and attitudes that accompany one's behavior (Allgeier and Allgeier, 1991; Kaplan, 1974; Kaschak and Tiefer, 2001; Leiblum and Rosen, 2000; Leiblum and Sachs, 2002; Whelehan and Moynihan, 1984). Intimacy necessitates an acceptance of interdependency. U.S. values on independence and individuality can work against intimacy. At this point, we are ambivalent about issues of intimacy and independence; masculinity/femininity as defined before the "Sexual Revolution" of the 1960s; androgyny, commitment, and autonomy. Concerns with AIDS and other STDs that impact on fertility and the quality of life intensify this ambivalence and confusion.

A survey of the Kinsey Institute's library holdings on sexual dysfunction revealed 1,024 titles on this topic alone (Kinsey Institute for Research in Sex, Gender, and Reproduction, 2006).

Changing gender roles cross-culturally

The interest in and concern over changing gender roles and relationships is not limited to either industrialized societies or ethnic and sexual communities within those societies. The effect of culture change on gender roles, sexuality, and relationships can be exemplified by looking at the *Mosuo*, a group located in western China near the Tibetan border; the twenty-first-century Sambia; and the residents of *Pohnpei* (formerly spelled *Ponape*), a group of islands in Micronesia. Traditionally, the *Mosuo*, a matrilineal and matricentered society, practiced a form of polyandry, called "walking marriages," where women had a number of sexual partners. Sexuality was viewed positively among the *Mosuo*, particularly for women, who could openly discuss their own sexuality and were expected to have many sexual partners. In the anthropological biography *Leaving Mother Lake: A Girlhood at the End of the World,* by Yang Erche Namu and Christine Mathieu, Namu, the protagonist who now lives in San Francisco, discussed the changes in her village and among the *Mosuo* after Mao Zedong (*Tse-Dong/tung* alternate spelling) came into power. Chairman Mao introduced radical social and economic changes in China, including those related to sexuality. Traditional villages were disbanded, people were sent to forced work camps, and a strict sexual morality of monogamy, an abolition of premarital sex, and a one child per family policy were instituted. The sexual freedom previous generations experienced all but disappeared from public view (Namu and Mathieu, 2003).

Among the Sambia, extensively studied by the anthropologist Gilbert Herdt, and discussed in Chapter 10, there have been radical changes in both male socialization and the expression of male and female gender roles (2006). Currently, Sambian young adults are leaving their villages, moving into their own apartments away from extended kin, and adult spouses and lovers are living together. Heterosexual couples are sharing household responsibilities and women are demonstrating more authority in their relationships. Some younger adult Sambian males even deny that the male insemination ceremonies ever occurred (Herdt, 2006; Knauft, 2003).

Martha Ward's work among the residents of Pohnpei provides a third example of changing gender roles and expectations (2005). "Night crawling," carried out by adolescents who were attracted to each other has been replaced by dating. The traditional diet, which was largely provided for by women, is being replaced by convenience and highly processed foods from the United States and Europe, resulting in health problems such as diabetes, high blood pressure, and obesity. Traditional pregnancy, birth, and postpartum practices, which focused on the extended female kin group and which allowed women to rest and regain their energy after pregnancy and birth, are being replaced by "modern" biomedical obstetric practices that include increasing use of drugs and monitoring during pregnancy, a reduction in home births, and an extended postpartum period. Ward was pregnant during her field work and gave birth in a United States hospital. She notes the differences in pre- and postnatal practices, especially those in the United States, which did not include a strong, female-centered basis of psycho-emotional support. The full impact these gender role and sexual changes will have for individuals and groups in both in the United States and cross-culturally is yet to be realized. Without romanticizing traditional ways of life, these changes can have serious consequences for the kinds of social, psychological and economic support individuals and groups experience.

BIOLOGICAL, PSYCHOLOGICAL, AND CULTURAL ASPECTS OF AGING AND SEXUALITY

Dealing with gender identity, gender role concerns, and sexuality carries across the life cycle. As we age (which is a "normal" physiological process for all animal species), our physical and socio-psychological expressions of sexuality change as well. Although there are issues in how aging and sexuality are defined and conceptualized, we will emphasize the process of aging and the research on sexuality in older populations. Ideas and definitions of what constitutes "older" vary with the particular study under consideration.

Through the aging process certain physiological changes occur that will affect how people express and experience their sexuality. But we must bear in mind that the aging process of sexuality is as much shaped by cultural norms, values, and expectations including concepts of personhood and the body as it is by the physiology of the aging process. In addition, class, status, ethnicity, and gender are all intervening variables which may intersect with health and illness during aging. Cultural features intervene in the biological process of aging and influence how humans experience their sexuality through the life course.

Unfortunately, there are a number of methodological issues in studying the aging process, particularly as it applies to the elderly. One problem is in defining what we mean by a particular point/age in the life cycle. Is fifty "middle age?" What age groups constitute middle age? How do we define elderly and old age? We know that aging is a biological, psychological, and cultural process that is related to cultural expectations about the life cycle and beliefs about aging. In the United States "elderly" is usually (but not invariably defined) age sixty-five or older and mandated by government issues of subsidy and retirement. Not only do studies of aging and sexuality differ regarding at what age elderly starts, this also varies cross-culturally. For Kinsey and colleagues, old age started at sixty; however some would vehemently disagree that sixty is "elderly." The Euro-American and industrial view of aging and the life course uses a temporal/age-based model that reflects the U.S. concerns with time, the future, newness, and youth (Clark and Anderson, 1975: 335; Robbins, 2006).

Other problems that occur in framing the study of aging, sex, and elders is that cross-culturally it may be difficult to ascertain exact chronological age. For example, a consultant (collaborator, informant) may not actually know her/his chronological age; furthermore adulthood, including U.S. definitions of middle age and old age, may be culturally codified in ways other than chronological (Lamb, 2005). The cross-cultural record illustrates the diverse ways that the life cycle may be segmented. Messenger notes that on the Irish island of Inis Beag, "a man is a 'boy' or 'lad' until forty, an adult until sixty, middle-aged until eighty, and aged after that..." (1971: 33). According to Marshall, for Mangaians aging is not experienced as a distinct phase but as continuation (1971: 145).

Even our scholarly approach to life stages such as childhood, adolescence, adulthood, middle age, and maturity is a culture-specific one as we have discussed earlier. Brandes (1987) argues that our industrial concepts of life span stages are permeated by our Euro-American cultural assumptions and notions of age. For example, the age of forty in the United States is regarded as a major transitional phase often associated with mid-life crises, which the media has helped to perpetuate (Brandes, 1987). In contrast, the Kgatla (Botswana) life cycle for women has its own context-specific definitions. Menopause, which marks the loss of reproductive ability, is regarded as a period in which a woman is at the height of her knowledge and competence, continuing her role as a mother, caretaker of home and family, and worker. However, menopause brings with it the first signs of the beginnings of Kgatla old age. In contrast to industrial societies, old age is not defined chronologically. Rather old age, *"mosadi mogolo,"* is defined by increasing infirmity and the inability to work or manage a household, not necessarily by age. It is associated with increasing dependence and marks a loss of status as a result (Suggs, 1993).

Issues in the definition of sexuality in the aging process are problematic as well. As elaborated in Chapter 11, how one defines and "counts" what sexual activity is may differ throughout the life course (Lancaster, 2003; Tiefer, 2004). If one defines sex primarily by heteronormative standards of penile-vaginal intercourse, then a range of sexual behaviors, needs and desires are excluded from analysis leading to a very narrow view of aging and sex over the life course (DeLamater and Sill, 2005). This leads to an industrial model of sexuality that eliminates the great variety of nonintercourse behaviors across the life span in what Riportella-Mueller (1989: 213) refer to as an all-or-none paradigm (also Tiefer, 2004 among others).

In addition, industrial/Euro-American research on sex and aging has not only emphasized biological and medicalized definitions of sexual "functioning" (defined as physiological responses: erection, lubrication), but are also based on data from U.S./industrialized societies (Kinsey et al., 1948, 1953; Masters and Johnson, 1966), which may reflect cultural expectations about aging rather than physiological capability (DeLamater and Sill, 2005; Tiefer, 2004).

Kinsey et al. (1948, 1953) were among the first sex researchers to claim that age made the biggest difference in human sexual response. Kinsey et al. (1948, 1953) found lower levels of sexual activity after sixty, but later studies by Masters, Johnson, and Kolodny (1985) and Greeley (in Cross, 1993) found much higher levels in the United States. This may reflect changes in societal attitudes toward sex in general and sex in the elderly. Marshall and Katz (2002: 53) note that sex researchers from the 1960s through the 1980s advised that "sexual activity, particularly sexual intercourse, [was] a healthy and necessary component of successful aging. Indeed, the passive acceptance of age-related changes in sexual capacity that had characterized the professional advice of the past, now became viewed as ... pathological ... " However, there were some real problems in sampling bias in this earlier sex research with aging populations. Some researchers have relied on reports from senior centers and others only from married partners (Riportella-Mueller, 1989: 214). There is also a bias in the literature on Caucasians that still occurs with even the more contemporary inquiries (DeLamater and Sill, 2005).

The more recent research has taken more sophisticated perspectives, although the findings confirm that there is a decline in sexual activity as people age and that desire and interest decline as well; this does not mean that older people are not having sex or that the kind of sex they are having isn't pleasurable. Extrapolating from Tiefer (2004, 2006a) and emphasizing some of the points made by DeLamater and Sill (2005), we can offer some of the bio-psycho-cultural influences likely to affect desire, experience and behavior in the elderly. These may be applied to aging populations as well as general influences on the quality and expression of sexuality:

- Biological factors: health, physical fitness, and illness in both the individual and/or partner, including local or systemic conditions such as the endocrine system, the vascular system, arthritis, cancer, disability, the side effects of medications and medical treatment, substance abuse.
- Psychological factors: past sexual experiences, emotional well-being, personality characteristics, beliefs/feelings/attitudes about sex and aging.
- Partner factors: quality and length of the relationship, opportunity for sex with a partner. The sex ratio for single women to single men over sixty makes it more difficult for heterosexual women and gay men

to find a partner since women outnumber men significantly in aging populations (women outlive men by around seven years).

- Socio-cultural factors: cultural beliefs about aging and sex, including the influence of ethnicity, religion, sexual cultures, gendered norms, sexual norms, ideologies of the body including the aging body, income level, etc.

Only more recently have cross-cultural and international comparative data of aging men and women become available. *The Global Study of Sexual Attitudes and Behaviors* funded by Pfizer includes in-person and telephone interviews with 27,500 men and women aged forty to eighty years old from twenty-nine countries (Laumann et al., 1994, 2006). This research will be discussed. Several other large surveys have been conducted in the United States. The American Association of Retired Persons (AARP) has undertaken two major studies on midlife and aging, both for AARP's *Modern Maturity Magazine,* which includes representative samples. One was reported in 1999 (see Jacoby, 1999) and the other in 2004, "Sexuality at Midlife and Beyond: 2004 Update of Attitudes and Behaviors." This 2004 sexuality research surveyed 1,682 men and women forty-five and older and an "augment" sample of 1,248, yielding 2,930 respondents, including information from 627 African Americans, 339 Hispanics, 263 Asians, and 1,660 non-Hispanic whites. As a consequence of this survey, comparative data with the AARP 1999 representative sample was provided (Delamater and Sill, 2005). Yet another study was conducted by the National Council on Aging (Dunn and Cutler, 2000). Clearly sexuality and aging is an expanding field for research since the number of U.S. elderly has grown exponentially as the baby boomers have aged. For a comparison of the findings of the 1999 AARP Survey and the National Council on Aging survey (2000) consult the Association of Reproductive Health Professionals: http:// www.arhp.org/.

Highlights of the AARP's "Sexuality at Midlife and Beyond: 2004 Update of Attitudes and Behaviors" (2005) are presented along with data comparing the 2004 research with the 1999 AARP sex survey (Jacoby, 2005: 1–3). This information targets the ages of forty-five through seventy-plus years. It is excerpted from Jacoby (2005: 1–3) and "Sexuality at Midlife and Beyond: 2004 Update of Attitudes and Behaviors" (2005: 1–6). Additional information on sexual desire compared by gender and age follow these findings.

- Forty-nine percent of all respondents (with a sexual partner) have intercourse at least one time a week.
- Two-thirds of the respondents are living with a partner or are married; 4 percent of the males and 1 percent of the females report a same-sex partner.
- The 2004 respondents report more self-pleasuring (20 percent) in contrast to the 1999 survey (12 percent).

- Fifty percent of the respondents report they are satisfied with their sex life; this varies by age with those that are younger reporting more satisfaction, and men more dissatisfied than women.
- Slightly more than half the respondents engage in sexual touching and two-thirds hug or kiss regularly.
- People aged forty-five to fifty-nine are more sexual than those over sixty; they think about sex more, and have more sexual encounters than older respondents.
- Sexual satisfaction is associated with better health and physical activity; those with partners are more satisfied with their sex lives and life in general across the ages and genders.
- Men aged seventy and women aged sixty have a more positive outlook than younger respondents.
- Only half of African American respondents have a sexual partner, compared with two-thirds of all other groups.
- Asians are the least likely to report satisfying sex lives; Hispanics report the greatest satisfaction; whites and Asians have similar levels of sex satisfaction.
- Use of medicine, hormones, or other treatments has increased among both men and women since 1999.
- More than twice as many men as in 1999 report ever using some type of drug or treatment to address problems with sexual performance (22 percent, up from 10 percent in 1999).
- Men are more likely to use a sexopharmaceutical than women to improve sexual functioning.
- More respondents now agree that sexual activity is a critical part of a good relationship—60 percent compared with 55 percent in 1999.
- Thirty-one percent of males report they experience moderate or extreme erectile problems.
- Sex is more important to men's quality of life than women's.
- Only 3 percent of men say they don't enjoy sex compared with 15 percent of the women (gender differences are discussed in more detail) (Jacoby, 2005: 1–3 and "Sexuality at Midlife and Beyond: 2004 Update of Attitudes and Behaviors," 2005: 1–6).

Men in the United States

There are a number of changes that occur in the experience of sexuality as men age that reflect biological, psychological, and cultural influences on the individual. Sexual functioning and desire/sexual interest represent two major areas of sexuality that undergo change as men age. These are interrelated, and have been translated into hetero-normative mechanistic approaches and have been phallocentrically defined in terms of erection and penetration (i.e., number of times penile-vaginal intercourse occurred), rather than more nuanced approaches that are explored more recently (DeLamater and Sill, 2006; Tiefer, 2006).

Masters, Johnson, and Kolodny (1982: 170) reported some of the following changes in men over the age of fifty-five, representing their more biological emphasis on human sexual response.

- It usually takes a longer time and more direct stimulation for the penis to become erect.
- The erection is less firm, less full and less vertical.
- The amount of semen is reduced, and the intensity of ejaculation is lessened.
- There is usually less physical need to ejaculate.
- The refractory period—the time interval after ejaculation when the male is unable to ejaculate again—becomes longer.

As a result of the medicalization of men's sexual dysfunction, an increasing number of aging men are interpreting changes in erectile functioning as a disorder or dysfunction (Marshall and Katz, 2002; Tiefer, 2004, 2006a). It is very important for individuals to have some awareness of the physiological changes in the sexual aging process and to understand the diverse influences on desire, erectile capability, and sexuality. The process of aging sexual expression is tied into the general features of the physiology of aging in which the body experiences an overall slowing down. The concomitant slowing down of sexuality should not be looked upon as an end to sex or as a dysfunction (although for some it may be viewed as a problem), but as a change in one's sexual expression and behavior. In Chapter 11 we discussed the medicalization of male sexuality as well as the nexus of sexopharmaceuticals such as sildenafil, vadenafil, and tadalafil (Viagra, Levitra, and Cialis) and related products. In the 1999 AARP sexual survey only 5 percent of the men had tried Viagra (it had been available only less than a year). By 2004, with Cialis and Levitra, as well as other new technologies, the use of erectile aids had more than doubled. Sixty-eight percent of the men in the AARP 2004 survey noted that their sexual satisfaction has been increased as a result of the availability of sexopharmaceuticals and recent erection-enhancing technologies (Jacoby, 2005). Jacoby (2005: 1) argues that Baby Boomers have created yet another sexual revolution, embracing an attitude that "health- and age-related physical problems should be treated and overcome rather than accepted as part of growing older" (also Marshall and Katz, 2002).

Viagra and its cohorts can be life-threatening for men with low blood pressure taking nitrate medications. Other side effects include headaches, upset stomach, and visual problems. Prior to Viagra, men's choices for erectile problems included vaccum devices (pumps), injections, and penile implants of various sorts.

We recognize that for many men and their partners, these drugs and/or the various technologies to facilitate erection have reinvigorated their sexual relationships. While there is literature that debates how female partners respond to sildenafil, vadenafil, and tadalafil (the literature is relatively silent on same-sex partners), the 2004 AARP survey indicated that women of all ages reported their own satisfaction was enhanced with the partner's use of sildenafil and its cohorts, with some increase in amount of sexual activity as well. It must be remembered that desire and sexual interest are not impacted by these drugs; they have no influence on psychological and socio-cultural dimensions, which according to Jacoby (2005: 1–3) is probably why 42 percent of the men discontinued using sildenafil and its cohorts.

At this point, we should recall a few points about the history of "impotence," or erectile problems and its relations to men's norms. Generally speaking, before the invention of Viagra and its successors, Tiefer (2004, 2006a), Marshall and Katz (2002), among others, have argued that a gradual decline in desire and erectile capability was regarded as a normal part of the aging process. Couples in intimate relationships adjusted their sexuality in various ways, focusing more on the total body experience. However, the last twenty years have witnessed an escalation of the notion of "an ageless sexual vitality" embedded in trends in medicalization of both age and sex, including the invention of sildenafil and its cohorts, contributing to a continued emphasis on sexual performance for men (Tiefer, 2004, 2006a: 7).

As a voice of resistance to these views, Castleman's Great Sex: A Man's Guide to the Secret Principles of Total-Body Sex *(2004: 2) exhorts men to: "Stop trying to imitate what you see in pornography—the rushed, mechanical sex that's entirely focused on the genitals. Instead, cultivate the opposite of porn: leisurely, playful, creative, whole-body, massage-based lovemaking that includes the genitals, but is not obsessed with them."*

The latter part of the twentieth century and the new millennium have witnessed the growing hegemony of masculine gender norms that equate sex with performance and an unrelenting and unfailing sexual desire. Viagra and its cohorts have had a tremendous impact on aging men who have experienced changes in erectile functioning. And these changes have more recently been interpreted as sexual dysfunctions rather than as part of the process of sexual aging in which libido and erectile functioning decrease (Marshall and Katz, 2002). This should not be interpreted to mean that sexual dysfunctions are not real to men. Rather, it is suggested that a more multidimensional approach is required to understand men who experience serious problems with sexuality and erection related to lifestyle, health, disease, disability, and medications such as antidepressants. Suffice it to say that there are psychological, relational, and cultural factors in sexual problems throughout the life course, not just among aging men (Tiefer, 2006a, in particular refer to the section, "A New View Classification of Sexual Problems"). In addition to issues related to aging erectile functioning, a separate but related matter is sexual desire throughout the life course.

Changes in sexual desire are also part of the aging process for men as well as women that are best viewed from the holistic stance of a biological, psychological, and cultural perspective (DeLamater and Sill, 2005). Desire has also been medicalized as we discussed in Chapter 11 (hypoactive sexual desire disorder (Meuleman and Van Lankveld, 2005). In contrast to men, the aging process for women's sexual and reproductive life is marked by a clear physiological change that culminates in the cessation of menses (menopause). However, a male counterpart to menopause has recently been identified and "named" in late twentieth-century Euro-American scholarly and media discourses. This has been variously designated as the **male climacteric, male menopause**, and/or **andropause**. Sperm production gradually declines through the male life course so that by age seventy-five a man may be producing only 10 percent of the sperm he produced before age thirty (Kelly, 1990: 58). Although women lose significant amounts of estrogen and progesterone as they age, and men's levels of testosterone do decline, how much and with what impact does the decline in testosterone have on sexual desire and interest? In addition, there is a great deal of variation among men that may include genetic as well context-specific factors such as medications (Angier, 1992; Marino, 1993; Vermeulin, 2000). With the FDA approval of a testosterone gel (Androgel) in 2002, there has been a substantial increase in men being treated with testosterone therapy for low sexual desire/interest, and for other related reasons including mood, energy levels, etc. Testosterone "therapy" has been escalating in the United States since the introduction of user-friendly gels and patches, as opposed to injections, and has led the National Institute of Aging to register concerns about the risks and benefits of testosterone treatments ("NIA Statement on IOM," 2003).

Studies offer conflicting views on testosterone production in aging men. Vermeulin (2000) notes that by seventy-five years old, average testosterone levels are only 65 percent of those of young adults; however 25 percent of the men over seventy-five still have testosterone levels in the upper range for young men. Tan and Culbertson (2003) assert that between the ages of twenty and eighty men's testosterone levels decline by about 35 percent. The Baltimore Longitudinal Study of Aging (Harmon et al., 2001) on 890 older men found age-related reduction in testosterone levels but these lower levels were not universal, affecting about 20 percent of men aged sixty, 30 percent of men over seventy years old and 50 percent of the men over eighty years old. Evidence suggests that low testosterone is not that common. For example, the National Institute on Aging ("Frequently Asked Questions about Testosterone," 2003) states:

> There is scant evidence that "male menopause," a condition supposedly caused by diminishing testosterone levels in aging men, exists. As men age, their testes often produce somewhat less testosterone than they did during adolescence and early adulthood, when production of this hormone peaks. But it is important to keep in mind that the range of normal testosterone production is large. Many older men have testosterone levels within the normal range of healthy younger men. Others have levels well below this range. However, the likelihood that a man will ever experience a major shut down of hormone production, similar to a woman's menopause, is remote.
>
> In fact, many of the changes that take place in older men often are incorrectly blamed on decreasing testosterone levels. Some men who have erectile difficulty (impotence), for instance, may be tempted to blame this problem on lowered testosterone. However, in many cases, erectile difficulties are due to circulatory problems, not low testosterone.

Changes in men's sexual desire as they age may be highly variable and interconnected to a number of factors which may include physiological influences related to the endocrine system, health and illness, medications and medical treatments. DeLamater and Sill's (2005) research using data from the AARP 1999 survey of people over age forty-five found that the chief influences on sexual desire for men were age, education, and the importance of sex to the individual. For both men and women, DeLamater and Sill conclude "attitudes are more significant influences on sexual desire than biomedical factors" (2005: 138).

Though there may be no profound and documented major changes in hormone levels before eighty years old, this does not mean that the masculine climacteric in the United States is a myth. A male climacteric or midlife crisis is a culturally acknowledged period in the industrialized man's cycle where he may experience a variety of symptoms including anxiety and depression (Henker, 1977 in Kelly, 1990: 58; Masters, Johnson, and Kolodny, 1982: 170; Moss, 1978, Vermeulen, 2000). The "male menopause" may in fact be a response to the cultural conception of aging dominant in the United States. This is a period where the male, whose patriarchal culture has encouraged, advantaged, and celebrated him, confronts a mitigating cultural feature: the youth orientation of U.S. society. The aging man must face the inevitability of aging and the profound changes in status and prestige that may accompany it. The "male menopause" may well be a response to this male dilemma, for ours is not a society that venerates the elderly. Whether a man experiences a social phase like "andropause" will vary cross-culturally, depending on the cultural meanings embedded in the particular society's ideology of aging, and the definitions and expectations regarding masculinity (Winn and Newton, 1982).

Societal attitudes about "dirty old men" may do much harm to the aging man's self-esteem. Industrialized society's ideal cultural standards set a very narrow age range for socially approved periods of sexual behavior. Sexuality is denied to the young as well as the very old in the United States in the ideal cultural norm. This reflects the traditional value on sex for procreation. If our model of sexuality was purely recreational, and not so phallocentric, elderly sexuality would probably be championed for the changes it produces. The elderly man as well as woman who wishes to continue to experience his or her sexuality may be the brunt of jokes and other sanctions among industrialized Anglos. Ageist attitudes regard sex as if it is something that should be outgrown among the elderly. That this damage may be first expressed through the ideologies of a male climacteric in anticipation of these cultural attitudes also reflects the reproductive success model of sexuality.

Industrial women: menopause

In the United States by the year 2015, 50 percent of American women will be in menopause ("Alternatives to HRT for Treatment of Menopausal Symptoms," 2005). The majority of U.S. and European women experience menopause between the ages of forty-five and fifty-five, with a median age fifty to fifty-two (Avis et al., 2007). The time period surrounding menopause includes the period of perimenopause, also referred to as the climacteric. It usually begins around five years prior to and after the last menstrual cycle, covering a period of about ten years (Northup, 2001; North American Menopause Society). Menopause is the cessation of menstruation that occurs as a result of decreasing hormone production of estrogen and progesterone by the ovaries; production of testosterone by the adrenals eventually decreases along with other age-related endocrine and other system changes. Over a period of time, a woman's menstrual cycle becomes increasingly irregular, although there are some women whose menstrual cycle just stops. However, because the climacteric is generally a period of irregularity, using birth control for a year after the cessation of menstruation is advised ("Menopause—Another Change in Life," 2006; North American Menopause Society; Planned Parenthood of America).

In industrialized Anglo populations, menopause is associated with a variety of psychological and physical changes. It is difficult to separate cultural myth from reality regarding the psychic and emotional changes reported with perimenopause and menopause given the industrialized fascination with raging hormones. A number of issues and factors have been identified with perimenopause. Menopause has been increasingly medicalized in the twentieth and twenty-first centuries, so it is not surprising that menopause has been concomitantly considered a syndrome with symptoms (Tiefer, 2004). Medicalization may be regarded as part of the Euro-American industrialized lens that shapes how women experience menopause. We have listed some of the more prominent health and psychological effects associated with perimenopause and menopause in United States society. This list is often referred to in the literature as "symptoms." A medicalized perspective attributes these "symptoms" to the decline in female hormones, specifically estrogen and progesterone. This list that follows was created from a number of sources including: Avis et al., 2001, 2003; "Fact Sheet: Hot Flashes," 2006; King, 2005; "Menopause—Another Change in Life," 2006; Vilet, 1993: 14–16; Ward, 2005). Complaints and physiological changes of industrialized menopausal women include the following:

- Headaches.
- Difficulty concentrating/changes in memory.
- Joint pain.
- Palpitations.
- Frequent urination.
- Night sweats.
- Insomnia/disrupted sleep.
- Vaginal dryness (lubrication is significantly reduced).
- Thinning of the vaginal walls and loss of vaginal elasticity.
- Lack of energy.
- Decline in sexual desire.
- Changes in sexual response with fewer orgasmic contractions.
- Increased risk for osteoporosis.

Keep in mind as you view this list that there is compelling research to suggest that many of the physical changes and "symptoms" of menopause as well as how women experience menopause, are in fact influenced by socio-cultural variables linked to women's status, the meaning of aging, sex, and reproduction (Avis, et al., 2001; Richters, 1997; Ward, 2006). For example, the Inis Beageans, an Irish community noted for their repressive sexual attitudes, believed that one of the consequences of menopause is mental illness, so that some of the physiological symptoms reported among industrialized women such as hot flashes and mood swings were regarded as signs of insanity. According to Messenger who studied this community some women have "retired from life in their mid-forties and, in a few cases, have confined themselves to bed until death, years later" (1971: 15). Psychological and physical changes associated with menopause are not experienced uniformly across cultures (Ward, 2005). We shall return to this topic shortly.

It is sometimes difficult to assess whether some of the uncomfortable sensations older women experience are related to the cessation of fertility and decline in estrogens, progesterone or with aging generally. Nevertheless, medicalization of menopause has been escalating since the first "treatments" for menopause with estrogen and progesterone, referred to initially as estrogen replacement therapy (ERT) and later coming to be known as HRT, hormone replacement therapy. HRT has more recently been called menopausal hormone treatment (MHT) by the National Center for Complimentary and Alternative Medicine, the National Institutes of Health.

Robert Wilson's (1962) research on prescribing estrogen and progesterone for menopausal women jump-started the U.S. and industrialized use of MHT (King, 2005). Wilson claimed MHT was a miracle drug and pronounced "Stepford Wife" results, claiming MHT would preserve women's youth and sexual vitality: "[e]strogen makes women adaptable, even-tempered, and generally easy to live with" (in King, 2005: 320). The widespread use of MHT contributed to the medicalization of menopause as a syndrome with symptoms that can be "fixed" with medication. One of the consequences is that these symptoms contribute to a negative view of women's aging, one that is exacerbated by U.S. and industrialized emphasis on youth culture and women's lower status vis-à-vis men. In addition, according to Tiefer (2004), the medicalization of menopause has been escalated by the growth of capitalism and the expansion of pharmaceutical companies and health care nationwide and internationally (Tiefer, 2004). This is certainly not the "menopausal zest" that Margaret Mead associated with women's renewed sense of energy that occurred in some societies as women experienced freedom from fulltime duty as mothers/spouses (in Ward, 2006: 75). We shall return to the topic of the influence of culture on the menopausal experience.

Hormone replacement therapy/menopausal hormone treatment (MHT)

Since the mid-1960s, hormone replacement therapy was widely prescribed to industrial women to intercede in the "symptoms" of menopause. Wide claims were made as to the benefits of MHT for hot flashes, sleeplessness, lack of lubrication, painful intercourse related to lack of lubrication, the thinning and loss of elasticity of the vaginal walls, diminished libido, hair loss and thinning, osteoporosis (the thinning of bones), loss of memory and concentration, and mood. It also promised health benefits such as the reduction in cholesterol (which it does do) and reducing the risk of heart attack (which it doesn't and actually may put users at higher risk). Research demonstrates that MHT does improve some of the menopausal effects associated with declining sex hormones associated with aging ("Fact Sheet: Hot Flashes," 2006). According to the National Institute on

Aging ("Age Page: Hormones after Menopause," 2005) it does ease symptoms of hot flashes, vaginal dryness, reduces the risk of osteoporosis and colorectal cancer. However, a 2002 report by the Women's Health Initiative (WHI) challenged whether these benefits were worth the health risks posed by MHT. In 1993 less than 15 percent of menopausal women used MHT (Utian et al., 1993: 16), but by 2002 about 38 percent of the women were using MHT ("Menopause Management in Light of the Women's Health Initiative," 2006).

Sponsored by the National Institutes of Health, the Women's Health Initiative was a large study launched to investigate the use of MHT, since research had begun to link estrogen replacement therapy with risks for breast and uterine cancer (Boston Women's Health Collective, 1992; Utian et al., 1993). This was a nationwide randomized and controlled study of 27,347 menopausal women using MHT including estrogen-only therapy, and those using combined estrogen and progesterone over a period of eight to twelve years. The combined MHT approach was developed for women with a uterus to offset the potential for uterine cancer as a result of prolonged exposure to estrogen. In 2002 the WHI study was abruptly stopped after only 5.6 years in order to report to the United States public empirical findings of the increased health risk MHT posed to women. Subsequently the estrogen-only study was stopped in 2004 after a little over seven years. The risks for MHT combined treatment included: heart disease, breast cancer, stroke, and blood clots among women who had long-term use of these treatments. The estrogen-only research found increased risk for stroke, a similar risk to the combined study ("Fact Sheets: Menopause and Heart Disease," 2006). According to the WHI the risks for every 10,000 women using a combination estrogen/progestin MHT are:

- Eight more cases of breast cancer than in women not using MHT.
- Seven more cases of heart disease.
- Eight more cases of stroke.
- Eight more cases of blood clots in the lungs ("The Age Page Hormones after Menopause," 2005).

In addition, the WHI (2003) memory study of women over sixty-five using MHT found twenty-three more cases of dementia per 10,000 women using combined MHT than in older women not using MHT ("The Age Page: Hormones after Menopause," 2005).

As a result of the WHI studies, medical practitioners became alerted to possible health risks and consequently carefully began to monitor MHT for clients. FDA guidelines recommend that the lowest dose for the shortest period of time is the best way to proceed. Even with low dosages the health risks are not known. Some women have switched to what are called bio-identitical hormones, chemically tweaked estrogens and progestins that are akin to the naturally occurring ones (Northrup, 2001); however, the health risks of using bio-identical hormones have not been established.

In addition, the health effects of "natural" supplements derived from plant estrogens that are not under FDA control have not been studied scientifically. Women are advised to consult with their health care providers and to weigh the risks and benefits of MHT. If they do decide to use MHT, then it should be regarded as a short-term and temporary treatment (Barclay and Vega, 2005).

As a result of the WHI findings, U.S./industrialized women and their medical practitioners have gone in quest of alternative and "natural" treatments, as well as lifestyle changes, including diet, exercise, the use of vitamins and supplements to reduce some of the more uncomfortable effects of menopause. However, a cache of other pharmaceuticals is also currently prescribed in place of MHT to counteract menopausal effects including antidepressants used off label to reduce hot flashes and anti-inflammatory drugs for joint pain, among others. These drugs also have detrimental side effects that must be considered when weighing the decision regarding menopausal effects and treatments (Parker-Pope, 2006). The natural and alternative approaches including vitamin therapy suggest that to reduce the risk of osteoporosis, menopausal women should take calcium and vitamin D. Regular weight-bearing exercise is also advocated for strengthening bones. In addition women and their health care providers are pursuing CAM: complementary and alternative medicine. The following points regarding menopause and treatments to alleviate symptoms are made by the National Center for Complementary and Alternative Medicine of the National Institutes of Health ("Do CAM Therapies Help Menopausal Symptions?" 2005).

- Many women have few or no symptoms related to menopause or feel that their symptoms are not enough of problem that they need to seek treatment. Some symptoms traditionally seen as menopausal may be related to aging in general.
- Menopause should not be viewed as a disease.
- For many years, menopausal hormone therapy was the primary treatment for troubling menopausal symptoms. Recent studies have found increased risks, however, for certain serious health problems from prolonged use of MHT.
- Women with severe or long-lasting symptoms of menopause that have not been adequately relieved in other ways should consult their health care providers about their personal risks and benefits for using MHT. Certain lifestyle changes can also be helpful.
- There is very little high-quality scientific evidence about the effectiveness and long-term safety of CAM therapies for menopausal symptoms. More research is needed.
- It is very important for women who are considering or using CAM therapies for any health concern to discuss them with their health care provider. This is to help ensure safety and a comprehensive treatment plan.

Since the Women's Health Initiative results were first reported in 2002, closer scientific scrutiny of the research findings has offered challenges to the study for its flawed design (Klaiber, Vogel, and Rako, 2005). For example, the health risks of MHT were primarily associated with the much older women (ages fifty to seventy-nine years old) who began taking hormones with little or no prior history of MHT. This biased the results of MHT because the older population was more at risk for coronary and cerebral atherosclerosis due to their age. The younger women who began MHT at menopause had far less risk, with some evidence that MHT may actually offer some safeguards for heart health (Klaiber, Vogel, and Rako, 2005; Parker-Pope, 2006). At this point the evidence is still inconclusive and menopausal women are encouraged to weigh their options carefully and to consider the risks and benefits of not only MHT but other prescription treatments as well as the use of supplements that are not scrutinized by the FDA for safety (Parker-Pope, 2006).

Biological, psychological, and cultural perspectives on menopause and its embodiment

One of the consequences of the WHI report is that by declaring the dangers of MHT (although the results have been critiqued), it has enhanced the position that menopause is a normal part of the aging process. Again a biological, psychological, and cultural lens allows us to see how physiology intersects with the individual through culture. The Boston Women's Health Collective has argued that the only universal physiological changes in menopause are loss of fertility, vaginal thinness, and loss of lubrication and vasomotor changes or "hot flashes" (1992; also Greer, 1992), while other research has included long lists of menopausal "symptoms." These "symptoms" reflect the confluence of the process of medicalization as well as United States cultural beliefs about aging in a society with an imposing youth culture. In reviewing this literature Avis et al. (2001: 4) note that the research includes lists of symptoms of menopause ranging from twenty to thirty-six characteristics.

Two lines of evidence argue against a medicalized view that menopausal effects on the body are due primarily to decline in "female" hormones and that menopause is a medical syndrome with associated symptoms. Cross-cultural research of nonindustrialized menopausal women and research including ethnicity has interrogated these notions. Research from India by Flint (1975) reported none of the problems with menopause that industrial women reported (in Avis et al., 2001). Research on Japanese women by Lock (1993) and Avis et al. (2001) found a low occurrence of hot flashes and night sweats, along with lower numbers of other somatic and psychological effects in comparison to Canadian and U.S. women (Avis et al., 2003). Variation in the experience of women globally argues strongly that the meaning of menopausal effects (psychological and physical) is interpreted through a cultural lens. For example, Beyene's (1989) study of Greek and Mayan women suggests that hot flashes are not regarded as necessarily problems to be treated. While hot flashes are viewed as a common "symptoms" of industrialized women's menopause, cross-cultural studies indicate that hot flashes and other effects are not as pronounced among Japanese, Indian women (Avis et al., 2001), Mayan women (Beyene and Martin, 2001), and Greek Women (Beyene, 1989). For women cross-culturally, what hot flashes mean is given a cultural message (Ward, 2006). We shall discuss the cross-cultural record in more depth at the end of this section.

Another line of evidence that challenges medicalized views of menopause is Avis et al's., (2001) research of the "symptom groupings" associated with menopause. Until Avis's research, the literature on menopause had supported a view that symptoms of menopause group together to create a universal menopause syndrome. Unfortunately the evidence for this view was from a primarily Caucasian sample. Avis et al. (2001) conducted research across five racial/ethnic groups to investigate how "symptoms" associated with menopause cluster (i.e. irritability, forgetfulness, etc). In this research, Avis and colleagues extrapolated ten symptoms from the literature on menopause and investigated these among a sample of 14,906 women from the ages of forty through fifty-five including those who self-identified as Caucasian, African American, Chinese, Japanese, and Hispanic. This research was designed to test empirically whether or not there are associations between symptoms of menopause and how these vary by race/ethnicity.

This research asserts that there is an incredible diversity in how women experience menopause and that there are some ethnic (cultural) differences as well; for example Asian women reported the fewest symptoms of all the ethnic groups. Further investigation to determine if this might be due to a soy rich diet has been suggested. Avis et al. (2001) concluded that "[t]he lack of a single set of menopausal symptoms and the findings that the type and number of symptoms vary with race/ethnicity attest to the need to continue to explore the complex relationship between the physiological changes occurring during menopause and the symptoms experienced by women" (2001: 16). Avis and colleagues' findings by ethnicity/race are:

- African American women were more likely to have surgical menopause.
- MHT was highest among Caucasian and lowest among African American and Hispanic women.
- Chinese and Japanese women were less likely to report feeling tense, depressed, irritable, with headaches and stiffness.
- Compared with Caucasian women, all other racial/ethnic groups of women report far fewer symptoms (2001: 345–356).

In assessing the interaction of biological, psychological, and cultural influences on menopause, hormones alone cannot explain the diversity as well as systematic differences in how women experience menopause across ethnicities and cultures. Regretfully, Avis et al. (2001) did not explore the issue of sexuality. There is a great deal of cultural heterogeneity in how women interpret the body's response to diminished hormones in regard to sexuality (as we shall discuss further in the section "Aging and sex: international and cross-cultural evidence").

How can we account for the negative symptoms associated with perimenopause and menopause among Caucasian women? Judith Brown argues that this is related to the general status of women in industrialized societies. She argues that industrial women have few restrictions in early life, so there is less to look forward to in old age. An increasingly youth-oriented culture structures our experiences of menopause as negative. In fact, a number of menopausal somatic and psychological effects can be explained by the other changes occurring in the industrialized woman's life coterminously including stress about aging and increasing invisibility in a culture that has no mature models of sexual beauty and attractiveness. Additional factors impacting menopausal women's stress is that American society emphasizes instant gratification (aided by technology), has little tolerance for discomfort and inconvenience, and expects fifty-year-old people to perform at the same level as they did in their twenties and thirties. We shall discuss specifically how these relate to issues of sexuality among aging and menopausal women separately.

Sexuality and menopause in the United States

To understand women's menopausal sexual experiences requires that we approach the topic from a bio-psycho-cultural perspective that integrates "A New View of Women's Sexual Problems" in the analysis (Kaschak and Tiefer, 2001; Tiefer, 2004). We have described "A New View" and the medicalization of sexual problems in Chapter 11. This perspective is also applicable to understanding menopausal women's sexual expression and experience. For example, a menopausal woman's lack of desire for penetrative sex and the cessation of penetrative sex behaviors must be considered holistically. One consequence of declining estrogen levels is that thinning of the vaginal walls occurs along with reduction in elasticity and a substantial reduction of vaginal lubrication. Both these factors may result in painful intercourse and consequently the decline and loss of a desire to have penetrative sex. However, external lubricants and a leisurely and whole-body approach to sex can make a huge difference. There are a number of over-the-counter lubricants available ("CME Alternatives to HRT for Treatment of Menopausal Symptoms," 2006). Finally, a perspective that emphasizes the multiple dimensions of women's sexuality is especially important. Declining frequency of penetrative sex does not mean that menopausal women are not encountering pleasure in sexual expression but may be finding that pleasure in other not so genitally focused ways. This perspective emphasizes more humanistic approaches that consider menopausal women's sexual experience in a holistic context including the partner and the relationship, socio-cultural factors, and psychological components including past sexual experience and medical conditions. We must be alert to critique a medicalized and biocentric model that looks at menopausal women as having a syndrome that is related to a nosology of sexual dysfunctions that is consequently treated with medication/hormones (FSD-Alert; Tiefer, 2004). Menopause is not "estrogen deficiency" disease.

A more recent trend in pathologizing menopausal women has been through the search for a "female Viagra." Although a woman's sexual response has proven too complicated for a "quick fix" like Viagra, the trend has been to explore drugs to enhance women's sexual desire, rather than genital blood flow (Hartley, 2005). This strategy has emphasized hypoactive sexual desire disorder and turned to testosterone "treatment" as a solution. With a huge Baby Boomer population in menopause, and with decreasing testosterone as part of the endocrine changes occurring in menopausal women, this line of investigation proved very promising for pharmaceuticals. With the potential for a very large number of menopausal women with a medicalized "testosterone deficiency syndrome" in the offing, the development of testosterone replacement therapies began. This has resulted in an increase in off-label prescription of male testosterone therapies (e.g., AndroGel, Testim) for menopausal women complaining of low libido. It has been estimated that one-fifth of all off-label prescriptions for testosterone are for women, reflecting the influence of pharmaceutical companies (also FSD-Alert; Hartley, 2005). In 2004, Proctor & Gamble tried to get approval for Intrinsa, a testosterone patch for women. The FDA unanimously turned down approval on the basis that there has been no empirical research demonstrating a clear link between low sexual desire and low testosterone in women. There was insufficient evidence of the health risks posed to menopausal women who were the prime target market, and no data on long-term use ("Concerns About New Hormone Treatments for Women," 2004; DeLameter and Sill, 2005; Hartley, 2005). Methyltestosterone with estrogen is a combination pill that blends estrogen and testosterone. This treatment has come under increasing scrutiny as well since the FDA has not approved this drug. The Women's Health Network has called for the FDA to disallow prescriptions of Solvay's Estratest and Breckenridge's Syntest since there is no evidence documenting safety and effectiveness in relieving hot flashes ("Group Asks U.S. FDA to Stop Sales of Hormone Combo," 2006). Off-label prescription of methyltestosterone with estrogen includes treatment for low sexual desire in menopausal women as well. Bancroft, Loftus, and Long (2003) report that there is a great deal of variation among menopausal women in the levels of circulating testosterone and in their reported interest in sex ("Concerns About New Hormone Treatments for Women," 2004).

Reports of menopausal problems in sexual desire and a related decline in penetrative sexuality are debated in the scientific literature. According to some earlier research on industrialized women, some decline in sexual interest is indicated. However, Butler and Lewis (1988) note that less than 20 percent of the postmenopausal women in their study experienced any significant drop in sexual interest, while Rienzo (1985) and Marron (1982) found that women's sexuality was enhanced by not having to be concerned about pregnancy at a time when the "nest" had been emptied (Riportella-Mueller, 1989: 216). More recent research also offers conflicting information (Koch, 2004). A 2000 report by Avis et al. found that menopausal women had lower sexual desire compared with when they were in their forties (in DeLameter and Sill, 2005: 142). Yet others record either an increase in specific sexual responses or no noticeable changes (Koch, 2004).

DeLameter and Sill (2005) found a number of factors that impact desire and sexual behavior in the older population of women. The literature supports a number of findings about women, age, and sexual desire. Psychological factors interact with cultural beliefs about aging and gender. Relational issues are important as well as intimacy. In the United States, women's postmenopausal age and the presence of a sexually attentive partner are also important considerations given the gender gap in mortality of 5.7 years between women and men (Brooks, 1993: 27–28; Renzetti and Curran, 2003). "Predictability of sexual activities and over-familiarity with the partner may also contribute to a loss in sexual desire" (Levy in DeLameter and Sill, 2005: 142). Lack of interest in sex may be a coping strategy among menopausal women without a partner as well. Other contextual factors are the physical and mental health of the individuals and their partners. Income is also important as a quality of life issue and potential life stressor in the sexual desire of menopausal women (DeLameter and Sill, 2005; Koch et al., 2005; also Tiefer, 2004 among others).

Using a large sample of 1,384 men and women, DeLameter and Sill (2005) explored the relationships among these variables in a population forty-five years old and older. They found that desire decreases with age, but it was not until women reach seventy-five years old that the majority report a low level of sexual desire. Desire is also related to attitudes toward sex and education; education may impact negative attitudes toward sex in a more positive direction. For aging women, absence of a partner was more of a predictor of desire than it was for men: 78 percent of the women without a partner indicated low levels of desire, while more than 83 percent of the women with a partner ranked their desire as high. Illness and medications also play a small role in women's desire. This research was biased towards Anglos and did not include the influence of sexual history or the role of culture in framing sexual desire among women. These findings are confirmed by the 2004 AARP Sexual Survey, "Sexuality at Midlife and Beyond: 2004 Update of Attitudes and Behaviors," 2005.

One of the gender differences reported by the 2004 AARP Sex Survey is that sex is more important to men's quality of life than it is to women's. In addition, 15 percent of the women say they don't particularly enjoy sex. This confirms that men have engaged in more sexual behaviors and think about it more than do women, and non-partnered women engage in fewer sexual activities than men as well. However, loss of lubrication and thinning of vaginal tissues and consequent discomfort may be implicated in this gender difference ("Sexuality at Midlife and Beyond: 2004 Update of Attitudes and Behaviors," 2005). Koch et al.'s research on body image and sexuality in middle-aged women (ages 35–55) found that sexual satisfaction was not related to body image. Although they experienced body image concerns, 72 percent of the women in her research reported they still enjoyed sex and that they were satisfied with their sexual relationship, confirming research (e.g., Trudel, 2002) that older sexually active women tend to report that they are satisfied with their sexual relationships despite changes in response and activity. However, desire and amount of activity were found to be correlated with body image (see discussion that follows) (Koch et al., 2005).

Cultural context: ideologies of aging

Contemporary approaches to understanding the sexual experiences of middle-aged, perimenopausal and menopausal women emphasize the importance of psycho-cultural influences on menopause. This approach, while relatively recent in sexology, psychology, and related disciplines, is not new to anthropological research on aging and sexuality. The anthropological perspective accents the socio-cultural context and the meanings of sexual desire and activity. The psychological and physical dimensions of embodiment are attributed with meaning by individuals who actively interpret the messages their culture provides, including ideologies, beliefs and practices.

Women, like men in industrial society, experience a dramatic drop in status associated with aging. Although the U.S. focus on youth affects both aging women and men, unlike men, who may be compensated for the effect of aging on their appearance by an increase in power, women as they age will be perceived as less attractive since beauty is equated with youthfulness. Currently, there are not many models available for elderly or mature beauty (although this might change with the relative proportions of menopausal women to reproductive women increasing over time). How can we explain the relative devaluing of older women in the United States and some other industrialized nations? This is related to gender differences in social roles for women and men. The industrialized gender roles break down into a gender-biased dichotomy: an instrumental and action orientation for men, and expressiveness and relationship orientation for women. Though gender roles are changing, the cultural messages supporting this dichotomy still prevail in a variety of arenas. We can summarize this dichotomy by say-ing men "do" while women "display." Women have come to be primarily defined in terms of beauty and allure, highly visible adornments and demon-strations of men's success (Bolin, 1992: 79–99). Sexual attractiveness and beauty norms in the United States are generally associated with youth dur-ing the reproductive years (Koch et al., 2005). As noted earlier, unlike many European countries and other societies cross-culturally, the United States does not have an ideology of mature beauty and sexual attractiveness. Our notions of beauty emphasize those in the reproductive years, neither too young nor too old.

In the film, The First Wives' Club, *Goldie Hawn's character laments: "There are only three ages for women in Hollywood: babe, district attorney, and driving Miss Daisy" (Lauzen and Dosier, 2005: 437).*

Research has only just begun to explore the relationship of decreased sexual desire and body image. This is an underreported area for sex research and indicates the importance of cultural attitudes on sexual desire (Koch et al., 2005). In a study of 307 (mostly white) heterosexual women aged thirty-five to fifty-five Koch and colleagues assert that women's loss of sexual desire is due more to their self-image than to hormones. Declines in sexual desire were directly linked to self-perception as unattractive. All women perceived themselves as less attractive than they were a decade earlier. The more a woman perceived herself as less attractive, the more she was likely to report a decline in desire and sexual activity and the more attractive she perceived herself the more likely she was to report an increase in sexual desire and activity. Two-thirds of women reported that over the last ten years that they had experienced either a loss of desire or less sexual activity with about one-third stating they enjoyed sex more. Thus, change was also in a positive direction, with an increase in desire and sexual response, which Koch et al. (2005) recommend bears further investigation. Recall as well that three-quarters of a research population reported they were sexually satisfied regardless of changes in activity and response.

This loss of status for women as they age can weigh dramatically upon women's self-concepts as being attractive and sexual. In addition, the same age and sex norms are applied to women that are applied to men as they mature toward the elderly age category. In fact Bancroft, Loftus, and Long (2003) found that age affected women's sexual desire and activity more than menopause per se, illustrating the importance of age norms in framing sexual experiences (Koch et al., 2005). Though there is no "dirty old woman" concept in the United States, there are cultural dis-courses that emphasize negative aspects of mature womanhood including "old bag," "grandma" (said with a snarl by a daughter-in-law in many media portrayals), and notions of the prim and proper matron (the "Church lady" of *Saturday Night Live* comes to mind); these are some of the archetypes that regard aging women as unattractive and sexually unappealing. Like men, women are also stigmatized for their interest in mature sexuality; this may be presented humorously, but the message indicates a discomfort with aging sexuality. Gay men may also face a similar stigma due to the youth orientation of the bar culture, although the degree to which this is true for those outside this scene and lesbians remains to be determined (in Riportella-Mueller, 1989: 222).

Elderly women may also buy into cultural notions that sex is something they should give up. Kaas (1978) has identified this as the "geriatric sexuality breakdown syndrome" defined as a self-fulfilling prophecy for many elderly who are responding to negative societal norms against elder sexuality. The aging individual may come to feel guilty or even that they are deviant for their continued interest in sexuality (in Brooks, 1993: 27, 31, 34; Riportella-Mueller, 1989: 219). However, the medical evidence contradicts this social norm. In fact, the reverse is true according to Cross (1993: 177) who quips one must "use it or lose it." Sex is good for the sexual organs which will shrink in size if not utilized; for example women who continued to experience their sexuality after sixty had less trouble with self-lubrication of the vagina (Riportella-Mueller, 1989: 216).

Because women in the United States live about 5.7 years longer than men do, this has ramifications upon the sex lives of heterosexual women who are married to men of the same age or older. There is an "imbalance in the sex ratio for those over 65; there are more women than men, and more women left without partners" (DeLameter and Sill, 2005; Riportella-Mueller, 1989: 212). This problem may be compounded by institutionalization, where sex may be discouraged among unmarried residents by formal administrative policies and by informal practices of employees in such institutions (Walker and Harrington, 2002). Only about 5 percent of the elderly are in homes for the aged at any given time (Riportella-Mueller, 1989: 212), although this should not dissuade us from concern over the effects of institutionalization on the sexual health of the elderly.

Aging and sex: international and cross-cultural evidence

Sociologist Edward Laumann and colleagues' "Global Study of Sexual Attitudes and Behaviors" (Pfizer 2002) is a massive undertaking that includes 27,500 women and men from twenty-nine countries around the world. The survey includes attitudes, behaviors, beliefs, information on sexual desire, and sexual problems among men and women from forty to eighty years old. This research has been funded by Pfizer, the makers of Viagra. Though Laumann is a highly esteemed sex researcher, questions have been directed about Pfizer's motives (e.g., expanding their market for Viagra) by feminist scholars, those subscribing to the "New View of Female and Male Sexual

Problems" (Tiefer, 2006a; Tiefer, Brick, and Kaplan, 2003) and other researchers concerned about the potential for expanding medicalization of sexual problems in the international sector.

Various articles, reports, and papers have been presented utilizing data collected from this project; for example Laumann et al. (2006) have analyzed sexual satisfaction across the twenty-nine countries. These countries were divided into three groups based on Laumann's concept of sexual regimes, defined as the way gender differences are understood in a culture. The first grouping of countries was identified as gender-equal regimes, including Western European countries, Mexico and non-European English-speaking countries. The second grouping included Brazil, Islamic (Mediterranean), and selected Asian countries (such as the Philippines); these were identified as male-centered regimes or patriarchal regimes. The third grouping included all East Asian countries which were also identified as male-centered. This grouping system allowed for comparisons across nations and across gender regimes.

Laumann et al. (2006) found a gender gap in sexual well-being, with men reporting higher levels of sexual satisfaction than women across all the countries; this was true even in alleged gender-equal regimes (although these countries are gender equal only in ideal not necessarily practice, like the United States). The highest levels of sexual satisfaction were associated with the gender-equal societies that endorsed forms of the companionate marriage. The two other male-centered groupings of nations had lower levels of sexual satisfaction, reflecting, according to Laumann et al., the de-emphasis of the relational aspects of sex and an emphasis on the reproductive aspects of sex. All the Asian countries were distinguished by low levels of sexual well-being, moderate to low levels of satisfaction with their relationships, and the importance of sex in comparison with other countries. Israeli women placed the highest value on sex, while lowest scores were from Taiwan; Brazilian men placed the highest value on sex, while Thai men placed the lowest on the importance of sex.

Other findings focused on related but distinct sexual issues have also been presented by colleagues of Laumann. Key points made by Laumann and associates are summarized collectively (Pfizer Global Study of Sexual Behaviors, 2002; Laumann et al., 2006):

- Women were reported to be much less likely to have age-related sexual "dysfunction" (Pfizer Global Study of Sexual Attitudes and Behaviors terminology) than men whose erectile dysfunction increases with age.
- Women's sexual "dysfunction" is related to psychological and social factors.
- Pooled data indicated that 31 percent of women lacked interest in sex, 22 percent were unable to orgasm, 21 percent found sex unpleasurable and 20 percent had trouble lubricating, and 14 percent had pain with sex.
- Only trouble with lubrication had significant age effects for women.

- Pooled data found that 80 percent of the men and 60 percent of the women aged forty to eighty said sex was an important part of their lives.
- More than 70 percent of Italians reported having p-v sex at least one to six times a week, compared with 21 percent of the Japanese surveyed.
- More people from Belgium and Spain report having sex at least once a day than any other nation.
- Excellent health and emotional well-being were associated with pleasurable sexual relationships.
- Eighty-six percent of the respondents engaged in sexual foreplay.

Turning now to the cross-cultural record, we will examine some of the evidence around the issue of aging and sexuality from the middle years through later years of the life cycle. Cross-culturally the period of the middle years is defined as the period in which one is not yet old and defined functionally as a period when one's children have reached adulthood (Brown and Kerns, 1985). Although cross-cultural research is limited on this period, Judith K. Brown and Virginia Kerns' *In Her Prime: A New View of Middle-Aged Women* offers an excellent overview of this subject. Brown and Kerns' work contains articles focusing primarily on women. There are unfortunately no "systematic cross-cultural studies of men in their middle years" (Oswalt, 1986: 161). However, Stanley Brandes' *Forty: The Age and the Symbol* (1987), mentioned earlier, offers an important cultural analysis of the meaning of forty in industrialized society. According to Brandes (1987: 85), one of the weaknesses in the adult life span literature is its focus on universals to the detriment of class, cross-cultural (author's addition), and ethnic differences. The perceptions of when one is aging and at what point transitions and stages are demarcated are largely cultural constructs overlying a biological continuum of changes. A person's appearance, position, stage in rites of passage, and reproductive roles demarcate one's "age" in society (Winn and Newton, 1982). Thus, Glascock and Feinman (1981 in Oswalt, 1986: 165) note that maturity and aging are not clearly identified by physiological changes, but rather by other transitions in the life course including changes in occupation and work effort, status of children, passing on of inheritance, etc.

Preindustrial societies do not show the expected variation in what we conceive of as the midlife experiences of women. In fact "[t]he changes in a woman's life brought about by the onset of middle age" appear to be somewhat positive in nonindustrialized societies (Brown and Kerns, 1985: 2). Three changes accompany transition into the middle years: restrictions may be lifted, authority over certain younger relatives may be expected, and women may become eligible for special nondomestic status (Brown and Kerns, 1985: 2–3). When women undergo menopause in societies in which menstruation is regarded as polluting or taboo, the postmenopausal woman may gain a great deal more freedom of movement and flexibility in interaction. For example, they may be free to talk with nonkin males and act in more indelicate and indecorous ways in societies in which propriety in young women is demanded (Brown and Kerns, 1985: 3).

Richard Lee (1985: 23–35) reports that Ju/wasi (formerly known as the !Kung) women between the ages of twenty to forty years old were required to project a nonsexual image of "shy sweetness." After age forty, Ju/wasi women are given much more sexual freedom. An older woman may have an affair with a young man that may be common knowledge among her cohorts or she may engage in open sexual joking with men (if over about fifty years old). Women's status among the Ju/wasi, which is high to begin with, becomes increasingly higher as they age so they have greater influence in arranging marriages, participating in gift exchanges, and acting in the role of kinship expert.

Cross-culturally, older women may be given the opportunity to be more influential and exert more authority; including increased access to the labor of children and their spouses, as well as a more managerial role in food getting and distribution activities. Control over the distribution of food is one way that informal power of older women is expressed. Finally, aging may provide women access to extra domestic positions such as that of shaman, holy or sacred roles, ceremonial planner, and midwife, among others. The obligations and taboos around fertility are no longer in effect with menopausal status and women can command respect, and exert more influence and power. For example, by becoming a mother-in-law she can gain status she never had with maidenhood (Brown and Kerns, 1985: 4–5; Ward, 2006).

The cross-cultural spectrum is broad concerning the issue of sexuality among older women and men. For example, Vatuk (1985: 147–148) notes in her research in Western Uttar Parades and Delhi that men and women are expected to give up sexual relations upon the marriage of the son. In contrast, for the Ju/wasi, a healthy sexuality is accorded even more leeway for the aging woman. Lee notes an interesting marriage pattern of older Ju/wasi women and younger men, a pattern sanctioned negatively in United States society (except for Hollywood movie stars). Approximately 20 percent of all marriages at /Xai/xai waterhole were between older women and young men. Following divorce or widowhood it is not uncommon for an older woman to take a younger man as a spouse (Lee, 1985: 30). It would be interesting to explore further the beliefs about older women as sexual partners in these kinds of relationships.

Information on sexuality among the elderly cross-culturally is not extensive and it is subject to the same methodological dilemmas of sex research in general. For example, while human sexuality textbooks may include a cross-cultural discussion of sexuality in childhood and adolescence, like the subject of "middle age," there is little available on the transition to older age. This is true for the anthropological literature as well, although there is a growing body of research on this subject, including some cross-cultural correlational approaches, some comparative approaches, and ethnographic perspectives. In contrast to the ageism found in the United States regarding sex among older people, the cross-cultural record shows more acceptance of sex as an activity and desire that continues throughout the life course as demonstrated in Win and Newton's (1982) cross-cultural correlational study of sexuality and aging among 106 traditional cultures using the HRAF files. This research identified common themes and patterns related to aging and sex.

• In 70 percent of the societies (in which data were available) older males continue to engage in sexual behavior.
• A common ideology in these societies was the expectation that men's sexual capabilities were not influenced by age.
• In 84 percent of the societies (in which data were available) older females continued to have an interest and engage in sexual activities.
• In these societies reports of strong sexual interest by older women were common.
• In 50 percent of these societies, older women's sexual expression was related to their change in reproductive status.
• In 22 percent of the 106 societies older females were permitted to engage in sexual conversation, sexual humor, and sexual gestures.
• The lessoning of prohibitions in sexual conversation was associated with older women in 74 percent of the societies.
• Only at very old ages do expectations decrease concerning sexual interest/activity.
• In only three societies (Taiwan, Northern Greece, and the Philippines) was disapproval of elderly sex a cultural norm held by young people.

In a study of Greek and Mayan peasant women, Beyene (1989) found none of the symptoms associated with menopause in industrialized societies. Both Greek and Mayan women looked forward to it as an end to fertility and reported more interest in sex and improved sexual relations with their husbands. We can see how biology and gender interact through the cultural system, as loss of reproductive roles for women often offers them more opportunities.

In this regard Davenport (1977: 115–163) cites some intriguing evidence from the peasants of Abkhasia who live in the Caucasus region. These peoples are known for their longevity and continued sexual functioning "long after 70, and even after 100" (1977: 118). The indigenous Abkhasians illustrate the nexus of biology and culture in the aging process, including reproduction and sexual expression. The Abkhasians represent an enclaved genetic population, so there are obviously genetic factors involved in their longevity. Notably, 13 percent of the women continue menstruating after age fifty-five. According to Davenport (1977: 118), "[o]ldsters continue to work, enjoy their food and have heterosexual relations in diminishing amounts well beyond ages at which Western Europeans and North Americans consider such activities to be almost impossible." However, the cultural factors are very important in understanding the Abkhasian sexual vigor at advanced ages. These peasants have no concept of retirement and change at old age. People continue through life doing everything they have always done, including having sex, but to a lesser extent. There are no specific negative sanctions concerning sex among the elderly in contrast to the industrialized societies. The variety of perspectives regarding sexual interest and activity among middle- to older-aged people continues to illustrate the richness and diversity of human sexuality throughout the life cycle and the importance of understanding the influence of culture upon bio-psychological dimensions of being human.

SUMMARY

1   Gender role is an expression of gender identity.
2   Gender role is culturally defined and expressed.
3   The cross-cultural expression of gender variance is explored.
4   U.S. transgender identity is presented from a historical and cultural perspective.
5   The concepts of androgyny and scripts were developed in the 1970s to explain gender role expression in U.S. culture. The concept of and desire for androgyny may be culture specific.
6   Intimacy, bonding, and male-female sexual relationships are of great interest and concern to many researchers in late-twentieth/early-twenty-first-century U.S. culture.
7   The bio-cultural aspects of aging sexuality are presented in the United States, internationally and cross-culturally. As with other aspects of sexuality, the cultural responses to an older person's sexuality vary widely and differ from those in the United States.

Thought-provoking questions

1   To what extent are fundamentalist social and religious movements within the United States and cross-culturally a backlash to the changes in sexuality, gender roles, and relationships that have been occurring since the late twentieth century in industrialized societies, particularly the United States?
2   Based on what you have read about the U.S. transgender identity and cross-cultural gender variance, how do you weigh in on the issue of biology and gender in gender variance?
3   What are your beliefs and attitudes about the sex among middle-aged and aging populations? At what age do you think people are middle

aged and old? What specific messages about aging people and sex have you seen in the media?
4   Imagine you are a menopausal women or aging man: given what you know about them would you use Viagra or MHT? Why or why not? How would you find more information on the subject?

SUGGESTED RESOURCES

Books

Barbach, Lonnie. 2000. *The Pause: Positive Approaches to Premenopause and Menopause.* Bergenfield: Plume Books.
Blackwood, Evelyn and Saskia Wieringa, eds. 1999. *Female Desires: Same-Sex Relations and Transgender Practices across Cultures.* New York: Columbia University Press.
Cromwell, Jason. 1999. *Transmen and FTMs: Identities, Bodies, Genders and Sexualities.* Urbana: University of Illinois Press.
Green, Jamison. 2004. *Becoming a Visible Man.* Nashville: Vanderbuilt University.
Herdt, Gilbert, ed. 1996. *Third Sex/Third Gender: Beyond Sexual Dimorphism in Culture and History.* New York: Zone Publishing

Journal

Anthropology and Aging Quarterly (http://www.slu.edu). Last Accessed 11/09/07.

Web sites

A New View Manifesto: Challenging the Medicalization of Sex. www.fsd-alert.org. Accessed 11/09/07.
Association for Anthropology and Gerontology (www.slu.edu). Last accessed 11/09/07.
Health and Age (http://www.healthandage.com). Last accessed 12/19/06.
Medline Plus Hormone Replacement Therapy (http://www.nlm.nih.gov/). Last accessed 12/19/06.
National Center for Complimentary and Alternative Medicine. The National Institutes of Health (http://nccam.nih.gov). Last accessed 11/09/07.
North American Menopause Society (http://www.menopause.org). Last accessed 11/19/07.

14 Sexual orientations, behaviors, and lifestyles

CHAPTER OVERVIEW

1 Defines and describes various sexual orientations.
2 Distinguishes between sexual orientation and sexual behavior.
3 Defines heterosexism and homophobia.
4 Discusses known sexual behaviors as a continuation of what is found in the mammalian and primate world.
5 Argues for a greater awareness of all forms of culturally defined sexual orientations.
6 Presents various theories which attempt to explain nonheterosexual orientation.
7 Discusses sexual orientations cross-culturally.
8 Presents a variety of partnering and parenting relationships.
9 Discusses the range of gender role behavior.

SEXUAL ORIENTATIONS

A discussion of sexual orientations and relationships confronts biases and assumptions about sexuality. In many societies presently, including the United States, heterosexuality is assumed and perceived as a "given." For those people who are heterosexual, this seems "normal and natural." For people who identify as gay, bisexual, or lesbian, this assumption of heterosexual "normalcy" appears to be biased and based in heterosexist ethnocentrism. As part of our exploration of human sexuality, we must seriously examine the range of sexual orientations, their possible expressions, and relationship forms.

Some basic definitions are needed. Sexual orientation refers to one's attraction to sexual and romantic love partners. Currently, this orientation is structured in the United States as being either **homosexual, bisexual,** or **heterosexual**. A homosexual orientation denotes sexual and romantic attraction toward individuals of one's own sex. A bisexual orientation denotes sexual and romantic attraction toward both one's own and the other sex, sometimes referred to as ambisexual. A heterosexual orientation is sexual and romantic attraction toward individuals of the other sex. Relatively nonjudgmental terms used to describe each of these orientations include "**straight**" for male and female heterosexuals, "**gay**" for male, and "**lesbian**" for female homosexuals, particularly for those who are open or "**out**" about their orientations, and "**bi**" for male and female bisexuals. These terms will be used in this chapter.

Sexual orientation is not synonymous with **sexual behavior**; these are discrete entities. As with sexual orientation, sexual behavior may be homosexual, bisexual, or heterosexual. Given our culture's assumptions about heterosexuality, lesbians, gays, and bis may experience confusion and rejection in establishing their identity. Comments illustrating this include:

"I always knew I was different."

"Something wasn't 'right or normal,' but for a long time I didn't know what it was."

"I always had girlfriends, but I was always interested in and attracted to boys." (Whelehan's files)[1]

Since the late twentieth century a number of groups and events have helped people become more comfortable with and accepting of sexual orientations. These include the Gay Rights Movement and **Gay, Lesbian, Bisexual, and Transgender Pride Parades (pride parades)** (Blackwood and Wieringa, 1999b).

The mayor of Moscow, Russia, Yuri Luzhkov, tried to ban the first-ever Gay Pride Day in the city in February 2006. Human Rights Watch, among other international groups, called on the mayor to allow the parade as an example of tolerance and acceptance of "universal" human rights (Human Rights Watch, 2006).

A person's sexual orientation and behavior may or may not be consonant. This can occur for example, when one's sexual partner of choice is not available, as in sex-segregated institutionalized populations such as prisons or all-boys' or all-girls' schools, or where one's choice is culturally proscribed. This latter situation frequently occurs in the United States which is overtly homophobic. **Homophobia** is the fear, prejudice, and negative acting-out behavior toward people who self-identify or are believed to have a homosexual orientation. Researchers such as Boswell (1980), Greenberg (1988), and Johansson, Dynes, and Lauritsense (1981/1985) believe that the presence of homophobia in most twentieth- and twenty-first-century societies is a continuation of practices and beliefs derived from Judaism and the Old and New Testaments. These beliefs have been perpetuated by Christianity and the Catholic Church since the Middle Ages.

In part, these homophobic positions are a reaction to the nonreproductive aspects of same-sex sexual relations, and their accompanying sex-for-pleasure aspects. The repercussions of this prejudice have been felt politically, economically, socially, and religiously to the present. In a homophobic society such as ours, for example, a same-sex sexual orientation may be hidden—it "passes." The behavior may be heterosexual and those involved pass (i.e., appear to be straight in public). Alternatively, a same-sex orientation may be expressed openly in communities where it can find support and relative degrees of acceptance and safety, e.g., "gay communities" such as Key West in Florida, West Hollywood in Los Angeles, the Castro in San Francisco, or the Village in New York (Blumenfeld and Raymond, 1989; Kelly, 1988; Kirk and Madsen, 1989).

We take extreme positions about nonheterosexual behavior and orientation in the United States.. On the one hand, we have organizations and events that celebrate gay, lesbian, bisexual, and transgendered people. GLBTQ (Gay, Lesbian, Bisexual, Transgender, Queer/Questioning) organizations can be found on a number of college campuses around the country. On the other hand, President Bush has proposed a constitutional amendment to ban same-sex marriages, an act that separates us from the policies of other industrialized nations such as Canada, Belgium, Holland, and Spain. These countries have all legalized same-sex marriages (Duff-Brown, 2005; Weber, 2005).

CAUSES OF SEXUAL ORIENTATION

The cause of anyone's sexual orientation is unknown. Over the past hundred years in industrialized cultures, volumes have been written in the professional and lay literature to explain the roots of one's sexual orientation, particularly if it is homosexual or bisexual (Bailey and Pillard, 1991; Hamer and Copeland, 1994; Rust, 1999). Heterosexuality is assumed to be "normal" and therefore needs no causal explanation (Allgeier and Allgeier, 1991). If we examine sexual behavior and orientation from cross-cultural, evolutionary, and interspecies perspectives, we find a wide variety of sexual expression (Vance as cited in *SOLGAN*, 1992).

Anthropologists conduct research about sexual orientations. Ford and Beach (1951) and others document a range of sexual expression in the mammalian and nonhuman primate world that includes hetero-, bi-, and homosexual behavior (Ford and Beach, 1951; Herdt, 1981, 1982,

1984a, 1984b, 2006; Weinrich, 1987). Williams (1986), Gregersen (1983, 1992), Marshall and Suggs (1971), and Frayser (1985) have documented the widespread nature of homosexual, bisexual, and heterosexual orientations and behavior cross-culturally and through time (Vance cited in Roscoe, 1998; *SOLGAN*, 1992).

Ford and Beach's research documents at least 76 out of 141 societies where homosexuality is acknowledged and receives varying degrees of acceptance for those who identify or behave as such (1951). In addition, Williams' and Roscoe's research clearly shows that **third-sex, two spirit,** or other forms of sexual identities are well integrated into some cultures worldwide (Roscoe, 1998; Williams, 1986). These identities do not translate smoothly into industrialized societies, such as the U.S., worldview due to homophobia, heterosexism, and cognitive rigidity in the formation of sexual identity boundaries. These identities, such as those discussed in Chapter 12, have meaningful, respected roles in their own cultures.

Dr. Jill Weiss conducts research on what she terms the "borderlands" of lesbian and transgender identity. Her research indicates the current generation of lesbians is challenging both what it means to be lesbian and transgendered. Some of these lesbians see more fluid boundaries between gender and sexual orientation than does either the larger society or many researchers (Weiss, 2005).

A variety of Melanesian groups provide a wealth of data that contradict our industrialized notions of sexual identity, orientation, and behavior. In Herdt's *Ritualized Homosexuality in Melanesia* (1984a) and his most recent work on the Sambia (2006), ritualized homosexual behavior, what he refers to as "boy-inseminating rites," is examined from spiritual, social, male identity, and gender relations perspectives (2006: xv). Our ideas about sexual orientation and behavior may be culture-bound when compared with sexual behavior that is perceived to be related more to concepts of spirituality, generativity (perpetuating oneself and the group), adult male-female systems of balance and order in the world, and the cycle of life and death. The Sambia from New Guinea will once again be used as an example of an alternative view on sexuality and male-female relations. (See Chapter 13 for further discussion.)

Data about the Sambia people in New Guinea reveal a radically different approach to homosexuality than found in our culture. Our conceptualization of homosexuality does not neatly apply to Sambian sexual practices. The horticultural Sambia live in an impacted habitat of perceived limited resources of which ejaculate is also seen as a scarce, precious commodity. As with other "spermatic economies" (Barker-Benfield, 1975), semen (more accurately ejaculate), a vital life fluid, is believed to exist in finite quantities. Since semen is seen as life enhancing and a source of male strength, pre-adolescent and adolescent boys engage in fellatio with other older males to nourish and build their strength and vitality. Male-to-male fellatio is seen as essential for healthy male psychosexual and physical development and pre-paration for heterosexual marriage and procreation (Herdt, 1984, 1993). Women, however, for a number of reasons, are seen as a potential drain in this vital life essence. Therefore, as we discussed in Chapter 8, male-female sexual contact, particularly p-v intercourse, is carefully controlled and channeled to protect the male from "losing" his energy *(jerungda)* and to ensure the healthy development of the fetus (Herdt, 1984, 1993). Herdt's most recent book on the Sambia indicates changes in these practices. Due to the influence of culture contact and change, Sambians of the current generation are starting to adopt sexual and relationship patterns that more closely resemble those of industrialized societies than those of their parents and grandparents (Herdt, 2006).

As with research done on sexual orientation in the United States, there is less cross-cultural research on bisexuality and lesbianism (Rust, 1999; *SOLGAN*, 1992: 9–10). This may be due to several reasons. First, male researchers have less direct access to women and their daily, intimate lives cross-culturally. The potential for sexual behavior that could disrupt indigenous patrilineal and bilineal descent systems makes both sexual and nonsexual access to females by male researchers taboo. Second, in industrialized societies, there is more interest in male homosexuality than either female homosexuality or bisexuality. Third, gender role boundaries are more rigid for males than for females in many societies. For example, the same behavior engaged in by two men as by two women in our culture is more likely to be interpreted as "homosexual" for the men, but not for the women. Two men walking arm in arm solicit different labels and responses in this culture than two women walking arm in arm. A similar kind of tunnel vision may be operative in examining female homosexuality cross-culturally. Research attempts to fill in this gap (Blackwood, 1986; Blackwood and Wieringa, 1999a; Kendall, 1999). Blackwood's and Wieringa's edited book explores female same-sex relationships historically and cross-culturally. Their book challenges ideas of female sexual passivity and gender conformity (Blackwood and Wieringa, 1999a).

Minimally, the nature of our sexual orientation and behavior is a complex interaction of a number of socio-cultural, psychological, and biological factors. Our sexual behavior is probably one of the more plastic or malleable behaviors we engage in as a species. Numerous theories and arguments proposed by researchers suggest that biological, genetic, *in utero,* psychoanalytic, and socio/environmental elements are involved in forming sexual orientations and behaviors that are *not* heterosexual. In the United States, we have a difficult time accepting ourselves as sexual beings and that a variety of sexual orientations and behaviors are part of human sexuality. The only difference in other- and same-sex sexual behavior is one of reproductive success: other-sex sexual behavior may lead to production of viable offspring; same-sex behavior does not. However, as discussed in Chapter 3, not all other-sex sexual behavior is reproductive. Deep kissing (referred to as "French Kissing"), masturbation, oral genital contact, anal penetration, and effective birth control with penile-vaginal intercourse do not make babies. At various times in this and other cultures, all these behaviors have been seen as "unnatural," "abnormal," or "sinful" in certain religious contexts (Bullough, 1976).

Biological theories to explain sexual orientation examine hormone levels pre- and postnatally, and differences in the size of brain structures as well as the sexual differentiation process *in utero* (e.g., Gladue, Green and Hellman, 1984; Green, 1987; Kelly, 1988; LeVay, 1991; Money, 1988a; *SOLGAN*, 1992). More recently, a genetic basis for *male* homosexuality has been proposed (Bailey and Pillard, 1991; Hamer and Copeland, 1994). All of these theories attempt to explain the cause of homosexual orientation, particularly for men. These theories speculate on delays or differences in release of androgens, LH, relative levels of estrogen and testosterone pre- and postnatally, genetic predispositions carried on the X chromosome, or the size of the hypothalamus as predispositions to a homosexual orientation. These theories gain some level of support from the self-descriptions of gays who believed from an early age they were more comfortable with and more attracted to members of their own sex. They are biased in that they only look at male homosexuality, not lesbianism, and they do not explore sexual orientations as social phenomena (see also Vance's comments in *SOLGAN*, 1992).

Psychoanalytic theories about sexuality often are misinterpretations of Freud's view that we are essentially bisexual in nature, and that society suppressed and channeled heterosexually (Freud, 1920 and 1959 [1929]; Kelly, 1988). These theories frequently posit a bi- or homosexual orientation as "deviant." It is depicted as "arrested psychosexual development" or viewed as a function of a poor parent-child relationship. The American Psychiatric Association (APA), after intensive lobbying efforts by members of the gay communities, removed homosexuality from its list of "personality-sexual disorders" in 1973. The formal removal of this category from the *Diagnostic and Statistical Manual of Mental Disorders* (DSM-III), however, does not necessarily change the beliefs of members of both the medical and lay communities who do not accept the behavior (American Psychiatric Association, 1973; Bjorklund and Bjorklund, 1988). For example, in 2005, the federal government posted a controversial Web site that discusses how parents "should" address their children's sexual orientation and sexuality. If interested in its contents, you can access this site at: http://www.4parents.gov/.

Discussions about the origins of sexual orientation and the sex of one's sexual and romantic love partners are emotionally and legally charged in the United States. The Supreme Court decided in 2003 that adult, consensual, same-sex behavior in the privacy of one's home was not a crime. It overturned a case of two men who were arrested for engaging in sex at home.

Socio-psychological, environmental, and learned behavior theories about sexual orientations also focus on homosexuality, thereby assuming hetero-sexuality as the norm. They primarily discuss gay men, not lesbians or bisexuals. This kind of bias implies a negative difference if one is anything except straight in behavior and orientation. These culture-specific theories relate sexual orientation and behavior to childhood and adolescent sexual experience, role models, and learned pleasurable and unpleasant sexual activities (Kelly, 1988; Rust, 1999).

Although acknowledging and recognizing these explanations about sexual orientation, this chapter posits that human sexuality is part of what makes us human, that it is an interaction of biological and learned experiences whose boundaries are currently unknown to us. Our sexual orientation is part of our socio-psychological and biological makeup. Increasingly, we will probably learn that orientation itself has a biological component (Money, 1988a; Small, 1993). Yet each society channels sexual behavior into culturally defined appropriate outlets. The following sections examine straight, gay, bi, and lesbian lifestyles as functions of their cultural milieus and as dimensions of the richness, adaptability, and diversity of the human sexual repertoire.

Bisexuality

There is increasing research on bisexuality, but less than exists for gays and straights (Klein, 1978; Paul, 1984; Rust, 1999; Tielman, Carballo, and Hendriks, 1991). A bisexual orientation is a romantic and sexual attraction toward both males and females. Both men and women can self-identify as bisexual. Bisexuals may choose only same-sex partners, partners of the other sex only, or of both sexes. (Bisexuality is *not* synonymous with group sex where people have multiple partners concurrently.) The following statements come from one of your author's files (Whelehan):

> "I am a self-identified [male] bisexual who generally acts out on my attraction to men. However, every once in a there is a woman to whom I'm strongly emotionally and sexually attracted and I decide to pursue that interest."

> "I believe everyone is pansexual [open to a variety of sexual experiences]. I am attracted to both men and women and don't care about society's labels." (Female)

"It's natural. It's an extension and expression of the love I feel for some of the people in my life, both men and women." (Female)

Of all the sexual orientations discussed, bisexuality appears to receive the least acceptance, even though bisexual behavior has been estimated to be as high as 45 percent (Klein, 1978; Rust, 1999). On Kinsey's scale, which is a measure of behavior, not orientation, bisexuals are a 2 to 5 clustering in the 3 to 4 range (Kinsey et al., 1948, 1953; see Table 14.1).

Bisexuals, on average, tend to be closeted, and are often most comfortable with other bis since both the straight and homosexual communities have difficulty understanding and accepting them. Gays, lesbians, and straights often pressure bis to choose a straight, or gay, or lesbian behavior and identity, possibly so that the non-bis are more comfortable. Frequently, gays and lesbians perceive bis as closeted homosexuals who "pass." The homosexual community politically may perceive bis as similar to the perceptions of so-called "Oreos" in the black community (i.e., African Americans who basically hold Anglo views and beliefs) (Bolin, 1974). Straights can see bis as "playing a game," "going through a stage," as being indecisive, or as being homosexual. Since some closeted gays and lesbians do engage in heterosexual relations, this behavior further reinforces misperceptions about bisexuals. In addition, since this culture only accepts a heterosexual orientation and behavior as "normal," people can be confused, trying to sort out their feelings and behavior. They may experiment sexually with members of their own and the other sex as part of psychosexual growth (Klein, 1978; Rust, 1999). One of the more unfortunate aspects of bisexuality, which is also shared with homosexuality, is the hiding and passing some bis engage in because of nonacceptance by the larger society. As Paul posits, bisexuality is part of the range of human sexual behavior (1984). It is probably the most inclusive of the orientations and one that can directly contribute to reproductive success.

Homosexuality

A homosexual orientation is the romantic and sexual attraction to members of one's own sex, frequently called gay, when the attraction is openly acknowledged between men, and lesbian when it occurs between women. Kinsey et al. estimate that at least 10 percent of the U.S. population is exclusively homosexual (1948). However, Kinsey's figure may be underreported since the scale does not clearly distinguish between orientation and behavior; research from other sources including cross-cultural material would support at least that percentage (Bell and Weinberg, 1978; Ford and Beach, 1951; Kirk and Madsen, 1989; Walters, 1986). Same-sex experience or behavior is higher, probably 50 percent for boys by the time they are eighteen years old and 33 percent for girls (Elias and Gebhard, 1969). A more recent survey from the Kinsey Institute also indicates the incidence to be closer to 50 percent for boys and girls collectively ("Sex Quiz," 1991: 4). Research published in 1994 stating that homosexuals comprise only 2 percent of the population is questionable since orientation and behavior were confused, and criteria by one of the researchers included that his subjects were out to their family, friends, and the researcher (Michael et al., 1994).[2]

As part of sexual culture change since the 1960s, many gays and lesbians have become more open and more desirous of formal social recognition for themselves and their relationships (Bell and Weinberg, 1978; Kirk and Madsen, 1989). Gays and lesbians want to live and work openly with their partners, be part of extended kin groups as couples, and receive comparable economic and social recognition and acceptance as do straight couples. Nowhere is this more obvious than in the controversies surrounding gay marriages. Massachusetts legalized same-sex marriages in 2004. Vermont and Connecticut legally recognize same-sex unions, but not marriages. San Francisco married same-sex couples in 2004, but those marriages were contested by the governor and the state (Marshall, 2004; "Opinion: U.S. Requirement that AIDS Group Sign Pledge Against Sex Work," 2005). Several states passed legislation either banning same-sex marriages or refusing to recognize those marriages performed in Massachusetts. This issue is so contentious that President George W. Bush proposed a constitutional amendment to ban same-sex marriages. That the federal government would seek to formally and legally deny entire groups of people rights that are granted to others is further evidence of our discomfort with sexual orientations and with sexuality that is not potentially reproductive (Buchanan, 2005a).

As people with varying degrees of formal acceptance in our culture, gays and lesbians have also established flexible, adaptable gender roles and divisions of labor relative to economics, household management, and social behavior. Straight couples struggling to redefine gender role expectations and behaviors may be able to use the flexibility of stable gay and lesbian relationships as models (Blumstein and Schwartz, 1983; Bryant and Demain, 1990; Kirk and Madsen, 1989). As a recent survey indicates, a large number of homosexual couples live in stable, satisfying, long-term relationships. They have worked out economic, social, and sexual issues. As with many heterosexual couples, homosexual couples can have similar problems with communication (Bryant and Demian, 1990).

The Stonewall riots in June 1969 were the formal marker of the Gay Rights movement. Customers of the Stonewall, a bar in the Village in New York City, refused to be arrested or evicted from the bar when police arrived on a sweep, and rioted instead against police arrests of patrons solely because they were in a gay bar (Kelly, 1988; Kirk and Madsen, 1989). Gays and lesbians as a group in this culture have become more organized and vocal in demanding equal legal, economic, and social treatment in their personal and professional lives. This involves an end to discrimination and harassment relative to service in the military (another heated controversy), in housing, employment, medical care, and in their interpersonal relationships (*Lambda Newsletter*, 1990; "Opinion: U.S. Requirement that AIDS Group Signs Pledge Against Sex Work," 2005a). It encompasses respect for them as individuals and the range of roles they fulfill in society, including their roles as parents, friends, and family members.

During his first administration, President Clinton endorsed a "Don't Ask, Don't Tell" policy concerning sexual orientation in the military. Under this policy, people could not be asked about their sexual orientation in the military, but they also were not permitted to be open about either their orientation or behavior unless it was heterosexual.

Lesbianism

Although there is a growing awareness and increasing body of literature in this culture on lesbianism (cf. Blumenfeld and Raymond, 1989) and cross-cultural documentation of lesbian relationships (Blackwood, 1986; Blackwood and Wieringa, 1999a), lesbian relationships and life-styles, like bisexual relationships, are less well known and discussed than those for gays (*SOLGAN*, 1992). There may be several reasons for this bias. Lesbian relationships tend to be less formalized and ritualized. Females in general have greater flexibility to form female-female bonds and be demonstrative than do males. Thus, lesbians may "pass" intentionally or unintentionally more readily than gays or bi males. Third, female sexuality is structured differently from male sexuality. Unless it threatens known paternity, female sexuality is not seen as having the same kind of force, power, visibility and possible threat as does male sexuality, particularly in industrialized societies which generate most of the researchers and research (Blackwood, 1986; Blumenfeld and Raymond, 1989; Kelly, 1988). Evelyn Blackwood and Saskia E. Wieringa's edited work on lesbian sexuality cross-culturally challenges European models of lesbians and research on women who identify as lesbian. They see the lack of data on lesbians as due to: "problems in collection and interpretation as well as to the silence of Western observers and scholars on the topic of female sexuality" (Blackwood and Wieringa, 1999a: 39).

Cross-culturally and in the United States, lesbian relationships manifest a great deal of flexibility and tend to emphasize the interpersonal dimensions of the interactions (Blumenfeld and Raymond, 1989; Blumstein and Schwartz, 1983; Bryant and Demian, 1990; Herdt, 1984b; Weil, 1990). As with gays, lesbians are parents who have well-adjusted children, friends, colleagues, and neighbors. Lesbians overall show no greater psychological problems than do straight women. In fact, research indicates that homosexuals who accept and are comfortable with each other have high levels of self-esteem and may have more stable relationships than the average heterosexual (Blumenfeld and Raymond, 1989; Blumstein and Schwartz,

1983; Bryant and Demian, 1990; Herdt, 1984b; Kirk and Madsen, 1989; Weil, 1990). Lesbians and gays may have had to learn to be psychologically strong to confront the discrimination they experience from the larger culture in a healthy way.

Homosexual youths

Homosexual adolescents in the United States tend to live in non-accepting, potentially hostile, and rejecting environments if they self-identify or are perceived to be homosexual. Homosexual adolescents in this culture have issues to resolve as well. Not only do they share common adolescent concerns about appearance, peer acceptability, sexual and drug decision making, and about communicating with adult authority figures, they also need to recognize and accept their sexual orientation. In a society that places much emphasis on conformity and normalcy, bringing a same-sex date to a public event, not concealing pronouns when referring to boyfriends and girlfriends, and not wanting to appear "queer" or "faggy" can create considerable stress for a gay or lesbian adolescent. Our homosexual youths have a relatively high suicide attempt rate (Whitaker, 1990). Parental and other adult support, validation of the worth of the person, location of support, and homosexual adolescent groups can help gay and lesbian youths accept and flourish as who they are.[3] One benefit of gay liberation is that homosexual youths are beginning to have their own support groups and organizations. These are "safe" places to be themselves and interact (Sullivan, 1998). Given this support, homosexual youths do accept themselves and can develop into well-adjusted, functioning adults (Boxer and Cohler, 1989).

Heterosexuality

The degree of heterosexual bias in our culture is illustrated by the number of heterosexual inventories that exist and the assumption that people are heterosexual in both orientation and behavior. Although there have been some inroads made in the area of popular culture with television shows such as *Queer Eye for the Straight Guy, Will and Grace,* and *Queer as Folk* as well as movies such as *Priscilla, Queen of the Desert, The Birdcage,* and the 2006 blockbuster movie, *Brokeback Mountain,* we continue to have trouble recognizing different lifestyles in our own and other cultures. As Vance has stated, our concept of homosexuality is "*only* found in modern, Western societies" (*SOLGAN,* 1992: 9). For example, in some books on orientations, behaviors, and genders cross-culturally, it is difficult to find vocabulary to label and describe the *manly-hearted women* among Plains Indians, the *nadle* among the Navaho, and other forms of identity and behavior that is common, accepted, and valued elsewhere (Roscoe, 1998; Williams, 1986).

In the post-WWII era in the United States, the ideal adult sexual standard was that of a heterosexual, middle-class, monogamously married couple with a minimum of two children—a boy and girl, in that order of preference. The couple owned their own home where the woman worked full time without monetary compensation and the man worked outside the home with paid full-time employment (Blumstein and Schwarz, 1983; Frayser, 1985; Kinsey et al., 1948, 1953). This ideal persisted until the Sexual Revolution of the mid-1960s (discussed in Chapter 13) when these values and behaviors that were labeled "traditional" were behaviorally challenged and questioned. During the Sexual Revolution many people's behaviors, but not necessarily their attitudes changed. The changes in behavior but not attitudes led some researchers to question whether there was a sexual revolution (Kelly, 1988; Weil, 1990).

Behavioral changes include more open sexuality outside of marriage, cohabitation, open marriage (O'Neill and O'Neill, 1972), and higher divorce rates as well as the continuation of the traditional marriage (Blumstein and Schwartz, 1983). At the beginning of the twenty-first century, there are numerous relationship patterns:

- Although over 90 percent of the adult population marries at least once, the "traditional" marriage comprises about 13 percent of relationships.
- Over 4.2 percent of people formally cohabitate.
- About 50 percent of marriages end in divorce; about 75 percent of divorcees remarry.
- Over 25 percent of the households are single-parented, generally female-headed.
- Serial monogamy is the dominant relationship pattern (Blumstein and Schwartz, 1983; U.S. Bureau of Labor Statistics, 1985; U.S. Census Bureau, 1980, 1990, 2000; Weil, 1990).

There was a slight drop in the divorce rate in the 1980s. This was attributed to: the fear of AIDS and other sexually transmitted diseases; the economic benefits of staying married contrasted with the economic hardship of separation, divorce, single parenting and child support; and the realization that being an older single adult can lead to sociosexual isolation (Weil, 1990). Ironically, the decrease in divorce is not attributable presently to couples' love for each other or their desire to be together as a socio-psychological unit.

Although heterosexual marriage continues as a statistical norm, an increasing number of people, greater than 10 percent, choose to be single. People are marrying slightly older—in their mid-twenties for both men and women; there is a bimodal distribution relative to the onset of pregnancy—one in the twenties and one in the thirties (U.S. Census Bureau, 1980, 1990, 2000). These variations can be attributed to a variety of factors. They include greater educational, career, and economic opportunity and flexibility for both men and women; behavioral changes in gender-role expression and expectations, and greater materialism. There is also a generation of children of divorced parents who are now adults, and who may be postponing marital commitment based on their experiences as children in custodial situations.

Interestingly, when men and women in this culture are asked how sexuality fits into their life and relationships, there tends to be both consistency and diversity through time between them regardless of their sexual orientation. Women, both lesbian and straight, tend to see sexuality as part of and an expression of the relationship. Men, both gay and straight, tend to see sexuality as a physical pleasure, and a release of sexual tension (Blumstein and Schwartz, 1983; Critchlow-Leigh, 1989; Hite, 1976, 1981, 1987; Kinsey et al., 1948, 1953; Shilts, 1987). Both men and women are orgasmic, enjoy sexual release, and enjoy sex in the context of a love relationship regardless of orientation (Blumenfeld and Raymond, 1989; Blumstein and Schwartz, 1983; Bryant and Demian, 1990; Critchlow-Leigh, 1989; Farrell, 1986; Goldberg, 1984; Hite, 1976, 1981, 1987).

PARENTING STYLES

Regardless of group structure and sexual orientation, the socialization of children is an ongoing concern in all societies. Parenting within mainstream U.S. culture is undergoing rapid behavioral and attitudinal changes. The average marriage in this culture lasts seven years, comparable to medieval Western European marriages. However, our marriages usually end through separation or divorce in contrast to the death of a spouse as occurred in medieval times (Stone, 1977). At the same time, American longevity continues to increase, with an average life expectancy of about eighty years for a middle-class white male and about eighty-three years for a middle-class white female (U.S. Census Bureau, 2000). In addition, nuclear family size is decreasing largely due to economic and subsistence reasons— it's expensive to raise children to adulthood in a highly technical, postindustrial society. The demography of parenting is also shifting. At one end are young (under fifteen years old) female teenaged parents who encounter socioeconomic problems since teenagers are not recognized as legal, social, or economic adults. At the other end are "older" adult parents, women older than thirty-five experiencing their first pregnancy. The overall average age of first pregnancy in this culture is about twenty-four years (U.S. Census Bureau, 2000).

The ideal post-WWII nuclear family is the least common family structure; more than 25 percent of households are headed by single parents. Although over one million men are full-time single parents, the majority of single parents are women, either by circumstance—divorce, separation, or desertion—or by choice (Hochschild, 1989; U.S. Bureau of Labor Statistics, 1985; U.S. Census Bureau, 1980, 1990, 2000).

Currently, in two-parent households, generally both parents work outside the home full-time. This creates a need for child care— largely in the form of paid, nonkin-based arrangements such as daycare centers based on class, not ethnicity. In-home division of labor and time spent parenting are highly variable in these situations. Frequently, the presence of a child restructures the adult relationship along more "traditional" lines, where the female assumes primary responsibility for housework and child care responsibilities in addition to full-time paid involvement. Although fathers are emotionally and socially bonded to their children, their in-home responsibilities usually are not equally shared with their female partners (Hochschild, 1989). Hochschild's research *(The Second Shift)* indicates that women in two-income families work an equivalent of an extra month a year with their additional household responsibilities (1989).

Parenting and gender role options are becoming more flexible as indicated by the greater availability of assisted reproductive technology (ART) (see Chapters 6 and 7), more educational and career opportunities for women, a rise in divorce rates, and greater numbers of single heads-of-households (AAUW, 1989: 5; U.S. Bureau of Labor, 1985; U.S. Census Bureau, 2000). With increased tolerance and visibility of alternative lifestyles, more gays and lesbians are more openly involved in parenting. Although increasing numbers of gays or lesbians are adopting children or having their own through ART, it is still difficult for them to obtain custody or reasonable visiting rights of children from their marriages (Boston Women's Health Collective, 1976, 1984, 1992, 2005; Douglas, 1990; *Lambda Legal Newsletter*, 1990; Whelehan, 1987). However, a few legal decisions have allowed gay and lesbian parents to maintain contact with their minor children. In Virginia, a lesbian mother was awarded custody (*Lambda Legal Newsletter*, 1990; *Morning Edition: Lesbian Mother in Custody*, 1994; *SOLGAN*, 1992; "The Courts Are Again Asked to Redefine Families," 1990). Lesbians also have the legal option of AI-D, which is available to them through clinics in urban areas or more informally through arrangements made with male friends. Lesbians stand a greater chance of parenting their biological children than do gays. For gays to do so, they must either "pass" in a heterosexual marriage, hope to receive visitation rights if they divorce, or find a woman willing to bear their child and let them raise the child. This latter option, known as surrogate mothering, is a difficult situation for gays or straights, married, or single men. It is probably not a viable option for most gay, bisexual, or straight men in this culture currently.

A lesbian in Southern California who wants to be artificially inseminated and bear a child is suing her doctors for discrimination. The doctors are refusing to perform the procedure. The legal question is whether the doctors are refusing based on the woman's sexual orientation (which would be illegal in California) or based on her being unmarried (which would be legal grounds for refusal in California). The California Medical Association currently is siding with the doctors. To what extent can doctors make decisions based on their own values rather than based on science and medicine (Buchanan, 2005b)?

From research conducted in the 1970s (e.g., Green, 1978, 1979a, 1979b), children of homosexual parents are as likely to be homosexual as are children of heterosexual parents. More recent research, which surely needs more follow-up, suggests possibly a familial tendency toward male homosexuality (Bailey and Pillard, 1991; Hamer and Copeland, 1994). Lesbians do not create man-hating daughters and sexually confused sons any more than gays create misogynist sons and sexually confused daughters. One gay man says of his daughter and son, "They're so normal," a statement many of us who are parents would like to make about our children. His children are proud and accepting of who their father is. Their conflicts, shared closeness, and confidences are what many parents in the United States hope to achieve with their children (Whelehan's files).

Single-parent households, which are primarily headed by women, frequently function under severe economic restrictions unless the woman is a middle-class career person who chose single parenting (Crooks and Baur, 1987; Hochschild, 1989). In female-headed single-parent households, there are a variety of parent-child interactions and male role models available to the children in the form of extended kin relations such as the mother's brothers or the mother's father, nonsexual male friends, and sexual partners (Dugan, 1988). This is a well-established, adaptive pattern in many lower income African American and *Latino* households (Dugan, 1988; Stack, 1974).

In single-parent, male-headed households, the economic situation is usually more stable, more secure, and more comfortable (AAUW, 1989: 5). Men earn approximately 28 to 34 percent more than women in comparable positions, and after divorce experience about a 43 percent increase in disposable, or available, income; however, women often experience a drop in disposable income of almost 33 percent (Boston Women's Health Collective, 2005; Faludi, 1991: 22).[4] It is also more socially acceptable for a male as a single person and parent in U.S. society to seek a relationship with a woman than for a female single parent to seek a relationship with a man. As with women, men rely on paid child care, extended kin, and nonsexual friends of both genders for support and to be female role models for their children. Use of extended kin and nonkin as a means of socioeconomic support and socialization of children is a continuation of our hominid behavior of **alloparenting,** where nonhuman primate "sisters" and "aunts" care for the young as well as the biological parents.

Since a significant proportion (25 percent) of families in the United States comprise single-parent households, this involves qualitative shifts in parenting and child care similar to those mentioned for dual-income families. In nonindustrialized societies and for some ethnic groups in industrialized societies, child care can be managed within extended kin and clan relationships. For the middle class in the United States, extended kin relationships have been attenuated since the beginning of the twentieth century. Increasingly, middle-class parents, both single and dual, turn to paid, nonkin-based child care, professional child care "experts"—counselors, educators, pediatricians, how-to advisors—and literature for information, support, and help in raising children. Blue-collar and lower-class kin groups tend to tie into Social Service agencies and extended kin for help in child rearing (Rubin, 1976).

In the southern United States, there is the practice of courtesy aunts/uncles for parenting children not related by blood or marriage.

The present generation of children is also the first generation as a group to be raised in either single-parent or **blended families** (i.e., step-parent households) on a large-scale basis. They grew up as children in kin groups, which lived through and with the Sexual Revolution, changed gender roles, sexual behaviors, and divorce. It will be interesting to observe what decisions these children make as adults about finances and careers, marriage, childbearing and rearing, and relationships.

Teenaged parents

A parenting situation defined in this culture as highly problematic is teenaged parenting, particularly for those teens younger than fifteen. We (in the United States) have the highest rate of teenaged pregnancy of any industrialized society (*The Alan Guttmacher Institute; Wattleton, 1990; World Health Statistics Annual*, 1988). Over 1 million teenagers get pregnant each year in this culture. Yet, teenagers in the United States are not culturally recognized adults physically, socio-psychologically, economically, legally, or politically. Most of these teenagers give birth to their children and many decide to keep and raise them. It is a cultural situation of "children having children." These teenagers have a high rate of complications during pregnancy and childbirth including premature births, low birth-weight babies, or spontaneous abortions. Often, the fathers of the babies, many of whom are men in their twenties, not teens, cannot and do not economically and socially support the nuclear families they have created (Males, 1992: 525). There was a decrease in the overall number of teenaged pregnancies during the 1990s with both sides of the sex education controversy claiming success for this decline (The Alan Guttmacher Institute).

Younger teenaged parents often become dependent on the social service system, which varies greatly by state relative to how much economic, social, and emotional support is available. These teens can have a difficult time gaining the culturally appropriate skills such as job training, high school, or college education. Survival mechanisms include support from extended kin networks, particularly in economically poorer, white, African American, and *Latino* families, and reliance on Aid for Families with Dependent Children, referred to as TANF (Temporary Assistance to Needy Families). Larger societal institutions perceive teenaged pregnancy and parenting as an unresolved crisis situation (The Alan Guttmacher Institute; Wattleton, 1990).

SEXUAL ORIENTATIONS CROSS-CULTURALLY

As with discussions of gender in Chapter 13, explorations of sexual orientations are culture specific. Industrialized societal ideas and terms for sexual orientations may have little meaning cross-culturally, either for ethnic subcultures in industrialized societies or elsewhere (Buhgra, 1997). This does not mean that sexual behavior other than heterosexuality does not exist or that it is not recognized, but that the structure and expression of nonheterosexual relationships and behavior are highly variable.

Same-sex sexual behavior is historically and culturally prevalent. It, as with many sexual behaviors, has been impacted by culture contact with Euro-Americans and has significantly changed as a result of that contact. For example, same-sex sexual behavior for both men and women is well documented in precontact sub-Saharan Africa, China, India, Japan, and Thailand (AFROL, 2003; Blackwood and Weiringa, 1999a; Kahn, 2001; Nanda, 1999; Ruan, 1991; Ruan and Bullough, 1992; Ruan and Tsai, 1988; Wikan, 2000). Indigenously, this behavior was integrated into the culture, and generally was less stigmatized than it is currently. Same-sex behavior was accepted in China, Japan, India, and among the Lesotho in sub-Saharan Africa. Acceptance of same-sex relationships cross-culturally relates to larger societal views about maleness and femaleness, balance and harmony, sexuality and spirituality, as well as the nature of heterosexual relationships and reproduction (Bullough, 1976, Kahn, 2001; Nanda, 2000; Ruan and Bullough, 1992; Whitam et al., 1998). People in these societies, however, generally did not develop an identity based on these behaviors and relationships; that is a uniquely industrial and recent phenomenon.

Culture contact and colonization changed indigenous sexual practices and views as it did other aspects of society (AFROL, 2003; Kahn, 2001; Ruan and Bullough, 1992; Whitam et al., 1998). The widespread prevalence of homophobia currently is largely a function of culture change. Globally, most societies are overtly homophobic as indicated by formal social and legal sanctions. Despite this, same-sex relationships exist and there are international organizations that support them (Blackwood and Weiringa, 1999a; Carillo, 1999; Whitam et al., 1998).

There are a variety of ways cultures respond to same-sex sexual behavior. Within nonassimilated *Latino* subcultures in the United States and in Latin America, for example, men who take the insertive role in sex retain their identity as male and heterosexual, regardless of their sexual behavior or the sex of their partners (Aggleton, 1994; Halperin, 1994, 1999; Parker and Aggleton, 1997). In these cultures, if the man is sexually discreet, his family is relatively accepting of him. Closeted African American men who engage in same-sex sex, referred to as being "on the down low," face potential rejection from families, their church, and the community, and thus may keep this part of their lives secret (Clay, 2002). In Asian-American communities, "maintaining face" is important. "Face" is a public behavior that honors the family and its values. Therefore, same-sex behavior may be hidden among this group as well. Generally, the less acculturated the group, the more people's behaviors are hidden (Choi et al., 1995). Outside the United States, stigmatization and sanctions can make it difficult or dangerous for people in same-sex relationships to be "out." Since the late twentieth century, movements in China and India are trying to create more accepting conditions for same-sex relationships.

GENDER ROLES

Parenting and relationship forms are based on cultural patterns of gender role behaviors and expectations. Gender role behaviors and expectations are learned, patterned, and symbolic. They are given cultural validity through both verbal and nonverbal forms of expressions. They relate to the culturally appropriate affect, behavior and perceptions ascribed to males and females, comprising in large part what we define as masculine or feminine. Cultural patterning of gender roles is ethnographic (i.e., culture specific). Each culture defines what is acceptable as male or female behavior; thus there is much variety as well as continuity cross-culturally. For example, although women are the primary child caretakers from infancy through early childhood, illustrating interculture continuity, the forms of dress, mannerisms, and speech patterns expected of males and females can vary greatly from one culture to another, and within cultures from one point in their history to another. Margaret Mead's work in this area, as discussed in Chapter 1, is particularly explicative of the variety of gender role behaviors and expressions of masculinity and femininity (e.g., 1949, 1963 [1935]). (See also Chapter 14.)

Over the past forty to fifty years in this culture, much research has addressed the causes and expressions of gender role behaviors and expectations. Explanations include the spurious nature/nurture controversy, the range of behaviors, behavioral variations intra- and interculturally, continuity and change, and nonconforming behavior. Research into this field is interdisciplinary, cross-cultural, and composed of male-female teams from the social and biological sciences. There is a large men's and women's literature available about this topic (e.g. Bem, 1974; Blumstein and Schwartz, 1983; Nanda, 2000; Sherfey, 1972; Symons, 1979). Conceptually, gender roles are often categorized as **traditional, nontraditional,** or androgynous. These terms are value laden and take on political connotations.

The scale of traditional, nontraditional, and androgynous gender roles can roughly be conceptualized as a fluid continuum with traditional and liberated (i.e., nontraditional) as more opposed than symmetrical to each other, and androgynous as comprising a wide, gray midsection as explained in Chapter 13. It may be analogous to Kinsey's scale of sexual behavior relative to labeling it as homosexual, heterosexual, or bisexual (Kinsey et al. 1948). Table 14.1 compares gender role categories on a continuum to Kinsey's sexual (behavior) orientation continuum. Perception is probably as important in interpreting this continuum as is the individual's behavior. Again, behavior (what you do) does not equal orientation (who you desire) relative to Kinsey's scale. As with traditional gender roles, nontraditional and androgynous refer to both gender role behaviors and attitudes. The men's and women's literature gives full breadth to what constitutes a nontraditional or "liberated" individual (Boston Women's Health Collective, 2005; Farrell, 1974, 1986; Hite, 1976, 1981, 1987; Goldberg, 1979, 1984; Greer, 1971; Zilbergeld, 1978). "Liberated" is a highly relative idea, most consistently correlated with the concept of choice, itself an industrialized society, middle-class concept. Liberated connotes rebellion. It refers to a state of being culture free of negatively perceived gender role expectations; that is, traditional roles, regardless of one's gender. It is individually oriented and defined, another phenomenon characteristic of the United States. Since we are all creatures of our culture, "liberated" is probably more realized in theory than in actuality. It is a state of mind which may be

Table 14.1 Gender role categories

Gender roles*			Sexual behavior**		
Traditional	Androgynous	Nontraditional	Heterosexual	Bisexual or ambisexual	Homosexual
1	2–5	6	1 Exclusively	2–5	6 Exclusively

Notes:
* The gender role scale adapts the Kinsey et al. scale for sexual behaviors (1948). One refers to following and emulating traditional mid-twentieth-century gender roles for middle-class people in the United States. Six refers to emulating and following gender roles that were seen as alternative by some groups in late twentieth- and early twenty-first century United States culture. This could include stay-at-home dads and women earning more than their male partners.
** The 1–6 scale for sexual behaviors refers to Kinsey et al.'s (1948) scale; see Chapter 13.

reflected behaviorally and attitudinally by choosing gender role behaviors that are positive for oneself and one's relationships. "Liberated" is difficult to measure objectively; however, various scales and measures exist to assess androgyny (Bem, 1974; see Chapter 13).

Regardless of the form of gender role behavior, there are several consistent variables. These exist as preferred states, and there may be considerable variance behaviorally and attitudinally from the preferred state. Few individuals consistently fit neatly into one ideal state: traditional/nontraditional, liberated, or androgynous. Culture lag, a situation where behavior changes more rapidly than the supporting belief system, can be found with each of these gender role patterns. A person may act one way yet feel very differently about the appropriateness of their actions; for example, a traditional male may be uncomfortable with the degree of emotional restrictiveness that is culturally expected of him. Not any one ideal state is inherently positive or negative. Depending on the situation, the actualization of any of the preferred states may have positive or negative consequences for the individual and group.

Gender role categories overlap. There is a wide middle ground in our behavior and affect that incorporates all of them. As theoretical constructs, these may be useful analytic tools; behaviorally, people live the reality of their everyday lives, not theory. Last, these categories are culture-bound; the context for their expression varies. Although all cultures have concepts of maleness and femaleness, the actual definitions and expectations of male and female behaviors vary widely intra- and interculturally (see Chapter 13).

This chapter emphasizes the diversity in human sexual orientations, behaviors, and lifestyles. It does so within the context of the range of known sexual behaviors among mammals, primates, and humans. It seeks an understanding, appreciation, and acceptance of the forms of sexual identities and their expression as inherent in human sexuality. Sexual orientation and behavior, in their most positive sense, enhance who we are and allow for talents in other areas of our lives to be developed. Finally, the chapter looks at relationships as an attempt to meet a larger primate need for bonding and connection, regardless of one's gender choice of partner.

SUMMARY

1 There are several forms of sexual orientation—homosexual (gay or lesbian), bisexual, and heterosexual.
2 Sexual orientation is not synonymous with sexual behavior.
3 We do not know what causes anyone's sexual orientation. However, heterosexuality is assumed to be normative in the United States, and thus is unexplained. In contrast, homosexuality and bisexuality often are seen as stigmatized or variant orientations and have been explained by a number of theories.

4 There is a wide continuum of sexual behaviors in the animal and human worlds.
5 Heterosexism and homophobia are widespread in the United States; definitions and expressions of sexual orientations vary by society and are influenced by culture change.
6 There exists a wide range of partnering relationships found within the United States.
7 Female and single-parent households are increasing in the United States.
8 Teenaged pregnancy is a common and serious problem in the United States.
9 Blended families or step-parent families are increasing in the United States.
10 Reproductive technology is changing the forms of parenting options available.
11 The Sexual Revolution of the 1960s in the United States was a time of testing traditional sexual boundaries and rules.
12 Culture lag exists in the United States between sexual behavior and values, creating confusion for individuals and groups and giving rise to a variety of gender role behaviors.

Thought-provoking questions

1 How does an ongoing value of sex for reproduction affect our attitudes towards relationships and sexual behavior that are not heterosexual?
2 How are sexual orientation and gender culturally constructed and expressed, and what changes have occurred since the Sexual Revolution of the 1960s?

SUGGESTED RESOURCES

Books

Blackwood, Evelyn, and Saskia Wieringa, eds. 1999. *Female Desires: Same-Sex Relations and Transgender Practices Across Cultures.* New York: Columbia University Press.
Rust, Paula C., ed. 1999. *Bisexuality in the United States: A Social Science Reader.* New York: Columbia University Press.

Web sites

Kaleidoscope (http://www.uky.edu/Kaleidoscope/fall2003/meyer/page3.htm). Last accessed 12/26/06.
Lambda Legal Defense Fund (http://www.lambdalegal.org). Last accessed 11/09/07.
4Parents.gov (http://www.4parents.gov/). Last accessed 11/09/07.

15 HIV and AIDS

INTRODUCTION

Sexuality is one of the more complex dimensions of our humanity. Probably nowhere is this complexity more obvious than when we explore the topic of sexually transmitted infections (STIs) and sexually transmitted diseases (STDs), specifically **HIV/AIDS**. This chapter highlights HIV/AIDS as one of the most significant challenges currently confronting human societies.

STIs are the organisms that infect people through unprotected sexual behavior. They can be viral, bacterial, fungal, or parasitic. STDs are the physical effects that happen to one's body once infected with an STI. These can include fevers, sores, fertility problems (particularly for infected females), and for those untreated STIs such as HIV and syphilis, death at their end stages.

STIs/STDs such as syphilis have an older history than HIV/AIDS. Syphilis, chlamydia, and the human papilloma virus (HPV), or genital warts, are all more common in terms of their **incidence** (number of new cases) and **prevalence** (how widespread a disease is in a population). However, syphilis and chlamydia are both treatable and curable. Chlamydia is not fatal, although if left untreated it can cause infertility in women. HPV and Herpes Simplex 2 (HS2) are both viruses as is HIV. But HPV and HS2, while incurable, are not fatal, and are easily treatable. Treatments for these other STIs generally involve a short course of antibiotics or other therapies, not a daily, lifelong regimen of treatment. There has been significant progress made in developing a vaccine for HPV which is currently being considered for approval by the Food and Drug Administration (Koutsky et al., 2002; "National Politics and Policy," 2006).

HIV is neither the most common sexually transmitted infection and AIDS is not the oldest, recorded, sexually transmitted disease. There is neither a cure nor a vaccine for HIV/AIDS, and it is fatal if left untreated. HIV infection can be treated with **anti-retroviral medications (ARVs)**, sometimes referred to as **HAART (Highly Active Anti-retroviral Therapy)** with dramatic improvement in people's health and their lives. But these drugs are expensive, are not widely available outside of industrialized societies, and can have serious side effects. People who take the drugs must adhere to a strict daily schedule of drug dosage in order for the drugs to be effective. In addition, other STIs such as syphilis and gonorrhea can act as **co-factors** in HIV infection. This means that having one of these other STIs increases one's risk for HIV either by impairing one's immune system or causing sores that make HIV more readily transmissible.

Aside from the biological differences between HIV and other STIs, there are socio-cultural, political, and economic factors that impact the course of HIV/AIDS. As will be discussed, HIV/AIDS is global (**pandemic**) and is found on all inhabited continents with devastating consequences for the individuals, groups, and societies. Poverty, local and international political decisions, and practices that are based more on "morality" and ideology than science affect risks for infection and the course of the disease once infected. The stigma that accompanies the HIV/AIDS pandemic shapes societal response to it to a greater degree than with other STIs. For these reasons, this chapter focuses on the HIV/AIDS pandemic. Table 15.1 compares HIV to other STIs.

Diseases such as the bubonic plague during the Middle Ages, syphilis, and leprosy have played an important role in the physical, social, economic, political, and psychological responses of societies over the past several hundred years. Today, the disease confronting us with global and culture-specific significance affects both affluent and poor nations. This disease, first identified by the media in the United States in 1981 as **GRID (Gay-Related Immune-deficiency Disease)**, a misnomer, is now identified as AIDS (Acquired Immune-deficiency Syndrome).[1] Currently believed to be caused

Table 15.1 Common sexually transmitted diseases (STDs): mode of transmission, symptoms, and treatment

STD	Transmissions	Symptoms	Treatment
Bacterial vaginosis	The most common causative agent, the *Gardnerella vaginalis* bacterium, is transmitted primarily by coitus.	In women, a fishy or musty smelling, thin discharge, like flour paste in consistency and usually gray. Most men are asymptomatic.	Metronidazole (Flagyl), ampicillin, or amoxicillin.
Candidiasis (yeast infection)	The *Candida albicans* fungus may accelerate growth when the chemical balance of the vagina is disturbed; it may also be transmitted through sexual interaction.	White, "cheesy" discharge; irritation of vaginal and vulvar tissue in women. Men rarely get yeast infections; uncircumcised and men with diabetes most susceptible. Inflammation, discharge possible.	Vaginal suppositories or cream, such as clotrimazole, nystatin, and miconazole. Men receive similar topical treatments.[1]
Trichomoniasis	The protozoan parasite *Trichomoniasis vaginalis* passed through genital sexual contact or less frequently by towels, toilet seats, or bathtubs used by an infected person.	White or yellow vaginal discharge with an unpleasant odor; vulva is sore and irritated. Most men with trichomoniasis are asymptomatic. Those with symptoms may have an urethral discharge, urge to urinate and burning sensation upon urinating.[2]	Metronidazole (Flagyl), effective for both sexes.
Chlamydial infection	The *Chlamydia trachomatis* bacterium is transmitted primarily through sexual contact. It may also be spread by fingers from one body site to another.	In men, chlamydial infection of the urethra may cause a discharge and burning during urination. Chlamydia-caused epididymitis may produce a sense of heaviness in the affected testicle(s), inflammation of the scrotal skin, and painful swelling at the bottom of the testicle. In women, PID caused by Chlamydia may include disrupted menstrual periods, abdominal pain, infertility, elevated temperature, nausea, vomiting, and headache.	Tetracycline doxycycline, erythromycin, or trimethoprim-sulfamethoxazole.

Table 15.1 (Continued).

STD	Transmissions	Symptoms	Treatment
Gonorrhea ("clap")	The *Neisseria gonorrhoeae* bacterium ("gonococcus") is spread through genital, oral-genital, or genital-anal contact.	Most common symptoms in men are a cloudy discharge from the penis and burning sensations during urination. If disease is untreated, complications may include inflammation of scrotal skin and swelling at base of the testicle. In women, some green or yellowish discharge is produced but commonly remains undetected. At a later stage, PID may develop.	Tetracycline or doxycycline is usually effective.
Nongonococcal urethritis (NGU)	Primary causes are believed to be bacteria *Chlamydia trachomatis* and *Ureaplasma urealyticum*, most commonly transmitted through coitus. Some NGU may result from allergic reactions or from Trichomonas infection.	Inflammation of the urethral tube. A man has a discharge from the penis during urination. A woman may have a mild discharge of pus from the vagina but often shows no symptoms.	Tetracycline, doxycycline, or erythromycin.
Syphilis	The *Treponema pallidum* bacterium ("spirochete") is transmitted from open lesions during genital, oral-genital, or genital-anal contact.	Primary stage: A painless chancre appears at the site where the spirochetes entered the body. Secondary stage: The chancre disappears and a generalized skin rash develops. Latent stage: There may be no observable symptoms. Tertiary stage: Heart failure, blindness, mental disturbance, and many other symptoms may occur. Death may result.	Benzathine penicillin, tetracycline, or erythromycin.
Pubic lice ("crabs")	*Phthirus pubis*, the pubic louse, is spread easily through body contact or through shared clothing or bedding.	Persistent itching. Lice are visible and may often be located in pubic hair or other body hair.	Preparations such as A-200 pyrinate or Kwell (gamma benzene hexachloride).

	Transmission	Symptoms	Treatment
Herpes	The genital herpes virus (HSV-2) appears to be transmitted primarily by vaginal, oral-genital, or anal sexual intercourse. The oral herpes virus (HSV-1) is transmitted primarily by kissing.	Small, red, painful bumps (papules) appear in the region of the genitals (genital herpes) or mouth (oral herpes). The papules become painful blisters that eventually rupture to form wet, open scores.	No known cure; a variety of treatments may reduce symptoms; oral acyclovir (Zovirax) promotes healing and suppresses recurrent outbreaks.
Viral hepatitis	The hepatitis B virus may be transmitted by blood, semen, vaginal secretions, and saliva. Manual, oral, or penile stimulation of the anus are strongly associated with the spread of this virus. Hepatitis A seems to be primarily spread via the fecal-oral route. Oral-anal sexual contact is a common mode for sexual transmission of hepatitis A.	Vary from nonexistent to mild, flulike symptoms to an incapacitating illness characterized by high fever, vomiting, and severe abdominal pain.	No specific therapy; treatment generally consists of bed rest and adequate fluid intake.
Genital warts (venereal warts)	The virus is spread primarily through genital, anal, or oral-genital interaction. Most are caused by some strain of the human papilloma virus (HPV).	Warts are hard and yellow-gray on dry skin areas; soft pinkish red, and cauliflower-like on moist areas.	Topical agents like podophylin: cauterization; freezing; surgical removal; or vaporization by carbon dioxide laser. Vaccines have been developed to prevent infection with some strains of HPV. Controversies exist about who should get the vaccine and when.

Table 15.1 (Continued)

STD	Transmissions	Symptoms	Treatment
Acquired Immuno-Deficiency syndrome (AIDS)	Blood and semen are the major vehicles for transmitting the AIDS virus, HIV, which attacks the immune system. It appears to be passed primarily through sexual contact or needle sharing among injection drug abusers. Can be passed perinatally from mother to fetus or during breastfeeding.	Varies with the type of opportunistic infections (OIs) that affects someone with HIV. Common systems include: fevers, night sweats, weight loss, loss of appetite, fatigue, swollen lymph nodes, diarrhea and/or bloody stools, atypical bruising or bleeding, skin rashes, headache, chronic cough, a whitish coating on the tongue or throat.	At present, therapy focuses on specific treatments of opportunistic infections and tumors. Since 1996, combination therapy has increased survival rates and decreased progression to AIDS and susceptibility to OIs in those people who have access to the drugs and can tolerate their side effects.

1 Information can be fount at http://www.bbc.co.uk/health/mens_health/issues_thrush.shtml.
2 Information can be fount at http://www.cdc.gov.ncidod/dpd/parasites/trichomonas/factsht_trichomonas.htm.

by the retro-virus **HIV-I** in this country, and **HIV-2** (a variant of HIV-1) in parts of West Africa, human immunodeficiency virus (HIV) is a worldwide phenomenon. It is one of our most serious health threats ("Declaration of Commitment on HIV/AIDS," 2001; "U.N. Report on the Global AIDS Epidemic," 2004).

Anthropology and medical anthropology have definite roles to play in resolving the AIDS pandemic. At the beginning of the twenty-first century, HIV/AIDS is a global problem. As such, HIV/AIDS is described as a disease and topic of study that fits well with an anthropological perspective. The physical, biological, socio-cultural, political, and economic aspects of HIV/AIDS filter through each society's values, beliefs, and institutions in relation to health, illness, disease, sexuality, men and women, life and death. Since anthropologists have a history of qualitative as well as quantitative research, we have the ability to discern the symbols and constructs underlying people's behaviors, and we work in intercultural health settings (AIDS and Anthropology Research Group, 1988, Herrell, 1991; Carrier and Bolton, 1991; Herdt et al., 1990; "National Institutes of Health Consensus Development Conference on Interventions to Prevent HIV Risk Behaviors," 1997). HIV/AIDS affects industrialized and nonindustrialized groups across the life cycle. The anthropological perspectives of cultural relativism, cross-cultural comparison, and a holistic approach to data are helpful in understanding the cultural complexities of this disease.

Please note that the material in this chapter is current through 2006. While some information about **HIV infection** and AIDS such as modes of transmission, risk reduction strategies, and safer sex has remained relatively constant over the past several years, other aspects such as treatment modalities, incidence rates, and prevalence patterns are changing rapidly. Please contact your local department of public health, AIDS task force, campus AIDS coordinator, or the CDC (Centers for Disease Control and Prevention) reports for the most up-to-date information.[2]

EPIDEMIOLOGY OF HIV/AIDS

A basic knowledge of **epidemiology,** which is the study of the patterns of disease, helps us understand HIV/AIDS anthropologically. Knowing how many people and who are infected with or at risk for HIV can help to develop intervention programs from prevention and testing to treatment and care. In addition to being a pandemic, HIV/AIDS is also **endemic,** meaning that it is well-established in the populations where it is found. For example, about 40 percent of Swazilanders in South Africa have AIDS ("Fact Sheet: The Global HIV/AIDS Epidemic—2005 Update," 2005). HIV/AIDS seems to have appeared rather suddenly among men who have sex with men (MSM) in Los Angeles, New York, and San Francisco during the summer of 1981 (Shilts, 1987). The sudden appearance of a disease that spreads relatively quickly through a population is referred to as an **epidemic**. The number of new cases of HIV/AIDS is referred to as the incidence rate. There have been between 40,000 and 42,000 new HIV infections every year in the United States since 1990 ("HIV and AIDS—United States, 1981–2001," 2001a). HIV/AIDS is an epidemic, a pandemic, and endemic in societies where it occurs.

HIV/AIDS also takes on **acute, chronic, and terminal aspects of disease and illness**. Acute diseases have a sudden onset and a relatively rapid course of infection. Colds and the flu are examples of acute diseases. About 50 percent of people with HIV experience flulike symptoms within the first two to three weeks of being infected (Bartlett, 2002, 2006). Chronic diseases, those which are incurable, can affect people's functioning, but may be treatable. Arthritis and diabetes are examples of chronic diseases. HIV/AIDS is incurable, but those people who have access to and can afford anti-retroviral therapy (ARVs/HAART) live longer and function reasonably well. Terminal diseases are those that kill you. Some cancers and some forms of heart disease are terminal. HIV/AIDS is terminal for those who do not have access to HAART/ARVs. This includes most of the people outside industrialized countries who have the disease. Disease refers to the clinical and physical manifestations of being sick: fevers, night sweats, and weight loss are all the other physical aspects of HIV/AIDS. Illness refers to the socioeconomic, psychological, and political aspects and consequences of having a disease. For people with HIV/AIDS, these aspects can include stigma and isolation from kin groups and friends, inability to work, with resulting economic problems, as well as the effects that grief and the loss of productive members of society have on the rest of the group. HIV/AIDS exemplifies the core of epidemiological work. (See Table 15.2 and Figure 15.1.)

Table 15.2 Regional/global HIV/AIDS statistics

Region	Adults (age 15+) and children living with HIV/AIDS, end 2006	New HIV infections among adults (age 15+) and children, end 2006	Adult (age 15–49) prevalence (%), end 2006	Adult (age 15+) and child deaths due to AIDS in 2006
Sub-Saharan Africa	24.7 million	2.8 million	5.9%	2.1 million
South/Southeast Asia	7.8 million	860,000	0.6%	590,000
Latin America	1.7 million	140,000	0.5%	65,000
East Asia	750,000	100,000	0.1%	43,000
North America	1.4 million	43,000	0.8%	18,000
Eastern Europe/ Central Asia	1.7 million	270,000	0.9%	84,000
Western/Central Europe	740,000	22,000	0.3%	12,000
Caribbean	250,000	27,000	1.2%	19,000

Table 15.2 (Continued)

Region	Adults (age 15+) and children living with HIV/AIDS, end 2006	New HIV infections among adults (age 15+) and children, end 2006	Adult (age 15–49) prevalence (%), end 2006	Adult (age 15+) and child deaths due to AIDS in 2006
Middle East/North Africa	460,000	68,000	0.2%	36,000
Oceania	81,000	7,100	0.4%	4,000
Global	39.5 million	4.3 million	1.0%	2.9 million

Source: "Distribution of reported AIDS cases, all ages by sex, cumulative through 2005," (http://www.stathealthfacts.org); Centers for Disease Control and Prevention, Division of HIV/AIDS Prevention-Surveillance and Epidemiology, Special Data Request, November 2006; maps provided by The Henry J. Kaiser Family Foundation. This information was reprinted with permission from the Henry J. Kaiser Family Foundation. The Kaiser Family Foundation, based in Menlo Park, California, is a nonprofit, private operating foundation focusing on the major health care issues facing the nation and is not associated with Kaiser Permanente or Kaiser Industries.

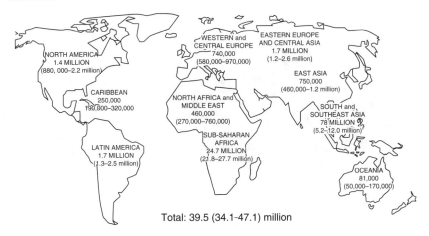

Figure 15.1 Adults and children estimated to be living with HIV in 2006. (*Source*: Provided by Sylvia A. Macey from information provided by UNAIDS [2006].)

Demographics of HIV/AIDS

Age

Demographic variables of age, gender, socioeconomic status, ethnicity, and location are also important in understanding the risks for and the manifestations of HIV/AIDS in a population. HIV/AIDS is classified as either pediatric when it is found in people younger than twelve years old, or adult when it is found in people older than twelve. Currently, most pediatric HIV/AIDS cases are a result of mother-to-child-transmission. A mother can transmit HIV to her child during pregnancy, childbirth, or breastfeeding if her HIV-positive status is unknown and/or she does not or cannot receive drugs to prevent transmission. (See Table 15.3 and Figure 15.2.)

Table 15.3 United States HIV/AIDS statistics 2005

U.S. HIV/AIDS Statistics	
People living with HIV/AIDS, U.S.	1.2 million
People newly infected with HIV, U.S.	40,000
African Americans as a proportion of new AIDS diagnoses in the U.S. (and their percentage of the U.S. population)	50% (12%)
Latinos as a proportion of new AIDS diagnoses in the U.S. (and their percentage of the U.S. population)	19% (14%)
Whites as a proportion of new AIDS diagnoses in the U.S. (and their percentage of the U.S. population)	29% (67%)

Source: Kaiser Family Foundation, Fact Sheet: The HIV/AIDS Epidemic in the U.S., November 2006. U.S. Centers for Disease Control and Prevention, U.S. Census Bureau.

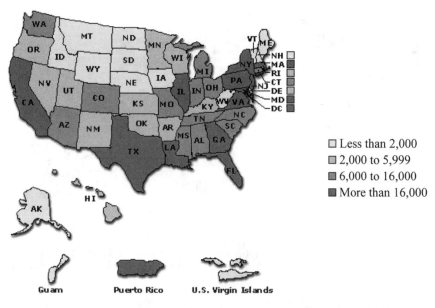

☐ Less than 2,000
◫ 2,000 to 5,999
◼ 6,000 to 16,000
◼ More than 16,000

Figure 15.2 Reported number of AIDS cases, all ages, cumulative through December 2005. (*Source:* "HIV/AIDS at a Glance;" "Distribution of reported AIDS cases, all ages by sex, cumulative through 2005," www.statehealthfacts.org; Centers for Disease Control and Prevention, Division of HIV/AIDS Prevention-Surveillance and Epidemiology, Special Data Request, November 2006; maps provided by The Henry J. Kaiser family Foundation. This information was reprinted with permission from the Henry J. Kaiser Family Foundation. The Kaiser Family Foundation, based in Menlo Park, California, is a nonprofit, private operating foundation focusing on the major health care issues facing the nation and is not associated with Kaiser Permanente or Kaiser Industries.)

Although HIV/AIDS is generally seen as a younger person's disease with most people worldwide infected in mid-to-late adolescence and early adulthood (fifteen to twenty-four years old), at least 14 percent of AIDS in the United States is diagnosed among people older than fifty (Edwards, 2005). It is increasingly found in older people in Thailand as well ("HIV and AIDS–United States 1981–2001," 2001; Im-em, 2002; Im-em et al., 2002). Reasons for this include increased longevity for people who have access to ARVs, changing sexual mores, a value on sexuality across the life cycle as part of Thai culture, and denial about risk for HIV among divorced, widowed, or separated middle-aged people who find themselves single and dating (Im-em et al., 2002). (See Figure 15.3 and Table 15.4.)

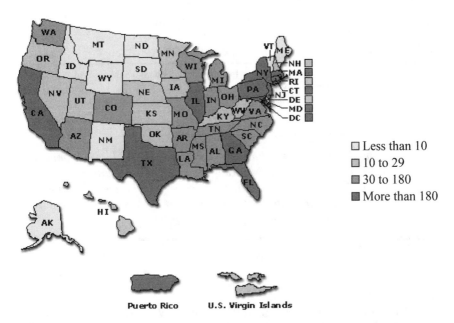

☐ Less than 10
◩ 10 to 29
▨ 30 to 180
■ More than 180

Puerto Rico   U.S. Virgin Islands

Figure 15.3 Reported number of AIDS cases in children <13, cumulative through December 2005 (Sources: "HIV/AIDS at a Glance;" www.statehealth facts.org; Centers for Disease Control and Prevention, Division of HIV/AIDS Prevention-Surveillance and Epidemiology, Special Data Request, November 2006; maps by The Henry J. Kaiser Family Foundation. This information was reprinted with permission from the Henry J. Kaiser Family Foundation. The Kaiser Family Foundation, based in Menlo Park, California, is a nonprofit, private operating foundation focusing on the major health care issues facing the nation and is not associated with Kaiser Permanente or Kaiser Industries.) (Notes: Includes persons with a diagnosis of AIDS, reported from the beginning of the epidemic through 2005. U.S. totals include data from the United States [50 states and the District of Columbia] and from U.S. dependencies, possessions, and independent nations in free association with the U.S., and persons whose state or area of residence is unknown.)

Table 15.4 AIDS cases by age

Age	Estimated # of AIDS cases in 2005	Cumulative estimated # of AIDS cases, through 2005*
Under 13	58	9,089
Ages 13–14	66	1,015
Ages 15–19	476	5,309
Ages 20–24	2,004	34,987
Ages 25–29	3,739	114,519
Ages 30–34	5,635	194,529
Ages 35–39	7,867	209,210
Ages 40–44	8,925	165,497
Ages 45–49	6,953	103,326
Ages 50–54	4,277	57,336
Ages 55–59	2,237	30,631
Ages 60–64	1,068	16,611
Ages 65 or older	894	14,606

Source: From CDC, http://www.cdc.gov. *Includes persons with a diagnosis of AIDS from the beginning of the epidemic through 2005.

Miami-Dade, Broward, and Palm Beach Counties in Florida have the highest incidence of HIV/AIDS among senior citizens of any place in the United States. Reasons given include the number of widowed and divorced senior citizens who believe that HIV/AIDS is not a concern for people their age and in their circumstances (Freidenreich, 2003).

Gender

Gender is a major risk factor for HIV/AIDS. HIV is primarily transmitted through unprotected penile and anal intercourse worldwide. While initially HIV/AIDS was seen as a disease of "middle-class 'gay' men" in Western industrialized societies (and thus the early misnomer of GRID), and the elite in both Brazil and some sub-Saharan African societies in the 1980s, it has become a gendered epidemic in the twenty-first century. For example, the male-to-female ratio of HIV/AIDS in the United States has changed from eleven males for every one female in the 1980s to about two males to every one female currently (Edwards, 2005: 7). In most of sub-Saharan Africa where more than 70 percent of the world's AIDS cases are found, most of the infections occur among reproductive-aged women and girls as a result of unprotected penile-vaginal intercourse (Ditmore, 2005; "Fact Sheet: The Global HIV/AIDS Epidemic—2005 Update," 2005; McGrath et al., 1993, Varga, 1999). (See Figures 15.4a and 15.4b and Table 15.5.)

Males

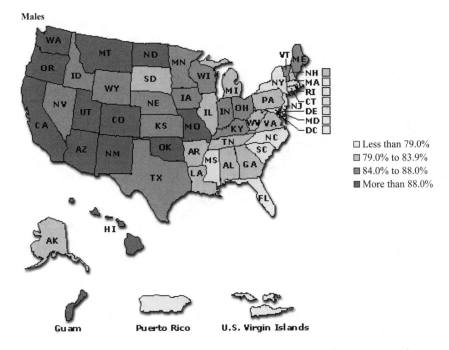

☐ Less than 79.0%
▨ 79.0% to 83.9%
▩ 84.0% to 88.0%
■ More than 88.0%

Guam   Puerto Rico   U.S. Virgin Islands

Figure 15.4a Distribution of reported AIDS cases, all ages by sex, cumulative through 2005: males.

Socioeconomic status

HIV/AIDS rapidly moved in the 1980s from an epidemic of the middle class in various parts of the world to a disease of the poor and disenfranchised by the 1990s and early twenty-first century. In the United States, it is increasingly a disease found among poor, urban, ethnic minorities. Cross-culturally, from sub-Saharan Africa to India and Southeast Asia, most of the people infected and affected by HIV/AIDS are poor. Most of the people in sub-Saharan Africa earn less than U.S. $2/day, with women, on average, earning less than that. The cheapest ARVs available cost U.S. $1/day, making them unaffordable to most of the people who need them (Farmer, 2000; Farmer, Walton, and Furin, 2000). This aspect of HIV/AIDS has led activist anthropologist/physician Paul Farmer and others to call AIDS a disease of poverty.

Ethnicity

Ethnicity is another salient variable when discussing HIV/AIDS. Most of the people with HIV worldwide are People of Color. Proportionately, most of the people in the United States with HIV/AIDS are African

Females

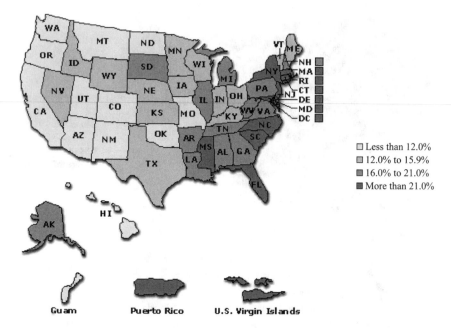

☐ Less than 12.0%
☐ 12.0% to 15.9%
■ 16.0% to 21.0%
■ More than 21.0%

Guam   Puerto Rico   U.S. Virgin Islands

Figure 15.4b Distribution of reported AIDS cases, all ages by sex, cumulative through 2005: Females (*Source:* "HIV/AIDS at a Glance;" "Distribution of reported AIDS cases, all ages by sex, cumulative through 2005," www.statehealthfacts.org; Centers for Disease Control and Prevention, Division of HIV/AIDS Prevention-Surveillance and Epidemiology, Special Data Request, November 2006; maps provided by The Henry J. Kaiser Family Foundation. This information was reprinted with permission from the Henry J. Kaiser Family Foundation. The Kaiser Family Foundation, based in Menlo Park, California, is a non-profit, private operating foundation focusing on the major health care issues facing the nation and is not associated with Kaiser Permanente or Kaiser Industries.) (*Note:* Maps may be broken into the four Census regions as defined by the 2000 U.S. Census: 1. Northeast; 2. Midwest; 3. South; 4. West.)

American and *Latino*, with Native Americans and Asian-Pacific Islanders also disproportionately affected given their prevalence in the population. African Americans and *Latinos* combined make up about 25 percent of the United States population, but account for more than 50 percent of the cases of AIDS. About 83 percent of the women with HIV/AIDS in the United States are African American or *Latina*. It is no coincidence that most of these people are also poor, and that their overall health, nutrition, and living conditions become co-factors for infection (Cummings et al., 1999; "Fact Sheet: The HIV/AIDS Epidemic in the U.S.—2005 Update," 2005; Farmer et al., 1996). (See Figure 15.5.)

Table 15.5 Simple comparison of men and women living with HIV/AIDS

United States	Percent
Male	80.5%[1]
Female	19.5%

[1]U.S. totals include two males in the Pacific Islands and one person from New York whose sex is unknown.

Source: "HIV/AIDS at a Glance;" "Distribution of reported AIDS cases, all ages by sex, cumulative through 2005," www.statehealthfacts.org; Centers for Disease Control and Prevention, Division of HIV/AIDS Prevention-Surveillance and Epidemiology, Special Data Request, November 2006; maps provided by The Henry J. Kaiser Family Foundation. This information was reprinted with permission from the Henry J. Kaiser Family Foundation. The Kaiser Family Foundation, based in Menlo Park, California, is a nonprofit, private operating foundation focusing on the major health care issues facing the nation and is not associated with Kaiser Permanente or Kaiser Industries.

Notes: Includes persons with a diagnosis of AIDS, reported from the beginning of the epidemic through 2005. U.S. totals include data from the United States (50 states and the District of Columbia) and from U.S. dependencies, possessions, and independent nations in free association with the U.S., and persons whose state or area of residence is unknown.

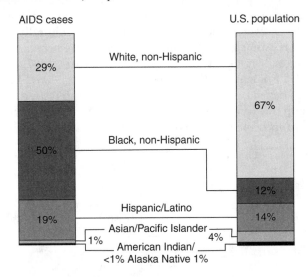

Figure 15.5 Estimated AIDS diagnoses and United States population by race/ethnicity, 2005. (*Source: HIV/AIDS Policy Fact Sheet: Black Americans and HIV/AIDS*, December 2006. Kaiser Family, reprinted with permission.)

Location

Location plays a role in HIV/AIDS. As stated, 70 to 80 percent of the AIDS cases occur in sub-Saharan Africa, and if the current infection rate continues, India and China will have epidemics and endemics of HIV/AIDS among their populations that surpass those of sub-Saharan Africa by 2010 ("Fact

Sheet: The Global HIV/AIDS Epidemic—2005 Update," 2005a; "UN AIDS 2004 Report on the Global AIDS Epidemic 2004," 2004). The reasons for this are largely economic and political and are discussed in other sections.

Epicenters of HIV/AIDS in the United States refer to those cities that are AIDS "dense" (i.e., have high incidence and prevalence rates of HIV/AIDS). New York City and New York State, for example, are the city and state with the highest incidence and prevalence of HIV/AIDS in the United States ("Fact Sheet: The HIV/AIDS Epidemic in the United States 2005," 2005). Cities tend to have higher incidence and prevalence rates than rural areas in the United States for reasons of population density, greater access to HIV testing and treatment that provide the basis for reporting and statistics, more population diversity, and a greater overall tolerance for a variety of lifestyles and behaviors than occur in more rural areas. United States epicenters tend to cluster on the coasts and in major industrial areas. (See Figure 15.6.)

In both the United States and in nonindustrialized societies the incidence and prevalence rates for HIV/AIDS are probably under-reported. There are several reason for this. One, reporting is based on HIV test results and AIDS diagnoses. As a highly stigmatized disease and illness, not everyone who is at risk for infection or who is infected gets tested and diagnosed. For example, only about 10 percent of the people with HIV cross-culturally know their HIV status. It is estimated that about 25 percent of the people with HIV in the United States do not know they are infected (Bartlett, 2002; "Fact Sheet: The HIV/AIDS Epidemic in the United States 2005," 2005). Two, testing and diagnosis depend on having an infrastructure and resources available within a group to carry out the tests and diagnosis. That is expensive and unavailable to most people at risk and with HIV/AIDS worldwide. Last,

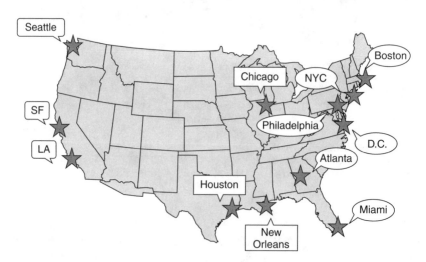

Figure 15.6 Incidence and prevalence of AIDS in the U.S. by epicenters. (*Source*: Provided by Sylvia A. Macey.)

since HIV/AIDS is stigmatized, there are political reasons for individuals, groups, and societies neither to know their HIV status nor to keep records. Active discrimination against people with HIV, moral condemnation from some fundamentalist religious groups, and loss of employment and health insurance can contribute to inaccurate epidemiological data.

MODES OF TRANSMISSION AND CO-FACTORS

Modes of transmission and co-factors for HIV risk are part of the epidemiology of HIV/AIDS. Modes of transmission refer to how HIV is spread. There are four basic modes of transmission: (1) through blood and any of its products, (2) through semen and vaginal fluids, (3) through breast milk, and (4) from **mother-to-child (MTCT)** during pregnancy or childbirth. The behaviors that can transmit these fluids include unprotected anal, vaginal, and to a significantly lesser extent, oral intercourse; sharing HIV-infected blood through needle usage; and during the peri- and postnatal period, including breastfeeding (Bartlett, 2006). The **Centers for Disease Control and Prevention (CDC)** and the **World Health Organization (WHO)** keep track of the modes of transmission of HIV.

Risk co-factors for HIV are those variables that do not transmit the virus, but which may increase one's risk for infection. They include other STIs which impair one's immune system or which may create sores or blisters that make it easier for HIV to pass through the skin. Other factors that can impair a person's immune system include using drugs that can also affect one's decision making, malnutrition, and overall poor heath that may leave a person with sores that ease the passage of the virus, and poverty. Poverty creates the foundation for these other co-factors to flourish. Poor people do not have the same kinds of "choices" that middle-class and wealthy people do relative to food, clean water, preventive medical care and treatments, and safer sex. The modes of transmission and co-factors have a synergistic effect in increasing one's risk for infection with HIV.

BIOMEDICAL ASPECTS OF HIV/AIDS

HIV/AIDS is one of the more recent diseases in human history, and its incidence and prevalence indicate that it may be one of the most serious diseases encountered. While not the most common or most easily transmitted STI or virus (colds, measles, and the flu are all caused by viruses that are much more readily transmitted than HIV), HIV has had a horrific impact on those groups where it is found. HIV is a **retrovirus** for which currently there is no vaccine and no cure. A retrovirus is one in which its genes are in the form of RNA; generally viruses have their genes in the form of DNA which transfer to RNA. With HIV and other retroviruses, this process acts in reverse. This means that HIV is transferred into the DNA of a cell. Since HIV inserts itself into the DNA, it continues to replicate itself. This is one of the reasons that developing a preventive vaccine is so challenging. There are two major forms of HIV, HIV-1 and HIV-2. HIV-1 is the most virulent form found worldwide; HIV-2 is less virulent and largely found in parts of West Africa (Alcamo, 2003; Stine, 1997).

HIV is a bloodborne, not airborne virus and mutates rapidly in the human body. This is one of the reasons why finding a preventive vaccine is so difficult and why it is so important for people with HIV to take their ARVs consistently in order to avoid having the virus develop resistance to the drugs. HIV slowly destroys the body's immune system, and in doing so makes the person with HIV susceptible to a number of **opportunistic infections (OIs)**. OIs are diseases caused by bacteria, fungi, or protozoa such as TB, *Pneumocystis carinii* pneumonia (PCP), or thrush that usually do not occur in people with healthy immune systems.

Within two to three weeks of being infected with HIV, about 50 percent of people develop flulike symptoms. Since these symptoms are vague and similar enough to the flu, most people do not associate them with being HIV infected. After about one month of being infected, about 50 percent of people develop a sufficient number of antibodies to the virus that they can be detected with an HIV test. After three months, more than 95 percent of the people who are infected will have detectable antibodies, and after six months, more than 98 percent of infected people will have detectable antibodies (Bartlett, 2002: 68).

Susceptibility to infection and progression of HIV from infection to AIDS are a function of a number of co-factors. Other STIs, use of recreational drugs that impair the immune system, malnutrition, other diseases such as tuberculosis (TB) or malaria weaken the immune system, or create their own portals of entry in the case of STIs, and increase the risk for infection. Poverty (which underlies poor nutrition), the presence of other diseases, and risky sexual behavior that includes multiple partners, early age of marriage to polygynous men, lack of power in or control over decision making, and lack of access to resources that occur in many nonindustrialized societies also increase the risk of infection.

The time from HIV infection to AIDS varies, but averages about 10.8 years. The 1993 CDC criteria for an AIDS diagnosis is the one currently accepted in the United States and by the WHO. AIDS requires an HIV positive antibody test (see "HIV testing" section), and the presence of either a T-cell count of < 200 and/or one or more OIs. In nonindustrialized societies where HIV testing is largely unavailable, inaccessible, or fraught with sociopolitical risks for many of the people being tested, most people find out they have AIDS when diagnosed with an OI ("UN AIDS 2004 Report on the Global AIDS Epidemic 2004," 2004). (See Table 15.6.)

AIDS can be treated, but not cured. Those people who have access to HAART or other forms of anti-retrovirals can experience a strengthening

Table 15.6 HIV continuum through 2007

HIV+, HIV infection/disease (formerly referred to as ARC-AIDS Related Complex)	AIDS diagnosis (generally occurs 10.8 years after infection with the virus)
Some people develop flu-like symptoms within a few weeks of infection. Viral load is high and people are infectious. Symptoms begin on average 10.8 years after infection, with the range from several months to a few people who are infected, but not symptomatic. Some or all of the following may appear: • HIV+ antibody test confirmed by ELISA and Western Blot • T-cell count above 200 (normal range is 800 to 1,200) • Night sweats • Swollen lymph glands, without other pathology • Fatigue, malaise • Chills • Loss of appetite, nausea • > 10% loss of body weight without dieting or other known causes • Gynecologic problems such as recurrent uncontrollable yeast infections, Pelvic inflammatory Disease (PID), CIN (cervical cancer in situ) and oral or vaginal thrush* • Body cavity infections such as thrush, acute or chronic illness episodes, herpes virus infection such as CMV (cetamegolo virus)	HIV+ antibody test—ELISA confirmed by Western Blot, and T cell count at or below 200, and/or one or more opportunistic infections (OIs): • Kaposi's sarcoma (KS) decreasing in frequency in the United States • *Pneumocystis carinii* pneumonia (PCP), most common OI in the United States, recurrent viral or bacterial pneumonias • Tuberculosis (TB) increasing incidence in United States, a co-factor of infection in many nonindustrialized societies, particularly drug-resistant forms of TB • Invasive cervical cancer—common in HIV+ women. Added by CDC as of January 1, 1993. Since then AIDS stats for women in the United States increased. Those diagnosed with invasive cervical cancer now included. • AIDS dementia—physical, psychological, and cognitive deterioration. May resemble some symptoms of Alzheimer's Disease
Some people do not progress beyond this point, have chronic problems with these symptoms, or gradually become weakened and debilitated to the point of death. A few individuals go into remission.	Most people with AIDS in the United States die within 4 years of diagnosis if they do not receive HAART/ARVS. Longevity varies by age, gender, and ethnicity. People do not die of AIDS per se, but due to one of the OIs, general debilitation, or heart or kidney failure.

* In Sub-Saharan Africa, these constitute a wasting phenomenon referred to as "the slims."

of their immune system as their T-cell count increases, a reduction of their viral load (how many particles of HIV are detectable in their blood), and resistance to OIs. HAART/ARVs are expensive, costing between $12,000 and $14,000/year, have side effects, and must be taken consistently to be effective. The prevalence of AIDS diagnoses (but not HIV infection) and AIDS deaths have dramatically decreased with the advent of these drugs in industrialized societies and their availability to insured, generally middle-class people in the United States since 1996 ("Advancing HIV Prevention," 2003). Taking these drugs can produce dramatic improvements in people's health. However, the efficacy of the drugs can decrease after about two years for about half the people taking them, and their availability in the United States is based on political and economic factors ("Global Challenges: Brazil, Abbott Close to Deal to Lower Price," 2006; Institute of Medicine, 2001). These include budget cuts to states that are epicenters of HIV/AIDS, the stigma of HIV/AIDS that makes it a lower priority for funding than other "lifestyle diseases" such as some heart disease or many lung cancers, and the overall poorer quality of health and health care for most of the **People Living With HIV/AIDS (PLWH/A)** currently in the United States. Most of these people are poor and ethnic, African American or *Latino* ("Fact Sheet: The HIV/AIDS Epidemic in the U.S.—2005," 2005).

In those nonindustrialized societies in sub-Saharan Africa, the Caribbean, and Southeast Asia that are heavily impacted with HIV/AIDS, people's access to prevention, testing, and treatment is determined by politics and economics. Poverty, stigma, lack of societal infrastructures relative to land, water, and access to resources that either do not exist or are only available for the elite in the society, and international trade agreements that concern the kinds, availability and cost of ARVs mean that the incidence, prevalence, and death rates from AIDS are high (Desclaux et al., 2003; Jooma, 2006).

AIDS is the end point of HIV infection. People do not die of AIDS per se, but usually from one or more of the OIs that are ecologically related, and a function of other diseases in the population and people's overall state of health. One way to forestall an AIDS diagnosis and possibly serve as a prevention mechanism is HIV testing.

HIV TESTING

As an intervention effort, **HIV testing** can be either a prevention tool or the basis for an initial diagnosis of HIV infection and AIDS. For people who test negative, education and support about prevention can result in fewer people becoming infected. For people who test positive, education and support can occur to prevent transmission to others and to keep themselves from being reinfected with another strain of the virus. HIV positive pregnant women who know their HIV status can take anti-retrovirals during their second and third trimesters as well as during labor and birth to reduce the chance of transmitting the virus to their fetus. After birth, they can reduce transmitting HIV to their infants if they can bottle feed instead of breastfeed. Bottle feeding, however, requires affordable formula, clean bottles, clean water, and a lack of stigmatization for not breastfeeding ("Bush's Global AIDS Plan," 2004; "UN AIDS Report on the Global AIDS Epidemic," 2004; "Woman and AIDS: Confronting the Crisis," 2004).

There has been an HIV antibody test available since 1985 (Shilts, 1987; Thomas, 2001). There are a number of types of HIV tests currently available in the United States; the general test is based on a blood test to detect antibodies to the virus. Other more recent tests include a buccal membrane test, which examines cheek cells for the virus (the virus is present in all cells in the body), finger-prick tests that comprise the at-home HIV tests, and the OraQuick, a blood or buccal membrane test that can give initial test results within twenty minutes ("Advancing HIV Prevention," 2003; Bartlett, 2002). It is hoped that the OraQuick test will be used on "hard to reach populations" such as the homeless and isolated individuals living in rural areas of the United States, as well as in nonindustrialized societies where one visit to a health center is acceptable, but repeat visits may raise suspicion that the tester has AIDS.

The standard HIV test procedure, which is *not* an AIDS test, involves clearing the **window period** (i.e., the time from infection to when antibodies are detectable). As stated in the previous section, this entails a minimum of thirty days, and generally occurs within three to six months. HIV testing can either be **anonymous** or **confidential**. Anonymous testing means that no identifying information such as name or address is given; anonymous testers receive a code number during the pretest counseling and receive their results by showing their code number. Because there is no way to trace who had a test, people are protected from the economic, political, and/or social discrimination they could be subjected to if their test results were known. However, if anonymous testers test HIV positive, unless they agree to convert to confidential status, there is no way to provide counseling, medical care, or other forms of support to them.

Confidential testing leaves a paper trail. People who choose confidential testing provide their names and addresses during pretest counseling. Since 2000, in most states in the United States, if people test positive with a confidential HIV test, their names, location, ethnicity, age, gender, and mode of transmission are then reported to their state department of health and then on to the CDC. This procedure is known as **mandatory name reporting**. The CDC requires this of states in order to provide a database of prevalence. States that do not comply with this requirement risk losing CDC funding. With this database, the CDC determines the need for interventions from prevention to testing to treatment and allocation of resources.

Some states, such as New York, also have **mandatory contact tracing** if people receive HIV positive confidential test results (but not for HIV positive anonymous test results). (Remember, there is no way to trace and track someone from an anonymous HIV test.) Mandatory contact tracing means that the sexual and needle-sharing partners of the HIV positive person are contacted through one of several interventions. The infected person can notify his/her partners (and this is seen as a "good faith" behavior); someone who works for the Department of Health can notify the partners, or the HIV positive person can bring in his/her sex and needle-sharing partners to the HIV test counselor and discuss the situation with the counselor. This is done as a preventive strategy and is a relatively common public health measure. The concern with mandatory contact tracing in regards to HIV testing rests with the stigma and discrimination that still exist for people who are HIV positive. The advantage of confidential HIV testing is that if people test positive, they can (ideally) be referred for medical, psychological, and financial care and help. Since anonymous and confidential testing have different consequences for people who test positive, it is important for them to make carefully reasoned decisions about which form of testing they want.

Both tests require adequate pre- and post-test counseling, informed consent, and a signed consent form. (Anonymous testers sign with their code number.) Pretest counseling determines: the window period and the potential risk factor; type of unprotected sex or risky needle usage; an assessment of how a person would respond to HIV positive test results; whether the person understands the difference between anonymous and confidential testing, and whether the person is being tested voluntarily.[3] After all questions are answered and the consent form is signed, the person has his/her blood drawn. Standard HIV test results generally are available within two weeks. (See Figure 15.7.)

HIV test results can be positive or negative, or indeterminate. The first test performed on the blood sample is an **ELISA** test. ELISA stands for enzyme-linked immunosorbent assay and is a general screening for HIV. If the blood tests HIV negative on the ELISA, the blood is considered HIV negative. If, however, the blood tests positive, a second ELISA is performed to ensure there was no lab error. If that second sample is negative, the blood is considered HIV negative. However, if the second sample tests positive, a third test, the **Western Blot Test** must be performed to provide an accurate result. ELISAs can detect other viral activity that is not HIV and are designed to test for more false positives than false negatives. The Western Blot Test is more discriminating, selecting for HIV specifically. If the blood tests negative on the Western Blot, it is considered HIV negative. If it tests positive on the Western Blot, it is considered HIV positive and the person will be told that she or he is HIV positive. If the blood tests HIV indeterminate, it means that a clear result is not available. Often, this means that the

Figure 15.7 Why should I worry about HIV?

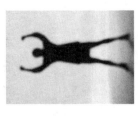

WHY SHOULD I WORRY ABOUT HIV?

Knowing Your Status

Could Save Your Life!

I HATE TESTS! WHAT DOES THIS ONE INVOLVE?

An HIV test looks for antibodies to the virus in your body. Your health care provider has different tests that he/she uses. Here are the more common ones:

Blood test – This test is just like any other blood test you take at the doctors. A small amount of blood is taken to the lab and the antibody test is run.

Oral test – No needles are involved. The health provider takes a cotton swab and runs it against your cheek to collect the cells necessary for the test.

Rapid test – This test involves a needle prick or an oral swab. Initial test results come back within 20 minutes.

Home based test – If you do not feel anonymous enough, you may purchase a home testing kit. With this, you prick your finger, draw blood, and send the kit to the lab which runs the test and gives you the results over the phone. It takes about a week for these results to come back. The Food and Drug Administration has approved an HIV home testing kit and it can be obtained through their website (www.fda.gov).

Most HIV tests done at public health care centers are free, but there will be a charge at your family physician or by using the HIV home testing kit. Also cost is dependent on the type of test you want to take.

WHERE CAN I GO FOR THE TEST?

The tests are given at most doctors' offices, hospitals, family planning clinics, county health departments, drug treatment facilities, and even some university health care centers. Call your local health department for the testing center nearest you.

SHOULD I RELY ON THE FIRST TEST RESULTS?

If your first test results were negative, but you think you have been exposed, you may be in what experts call the "window period." The window period is a time when you have been exposed to HIV, but do not have sufficient number of antibodies to be detected. The window period can be as early as 3 weeks after exposure to 6 months.

HOW DO I ENCOURAGE MY PARTNER TO BE TESTED?

It is always a good idea for you and your partner to be tested so you both know your status. By both being tested, you are not only protecting yourself but your partner also.

1. Have an open discussion early in your relationship about the need for testing. This ensures that both of you are aware of the possible risks of infection
2. Have the discussion away from your friends and relatives in a quiet location.
3. Plan what you will say. Make it simple, but direct.
4. Go together. There is strength in companionship.

To learn more about HIV and other sexually transmitted disease, contact your local health department, your family physician, or call:

CDC NATIONAL STD AND AIDS HOTLINE
(800) 227-8922 OR (800) 344-7432 (24 HOURS A DAY)

CDC NATIONAL HIV TESTING RESOURCE
WWW.HIVTEST.ORG

AMERICAN SOCIAL HEALTH ORGANIZATION
222.ashastd.org/stdfaqs/index.html

*INFORMATION PROVIDED BY American Social Health Association.
Other sources include AVERT and The Body.

Figure 15.7 (Continued).

WHY SHOULD I WORRY: THE NEED FOR HIV TESTING*

HIV (Human Immunodeficiency Virus) can infect anyone, of any age, race, ethnicity, or sexual orientation. While people with the virus can look and feel healthy for years, they can still infect others, and HIV can damage their immune systems, even when they feel well. The only way to know if you have the virus is to take an HIV test. While the test will not protect you from HIV, the process of taking it can provide you with information and the motivation to make healthy choices.

WHAT IS HIV?

HIV is a retrovirus that leads to a depletion of immune cells and eventually a diagnosis of AIDS.

WHAT IS AIDS?

AIDS (Acquired Immune-deficiency Disease) is the latter stages of HIV infection characterized by a positive HIV antibody test, and/or low or absent T-cells, and one or more Opportunistic Infections. It can lead to death.

I CAN'T GET HIV OR AIDS! I'M NOT GAY!

HIV and AIDS is not a "gay" disease. While first considered a disease that was based in the homosexual community, it is now found in a number of communities, including college students. This is a disease caused by a virus and transmitted by specific sexual and needle sharing behaviors.

HAVE YOU EVER?*

had unprotected sex (anal, vaginal)?
_____ Yes _____ No
had unprotected sex (oral)?
_____ Yes _____ No
shared needles or works (for drugs, tattoos, body piercings, steroids, hormones)?
_____ Yes _____ No
had a Sexually Transmitted Infection (STI)?
_____ Yes _____ No

If your sexual partner can answer "yes" to any of the questions above, especially to *anal or vaginal sex*, then you should think about getting tested for HIV. Unprotected anal or vaginal sex puts you more at risk than oral sex. A test would be wise even if you answer "no" to all three questions.

WHY SHOULD I BE TESTED?

For many, HIV will not be a concern in your lifetime. For others, HIV will develop and you may not even know you have it, as it is not a visible condition.

* As a college student, the need for testing lies in not only your personal health, but that of any sexual partners you may have. Whether you realize it or not, people you have had unprotected anal or vaginal sex with could have exposed you to the risk of HIV. Getting tested in a relationship can help make decisions about safer sex and birth control.

* Another reason is that you may decide you want to have a child. By becoming pregnant without knowing your status, you are exposing yourself and your child to potentially dangerous health risks.

* If you have shared a needle with anyone, you run the risk of catching the HIV virus from the needle or equipment.

* To alert your health provider to special needs that may develop and to get you any necessary medication or additional treatments that may be needed.

WHAT IF SOMEONE FINDS OUT THAT I WAS TESTED?

Your HIV test results can be confidential or anonymous. In an anonymous HIV test, you are assigned a number which identifies your test. When you contact your health provider for your results, you would give him/her the identification number and s/he would then give you the results. No one will know unless you feel the need to inform others of your results in an anonymous test. In the confidential test, your name appears on the test results and the administering health provider gives you the results.

It is wise though to alert your sexual and needle using partner, and your doctors (including dentists) to your status so they are aware of your condition.

WHAT DOES A NEGATIVE RESULT MEAN?

A negative result means two things.
1. There is no sign that you have HIV at the time of the test.
   There is still a chance you could get the virus in a future.
2. You have HIV but the virus hasn't shown up yet. You may still develop the antibodies and infect others.

WHAT DOES A POSITIVE TEST RESULT MEAN?

A positive result means that you have the HIV antibodies in your system. You can pass the virus on to others. It does not mean you have AIDS but that the virus is there that causes the disease. You can become immuno-compromised and you should seek medical care for continued monitoring.

person is HIV positive, but has not passed the window period and should consider getting another test later (Bartlett, 2002 and 2006).

Post-test counseling is legally required in order to get test results. In New York and California post-test counseling and results must be conducted in person; they cannot be given over the phone or to a third party. Post-test counseling involves explaining the test results and discussing ways to remain HIV negative if that is the case, suggestions of how to proceed if results are HIV indeterminate, and options if the results are HIV positive. Getting an HIV test is serious; making the decision to get tested involves a careful consideration of not only risky behavior and adherence to HIV test guidelines, but an acceptance of and preparedness to receive HIV test results. (See Figures 15.8 and 15.9.)

Patricia Whelehan has provided HIV test counseling to students on her campus through Student Health since 1995. Students can get either a confidential or anonymous test; about half choose to test anonymously and half test confidentiality. The students she sees give one of three reasons why they are getting an HIV test:

- *To "know" and be sure of their status as part of general health knowledge and awareness.*
- *To determine what form of birth control and safer sex practices they will use as they decide to pursue a long-term, monogamous relationship.*
- *To learn their status because of risky sex or needle-using behavior in which they have engaged.*

There are a number of controversies and ethical debates in the United States and cross-culturally about HIV testing, and certain groups are more affected by these controversies than others. The controversies center on confidentiality concerns and voluntary versus mandatory testing. These concerns are most readily seen when looking at the situation of testing women in this culture and elsewhere.

Since 2003, the CDC has recommended **opt-out** HIV **testing** for pregnant women. Prior to 2003, it recommended **opt-in testing** for this group. Opt-out consent means that a test, in this case an HIV test, will be given to pregnant women unless they specifically decline it. Opt-in consent means that consent has to be obtained in advance with notification of an HIV test. It is important to state strongly that women do not want to be HIV infected and do not want to infect their fetuses and infants if at all possible. That is not the issue. Why, then, is opt-out testing such a concern? Discriminatory

Figure 15.8 Being HIV negative.

HIV AND OTHER SEXUALLY TRANSMITTED DISEASES

While you have tested negative for HIV, you need to be aware that if you are exposed to other sexually transmitted diseases, you have a stronger chance of developing HIV in the future. Be aware that the sores or rashes caused by an STD leave you more vulnerable to HIV.

WHERE CAN I GET MORE INFORMATION?

To learn more about HIV and other sexually transmitted disease, contact your local health department, your family physician, or call:

CDC NATIONAL STD AND AIDS HOTLINE
(800) 227-8922 OR (800) 344-7432 (24 HOURS A DAY)

CDC NATIONAL HIV TESTING RESOURCE
WWW.HIVTEST.ORG

AMERICAN SOCIAL HEALTH ORGANIZATION
www.ashastd.org/stdfaqs/index.html

*INFORMATION PROVIDED BY American Social Health Association.

Information provided by the American Social Health Association (ASHA), the Centers for Disease Control and Prevention, AVERT.org, and The Body.

SO WHAT DO I DO NOW?

Now you need to take steps so you won't be faced with the possibility of becoming HIV infected. So, here are some suggestions:

* use a latex, lubricated, non-spermicidal condom during anal and vaginal sexual intercourse.
* use a dental dam during oral sex.
* talk with your partner about how to practice safer sex and needle-usage.
* be tested if risky sex or needle-usage happens.

WHAT ABOUT MY PARTNER?

Remember, in many instances people are unaware of their HIV status. You can't see the disease because the symptoms do not become obvious until you develop full-blown AIDS. The only way to be sure that your partner is HIV negative is for him or her to be tested too!

The main thing you need to do is to talk to your partner about the HIV risk you both face. It may be difficult but this type of openness will save you from the fear in the future. Be proactive and find out! Be honest yourself. After all, it is ultimately your health and life!

Figure 15.8 (Continued).

WHAT IS HIV?

HIV stands for human immuno-deficiency virus. Your immune system keeps you healthy through CD4 cells that fight diseases to which you are exposed. If you are HIV Positive, your immune system will start to fail as the CD4 cells are destroyed. You will no longer be able to fight infections or diseases.

HIV can lead to AIDS (Acquired Immune Deficiency Syndrome). When you are HIV+, your CD4 cells fall to a count of less than 200, and/or you have an Opportunistic Infection, you have developed full-blown AIDS. There are ways of keeping yourself healthy and slowing down the onset of AIDS, but you need to know your status and for you this you need to be tested!

WHY SHOULD I WORRY: THE NEED FOR HIV TESTING*

HIV (Human Immunodeficiency Virus) can infect anyone, of any age, race, ethnicity, or sexual orientation. While people with the virus can look and feel healthy for years, they can still infect others, and HIV can damage their immune systems, even when they feel well. The only way to know if you have the virus is to take an HIV test. While the test will not protect you from HIV, the process of taking it can provide you with information to make safer choices.

WHY SHOULD I BE TESTED? I'M CAREFUL!

Have you . . .

... had unprotected anal or vaginal sex (no condom)?

... shared a needle, syringe, or other drug paraphernalia?

... had sex with more than one partner?

... had sex with a partner who has had sex with others or shared drug paraphernalia?

... had a sexually transmitted disease?

... had a blood transfusion before 1985.

... been raped or didn't know your partner?

... questioned your possible exposure?

Are you . . .

... a man or woman who has had unprotected anal sex with another man?

... a health care provider who may have been exposed to someone else's blood through a needlestick injury or other medical procedure.

If you can answer yes to any of these questions, then it could be good to be tested to be sure that you haven't been exposed to HIV.

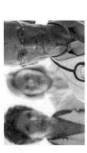

WHERE CAN I GO FOR THE TEST?

The tests are given at most doctors' offices, hospitals, family planning clinics, county health departments, drug treatment facilities, and even some university health care centers. Call your local health department for the testing center nearest you.

I HATE TESTS! WHAT DOES THIS ONE INVOLVE?

An HIV test looks for antibodies to the virus in your body. Your health care provider will help you determine which test suits your needs. Common ones include:

Blood test – You have these at the doctors during physicals. They will take a sample of your blood and run an antibody test on it.

Oral test – This one involves no needles. A cotton swab is wiped inside your cheek to collect cells for the test.

Rapid test – The test involves a needle prick or oral swab. Initial test results come back within 20 minutes.

Home based test – For anonymity, a home testing kit may be purchased. You prick your own finger and draw the blood. The test is sent to a lab and results come to you by calling a telephone number in about a week.

AND THE TEST RESULTS ARE . . . NEGATIVE!

Congratulations on being HIV negative. These results are only accurate as of the day the test was taken. You should consult with your health provider to see about whether you should be retested if you engage in risky sex or needle usage after your test was done. There is usually a three month "window" period where the virus can be dormant. They will probably recommend that you be retested after the three month window period.

Figure 15.9 Being HIV positive.

SO WHAT DO I DO NOW?

Make an appointment with a health care provider to discuss treatment options. If your personal care provider feels the need, s/he will send you to an HIV specialist. The important thing is to get help in evaluating your options and choosing the right treatment for you.

Ask your doctor about:
* HIV treatments and their risks;
* other diseases you may be vulnerable to;
* lifestyle modifications for healthy living;
* how to prevent yourself from infecting others.

WHAT IS THE TREATMENT AND HOW LONG WILL IT LAST?

Your health care providers will have guidelines which will help them determine the best course for your treatment. They may want to wait until your CD4 cells reach a certain level. In most instances when you are put on a drug regimen, it will be HAART (Highly Active Antiretroviral Therapy), i.e., the cocktail. You and your health care provider should consider the following:
* the results from various tests to measure how much virus there is in your body and the number of T-cells you have;
* the number of pills and when they are to be taken;
* the HIV drugs' interaction with your other medications;
* whether you are pregnant.

HIV treatment will continue for the rest of your life.

WHAT ELSE DO I DO?

It is important to contact sex and needle-sharing partners and encourage them to be tested. Either you can do that yourself, or a counselor can contact them and protect your identity.

Also learn ways to keep yourself healthy.
* Consistently practice safer sex!
* Take all medications you are given!
* Reduce the risk of exposure to other STDs!
* Eat healthy and exercise!
* Get enough sleep!
* Practice stress reduction techniques and think about joining a support group for people with HIV.

WHERE CAN I GET MORE INFORMATION?

To learn more about HIV and other sexually transmitted disease, contact your local health department, your family physician, or call:

CDC NATIONAL STD AND AIDS HOTLINE
(800) 227-8922 OR (800) 344-7432 (24 HOURS A DAY)

CDC NATIONAL HIV TESTING RESOURCE
WWW.HIVTEST.ORG

AMERICAN SOCIAL HEALTH ORGANIZATION
www.ashastd.org/stdfaqs/index.html

*INFORMATION PROVIDED BY American Social Health Association.

Information provided by the American Social Health Association (ASHA), the Centers for Disease Control and Prevention, AVERT.org, and The Body.

Figure 15.9 (Continued).

WHAT IS HIV?

HIV stands for human immuno-deficiency virus. Your immune system keeps you healthy through CD4 cells that fight diseases to which you are exposed. If you are *HIV- positive*, your immune system will start to fail as the CD4 cells are destroyed. You will no longer be able to fight infections or diseases.

HIV can lead to AIDS (Acquired Immune Deficiency Syndrome). When you are HIV+ and your CD4 cells fall to a count of less than 200 *and/or you have an Opportunistic Infection (OI)*, you have developed full-blow AIDS. There are ways of keeping yourself healthy and slowing down the onset of AIDS, but you need to know your status and for you this you need to be tested!

WHY SHOULD I WORRY: THE NEED FOR HIV TESTING*

HIV (Human Immunodeficiency Virus) can infect anyone, of any age, race, ethnicity, or sexual orientation. While people with the virus can look and feel healthy for years, they can still infect others, and HIV can damage their immune systems, even when they feel well. The only way to know if you have the virus is to take an HIV test. While the test will not protect you from HIV, the process of taking it can provide you with information to make safer choices.

WHY SHOULD I BE TESTED? I'M CAREFUL!

Have you . . .

... had unprotected anal or vaginal sex (no condom)?
... shared a needle, syringe, or other drug paraphernalia?
... had sex with more than one partner?
... had sex with a partner who has had sex with others or shared drug paraphernalia?
... had a sexually transmitted disease?
... had a blood transfusion before 1985.
... been raped or didn't know your partner?
... questioned your possible exposure?

Are you . . .

... a man or woman who has had unprotected anal sex with another man?
... a health care provider who may have been exposed to someone else's blood through a needlestick injury or other medical procedure.

If you can answer yes to any of these questions, then it could be good to be tested to be sure that you haven't been exposed to HIV.

WHERE CAN I GO FOR THE TEST?

The tests are given at most doctors' offices, hospitals, family planning clinics, county health departments, drug treatment facilities, and even some university health care centers. Call your local health department for the testing center nearest you.

I HATE TESTS! WHAT DOES THIS ONE INVOLVE?

An HIV test looks for antibodies to the virus in your body. Your health care provider will help you determine which test suits your needs. Common ones include:

Blood test – You have these at the doctors during physicals. They will take a sample of your blood and run an antibody test on it.

Oral test – This one involves no needles. A cotton swab is wiped inside your cheek to collect cells for the test.

Rapid test – The test involves a needle prick or oral swab. Initial test results come back within 20 minutes.

Home based test – For anonymity, a home testing kit may be purchased. You prick your own finger and draw the blood. The test is sent to a lab and results come to you by calling a telephone number in about a week.

AND THE TEST RESULTS ARE . . . .
POSITIVE!

Don't panic! The results do not mean you have AIDS. Your body has the virus that can lead to AIDS. There are treatment options available.

health, social, and legal practices have occurred against those women who test HIV positive. In addition:

- Most HIV positive women in this culture are poor and either African American or Latina. They fear that they may be blamed for being HIV infected, encouraged to have an abortion, or be given poor prenatal care if they refuse to be tested.
- The primary concern is for the fetus in this situation, not the woman's health or well-being. This is referred to as a **pronatalist** stand. With opt-out procedures, if a woman tests negative, she may not be told her results; there may not be a discussion about how she can maintain her HIV negative status, or about her risks for becoming infected in the future.
- HIV testing is supposed to be conducted voluntarily, without pressure, and with appropriate pre- and post-test counseling. There is concern that with opt-out testing, the HIV test will be folded in with other prenatal blood work and that the pre- and post-test counseling will not be done or will be done incorrectly. There needs to be a separate informed consent for an HIV test.
- It places the burden of responsibility on the pregnant woman, not her sex partner. If she tests negative and there is a lack of adequate counseling, her actual risk for infection is difficult to assess. Since a woman could be infected at any point in her pregnancy and there is a window period before antibodies are detected, when and how often are women tested? Who conducts the test and the counseling? How is confidentiality maintained, particularly with reporting claims to insurance companies which can charge higher premiums or drop clients who have HIV/AIDS?
- Recommendations made by the American Medical Association and the American College of Obstetricians and Gynecologists are that women whose sero-status is unknown before she goes into labor be given the OraQuick rapid test when she enters the hospital or birthing center to give birth. This hardly provides an atmosphere of confidentiality or informed consent ("Advancing HIV Prevention," 2003; Banks, 1996; Bennett, 1999).

These concerns are not isolated to pregnant women in the United States. HIV testing in nonindustrialized societies raises a number of ethical concerns for women and for men. One concern is confidentiality. United States culture values privacy, the individual, and confidentiality (i.e., who knows and controls the release of data).

Cross-culturally, confidentiality may rest with the kin group, or minimally the women's male relatives—their husbands and fathers or their brothers—and not with the women themselves. Women are the focus of testing because they are the ones who receive prenatal care, have most of the health care visits, and receive most of the contraceptive services in many societies. Research has found that women are willing to have an HIV test if they can be assured they will receive the results in a private area, and decide when, how and to whom results are given (Blankenship, 1999; Coodvadia, 2000; "Women's Experience with HIV Serodisclosure in Africa," 2003). In some sub-Saharan African groups married couples get tested, but it is usually the husband who makes the decision about getting tested for both himself and his wife. Decisions about having an HIV test are serious given that women bear the brunt of HIV care giving, are usually the ones blamed if they, their partners, or their children are infected, and are the ones who are most often more severely stigmatized and ostracized for being HIV positive.

When considering HIV testing outside industrialized countries, there are a number of factors to consider:

• What does confidentiality mean in this society? Who controls and has access to information? Who will receive HIV test results and who else will know?
• Where and how are HIV tests administered? If travel is required to a health clinic, is the clinic accessible and affordable? OraQuick or other rapid HIV tests could be helpful in situations where people may only be able to travel to a clinic once to have a test and need to get tested and their results in the same visit.
• What are the psychological, social, financial, and political costs of having an HIV test? If there are no treatments for those who test positive, if people lose their employment, are ostracized from family and community, beaten, killed, or have their children taken from them, is testing appropriate in these situations with the resources available?
• What kinds of community involvement, participation, and education are there about HIV/AIDS in general, safer sex, and testing? Are local leaders involved (de la Gorgendière, 2005; Mariano, 2005)?

HIV testing can be a valuable intervention effort. It can serve as a prevention strategy or as part of getting people into early treatment if they are HIV positive. However, for it to be effective and safe, the structure and values of the communities in which people live need to be considered first, resources need to be available if people test positive, and safeguards need to be in place to protect people.

SEX AND HIV/AIDS

From the information in previous chapters, we know that sexuality is a highly complex phenomenon that is socially constructed and expressed through individual behavior. This knowledge is crucial to understanding the sexual transmission of HIV. Worldwide, 80 percent of HIV is transmitted sexually. Most of that transmission is through unprotected heterosexual behavior ("Fact Sheet: The Global HIV/AIDS Epidemic—2005 Update," 2005; "UN AIDS Report on the Global AIDS Epidemic – 2004," 2004). However, not all sexual behaviors are equally risky. The sexual risk for contracting HIV exists along a **sexual risk continuum**. In descending order of risk, those sexual behaviors that can transmit HIV most easily are unprotected receptive anal intercourse and unprotected receptive vaginal intercourse, and insertive anal and vaginal sex. Unprotected oral sex can transmit HIV, but it is much less risky (Bartlett, 2006). (Less risky *does not mean no risk*.) This continuum can be confusing as it lists behaviors from the riskiest to the least risky, so that **safer sex** is actually riskier than **safe sex**.

Safer sex

Risky sex entails any sexual behavior where people may come into contact with infected blood, semen, or vaginal fluids. To make these behaviors safer (i.e., to reduce the risk of transmitting HIV), safer sex can be practiced. Safer sex includes the proper, consistent use of lubricated, nonspermicidal latex male and female condoms (but not together) for anal and vaginal intercourse; vaginal dams for oral sex on a female and rimming (oral-anal contact); and finger cots and gloves for anal and vaginal fisting (fingers or hands inserted into the rectum or vagina). Practicing safer sex whenever you engage in any of these behaviors will significantly reduce the risk of contracting or transmitting HIV and most other STIs.[4] This is supported by research documenting the lack of HIV transmission among heterosexual **sero-discordant couples** (one person is HIV positive, the other HIV negative) who consistently practice safer sex and by the sharp decline in HIV/AIDS in the later 1980s among men who have sex with men (MSM) ("HIV and AIDS—United States 1981–2001," 2001; Padian, Shiboski and Jewell, 1991). (See Figure 15.10.)

Safe sex

In contrast to safer sex, safe sex means that there is no chance of transmitting or contracting HIV between partners. There is a variety of safe sex behaviors that people can engage in. **Abstinence**, defined as not having sexual contact with another person, will prevent HIV, other STIs, and pregnancy. Abstinence is a viable choice and may be suitable for a number of people at various stages in their life or circumstances.

Masturbation, fantasy, use of erotica or pornography, and any sexual behavior that does not potentially expose people to others' semen, vaginal fluid, or blood are safe sex behaviors. If people agree to a mutually monogamous relationship and test negative for HIV following window period guidelines, they can engage in whatever sexual behaviors they want

AIDS HOTLINE
1-800-541-AIDS
Toll-free and confidential

For information, referral and support call your regional hotline and ask for the HIV counselor. This is a confidential service.

REGIONAL AIDS HOTLINES

Rochester area	585-423-8081
Syracuse area	315-475-2437
Buffalo area	716-847-4520
Suffolk County	800-462-6786
Northeastern NY	800-962-5065
Bronx	212-447-8200
Harlem	212-369-8378

Condoms, water-based lubricants, latex gloves, vaginal dams and fingercots are in this kit and can be purchased in drug stores and some grocery stores.

Condoms and safer sex kits can be obtained free from Student Health Services on campuses.

For more information visit:
www2.potsdam.edu/clubs/paeg/Index.html

SAFER
SEX...

It's fun,
It's easy,
and
it may save
your life.

Don't Die
of
Embarrassment

Don't be too embarrassed to talk about condoms. Condoms can help prevent AIDS. Insist on the use of a condom if you have sex with a person whose health and drug history cannot be guaranteed to be HIV negative.

The materials in this kit are provided to help you maintain your health. The pamphlet is graphic and explicit in explaining ways of reducing your risk of contracting or transmitting HIV. These materials are not meant to shock anyone. The goal is to encourage responsible behavior and decision-making relative to your sexuality and to keep you and your partner(s) safe and infection free.

Figure 15.10 Safer sex brochure—"Don't Listen to Rumors about AIDS: Get the Facts".

Safer sex involves reducing your risk of contracting the HIV virus as well as enhancing your sexuality. Once one decides to have genital sexual contact with a partner, one moves from safe sex to the safer-to-risky continuum. Only you can decide what level of risk and trust are acceptable to your health. If a person lies to you about their HIV status, your life is at risk. Remember, PEOPLE LIE TO GET LAID, unfortunately. You are solely responsible for your decisions.

If you decide to become sexually active with a partner in which semen, blood or vaginal fluids could be exchanged, your behavior enters the realm of risk-taking. Safer sex is for anyone-male or female- who is sexually active with males and/or females. Safer sex practices that reduce the risk of infection are encouraged. It is recommended to use as many different forms of protection as possible: lubricated condoms for penetrative anal and vaginal intercourse; unlubricated, nonspermicidal condoms for fellatio (oral sex on a male) and vaginal dams for cunnilingus (oral sex on a female) or any oral-perineal or perianal activity.

Cuts, scratches, scrapes on fingers, hands, lips, any broken skin surface may be a potential entry for infection. Therefore, finger cots and gloves are recommended in this situation. A glove can be turned into a vaginal/perineal dam by leaving the thumb intact for a finger cot and cutting open the rest of the glove. An unused unlubricated condom can also be used as a similar barrier by cutting it lengthwise.

In this pamphlet is a list of behaviors that are considered high-risk and absolutely unsafe. Most of the behaviors on the list you will probably recognize, but there are some that may be unfamiliar to you. By listing these, the editors of this pamphlet are neither condoning nor condemning them. But to be safe, you must have as much information as possible. It is important to remember that you must choose behaviors that are right for you, and you need not participate in any activity that you are uncomfortable with. Consider your own values carefully so you know how you feel before you find yourself in a situation that requires a decision about sex.

ABSTINENCE IS A PERFECTLY ACCEPTABLE, HEALTHY CHOICE TO MAKE

Figure 15.10 (Continued).

The following information from:
1989 San Francisco AIDS Foundation, San Francisco
Our Bodies, Ourselves, Boston Women's Health Collective

CONDOM USAGE

Befriend your condom. You might want to buy some cheap ones and play with them. Get used to how they look, feel, smell and taste and how to open the package before you want to use them. They are awkward at first, but so is riding a bike, learning how to use tampons, shaving, anything that is new and different.

How to put the condom on

Do retract (pull back) the foreskin if you are uncircumcised (uncut) before putting on the condom.

Do remove rolled condom from package.

Do roll condom down penis as soon as it is hard, before you start to make love (foreplay).

Do leave ¼ - ½ inch extra space at the tip of the condom to catch the ejaculate if the condom has no nipple.

Don't unroll the condom before using it. Instead carefully roll the condom down the erect penis toward the base.

Don't wait to put the condom on until you are ready to enter your partner- it may be too late. Drops of semen- precum- may drip from the uncovered penis before ejaculation, and may infect or impregnate your partner.

Don't twist or bite or prick the condom with a pin- this will damage it and allow fluid to leak out, possibly infecting your partner.

Don't use two condoms at once or the male and female condom at the same time. Double bagging can create friction that can cause tears in the condoms.

After ejaculating, hold the condom at the base of the penis and withdraw immediately. Unroll the condom from the penis and discard it.

A NEW CONDOM MUST BE USED EACH TIME ANAL, ORAL OR GENITAL CONTACT OCCURS. A USED CONDOM OFFERS NO PROTECTION FROM AIDS OR OTHER SEXUALLY TRANSMITTED DISEASES.

Pictures courtesy of http://www.metro-mate.org.uk/sah put-condoms.phtml

Figure 15.10 (Continued).

VAGINAL DAM USE

Vaginal dams are difficult to find here. They come in a variety of sizes, thickness, colors, tastes, and smells. Generally, they take more accommodation than do condoms. Vaginal dams are needed when performing oral sex on a woman, oral-perineal stimulation, and any kind of oral-anal contact. Vaginal dams are placed over the genitals, perineum, or anal area before and during any oral contact. Stimulation is through the vaginal dam. Because vaginal dams are difficult to obtain, we are including a vaginal dam in the Safer Sex Kit.

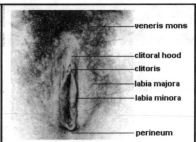

Picture courtesy of http://www.luckymojo. com/faqs/ altsex/vulva.html

A NEW VAGINAL DAM MUST BE USED EACH TIME ANAL OR GENITAL CONTACT OCCURS.

HIGH RISK, UNSAFE SEX PRACTICES

• Multiple genital partners without using condoms or vaginal dams
• A single genital sex partner without using condoms or vaginal dams unless monogamy and HIV-status can be guaranteed now and in the future
• Oral genital (male or female) contact, anal penetration, vaginal penetration, without condoms and vaginal dams; or sharing sex toys
• Rimming (oral-anal contact) without a vaginal dam
• Fisting (finger-hand vaginal-anal penetration)
• Oral-perineal contact without a vaginal dam

(the perineum is the soft skin between the genitals and the anus)
• S/M (sado-masochism), B/D (bondage-discipline), tying up, spanking, M/S (master-slave) behavior that breaks the skin or deeply bruises it
• Sharing sex toys such as vibrators or dildoes with a partner
• Water sports (playing with urine) on broken skin and, possibly, internal water sports

Engaging in any or all of the behaviors in this group even once jeopardizes your own and your partner's health.

CO-FACTORS: NON-SEXUAL BEHAVIORS WHICH MAY INCREASE YOUR RISK

Using alcohol and other drugs may impair your judgment or lower your inhibitions and may cause you to behave unsafely

SAFER SEX GUIDELINES

Always use lubricated condoms for anal and vaginal sex
Don't get semen or vaginal fluids in your mouth. Use a condom or vaginal dam for any oral sex. Unlubricated condoms may be used, if preferred, for oral sex.
Don't have mouth to rectum contact without using a latex barrier.

Figure 15.10 (Continued).

with each other and neither transmit or contract HIV. However, a mutually monogamous relationship and a negative HIV test do not mean they are protected from passing on other STIs, impregnating or becoming pregnant if their behavior is heterosexual. If all people need to do to prevent HIV is either be abstinent, monogamous, or practice safer sex, what is the problem? The answer is as simple and as complicated as culture.

Since people's behavior occurs and is expressed through their cultures' norms, values, and structures, the disparate socioeconomic and political situations that exist within and between societies all influence the risk for HIV. These disparities have been created and maintained through colonialism, global markets, and culture change. Socially, we have seen throughout this book that sexual behavior is influenced by the forms of descent and residence that exist, the degree of patricentricity within a society, and the role extended kin groups play in people's lives. Euro-American colonial practices changed sexual mores and norms, generally lowered women's status in societies and made them dependent on males, and created economic and political practices that benefitted colonial powers to the detriment of indigenous groups (Blackwood and Wieringa, 1999a; Farr, 2005; Kempadoo and Doezema, 1998). In the grand mix of culture contact and change with vast discrepancies in access to goods and services, sexual behavior has become the major conduit for HIV worldwide. Specific examples from subcultures in the United States and from nonindustrialized societies can highlight what has happened.

The demographic profile of PLWH/A in the United States has changed dramatically over the past three decades of the epidemic. Currently, HIV/AIDS increasingly occurs among poor, ethnic, and female populations. African Americans, *Latinos*, and Native Americans comprise a disproportionate percentage of HIV/AIDS in the United States. Socially, preventive programs that worked for MSM are not appropriate for other groups, as they do not reflect these groups' norms and values. Economically and politically, African Americans, *Latinos*, and Native Americans have experienced and continue to experience discrimination relative to employment, health services, and self-determination. Fewer preventive and treatment resources have been directed towards people in these communities than for middle-class people. Within these groups, homophobia and double standards of sexual behavior can increase the risk for sexual transmission (Brooks, Rotheram-Borus, and Bing, 2003; Burhansstipanov et al., 1997; Clay, 2002; Diaz, 1998, 2000; Vernon, 2001).

"Down low" behavior, as it is referred to among African Americans, involves those MSM who also have sex with females. These men, who do not identify themselves as gay or bisexual, generally hide their behavior from female partners and family, fearing ostracism and criticism by others in their community, and may not practice safer sex with their female or male partners (Clay, 2002). A strong value among African American women is to "stand by your man," particularly in the face of real and perceived discrimination from the larger society. That value may be stronger than insisting on safer sex.

Latinos in the United States come from Latin America, the Caribbean, and Spain. Even with the variety of *Latino* subcultures in the United States, there are common values such as *la familia* and *machismo* which support multiple sex partners for men and monogamy for women, and *respeto*, or respect for family and cultural traditions. Within this system of values, same-sex behavior between men or between women must occur discreetly. Marriage is expected and women are supposed to defer to their husbands. A woman who insists on using condoms raises questions not only about her behavior, but the integrity of her male partner as well. Men are reluctant to use condoms with their wives, the mother of their children. To do so would be a symbolic and behavioral gesture of disrespect (Carrier, 2001; Diaz, 1998, 2000).

Native American populations are equally diverse, but they share some of the poorest living conditions and health care of any group in the United States (Burhansstipanov et al., 1997). Many Native Americans struggle to maintain traditions they value, and adapt to larger cultural values as well. This can be shown with multiple genders such as Two Spirits discussed in Chapter 13. Two spirit or other third- or fourth-gendered people were common among many Native groups prior to European contact (Blackwood and Wieringa, 1999a; Rosoce, 1998). European contact stigmatized, penalized, and tried to eradicate these phenomena. Currently, there is a resurgence of third and fourth genders among some groups, but these people receive varying degrees of acceptance. Lack of acceptance can and does lead to risky sexual behavior due to denial and shame (Bockting and Kirk, 2001).

The highest rates of AIDS globally occur in sub-Saharan Africa. Women are at particular risk of HIV in sub-Saharan Africa. This is due to sexual, economic, and political factors (Barnett and Whiteside, 2002). Traditional farming, inheritance, and decision-making practices have been lost due to not only colonialism, but also global political and economic decisions over the past twenty years. These decisions disrupted local agricultural practices, encouraged or forced men to migrate to find work, particularly to places such as the diamond mines in South Africa, and disrupted social relations. To combat poverty and the malnutrition and diseases that accompany these changes, prostitution has flourished. Safer sex is generally not an option; for women and girls in polygynous relationships, it is not their decision to make.

In addition, regardless of where we discuss sexual practices and risks, the effects of fundamentalist conservative beliefs that either mandate or support abstinence-only sexual behavior contribute to the risk for HIV. This is clearly shown in President George W. Bush's **PEPFAR** program. PEPFAR stands for President's Emergency Plan for AIDS Relief. This plan provides resources for fifteen countries seriously impacted by HIV. However, the plan also mandates that 30 percent of prevention efforts go towards abstinence-only programs, and that condoms are only for prostitutes, gay men, injection-drug users, and those who "can't be abstinent." This policy increases the stigma associated with condoms and ignores the reality of people's sexual behavior. President Bush implemented an international gag rule that withdraws funding from any agency or group that provides abortion information as part of its services. In 2004, he also withdrew funds from any international group that provided services to prostitutes. These kinds of policies increase, rather than decrease, the risk for HIV transmission ("Bush's Global AIDS Plan," 2004; "Sex Workers," 2005; "SIECUS PEPFAR Country Profiles," 2005; UNIFEM, 2005).

DRUGS, NEEDLES, AND HIV

President Bush's PEPFAR plan also affects the risk of contracting HIV from infected needles and drug usage. His plan withdraws money from international groups that have needle-exchange programs to reduce HIV transmission; within the United States, these programs are highly controversial and operate under various legal restrictions. **Injection drug usage (IDU)** and other forms of "dirty needle" usage are the second most common form of HIV transmission in the United States, India, parts of Southeast Asia, and Brazil in the early stages of its epidemic (Brimlow and Ross, 1998; Francis and Cargill, 2001; "HIV and AIDS—United States, 1981–2001," 2001; Marins et al., 2000; Singer, 2005). It is the most common form of HIV transmission in Eastern Europe, China and Vietnam (Choi et al., 2000; Somlai et al., 2002; Stimson et al., 1998; Stimson and Choopanya, 1998; Thuy et al., 2000). PEPFAR's policies negatively impact harm reduction efforts in these areas (Buchanan et al., 2004; "Bush's Global AIDS Plan," 2004; DesJarlais et al., 1998; "Sex Workers," 2005; "SIECUS PEPFAR Country Profiles," 2005; Singer, 2005; UNIFEM, 2005; "Woman and AIDS: Confronting the Crisis," 2004).

HIV infection from "dirty needles" can originate from injection drug usage, body adornment such as piercing and tattooing, or needle usage during medical procedures. It is estimated that about 5 percent of HIV infection in nonindustrialized societies occurs through HIV-infected blood transfusions or needle usage during medical procedures (SciDev Net, 2003). In the United States, the blood supply is considered "statistically safe," and the American Red Cross has a number of (discriminatory) practices involved in donating and screening blood that increase the safety of the blood supply (American Red Cross, 2004). Donating blood is safe; new equipment is used for each blood draw in the United States. Medically, the use of universal precautions in which latex and other barriers are used to keep blood from skin and mucosal surface contact, and in which needles and other instruments are disposed of in hazardous waste containers significantly decreases the risk of HIV transmission between health care workers and patients. For example, between 1981 and 2002, 105 health care workers have been HIV infected from medical procedures ("Surveillance of Health Care Personnel with HIV/AIDS," 2002). Over the past several years, **postexposure pro-phylaxis (PEP)** has been available to health care workers who experience needle-stick injuries or other blood exposure in health care settings. PEP is a fourteen to thirty-day regimen of ARVs to prevent HIV. To date, only six of the health care workers who have received PEP have become HIV positive as a result of occupational exposure (Bartlett, 2006: 78; "Surveillance of Health Care Personnel with HIV/AIDS," 2002). (See Figure 15.11.)

Figure 15.11 Safer needle/razor brochure—"Don't Die of Ignorance: Get the Facts".

___Sharing Needles___

The HIV virus can be transmitted by infected blood and blood products, semen, vaginal fluids, breast milk, and *in utero*—from mother to fetus. While unprotected penetrative sex—penile, vaginal or anal—is the most common means of transmitting HIV, sharing needles which carry HIV-infected blood is the second most common means of transmitting HIV, the virus which causes AIDS.

Sharing needles of any kind in any behavior is risky.

Sharing needles includes:

Medical and Body Decoration Uses	Drug Usage
◆ insulin injections for diabetics	◆ injection steroid use
◆ tattooing	◆ heroin (smack)
◆ scarification	◆ cocaine
◆ ear and body piercing	◆ speed

Sharing needles in any of these activities is risky and potentially enables you to become HIV infected.

Don't use needles.
If you do, don't share.
If you share, clean your needles.

San Francisco AIDS Foundation

___Cleaning Needles___

Safer needle cleaning involves using a ten-to-one water-to-bleach solution. Needles need to remain in the solution for at least 30 seconds. In hollow needles— the ones used for injection—the needle, syringe, and cotton need to hold the bleach solution for 30 seconds. This procedure must be repeated at least four times.

| Ten parts water One part bleach | + | Needle Syringe Cotton | + | 30 second soak time | + | Repeat four times | = **SAFE** |

Figure 15.11 (Continued).

Most of the needle-based transmission of HIV occurs from drug usage. We are a drug-using society in the United States. We use drugs recreationally— alcohol, "party drugs" such as Ecstasy and crystal (crystal meth), and marijuana—and medically in over-the-counter and prescription drugs. Our drug usage is both legal and illegal. We use drugs that we do not classify as drugs, such as the caffeine found in chocolate, coffee, and tea. Our culture structures drugs as "good" or "bad" drugs based on how they are used and obtained. For example, prescription drugs are "good drugs"; recreational drugs may be accepted for some people as alcohol is for adults in this society, or unacceptable and illegal for others such as heroin, cocaine, or "speed" (Singer, 2005; Weil, 2004). Much of the risk for HIV from drug usage is based on either the effect on judgment that a drug can have (e.g., getting drunk or high and making decisions in that frame of mind); the effect on the immune system or organs that the drug can have (e.g., smoking crack can cause mouth sores or breaks in the skin); or from directly injecting drugs with needles or syringes that may contain HIV-infected blood (e.g., heroin injection, speedball injections of heroin and cocaine) (DesJarlais et al., 1998; Singer, 2005).

The reasons that people use drugs and risk HIV from drug usage are varied. We evolved with the neurobiology for our brains and bodies to be receptive to chemical substances. Drugs make people feel good, reduce anxiety and pain, alleviate fear, and can be an escape from the often desperate reality of some people's existence (DesJarlais et al., 1998; Singer, 2005; Singer et al., 2000). When people become addicted to drugs, their response to addiction is largely based on the socioeconomic circumstances of the addict. Drug rehabilitation programs can be very successful; they also are most available to middle-class, insured Anglos (Anderson, 2001; Francis and Cargill, 2001; Singer, 2005). These people more often have their addiction diagnosed as an illness; poorer people, those without insurance, the homeless, and poor African Americans and *Latinos* who are addicted more often have their addiction diagnosed as a crime (Francis and Cargill, 2001; Singer, 2005).

Needle exchange programs (NEPs) in the United States and other industrialized countries have been successful in reducing the rates of HIV transmission for IDUs. They are also very controversial in the United States, receiving varying degrees of support and acceptance. For example, NEPs are legal in New York City and San Francisco, but repeatedly are not accepted in parts of New Jersey (The Body Pro, 2007).

Patricia Whelehan worked in a needle-exchange program in San Francisco in the late 1980s to 1990. Twice a week at a designated area in one of the poor neighborhoods in San Francisco, the Tenderloin, she, her husband, and several others would collect used syringes in a hazardous waste container and provide clean needles. The people who exchanged needles represented a cross-section of the city. There were homeless people, wealthy women in furs who drove up in chauffeured limousines, middle-class people, and the rainbow of ethnic and sexual diversity found in the city.

Research indicates that people will change their needle-using behavior more readily than their sexual behavior (Friedman et al., 1999; McKeganey et al., 1998). Therefore, interventions designed to reduce HIV transmission from needle/drug usage increase their effectiveness if they also address people's sexual behavior.

Cross-culturally, the highest rates of HIV transmission from drug/needle usage occur in those parts of the world undergoing rapid economic, political, and social change, and experiencing direct effects of globalization (see Chapter 16). The linkages between drugs and needles and risk for HIV are complex. Medical and injection drug usage for a variety of drugs is traditional in many Southeast Asian cultures (Stimson and Choopanya, 1998). In South Vietnam in particular, IDU is the major mode of transmission for HIV. Injuries incurred during the Vietnam War increased drug usage as a treatment for pain and disability (Stimson and Choopanya, 1998). The use of injection drugs increased after the Vietnam War, due to the easy availability of heroin from Myanmar, and the burgeoning tourist industry (Thuy et al. 2000).

South Vietnam is also undergoing rapid economic, political, and social change. The tourist industry provides significant economic resources. Tourists bring in their ideas about sex and drugs and know that drugs are relatively easy to obtain in Vietnam. Drug usage becomes part of social networks, garnering individual economic gain, and facilitating personal relationships (McKeganey et al., 1998; Stimson and Choopanya, 1998). In other parts of Southeast Asia such as Thailand and Myanmar, HIV infection attributable to IDU is rising (Stimson and Choopanya, 1998). These areas are major tourist attractions.

The relative availability of sex and drugs, low prices for drugs, social networks that foster drug usage, and the tourists' desire for the exotic encourage the desire and acceptability of drug usage in these areas (DesJarlais et al., 1998; Stimson and Choopanya, 1998). In the earlier stages of the epidemic, drug-and needle-sharing occurred. Needle sharing fostered rapid transmission of HIV within these drug-using social networks (DesJarlais et al., 1998).

In Latin America, Brazil is one country where IDU is the second major means of contracting HIV (Andrade et al., 2001; Marins et al, 2000). Twenty-one percent of Brazil's AIDS cases are attributable to IDU (Andrade et al., 2001). As in the United States and parts of sub-Saharan Africa, Brazil's HIV epidemic began within the middle- and upper-middle classes, eventually moving downward to include the poor and disenfranchised (Andrade et al., 2001). Recreational IDU and unprotected sex with multiple partners were initial modes of HIV transmission (Andrade et al., 2001; Marins et al., 2000).

Since the dissolution of the USSR, Eastern Europe represents "the fastest [growing] incidence rate of HIV in the world" (Somlai et al., 2002: 295). Having undergone rapid economic, social, political, and sexual changes in the past decade, rates of HIV and other STIs are increasing exponentially, particularly among females (Somlai et al., 2002). While unprotected sexual behavior is the primary route of transmission, IDU is a secondary causal factor. NEP programs are relatively new, with about 50–60 percent of IDUs no longer sharing needles (Somlai et al., 2002).

There are a number of factors that affect the success of reducing needle/drug transmission of HIV. Successful programs outside the United States incorporate these components:

- They develop programs at a grass-roots level.
- They use community and nongovernmental groups that take advantage of human and local resources to implement programs.
- They work with local law enforcement agencies to establish safe zones for needle exchange in areas where needle exchange is illegal.
- They use peer educators and people from the community in education and outreach efforts.
- They establish programs that meet the linguistic, sexual, and economic needs of the target group.
- They incorporate safer sex messages into harm-reduction models.
- They use harm-reduction messages that are less judgmental, more realistic, developed locally, and are less authoritarian.

WOMEN AND HIV/AIDS

Throughout this chapter, we have referred to women and their risk for HIV. Women's experience with HIV is unique in many ways. First, they are more at risk for infection in penetrative sex since they are generally the receivers. Second, women who have sex with other women (WSW) are invisible in this epidemic (Kwakwa and Ghobrial, 2003). There are few programs specifically designed to address their needs and concerns; the CDC does not have a risk exposure category for WSW. This omission can feed denial about risk and also does not reflect the number of infected WSW (Chapkis, 1997; Goldstein, 1997; Gomez, 1995; Herek and Greene, 1995). Third, women face the risk of transmitting HIV to their fetuses and infants during pregnancy, childbirth, or nursing.

Mother to child transmission (MTCT) in industrialized societies, specifically the United States, has decreased significantly since 1994. Since 1994, ARVs have been administered to HIV positive pregnant women from the second trimester through the birth of their children and to the children immediately after birth. In addition, most HIV positive women in industrialized societies can safely bottle feed their babies to prevent transmission through breast milk. Currently in the United States, MTCT is "statistically insignificant" ("Pregnancy and Childbirth," 2005).

This reduction in MTCT, however, is not replicated in much of the nonindustrialized world where only 10 percent of the people know their HIV status; prenatal care and access to ARVs by women are irregular at best, and breastfeeding may be the only or best way to insure an infant survives (Harder, 2005). Where nevirapine, an anti-retroviral, is available to pregnant women, it greatly reduces perinatal transmission, although there is the possibility of the mother developing resistance to it ("Fact Sheet: The Global HIV/AIDS Epidemic 2005 Update," 2005; "Fact Sheet: The HIV/AIDS Epidemic in the United States 2005 Update," 2005; Gender-AIDS eForum, 2004/2005).

As a group, women are poorer than men and have worse overall health than do men. In addition, double standards of sexual behavior are applied more often and more negatively to women than to men in most of the world. All of these factors combine to increase their risk for HIV and the way the virus affects them once infected. The cultural construction of sexuality generally holds women responsible for "morality," and allows them a narrower range of sexual behavior before they are ostracized and stigmatized for it. In societies where patrilineal or bilateral, patricentered kin groups make decisions for them, women have little "choice" or "negotiating power" about when, with whom or how they have sex, let alone whether or not to practice safer sex. In addition, early marriage of girls, the belief that having sex with a virgin will either prevent or cure diseases, including HIV/AIDS, widow inheritance, and sexual practices that leave the vagina dry or irritated can all increase the risk for infection.

Larger political and economic policies that disenfranchise women make them more vulnerable to infection. Wars, migration, interpersonal violence and partner abuse, loss of farmable land, colonial rule that ended women's political and economy autonomy and gave it to their male kin, all increased women's dependency on men and therefore their risk for infection. Much female prostitution in nonindustrialized societies involves **survival sex**. Survival sex is the exchange of sexual behaviors for money, food, shelter, and protection for the woman and her family. It may be the only or best way for a woman to provide for herself and her family (see Chapter 16).

Once infected, women tend to receive less care, experience more discrimination for their HIV status, and die sooner than do HIV positive men. Again, poverty, stigma, double standards of sexual behavior (women are blamed for having HIV, having contracted it through "immoral" behavior, and for passing it on to their partners and babies) interact, contributing to women's shorter life spans with HIV/AIDS. In areas where ARVs are available, men and children may receive them before women ("SIECUS PEPFAR Country Profiles," 2005). Women have a different experience with HIV/AIDS than do others (Desgrees de Lou, 1999).

POLITICAL AND ECONOMIC DIMENSIONS OF HIV/AIDS

Political and economic structures and decisions are inextricably tied to the risk for HIV infection and intervention efforts to prevent infection and treat HIV/AIDS. Political decisions in the United States and internationally impact safer sex interventions, access to HIV testing, treatment, and stigma. As with other aspects of the epidemic, the political-economic situations differ greatly between industrialized and nonindustrialized societies.

The politics and economics of AIDS in the United States

Although there are fewer cases of AIDS and AIDS deaths in the United States since the advent of HAART in 1996, the HIV incidence rate has remained at approximately 40,000–42,000 new infections yearly since the 1990s ("Advancing HIV Prevention," 2003; "Fact Sheet: The HIV/AIDS Epidemic in the United States 2005 Update," 2005; "HIV and AIDS—United States 1981–2001," 2001). Prevention of infection is much cheaper than testing for and treating HIV disease and AIDS (Mayer and Pizer, 2000; Barnett and Whiteside, 2002). If we know this, then what is the problem with reducing the incidence rate in the United States? The answer is political-economic factors.

HIV/AIDS was first diagnosed in the United States in 1981 among young, middle-class, Anglo, gay men. This proved to be both a curse and a blessing. The CDC and governmental interventions were slow in responding to a sexually transmitted disease that affected a stigmatized group. President Reagan, at the time, didn't publicly mention AIDS until the death of Ryan White, a teenager who contracted HIV from a blood transfusion and who had been ostracized by his community for having the virus. Initially labeling AIDS as GRID put blinders on researchers and other people as to the modes of transmission, the individuals at risk, and the communities affected by the virus (Shilts, 1987; Thomas, 2001).

From an activist perspective, middle-class gay men and groups support-ive of them had the resources and political clout in some circles to push for research, development of an HIV antibody test, and treatments. A num-ber of people active in the AIDS epidemic believe that if HIV/AIDS had been initially found among poor, disenfranchised, ethnic, and/or female communities, progress made about the risks for infection, course of the dis-ease, and treatments would have been even further delayed (Shilts, 1987; Thomas, 2001). Since 1981, we have seen great strides made towards treat-ment, reduced levels of discrimination in some parts of the country towards people with HIV/AIDS, and greater awareness of HIV/AIDS nationally.

However, conservative federal administrations and Congress have also cut funding for **AIDS Drug Assistance Programs** (**ADAPs**) in a number of states, advocated for abstinence-only sex education, and periodically have asked for such policies as mandatory testing and quarantines for people with HIV/AIDS. As discussed, ethnic minorities and poor people are par-ticularly affected by these decisions ("Fact Sheet: The HIV/AIDS Epidemic in the United States—2005 Update," 2005). In 2003, the National Insti-tutes of Health warned researchers that their funding could be denied or cut if they submitted proposals with "homosexual," "anal sex," or "condoms" in them. That members of the social and biological scientific communities protested this warning does not mitigate the effects it had on research (Goode, 2003). However disturbing these policies may be in the United States, the political and economic situation is even more dire in nonindustrialized societies.

The politics and economics of AIDS cross-culturally

Only 12 to 15 percent of the people worldwide who need and could benefit from ARVs/HAART receive them (World Health Organization, 2004). Most of the people who receive them live in industrialized societies (World Health Organization, 2004). Seventy percent of HIV/AIDS occurs in sub-Saharan Africa alone, one of the least densely populated areas of the world. Sixty percent of the world's population lives in Asia and India, both projected areas of the next wave of HIV/AIDS (Kaiser Family Foundation, 2005a). Economics and politics again play a major role in incidence and prevalence rates in these areas and in risks for infection. Poverty accounts for overall poorer health, compromised immune systems without having HIV, malnutrition, and risky sexual behavior for many people worldwide. These factors comprise major co-factors for HIV infection (Basu et al., 2000). As discussed, women are particularly vulnerable, and their risk extends to the potential for transmitting HIV to their fetuses and infants.

Societal infrastructures that have been impacted by colonial rule, global markets, and the **brain drain** of indigenous health care practitioners, engineers, and scientists increase the seriousness of the situation. Brain drain is the movement of skilled people from their native lands to industrialized societies where pay, working and living conditions, and the opportunities for advancement are higher and better than in their home countries (GenderAIDS e-Forum, 2004/2005; "Global Challenges: Shortage of Health Workers," 2006). Deaths from HIV/AIDS and other diseases mean that there are fewer adults and more orphans who do not possess the skills to maintain their cultures. Inter- and intracultural conflict depletes populations, drains resources, and can increase risk as people are forced to move to other areas, and women are raped as part of the wars (GenderAIDS e-Forum, 2004/2005; Human Rights Watch, 2004; Schoepf, 2001).

Access to drugs and international relief for people with HIV/AIDS in these situations are also mired in politics and economics. Although Brazil, Thailand, and India produce their own ARVs and generic drugs for their own infected populations and for export to places in sub-Saharan Africa, the quantity and access to the drugs are insufficient to meet the needs. In addition, international trade and patent laws and international drug conglomerates such as **PhRMA** restrict the development and availability of drugs to affected populations. Recently, after months of negotiations, Brazil brokered a deal with Abbott Laboratories to sell one ARV at a reduced rate to its AIDS population ("Global Challenges: Brazil," 2005).

President George W. Bush's PEPFAR plan provides for ARVs to fifteen different countries heavily impacted by HIV/AIDS. However, there are stipulations about how many of these drugs can be generic drugs. The WHO and other groups have challenged this policy, and some changes in access are being made ("Bush's Global AIDS Plan," 2004; World Health Organization, 2004). The PEPFAR plan also incorporates conservative policies about condom use, services provided to sex workers, and substance use. Thirty percent of all prevention funding must go to abstinence-only programs. Service organizations that work with sex workers risk losing funding if they do not take an open stand against prostitution. Needle-exchange programs are not supported for substance users, despite their proven efficacy ("Sex Workers," 2005; "SIECUS PEPFAR Country Profiles," 2005; Singer, 2005).

Intragroup social, sexual, and inheritance practices can affect people's risks for contracting HIV. Widow inheritance and cleansings, economic dependence, and migration can all serve to increase the risk. Migration for work and economic survival often means prolonged separation from spouses and regular sex partners, entry into low paying employment in the destination country, and discrimination from various sectors of the destination country. The combination of these factors can result in risky sex or drug use behavior (Wolffers and Bevers, 1997; Wolffers and Josie, 1999). Political and economic conditions serve as co-factors for infection and impact the course of the disease among those infected.

The socio-psychological dimensions of HIV/AIDS

HIV/AIDS is a debilitating situation for the people infected, their loved ones and families, and the cultures affected. The socio-psychological dimensions of this epidemic include stigma, grief, and loss at the individual, group, and societal level. Stigma itself can be considered a co-factor in the epidemic. Stigma entails isolation, shame, fear, and the assumption of an identity totally centered on having HIV/AIDS. Stigma fuels reluctance to get tested, nondisclosure of one's status, ambivalence about practicing safer sex, and prejudice. Individuals, families, and groups in both industrialized and non-industrialized societies have experienced stigma and guilt by association from having HIV/AIDS as part of their lives and communities.

Loss is another aspect of the HIV/AIDS epidemic. The sense of loss is not only related to the sheer number of people who have died, but to the loss of entire kin groups and communities due to this disease. Worldwide, the number of AIDS orphans is about fifteen million children and increasing ("Fact Sheet: The Global HIV/AIDS Epidemic 2005 Update," 2005; World Health Organization, 2004). Since HIV/AIDS is largely a younger person's disease, communities lose people in the most productive years of their lives, and thus suffer economic hardship from the disappearance of a large section of the work force (Kruger and Richter, 2003). OIs can leave people disfigured, contributing to a visible loss of bodily integrity and a further source of stigma as people become thinner, marked with visible lesions or other physical signs of their illness.

Grief is a universal aspect of HIV/AIDS. There is the grief of loss of life, but also the grief that comes with death early in life. Families, caretakers, and health care workers who tend for people with HIV/AIDS share this grief. HIV/AIDS could be the worst epidemic in human history.

Responses to the HIV/AIDS epidemic need to be holistic, interdisciplinary, integrated, and humane. Political agendas, ethnocentrism, and lack of cultural awareness contribute to the continuation of this disease. Anthropology offers unique contributions to addressing the problem. Our discipline's appreciation of culture-specific factors, an emic perspective, and a history of bridging theory and academic discourse with reality-based and applied activities can serve to reduce risk and implement culturally-sensitive interventions.

SUMMARY

1   HIV/AIDS is a global health problem.
2   HIV is caused by a retrovirus which eventually destroys the immune system and results in death for almost everyone who does not receive treatment.
3   HIV testing can be both a preventive and first-line treatment option. Most people worldwide do not know their HIV status.
4   Globally, 80 percent of HIV is transmitted sexually, and primarily through unprotected heterosexual behavior. Women are more at risk for HIV than are men in any given act of unprotected penile-vaginal intercourse.
5   Safer sex that includes the correct use of lubricated, nonspermicidal condoms and other latex barriers can significantly reduce the risk of HIV and other STIs.
6   Injection drug use and "dirty" needles are the second most common means of transmitting HIV in the United States and cross-culturally.
7   Women have become the most at-risk group of people for HIV infection globally. The reasons for this are biological vulnerability, and social, political, and economic policies and practices that place women at risk.
8   Global and local economic and political factors increase the risk for HIV, including international pharmaceutical and trade practices that perpetuate global poverty and lack of access to ARVs. PEPFAR places restrictions on both preventive and treatment efforts to the people seriously in need of intervention.
9   The socio-psychological challenges associated with HIV/ AIDS include stigma, discrimination, and grief for those who are infected, their loved ones and the larger society.
10 The holistic, relativistic, and culture-specific approach of anthropology is a valuable perspective in responding to the HIV/AIDS epidemic.

Thought-provoking questions

1　Why do researchers and activists believe that HIV/AIDS could be the worst human health problem ever?

2　How do socio-economic, sexual, and political factors affect risk for infection, HIV testing decisions, and treatment?

SUGGESTED RESOURCES

Books

Shilts, Randy. 1987. *And the Band Played On: Politics, People, and the AIDS Epidemic*. New York: St. Martin's Press.

Vernon, Irene, S. 2001. *Killing Us Quietly*. Lincoln: University of Nebraska Press.

Videos/Movies

A Closer Walk
And the Band Played On
It's My Party
Philadelphia
Yesterday (HBO)

Web sites

CDC (http://www.cdc.gov/). Last accessed 8/7/06.

PAEG (http://www.potsdam.edu/content.php?contentID=E9CABAC 13BFD227A 43FF1BE205B2B184). Last accessed 11/09/07.

The Body (http://www.thebody.com/). Last accessed 8/7/06.

UNAIDS (http://www.unaids.org/en/default.asp). Last accessed 8/7/06.

WHO (http://www.who.int/en/). Last accessed 8/7/06.

16 Globalization and sexuality
The meaning and issues of "sex work"

CHAPTER OVERVIEW

1   Places globalization in a cultural-historical context.
2   Discusses the globalization of sexuality relative to social, political, and economic factors.
3   Discusses globalization and sex work/prostitution.
4   Examines the relationship between globalization, sexuality, and HIV.

GLOBALIZATION

Since the late twentieth century, we have heard a lot about "**globalization**" and the "global village." What do these terms mean and how do they apply to sexuality? This chapter addresses the globalization of sexuality.

Globalization is a new term for an old phenomenon. It is actually a continuum of centuries of intergroup contact, trade, and change that has occurred among indigenous groups worldwide as well as between European societies and traditional peoples since the fifteenth century, including those in the Americas (Dalby, 2000). For example, precolonial Southeast Asians such as the Macassans from Sulawesi traded with aboriginal people of Northern Australia when fishing for trepang that they then traded to China (Reid, 1999).

Currently, globalization includes bidirectional contact between industrialized and nonindustrialized societies. Since the late twentieth century, however, wealthy industrial nations such as the United States, Great Britain, and Japan have significantly impacted the kinds of social, political, and economic changes that have occurred. These changes reflect capitalism's influence on the economies of nonindustrialized societies. The effect industrialized countries have on other countries and groups cannot be overemphasized.

These effects are global, can be irreversible, and are a definite shift from previous culture contact and change. Although changing the econiche is part of human exploitation of resources, there are qualitative differences between how and what nonindustrialized societies and industrialized societies have done to and with the environment and one another. For example, the precontact Mayans overworked the land which resulted in soil depletion. These effects, however, were local and not global. Industrialized societies have irreversibly changed the econiche of rainforests around the world, and have transformed local economies into sources of production that primarily benefit industrialized societies, not their own (Robbins, 2005).

The changes from industrialization are extensive. They range from pollution that has led to global warming to the destruction of the rainforests in South America, to control over the production and distribution of drugs by pharmaceutical conglomerates such as PhRMA (an international drug cartel). Changes also include the consequences economic decisions made by the World Bank have had on small-scale farming. Anthropologists do not see globalization as a process that creates a uniform middle-class Euro-American value system worldwide, but instead see it as a phenomenon that engenders qualitative change. Although these changes primarily benefit those living in industrialized societies, they do not totally eliminate other societies' core cultural values. For example, a core value in Latino culture is *la familia*. *La familia* places the nuclear family and extended kin group at the center of daily life. This value can take on different manifestations depending on location and degree of assimilation, but it persists.

From the beginnings of the Industrial Revolution in the 1700s to the present, globalization has involved the colonization of the people in Southeast Asia, India, sub-Saharan Africa, and the Pacific. The subsequent independence of these groups from colonial rule during the twentieth century does not isolate them from current international trade and communication or the effects of capitalism on their local economies. The often irreversible changes resulting from colonialism and twentieth-century economic, political, and social policies extend to sexuality as well. Globalization and the global village refer to the interconnectedness and expanse of industry, travel, and sexuality that belie the existence of "purely" traditional behaviors and beliefs almost anywhere in the world. These concepts are embedded in culture contact and change, which form the heart of globalization (see Figure 16.1).

Since the late twentieth century, however, the rapidity and nature of culture contact and change have increased exponentially. This is largely due to the growth of technology such as computers and the Internet, airline travel with destinations around the world, the end of European colonial rule, and the worldwide impact of U.S. foreign policies. The general effects

Figure 16.1 Globalization in Japan. (*Source*: Courtesy of *Art Explosion 600,000 Images*, Nova Development Corporation.)

(See color plates, between pp. 168–169)

of globalization, aside from their impact on sexuality, appear in a number of ways:

- a dramatic increase in the variety of food, clothing, art, and cars available all over the world.
- outsourcing of work from the United States to nonindustrialized societies and **sweatshop** industries in places such as Thailand and India that provide much of our clothing and other products. Sweatshops exist in both industrialized and nonindustrialized societies and are characterized by low wages, unsafe working conditions, long workdays without breaks, and lack of benefits for the employees (check the labels of your clothes and other goods to see where they were made!).
- international student exchange programs.
- the development of generic drugs in Brazil, Thailand, and India, which are available both in these countries and in sub-Saharan Africa.
- the prominence and influence of the World Trade Organization (WTO), the World Bank, and PhRMA, which affect world markets.
- "brain drain," which occurs when industrialized countries hire professionals from nonindustrialized countries in fields such as medicine and engineering. These people leave their homelands, thereby reducing the number of available professionals in their fields there. The professionals who leave their home countries may receive lower salaries and benefit packages compared with the residents and citizens of the hiring

companies (GenderAIDS e-Forum, 2004/2005; "Global Challenges: Shortage of Health Workers," 2006).
- a worldwide increase in tourism, including sex tourism.

Kathryn Farr, a sociologist, has studied sex trafficking globally. Geographically, she categorizes trafficking according to "source countries," which supply people, primarily girls and women, and "destination countries," where the girls and women go to work. A partial list of source and destination countries includes:

Source countries: Thailand (both source and destination), Croatia, Ghana, Dominican Republic
Destination countries: Japan, United Arab Emirates, South Africa, Scandanavia, Canada, and the U.S. (Farr, 2005: 142–154).

These examples reflect both positive and negative effects of globalization and contribute to it.

Technological examples of globalization abound. They include Bollywood, the Indian film industry (e.g., Monsoon Wedding), worldwide, urban Internet cafes, the availability of MTV, and international broadcasting (e.g., BBC). Baywatch and Oprah are two of the most popular U.S. television programs cross-culturally. People often form their perceptions of women, men, sexuality, and relationships in the United States from watching these shows. How accurate a reflection of us is this? Conversely, how accurate and holistic a portrayal of other cultures and peoples do we get from our media?

GLOBALIZATION AND SEXUALITY: TRAFFICKING

Globalization also impacts sexuality. In some ways, the globalization of sexuality parallels our previous discussion. International travel, student exchange programs, commerce, the Internet, media, and migration for work including the tourist industry or for political asylum all have a sexual component to them. Although this can have positive results, such as greater tolerance for diversity and exchange of resources, it can be problematic as with trafficking.

Trafficking is not a recent phenomenon as evidenced by the British and U.S. "White Slave Trade" scare and laws governing prostitution during the nineteenth and twentieth centuries (Fisher, 1997, 2001; Human Rights

Watch, 2004; "World AIDS Day," 2002). Trafficking constitutes a broad range of activity, although currently most attention is paid to sex trafficking. Trafficking is largely illegal and refers to the movement of individuals and groups within and across borders for work that is generally exploitative and underpaid (Farr, 2005; "Sex Workers," 2005). Trafficking can involve both children and adults, most of whom are women; it may be coerced or voluntary; it can entail sex work as well as sweatshops in factories or indentured servitude in wealthy people's homes or businesses (Farr, 2005; Kempadoo and Doezema, 1998).[1]

In the twentieth and in the twenty-first centuries, trafficking has been closely related to changes in international and interethnic socio-political and economic conditions and the resulting migrations of groups. These changes are global phenomena. Examples of migration include "undocumented workers" who are brought across the United States-Mexico border to work in agricultural and industrial areas, the movement of people from Malaysia to other parts of Southeast Asia and Asia to find work, the "fall" of the Berlin Wall and the dissolution of the Union of Soviet Socialist Republics (USSR), and the changes in political states in sub-Saharan Africa (Wolffers and Bevers, 1997; Wolffers and Fernandez, 1999). Economic inequality often leads to migration. It did for many immigrants who came to the United States from Europe in the nineteenth and twentieth centuries, as well as for those who now migrate across Southeast Asia and in Africa in search of employment. In this chapter, we are going to focus on how trafficking and larger socio-political and economic changes have impacted sexuality, particularly sex work as it affects women and children.

In examining the globalization of sexuality, it is important to understand how culture contact and change have impacted indigenous sexuality over the past several hundred years. First, currently there are no cultures that are totally isolated from industrialized societal influence. What are presented as "traditional" practices are a function of culture contact and change, colonization and industrialization, and this is particularly true for sexual, marital, and familial behaviors. For example, homophobia and attitudes towards *hijras* in India and legal policies towards same-sex sexual behavior are a function of British Colonial law, not of "traditional" beliefs and practices (Kahn, 2001; Nanda, 2000; "A Perspective from India," 2004). Similar changes can also be seen in China and Africa (AFROL, 2003; Ruan and Bullough, 1992; Ruan and Tsai, 1988; see Chapter 14). In many sub-Saharan African societies prior to European contact, women had control over not only their sexuality, but over their profits from market exchange as well (Setel, 1999). They could refuse sex during menstruation and during the postpartum period; they kept what they earned in trading. British Colonial law changed that by transferring women's economic and sexual rights over to their husbands and male family members. Consequently, their overall loss of status and loss of sexual and economic autonomy have resulted in increased risks for HIV among a number of women in sub-Saharan Africa (Gender-AIDS eForum, 2004/2005; see Chapter 15). So, in discussing globalization and sexuality, we need to be aware of both traditional and culture change practices to fully understand its impact. To do so, we take a **deconstructionist** approach in this chapter. Deconstructionism is a way of collecting and analyzing data that challenges androcentric, industrialized, etic perspectives while focusing on emic interpretations.

There are highly visible aspects of the globalization of sexuality. They include multiethnic families and emic and etic controversies over both male and female circumcision globally. Health care and legal systems are developing ways to address female migrants who have been circumcised, as well as how to respond to families who have migrated to industrialized societies and want to have their daughters circumcised (Boston Women's Health Collective, 2005; Stewart and Spencer, 2002). The globalization of sexuality is evident in the number of Internet pornography sites and the prevalence of sex work around the world. A Google search of "international pornography" on July 12, 2005, resulted in a list of 1,730,000 sites!

Multiethnic families are evident in the U.S. Census. For the 2000 Census, the number of ethnic identity categories increased, but still was not inclusive of the variety of identifications that exist in the United States. The basic categories include American Indian or Alaska Native; Asian; black or African American; Native Hawaiian or Other Pacific Islander; and white. A new category, "some other race," was added in 2000. The two minimum categories are "Hispanic or Latino or not Hispanic or Latino" (U.S. Census, 2000).

SEX WORK

Sex work is a broad category that encompasses prostitution, pornography, phone sex operators, exotic dancers (strippers), massage parlor workers, and dominatrix workers. It includes those services offered over the Internet, those that occur in brothels, on the street, and through "call work" (Delacoste and Alexander, 1987; Whelehan, 2001a). Sex work involves males, females, and transgendered persons, but is primarily engaged in by females. In industrialized societies, sex work is usually an adult activity; in nonindustrialized societies, there are more children involved (Farr, 2005; Kempadoo and Doezema, 1998; see Chapters 9 and 10 for cultural definitions of childhood and adolescence). The legality and types of sex work found vary widely within and between societies. For example, pornography by and for adults is legal in the United States. Prostitution is illegal everywhere in the United States except for counties in Nevada with fewer than 100,000 people. Prostitution is legal in Canada while solicitation is not. The "red light" district of Amsterdam, Holland, is well-known worldwide. Regardless of the legal status of sex work, those who work in the industry are almost universally stigmatized for doing so, although their (male) clients experience less stigma (Whelehan, 2001a).

Prostitution is the most common and well-known form of sex work. In the United States, prostitution is the exchange of sex (left undefined) for money, goods, or services (goods and services are unspecified) (Whelehan, 2001a). Since prostitution is the most common form of sex work globally, and 80 percent of sex workers are female, this discussion will focus on female prostitution. "Prostitution" evokes strong legal, social (moral), and emotional responses from people. The structure and expression of prostitution are deeply embedded in larger cultural constructions of sexuality, particularly female sexuality. The cultural construction of prostitution rests on several assumptions about sexuality:

- Sex is defined as largely heterosexual, penetrative, relationship-centered and potentially reproductive.
- Sexuality is defined as male: men need and want sex; men are the sexual beings.
- Male sexuality is defined primarily as sex for pleasure and not primarily for reproduction.
- Female sexuality is defined primarily as reproductive and not as sex for pleasure.
- Females are less sexual and more monogamous than males.

When these assumptions are integrated with patrilineal and bilateral descent (paternity certainty), in rigidly socio-economically hierarchical societies, they lay a foundation for the existence of double standards of sexual behavior and female prostitution.

Despite the public noise about sexuality (i.e., its high visibility in the media, in advertising, in the availability of human sexuality classes), we still have a very deeply held view that sex is primarily for reproduction. At various times and in many cultures same-sex sexual behavior, masturbation, oral sex, and anal sex have all been seen as "immoral, deviant, perverse, unnatural, sinful, or dirty." These behaviors all have two things in common. They can produce intensely pleasurable sensations without resulting in reproduction. The brunt of censure for engaging in these behaviors is often harsher on women who are largely defined by their reproductive ability than on men who are largely defined by their sexual behavior.

Discussions of prostitution tend to be polarized. Sex workers' rights groups advocate for sex work as a form of employment, for clean, safe, and regulated work conditions, and are against child prostitution and coercion (Delacoste and Alexander, 1987; Ditmore, 2005; ICPR, 1985; Kempadoo and Doezema, 1998; Maticka-Tyndale, Lewis and Street, 2005; "Sex Workers," 2005). This position contrasts sharply with most other lay and professional depictions of prostitutes as victims and deviants and of the act of prostitution as furthering victimization and deviance (e.g., Farr, 2005). Although there are qualitative and significant differences between prostitution in industrialized and nonindustrialized societies, there are commonalities within sex work/prostitution. These similarities include:

- Sex work/prostitution is primarily a female endeavor.
- The common denominator is money: females can earn more money from sex work than in "straight" employment that is comparable relative to their age, education, and skills.
- Prostitution is *not* the "world's oldest profession." It developed from disparate economic, political, and social conditions that accompanied the development of agriculture and agrarian societies (Bullough and Bullough, 1987; Whelehan, 2001a).
- Prostitution did not exist indigenously in foraging and horticultural societies. Currently, prostitution is global.
- Most of the clients of sex workers are male.
- Prostitutes usually will practice safer sex if they are allowed to with their clients; as with other people, they tend not to practice safer sex with spouses and lovers.

The differences, however, between the expression of sex work in industrialized and nonindustrialized societies are vast.

SEX WORK IN INDUSTRIALIZED SOCIETIES

As a largely female-based endeavor, sex work, specifically prostitution, reflects the structure of female sexuality and heterosexuality in patrilineal and bilateral descent societies where known paternity is important to social and economic functioning and to reinforcing patriarchy. This applies to both industrialized and nonindustrialized societies. The expression of female sexuality and heterosexuality underlies this discussion of prostitution worldwide.

Double standards of sexual behavior are prevalent in many societies, including the United States (Crawford and Popp, 2003; Parker and Aggleton, 1997). Men's sexuality is seen as innate, the norm; heterosexuality is assumed and unquestioned. In contrast, women's sexuality is rewarded and accepted when it is potentially reproductive: in an adult, heterosexual, committed (marital or other recognized partnership), monogamous, and penetrative relationship (Parker et al., 1999; Parker, 2001; Parker and Aggleton, 1997; Whelehan, 2001a, 2001b). The further from this model the women's real or perceived sexual behavior is, the more they are subject to rejection, stigma, and ostracism. The Latino and Mediterranean concept of *machismo* illustrates this point. *Machismo* connotes virility and the willingness for men to protect their family's honor. The idealized counterpart for women is to be "good wives and mothers" and to be sexually faithful; women desire sex to have children and please their mates. In societies that have sexual double standards, overtly sexual women risk having their moral worth called into question as "whores, sluts, and bad girls." In gendered social hierarchies, double standards serve to reinforce the expected sexual behaviors for both men and women, and keep women "in their place."

The movie, The Stepford Wives, *is an example of keeping women "in their place." Men in an upper-middle-class suburb turn their wives into robots who are attractive, maintain an immaculate house and well-behaved children, and who cater to their husbands sexually and nonsexually.*

The persistence of double standards, especially for women, permeates the conceptualization of prostitution. Prostitution provides (male) sexual pleasure without either commitment or the intent of reproducing legally recognized offspring, and disrupts the social order for acceptable female sexuality. Since men are the sexual beings, female prostitutes are the "bad girls" who undermine the structure of the (monogamous) family, separating female sexuality from reproduction and a committed relationship (Thornhill and Palmer, 2000; Whelehan, 2001a).

Given this construction of female sexuality, the predominant view of sex work and prostitution in industrialized societies is that the women involved could not consciously choose this work. This view perpetuates the shame and stigma associated with prostitution. Stigmatizing sex work maintains the status quo around female sexuality and heterosexual relationships, perpetuating the "good girl/bad girl" dichotomy. It keeps women in line, and reinforces men as the people who need sex and women as the people who provide sex. This model obscures the economic and political factors underlining prostitution in industrialized societies and ignores the literature from sex workers' rights groups (Kempadoo and Doezema, 1998; Maticka-Tyndale, Lewis, and Street, 2005).

Sex work reflects the political and economic structures of the societies where it is found. From an activist perspective, sex work challenges the status quo. International sex workers' rights groups advocate for sex work to be recognized as a legitimate occupation (ICPR, 1985). These groups, which include COYOTE ("Call Off Your Old Tired Ethics") in the United States; "The Red Thread" in Holland; SPOC ("Sex Professionals of Canada") and CORP ("Canadian Organization for the Rights of Prostitutes") in Canada; and the Scarlet Alliance in Australia, want a number of legal, social, and political changes to occur. Their efforts are primarily directed toward:

- decriminalization of prostitution and other forms of sex work globally.
- clean, safe working environments.
- prosecution of people who abuse sex workers.
- health care for sex workers, including drug rehabilitation for women who exchange sex for drugs or drug money.
- consensual entry into, involvement in, and exit from sex work.
- protection of children from recruitment into child prostitution and child pornography (see also Ward and Edelstein, 2006; http://www.walnet.org/csis/groups/icpr_charter.html).

Sex workers' rights groups also work to change attitudes about prostitution. Even in Holland and Australia where prostitution is legal, workers are stigmatized. Decriminalizing prostitution, advocating for decent and safe working conditions, and educating the public about sex work are attempts to reduce the stigma associated with it, address beliefs supporting sexual double standards, and challenge the negativity which surrounds women's sexuality in general.

Patricia Whelehan published an ethnographic study about sex workers who live and work in urban areas of the United States. The biological men, women, and transgendered individuals in this book made several points about themselves and their work. First, most of them wanted sex work decriminalized to make it safer, to promote education about the industry, and to create a legal venue where abuses can be addressed. Second, most of them found the stigmatization to be one of the most difficult things for them to deal with as sex workers. The stigma associated with sex work is what Goffman (1963) refers to as a "master status." Sex work defines who and what you are and it also carries over to other areas of your life. For example, if you are a sex worker, then you *must* be dishonest, a bad neighbor, wife, and mother. Every aspect of your life is suspect and questioned. Third, sex workers want to be seen as people for whom their work is one part of their life, but which does not define them. This is similar to statements made by people in the lesbian-gay-bisexual-trans-gendered-Queer communities. Fourth, sex workers want their profession seen as a means of legitimate work. The majority do not see themselves as victims or deviants. Universally perpetuating the view that they are only adds to the problems they face and reinforces the sexual double standard (Kempadoo and Doezema, 1998; Whelehan, 2001a).

Finally, sex workers in industrialized societies recognize that they have a privileged position relative to many prostitutes in nonindustrialized societies. As such, a number of them work to improve the conditions existing elsewhere, including changing larger socioeconomic situations and advocating for an end to the exploitation of sex workers globally (Kempadoo and Doezema, 1998).

SEX WORK IN NONINDUSTRIALIZED SOCIETIES

Prostitution developed from agrarian societies in places such as ancient and medieval Europe, India, Southeast Asia, China, and Japan. Agrarian societies, which began 5,000 to 8,000 years ago, are characterized by hierarchical social, political, and economic systems that have unequal access to and distribution of resources. The rationale for inequality in these societies can either be secular, as in class systems, or religious, as in caste systems. In class-based societies for example, the ideology embraces upward mobility and "working hard is its own reward. Anyone can become president if they [sic] work hard enough." This is referred to as **achieved status.**

Caste-based societies justify unequal access to authority, power, and resources with such constructs as karma or beliefs in reincarnation. One's caste is set at birth and is referred to as **ascribed status.** In both caste- and class-based societies, gender is generally perceived as an ascribed status. (See Chapter 13 for a discussion on gender as a social construction.) Historically, the forms of prostitution found in these societies over the past 5,000 to 8,000 years reflect not only their socioeconomic/political structures, but their beliefs about the relationship between sexuality and religion as well. For example, prostitution has existed in Europe since the Middle Ages, and was often found on the outskirts of towns with prostitutes paying tithes to the church (Bullough and Bullough, 1987). Prostitution in ancient Rome gave us our modern word "fornication" (sex outside marriage), derived from the Latin word for the outside structure where street prostitutes solicited customers. In ancient Greece, the *hetarae's* clients were upper-class Greek men. In India, the *devi dasi* were sacred temple prostitutes (Bullough and Bullough, 1987). Prostitution was widespread in other Old World areas as well, such as China, Japan, and Thailand (Ruan, 1991).

In examining the impact of globalization on sex work in general and prostitution specifically, it can be helpful to explore the structure of prostitution in several societies prior to Euro-American contact. The preindustrial nation states of China, Japan, and Thailand all had indigenous forms of prostitution. In China and Japan, both highly stratified societies, men could have a variety of sexual relationships with women. They could have wives, mistresses, concubines, particularly for the emperors, and patronize prostitutes. In general, prostitutes had the lowest status of any of these women, but they were a recognized sexual contact (Ruan, 1991; Whelehan, 2001b).

China has a rich sexual history. The emperors in particular could have a variety of and a number of sexual relationships with both women and other men. Male and female prostitutes were both common and relatively accepted during the Han dynasty (206 BC – AD 24) (Ruan, 1991). Sex was seen as "a natural need" to be filled. Taoist beliefs emphasize balance and harmony through *yin* and *yang*, female and male essence, respectively. Prostitutes were believed to balance an oversupply of male *yang* with their *yin*, and thus maintain harmony (Ruan, 1991).

Japan also had *geishas*. Geishas were not prostitutes but a group of women who were selected prior to puberty and educated to be highly skilled entertainers. Only a few girls actually became geishas with even fewer becoming owners of geisha houses, a position of status and respect in Japanese society. Geishas were conversant and skilled in politics, current events, art, music, dance, the preparation of Japanese tea ceremonies (an elaborate and time-consuming ritual), and drama. Geishas' clients were wealthy Japanese businessmen who came to the houses to be pampered and entertained. If a geisha had a sexual relationship with a client, she arranged that independently with him; it was not an expected part of working as a geisha. These sexual relationships could significantly increase her wealth and social standing (Golden, 1997).

As a society, Thailand's views on sexuality are radically different from Euro-American perspectives. Thailand had an indigenous system of prostitution dating back to at least the fourteenth century BCE that provided a source of income to peasant females and served as the sexual initiation for Thai males (Nadeau, 2005; Seabrook, 2001). Prostitution was a part of Thailand's economic structure. As part of the socioeconomic structure of a number of agricultural societies, prostitution also served as a boundary marker for female sexual morality. Since almost all of the cultures where prostitution existed and exist are **patricentered** (focused on the male), and have either patrilineal or bilateral descent, perceived or known sex outside of a monogamous marital context exposed women to potential censure as "sluts, bad girls, fallen women, or whores."

Contact with Euro-Americans perpetuated indigenous systems of prostitution, altered the nature of a number of existing ones, and created the economic environment for it to appear in places where it had not existed previously (cf. Nadeau, 2005; White, 1990). Colonization changed precontact socio-economic and political structures, including concepts of sexuality and morality and sexual relationships (Kahn, 2001; "A Perspective from India," 2004; White, 1990). These changes particularly affected women in places such as India and sub-Saharan Africa where British colonial rule altered inheritance, property, and ownership practices, making women essentially the economic and legal property of their male kin (Kahn, 2001; White, 1990).

An example from *The Comforts of Home: Prostitution In Colonial Nairobi* will illustrate this (White, 1990). Prostitution existed in this area prior to WWII. Some women migrated to the cities before the war and established comfort houses that they owned and operated. Comfort houses more resembled what we consider an inn than a brothel. Men traveling along trade routes found lodging, food, and company at these comfort houses. Sex was negotiable with women setting the terms and prices. Often, income from the houses was sent back to the villages to support the kin group.

When Allied soldiers arrived in Africa, they brought their own ideas of sexuality and relationships. Over time, these views transformed the nature and control of the comfort houses. Women were judged by Allied standards of morality, and the men took over the houses, leaving the women to either work in them or become street prostitutes. The focus of the houses shifted away from comfort to sex (White, 1990).

Globalization since the mid-twentieth century has drastically altered prostitution. This is most noticeable in what the anthropologist Robbins (2005) refers to as "peripheral" societies. (See Table 16.1.) These societies include the former Soviet Bloc countries in Eastern Europe, Southeast Asia, and sub-Saharan Africa.

Prostitution in these areas is often radically different from that in industrialized societies for a number of reasons. First, sex work and prostitution in industrialized societies are often a matter of choice, of earning more in sex work than in other venues. In peripheral societies, it is often a function of economic survival for the worker and her family. Second, younger females—preadolescent and early adolescent—are often involved, a practice which is opposed by sex workers' rights groups. Third, the stigma associated with Euro-American sex work extends globally; the stigma attached to prostitution is almost a universal.

Fourth, prostitution frequently accompanies migration in these societies. Women often migrate within and across borders throughout Southeast Asia, Malaysia, to the Middle East, from Eastern to Western Europe and in sub-Saharan Africa only to learn that they can make more money in prostitution than they can in factories, as domestic workers, or in other venues (Farr, 2005; Wolffers and Bevers, 1997; Wolffers and Fernandez, 1999). They may also believe that they have work waiting for them in their new country and find out upon arriving that the work is coerced prostitution.

Fifth, culture contact and change do not occur in a smooth trajectory or systematically. What currently appear to be "traditional" sexual mores and behavior are a result of ongoing contact and change, which have been transformed into something new and different from either the pre- or early contact period. As such, sexual expectations between clients and prostitutes can differ radically (Kempadoo and Doezema, 1998). For example, Seabrook's *Travels in the Skin Trade* discusses the expectations that European men have of the female prostitutes they hire in Thailand. Thai women take

Table 16.1 Sexual tourism

Country	Sexual tourists live/depart	Sexual tourist destinations
Australia	Yes	
Bangladesh		Yes
Brazil		Yes
Cambodia		Yes
Canada	Yes	
China	Yes	
Costa Rica		Yes
Dominican Republic		Yes
France	Yes	
Germany	Yes	
Great Britain	Yes	
Hungary		Yes
India		Yes
Indonesia		Yes
Japan	Yes	
Kenya		Yes
Kuwait	Yes	
Morocco		Yes
Norway	Yes	
The Philippines		Yes
Saudi Arabia	Yes	
Singapore	Yes	
Sweden	Yes	
Thailand		Yes
United States	Yes	
Vietnam		Yes

Source: Adapted from Joni Seager, *The State of Women in the World Atlas, New Edition*. London: Penguin Books, 1997: 54; Martha Ward and Monica Edelstein, *A World Full of Women*, Pearson Education, 2006.

"very good care of men," resulting in their clients "falling in love" with them. Sometimes clients provide the women with apartments, food, clothing, jewelry, and cash. The clients become surprised and angry, however, when the women see the "relationship" as a business relationship. The women's loyalties lay with their families. Gifts, money, and other valuables can be used to support their families, not to fulfill the client's idea of a "relationship" (Seabrook, 2001).

In Eastern Europe, the dissolution of the USSR and the fall of the Berlin Wall dramatically affected prostitution in this area. Rapid economic and political changes accompanied these events; most notable has been the change of the infrastructure from a communist state where much of the requirements of daily living such as housing, transportation, food, and medical care are provided for, to a capitalist market. There has been much political and economic unrest as a consequence, including the development of an extensive sex trade. The sex trade in Eastern Europe involves both coercive and noncoercive trafficking within and across European borders as people grapple for economic survival (Human Rights Watch, 2004; "Sex Workers," 2005).

Sex work can comprise a specialized form of tourism, **sex tourism**, where people travel to specific areas of the world to engage in paid sex. Although sex tourism exists in various parts of the world, one of the most well-known sex tourism areas is in Southeast Asia, specifically Thailand.[2] Thai attitudes toward gender, sexual orientation, and age of consent are radically different from in many Euro-American societies. Coupled with a struggling economy and a strategic geographic location for R&R (rest and relaxation) for United States and East Asian military personnel stationed in places such as the Philippines, the area is ripe for a thriving sex industry. Thailand's sex trade provides incomes for individuals and their families as well as for the overall economy (Seabrook, 2001).

Sex junkets to Thailand by Euro-American and Japanese businessmen are popular. Rules about same-sex sex, sex with minors, and "kinky" sex (i.e., nonmissionary position p-v intercourse or oral sex) are looser than in people's home countries or are nonexistent. If these sex contacts were truly consensual, were under the control of the sex worker, did not involve minors, and were protected from HIV and other STIs, there might be less concern about people's behavior. However, since market conditions and disposable income tend to set the working conditions—place, worker age and gender, and behavior—there are considerable concerns raised about sexual and economic exploitation. Since the 1980s, sex workers' rights groups have consistently advocated for safe working conditions including enforced safer sex practices and sex worker input concerning venues and salaries (Farr, 2005; ICPR, 1985; "IXth International Conference on AIDS in Affiliation with the IVth STD World Congress," 1993; "XVth International AIDS Conference (IAC)," 2004).

A CRITICAL REVIEW OF TRAFFICKING

When discussing trafficking as an entity in the context of globalization, much of the focus centers on prostitution. In some ways, this is misguided. Trafficking involves a number of activities from drugs (think of the cocaine drug cartels in South America, Southeast Asia, and Afghanistan) to sweatshop labor and domestic servitude to coerced child prostitution. Equating trafficking with prostitution presents several problems.

One, it overlooks the other forms of trafficking, and by doing so does not address the exploitation and inherent problems in these other activities. Two, it strongly implies that all forms of sex work are coercive and all sex workers are victims and exploited. This is often, but not always, the situation as discussed in the section on sex work in industrialized societies. It also blurs the differences between sex work in industrialized and nonindustrialized societies, and diminishes the charter and work of sex workers' rights groups. Three, equating trafficking with prostitution presents sex work as the most horrific form of trafficking. That assertion may be arguable when there are six-year-old children in India and Pakistan who are blind from making finely woven "oriental" rugs in sweatshop factories. Four, focusing exclusively on sex work perpetuates the double standard, good girl/bad girl/madonna/whore dichotomies and sex as a commodity given by women to men. Last, focusing on prostitution and prostitutes as the totality of trafficking does not consider the larger socioeconomic and political conditions that create and perpetuate sex work as it exists in the twenty-first century. Consideration of these larger conditions is important when we look at sex work, globalization, and HIV.

SEX WORK, GLOBALIZATION, AND HIV

Globalization, sex work, and HIV are inextricably linked epidemiologically and perceptually. As discussed in Chapter 15, HIV is primarily sexually transmitted. Risk for contracting the virus is higher for the recipient than the inserter in penetrative sex, which means that men are more likely to transmit HIV to women than women are to transmit it to men. We've also discussed in Chapter 15 how women's vaginal mucosa is more vulnerable to the virus depending on her age, overall state of health, other diseases, and cultural practices that may tighten or dry the vagina. The common perception is that women are "the vectors of (HIV) transmission." However, epidemiological and statistical studies indicate that women are more often infected by their male partners than the men are by their female partners (Anderson, 2001; Bailey, 1999; Padian, Shiboski, and Jewell, 1991).

The stigma surrounding sex work extends to and couples with the stigma surrounding HIV and AIDS. Therefore, female sex workers incur a double stigma globally: they are sexually "promiscuous" and they transmit disease. What are the risks for HIV transmission to and by sex workers?

First, not all sex work, just as not all sexual behavior, is equally risky. Phone sex operators, exotic dancers, and dominatrixes are not at risk for HIV in those capacities since they do not exchange semen, blood, or vaginal fluids with their clients. Prostitution involving unprotected anal, vaginal, and to a lesser extent oral sex are primarily risky to the prostitute since it is her mucous membranes that are abraded. Making pornographic movies can be risky if the actors do not practice safer sex. There have been voluntary quarantines and controversy within the porn industry about risky sex and HIV-infected actors (The Body, 2004).

Generally, if sex workers have the option, they will practice safer sex with their clients for several reasons. One, it is a good business practice.

STIs and pregnancy are expensive. (Doctor's visits, medical bills, and anti-biotics require time away from work, a financial investment, and loss of income.) Two, practicing safer sex provides a physical and psychological barrier between the prostitute and client. Protected sex is business sex; unprotected sex is lover/partner/spouse sex. The primary obstacles to prac-ticing safer sex with clients are financial and political. Clients will often pay more for unprotected than safer sex. Particularly for women who engage in prostitution as a survival strategy, unprotected sex can mean the difference between paying for food, lodging, or health care for her and her family.

Sociopolitical obstacles involve the culturally loaded term "choice." Choice is a cultural construct highly valued in the United States. It is not a universal. Coerced sex work, brothel sex work in which the brothel own-ers, not the prostitutes, decide what the working conditions and safer sex practices are, and survival sex work rarely involve choice. When decisions about sexual behavior rest with the male kin group or employer, women have very little say over what happens to them sexually. Before imposing the idea of "choice" onto sexual decision making, the ability to choose must be present (Farr, 2005).

Sex work and HIV in the United States

According to Cohen (1999), Padian (1998), and the Centers for Disease Control and Prevention (CDC) ("Advancing HIV Prevention," 2003) about four one-hundredths of one percent (0.04 percent) of HIV in the United States is transmitted by female prostitutes to their male clients. This statistic seriously questions the perception of sex workers as diseased and challenges us to look at the relationship between sex work and HIV in the United States. Emically, sex workers do not see themselves as responsible for infect-ing their clients. Depending on the definition of sex work, this assertion is supported etically as well. Sex workers define women who exchange sex for drugs or drug money as substance users, not sex workers or prostitutes. Women who exchange sex for drugs or drug money do not necessarily define themselves as prostitutes (Whelehan, 2001a). Who does then? The answer: the CDC. The CDC does not distinguish between these emic categories, labeling women substance users who trade sex for drugs or drug money as "prostitutes" ("Advancing HIV Prevention," 2003a; Cohen, 1999; Padian, 1998).

Blurring emic and etic categories potentially skews statistics and rein-forces stereotypes about prostitutes, disease, and HIV transmission. It can also impact the effectiveness of intervention programs for these women if etic categories underlie the creation and implementation of prevention and outreach programs. Statistically in the United States, sex work, when sep-arated from drug use, is not a significant mode of transmission of HIV from prostitute to client. The situation in what Robbins calls "peripheral societies," however, can be very different (2005).

HIV and sex work in nonindustrialized societies

Where sex workers' rights organizations and HIV intervention groups have been able to establish, implement, and support safer sex practices between prostitutes and their clients, HIV risk is reduced and infection rates fall. This was clearly demonstrated in Thailand during the 1980s–1990s. A campaign by groups such as Empower, a sex workers' rights organization there, encouraged clients to use condoms and was highly successful in reducing incidence rates ("XVth International AIDS Conference (IAC)," 2004; Kempadoo and Doezema, 1998).

Unfortunately, for prostitutes in much of sub-Saharan Africa, India, China, and Malaysia, this kind of support generally does not exist. Most of the prostitution in these areas constitutes survival sex and many prostitutes are coerced into the work (Farr, 2005). Choices are not an option for many female sex workers who engage in survival sex in nonindustrialized societies. The results are that these women are then stigmatized and blamed for both the work they do and as being the source of HIV. Some are forced into sex work after receiving an HIV-positive diagnosis. Their families and communities reject them for being HIV positive and "bringing the disease into their homes." Prostitution becomes the survival option (Morrison and Fleishman, 2005). Additionally, these women may have other health issues such as malnutrition or malaria that act as co-factors for HIV infection. Control over safer sex does not exist for them, nor do other economic options (Farr, 2005). Literally removed from their communities by their families, they may be ostracized further for engaging in prostitution. Health care options may be less available to them than to others (Morrison and Fleishman, 2005).

International AIDS plans can contribute to this conundrum. President George W. Bush's PEPFAR plan calls for abstinence except for "high risk groups such as prostitutes and homosexual men," for whom condom use is acceptable. This both stigmatizes condom use and restricts the availability of condoms to the general population. The plan also overlooks the lack of choice women and girls have economically and sexually, both of which put them at risk for HIV. In 2004 and 2005, President George W. Bush placed a gag rule on international aid agencies that work with sex workers. These agencies must openly oppose prostitution or risk losing their funding. He imposed this rule on U.S.-based groups as well and was challenged on First Amendment rights ("Opinion: U.S. Requirement that AIDS Groups Sign Pledge Against Sex Work," 2005; "SIECUS PEPFAR Country Profiles," 2005). These moralistic policies have been criticized widely.

Recommendations to reduce risk

To reduce coerced sex work and trafficking in sex as well as the risk for HIV, larger societal, economic, political, and social beliefs and practices need to change as well as individual and group behavior. Societies need an infrastructure of sustainable agriculture or other food sources, roads, water, and health care. Economically, people need viable sources of income and access to resources. This involves educating girls and providing them with marketable skills, preventing infectious diseases such as malaria and tuberculosis that serve as co-factors for HIV infection, and having available a nutritious diet.

Politically, inter- and intragroup warfare needs to be addressed so that the infrastructure of the society can be maintained and daily life can occur free from displacement and death. Laws need to change so that economic decision making/autonomy is returned to women, not left to the state and kin group. For example, legal protections need to be made for women to be able to go to school, learn a trade, and keep what they earn from their trades, rather than turning over their incomes to their male relatives. When their husbands die, women need to retain their rights to property and their children, rather than having those rights and her child transferred to her husband's relatives. Ritual sexual cleansings of widows can be symbolic rather than behavioral; this will reduce the risk for HIV infection (Outwater, 1996; Setel, 1999).

Concomitantly, men need to be held responsible for their sexual behavior. Polygyny and having multiple sex partners can be made safer by educating, encouraging, and supporting men in safer sex practices, encouraging later onset for sexual activity with a partner, and reducing the number of partners. This can be incorporated into male initiation ceremonies, so that boys enter manhood with different ideas about sexuality. Support groups for people who are HIV positive need to be developed at the grass-roots level, and intervention efforts need to present accurate information about transmission, HIV testing, and treatment. These are not new recommendations. The World Health Organization (WHO) and **nongovernmental organizations (NGOs)** have been requesting this for more than two decades ("Declaration of Commitment on HIV/AIDS," 2001; WHO, 2004a, 2004b; "Woman and AIDS," 2004).

The risk of HIV for sex workers globally requires an interdisciplinary, holistic, and multifaceted approach. (This is what anthropologists are good at!) All structures of society are involved: from the individual to group to larger society, across the life cycle, and encompassing the socioeconomic, political, and symbolic behaviors and beliefs. This entails support or creation of an economic and political infrastructure that allows people to survive economically without putting themselves at sexual risk. Examples of this include village banking efforts in Zambia that help women economically and also disseminate health information, and Women Fighting AIDS in Kenya, a grass-roots group that provides support to home care givers (Morrison and Fleishman, 2005).

Challenging gender and sexual norms that allow men to be sexual without responsibility and which denies women their sexuality and ability to say no needs to occur as well. The approach addresses double standards of sexual behavior and offers alternatives to risky behavior. Accurate HIV information and support from NGOs, CBOs (Community Based Organizations), and FBOs (Faith Based Organizations) can help to lessen the stigma around HIV. A holistic approach further supports keeping professionals such as doctors, nurses, and engineers in their countries of origin and making it safe and feasible for them to practice there (Gender-AIDS eForum, 2004/2005).

These changes cannot be made by individual societies alone. International agencies such as WHO, Doctors Without Borders, and the Global Fund to Fight Malaria, Tuberculosis and HIV continue to work in areas heavily impacted by these problems. The wealthy industrialized societies could alleviate the problems created by globalization if they would critically examine and change their international business and political practices that contribute to economic and political disenfranchisement. PhRMA can work with other countries to make drugs more accessible and affordable. It is not a hopeless situation, but solutions require concerted, interdisciplinary effort.

In conclusion, globalization is not a recent phenomenon, although the magnitude of commercial capitalism's impact on nonindustrialized countries has escalated since the late twentieth century producing irreversible changes in the environment and the economic lives of people living in nonindustrialized nations. Globalization is defined in this chapter as bidirectional contact between industrialized and nonindustrialized nations and does not necessarily mean that all cultures will become homogenized versions of U.S. society; indeed core cultural features may persist such as the Latino cultural value of *la familia*. However, the influence of industrial capitalism on nonindustrialized societies is extensive. This has been discussed in this chapter through the globalization of sexuality and trafficking. Although a broad term, trafficking generally refers to the movement of people across borders for work that is exploitative and underpaid. Trafficking is discussed as a product of global economic trends that have led to the escalation of migration.

Sex work/prostitution is at the intersection of globalization and sexuality, and is the emphasis of this chapter. However, it is not the only way that sexuality is affected. In this and previous chapters, we have discussed the exportation of industrialized versions of homophobia, the change in sub-Saharan African women's status that came with colonization, female genital cutting as it becomes an international issue through migration, and the expansion of Internet pornography among other issues impacting women and children specifically. Because approximately 80 percent of sex workers are female, the emphasis is placed here on women (and children) as sex workers.

Sex work in industrialized nations and nonindustrialized nations is compared and contrasted. Prostitution/sex work is associated with the development of agrarian, stratified, hierarchical societies 5,000 to 8,000 years ago that are characterized by unequal access to power, prestige and resources. Sex work did not occur among traditional foragers or horticulturalists.

Cultural views of prostitution include strong legal, social, and emotional responses which are embedded in assumptions about sexuality generally and women's sexuality in particular. In industrial societies, a double standard of women's sexuality is linked to patrilineal and bilateral descent systems, concern with paternity certainty, and patriarchy as it is embedded in socio-economic institutions. This double standard is expressed in negative attitudes towards sex workers who violate cherished notions of women's sexuality as legitimate only in the context of a potentially reproductive, heterosexual, committed, monogamous relationship. Thus, sex work challenges the status quo. Sex workers' rights groups advocate for better conditions for sex workers including decriminalization, better working environments, protection of children from recruitment, and destigmatization of prostitution among other issues. Sex workers in industrialized nations are aware that they have a privileged position in comparison with sex workers in nonindustrialized nations.

Examples of sex work in preindustrial nation states prior to Euro-American contact illustrated the various positions of sex workers historically. Patrilineal/bilateral decent systems in patricentered societies created the dichotomy of good girl, married woman and the fallen woman, the whore.

The influences of globalization, including colonization, impacted extant indigenous systems of prostitution as well as creating the economic conditions that fostered its appearance in new places, especially peripheral societies such as the former Soviet Bloc countries, Southeast Asia and sub-Saharan Africa.

As discussed, sex work in these areas is distinctive from industrialized sex work in that it:

- Often is not a matter of choice but of survival.
- Often involves preadolescent and early adolescents.
- Has incorporated the stigma associated with Euro-American sex work conditions.
- Has become global.
- Often accompanies migration.
- Illustrates that culture contact and change do not occur in a smooth trajectory and can create diverse sexual expectations between clients and prostitutes.
- Can become a specialized form of tourism, sex tourism. Because the market conditions tend to set the working conditions, sex tourism raises special concerns about sexual and economic exploitation.

A critical review of trafficking argues that prostitution is not the only form of trafficking in which exploitation occurs. In addition, such a view implies that all sex work is coercive and overlooks other forms of sex work in industrialized nations where prostitution may be a choice selected from other forms of work, particularly when viewed from an emic perspective (Whelehan, 2001a). The current construction of trafficking and the conflation of trafficking with prostitution perpetuates a double standard, and overlooks the larger socioeconomic and political conditions that create and sustain sex work as it currently exists.

Globalization, sex work, and HIV are linked both epidemiologically and perceptually in a number of ways. Discussion exploded several myths about HIV, women, and sex work. First, women are more often infected by male partners than the reverse. Second, sex workers will practice safer sex if they are given the option or the choice. This comes down to whether women are given the ability to choose by male kin groups or employers. Data from the United States indicate that only 0.04 percent of HIV in the United States is transmitted by female prostitutes to male clients. It is important to remember that clarification of emic and etic categories of sex work is important for statistics related to prostitution, disease, and HIV transmission.

The evidence of HIV and sex work in nonindustrialized nations suggests that support for safer sex practices results in the reduction of HIV risk and infection rates as occurred in Thailand during the 1980s and 1990s. This kind of support, however, is rare globally and undermined, for example, by the PEPFAR plan and its lack of support for condom availability. The gag rule on international aid agencies that work with sex workers further undermines safer sex practices.

In order to reduce the risk of HIV for sex workers, a variety of recommendations are suggested. These include: (1) the need for an infrastructure of sustainable food sources; (2) viable sources of income and access to resources, including educating girls, access to a healthy diet, and prevention and treatment of diseases that are co-factors for HIV infection; (3) development strategies to enhance women's status including legal protections, educational and economic approaches; (4) support of men in practicing safer sex and holding them accountable for their sexual behavior; (5) development of an interdisciplinary, holistic, and multifaceted approach that challenges double standards, offers safer alternatives; and (6) reduction of the brain drain of professionals. This approach includes developing economic and political infrastructures that allow for economic survival without engaging in risky sexual behavior.

SUMMARY

1   Globalization is an expansion of centuries of intercultural contact and change.

2   Globalization of the twentieth and twenty-first centuries is primarily directed by the political and economic policies of the wealthiest nations.

3 Globalization impacts sexuality in a variety of ways from changes in dress and marriage practices to sex tourism.
4 The current HIV epidemic reflects global sexual, economic, political, and social policies.

Thought-provoking questions

1 What changes have occurred in sexuality as a result of globalization over the past century?
2 How do the economic, political, and social policies of industrialized nations impact sex work in their own and nonindustrialized societies?

SUGGESTED RESOURCES

Books

Farr, Kathryn. 2004. *Sex Trafficking: The Global Market in Women and Children*. New York: Worth Publishers.
Kempadoo, Kamala and Jo Doezema, eds. 1998. *Global Sex Workers: Rights, Resistance, and Redefinition*. New York: Routledge Publishers.
Robbins, Richard. 2005. *Global Problems and the Culture of Capitalism*. 3rd ed. Boston: Allyn and Bacon.
Seabrook, Jeremy. 2001. *Travels in the Skin Trade: Tourism and the Sex Industry*. 2nd ed. Sterling: Pluto Press.
Whelehan, Patricia. 2001. *An Anthropological Perspective on Prostitution: Mellen Studies in Anthropology*. Vol. 4. Lewiston: Edwin Mellen Press.

Web sites

ICPR (International Committee on Prostitutes Rights) (http://www.walnet.org/csis/groups/icpr_charter.html. Child)
Trafficking (http://www.childtrafficking.com/)

17 Summary and conclusion

CHAPTER OVERVIEW

1   Restates the biological, psychological, and cultural perspective, its embeddedness in anthropological understandings and how this applies to an exploration of human sexual behavior.
2   Reiterates the distinction between universal human sexuality and that which is culture specific.
3   Puts sexual behavior in a socio-cultural context and emphasizes the effects of culture change on traditional sexual behavior and values.
4   Makes a concluding statement about the potential for changes in hominid sexuality based on late twentieth and twenty-first-century sexual and reproductive technology.
5   Places AIDS in a global context relative to its threat and the potential for responding to it in a human way.
6   Places sex work currently in the context of globalization.

An anthropological perspective, including evolutionary, holistic, cross-cultural/comparative, and relativistic approaches, has been used in this exploration of human sexuality. We have framed this as a biological, psychological, and cultural approach, stressing the interdisciplinary nexus of anthropology and sexology as well as the multidimensional aspects of human sexual expression. This approach accents the importance of the individual in society by emphasizing her/his relationship to the broader cultural context, yet recognizes the importance of social systems and cultural meanings in shaping human sexual experience. We have recognized that a broad lens includes an examination of human sexuality through space and time as a human phenomenon. This evolutionary perspective provides a framework for understanding bio-behavioral aspects of sexuality as it has developed and changed through time and adapted to particular environments. It also allows us to explore continuities in our sexuality through our evolution as primates. Holism allows for examining sexuality in the context of group behavior and institutions. It relates various aspects of sexuality such as marriage forms to other dimensions of society such as the economic and political spheres. Rather than viewed as separate from society, sexual attitudes and behaviors are discussed as integrated into the fabric of the culture.

By aiming for a culturally relativistic or nonjudgmental perspective on sexuality, the comparative approach can be utilized. Generally the comparisons are cross-cultural and international (i.e., inter-societal, but can be extended to include the higher primates, our closest nonhuman relatives). Through a comparative perspective, a better understanding of that which is universal human sexual behavior (e.g., bonding) and what is culture-specific sexual behavior (e.g., marriage form) can be achieved. The striking similarities and rich diversities of human sexuality emerge. These perspectives provide a basic foundation for exploring continuity and change, our uniqueness as humans, and the impact that industrialization, globalization, and recent technological developments have had on sexuality.

As primates and hominids, we have evolved certain bio-behavioral characteristics that affect our sexuality. A crucial characteristic is bipedalism and the accompanying pelvic and brain changes that affected pregnancy, birth, and survival of the young. Our young are born immature and have a prolonged infant dependency on adults. The major human survival strategy is to adapt through learned behavior. Certain behavioral patterns adapted to specific econiches have developed to promote reproductive success. These include culture-specific socialization patterns, definitions of acceptable sexual behavior, and birth practices.

In the late twentieth century and the new millennium in the United States and other industrialized cultures, technical developments have become available which can drastically change our hominid sexuality. Since 1978, the availability of technological innovations such as *in vitro* fertilization, embryo transplants, chromosomal sex selection, sperm banks, and artificial insemination donor, fetal reduction, and surrogate motherhood have the potential to qualitatively alter our means of reproduction, alter our definitions of parenthood, our concepts of kinship, and of relationships. Most simply, penile-vaginal intercourse is no longer required for reproductive success. Although societies have needed fewer adult males than adult females to survive for most of our evolution, this sex ratio can be altered further with the technical ability to store sperm indefinitely in sperm banks and to predetermine gender through chromosomal selection. Amniocentesis and chorionic villi sampling (CVS) also allow for gender selection *in utero*. For example, while developed in the industrialized countries, amniocentesis is used in some societies such as China and India to select for boys (Ward and Edelstein, 2006).

Paralleling the technological changes are socioeconomic shifts. In the 1950s, in the United States, mostly men worked full-time outside the home in the labor force while women stayed home (in two-thirds of American families). Currently fewer than 20 percent of all U.S. households practice this earlier twentieth-century traditional arrangement. Dual-career couples are now the norm. Single-parent families have increased and subsequently leveled off since the 1970s into the new millennium with the proportion of the single-parent mothers increasing from 12 to 26 percent, and single-parent fathers increasing from 1 to 6 percent, including an increase in never-married couples. Among twenty to twenty-four-year-old women, the proportion of never-married doubled from 36 to 75 percent between 1970 and 2003, and never-married twenty to twenty-four-year-old men increased from 55 to 86 percent in that same time frame ("America's Family and Living Arrangements," 2003).

The United States has the highest rates of teenaged pregnancy, birth, abortion and STIs (not HIV/AIDS) in the industrialized world ("Facts in Brief: Teenagers' Sexual and Reproductive Health: Developed Countries," 2006), as well as the second highest infant mortality rate of industrialized countries for newborns (only Latvia exceeds us) ("Saving the Lives of Mothers and Newborn, 2006: State of the World's Mothers 2006"). Divorce is on the decline in America, falling since the 1980s from 22.6 per 1,000 married women to 17.7 in 2004. But the marriage rate has also dropped by 50 percent from 1970 when it was 76.5 per 1,000 unmarried women representing a shift from marriage to cohabitation, currently practiced by 8.1 percent of heterosexual coupled households. About 40 percent of cohabiting couples bring children into the relationship. There are numerous journals, books, and self-help groups that inform us about how to be attractive, successful, find a mate, and achieve intimacy. There are a comparable number of books that instruct us on parenting. Behaviors, values, and courting patterns which previously occurred in the context of extended kin groups or neighborhoods are now the arena of sex professionals, educators, counselors, and therapists. Simultaneously, industrialized cultures are cognitively more knowledgeable about sexuality, more openly sexually active, and more openly engaged in lifestyles which include singlehood, serial monogamy, cohabitation, bisexuality, and homosexuality.

At the same time that industrialized people are more open about certain sexual behaviors and lifestyles, we continue to hold rather rigid concepts concerning sexual orientation, gender, and gender role/identity; witness attempts to legislate against same-sex marriage. Concurrently, however, to balance some of that rigidity in our own culture, a greater interest in the study of orientation and gender identity is occurring in the scholarly sectors of society. An escalating body of literature on gender variance cross-culturally is being developed as the internet and tourism introduce and infuse traditional notions of gender variance with industrialized views of transgender and broader GLBTQ sensibilities, creating new possibilities and meanings for gender. The combination of these developments may heighten our awareness of human sexual diversity and lead us to a more accurate, realistic, and accepting comprehension of identities and orientations.

Human sexuality is further explored from a life cycle developmental context. Using cross-cultural and industrialized perspectives, attitudes, and behaviors regarding pregnancy and childbirth, early childhood and adolescence, adult, and aging sexuality are examined. The bio-behavioral aspects of sexuality are reinforced through discussions of the universalistic and culture-specific aspects of these topics as well as human sexual response and birth control.

Globally, we are presented with severe population pressures relative to the available resources; conflicts between industrialized and indigenous sexual behaviors and values in acculturating societies and among assimilating individuals; AIDS, and the increase in sex work and trafficking. Sex work and trafficking are escalated by globalization and the resultant increase in transnational movement by peoples, as their socioeconomic situations are worsened. AIDS could easily be our most serious health and sexual problem we face as a species. The disease has spread worldwide, with devastating effects on the individuals and groups involved. It may also serve to unite us in our humanness. Sex work is inextricably tied to HIV/AIDS epidemiologically and perceptually as well as embedded in assumptions about sexuality generally and women's sexuality in particular. Issues such as sex work, trafficking, and AIDS requires a cooperative, culturally relativistic and culturally sensitive approach. This position is particularly urgent as the very first global study of sexual and reproductive health coordinated by the World Health Organization documents some particularly disturbing trends:

> . . . the level of disability and premature death due to sexual and reproductive health is huge and increasing. Unsafe sex is the second most important cause of illness and death in developing countries and ninth in developed countries. The analysis reveals a picture of growing unmet needs and neglect. More than half a million women die as a result of complications in pregnancy and childbirth every year. Access to contraception has increased worldwide but there are still an estimated 120 million couples who do not get the contraceptives they would like or need. An estimated 80 million women have unintended or unwanted pregnancies each year, 45 million end in abortion. WHO figures quoted in the survey show that there are 19 million unsafe abortions carried out each year, resulting in around 68 000 deaths and millions of injuries and permanent disabilities. ("Future of Sexual and Reproductive Health at Tipping Point According to Global Study," 2006)

As we encounter this evidence of human tragedy and suffering, it has the potential to elicit from us hominid characteristics such as bonding, flexibility, and the ability to change and adapt to new surroundings and challenges. In the past generation, changes in our sexuality are probably as significant to us now as bipedalism was to our early ancestors.

Human sexuality has evolved over several million years. Its richness, diversity, complexity, and commonality are a reflection of us as a species. Fear, prejudice, and ethnocentrism can limit our appreciation of its depth and scope. Respect, cooperation, and an integration of the cognitive and affective dimensions of our sexual selves may help us to address the challenges we have created for ourselves as sexual beings.

Notes

Chapter 1

1 We would like to thank Dr. Jane Granskog, Department of Anthropology, California State University at Bakersfield, for conceptualizing this model. Although it has been modified to meet the needs of our text and been given a new metaphor, Dr. Granskog was instrumental in providing the foundation for this approach.

Chapter 2

1 Sue-Ellen Jacobs states in "Native American Two Spirits":

> The term *"berdache"* [sic] as used by anthropologists is outdated, anachronistic, and does not reflect contemporary Native American conversations about gender diversity and sexualities. To use this term is to participate in and perpetuate colonial discourse, labeling Native American people by a term that has its origins in Western thought and languages.
>
> The preferred term of Native Americans who are involved in refining understanding about gender diversity and sexualities among Native American peoples is "two spirit" . . . or terms specific to tribes (1994: 7).

We have adopted this usage where it seems appropriate to refer to gender-transformed/alternative genders throughout the Native American ethnographic record and to use the appropriate indigenous term or the more generic usages such as gender variance elsewhere.

Chapter 3

1 Some scholars prefer to use the term "hominin" to refer to humans and their ancestors (*Homo* and *Australopithecus* species) as a reflection of the close evolutionary similarity of humans, chimpanzees, and gorillas. In this text, however, we will use the more common and historically older term "hominid" to refer to the group that includes humans and their ancestors.

2 There are several classical and contemporary theories as to the conditions that may have led to the development of the visual center of the brain as well as the grasping hand. Collins (1921) has proposed that binocular vision would be favored in species that have to leap from branch to branch as in the conditions encountered by the earliest tree dwellers. Cartmill's (1974) visual predation theory suggests that diet may have selected for the grasping hand in tandem with binocular vision

in situations where prey, such as insects, were found on slender vines. Sussman (1978) is of the opinion that grasping hands would be adaptive for an arboreal niche where early primates traveled on small branches. In this theory, reliance on vision occurred because these early primates were probably nocturnal and they had to be able to locate plant foods in the dark (Ember and Ember, 2005: 77–78).

3 Evidence for large game hunting appears relatively late in human history and may represent one of several possible strategies for hunting and survival. In fact, microscopic analysis of the earliest tools dated between two and two-and-a-half million years ago reveals that these were not used in actual hunting. Wear patterns indicate use in modifying plant materials, scraping, and cutting up animal skins (Zihlman, 1989).

Chapter 5

1 Baldness tendencies are a genetic trait in men carried by females.
2 This does not include taking steroids by some male and female athletes in order to increase muscle size.
3 Muscle mass and standards of leanness are culturally defined. Men need a minimum of 4 to 6 percent body fat to reach puberty.
4 Sex hormones can stimulate certain cancers.
5 This is *not* recommended as a means of contraception.

Chapter 6

1 Aspirin dissipates prostglandins. It also is an anti-clotting agent. If a woman has blood clotting disorders or is to undergo surgery, she should limit her aspirin intake and inform medical personnel as to how much and when she last took aspirin.
2 The craving for chocolate may be related to phenylethylamine. One of its chemical compounds is related to phenylalanine, an amino acid. These compounds may serve as mood elevators in humans.
3 Currently, regulated sperm banks test donations for HIV, since the virus is carried in semen.

Chapter 7

1 It takes about twenty-four to thirty hours to replenish the supply of sperm after ejaculation (Stewart et al., 1979).
2 Medical terminology for various sexual and reproductive conditions frequently has pejorative connotations. These connotations, while not consciously intended to hurt clients, may inflict psychological and emotional discomfort or harm a client. A distraught, infertile couple does not need to hear about "hostile" cervical mucous or "incompetent" cervices in their attempt to remedy their situation.
3 As of 2005, the FDA (Food and Drug Administration) requires that AI-D donations are screened for HIV, since the virus is carried in the semen of an infected person.
4 The role of H-Y antigen in male sexual differentiation is controversial.
5 Later differentiation may occur in the female so that Wolffian duct development of the urinary tract can take place.
6 They have been referred to as "degenerate testicles." See note 2.
7 Efforts have been made to adjust the language usage in reference to the terms transsexual, cross-dresser and transgender so as not to suggest clinical syndromes

but rather cultural and social identity (e.g., instead of transsexual, the terminology transsexual people is adopted). Unfortunately, not all instances could be eliminated due to stylistic requirements and/or clinical usage.

8 Relative to specific sexual activity, the major difference between heterosexual and homosexual behavior is that homosexual behavior is nonreproductive; heterosexual behavior can be. In terms of its evolution, most of the heterosexual acts themselves are nonreproductive.

Chapter 8

1 This is starting to change since about 30 percent of the currently trained obstetricians and gynecologists are female. However, these women are socialized into a biomedical, interventionist model and tend to carry that into their practice (Arms, 1975; Davis-Floyd, 1992 and 2001; Jordan, 1988; Sargent and Stark, 1989).

2 Even the term "coach" implies some form of external management akin to an athletic event.

Chapter 9

1 The interested reader is encouraged to explore the works of Cohen (1978), Fox (1980), Levi-Strauss (1969), Livingstone (1969), Murdock (1949), Phelan (1986), White (1948), among others too numerous to mention. Recent reviews of the incest taboo include Meigs and Barlow (2002: 38–49) and Patterson (2005: 1–18).

Chapter 11

1 The meanings that sex is given in a society are embedded and expressed in complex ways through the social structure and the ideological system. For example, how people experience their sexuality is linked to the ideological system such as beliefs about reproduction, menstruation, and pollution. All are part of shaping sexuality at the personal and cultural level. Indeed human sexuality "is embedded in a complex web of shared ideas, moral rules, jural regulations, obvious associations and obscure symbols" (Davenport, 1977: 117). Our sexuality is ultimately part of "worldwide economic, social, political and cultural systems" (Ross and Rapp, 1983: 57) which have diverse histories, trajectories and encounters (Herdt, 1999, 2004). The ethnographic spectrum offers an array of sexual practices and beliefs that are testimony to the flexibility of humans in their ability to adapt to different cultural milieus and environments.

2 Anthropologists have also devoted considerable time and increasing attention to studying sex in industrialized societies.

3 This may be contrasted with Judaic traditions that have a generally positive view of sex regarding it as a gift from God if practiced in the appropriate moral context (Stein, 2005).

Chapter 13

1 Transgender has several meanings within (emic) and outside (etic) the gender variant communities. Your authors recognize the different connotations associated with the transgender identity and transpeople. See note 7, Chapter 7.

2 Unfortunately at the time of Bolin's research, the term "*berdache*" was popular in the anthropological literature of the period. No disrespect is meant to the transcommunity by using this term here; it just represents the importance of "naming" and the temporal nature of cultural meanings. See note 1,

Chapter 2. Walter Williams has referred to the female gender variant individual as "Amazon" (1986), although this has been contested by some anthropologists for its Eurocentric bias.

Chapter 14

1 The sections of this chapter are based primarily on one of the author's (Whelehan) works since 1988 with individuals and groups in the gay and bisexual communities in northern and southern California and northern New York. These include "white bread" Americans and *Latinos*. She is deeply appreciative of the openness and acceptance she has found. She acknowledges that any misinterpretations of the individuals' and group's message to the straight world are solely her responsibility.

2 The research presented in the much-lauded book, *Sex in America* (1994), seriously questioned the 10 percent figure. However, these researchers did not clearly distinguish between sexual behavior and sexual orientation, only included same-sex sexual behavior in the year prior to their questionnaire, and conducted interviews with people in nonprivate settings.

3 Additional information on homosexual support groups and referral sources for gays, lesbians, their friends, and loved ones can be obtained from the Lambda Legal Defense Group, Lambda Rising and PFLAG. These groups have chapters around the country.

4 Faludi's (1991) research challenges an earlier statistic that women's disposable income after divorce drops almost 73 percent (AAUW, 1989: 5).

Chapter 15

1 GRID (Gay-Related Immune-deficiency Disease) was a misnomer that reflected the homophobia and sex phobia of the media, researchers, and the Centers for Disease Control and Prevention in 1981. That misnomer created the perception and belief that HIV/AIDS was a "gay" disease, something that has persisted among a number of groups to the present and which also contributed to the stigma associated with it.

2 The Centers for Disease Control (CDC) have been renamed the Centers for Disease Control and Prevention. As of July 1993, the commonly used acronym for this organization remained the "CDC" and will be used here. Statistics are updated biannually by the CDC.

3 Mandatory testing is required to enter and stay in the military, to be in the Job Corps, and can be court-ordered in the United States. Mandatory testing was proposed by some members of Congress in the 1980s with quarantine recommended for those testing positive. That did not occur.

4 To distinguish between sexual orientation and behavior, please see Chapter 14.

Chapter 16

1 As controversial as discussions of trafficking are, it is important to remember that what constitutes childhood and adolescence are culturally defined.

2 One of the major concerns with sex tourism is the coerced and exploitative nature of it particularly for women and children. Here are urls for two groups that specifically address sex tourism, trafficking, and children: http://www.children trafficking.com and http://www.ecpat.net/eng/index.asp.

Glossary

A-frame orgasm: An orgasm occurring as a consequence of stimulation of the Grafenberg Spot.

abstinence: For this book's purpose, the practice of refraining from anal, oral, and vaginal intercourse.

acculturation: The change which occurs in the original culture when two or more cultures are in contact with each other.

achieved status: One's rank in society based on one's efforts.

actual effectiveness rate: The statistical figure used to calculate accuracy in birth control. Since not all couples use birth control properly or consistently, this figure will be lower than the theoretical effectiveness rate.

acute aspects of disease: Sudden onset and relatively rapid course of infection.

adaptation: "The process by which organisms achieve a beneficial adjustment to an available environment, and the results of that process" (Haviland, 1989: 59). In evolutionary theory, referring to the principle that traits arise through natural selection.

adolescence: The period of life from puberty to maturity terminating legally at the age of majority.

adolescent sterility: The period that occurs between menarche and reproductive maturity when pregnancy is not likely to result from intercourse. It has been discussed among the Ju/Wasi people as a mechanism for controlling population.

adrenal glands: Two small glands located on top of each kidney that are responsible for much of the other sex hormone production in males (progesterone) and females (testosterone).

affinal kin/ties/relations: Those individuals who are related by marriage. For example, "in-laws" in United States culture.

age-grade: A grouping of individuals based on shared biological maturity. It includes responsibilities, rights, cultural practices, and obligations that change from age stage to age stage.

age of maturity: A marker established by Euro-American society where an individual gains the legal status of adulthood, conferring both rights and responsibilities. These include marriage, adult responsibilities for criminal actions, and the right to make personal choices.

age set: A "non-kin association in which individuals of the same group interact throughout their life" (Oswalt, 1986: 432).

AIDS (Acquired Immunodeficiency Syndrome): The latter stages of HIV infection characterized by a positive HIV antibody test, and/or low or absent T-cells, and one or more opportunistic infections.

AIDS Drug Assistance Program (ADAP): Federally funded programs that help PLWH/A be able to buy ARVs.

alliance theory: Theory that exogamy creates economic and political relationships between groups, some of which might otherwise be in conflict and/or forges broader social networks and economic ties providing greater integration.

alloparenting: Use of extended kin and nonkin as a means of socioeconomic support and socialization of children as a continuation of our hominid behavior.

ambilineal descent: The tracing of one's family through either the male or female parent or both.

amniocentesis: The surgical insertion of a hollow needle through the abdominal wall and uterus of a pregnant female, especially to obtain amniotic fluid for the determination of sex or chromosomal abnormality.

amnion: The bag of waters surrounding the embryo.

ampulla: The far end of the fallopian tube.

anal stage: Freudian psycho-sexual stage of development occurring at approximately two years of age when the child achieves control of bladder and anal sphincter and finds pleasure in this sensation.

analogous/analogues: Something that is similar in function to something else.

anatomy: Study of specific body parts or structures.

androcentric: Sexist, male-biased.

androgen(s): The hormones such as testosterone and adrosterone that produce or stimulate the male characteristics.

androgen insensitivity syndrome: The most common hormonal error that occurs in chromosomal XY males. The testes secrete amounts of testosterone that are generally defective so that these cells are unresponsive to testosterone. The fetus develops with partially feminized sex hormones.

androgynous gender role: On the scale of traditional, nontraditional, and androgynous gender roles can roughly be conceptualized as a fluid continuum with traditional and liberated (i.e., non-traditional) as more opposed than symmetrical to each other, and androgynous as comprising a wide, gray mid-section.

androgyny/androgynous: Greek word combining words for male, *andros*, and female, *gyne*. Refers to responding to the situation regardless of one's gender or gender-defined characteristics.

andropause: A male counterpart to menopause that has recently been identified and "named" in late twentieth-century Euro-American scholarly and media discourses. This has been variously designated as the male climacteric, male menopause and/or andropause.

anonymous HIV testing: Number coding for an HIV test where the person is only identified by a number, no name is given.

anorexia nervosa: Severe and dangerous eating disorder that is found primarily in middle-class adolescent females and that involves minimal intake of food and that can cause the cessation of menstruation and other health problems.

anthropology: The interdisciplinary approach that studies human and primate behavior evolutionarily and across cultures through the examination of paleo and archaeological data as well as the interaction of people in modern human groups.

anti-retrovirals (ARVs)/anti-ret medications: Also referred to as HAART (Highly Active Antiretroviral Therapy). Those drugs given to people with HIV/AIDS to decrease their viral load, boost their immune systems (T-cells), and prevent Opportunistic Infections.

arboreal: Adapted to life in the trees.

areola: Pigmented area surrounding the nipple.

arousal phase: Kaplan's combined term for Master and Johnsons's excitement and plateau phase.

artificial insemination by donor (AI-D): The use of ejaculate from a person other than the woman's husband or significant other to medically inseminate her. Generally done when the woman's partner produces no or insufficient or problematic sperm to be able to impregnate his wife/significant other.

artificial insemination by husband (AI-H): The use of the husband's ejaculate to medically inseminate his wife. This may be done for psychological reasons or when the husband's sperm is of low quantity and multiple ejaculate samples are concentrated and injected into the vagina.

ascribed status: One's rank in society based on birth or biological characteristics.

Assisted Reproductive Technology (ART): Any technology that increases the chances that conception will occur and the baby will be carried to term.

associated polyandry: The practice where a woman is allowed multiple related husbands. These men are referred to as "visiting husbands."

attractivity: A term proposed by Beach (1976) to describe aspects of female sexual behavior that refer to males' interest in mating with females.

autogynephilic: Transsexuals (male-to-female) who are sexually attracted to women.

autonomy theory: Reiss's theory that sexual permissiveness will increase in cultural contexts in which adolescents have greater independence in courtship and dating.

avunculocality: Unmarried couples residence.

Barrier Method: Contraceptive method that prevents pregnancy by placing a barrier between the egg and sperm so the sperm cannot reach the egg to fertilize it.

Bartholin's glands: Located at the base of the introitus, these glands secrete a clear liquid whose function is unknown.

basal body temperature: The body temperature at rest, usually taken before arising in the morning. Used to determine when a woman is ovulating and therefore may be used as a method of birth control.

berdache: Term used in early anthropological literature. It is no longer used and is a misnomer.

bi: Term used for those whose sexual and romantic interests are in people of their own and the opposite sex.

bilateral descent (nonunilineal, double descent): The practice of tracing one's descent through both parents with each lineage in control of different areas of activity and property.

bilateral kindred (kinship): The system of kinship structure in which an individual belongs equally to the kindred of both parents.

bilineal descent: Similar to ambilineal type in which descent is traced through both the patrilineage and matrilineage with each controlling different areas of activity and property.

Billings method: Birth control rhythm method based on evaluation of vaginal mucous to determine when ovulation takes place.

bilocality: Practice where the newly married couple may live near the bride's or groom's parents and follow the particular set of rules established by either the parents or the culture.

bio-cultural: An anthropological approach that incorporates an understanding of humankind as both biological and cultural beings.

biological, psychological, and cultural approach: Includes such fields as medical anthropology, biological anthropology, the anthropology of sex and gender, psychological anthropology, and clinical anthropology.

biological reductionism: The theoretical approach that reduces and interprets behavior to its biochemical and genetic basis.

biological relations (consanguineal): Kin related by descent or filliation rather than through marriage; "blood relatives."

biological sex: Generally considered the definition of one's sex as male or female but includes chromosomal, gender, hormonal, internal reproductive structures, sex characteristics, gender identity and role assignment and rearing, and legal sex.

bipedalism: The ability to maintain and walk in an upright position.

birth attendants: Those people, often women in traditional societies, who stay with a pregnant woman during her labor and birth.

birth control: Methods used to prevent conception and control fertility.

bisexual: Sexual and romantic attraction to people of your own and the opposite sex.

blended family: A household made up of two parents, their biological children, and any children from previous marriages and other relatives.

blended orgasm: Combines characteristics of the vulval and uterine orgasm.

blood ties: Blood relations; refers to those people related to you genetically, also referred to as consanguineal kin.

body fat: The amount of fat located beneath the skin.

bonding: The ongoing and continuous socio-emotional link between people.

brain complexity: Human reliance on learning is a significant aspect of our sexuality associated with the expansion of the neocortex.

brain drain: Hiring professionals from nonindustrialized societies for positions in industrialized societies, resulting in a lack of professionally-trained people to attend to the needs of their home country.

breastfeeding: Feeding an infant from the milk produced by the mammary glands of mammals.

broad ligament: A band of connective tissue across the lower abdomen that supports the uterus, fallopian tubes, and ovaries.

calendrical method: Based on a formula in which eighteen is subtracted from a woman's shortest cycle and eleven from her longest cycle observed over a minimum of eight cycles with day one being the first day of menstruation.

castration: Surgical removal of the testicles or chemical removal of the androgens produced by the testes.

caul: The amnion or "bag of waters" which envelops the developing embryo/fetus.

CC + HPG axis: Biochemical basis of human sexuality.

Centers for Disease Control and Prevention (CDC): The organization that tracks the incidence and prevalence of diseases within the United States, and makes recommendations about their prevention and treatment.

cerebral cortex (CC): The outer layer of the brain characteristic of humans and hominids involved in perception, analytic and logical thought, and learning.

cervical cap: A barrier method in which a small plastic or rubber cup is placed on the woman's cervix and which must be used in conjunction with spermicides.

cervical mucous: A thickish, sticky substance which covers the os prior to ovulation. At ovulation, the cervical mucous thins and stretches, allowing for sperm to pass through the os into the uterus.

cervical mucous checks: Birth control based on avoiding sexual intercourse during the time when the cervical mucous thins in order to allow sperm to pass through the os.

cervix: The lower section of the vagina.

childbirth: The bio-social process where a woman experiences labor and the expulsion of the fetus from the uterus.

chorion: The structure that eventually develops into the placenta. The chorion secretes hormones during the early stages of pregnancy that allow it to attach to the uterine wall and which are detected in pregnancy tests.

chorionic villi sampling (CVS): A technique for diagnosing medical problems in the fetus as early as the eighth week of pregnancy; a sample of the chorionic membrane is removed through the cervix and studied.

chromosomal filtration: Method of preselecting XX or XY chromosomes.

chromosomal sex: Also referred to as genetic sex, it is sex determined at conception, either XX for a girl or XY for a boy.

chronic aspects of disease: A medical condition that is incurable and can affect people's functioning, but may be treatable.

circumcision: In the female, surgical procedure that cuts the prepuce exposing the clitoral shaft; in the male, surgical removal of the foreskin from the penis.

clan: A group of people whose unilineal descent is established upon a belief that they have a common real or mythical ancestor even if the claim cannot be proven. While biological links cannot be traced due to the large number of people concerned, the group shares mutual economic security, social control, political and marriage relations, religious practices, and ceremonies.

climacteric: Sexual aging experienced by both men and women including physical and social change.

clitoral hood: In the female, the upper part of the labia minora that covers the clitoral glans.

clitoridectomy: Surgical removal of the clitoris practiced in some cultures.

clitoris: A female sexual structure involved directly or indirectly in sexual response that is homologous to the glans of the penis.

co-factor: A variable or other infection/disease/health status that can increase one's risk for HIV infection.

cognatic descent: The practice of tracing relations through both sides of the parental lineages, i.e., non-unilineal.

coital: The physical union of male and female genitalia accompanied by rhythmic movements, i.e., insertion of penis and vagina in heterosexuals.

coitus interruptus: A method of birth control in which the penis is withdrawn from the vagina prior to ejaculation.

Community-Based Organizations (CBOs): Those groups that are derived from, located in, and serve specific communities.

competence: What a person knows, both consciously and unconsciously, about her or his culture.

comprehensive sexuality education: Education that includes information on a variety of options over abstinence-only education.

conception: The union of the sperm and egg.

conceptus: The fertilized egg.

Confidential HIV Testing: HIV testing in which a person's name is recorded and known but kept private.

confinement: The period surrounding labor and birth when a woman's activities are restricted.

consanguineal (kin/ties/relations/family): Kin related by descent or filliation rather than through marriage; "blood relatives."

contraception: Any natural barrier, hormonal or surgical means, that prevents conception and pregnancy.

coronary heart disease (CHD): Blockage of the arteries to the heart that increases the chances of a heart attack.

corpora cavernosa: Hollow, spongelike cylinders of tissue within the penile shaft that become engorged with blood during sexual excitement.

corpus: The body of the uterus composed of several layers including the endometrium.

corpus luteum: Reddish yellow endocrine tissue that forms within a ruptured ovarian follicle. It produces progesterone.

corpus spongiosum: A spongy cylinder of tissue running through the underneath part of the penis shaft that also becomes engorged with blood causing erection.

couvade: The *couvade* is a culturally created bio-behavioral phenomenon in which the father shares pregnancy prohibitions and restrictions with the woman who is bearing his child.

Cowper's glands: Located beneath the prostrate on either side of the urethra, their secretions neutralize urine acid levels and lubricate the urethra during the emission (first stage) of ejaculation.

cremasteric muscle: A muscle located in the spermatic cord that elevates the testicles when contracted.

cremasteric reflex: The response of the cremasteric muscle.

cross-cousin: A relative who is the child of one's mother's brother or father's sister.

crura: The innermost tips of the cavernous bodies that connect to the pubic bones.

cuckolded: Generally applies to a man whose wife has had sex with someone else.

cultural constructionist/constructionism: The examination of human behavior as a function of socio-cultural factors.

cultural relativism: The concept that cultures operate within their own structures, values, beliefs, and symbols and that they are to be interpreted within that system.

cultural system: Patterned beliefs and meanings.

culture: The learned behavior, skills, attitudes, beliefs, and values of a particular society. These are learned by observation, imitation, and social learning.

culture-bound: Unique to a given culture.

culture lag: A situation that occurs when behavior changes faster than the belief system.

cunnilingus: Oral stimulation of the clitoris, vaginal opening, or other part of the vulva.

cyclic/cyclicity: The term used to refer to the female's pattern of hormone release during her reproductive life cycle.

cystitis: A nonsexually transmitted infection of the urinary bladder.

deconstructionism/ist: An approach to collecting and analyzing data that challenges etic, androcentric, industrialized perspectives and focuses on emic perspectives.

Depo-Provera: Hormonal birth control method in which injectable synthetic progesterone prevents the release of the ovum and interferes with implantation of an egg in the uterus lining.

descent: The tracing of one's relationship based on the parent/child connection that defines the social relationship. Often claims are based on common ancestry that may or may not actually exist. Descent may be based on the mother's, father's, or both parentage.

descent group: A set of relationships that cannot be changed by location or death.

descent theory: Endogamy as a vehicle for families to contribute to cohesion and solidarity by keeping wealth, power, and prestige within the group.

desire: Precursor stage to arousal; specific sensations that lead to an interest in having sex.

developmental level: Also known as the ontogenetic level of the three categories of explanation. This level causes external and internal experiences in the individual's lifetime.

Diagnostic and Statistical Manual of Mental Disorders (DSM): Published by the American Psychiatric Association, this handbook is used most often in the diagnosis of mental disorders in the United States.

diaphragm: Thin dome-shaped barrier that prevents sperm from entering the cervix that is used with a spermicidal gel or cream.

dilation and evacuation (D & E): Abortion method that combines the vacuum aspiration method with elements of dilation and curettage.

disease: The physical manifestations of being sick or having been infected with some microorganism.

division of labor: The basis on which work is decided, often by sex or gender.

dorsal lithotomy position: A position that is common in U.S. obstetrics and used during pelvic exams where the woman lies on her back with her legs apart and her heels resting on an elevated surface.

double descent (nonunilineal, bilateral descent): The practice of tracing one's descent through both parents with each of these in control of different areas of activity and property.

doula(s): Adopted from the Greek, *doulas* are women who provide socio-psychological support to women during pregnancy and the postpartum period.

"down low": The term used in the African American community to refer to men who have sex with men covertly, but do not practice safer sex or inform their female sex partners of their behavior.

Down's Syndrome: A chromosomal abnormality that can result in the birth of a child with cognitive and other physical problems.

duolocality: The living arrangement where a young married couple lives apart from one another so only blood relations make up a household.

dysmenorrhea: Painful menstruation.

dyspareunia: Painful intercourse for women.

econiche: A particular environment to which a species is adapted.

ectopic pregnancy: The implantation of a blastocyst somewhere other than in the uterus, usually in the fallopian tube.

effacement: The gradual softening of cervix during labor.

ego: The term used for a person or persons in determining and tracing kinship.

ejaculate: A substance containing semen, sperm, and other chemicals which aid in sperm transport and mobility.

ejaculatory duct/tract: Continuation of the vas deferens through the prostrate to the urethra.

Electra complex: The female version of the Oedipal complex. The young female sexually desires her father and thus regards her mother as a competitor.

ELISA (Enzyme-Linked Immunosorbent Assay): A general screening test for HIV.

embryo: Term used to refer to the fertilized egg after it implants in the uterus until the end of the eighth week of pregnancy.

embryo transplants: Procedures in which a woman other than the prospective mother is impregnated with the husband's sperm. After several days, the fertilized egg is removed from her womb and placed within the mother's uterus.

Emergency Contraception (EC): A form of postcoital contraception taken within seventy-two hours of unprotected p-v intercourse that prevents conception; e.g. morning-after pills.

emic: The perception of a phenomenon as seen and felt by a participant inside the system.

endemic: A disease that is well-established in a population.

endemic warfare: A practice of ongoing, ritualized conflict between horticultural groups which compete for limited resources.

endocrine glands: Glands that directly release hormones into the bloodstream. Sex hormones are released by endocrine glands.

endogamy: The rule that requires a member of a community to marry within their group, tribe, caste, or class. This allows the group to retain and maintain control of wealth, power, and prestige.

endometriosis: A clinical condition often found among middle-class, college-educated career women in the United States in their twenties and thirties consisting of patches of endometrial tissue which are found on ovaries, the external uterus, and other pelvic and abdominal organs and fallopian tubes. It can cause fallopian tube blockage and scarring and interfere with conception.

endometrium: Interior lining of the uterus, innermost of three layers.

epidemic: The rapid spread of a disease through a population.

epidemiology: The study of the incidence, prevalence, and patterns of diseases within and between populations.

epididymis: Tubular structure on each testis in which sperm cells mature.

episiotomy: A surgical incision in the vaginal opening made by the clinician or obstetrician if it appears the perineum will tear in the process of birth.

erotocentricity: The process whereby we allow our own culture's sexual attitudes, values, and mores to bias our understanding of sexuality in other cultures.

erogenous (erotogenic) zone: The parts of the body where touching or stroking results in sexual excitement. The areas usually include, but are not limited to, the breasts, lips, genital or anal regions, and buttocks.

erogenous zone sensitivity: Those parts of the body that produce sexual arousal when stimulated.

essentialist: A person who believes that most behavior is based on genes, hormones, and biochemical factors.

Essure Method: Sterilization method in which a tiny tube shaped like a spring is placed in each tube which causes the tubal lining to form scar tissue and results in the obstruction of the fallopian tubes and prevents passage of the egg.

estradiol: An estrogen that effects the development and maintenance of the female reproductive organs as well as all female secondary sex characteristics.

estrogen: Term given to a group of "female" sex hormones found in postpubertal males and females. It is largely responsible for primary and secondary sex characteristic development in girls.

estrus: The reproductive cycle in female non-human mammals, which is accompanied by physiological, anatomical, and behavioral changes.

ethnocentrism: The view that the cultural values and practices of one's own society are superior to all others.

ethnography: The descriptive study of a culture; the research method of participant-observation in which the anthropologist becomes entrenched in the lives of people in his/her research community.

ethos: Approved style of life.

etic: The interpretation of customs in a specific culture as seen by the outside observer. The use of descriptions and analyses in terms of conceptual schemes and categories associated with industrialized scientific perspective.

etiology: The origin of a disease or abnormal condition.

evolution: The process of irreversible, qualitative change from one form or another that occurs over time that allows species to adapt to their changing environments.

excision: Refers to genital cutting during women's rites of passage.

exogamy: The marriage rule that requires its members to marry outside their community, tribe, clan, or group.

explicit culture: The knowledge about ourselves that can easily be communicated. Examples include genealogies and marriages.

expressive gender roles: Refers to the emotional work of women in the family and in relationships circa 1950s middle-class nuclear families. In 1995, the sociologist Talcott Parsons contrasted women's expressive roles with the instrumental roles of men characterized by work and the breadwinner role.

extended family: A group of people consisting of parents, children, grandparents, aunts, uncles and other relatives. Relationships are consanguineal (blood) and/or affinal (marriage).

extramarital sex: Having sex with someone other than your spouse.

exudate: Vaginal lubrication.

Faith-Based Organizations (FBOs): Those organizations that are derived from, supported by, and implemented by religious groups.

fallopian tubes: Organ in the female which extends from the fundus of the uterus for about five to seven inches to the ovaries. Hollow with hairlike cilia along the inner walls, they are the size of a broom straw or strand of spaghetti. Homologous and analogous to the vas deferens in males.

family of orientation: The family into which a person is born or adopted.

family of procreation: The family created through childbearing or adoption.

fellatee: The recipient of oral stimulation of male genitals.

fellatio: Stimulation of the male genitals with the mouth.

fellator: Refers to the individual performing oral stimulation of male genitals.

female condom (FC1): Barrier method introduced in the 1990s; device made of a seven-inch polyurethane bag held in place by two flexible rings one of which is located outside vagina with the other against the cervix.

female condom (FC2): Barrier method; new version of the female condom made of synthetic latex that is cheaper to produce.

female hormone patterning: The cyclical release of estrogens and progesterone triggered by fluctuations in the H-P-G axis.

female-to-male (FTM) transgender: Person identified at birth as female but who desires to live as a man or in an androgynous role. See TRANSGENDER.

femininity: A set of behavioral and affective characteristics associated with the female gender role; can very often be stereotypic and culture-bound.

fertility: The ability of a person to produce offspring.

fertility awareness methods (FAMs): Methods of birth control where the woman's menstrual cycle is tracked to predict periods of safe and unsafe days for coitus.

fetal reduction: Selectively aborting a fetus in a multiple pregnancy so that the other fetuses have an increased chance of survival.

fetus: The embryo after eight weeks of development until birth.

fictive kin: People who are not related to you, but stand in a kinship relation to you.

follicle(s): Relative to human sexuality, the sacs in the ovaries which contain the eggs.

follicular phase: The first phase of the menstrual cycle during which egg maturation and development occur.

follicular stimulating hormone (FSH): A hormone produced or secreted by the anterior pituitary gland which stimulates sperm production in males and follicle and ovum development in females.

foreskin: Generally used to refer to the skin that covers the glans penis.

fraternal polyandry: The marriage of brothers to the same woman with whom they live patrilocally. All husbands take responsibility for the woman's children.

frenum/frenulum: Thin tightly drawn fold of skin on the underside of the penile glans; it is highly sensitive.

fundus: The rounded top part of the uterus.

G-spot model: The Grafenberg spot is an area of sensitive tissues located one or two inches inside and on the anteria wall of the vagina. It is debated whether it is involved in orgasm.

gamete: The egg or sperm.

gamete transplant: A form of assisted reproductive technology (ART) in which the sperm is transferred into the woman's egg.

gay: A biological male whose sexual and romantic attractions are to others of his sex.

Gay, Lesbian, Bisexual and Transgender Pride Parades (Pride Parades): Annual parades held nationally and internationally that celebrate the diversity of genders and sexual orientations.

Gay-Related Immune-deficiency Disease (GRID): The erroneous label first given to AIDS in the United States.

gender: A designation given to sexes in regard to biobehavioral and psychosocial qualities.

gender dysphoria: Dissatisfaction with one's gender.

gender identity: The sense that one is a male, female, or some other gender.

gender role: Often referred to as script or scripting of an individual. The internalization and acting out of culturally defined male/female behavior, affect, and attitudes.

gender schema: Shared belief system about sex and gender.

gender selection: A preference for males or females, sometimes selected before birth through chromosome filtration or abortion, or after birth as with female infanticide.

genetic entities: Refers to the unique genetic makeup of individuals.

genetic sex: See CHROMOSOMAL SEX.

gestalt: The concept used by Ruth Benedict by which the configuration of a culture is presented as a whole formation which connotes more than its component parts.

glans: The acorn-shaped end of the penis that is covered by the foreskin and which is highly sensitive to sexual stimulation; homologous to the glans clitoris.

GLBTQ: acronym for gay, lesbian, bisexual, transgender, and queer community.

globalization: A process of economic, political, and social exchange and change that has existed for millennia, but usually refers to the impact of culture change between industrialized and nonindustrialized societies in the twentieth and twenty-first centuries.

gonadotropic releasing hormone (GnRH): Hormone released by the hypothalamus which stimulates the production of the pituitary hormone.

gonadotropins: Generic term given for sex hormones. See SEX HORMONES.

gonads: Ovaries in female, testes in male. The gonads comprise one-third of the H-P-G axis. They are the primary sources of estrogen and progesterone production in females, and testosterone in males.

Grafenberg spot (G spot): The Grafenberg or G spot is located approximately one or two inches inside the opening of the vagina on the anterior wall about halfway between the outer labia and the cervix. It is named after Dr. Ernst Grafenberg, (1950) who first located and described the dime-sized spot in a 1950 report.

grasping hand: A hand with a thumb that is opposable to other digits, enhancing the ability to grasp (grab) objects.

group marriage: As practiced by the Oneida Utopian Christians in communal living, the practice where all members regard one another as spouses.

gynecomastia: Breast enlargement in the male.

heteronormative: The idea that everyone is heterosexual.

heterosexual: Sexual and romantic attraction to the other sex.

Highly Active Antiretroviral Therapy (HAART): A combination of drugs called anti-retrovirals given to people with HIV to reduce their viral load, increase their T-cells and prevent them from contracting an Opportunistic Infection.

hijras: Indian group recognized as third gender and usually born as men and become transformed through ritualized surgical emasculation in which genitals are removed.

HIV: See HUMAN IMMUNODEFICIENCY VIRUS.

HIV-1: Retrovirus associated with HIV in this country.

HIV-2: A variety of HIV-1 found in West Africa.

HIV infection: The state of being HIV positive, determined through an HIV antibody test.

HIV testing: A blood or buccal membrane test that can be a preventive tool or basis of an initial diagnosis of HIV infection and AIDS.

holism: An all-embracing outlook that "refers to the study of the whole of the human condition; past, present, and future; biology, society, language and culture" (Kottak, 2002: 4).

holistic approach: The view that all parts of a culture are interrelated; leads to the study of all aspects of a culture and how they are interrelated.

hominid: Humans and their direct ancestors

homologous/homologues: Structures that develop from the same embryological tissue.

homophobia: Strongly held negative attitudes and irrational fears of homosexuals.

homosexual: The sexual and romantic attraction to people of one's own sex.

hormonal method: Birth control method using estrogen and progesterone and other hormones.

hormone replacement therapy (HRT): The use of supplemental hormones during and after menopause, also referred to as menopausal hormone treatment (MHT).

hormone therapy (HT): Generally referring to drugs given to peri- and postmenopausal women to treat the symptoms of menopause such as hot flashes and vaginal drying.

hormones: Substances released by the endocrine (ductless) glands that affect anatomical development and functioning.

horticulture: Describing a farming community; a form of cultivation also referred to as hoe or digging stick agriculture in which wide areas of land are farmed until they are depleted and there is an absence of the use of irrigation, crop rotation, and fertilizer. Often associated with endemic warfare and impacted habitats.

H-P-G Axis: Composed of the hypothalamus, the pituitary, and the gonads. This is the hormonal basis of sex and reproduction. This axis forms a network for understanding puberty, sexuality, and reproduction.

H-Y antigen: Testosterone; a substance found in the *in utero* sexual differentiation of chromosomal males.

human chorionic gonadotropin (HCG): Produced by the chorion and often referred to as the pregnancy hormone; HPG is detected by standard at-home pregnancy and clinical pregnancy tests.

Human Immunodeficiency Virus (HIV): A retrovirus that leads to a depletion of immune cells and eventually a diagnosis of AIDS.

Human Relations Area Files (HRAF Files): Classification scheme developed by G. P. Murdock that serves as the basis for statistical comparison for anthropologists.

human sexuality: The evolutionary, biochemical, anatomical, and socio-cultural dimensions from birth to death that relate to sexual behavior, beliefs, values, and symbols.

hymen: Membranous tissue that can cover part of the vaginal opening.

hypothalamus/hypothalamic: A ductless gland located in the brain that contains neurosecretions used in controlling certain metabolic actions like the maintenance of the body's water balance, sugar and fat metabolism, the regulation of body temperature, and the secretion of FSH, LH, and LTH.

ideal culture: The normative expectation or behavior of individuals in a given culture.

illness: The socio-psychological and economic aspects of being sick that affect the individual, the family, and possibly the community.

immediate family: Term used in the United States to designate those with close family relationships (husband, wife, mother, father, children, grandparents, siblings).

impacted habitats: Econiches characterized by natural boundaries that set limits to a group's expansion. These boundaries can include volcanoes, mountains, or impenetrable forests.

Implanon: A 1.5-inch rod that is injected under the skin of the upper arm of a woman and offers protection against pregnancy for up to three years through delivery of progestin which prevents ovulation.

in vitro **fertilization (IVF):** A technological process whereby the union of the sperm and egg occurs outside the mother's body.

incest taboo: The universal prohibition against marrying or mating within the primary family. The prohibition of sexual relations exists between mother and son, father and daughter, and brother and sister.

incidence: The number of new occurrences of a disease in a population.

incorporation: In rites of passage, the phase in which the initiates are integrated back into their society/social group in their new status.

independent household: Also known as neolocality. A newly married couple moves away from both set of parents to make their home in a different area.

indigenous cultural integrity: Refers to the survival of indigenous core cultural features, patterns, beliefs, values, and systems.

indigenous sexual behaviors: Sexual behaviors specific to a particular group.

induction method: Abortion option used in late-term pregnancies and used only when a severe medical problem for the mother or the fetus exists. Medication is injected into the amniotic sac and vagina to cause contractions and the explusion of the nonliving embryonic tissues.

infant dependency: The period of time when the young are dependent upon adult caregivers for survival.

infanticide: Method used to control birth found in a variety of forms around the globe and involves infant death.

infertility: A couple's inability to conceive and bear a child after one year of trying.

infibulation: Surgical procedure, performed in some cultures, that seals the opening of the vagina and removes the clitoris.

initiation ceremonies: Public recognition that facilitates the movement from child-hood to adulthood. These may be stressful, often include rigorous tests, hazing, isolation from younger friends, and painful ordeals.

injection drug use (IDU): Intravenous or subcutaneous use of drugs that can be recreational and often are illegal.

inseminate: To deposit ejaculate (semen) in the body.

inseminatee: Among the Sambia, the inseminatee is a boy who is the fellator of other males as part of a rite of passage into manhood in which he must build up his supplies of semen through ingesting it.

inseminator: See FELLATEE.

instrumental gender role: Boys' traditional industrialized socialization into roles associated with acting or achieving, circa 1950s middle class.

interactionist approach: The interaction of both biological and environmental variables and the nature of this interaction in the study of human sexuality; also referred to as intergrationist approach.

interfemoral intercourse: Position where the penis is placed between the partner's thighs.

intermediate societies: Joint household domesticated food economies like pastoralists and horticulturalists.

intersex: Individual possessing sexual characteristics of both male and female. Also referred to clinically as hermaphrodite.

interstitial cell stimulating hormone (ICSH): Pituitary hormone that stimulates the testes to secrete testosterone. Also known as LH in females and males.

interstitial cells: Cells in the testes that are a major source of testosterone.

interventionist and noninterventionist: Describes the continuum that refers to the degree of active involvement of others, use of drugs and other technology in a woman's labor and birth.

intimacy: Late twentieth-century middle-class term for bonding. The deep, intense, psychological, social, and emotional bonds between individuals that may or may not include sexual behavior.

intrauterine device (IUD): Birth control method; a small metal or plastic device placed in the uterus.

introitus: The outer opening of the vagina.

involution: The return of the uterus after childbirth to its prepregnant size and shape.

***jerungda*:** The vital life force in men that the Sambia believe is found in ejaculate. *Jerungda* is potentially exhaustible, and therefore ejaculate is both an essential body fluid and believed to exist in finite quantities.

joint household residence: The practice of living with or near one of the couple's parents.

kin groups: Descent that is determined by social position and cultural meaning. These links are formed through marriages and reproduction.

Kinsey Report: One of the earliest formal studies in United States of sexual behavior which has generated controversy.

kinship: A method for ordering human social relations and creating groups and boundaries.

Klinefelter's Syndrome: A genetic condition represented chromosomally by an XXY combination and occurring in about 1/500 to 1/1000 live births.

labia majora: Major or large lips of tissue on either side of the vaginal opening.

labia minora: Smaller lips of tissue on either side of the vagina.

labor: The time during childbirth when the woman's os dilates and the baby passes through the cervix into the vagina.

lactation: The production of milk from the mammary glands of mammals.

laparoscopy: Surgical procedure that involves an incision in the abdomen where organs are viewed through a lighted tube or laparoscope.

Late Luteal Phase Disorder (LLPD): The medical term given to what is popularly referred to as Premenstrual Syndrome (PMS), also referred to as premenstrual dysphoric disorder (PMDD).

latency stage: A Freudian psychosexual stage from six years of age to puberty when children lose interest in sex.

Lea's Shield: Barrier method approved by the FDA; a dome-shaped rubber disk with a valve and loop which is held in place by the vaginal wall.

lesbian: A biological female whose sexual and romantic attractions are to others of her own sex.

levirate: A tradition practiced in some cultures where a man is required to marry a deceased brother's wife.

leydig cells: Cells located between the seminiferous tubules that are the major source of androgen in males.

liaisons: Unstable relationships based solely on sex.

liberated gender role: It refers to a state of being culture-free of negatively perceived gender role expectations; that is, traditional roles, regardless of one's gender. It is individually oriented and defined, another phenomenon characteristic of the United States.

libidinous functioning: General reference to one's sexual interest in relation to sexual expression.

libido: A desire for sex. Freud considered it natural, present at birth, and focused in various areas of the body.

life cycle: The course of life from birth through death.

liminality: In rites of passage, these are the threshold rites that prepare an individual "for his or her reunion with society" (Van Gennep, 1960 [1909]: 21, 46, 67). Also referred to as the transition phase.

luteal phase: The third phase of the menstrual cycle. Conception occurs during this phase.

lutenizing hormone (LH): Hormone secreted by the pituitary gland that precipitates ovulation in females and maintains the leydig cells in males.

luteotropic hormone (LTH): Hormone that helps maintain uterine tone, promotes progesterone production, directly involved in the lactation process and may be involved in testosterone production.

machine suction: Abortion method used between the six to twelve weeks after conception to remove endometrial tissue from the uterus.

mahu: Tahitian gender variant status for men.

maidenhood: Time frame in a girl's life between menarche and full adulthood.

Maithuna: Sexual union in Tantric doctrine; a way to approximate merging with the sacred.

male climacteric: Sometimes termed "male menopause." At about the same age that women experience menopause, men have decreased testosterone production and, in industrialized countries, often begin to question the direction their lives are headed.

male condom: Made of latex rubber, lamb intestine, polyurethane, or synthetic elastomers, this device covers the penis and contains ejaculated sperm.

male menopause: See MALE CLIMACTERIC.

mandatory contact tracing: A process where sexual and needle-sharing partners of HIV-positive people are contacted through one of several interventions. Notification can be made by the infected people to their partners (good faith), by the Department of Health to the partners of HIV-positive individuals, or by having the HIV-positive individuals bring their partners to a post-test counseling session.

mandatory name reporting: Procedure used in the United States since 2000. If a person tests positive in a confidential HIV test, their names, location, ethnicity, age, gender, and mode of transmission are reported to their state agency of health and the CDC.

manual vacuum aspiration method (MVA): Abortion method whereby tissues from the uterus are gently suctioned through a handheld device. This method is used as early as three to seven weeks after a missed menstrual period.

marital ties: Those individuals who are related by marriage. For example, "in-laws" in United States culture.

marriage: A public and social ceremony between two or more people which creates relationships, sexual and economic rights, and obligations within the union. It also provides a means for incorporating offspring into the group.

masculinity: A pattern of learned, verbal/nonverbal signs, symbols, and behaviors that reinforce the socially defined concepts of male gender; may reinforce stereotypes and be culture-bound.

master gland: Also known as the pituitary. An organ in the brain which, as one of its functions, releases hormones necessary for sperm formation and egg development.

masturbation: Sexual self-stimulation, generally of one's genitals.

mateship: A public and social ceremony between two or more people which creates relationships, sexual and economic rights, and obligations within the union. It also provides a means for incorporating offspring into the group.

matrescence: The sociological process of becoming a mother.

matricentered, matricentricity: Weighted toward the female, valuing a female perspective, structure, values and belief system.

matrilineal descent: The practice of tracing descent through the female line.

matrilocal residence: The practice in which a married couple moves to live near or with the bride's family.

matrilocality: This refers to living arrangements where a couple resides in the community of the wife's mother. Also referred to as matrilocal residence.

medicalization: The classification of health, illness, and normalcy into industrial medical categories that emphasize dysfunctions and disorders.

medication abortion: Hormonal method of abortion.

menarche: Onset of menstruation.

menarche rituals: Rites of passage related to females' first menstruation.

menopause: The period of cessation of menstruation occurring usually between the ages of forty-five and fifty-five.

menses: Menstrual blood composed of blood, tissue, and mucous.

menstrual cramps: Uterine contractions caused by prostglandins.

menstrual cycle: Primary sex characteristic in the female that involves maturation and release of an egg from the ovary, preparation of the endometrium for either implantation of a fertilized egg or sloughing of the endometrium if fertilization has not occurred, and discharge of the menses if there is no implantation.

menstrual synchrony: Eventual synchronization of menstrual cycles among women who live near one another and are in close contact.

menstruation: The fourth phase of menstrual cycle when the endometrium is shed as menses; generally lasts four to seven days.

midwives: Women trained in administering pre- and postnatal care and attending births.

mifepristone: Hormonal method of abortion which is also known as RU 486. This method induces menstruation by interfering with production of progesterone.

migration: The movement of people into a region where they seek permanent residence.

mini-pill: Hormonal method for females that contains only progesterone, which inhibits the development of the uterine lining.

misoprostol: Hormonal method of abortion used with mifepristone that causes the cervix to soften and the uterus to contract.

mittelschmerz: The release of the egg from the ovary which some women experience as a cramping sensation.

modes of transmission: Transmission of HIV through infected blood, semen or vaginal fluids, or from mother-to-child during pregnancy or birth and through breastfeeding.

moiety system: Society is divided into two large social groups.

monogamy: Marriage to only one partner.

mons, mons pubis, mons veneris: Cushion of fatty tissue located over the female's pubic bone.

mortality: The incidence of death rates.

Mother-To-Child-Transmission (MTCT): The mechanisms by which HIV can be passed from mother to her fetus, infant, or child.

Müllerian ducts: Found in both embryonic males and females. Prenatal structures that develop into the broad ligament uterus, fallopian tubes, and upper third of the vagina.

Müllerian Inhibiting Substance (MIS): A hormone released by embryonic males to close their Mullerian ducts.

mutual masturbation: Stimulations of one's partner's genitals, usually manually.

myometrium: The middle layer of the uterus; consists of smooth muscle, thereby aiding the pushing of the newborn through the cervix.

nadle: Third gender position ascribed on the basis of ambiguous genitals among the Navajo.

negative feedback cycle: A term used to refer to the release of hormones during the menstrual cycle where a decrease in one hormone triggers the release of another one.

negative feedback loop: A regulatory system that coordinates the production of gonadal hormones through the complex interaction of the gonads, the hypothalamus, and the pituitary gland.

neolocality: The practice where the young married couple lives apart from their parents in their own home, usually in a different area.

neonate: Newborn.

neonatal: Referring to the care of newborns.

"noble savage": Notion derived from early anthropological reports of "exotic natives" communing with nature in its unspoiled and pristine state continues in popular culture.

nongovernment organizations (NGOs): Organizations that are not sponsored or under the aegis of the government.

noninterventionist: When applying to childbirth, the practice of using minimal interventions during the labor and birth of the child.

nontraditional gender role: Concept developed in the 1960s to refer to people who challenged the accepted cultural norms and structures about how men and women were to behave.

nonunilineal descent (bilateral, double descent): The practice of tracing one's descent through both parents with each of these in control of different areas of activity and property.

Norplant: Hormonal birth control method placed under the skin of the arm that releases progestin and provides protection against pregnancy for five years unavailable in the U.S.

nuclear family: A grouping of individuals of a household made up of a married couple and their children.

Oedipal phase (phallic stage): The Freudian psychosexual stage that occurs between the ages of three and five, characterized by love, hate, envy, and guilt.

Oedipus (Oedipal) complex: Named for the tragic mythical hero, Oedipus, who unknowingly fell in love with and married his mother. Oedipus blinded himself when he realized what he had done. The Freudian term is used to refer to a young boy who covets his mother while competing with his father.

olfaction: Sense of smell.

olfactory cues: Sexual scent signals.

olfactory kiss: See SMELL KISS.

omnivorous: A diet composed of both meats and vegetables.

ontogenetic level: Also known as the developmental level of the three categories of levels of explanation; seeks causes in external and internal experiences in the individual's lifetime.

oophrectomy: Surgical removal of the ovary or ovaries.

open biogram: An extremely flexible genetic program that is shaped by learning experience.

opportunistic infections (OIs): Those bacteria, viruses, fungi, and protozoa generally found in someone with a compromised immune system. One of the defining criteria for an AIDS diagnosis.

Opt-In Testing: HIV testing that occurs by someone specifically agreeing to have the test.

Opt-Out Testing: HIV testing that occurs by someone specifically declining to have the test.

oral combined contraceptive: Pill that contains synthetic estrogen and levonorgestrel; taken within seventy-two hours of intercourse, it is 75 percent effective in preventing pregnancy.

oral contraceptive pill (OCP): Hormonal method that combines estrogen and progesterone which tricks the body into thinking it is pregnant and prevents the egg's release.

oral stage: The Freudian psychosexual stage of development that occurs from birth to one year of age in which an infant's interest centers on the mouth as a source of pleasure.

orchidectomy: The surgical removal of the testes. See CASTRATION.

orgasm: Sexual climax. The intensely pleasurable feeling that comes at the end of stimulation to the genital organs (clitoris, vagina, penis).

orgasmic platform: Reached during the stage when the vaginal opening is reduced in size because of engorgement of the surrounding erectia tissue.

os: The opening of the cervix.

osteoporosis: A degenerative bone disease common in older women and men.

out: Term used for male and female homosexual people who are open about their orientation.

ovary/ovaries: The organ in the female responsible for egg maturation, the release of estrogen and progesterone, and some testosterone.

overdetermination of women's selfhood: Rules of conduct that are more restrictive for women than for men and emphasize control over women's bodies that are usually associated with patricentric and patriarchal societies.

ovulation: The release of the egg from the ovary.

ovum/ova: The egg(s).

oxytocin: A labor-stimulating hormone.

paleoanthropologists: Scholars of human evolution.

pandemic: A disease that is found globally.

Papanicolaou smear (Pap smear): Part of a gynecological exam where cells are gently scraped from the cervix and analyzed to detect cervical normalcy and abnormalities including cancer.

parallel cousins: Children of one's mother's sister, father's brother.

parametrium: Outer covering of the uterus.

paraurethral glands: Glands on either side of the Grafenberg spot that secrete a fluid into the urethra upon sexual stimulation.

participant-observation: Research method in which an anthropologist becomes entrenched in the lives of the people in their research community.

passage ceremony: See RITE(S) OF PASSAGE.

patch, the: Hormonal contraceptive containing estrogen and progestin which is applied once a week for three weeks to the upper body, lower abdomen, or buttocks. It is removed during the fourth week for menstruation to occur.

paternity: Blood relationship traced to the male or father.

paternity certainty: Firm knowledge of the father of an offspring.

patrescence: A status change for the male after the birth of his child.

patriarchy: Reference to a society in which males have privileged access to prestige, power, and resources.

patricentered, patricentricity: Weighted toward the male, valuing a male perspective, structure, values, and belief system.

patrilineal descent: Tracing kin through the male line.

532   Human sexuality

patrilocality (residence): Postmarital residence where the couple lives near or with the groom's family.

penile-vaginal intercourse (p-v sex): Insertion and incorporation of the penis in the vagina; colloquially, what many people in the U.S. refer to and think of as "sex."

penis: A primary male sexual and reproductive organ.

People Living with HIV/AIDS (PLWH/A): Those individuals who are HIV infected or who have AIDS.

PEPFAR: Implemented under George W. Bush's Presidency, the President's Emergency Plan for AIDS Relief. This plan provides resources for fifteen countries seriously impacted by HIV, but the plan mandates 30 percent of the resources earmarked for prevention goes to abstinence-only programs and condoms are only for prostitutes, gay men, injection drug users, and those who "can't be abstinent."

performance: Socially acquired lifeways and patterned interactions; the things humans do and make.

perimenopause: Climacteric period which begins five years prior to last menustral cycle and covers a ten-year period.

perineum: Sensitive area of skin between the scrotum or vagina and the anus.

phallic stage: The Freudian model of psychosexual development occurring between the ages of three and five years. Often this is characterized by love, hate, envy, and guilt and fascination with one's genitals. See OEDIPAL PHASE.

phenotypic sex: The physical expression of either the XX or XY genotype including structures such as ovaries, labia majora and minor, or the penis, testes, scrotum.

pheromones: Chemical signals; hormones produced by the body that either attract or repel the other sex.

phratry: A large grouping of people of unilineal descent composed of several clans.

physiology: The function of an organ or body structure.

PhRMA: An international prescription drug cartel that sets prices and regulates access to and the distribution of drugs cross-culturally.

pituitary: Also known as the "Master" gland, an organ in the brain which, as one of its functions, releases hormones necessary for sperm formation and egg development.

placenta: That structure in female mammals, primates, and humans that attaches to the uterine wall during pregnancy, providing nutrients to the fetus and filtering fetal wastes.

Plan B: A hormonal option for emergency contraception; a progestin-only pill taken in two doses twelve hours apart or two doses taken at the same time.

polyandrous marriages: Unions that help maintain family landholding units against possible subdivision through individual inheritance and partition of lands.

polyandry: The practice where one woman has several husbands at the same time. A form of polygamy practiced in Tibet, Nepal, India, Sri Lanka, and by the Marquesans of the Pacific.

polygamy: Marriage to multiple partners (spouses) at the same time.

polygyny/polygynous: The practice where one man has several wives at the same time.

population control: Any means a group uses throughout the life cycle to control its size.

postexposure prophylaxis (PEP): ARVs given to someone immediately after exposure to HIV in order to reduce the chances of infection.

postpartum: The period after birth.

postpartum depression: A culture-specific, bio-cultural phenomenon found more often in women in the United States than elsewhere where they become depressed after giving birth.

pre-ejaculatory fluid: A clear, slippery fluid released from the Cowper's gland into the urethra before ejaculation that neutralizes the acidity of the urethra.

pregnancy: The time from implantation of the fertilized egg into the uterine wall until after the placenta has been born.

premarital sex: Sex before marriage.

premenstrual syndrome (PMS): A collection of symptoms that some women in industrialized societies experience the week before menstruation that can include food cravings, mood swings, and bloating. The existence and nature of PMS is controversial.

prepuce: In the female, the upper part of the labia minora that covers the clitoral shaft, known as the "clitoral hood." In males, the foreskin, a loose tissue covering the glans.

prevalence: How widespread a disease is in a population.

primary orgasmic dysfunction: Clinical term that refers to women who have never experienced an orgasm.

primary sex characteristics: Those structures in both the male and female related to the reproductive cycle and directly involved in sexual and reproduction function.

primates: An order in the phylogenetic tree characterized by large-brained, highly social creatures of which prosimians, monkeys, apes, and humans are members.

proceptivity: Actively seeking a mating opportunity.

progesterone: A "female" sex hormone found in postpubertal females and males and responsible for the development of certain primary sex characteristics.

prolactin (PRL): A hormone found in the pituitary gland that is involved with breast development and the production of milk during lactation (nursing or breast-feeding).

promiscuity: A highly value-laden term referring to the number of sex partners a person has; often applied to females.

pronatalism/pronatalist: The belief or practice of regarding the fetus as primary and/or more important than its mother.

prostate: A walnut-sized organ surrounding the male urethra which releases semen.

prostatitis: A localized or systemic infection or irritation of the prostate.

prostglandins: Hormones produced in the uterus which contract the uterus.

prostitution: A specific form of sex work that involves the exchange of sex (left undefined) for money, goods, or services (goods and services are undefined).

proximate level: One of the levels of explanation that seeks causes in the immediate external and internal environment.

psychoanalysis: Freudian technique used in treating personal and psychological disorders in which people explore their pasts to gain insights into their current behaviors and feelings.

puberty: The stage of life when a person develops secondary sexual characteristics and begins spermatogenesis or the menstrual cycle.

pubic bone (pubis): The pelvic bone that lies beneath the mons.

pubic hair: A secondary sex characteristic of hair distribution in males and females that covers the genitalia.

pubococcygeus muscles: Muscles encircling the vagina and the crura.

quickening: The time when a woman first feels the fetal movement.

ramage: Ambilineal descent in which groups are formed by household and common ancestors; may be stratified internally.

real behavior/culture: This term is usually used to contrast with the term "ideal" behavior/culture. Ideal culture is what is expected in contrast to what people actually do, which is termed "real" behavior/culture. This may be contrasted with "perceived behavior," what others think they are doing

receptivity: Willingness to engage in sexual activity with a partner.

recreational ideology: Industrialized men are socialized in a recreational model of sexuality to experience sex as conquest with the goal orientation of orgasm.

relational ideology: Industrialized women are socialized in a relational model to experience sex as intimacy and as a process of achieving closeness.

relatives: People linked to individuals through the kin of both sexes.

reliance on learning: the principle that most behaviors are learned rather than genetically determined for humans.

reproduce: To produce offspring.

reproductive cycle: That component of sexuality involved in the structures and behaviors that can result in offspring.

reproductive functions: Those functions that result in offspring and include spermatogenesis, ejaculation, the menstrual cycle, pregnancy, and birth.

reproductive structures: Those structures directly involved in reproduction.

reproductive success: The ability of a species to produce enough viable young who live to reproductive age to continue the species.

resolution: Final phase of human sexual response.

rete testes: The rudimentary structure that develops from the Wolffian ducts.

retrovirus: A virus whose genes are in the form of RNA.

rhythm method: A natural birth control method entailing abstinence during the ovulatory phase of the menstrual cycle.

rite(s) of passage: The symbolic or ceremonial observance that occurs when an individual moves from one stage in the life cycle to the next. This includes three stages: separation, transition (liminality), and incorporation.

ritual marriage: A relationship where a woman marries a man from a linked lineage. Associated with specific polyandrous forms of marriage.

ritual totemic meal: According to Freud, the occasional ritual eating of the totemic animal that is usually proscribed is evidence of the commemoration of the original primal scene in which the sons killed their father and is the origin of the incest taboo.

root: The part of the penis and clitoris that is attached to the body.

safe sex: Those behaviors which will not transmit HIV or other STIs.

safer sex: Those behaviors which reduce the risk of transmitting HIV or other STIs.

script/scripting: Gender role; the internalization and acting out of culturally defined male/female behavior, affect, attitudes.

scrotal sac/scrotum: The multilayered pouch of loose skin located between the penis and contains the testicles, epididymis, and spermatic cords.

secondary orgasmic dysfunction: Clinical term that refers to women who have once been orgasmic but who are no longer.

secondary sex characteristics: Those structures in both the male and female which are often directly involved in sexuality, indirectly involved in reproductive functioning, and are frequently used as cultural markers of physiological sexual maturity and gender signals.

semen: The fluid produced in the seminal vesicles and prostate that transports and nourishes the sperm.

seminal vesicles: Two structures that provide most of the semen.

seminiferous tubules: Tightly coiled tubes in the testes where the sperm develop.

separation: In rites of passage, the phase in which an individual is removed from his or her previous world or place in society.

sero-discordant couples: Couples in which one person is HIV-positive and one person is HIV-negative.

sex: As in male, female, intersex, or other, typically refers to biological attributes including chromosomes, external genitals, gonads, internal reproductive structures, hormonal states, and secondary sexual characteristics, among others.

sex drive: Sometimes referred to as the libido, the interest in behaving sexually that is, in part, a function of testosterone, but largely a function of socio-cultural factors.

sex-gender system: The sex-gender system refers to the relationship of the biological, the social, and the cultural system as mediating the expression of gender roles and sexuality. Sexuality and gender may be analytically distinct but intersect in the lives of humans in particular ways depending on cultural context.

sex hormones: Those hormones, specifically testosterone and its derivatives, estrogen in its varied forms, and progesterone, that are responsible for the development and expression of male and female primary and secondary sex characteristics respectively.

sex signal: Erotic symbol.

sex tourism: An international industry where people travel to specific countries in order to hire and engage in a variety of sexual activities.

sex work: An inclusive term referring to formal exchanges of money, goods, or services for various kinds of sexual behavior.

sexology: The study of sexual attitudes and behaviors by scientific means.

sexual addictions: Desire disorders of a "hypersexual" response, known popularly as sexual addiction. This "problem" is not included in the *DSM*, although it is included in the World Health Organization's *International Classification of Diseases* (ICD 10, 1992; King, 2005).

sexual behaviors: The type of behavior that one expresses; distinct entity from sexual orientation.

sexual cue(s): Visual clues of stimulation.

sexual culture: Defined by Gilbert Herdt as the "intrinsic or internal meaning, as well as extrinsic or environmental sources of sexual behavior" (Herdt, 1999: 100).

sexual cycles: Those behaviors and anatomical structures that primarily deal with sexual arousal and release.

sexual desire disorders: A broad category of sexual problems related to having an interest in behaving sexually.

sexual differentiation: The process by which male and female sexual and reproductive anatomy develops *in utero*.

sexual double standard: Sexual norms commonly found in bilateral and patrilineal descent societies where men and women's sexual behaviors are perceived and responded to differently.

sexual functions: The anatomical (e.g., clitoris), psycho-social, and emotional components of sexual desire, arousal, and orgasm.

sexual orientation: The sex to which one is sexually attracted.

sexual partnership: Two people who have sexual relations with each other.

sexual prohibitions: These are cultural rules defining appropriate and inappropriate categories of marriage and sexual partners.

Sexual Revolution: A part of the 1960s when a tremendous amount of time, energy, and attention was directed toward defining and elaborating the concepts of gender role, gender identity, and sexuality.

sexual risk continuum: The continuum of sexual behaviors from riskiest to least risky regarding sexual susceptibility for contracting HIV.

sexual scent signals: Pheromones.

sexual structures: Structures primarily involved in sexual arousal and release such as the clitoris.

sexual subjectivity: How we experience and express sexuality including individual activities like personalities, histories, and sense of self.

sexually transmitted infections (STIs)/sexually transmitted diseases (STDs): STIs are those bacteria, viruses, fungi, creatures such as pubic lice, and protozoa that are transmitted sexually. STDs are the physical manifestations of being infected with and STI.

shaft: The long part of the penis ending in the glans.

show: The mucous "plug" or substance that covers the os during pregnancy which is expelled as blood and mucous during the early stages of labor.

situational orgasmic dysfunction: Clinical term that refers to women's problems of achieving orgasm in certain contexts but not others.

Skene's Glands: Also known as the paraurethral glands. Glands on either side of the Grafenberg spot (G-spot) that secrete a fluid into the urethra upon sexual stimulation.

smegma: White, lubricating, cheeselike substance secreted underneath the foreskin of the penis and prepuce of the clitoris.

smell kiss: Nose is placed on the partner's face as one inhales.

social construction/constructionism: Theory of how societies produce and create sexual meanings, behaviors, and subjectivities.

social organization: Relationship seen through kinship and marriage and also through institutional structures such as religion and political organizations.

social structures: Used in reference to social systems and the impact of institutions and socioeconomic status factors on sexual behavior.

social system: A set of patterned interactions incorporating various institutions, including the sex and gender systems.

sororal polygyny: A situation where men marry their wives' sisters in the belief that this will contribute to household harmony and productivity.

sororate: The practice where a man marries his dead wife's sister. In some cultures this is required after the death of a spouse.

species: Defined as a "population or group of populations that is capable of inter-breeding but that is reproductively isolated from other such populations" (Haviland, 1989: 66).

spectatoring: A behavior in which an individual or couple monitor their sexual response, thereby detracting from the pleasure the individual or couple experiences.

sperm: Male sex gamete produced in the testes.

sperm banks: Repositories of donated ejaculate that have been medically and genetically screened and HIV tested, which are used for artificial insemination-donor.

sperm count: Any sperm count at or below 20 million per ejaculate renders a man "subfertile."

sperm count, motility, and form: The criteria used to determine a man's fertility.

sperm form: The head, midsection, and tail of sperm. All sections must be present for impregnation to occur.

sperm motility: The mobility or rapidity of sperm movement.

spermatic cord: Male organ located on the side of each testicle and extending to the pubis which contains several structures such as the cremasteric muscle, vas deferens, blood vessels, and nerves.

spermatic economy: A widely held nineteenth-century western belief that ejaculate exists in finite quantities in a man's life.

spermatogenesis: The formation of sperm.

sponge: A barrier method used with a spermicide; can be inserted up to twenty-four hours before penile-vaginal intercourse.

stereoscopic vision: The development of three-dimensional vision that occurred in primate and hominid evolution with the location of the eyes on the front of the face. Represents an adaptation related to primate arboreal and subsequent terrestrial environments.

steroids: A class of hormones that includes androgens.

straight: Argot for heterosexual people.

subfertility: See ADOLESCENT STERILITY.

subincision: Incision on the underside of the penis.

superincision: Incision on the upper side of the penis.

"Supermale Syndrome": Also known as the XYY syndrome, the genetic chromosomal makeup of XYY and occurs in about 1/1,000 live births.

survival of the fit: Those individuals who are better adapted to their environments will be more likely to reproduce surviving offspring than those who are not. Those individuals who reproduce themselves are more likely to pass on the traits they possess than those who are not so well adapted to their environments.

survival sex: Exchange of sexual behaviors for money, food, shelter and/or protection for a woman and possibly her family.

sweatshops: Factories and businesses in industrialized and nonindustrialized countries that pay very low wages, have unsafe working conditions, long work days without breaks, and offer no benefits such as sick leave, vacations, or health insurance.

syncretism: The blending and mixing of indigenous cultural elements with those introduced by other societies; the "interplay of local, regional, national and international cultural forces" (Kottak, 2002: 504).

tacit culture: Shared rules that an individual learns unconsciously from those around them regarding behavior.

Tantra: A sect of Hinduism practiced in India.

tenting orgasm: An orgasm that occurs with clitoral stimulation after which the inner portion of the vagina balloons as a result of the lifting up of the uterus.

terminal disease: A disease that is fatal.

testes: Primary source of testosterone and other androgens in the male, as well as where sperm are produced.

testicles: See TESTES.

testicular self-exam (TSE): A self-examination men can do to detect changes in their scrotal sac, testicles, and spermatic cord.

testosterone: Considered the "male sex hormone"; found in postpubertal males and females. Responsible for the libido or innate sex drive in people and primary and secondary sex characteristic development in the male.

theoretical effectiveness rate: The effectiveness rate of a given method of birth control based on laboratory conditions and correct and consistent practices.

third sex: A term applied to people identifying as something other than a male or female. There may be more than three referred to as supernumerary genders or gender variance.

threshold level: The amount of testosterone required to maintain the libido in men and women.

tonic: Ongoing releasing patterns.

tonicity: Refers to the pattern of male gonadotropic hormone release.

totem animal: Freudian concept in which the symbol that represents the father is ritually eaten in commemoration.

traditional gender role: Conforming to mid-twentieth-century U.S. structures and norms regarding appropriate behavior for males and females.

trafficking: The movement of individuals and groups within and across borders for economic purposes that can include prostitution, slave labor, sweatshop conditions in businesses or factories, or indentured labor in residences of wealthy people. Trafficking is generally illegal.

transition: See LIMINALITY.

transgender: A recent addition to industrialized gender-variant social identities. A community term that regards gender-variant identities as a continuum which includes the traditional transsexual and cross-dresser and identities that lie in between and beyond.

transsexual: An individual who has the phenotype of one gender, but the gender identity of another. See TRANSGENDER.

transurethral resection of the prostate (TURP): A surgical procedure to reduce benign (or noncancerous) enlargement of the prostate.

transvestic fetishism: Classified by DSM-IV-TR as a paraphilia (problematic sexual desire or behavior).

transvestite: A clinical term for an individual, usually male, who dresses in clothing of the other sex. Cross-dresser is the preferred term among the trans community.

tubal ligation: Sterilization method where surgical procedure cuts, cauterizes, bands or ties the fallopian tubes.

tubal patency: Having unblocked fallopian tubes.

Turner's Syndrome: Genetic anomaly represented by an X or XO combination and occurring in 1/4000 live births.

two spirit: Acceptable term for Native American gender-variant individuals.

Type I: Excision. See CLITORIDECTOMY.

Type II: Excision of clitoral hood, clitoredectomy and/or partial/total removal of labia minora.

Type III: See INFIBULATION. Surgical removal of external genitalis with sutering of vagina opening.

Type IV: Practice that includes various modifications of the female genital area, but not removal of, tissues.

ultimate level: The final level of the three levels of explanation; the evolutionary explanation seen as being the result of natural selection, as having adaptive significance.

umbilical cord: The cord that connects the fetus to the placenta.

unilineal (descent): Tracing descent through either the male or female line.

urethra: The tube running from the bladder to the outside of the body. The urethra transports urine from the bladder to outside the body in both males and females, and ejaculate in the male.

urethral sponge: Sheath of erectile tissue around the urethra which becomes engorged during sexual excitement and protects the urethra during sexual activity.

urinary meatus: Located between clitoris and introitus in females and the end of the glans penis in the male; it is the opening in the urethra in both sexes through which urine passes and ejaculate passes in the male.

urinary stress incontinence (USI): Involuntary leakage of urine.

urinary tract infection (UTI): An infection of the urethra more often found in women which can be caused by an abrasion of the urethra or infection by a pathogen.

uterine orgasm: According to Singer and Singer (1972: 259–260): "The 'uterine orgasm' does not involve any contractions of the orgasmic platform . . . this kind of orgasm occurs in coitus alone, and it largely depends upon the pleasurable effects of uterine displacement."

uterine tone: The muscular strength and integrity of the uterus.

uterus: A pear-shaped organ located in the female's pelvis that is both a primary and secondary sex organ. The uterus is the site of implantation and embryo/fetal growth.

vagina: Female organ that functions both sexually and reproductively.

vaginal contraceptive ring: Flexible ring that releases estrogen and progestin and is worn for three weeks and removed for one.

value system: System of meanings and beliefs in a culture including art, music, rituals, myths, folklore, and cosmology: sustains patterning of culture such as marriage norms, gender roles, courtships, etc.

vas deferens: Male reproductive structures which transport the sperm from the epididymis to the seminal vesicles.

vasectomy: Male sterilization procedure where each vas deferens is surgically blocked to prevent sperm from passing through.

vasocongestion: A physical condition occurring during sexual intercourse when blood vessels in the genitals engorge.

vernix: A waxy, protective substance covering the fetus.

viability: The ability of the neonate to live.

Victorian era: Historical period covering the rule of Queen Victoria of England (1837–1901). This era saw strict rules in regard to morality and valued the unspoiled or the pristine state. Sexual impulses were associated with shame and were suppressed or never publicly shared.

visiting husband: In polyandrous marriages, the woman does not live with her husband but he may visit her for sexual relations.

vulva: External sex organs of the female, including the mons, major and minor lips, clitoris, and opening of the vagina.

vulval orgasm: This is the type of orgasm described in Masters and Johnson's human sexual response cycle. It includes the reduction of the vaginal opening due to engorgement of the surrounding erectile tissues, with orgasm occurring three to twelve contractions at 0.8 second intervals.

Westermarck Effect: Theory of the lack of erotic desire that people who are raised in proximity feel toward one another, i.e.: "proximity breeds contempt."

Western Blot Test: A confirmatory HIV antibody test.

window period: The time between infection with HIV and when antibodies to the virus are detectable.

withdrawal: Coitus interruptus.

Wolffian Ducts: Embryonic structures that develop into male sexual and reproductive organs if male hormones are present and into part of the urinary tract system in both males and females.

Wolffian Inhibiting Substance: A nonexistent substance analogous to MIS.

woman marriage: The practice found in some cultures wherein two women marry. One may become the "social" male and makes arrangements for the wife to become pregnant by another man.

woman years: The number of failures for a given contraceptive method per 100 couples during a year of use called women years because women are the ones who are impregnated.

World Health Organization (WHO): An international organization located in Geneva, Switzerland, that addresses global health issues.

xanith: A third gender identity found among the Omani in the Middle East.

zygote: A fertilized egg.

zygote transplant: The implantation of the fertilized egg into a woman's fallopian tubes.

Bibliography

4Parents.gov. 2005. http://www.4parents.gov/. Last accessed February 9, 2006.

Aalbers, Manuel B. 2005. "Big Sister is Watching You: Gender Interaction and the Amsterdam Red-Light District." *Journal of Sex Research* 42: 54–62.

AAUW Briefs. 1989. May/June, 83(3).

"Abortion." 2005–2006. WebMD. http://www.webmd.com/hw/womens_conditions/tw1043.asp. Last accessed 1/20/2007.

"Abortion." 2006. Planned Parenthood Federation of America. http://www.plannedparenthood.org/mar-monte/abortion.htm. Last accessed 1/20/2007.

"Abortion: A to Z Health Guide." 2004. WebMD. http://www.webmd.com/hw/womens_conditions/tw1043.asp?pagenumber=3. Last accessed 1/20/2007.

"Abortion and Birth Control Polling Report" 2006. PollingReport.com. http://www.pollingreport. com/abortion.htm. Last accessed 1/7/07.

"Abortion in American History." 1990. *Parade Magazine*, April 22: 8.

"Abortion Information." 2006. Feminist Women's Health Center. http://www.fwhc.org/index.htm. Last accessed 1/20/2007.

"Abortion Law in Ireland: A Brief History." 2006. Irish Family Planning Association. http://www.ifpa.ie/abortion/hist.html. Last accessed 11/30/2006.

Abramson, Allan. 1987. "Beyond the Samoan Controversy in Anthropology: A History of Sexuality in the Eastern Interior of Fiji." In *The Cultural Construction of Sexuality*. Pat Caplan, ed. New York: Tavistock. Pp. 193–216.

Adelson, Joseph. 1980. *Handbook of Adolescence.* New York: John Wiley and Sons.

"Advancing HIV Prevention: New Strategies for a Changing Epidemic—United States, 2003." 2003. *Morbidity and Mortality Weekly Report (MMWR)*, 52: 329–332.

AFROL. 2003. *Legal Status of Homosexuality in Africa.* http://www.afrol.com/Categories/Gay/backgr_legalstatus.htm. Last accessed February 9, 2006.

"Age Page: Hormones After Menopause, 2005, The." 2005. National Institute on Aging. http://www.niapublications.org/agepages/. Last accessed 8/10/06.

Aggleton, Peter, ed. 1994. *Learning About AIDS: Scientific and Social Issues.* 2nd ed. New York: Churchill Livingstone.

AIDS and Anthropology Research Group. 1988. *The AIDS and Anthropology Research Group (AARG) Newsletter*, July–September, 1(1): 1–4.

Aitken, R. John, and Jennifer A. Marshall Graves. 2002. "On the Vulnerability of the Human Spermatozoon." *Nature,* 415: 963.

Aitken, R. John, Peter Koopman, and Sheena E. M. Lewis. 2004. "Public Health: Environmental Pollution and Male Fertility." *Nature,* 432: 48.

Alan Guttmacher Institute. http://www.agi-usa.org. Last accessed 3/28/06.

Alcamo, I. Edward. 2003. *AIDS: The Biological Basis*. 3rd ed. Boston, MA: Jones and Bartlett Publishers.

Alexander, Priscilla. 1987. "Prostitutes Are Being Scapegoated for Heterosexual AIDS." In *Sexwork: Writings by Women in the Sex Industry*. Frederique Delacoste and Priscilla Alexander, eds. Pittsburgh: Cleis Press. Pp. 248–263.

Allgeier, Elizabeth R. and Albert Richard Allgeier. 1991. *Sexual Interactions*. 3rd ed. Lexington: DC Heath and Co.

"Alternatives to HRT for Treatment of Menopausal Symptoms." 2005. Continuing Medical Education Program of the University of Florida, College of Medicine. http://womenshealth.ufl.edu/hrt_althome.htm. Last accessed 12/4/06.

Althof, Stanley E. and Patricia Schreiner-Engle. 2000. "The Sexual Dysfunction." In *New Oxford Textbook of Psychiatry*. Michael G. Gelder, Juan J. Lopez-Ibor and Nancy Andreasen, eds. Oxford: Oxford University Press.

Altman, Dennis. 2002. *Global Sex*. Chicago: University of Chicago Press.

Altman, Lawrence K. 1998. "U. N. Breast-Feeding Warning for Moms with AIDS." *San Francisco Examiner*, July 26: A19.

Altzate, Heli and Maria Ladi Londono. 1984. "Vaginal Erotic Sensitivity." *Journal of Sex and Marital Therapy*, 10(49).

Amadiume, Ifi. 1987. *Male Daughters and Female Husbands*. Atlantic Highlands: Zed Books.

"America's Families and Living Arrangements." 2003–2004. U.S. Census Bureau. Pp. 1–20. http://www.census.gov/prud/2004pubs/p20-553.pdf.

American Anthropological Association. 2006. http://www.aaanet.org. Last accessed 2/9/06.

American Association of Physical Anthropologists. 2006. http://www.physanth.org. Last accessed 6/8/06.

American Health. 1994. July/August: 8, 101.

American Heritage Dictionaries editors. 2004. *American Heritage Stedman's Medical Dictionary*. Boston: Houghlin Mifflin.

American Primatological Society. 2006. http://www.asp.org/. Last accessed 6/6/06.

American Psychiatric Association. 1973. *Diagnostic and Statistical Manual of Mental Disorders*. 2nd ed. Washington: American Psychiatric Association.

———. 1980. *Diagnostic and Statistical Manual of Mental Disorders*. 3rd ed. Washington: American Psychiatric Association.

———. 1994. *Diagnostic and Statistical Manual of Mental Disorders-IV*. 4th ed. Washington, DC: APA.

———. 2000. *Diagnostic and Statistical Manual of Mental Disorders-IV-TR*. http://www.behavenet.com. Last accessed 8/11/06.

American Psychological Association Committee on Aging. 2007. http://www.apa.org/pi/aging/cona01.html. Last accessed 11/9/07.

American Red Cross. 2004. http://www.redcross.org. Last accessed 2/9/06.

And the Band Played On. 1993. Directed by Roger Spottiswoode. USA: HBO Home Videos.

Andersen, Alan, Nyboe, Luca Gianaroli, and Karl Gösta Nygren. 2004. "Assisted Reproductive Technology in Europe, 2000. Results generated from European registers by ESHERE." *Human Reproduction*, 19(3): 490–503.

Anderson, Jean, ed. 2001. *A Guide to the Clinical Care of Women with HIV*. 2001 ed. Rockville: Womencare.

Anderson, Richard A., H. Shu, L. Cheng, and D. T. Baird. 2002. "Investigation of a Novel Preparation of Testosterone Decanonate in Men." *Contraception,* 66: 357–364.

Anderson, Sarah E. and Aviva Must. 2005. "Interpreting the Continued Decline in the Average Age at Menarche: Results from Two Nationally Representative Surveys of U. S. Girls Studied 10 Years Apart." *Journal of Pediatrics,* December, 147(6): 753–760.

Andrade, Tarcisio, Peter Lurie, Maria Guadalupe Medina, Kim Anderson, and Ines Dourado. 2001. "The Opening of South America's First Needle Exchange Program and Epidemic of Crack Use in Salvador, Bahai-Brazil." *AIDS and Behavior,* 5(1): 51–64.

Angeloni, Elvio. 1989/1990. *Annual Editions Anthropology.* Sluice Dock: Dushkin Publishers.

Angier, Natalie. 1992. "A Male Menopause? Jury Is Still Out." *New York Times,* 20 May 6.

Anon. 2005. "Baseball Objects to Congressional Subpoenas for Steroids: Canseco, Giambi, Sosa Among Those on List." KTVU.com. http://www.ktvu.com/sports/4267109/detail.html.

Answers.com. 2005. "Oxytocin." http://www.answers.com/topic/oxytocin. Last accessed 2/9/06.

Anthropology and Aging Quarterly. http://artsci.wustl.edu/~aage/quarterly.htm. Last accessed 11/2006.

Appignanesi, Richard. 1979. *Freud for Beginners.* New York: Pantheon Books.

Arcaro, Thomas and Jocelyn Drye, eds. 2002. *Understanding the Global Experience: Becoming a Responsible World Citizen.* 3rd ed. Elon: Carpe Viam Press. As a CD-ROM.

Arcaro, Thomas and Duane McClearn, eds. 2000. *Understanding the Global Experience: Becoming a Responsible World Citizen.* Elon College: Carpe Viam Press.

Archer, John and Barbara Lloyd. 2002. *Sex and Gender.* New York: Cambridge University Press.

Aries, Philippe. 1962. *Centuries of Childhood: A Social History of Family Life.* New York: Random House.

Arms, Suzanne. 1975. *Immaculate Deception: A New Look at Women and Childbirth in America.* South Hadley: Bergin and Garvey Publishers.

Aron, Arthur, Helen Fisher, Debra J. Mashek, Greg Strong, Li Haifang, and Lucy L. Brown. 2005. "Reward, Motivation, and Emotion Systems Associated with Early-Stage Intense Romantic Love." *Journal of Neurophysiology,* 94(1): 327–337.

"Asia: Discarding Daughters." 1990. *Time,* November 1, 136(19): 40.

Association for Anthropology and Gerontology, The. http://artsci.wustl.edu/~aage. Last accessed 12/2006.

Association for Feminist Anthropology. 2006. http://sscl.berkeley.edu/~afaweb/. Last accessed 3/27/06.

Association of Reproductive Health Professionals. https://www.arhp.org/. Last accessed 11/9/2007

"Attacking the Last Taboo." 1990. *Time,* April 14, 115(15): 72.

Ault, Alicia. 1988. "First Pill for Male Impotence Approved in USA." *Lancet,* April 4, 351(9108): 1037.

Austin, E. 1993. "Four New Improved Birth Control Pills." *Self*, 1993: 57.

"Average Age of Menarche in Various Cultures." 2003. The Museum of Menstruation and Women's Health. http://www.mum.org/menarage.htm. Last accessed 7/11/06.

Aydun, Hamdullah and Zeynep Gulcat. 2004. "Turkey." In *The Continuum Complete International Encyclopedia of Sexuality*. Robert T. Francoeur and Raymond J. Noonan, eds. New York: Continuum. 2004. Pp. 1054–1071.

Avis, Nancy E., Rebecca Stellato, Sybil Crawford, Joyce Bromberger, Patricia Ganz, Virginia Cain, and Marjorie Kaguwa-Singer. 2001. "Is There a Menopausal Syndrome? Menopausal Status and Symptoms across Race/Ethical Groups." *Social Science and Medicine*, 52(3): 345–356.

"Backgrounder: "Do CAM Therapies Help Menopausal Symptoms?" 2005. The National Center for Complimentary and Alterative Medicine. http://nccam.nih.gov/health/menopauseandcam/. Last accessed 8/11/06.

Badri, Amna el Sadik. 2000. "Female Circumcision in the Sudan." In *Human Sexuality: Cross Cultural Readings*. Brian M. du Toit, ed. New York: McGraw Hill. Pp. 95–106.

Baetens, Patricia M., Michel Camus, and Paul Devroey. 2003. "Should Requests for Donor Insemination on Social Grounds Be Expanded to Transsexuals." *Reproductive Biomedicine Online*, 6(3): 281–286.

Bailey, Michael. 1999. "Young Women and HIV: The Role of Biology in Vulnerability." In *The Impact of AIDS: Psychological and Social Aspects of HIV Infection*. Jose Catalan, Loraine Sherr and Barbara Hedge, eds. London: UCL. Pp. 159–169.

Bailey, J. Michael. 2003. *The Man Who Would Be Queen: The Science of Gender-Bending and Transsexualism*. Washington: Joseph Henry Press.

Bailey, J. Michael and Richard C. Pillard. 1991. "A Genetic Study of Male Sexual Orientation." *Archives of General Psychiatry*, 48: 1089–1096.

Baker, Diane and Sharon E. King. 2004. "Child Sexual Abuse and Incest in the United States." *The Continuum Complete International Encyclopedia of Sexuality*. Robert T. Francoeur and Raymond J. Noonan, eds. New York: Continuum. Pp. 1233–1237.

Bakwin, Harry. 1974. "Erotic Feelings in Infants and Young Children." *Medical Aspects of Human Sexuality*, 8(10): 200–215.

Bancroft, John, ed. 2000. *The Role of Theory in Sex Research*. Bloomington: Indiana University Press.

Bancroft, John, Jeni Loftus, and J. Scott Long. 2003. "Distress About Sex: A National Survey of Women in Heterosexual Relationships." *Archives of Sexual Behavior*, 32(3): 193–208.

Bandura, Albert. 1986. *Social Foundations of Thought and Action*. Englewood Cliffs, NJ: Prentice-Hall.

Bankole, Akinrinola, Susheela Singh, Vanessa Woog and Deirdre Wulf. 2004. "Risk and Protection: Youth and HIV/AIDS in Sub-Saharan Africa." *Alan Guttmacher Insititute*, January, Pp. 1–40. http://www.guttmacher.org/pubs/riskandprotection.pdf. Last accessed 7/11/06.

Banks, Taunya L. 1996. "Legal Challenges: State Intervention, Reproduction, and HIV-Infected Women." In *HIV, AIDS and Childbearing: Public Policy, Private Lives*. Ruth R. Faden and Nancy Kass, eds. New York: Oxford University Press. Pp. 143–177.

Barale, Michele Aina. 1986. "Review Body Politic/Body Pleasured: Feminism's Theories of Sexuality, a Review Essay." *Frontiers: A Journal of Women's Studies* 9(1): 80–89.

Barash, David P. 2005. "Let a Thousand Orgasms Bloom! A Review of *The Case of the Female Orgasm* by Elisabeth Lloyd." *Evolutionary Psychology*, 3: 347–354.

Barbach, Lonnie. 2000. *The Pause: Positive Approaches to Premenopause and Menopause*. Bergenfield: Plume Books.

Barcaly, Laurie and Charles Vega. 2005. "The U.S. Preventive Services Task Fork (USPSTF) Recommends Against Routine Use of Hormone Therapy for Chronic Disease Prevention." *Medscape*.

Barker-Benfield, Graham J. 1975. *Horrors of the Half-Known Life: Male Attitudes Toward Women and Sexuality in Nineteenth-Century America*. New York: Harper and Row.

Barnett, Theodore and Alan Whiteside. 2002. *AIDS in the Twenty-First Century: Disease and Globalization*. Houndmills and New York: Palgrave MacMillan.

Barnouw, Victor. 1985. *Culture and Personality*. 4th ed. Homewood: The Dorsey Press.

Bartlett, John G. 2002. *The Johns Hopkins Hospital 2002 Guide to Medical Care of Patients with HIV Infection*. 10th ed. Philadelphia: Lippincott, Williams & Wilkins.

———. 2006. "Pocket Guide. Adult HIV/AIDS Treatment." January 2006. The Johns Hopkins AIDS Service." http://www.hopkins-aids.org. Last accessed 5/12/06.

Basirico, Lawrence and Anne Bolin. 2000. "The Joy of Culture." In *Understanding the Global Experience: Becoming a Responsible World Citizen*. Thomas Arcaro and Duane McClearn, eds. Elon College: Carpe Viam Press. Pp. 79–106.

———. 2002. "The Joy of Culture." In *Understanding the Global Experience: Becoming a Responsible World Citizen*. 3rd edition. Thomas Arcaro and Jocelyn Drye, eds. Elon: Carpe-Viam Press. As a CD-ROM.

Basson, Rosemary. 2002. "Are Our Definitions of Women's Desire, Arousal, and Sexual Pain Disorders too Broad and Our Definition of Orgasmic Disorder too Narrow?" *Journal of Sex and Marital Therapy*, 28: 289–300.

———. 2005. "Women's Sexual Dysfunction: Revised and Expanded Definitions." *Canadian Medical Associational Journal*, 172(10): 1327–1333.

Basu, Sanjay, Kedar Mate, and Paul E. Farmer. 2000. "Debt and Poverty Turn a Disease into an Epidemic." *Nature*, September 7, 407(6800): 13.

Bates, David G. and Elliot M. Fratkin. 2003. *Cultural Anthropology*. Boston: Pearson Education, Inc.

Bateson, Gregory. 1958. *Naven*. Stanford: Stanford University Press.

Beach, Frank A., ed. 1976. "Sexual Attractivity, Proceptivity, and Receptivity in Female Mammals." *Hormones and Behavior*, 7: 105–138.

———. 1977. *Human Sexuality in Four Perspectives*. Baltimore: The John Hopkins University Press.

B.E.A.C.H.E.S Foundation. http://www.lalecheleague.org/bfinfo.html. Last accessed 1/20/06.

Becker, Gay. 1990. *Healing the Infertile Family: Strengthening Your Relationship in the Search for Parenthood*. New York: Bantam Books.

Beckerman, Stephen and Paul Valentine, eds. 2002. *Cultures of Multiple Fathers: The Theory and Practice of Partible Paternity in Lowland South America.* Gainesville: University Press of Florida.

Bell, Alan and Martin Weinberg. 1978. *Homosexualities: A Study of Diversity Among Men and Women.* New York: Simon and Schuster.

Bell, Alan, Martin Weinberg, and Sue Keifer Hammersmith. 1981. *Sexual Preference: Its Development in Men and Women.* Bloomington: Indiana University Press.

Bell, Diane. 1983. *Daughters of the Dreaming.* Sidney: McPhee Gribble/George Allen and Unwin.

Belzer, Edwin G., Beverly Whipple, and William Moger. 1984. "On Female Ejaculation." *Journal of Sex Research,* 20(4): 403–406.

Bem, Sandra L. 1974. *Bem Sex-Role Inventory.* Princeton: Educational Testing Service.

Benagiano, Giuseppe and Paola Bianchi. 1999. "Sex Preselection: An Aid to Couples or a Threat to Humanity?" *Human Reproduction,* 14: 868–870.

Benderly, Beryl Lieff. 1987. "Rape Free or Rape Prone." In *Conformity and Conflict: Readings in Cultural Anthropology.* James Spradley and David W. McCurdy, eds. Boston: Little, Brown and Company. Pp. 184–188.

Benedict, Ruth. 1934. "Anthropology and the Abnormal." *Journal of General Psychology,* 10: 59–82.

———. 1939. "Sex in Primitive Society: A Discussion of Dr. Worth's Paper." *American Journal of Orthopsychiatry,* 9: 570–574.

———. 1959. *Patterns of Culture.* New York: The New American Library.

Benjamin, Harry. 1966. *The Transsexual Phenomenon.* New York: The Julian Press.

Bennett, Rebecca. 1999. "Should We Routinely Test Pregnant Women for HIV?" In *HIV and AIDS: Testing, Screening and Confidentiality.* Rebecca Bennett and Charles A. Erin, eds. New York: Oxford University Press. Pp. 228–239.

Bennett, Rebecca and Charles A. Erin, eds. 1999. *HIV and AIDS: Testing, Screening and Confidentiality.* New York: Oxford University Press.

Berek, Jonathan S., Eli Y. Adashi, and Paula A. Hillard. 1996. *Novak's Gynecology.* 12th ed. Baltimore: Williams and Wilkins.

Berger, Gilda. 1993. *Alcoholism and the Family.* New York: Franklin Watts.

Berman, Laura, Jennifer Berman, and Elisabeth Bumiller. 2001. *For Women Only: A Revolutionary Guide to Overcoming Sexual Dysfunction and Reclaiming Your Sex Life.* New York: Henry Holt and Company.

Bernard, H. Rusell. 1994. *Research Methods in Anthropology.* Thousand Oaks: Sage.

Bernard, Richard J. 1983. *Beyond Objectivism and Relativism: Science, Hermeneutics and Praxis.* Philadelphia: University of Pennsylvania Press.

Bernstein, R.J. 1983. *Beyond Objectivism and Relativism: Science, Hermeneutics and Praxis.* Philadelphia: University of Pennysylvania Press.

Bersamin, Melina M., Samantha Walker, Elizabeth D. Waiters, Deborah Fisher, and Joel W. Grube. 2005. "Promising to Wait: Virginity Pledges and Adolescent Sexual Behavior." *Journal of Adolescent Health,* 36(5): 428–436.

Besnier, Niko. 1996. "Polynesian Gender Liminality: Through Time and Space." *Third Sex, Third Gender: Beyond Sexual Dimorphism in Culture and History.* Gilbert Herdt, ed. New York: Zone. Pp. 447–485.

Beyene, Yewoubdar. 1989. *From Menarche to Menopause: Reproductive Lives of Peasant Women in Two Cultures*. Albany: State University of New York Press.

Beyene, Yewoubdar and Mary C. Martin. 2001. "Menopause as a Measure of Population Health." *American Journal of Human Biology*, 13(4): 505–511.

Bhugra, Dinesh. 1997. "Coming Out by South Asian Gay Men in the United Kingdom." *Archives of Sexual Behavior*, 26: 547–557.

"Birth, Abortion and Pregnancy Rates for Developed Countries, Ages 15–19." 2004. *The Washington Post*. http://www.washingtonpost.com/wp-srv/health/daily/051606/indepth_teenagepregnancy.html. Last accessed 8/14/06.

"Birth Control." 2006. Planned Parenthood. http://www.plannedparenthood.org. Last accessed 8/11/06.

"Birth Control Comparisons." 2006. Feminist Woman's Health Center. http://www. fwhc.org/. Last accessed 1/20/07.

"Birth Control Comparisons (Our Bodies Ourselves)." 2006. Planned Parenthood Affiliates of New Jersey. February 21. http://www.plannedparenthoodnj.org/library/index.php?tid=17. Last accessed 8/11/06.

"Birth Control Guide." 2003. U.S. Food and Drug Administration: U.S. Department of Health and Human Services. http://www.fda.gov/fdac/features/1997/babyguide2.pdf. Last accessed 8/11/06.

"Births: Preliminary Data for 2003." 2004. *USDHHS/CDC*, November 23, 53(9).

Bjorklund, David and Barbara Bjorklund. 1988. "Straight or Gay?" *Parents*, October, 98: 93–96.

Blackless, Melanie, Anthony Charuvastra, Amanda Derryck, Anne Fausto-Sterling, Karl Lauzanne, and Ellen Lee. 2000. "How Sexually Dimorphic Are We? Review and Synthesis." *American Journal of Human Biology*, 12: 151–166.

Blackwood, Evelyn. 1984a. "Lesbian Behavior in Cross-Cultural Perspective." MA Thesis, San Francisco State University.

———. 1984b. "Sexuality and Gender in Certain Native American Tribes: The Case of Cross-Gender Females." *Signs: The Journal of Women in Culture and Society*, 10: 27–42.

———. 1986. "Breaking the Mirror: The Construction of Lesbianism and the Anthropological Discourse on Homosexuality." In *Anthropology and Homosexual Behavior*. Evelyn Blackwood, ed. Binghamton, NY: The Haworth Press.

———. 1998. "Tombois in West Sumatra: Constructing Masculinity and Erotic Desire." *Cultural Anthropology*, 14(4): 491–521.

———. 1999. "Sapphic Shadows: Challenging the Silence in the Study of Sexuality." In *Female Desires: Same Sex Relations and Transgender Practices Across Cultures*. Evelyn Blackwood and Saskia E. Wieringa, eds. New York: Columbia University Press. Pp. 39–66.

———. 2004. "Conference Report: The Women's Same-Sex Forum and African Women's Life History Project of Sex and Secrecy: The Fourth Conference of the International Association for the Study of Sexuality, Culture and Society." *Sexuality Research and Social Policy*, 1(1): 104–107.

———. 2005a. "Women's Intimate Friendships and Other Affairs: An Ethnographic Overview." In *Gender in Cross-Cultural Perspective*. Caroline B. Brettell and Carolyn F. Sargent, eds. Upper Saddle River: Pearson Prentice Hall. Pp. 268–276.

———. 2005b. "Women's Intimate Friendships." In *Cultural Anthropology: Tribes, States and the Global System*. John H. Bodley, ed. Boston: McGraw-Hill.

Blackwood, Evelyn and Saskia E. Wieringa, eds. 1999a. *Female Desires: Same-Sex Relations and Transgender Practices Across Cultures.* New York: Columbia University Press.

————. 1999b. "Sapphic Shadows: Challenging the Silence in the Study of Sexuality." In *Female Desires: Same-Sex Relations and Transgender Practices Across Cultures.* Evelyn Blackwood and Saskia E. Wieringa, eds. New York: Columbia University Press. Pp. 39–66.

Blanchard, Ray. 1989. "The Classification and Labeling of Nonhomosexual Gender Dysphorias." *Archives of Sexual Behavior,* August, 18(4): 315–334.

————. 1991. "Clinical Observations and Systematic Studies of Autogynephilia." *Journal of Sex and Marital Therapy,* 17: 235–251.

————. 1993. "Varieties of Autogynephilias and Their Relationship to Gender Dysphoria." *Archives of Sexual Behavior,* 22: 241–251.

Blankenship, Kim. 1999. "Social Context and HIV: Testing and Treatment Issues Among Commercial Sex Workers." In *The Gender Politics of HIV/AIDS in Women: Perspectives on the Pandemic in the U.S.* Nancy Goldstein and Jennifer L. Manlowe, eds. New York: New York University Press. Pp. 252–269.

Blumenfeld, Warren J. and Diane Raymond. 1989. *Looking at Gay and Lesbian Life.* Boston: Beacon Press.

Blumstein, Philip and Pepper Schwartz. 1983. *American Couples.* New York: Pocket Books.

Bock, Philip K. 1988. *Rethinking Psychological Anthropology.* New York: W. H. Freeman and Company.

Bockting, Walter O. and Sheila Kirk, eds. 2001. *Transgender and HIV.* Binghamton, NY: The Haworth Press.

Boddy, Elizabeth. 1989. *Wombs and Alien Spirits: Women, Men and the Zar Cult in Northern Sudan.* Madison: University of Wisconsin Press.

Bodley, John H. 2005. *Cultural Anthropology; Tribes, States and the Global System.* Boston: McGraw-Hill.

Body, The. 2004. http://www.thebody.com. Last accessed 8/8/06.

Bogoros, Waldemar. 1907. "The Chuckchee Religion." *Memoirs of the American Museum of Natural History.* Vol. II. Leiden: E. S. Brill.

Bohlen, Joseph G., et al. 1982. "Development of a Woman's Multiorgasmic Pattern: A Research Case Report." *Journal of Sex Research,* 18(2): 130–145.

Bolin, Anne. 1974. "God Save the Queen: An Investigation of Homosexual Subculture." MA Thesis. Boulder: Norlin Library, University Microfiche.

————. 1987a. "Transsexualism and the Limits of Traditional Gender Analysis." *American Behavioral Scientist,* 31(1): 41–65.

————. 1987b. "Transsexuals and Caretakers: A Study of Power and Deceit in Intergroup Relations." *City and Society,* 1(2): 64–79.

————. 1988a. *In Search of Eve: Transsexual Rites of Passage.* South Hadley: Bergin and Garvey Publishers.

————. 1988b. "Minds and Bodies: Gender Identity, Role and Body Rituals." Paper presented at the annual meetings of the American Anthropological Association, November 17–20, Phoenix, Arizona.

————. 1992. "Vandalized Vanity: Feminine Physiques Betrayed and Portrayed." In *Tattoo, Torture, Jultilation and Adornment: The Denaturalization of the Body in Culture and Text.* Francis E. Mascia-Lees and Patricia Sharpe, eds. Albany: State University of New York Press.

———. 1996a. "Transcending and Transgendering: Male-to-Female Transsexuals, Dichotomy and Diversity." In *Third Sex/Third Gender*. Gilbert Herdt, ed. New York: Zone Publishing. Pp. 447–485.

———. 1996b. "Traversing Gender: Cultural Context and Gender Practices." In *Gender Reversals and Gender Cultures: Anthropological and Historical Perspectives*. Sabrina Petea Ramet, ed. New York: Routledge. Pp. 22–52.

———. 1998 [1996]. "Transcending and Transgendering: Female-to-Male Transsexuals, Dichotomy and Diversity." In *Current Concepts in Transgender Identity Toward a New Synthesis*. Dallas Denny, ed. New York: Garland Publishing Company. Pp. 63–96

———. 2000. "Reinventing Gender in the New Millennium." In *Sexuality in the New Millennium*. E. M. L. Ng, J. J. Borras-Valls, M. Perez-Concillo and E. Coleman. Bologna: Editrice Compositori. Pp. 27–30.

———. 2004a. "French Polynesian Sexuality." *The Continuum Complete International Encyclopedia of Sexuality*. Robert T. Francouer and Raymond J. Noonan, eds. New York: Continuum Press. Pp. 431–448.

———. 2004b. "Genderscapes: Panoramas, Paradigms and Possibilities." Invited Speaker. The Institute of Ethnology. Academia Sinica. November 27, Taipei, Taiwan.

Bolin, Anne and Jane Granskog. 2003. *Athletic Intruders: Ethnographic Research on Women, Culture, and Exercise*. State University of New York Press.

Bolin, Anne and Patricia Whelehan. 1999. *Perspectives on Human Sexuality*. Albany: State University of New York Press.

———. 2004. *Perspectives on Human Sexuality*. Boston: The McGraw-Hill Companies, Inc.

Boonstra, Heather. 2002. "Teen Pregnancy: Trends and Lessons Learned." *The Guttmacher Report on Public Policy*, February, 5(1): 1–6. www.guttmacher. org/pubs/tgr/05/1/gr050107.html. Last accessed 8/14/06.

Boonstra, Heather D., Rachel Benson Gold, Cory L. Richards, and Lawrence B. Finer. 2006. "Abortion in Women's Lives." The Guttmacher Institute. http:// www.guttmacher.org/pubs/2006/05/04/AiWL.pdf. Last accessed 8/11/06.

Booth, Alan and Allan Mazur. 1998. "Testosterone and Dominance in Men." *Behavioral & Brain Sciences*, 21(3): 386–398.

Boston Women's Health Collective. 1976. *The New Our Bodies, Ourselves: A Book by and for Women*. New York: Simon and Schuster, Inc.

———. 1984. *The New Our Bodies, Ourselves: A Book by and for Women*. New York: Simon and Schuster, Inc.

———. 1992. *The New Our Bodies, Ourselves: A Book by and for Women*. New York: Simon and Schuster, Inc.

———. 2005. *Our Bodies, Ourselves: A New Edition for a New Era*. New York: Touchstone Publishers, Ltd.

Boswell, Holly. 1991. "The Transgender Alternative." *Chrysalis Quarterly*, 1(2): 29–31.

Boswell, John. 1980. *Christianity, Social Tolerance, and Homosexuality*. Chicago: University of Aldine Press.

Bower, Herbert. 2001. "The Gender Identity Disorder in the DSM-IV Classification: A Critical Evaluation." *Australian and New Zealand Journal of Psychiatry*, 35(1): 1–8.

Boxer, Andrew M. and Bertram J. Cohler. 1989. "The Life Course of Gay and Lesbian Youth: An Immodest Proposal for the Study of Lives." *Gay and Lesbian Youth.* Gilbert Herdt, ed. New York: Harrington. Pp. 315–355.

Boyd, Robert and Peter J. Richerson. 1989. "The Evolution of Ethnic Markers." In *Ideas in Anthropology.* Santa Fe: School of American Research.

"Brain Drain of Health Care Professionals from Southern Africa, The." 2005. IOM/HDN Project Team. AF-AIDSe Forum 2005.

Brainy Quotes. 2004. www.brainyquote.com. Last accessed 2/9/06.

Brandes, Stanley. 1987. *Forty: The Age and the Symbol.* Knoxville: University of Tennessee Press.

Breedlove, Marc. 1996. "The Chicken-and-Egg Argument as It Applies to the Brains of Transsexuals: Does It Matter?" *Psychologue: The Newsletter of the Psychology Department of the University of California at Berkeley.* Reprinted in *Psychology of Gender Identity and Transgenderism.* http://www.gender psychology.org/psychology/BSTc.html. Last accessed 6/26/06.

Brettell, Caroline B. and Carolyn F. Sargent, eds. 2005a. *Gender in Cross-Cultural Perspective.* Upper Saddle River: Pearson Prentice Hall.

———. 2005b. "Equality and Inequality: The Sexual Division of Labor and Gender Stratification." In *Gender in Cross-Cultural Perspective.* Caroline B. Brettell, and Carolyn F. Sargent, eds. Upper Saddle River: Pearson Prentice Hall. Pp. 135–141.

Brimlow, Deborah L. and Michael W. Ross. 1998. "HIV-Related Communication and Power in Women Injection Drug Users." In *Women and AIDS. Negotiating Safer Practices, Care, and Representation.* Nancy L. Roth and Linda K. Fuller, eds. Binghamton, NY: The Haworth Press: Pp. 71–80.

Broad, Kendal L. 2000. "Is It G, L, B and T? Gender/Sexuality Movements and Transgender Collective Identity (De)Constructions." *International Journal of Sexuality and Gender Studies,* 7(4): 241–264.

Brockman, Norbert. 2004. Kenya, In *The Continuum Complete International Encyclopedia of Sexuality.* Robert T. Francoeur and Raymond Noonan, eds. New York: Continuum International Publishing Group. Pp. 679–691.

Broderick, Carlfred B. 1972. "Children's Romances." *Sexual Behavior,* 2(5): 16–21.

Brooks, Ronald, Mary Jane Rotheram-Borus, and Eric G. Bing, eds. 2003. *HIV Prevention for Men of Color Who Have Sex With Men (MS) and Men of Color Who Have Sex With Men and Women (MSM/W): A Special Supplement to AIDS Education and Prevention,* 15 (Supplement A), 1–6: 1–138.

Brooks, T. R. 1993. "Sexuality in the Aging Woman." *The Female Patient,* 18(11): 27–28, 31–32, 34.

Broude, Gwen J. 1980. "Extramarital Sex Norms in Cross-Cultural Perspective." *Behavior Science Research,* 15: 181–218.

Broude, Gwen J. 1994. *Marriage, Family, and Relationships.* Denver: ABC-CLIO.

Broude, Gwen J. and Sarah J. Greene. 1976. "Cross-Cultural Codes on the Twenty Sexual Attitudes and Practices." *Ethnology,* 15: 409–429.

Broverman, Inge K., Donald M. Broverman, B. E. Clarkson, P. Rosenkrantz, and S. R. Vogel. 1970. "Sex Role Stereotypes and Clinical Judgements of Mental Health." *Journal of Consulting and Clinical Psychology,* February, 34(1): 1–7.

Broverman, Inge, Susan Vogel, Donald M. Broverman, Fran E. Clarkson, and Paul S. Rosenkrantz. 1972. "Sex-role Stereotypes: A Current Appraisal." *Journal of Social Issues,* 28: 59–78.

Brown, Donald E. 1991. *Human Universals*. New York: McGraw-Hill, Inc.

Brown, Jane D., Carolyn T. Halpern, and Kelly L. L'Engle. 2005. "Mass Media as Sexual Super Peer for Early Maturing Girls." *Journal of Adolescent Health*, 36(5): 420–427.

Brown, Judith K. and Virginia Kerns. 1985. *In Her Prime: A New View of Middle-Aged Women*. So. Hadley: Bergin and Garvey Publishers.

Brückner, Hannah and Peter Bearman. 2005. "After the Promise: The STD Consequences of Adolescent Virginity Pledges." *Journal of Adolescent Health*, April, 36(4): 271–278.

Bryant, Steve and Demian, eds. 1990. "Partners' National Survey of Lesbian and Gay Couples." *Partners' Newsletter for Gay and Lesbian Couples*, May/June: 1–6.

Buchanan, David, Susan Shaw, Amy Ford, and Merrill Singer. 2004. "Empirical Science Meets Moral Panic: An Analysis of the Politics of Needle Exchange." *Journal of Public Health Policy*, 24(3/4): 427–444.

Buchanan, Wyatt. 2005a. "Canada Expected to Pass Bill Approving Same Sex Marriage." *Pew Forum of Religion and Public Life*. http://pewforum.org/news/display.php?NewsID=4990. Last accessed 5/17/06.

———. 2005b. "When Rights Collide: Doctor and Patient Both Say Their Liberty Was Violated." *San Francisco Chronicle*, July 29: A1 and A12.

Buckley, Thomas and Alma Gottlieb, eds. 1988. *Blood Magic: The Anthropology of Menstruation*. Berkeley: University of California Press.

Buffum, John. 1982. "Pharmacosexology: The Effects of Drugs on Sexual Function." *Journal of Psychoactive Drugs*, 14: 5–44.

Bullough, Bonnie, and Vern L. Bullough. 1998. "Transsexualism: Historical Perspectives, 1952 to Present." In *Current Concepts in Transgender Identity*. Dallas Denny, ed. New York: Garland Press.

Bullough, Vern. 1976. *Sexual Variance in Society and History*. New York: S. Wiley and Sons.

———. 1979. *Homosexuality: A History*. New York: New American Library.

———. 1994. *Science in the Bedroom*. New York: Basic Books.

———. 2004. "Sex Will Never be the Same: The Contributions of Alfred C. Kinsey." *Archives of Sexual Behavior*, 33(3): 277–286.

Bullough, Vern and Bonnie Bullough. 1987. *Women and Prostitution: A Social History*. New Hyde Park: University Books.

Bullough, Vern L. and Fang Fu Ruan. 1988. "First Case of Transsexual Surgery in China." *Journal of Sex Research*, 25: 546–47.

Buhgra, D. 1997. "Coming Out by South Asian Gay men in the United Kingdom." *Archives of Sexual Behavior*, 26: 547–557.

Burhansstipanov, Linda, Carole la Favor, Shirley Hoskins, Gloria Bellymule, and Ronald M. Rowell. 1997. "Native Women Living Beyond HIV/AIDS Infection." In *The Gender Politics of HIV/AIDS in Women: Perspectives on the Pandemic in the U.S.* Nancy Goldstein and Jennifer L. Manlowe, eds. New York: New York University Press. Pp. 337–356.

Burleson, Mary H., Wenda R. Trevathan, and W. Larry Gregory. 2002. "Sexual Behavior in Lesbian and Heterosexual Women: Effects of Menstrual Cycle Phase and Partner Availability.' *Psychoneuroendocrinology*, 27: 489–503.

Burleson, Mary H., Wenda R. Trevathan, and M. Todd. In press. "In the Mood for Love or Vice Versa? Exploring the Relations among Sexual Activity, Physical

Affection, Affect, and Stress in the Daily Lives of Mid-Aged Women." *Archives of Sexual Behavior.*

Burley, Nancy. 1979. "The Evolution of Concealed Ovulation." *American Naturalist*, 114: 835–858.

Burnham, Dorothy. 1978. "Biology and Gender." In *Genes and Gender I*. Ethel Tobach and Betty Rosoff, eds. New York: Gordian Press: 51–59.

Burton, Roger and John W. M. Whiting. 1961. "The Absent Father and Cross-Sex Identity." Reprinted from *Merrill-Palmer Quarterly of Behavior Development*, 7(2): 86–95.

Burton, Sandra. 1990. "Condolences, It's a Girl." *Time*, 136(19): 36.

"Bush's Global AIDS Plan: Long on Rhetoric, Short on Science and Solutions. 'Smoke and Mirrors Strategy' Fails to Meet Needs of Women and Girls." 2004. Center for Health and Gender Equity (CHANGE). http://www.genderhealth. org/pubs/PR20040223.pdf. Last accessed 2/9/2006.

Buss, David M. 1989. "Sex Differences in Human Mate Preferences: Evolutionary Hypotheses Tested in 37 Cultures." *Behavioral and Brain Sciences*, 12: 1–49.

———. 1994. *The Evolution of Desire: Strategies of Human Mating*. New York: Basic Books.

Butler, Robert N. and Myrna I. Lewis. 1988. *Love and Sex after Sixty*. New York: Harper & Row.

Byer, Curtis O. and Louis W. Shainberg. 1991. *Dimensions of Human Sexuality*. Dubuque: William C. Brown Publishing.

Calderone, Mary. 1985. "Adolescent Sexuality: Elements and Genesis." *Pediatrics Supplement*, 699–703.

Caldwell, John C. 1999. *Resistances to Behavioural Change to Reduce HIV/AIDS Infection*. Canberra: Health Transition Centre.

Caldwell, John, Pat Caldwell, John Anarfi, Kofi Awusabo-Asare, James Ntozi, I. O. Orubuloye, Jeff Marck, Wendy Cosford, Rachel Colombo, and Elaine Hollings, eds. 2002. *Resistances to Behavioural Change to Reduce HIV/AIDS Infection in Predominantly Heterosexual Epidemics in Third World Countries*. Canberra: Health Transition Centre, Australian National University.

Callender, Charles and Lee M. Kochems. 1983. "The North American Berdache." *Current Anthropology*, 24(4): 443–456. See also comments and reply, Pp. 456–70.

Campbell, Meredith F. 1979. *Campbell's Urology*. Philadelphia: Saunders.

Caplan, Pat, ed. 1987. *The Cultural Construction of Sexuality*. New York: Tavistock.

Carillo, Héctor. 1999. "Culture Change, Hybridity and Male Homosexuality in Mexico." *Culture, Health, and Sexuality*, 1: 223–238.

Carlson, Margaret. 1990. "It's Our Turn." *Time*, 136(19): 16–18.

Carpenter, Laura. 2005. *Virginity Lost: An Intimate Portrait of First Sexual Experiences*. New York: New York University Press.

Carrier, Joseph. 2001. "Some Reflections on Ethnographic Research on Latino and Southeast Asia Male Homosexuality and AIDS." *AIDS and Behavior*, 5(2): 183–191.

Carrier, Joseph M. and Ralph Bolton. 1991. "Anthropological Perspectives on Sexuality and HIV Prevention." *Annual Review of Sex Research*, 2: 49–74.

Carrillo, Hector. 2002. *The Night Is Young: Sexuality in Mexico in the Time of AIDS*. Chicago: University of Chicago Press.

Carroll, Peter R. and William G. Nelson. 2004. "Report to the Nation on Pro-state Cancer: Introduction." *Medscape*. http://www.medscape.com. Last accessed 5/1/06.

Cashdan, Elizabeth. 1993. "Attracting Mates: Effects of Paternal Investment on Mate Attraction Strategies." *Ethology and Sociobiology*, 14: 1–24.

Cassell, Carol. 1984. *Swept Away: Why Women Fear Their Own Sexuality*. New York: Simon and Schuster.

Castro, Roberto. 2001. "'When a Man Is with a Woman, It Feels Like Electricity': Subjectivity, Sexuality and Contraception Among Men in Central Mexico." *Culture, Health and Sexuality*, 3(2): 149–165.

Catalan, Jose, Loraine Sherr, and Barbara Hedge, eds. 1997. *HIV, AIDS and Childbearing: Public Policy, Private Lives*. New York: Oxford University Press.

Centers for Disease Control and Prevention. 2006. http://www.cdc.gov. Last accessed 8/7/06.

Centers for Disease Control's Reproductive Health Information Source. 2005. *ART 2002 Report*. http://apps.nccd.cdc.gov/ART2002/clinlist02.asp?State=IL. Last accessed 2/9/2006.

Chagnon, Napoleon. 1983. *Yanomamo: The Fierce People*. New York: Holt, Rinehart and Winston.

Chalker, Rebecca. 2000. *The Clitoral Truth: The Secret World at Your Fingertips*. New York: Seven Stories Press.

Chang, Heewon. 1992. *Adolescent Life and Ethos: An Ethnography of a US High School*. Washington, DC: The Falmer Press.

Chapkis, Wendy. 1997. *Live Sex Acts: Women Performing Erotic Labor*. New York: Routledge.

Chappel, Eliot and Carleton Stevens Coon. 1942. *Principles of Anthroplogy*. New York: Holt.

Chaya, Nada, and Jennifer Dusenberry. 2004. "ICPD at 10. Where are We Now? A Report Card on Sexual and Reproductive Rights." *International Conference on Population and Development (ICPD)*. http://www.populationaction.org/news/press/news_083104_ReportCard.pdf. Last accessed 3/26/06.

Child Trafficking. http://www.childtrafficking.com. Last accessed 12/6/2006.

Chodorow, Nancy. 1974. "Family Structure and Feminine Personality." In *Woman, Culture, and Society*. M. Z. Rosaldo and L. Lamphere, eds. Stanford: Stanford University Press.

———. 1989. *Feminism and Psychoanalytic Theory*. New Haven: Yale University Press.

———. 1995. "Gender as a Personal and Cultural Construction." *Signs*, 20: 516–544.

Choi, Kyung-Hee, N. Salazaar, S. Lew, and Thomas J. Coates. 1995. "AIDS Risk, Dual Identity, and Community Response Among Gay Asian Islander Men in San Francisco." In *AIDS, Identity, and Community: The HIV Epidemic and Lesbians and Gay Men*. Vol. 2. Gregory M. Herek and Beverly Green, eds. Thousand Oaks: Sage Publications. Pp. 115–134.

Choi, Kyung-Hee, Zheng Xiwen, Qu Shuquan, Kevin Yiee, and Jeffrey Mandell. 2000. "HIV Risk Among Patients Attending Sexually Transmitted Disease Clinics in China." In *AIDS and Behavior*, 4(1): 111–119.

Chouinard Amy and Jacque Albert. 1990. *Human Sexuality: Research Perspectives in a World Facing AIDS*. Ottawa: IDRC.

Christensen, Damaris. 2000. "Male Choice: The Search for New Contraceptives for Men." *Science News*, 158: 222.

"Civil Unions in Connecticut." 2005. *New York Times*, March 7: Section A, p. 16.

Clark, M. and B. G. Anderson. 1975. "An Anthropological Approach to Aging." *Introducing Anthropology*. James R. Hayes and James M. Henslin, eds. Boston: Holbrook Press, Inc. Pp. 331–344.

Clay, S. B. 2002. "Villains or Victims?" *HIV Plus*, 5: 28–31.

Clement, U. 1990. "Surveys of Heterosexual Behavior." *Annual Review of Sex Research*. Vol. 1. John Bancroft, ed. Lake Mills. The Society for the Scientific Study of Sex. Pp. 45–74.

Clinton, Hillary. 1996. *It Takes a Village and Other Lessons Children Teach Us*. New York: Simon and Schuster.

Closer Walk, A. 2003. Directed by Robert Bilheimer. USA: Worldwide Documentaries.

"CME Alternatives to HRT for Treatment of Menopausal Symptoms." 2006. Continuing Medical Education Program of the University of Florida College of Medicine. http://womenshealth.ufl.edu/hrt_althome.htm. Last accessed 8/10/06.

Cohen, Eugene N. and Edwin Eames. 1982. *Cultural Anthropology*. Boston: Little, Brown and Company.

Cohen, Judith B. 1999. "Sexual Transmission of HIV in Prostitutes." In *The AIDS Knowledge Base: A Textbook on HIV Disease from the University of California, San Francisco School of Medicine, and San Francisco General Hospital*. Philip T. Cohen, Merle A. Sande, and Paul Volberding, eds. Philadelphia: Lippincott, Williams and Wilkins: 1.15–1–1.15–9.

Cohen, Philip T., Merle A. Sande, and Paul Volberding, eds. 1999. *The AIDS Knowledge Base: A Textbook on HIV Disease from the University of California, San Francisco School of Medicine, and San Francisco General Hospital*. Philadelphia: Lippincott, Williams and Wilkins.

Cohen, Susan. 2004. "Delayed Marriage and Abstinence-until-Marriage: On a Collision Course?" *The Guttmacher Report on Public Policy*, 7(2): 1–3.

———. 2006. "The Global Contraceptive Shortfall: U.S. Contributions and U.S. Hindrances." *Guttmacher Policy Review*, 9(2). http://www.guttmacher.org/pubs/gpr/09/2/gpr090215.html. Last accessed 8/11/06.

Cohen-Kettenis, Peggy and Willem A. Arrindell. 1990. "Perceived Parental Rearing Style, Parental Divorce and Transsexualism: A Controlled Study." *Psychological Medicine*, 20: 613–620.

Cohen-Kettenis, Peggy and Louis J. G. Gooren. 1999. "Transsexualism: A Review of Etiology, Diagnosis and Treatment." *Journal of Psychosomatic Research*, 46(4): 315–333.

Collaler, Marcia L. and Melissa Hines. 1995. "Human Behavioral Sex Differences: A Role for Gonadal Hormones During Early Development?" *Psychological Bulletin*, 118: 55–107.

Comfort, Alex. 1972. *The Joy of Sex*. New York: Crown Publishers.

"Compare Birth Rates, Abortion Rates and Number of Partners." 2004. *The Washington Post*. http://www.washingtonpost.com/wp-srv/health/daily/051606/teensex.html. Last accessed 8/14/06.

"Concerns About New Hormone Treatments for Women: A New View of Women's Sexual Problems for the FDA Advisory Committee Hearing on Intrinsa." 2004.

FSD-Alert. December 2. http://www.fsd-alert.org/intrinsa.html. Last accessed 8/11/06.

"Condom History, The." 2006. Avert.Com. http://www.avert.org/condoms.htm. Last accessed 8/11/06.

Constantine, Joan M. and Larry Constantine. 1973. *Group Marriage: A Study of Contemporary Multilateral Marriage.* New York: Macmillian Co.

"Contraceptive Pill for Men, A." 2006. *Medical News Alert.* http://www.news-medical.net/?id=17634. Last accessed 8/11/06.

Coodvadia, Hoosen M. 2000. "Access to Voluntary Counseling and Testing for HIV in Developing Countries." *Prevention and Treatment of HIV Infection in Infants and Children,* November, 918: 57–63.

Corey, Donald Webster, ed. 1956. *Homosexuality: A Cross-Cultural Approach.* New York: The Julian Press.

CosmeticSurgery.Com. 2006. http://www.cosmeticsurgery.com/essential_facts/cosmetic-surgery/Labiaplasty-(Labia-Rejuvenation)/. Last accessed 7/11/06.

Coste, Joël, Jean Bouyer, Sylvie Ughetto, Laurent Gerbaud, Hervé Fernandez, Jean-Luc Pouly, and Nadine Joy-Spira. 2004. "Ectopic Pregnancy Is Again on the Increase: Recent Trends in the Incidence of Ectopic Pregnancies in France (1992–2002)". *Human Reproduction,* 19: 2014–2018.

Cote, James. 2000. "Was Coming of Age in Samoa Based on a 'Fateful Hoaxing'?" *Current Anthropology,* 41(4): 617–622.

"Courts Are Again Asked to Redefine Family, The." 1990. *New York Times,* October 8: 28.

Cox, Sue, ed. 1981. *Female Psychology.* New York: St. Martin's Press.

Coyne-Beasley, Tamera and Victor J. Schoenbach. 2000. "The African-American Church: A Potential Forum for Adolescent Comprehensive Sexuality Education." *Journal of Adolescent Health,* 26(4): 289–294.

Crandon, Libbet. 1986. "Review of Reproductive Rituals: The Perception of Fertility in England from the Sixteenth Century in the Nineteenth Century." *American Anthropologist,* 88(2): 470–471.

Crapo, Richley H. 1987. *Cultural Anthropology: Understanding Ourselves and Others.* Sluice Dock: Dushkin Publishers.

Crawford, Mary and Danielle Popp. 2003. "Sexual Double Standards: A Review and Methodological Critique of Two Decades of Research." *Journal of Sex Research,* 40: 13–27.

Critchlow-Leigh, Barbara. 1990. "The Relationship of Substance Use During Sex in High-Risk Sexual Behavior." *Journal of Sex Research,* May, 27(2): 199–213.

Cromwell, Jason. 1999. *Transmen and FTMs: Identities, Bodies, Genders and Sexualities.* Urbana: University of Illinois Press.

Crooks, Robert L. and Karla Baur. 1987. *Our Sexuality.* 3rd ed. Menlo Park: Benjamin/Cummings.

Cross, Richard J. 1993. "What Doctors and Others Need to Know." *SIECUS Report,* 21(5): 7–9.

Cummings, Gayle, Robins Battle, Judith C. Barker, and Flora M. Krasnovsky. 1999. "Are African-American Women Worried About Getting AIDS? A Qualitative Analysis." In *AIDS Education and Prevention. An Interdisciplinary Journal,* August, 11(4): 331–342.

"Current Trends Ectopic Pregnancy—United States, 1990–1992." 1995. *MMWR Weekly*, January 27, 44(03): 46–48. http://www.cdc.gov/mmwrhtml/ 00035709. htm. Last accessed 6/12/06.

Dahlberg, Francis. 1981. *Woman the Gatherer*. New Haven: Yale University Press.

Dailard, Cynthia. 2003. "Understanding 'Abstinence': Implications for Individuals, Programs and Policies." *The Guttmacher Report on Public Policy*, December, 6(5): 4–6. http://www.guttmacher.org/pubs/tgr/06/5/gr060504.html. Last accessed 8/11/06.

———. 2006. "The Other Shoe Drops: Federal Abstinence Education Program Becomes More Restrictive." *Guttmacher Policy Review*, Winter, 9(1). http:// www.guttmacher.org/pubs/gpr/09/1/gpr090119.html. Last accessed 8/14/06.

Dalby, Andrew. 2000. *Dangerous Tastes. The Story of Spices*. London: The British Museum Press.

Daniels, Cynthia R. 1997. "Between Fathers and Fetuses: The Social Construction of Male Reproduction and the Politics of Fetal Harm." *Signs*, 22: 579–600.

Darling, Carol A. and Mary W. Hicks. 1982. "Parental Influence on Adolescent Sexuality: Implications for Parents as Educations." *Journal of Youth and Adolescence*, 11: 231–245.

Darroch, Jacqueline, Jennifer J. Frost, Susheela Singh and Study Team. 2001. "Teenage Sexual and Reproductive Behavior in Developed Countries: Can More Progress Be Made?: Occasional Report, Number 3." The Alan Guttmacher Institute, November. http://www.guttmacher.org/pubs/eurosynth_rpt.pdf. Last accessed 8/14/06.

Darwin, Charles. 1859. *The Origin of Species*. London: John Murray.

Darwin, Charles. 1874 [1871]. *The Descent of Man and Selection in Relation to Sex*. New York: Thomas Y. Crowell.

Darwin, Charles and Alfred Wallace. 1858. "On the Tendency of Species to Form Varieties: And on the Perpetuation of Varieties and Species of Natural Means of Selection." *Journal of the Proceedings of the Linnean Society*.

Davenport, William H. 1977. "Sex in Cross-Cultural Perspective." In *Human Sexuality in Four Perspectives*. Frank Ambrose Beach and Milton Diamond, eds. Baltimore: The John Hopkins University Press. Pp. 115–163.

Davidson, J. Kenneth, Sr., and Nelwyn B. Moore, eds. 2005. *Speaking of Sexuality: Interdisciplinary Readings*. Los Angeles: Roxbury Publishing Company.

Davies, Sharyn Graham. 2007. *Challenging Gender Norms: Five Genders among Bugis in Indonesia*. Belmont: Thomson Wadsworth

Davis, Dona. n.d.a "Draft of Article on Adolescence." Pp. 1–10.

———. n.d.b Personal communication.

Davis, Dona L. and Richard G. Whitten. 1987. "The Cross Cultural Study of Human Sexuality." *Annual Review in Anthropology*, 16: 69–98.

Davis, Susan, Sonia L. Davison, Susan Donath, and Robin J. Bell. 2005. "Circulating Androgen Levels and Self-Reported Sexual Function in Women." *Journal of the American Medical Association*, 294(1): 91–96.

Davis-Floyd, Robbie. 1988. "Birth as an American Rite of Passage." In *Childbirth in America*. Karen L. Michaelson, ed. Granby: Bergin and Garvey Publishers. Pp. 153–172.

———. 1989/90. "The Technological Model of Birth." In *Annual Editions Anthropology*. Elvio Angeloni, ed. Sluice Dock, Guilford: Dushkin Publishers. Pp. 163–171.

―――. 1992. *Birth as an American Rite of Passage*. Berkeley: University of California Press.

―――. 2001. "The Technocratic, Humanistic, and Holistic Paradigms of Child-birth." *International Journal of Gynecology and Obstetrics*, November, 75(Supplement #1): S5-S23.

de la Gorgendière, Louise. 2005. "Rights and Wrongs. HIV/AIDS Research in Africa." *Human Organization*, Summer, 64(2): 166–178.

de Waal, Frans. 1989. *Chimpanzee Politics*. Baltimore: Johns Hopkins University Press.

"Declaration of Commitment on HIV/AIDS." 2001. United Nations Special Session on HIV/AIDS. http://www.unaids.org/en/Goals/UNGASS/default.asp. Last accessed on 2/10/06.

Def Leppard. 1987. "Pour Some Sugar on Me." *Hysteria*. Mercury/Universal.

―――. 1999. "All Night". *Euphoria*. Mercury/Bludgeon.

"Defining Overweight and Obesity." 2005. Centers for Disease Control and Prevention (CDC). http://www.cdc.gov/nccdphp/dnpa/obesity/defining.htm. Last accessed 2/9/2006.

Delacoste, Frederique, and Priscilla Alexander, eds. 1987. *Sex Work, Writings by Women in the Sex Industry*. Pittsburgh: Cleis Press.

DeLameter, John. 1989. "The Social Control of Human Sexuality." In *Human Sexuality: The Societal and Interpersonal Context*. Kathleen McKinney and Susan Sprecher, eds. Norwood: Ablex Publishing Co. Pp. 30–62.

DeLameter, John D. and William N. Friedrich. 2005. "Human Sexual Development." In *Speaking of Sexuality: Interdisciplinary Readings*. J. Kenneth Davidson, Sr. and Nelwyn B. Moore, eds. Los Angeles: Roxbury Publishing Company. Pp. 75–80.

DeLameter, John D. and Morgan Sill. 2005. "Sexual Desire in Later Life." *The Journal of Sex Research*, 42(2): 138–149.

Delaney, Carol. 1991. *The Seed and the Soil: Gender and Cosmology in a Turkish Village Society*. Berkeley: University of California Press.

Demac, Donna A. 1988. *Liberty Denied: The Current Rise of Censorship in America*. New York: PEN American Center.

D'Emilio, John and Estelle Freedman. 1988. *Intimate Matters: A History of Sexuality in America*. New York: Harper and Row.

Denny, Dallas. 1991. "Dealing with Your Feelings." *AEGIS Transition Series*. Decatur: American Educational Gender Information Service, Inc. P. 6.

―――. 1992. "The Politics of Diagnosis and Diagnosis of Politics." *Chrysalis Quarterly*, 1(3): 10, 18–19.

―――. 1995. "Editorial: Paradigm Shift." *AEGIS News Quarterly*, 6(4): 9.

―――. 1998. *Current Concepts in Transgender Identity: Toward a New Synthesis*. New York: Garland Publishing Company.

Desclaux, Alice, Mounirou Ciss, Bernard Taverne, Papa S. Sow, Marc Egrot, Mame A. Faye, Isabelle Lancièce, Omar Sylla, Eric Delaporte, and Ibrahima Ndoye. 2003. "Access to Antiretroviral Drugs and AIDS Management in Senegal." *AIDS*, 17(Supplement 3): S95-S101.

Desgrees du Lou, Annabel. 1999. "Reproductive Health and AIDS in Sub-Saharan Africa: Problems and Prospects." *An English Selection*, 11: 61–87.

DesJarlais, Don and Andrew Ball, eds. *Drug Injecting and HIV Infection: Global Dimensions and Local Responses*. London: UCL Press.

DesJarlais, Don C., Katchit Choopanya, Peggy Millson, Patricia Friedmann, and Samuel R. Friedman. 1998. "The Structure of Stable Seroprevalence HIV-1

Epidemics among Injecting Drug Users." In *Drug Injecting and HIV Infection: Global Dimensions and Local Responses.* Gerry Stimson, Don DesJarlais, and Andrew Ball, eds. London: UCL Press. Pp. 91–100.

Devereaux, George. 1937. "Institutionalized Homosexuality of the Mohave Indians." *Human Biology,* 9(4): 498–527.

———. 1955. *A Study of Abortion in Primitive Societies: A Typological, Distributional, and Dynamic Analysis of the Prevention of Birth in 400 Pre-Industrial Societies.* New York: The Julian Press.

———. 1967. "A Typological Study of Abortion in 350 Primitive, Ancient and Pre-Industrial Socieities." In *Abortion in America.* Harold Rosen, ed. Boston: Beacon Press.

———. 1976. *A Study of Abortion in Primitive Societies.* New York: International University Press.

Devi, Kamala. 1977. *The Eastern Way of Love: Tantric Sex and Erotic Mysticism.* New York: Simon and Schuster.

Devor, Holly. 1989. *Gender Blending: Confronting the Limits of Duality.* Bloomington: Indiana University Press.

———. 1997. *FTM: Female-to-Male Transsexuals in Society.* Bloomington: Indiana University Press.

Diagnostic and Statistical Manual of Mental Disorders. 1973. 2nd ed. Washington: American Psychiatric Association.

Diagnostic and Statistical Manual of Mental Disorders. 1980. 3rd ed. Washington: American Psychiatric Association.

Diagnostic and Statistical Manual of Mental Disorders-IV. 1994. 4th ed. Washington, DC: APA.

Diagnostic and Statistical Manual of Mental Disorders-IV-TR. 2000. http://www. behavenet.com. Last accessed 8/11/06.

Diamant, Anita. 1997. *The Red Tent.* New York: St. Martin's Press.

Diaz, Rafael. 2000. "Cultural Regulation, Self-Regulation, and Sexuality." In *Framing the Sexual Object: The Politics of Gender, Sexuality, and Power.* Richard. Parker, Regina Maria Barbosa, and Peter Aggleton, eds. Berkeley: University of California Press. Pp. 191–215.

Diaz, Rafael M. 1998. *Latino Gay Men and HIV: Culture, Sexuality, and Risk Behavior.* New York: Routledge.

Dickermann, Mildred. 1990. "A Sister Reclaimed. A Review of Ruth Benedict: Stranger in This Land." *Solga Newsletter,* 12(2): 5–9.

Diiorio, Colleen, Maureen Kelly, and Marilyn Hockenberry-Eaton. 1999. "Communication about Sexual Issues: Mothers, Fathers, and Friends." *Journal of Adolescent Health,* 24(3): 181–189.

Ditmore, Melissa. 2005. "U.S. Funding Policies on Trafficking Affect Sex Work and HIV-Prevention Efforts Worldwide." *SIECUS REPORT,* 33: 26–29.

Divale, William T. and Marvin Harris. 1976. "Population, Warfare and the Male Supremacist Complex." *American Anthropologist.* 78: 421–538.

"Do CAM Therapies Help Menopausal Symptoms." 2005. The National Center for Complimentary and Alternative Medicine, The National Institutes of Health. http://nccam.nih.gov/health/menopauseandcam/. Last accessed 12/4/06.

Dolan, Kathleen A. and Phillip W. Davis. 2003. "Nuances and Shifts in Lesbian Women's Constructions of STI and HIV Vulnerability." *Social Science and Medicine,* 57(1): 25–38.

Dolance, Susannah. 2005. "'Whole Stadium Full?': Lesbian Community at Women's National Basketball Association Games." *Journal of Sex Research,* 42: 74–83.

Doskoch, Peter. 2006. "Skewed Sex Ratio of Birth in India May be the Result of Sex Selective Abortion." *Digest International Family Planning Perspectives*, 32(2): 1–2. http://guttmacher.org/pubs/journals/3210206b.html. Last accessed 8/11/06.

Douglas, Carlyle C. 1990. "Lesbian Child-Custody Cases Redefine Family Laws." *New York Times*. 7/8 Opinion 1.

Dowie, Mark. 1991. "Reluctant Crusader." *Annual Editions of Human Sexuality 91/92*. Ollie Pocs, ed. Sluice Dock: Dushkin Publishers. Pp. 137–140.

Downie, David C. and David J. Hally. 1961. "A Cross-Cultural Study of Male Transvestism and Sex-Role Differentiation." Unpublished manuscript. Dartmouth College.

Dr. Spock Company, The. 2004. "Dr. Benjamin Spock, 1903–1998." http://www drspock.com/about/drbenjaminspock/0,1781,00.html. Last accessed 5/12/06.

Dreger, Alice Dumurat. 1998. "'Ambiguous Sex'—or Ambivalent Medicine?" *The Hastings Center Report*, 28(3): 24–35. http://www.isna.org/articles/ambivalent_medicine. Last accessed 6/26/06.

"Drew Barrymore's Hairy Armpit Shocker." 2005. Female First. http://www.femalefirst.co.uk/celebrity/25012004.htm. Last accessed 2/9/2006.

"Drug Access. ADAP Watch Says 954 HIV-Positive People in 10 States are on Waiting Lists." 2006. Kaiser Daily HIV/AIDS Report. http://www.kaisernetwork.org/daily_reports/rep_index.cfm?DR_ID=35190. Last accessed, 2/3/06.

"DSM-IV." 2006. *Wikipedia*. http://en.wikipedia.org/wiki/DSM-IV. Last accessed 6/7/06.

du Toit, Brian, ed. 2000. *Human Sexuality: Cross-Cultural Readings*. 6th ed. New York: McGraw-Hill.

Duff-Brown, Beth. 2005. "Same Sex Marriage Gains in Canada." *Lincoln Journal Star*, June 29: 3A.

Dugan, Anna. 1988. "Compadorango as a Protective Mechanism in Depression." *Women and Health: Cross-Cultural Perspective*. Pat Whelehan, ed. Granby: Bergin and Garvey Publishers. Pp. 143–153.

Duggan, Lisa. 1990. "From Instincts to Politics: Writing the History of Sexuality in the U.S." *The Journal of Sex Research*, 27(1): 95–109.

Dunbar, Robin. 1996. *Grooming, Gossip, and the Evolution of Language*. Cambridge: Harvard University Press.

Dunn, Kate M., Kelvin Jordan, Peter R. Croft, Willem J. J. Asendleft. 2002. "Systematic Review of Sexual Problems: Epidemiology and Methodology." *The Journal of Sex and Marital Therapy*, 28(5): 399–422.

Dunn, M. and N. Catler. 2000. "Sexual Issues in Older Adults." *AIDS Patient Care & STDs*, 14(2), 67–69.

Dunn, Marian E. and Jan E. Trost. 1989. "Male Multiple Orgasm: A Descriptive Study. *Archives of Sexual Behavior*, 18(1): 377–387.

"E: Testicular Self Exam." 2005. National Cancer Institute. http://visualsonline.cancer.gov/. Last accessed 2/10/06.

Edwards, Michael W. E. 2005. "In Your Face." *HIV Plus*, December: 4–7.

Ehrenreich, Barbara and Deirdre English. 1978. *For Her Own Good: 150 Years of the Experts' Advice to Women*. Garden City: Anchor Press.

Ehrenreich, Barbara, Elizabeth Hess, and Gloria Jacobs. 1986. *Re-making Love: The Feminization of Sex*. New York: Anchor Press/Doubleday.

Ehrenberg, Margaret. 2005. "The Role of Women in Human Evolution." In *Gender in Cross-Cultural Perspective*. Caroline B. Brettell and Carolyn F. Sargent, eds. Upper Saddle River: Pearson Prentice Hall.

Eicher, Wolf, Marijan Spoljar, Hartwig Cleve, Jan-Dieter Marken, Wolfgang Eiermann, Kurt Hichter, and Sabine Stengel-Rutkowski. 1981. "Transsexuality and H-Y Antigen." Paper presented at the 7th International Gender Dysphoria Symposium. The Harry Benjamin International Gender Association. March 4–8, Lake Tahoe, Nevada.

Ekins, Richard. 1998. "On Male Femaling: A Grounded Theory Approach to Cross-Dressing and Sex Changing." In *Current Concepts in Transgender Idenitty*. Dallas Denny, ed. New York: Garland Publishing, Inc. Pp. 181–211.

Elias, J. and P. Gebhard. 1969. "Sexuality and Sexual Learning in Childhood." *Phi Delta Kappan*, 50: 401–405.

Ellison, Peter T. 2001. *On Fertile Ground: A Natural History of Human Reproduction*. Cambridge: Harvard University Press.

Elliston, Deborah A. 1999. "Negotiating Transitional Sexual Economies: Female Mahu and Same-Sex Sexuality in Tahiti and Her Islands." *Female Desires: Same Sex Relations and Transgender Practices Across Cultures*. Evelyn Blackwood and Saskia E. Wieringa, eds. New York: Columbia University Press. Pp. 230–252.

Else-Quest, Nicole, M., Janet Shibley Hyde, and John D. DeLamater. 2005. "Context Counts: Long-Term Sequelae of Premarital Intercourse or Abstinence." *The Journal of Sex Research*, 42(2): 102–112.

Elshtain, Jean Bethke. 1989. "Why We Need Limits." *Annual Editions: Human Sexuality, 1989–90*. Ollie Pocs, ed. Sluice Dock: Dushkin Publishers. Pp. 6–8.

Emanuele, Mary Ann and Nicholas V. Emanuele. 1998. "Alcohol's Effect on Male Reproduction." *Alcohol Health and Research World*, 22: 195–202.

Emanuele, Mary Ann, Frederick Wezeman, and Nicholas V. Emanuele. 1999. "Alcohol's Effects on Female Reproductive Function." *National Institute on Alcohol Abuse and Alcoholism*. http://pubs.niaaa.nih.gov/publications/arh26–4/274–281.pdf. Last accessed 7/5/06.

Ember, Carol and Melvin Ember, eds. 1988. *Anthropology*. 5th ed. Englewood Cliffs: Prentice Hall.

———. eds. 1990. *Anthropology*. 6th ed. Englewood Cliffs: Prentice Hall.

———. eds. 1994. *Research Frontiers in Anthropology*. Englewood Cliffs: Prentice Hall.

———. 2003. *The Encyclopedia of Sex and Gender*. Vol. 1. New York: Kulwer Press for the Human Relations Area Files.

Ember, Carol R., Melvin Ember and Peter N. Peregrine. 2005. *Anthropology*. Upper Saddle River: Person Prentice Hall.

Ember, Carol R., Melvin Ember, and Andrea Shaw, eds. 1994. *Research Frontiers in Anthropology*. Englewood Cliffs: Prentice Hall.

Ember, Melvin. 1985. "Evidence and Science in Ethnography: Reflections on the Freeman-Mead Controversy." *American Anthropologist*, 87(4): 906–910.

"Emergency Contraception: How to Take." 2006. Planned Parenthood Federation of America. http://www.plannedparenthood.org/birth-control-pregnancy/emergency-contraception/procedure-4366.htm. Last accessed 1/20/2007.

"Emergency Contraception: The Basics." 2005. Planned Parenthood of America. http://www.plannedparenthood.org/pp2/portal/files/portal/medicalinfo/ec/pub-emergency-contraception.xml. Last accessed 8/11/06.

Erick, Miriam. 1994. "Morning, Noon, and Night Sickness." *Parenting*, February: 72–78.

Erickson, Mark T. 1999. "Incest Avoidance: Clinical Implications of the Evolutionary Perspective." In *Evolutionary Medicine*. Wenda R. Trevathan, E. O. Smith, and James J. McKenna, eds. New York: Oxford University Press.

Eshleman, J. Ross, Barbara Cashion, and Laurence A. Basirico, 1988. *Sociology: An Introduction*. Boston: Scott, Foresmans and Company.

Esiet, Uwem Edimo, chapter coordinator. 2004. "Nigeria." In *The Continuum Complete International Encyclopedia of Sexuality*. Robert T. Francoeur and Raymond J. Noonan, eds. New York: Continuum. 2004. Pp. 752–780.

Estioko-Griffin, Agnes. 1993. "Daughters of the Forest." In *The Other 50 Percent: Multi-Cultural Perspectives on Gender Relations*. Mari Womack and Judith Marti, eds. Prospect Heights: Waveland Press, Inc. Pp. 225–232.

Estioko-Griffin, Agnes A. 1993. "Daughters of the Forest." *Natural History*, 1990. 95(5): 36–43. (Reprinted in *Anthropology: Contemporary Perspectives*, 5th ed., 1987. Phillip Whitten and David Hunter, eds., Pp. 234–237. Boston: Little, Brown, and Company.)

Estioko-Griffin, Agnes and P. Bion Griffin. 2005. "Woman the Hunter: The Agta." In *Gender in Cross-Cultural Perspective*. Carolyn B. Brettell and Carolyn F. Sargent, eds. Upper Saddle River: Pearson Prentice Hall.

Evans-Pritchard, Edward Evans. 1951. *Kinship and Marriage Among the Nuer*. Oxford: Clarendon Press

Evans-Pritchard, Edward Evans. 1970. "Sexual Inversion Among the Azande." *American Anthropologist*, 72(6): 1428–1434.

Eveleth, Phyllis B. and James M. Tanner. 1990. *Worldwide Variation in Human Growth*. Cambridge: Cambridge University Press.

"Exploring the Biological Contributions to Human Health: Does Sex Matter?" 2001. Institute of Medicine (IOM). http://www.nap.edu/books/0309072816/html/46.html. Last accessed 2/9/2006.

"Facts in Brief: Contraceptive Use." 2005. The Guttmacher Institute. March. http://www.guttmacher.org/pubs/fb_contr_use.html. Last accessed 8/11/06.

"Facts in Brief: Sexual and Reproductive Health: Women and Men." 2002. The Guttmacher Institute. http://www.guttmacher.org/pubs/fb_10–02.html. Last accessed 8/11/06.

"Facts in Brief: Sexuality Education: Sex and Pregnancy Among Teenagers." 2000. Guttmacher Institute. www.guttmacher.org/pubs/fb_sex_ed02.html. Last accessed 8/14/06.

"Facts in Brief: Teenagers' Sexual and Reproductive Health: Developed Countries." 2006. Guttmacher Institute. http://www.guttmacher.org/pubs/fb_teens.html.

"Facts in Brief: Teenagers' Sexual and Reproductive Health." 2002. The Alan Guttmacher Institute. http://www.guttmacher.org/pubs/fb_teens.html. Last accessed 8/14/06.

"Fact Sheet: The Global HIV/AIDS Epidemic—2005 Update." 2005. Kaiser Family Foundation. http://www.kff.org/hivaids/3030–05.cfm. Last accessed 12/26/05.

"Fact Sheet: The HIV/AIDS Epidemic in the United States—2005 Update." 2005. Kaiser Family Foundation. http://www.kff.org/hivaids/3029-05.cfm. Last accessed 2/9/2006.

"Fact Sheet: Hot Flashes." 2006. The National Women's Health Network. http://www.nwhn.org/publications/fact_details.php?fid=13. Last accessed 12/4/06.

"Fact Sheets: Menopause and Heart Disease." 2006. National Women's Health Network. http://www.nwhn.org/publications/fact_details.php?fid=2. Last accessed 12/4/06.

Faden, Ruth R. and Nancy Kass, eds. 1996. *HIV, AIDS and Childbearing: Public Policy, Private Lives.* New York: Oxford University Press.

Faludi, Susan. 1991. *Backlash: The Undeclared War Against America Women.* New York: Doubleday.

Family Care International. http://www.familycareintl.org/issues/unsafeAbortion.php.

Farmer, Paul. 2000. *Infections and Inequalities: The Modern Plagues.* Berkeley: University of California Press.

Farmer, Paul, Margaret Connors, and Janie Simmons, eds. 1996. *Women, Poverty, and AIDS: Sex, Drugs, and Structural Violence.* Monroe: Common Courage Press.

Farmer, Paul, David A. Walton, and Jennifer J. Furin. 2000. "The Changing Face of AIDS: Implications for Policy and Practice." In *The Emergence of AIDS: The Impact of Immunology, Microbiology and Public Health.* Kenneth H. Mayer and Hank F. Pizer, eds. Washington: American Association of Public Health. Pp. 139–161.

Farr, Kathryn. 2005. *Sex Trafficking: The Global Market in Women and Children.* New York: Worth Publishers.

Farrell, Warren. 1974. *The Liberated Male: Beyond Masculinity: Freeing Men and Their Relationships with Women.* New York: Bantam Books.

———. 1986. *Why Men Are the Way They Are.* New York: McGraw Hill.

———. 1993. *The Myth of Male Power.* New York: Simon and Schuster.

Faust, Betty B. 1988. "When Is a Midwife a Witch? A Case Study from a Modernizing Maya Village." *Women and Health: Cross-Cultural Perspectives.* Patricia Whelehan, ed. Granby: Bergin and Garvey Publishers.

Fausto-Sterling, Anne. 1993. "The Five Sexes: Why Male and Female Are not Enough." *The Sciences* March/April: 20–24.

———. 2000. *Sexing the Body: Gender Politics and the Construction of Sexuality.* New York: Basic Books.

"FDA Approves Long-Term, Implantable Birth Control." 2006. *Associated Press,* July 19, Washington. http://www.boston.com/business/globe/articles/2006/07/19/fda_approves_long_term_implantable_birth_control?mode=PF. Last accessed 8/11/06.

Federation of Feminist Women's Health Centers. 1995. *A New View of a Woman's Body: A Fully Illustrated Guide.* Los Angeles: Feminist Health Press.

"Female Condom FC2, The." 2005. World Health Organization: Joint WHO/USAIDS/UNFPA Statement. September 8.

"Female Condom: A Powerful Tool for HIV Prevention, The." 2005. Center for Health and Gender Equity. http://www.genderhealth.org/pubs/FemaleCondom.doc. Last accessed 8/11/06.

"Female Genital Mutilation." 2000. *Fact Sheet 241*. World Health Organization. http://www.who.int/mediacentre/factsheets/fs241/en/print.html. Last accessed 7/11/06.

Female Intelligence Agency. 2005. Normal Breasts Photo Gallery. http://www. 007b.com/breast_gallery.php. Last accessed 2/9/2006.

"Female Sexual Dysfunction: A New Medical Myth: Current Campaign Activities." 2006. FSD-Alert. http://www.fsd-alert.org/campaign.html. Last accessed 12/11/2006.

Feminist Woman's Health Center. 2004. http://www.fwhc.org/birth-control/ diaphram.htm. Last accessed 8/11/06.

Ferguson, Brian. 2001. "Materialist Cultural and Biological Theories on Why Yanomami Make War." *Anthropological Theory*, 1(1): 99–116.

Fernea, Elizabeth Warneck. 1965. *Guests of the Sheik*. New York: Doubleday.

Fernea, Elizabeth W. 1989. *Guests of the Sheik: An Ethnography of an Iraqi Village*. New York: Anchor Books.

Ferraro, Gary. 2004. *Cultural Anthropology: An Applied Prospective*. Belmont: Thomsom-Wadsworth.

"Fictive Kin." 2006. Adoption.org. http://www.glossary.adoption.com/fictive-kin. html. Last accessed 8/2/06.

Findlay, Steven. 1991. "Birth Control." In *Annual Editions of Human Sexuality 91/92*. Ollie Pocs, ed. Sluice Dock: Dushkin. Pp.126–129.

Finer, Lawrence B. and Stanley K. Henshaw. 2006. "Disparities in Rates of Unintended Pregnancy in the United States, 1994 and 2001." *Perspectives on Sexual Reproductive Health*, June, 38(2). http://www.guttmacher.org/pubs/journals/ 3809006.html. Last accessed 1/20/06.

Finkelhor, David. 1984. *Child Sexual Abuse: New Theory and Research*. New York: Free Press.

First Moravian Church. 2006. Greensboro, North Carolina. http://www.greensboro moravian.org/. Last accessed 5/12/06.

Fischer, I.V. and Eisenstein, T. 1984. "Current Approaches in Sex Therapy." In *Sexual Arousel*. M. Ficher, R. E. Fishkin, and J. A. Jacobs, eds. Springfield: Charles Thomas: 142–16.

Fisher, Helen E. 1983. *The Sex Contract: The Evolution of Human Behavior*. New York: Quill.

———. 1992. *Anatomy of Love: The Natural History of Monogamy, Adultery, and Divorce*. New York: W. W. Norton.

———. 2004. *Why We Love*. New York: Henry Holt and Company, LLC.

Fisher, Judith A., Marjorie Bowman, and Tessie Thomas. 2003. "Issues for South Asian Indian Patients Surrounding Sexuality, Fertility, and Childbirth in the U.S. Health Care System." *The Journal of the American Board of Family Practice*, 16(2): 151–155.

Fisher, Trevor. 1997. *Prostitution and the Victorians*. United Kingdom: Sutton Publishing Limited.

———. 2001. *Prostitution and the Victorians*. United Kingdom: Sutton Publishing Limited.

Fiske, Alan Page and Kathryn F. Mason. 1990. "Introduction." *Ethos*, 18(2): 131–139.

Ford, Clellan S. and Frank A. Beach. 1951. *Patterns of Sexual Behavior*. New York: Harper Torchbooks.

Foster, Lawrence. 1991. *Women, Family, and Utopia: Communal Experiments of the Shakers, the Onedia Community, and the Mormons.* Syracuse: Syracuse University Press.

Fox, J. Robin. 1962. "Sibling Incest." *British Journal of Sociology,* 13: 128–150.

Francis, Henry L. and Victoria A. Cargill. 2001. "Substance Abuse." In *A Guide to the Clinical Care of Women with HIV.* 2001 ed. Jean. Anderson, ed. Rockville: Womencare. Pp. 313–333.

Francoeur, Robert, ed. 1989. *Taking Sides: Clashing Views on Controversial Issues in Human Sexuality.* Guilford: Dushkin Publishers.

———. 1991a. *Becoming a Sexual Person.* New York: Macmillan Publishing Company.

———. 1991b. *Instructors' Manual for Becoming a Sexual Person.* New York: Macmillan Publishing Company.

———. 1991c. "Sex and Spirituality: The Relevance of Tantric and Taoist Experiences." *The Siecus Report,* 1–12.

———. 1992. "Sexuality and Spirituality: The Relevance of Eastern Traditions." *The Siecus Report,* 20(4): 1–8.

Francoeur, Robert T. 1993. *The Gender Rainbow: An Ancient Myth of Sexuality Reinterpreted for a New Millennium.* Rockaway: Robert T. Francoeur.

Francoeur, Robert T. and Raymond J. Noonan, eds. 2004. *The Continuum Complete International Encyclopedia of Sexuality.* New York: Continuum International Publishing Group.

Franzetta, Kerry, Elizabeth Terry-Human, Jennifer Manlove, and Erum Ikramullah. 2006. "Teens and Recent Estimates: Contraceptive Use among U.S. Teens." *Child Trends Research Brief.* 2006–04: 1–8.

Frayser, Suzanne G. 1985. *Varieties of Sexual Experience: An Anthropological Perspective on Human Sexuality.* New Haven: HRAF.

Frayser, Suzanne G. and Thomas J. Whitby. 1987. *Studies in Human Sexuality: A Selected Guide.* Littlejohn: Libraries Unlimited, Inc.

Freeman, Derek. 1983. *Margaret Mead and Samoa: The Making and Unmaking of an Anthropological Myth.* Cambridge: Harvard University Press.

———. 1996. *Margaret Mead and Samoa: The Making and Unmaking of an Anthropological Myth.* New York: Penguin Books.

———. 1999. *The Fateful Hoaxing of Margaret Mead: A Historical Analysis of Her Samonan Research.* Boulder: Westview Press.

Freidenreich, Marcia. 2003. "HIV a Topic at Pembroke Pines Health Fair for Seniors." *South Florida Sun Sentinel,* December 7.

"Frequently Asked Questions About Testosterone and the IOM (Institute of Medicine) Report National Institute on Aging." 2003. http://www.nia.nih.gov/NewsAndEvents/PressReleases/FrequentlyAskedQuestionsAboutTestosteroneand theIOMReport.htm. Last accessed 8/11/06.

Freud, Sigmund. 1920a. "Three Essays on the Theory of Sexuality." *The Complete Psychological Works of Sigmund Freud, VII.* Standard original ed. London: Hogarth Press.

———. 1920b. *Selected Papers on Hysteria and Other Psychoneurosis.* 3rd ed. New York: Nervous and Mental Disease Publishing Company.

———. 1959 [1929]. *Group Psychology and the Analysis of the Ego.* James Strachey ed. and translator. London: Hogarth Press.

------. 1950 [1913]. *Totem and Taboo*. New York: W. W. Norton and Company.

------. 1975 [1905]. *Three Essays on the Theory of Sexuality*. New York: Basic Books.

------. 1975 [1992]. *Beyond the Pleasure Principle*. New York: Norton.

Friday, Nancy. 1974. *My Secret Garden: Women's Sexual Fantasies*. New York: Pocket Books.

Friedan, Betty. 1963. *The Feminine Mystique*. New York: W. W. Norton.

Friedman, Richard C. et al., eds. 1974. *Sex Differences in Behavior*. New York: Wiley.

Friedman, Samuel R., Richard Curtis, Alan Neaigus, Benny Jose, and Don C. Des-Jarlais. 1999. *Social Networks, Drug Injectors' Lives, and HIV/AIDS*. New York, NY: Kluwer Academic.

Frisch, Rose. 1978. "Population, Food Intake, and Fertility." *Science*. 199: 22–30.

FSD-Alert. 2005. http://www.fsd-alert.org/. Last accessed 2/9/2006.

Fu, Haishan, Jacqueline E. Darroch, Taylor Haas, and Nalini Ranjit. 1999. "Contraceptive Failure Rates: New Estimates from the 1995 National Survey of Family Growth." *Family Planning Perspectives*, March/April, 31(2). http://www.guttmacher.org/pubs/journals/3105699.html. Last accessed 1/20/2007.

Fuller, Nancy and Brigitte Jordan. 1981. "Maya Women and the End of the Birthing Period: Postpartum Massage-and-Binding in Yucatan, Mexico." *Medical Anthropology*, Winter, 5(1): 35–51.

"Future of Sexual and Reproductive Health at Tipping Point According to Global Study." 2006. World Health Organization Media Centre. http://www. who.int/mediacentre/news/release/2006/pr63/en/index.html.

Gagnon, John H. 1977. *Human Sexualities*. Glenview: Scott Foresman.

------. 1978. "Reconsiderations." *Human Nature*, 1(10): 92–96.

------. 1979. "Sociological Perspectives: The Interaction of Gender Roles and Sexual Conduct." In *Human Sexuality: A Comparative and Developmental Perspective*. Herant A. Katchadourian, ed. Berkeley: University of California Press. Pp. 225–245.

------. 2004. *An Interpretation of Desire: Essays in the Study of Sexuality*. Chicago: University of Chicago Press.

Gagnon, John H. and Richard Parker, eds. 1995. *Conceiving Sexuality: Approaches to Sex Research in a Post Modern Era*. New York: Routledge, Inc.

Gagnon, John H. and William Simon. 1973. *Sexual Conduct: The Social Sources of Human Sexuality*. Chicago: Adline.

Gagnon, John H., William Simon, and A. J. Berger. 1970. "Some Aspects of Sexual Adjustment in Early and Late Adolescence." In *Psychopathology of Adolescence*. Joseph Zubin and Alfred M. Freedman, eds. New York: Greene and Stratton. P. 278.

Garden, G. M. and D. J. Rothery. 1992. "A Female Monozygotic Twin Pair Discordant for Transsexualism: Some Theoretical Implications." *British Journal of Psychiatry*, 161: 852–854.

Garrison, Omar V. 1983. *Tantra: The Yoga of Sex*. New York: Julian Press.

Gavey, Nicola, Kathryn McPhillips, and Virginia Braun. 1999. "Interruptus Coitus: Heterosexuals Accounting for Intercourse." *Sexualities*, 2(1): 35–68.

Geertz, Clifford. 1973. *The Interpretation of Cultures*. New York: Basic Books.

------. 1984. *The Interpretation of Cultures*. New York: Basic Books.

Gelder, Michael G., Juan J. Lopez-Ibor and Nancy Andreasen, eds. 2000. *New Oxford Textbook of Psychiatry*. Oxford: Oxford University Press.

Gender-AIDS eForum. 2004/2005. Email contact: af-aids@eforums.healthdev.org. Last accessed 2/9/06.

Gender Education and Advocacy. 2006. http://www.gender.org. Last accessed 6/7/06.

Gender Identity Reform Advocates. 2008. http://www.transgender.org. Last accessed 6/7/06.

Gender Inn. 2006. http://www.uni-koeln.de/phil-fak/englisch/datenbank/e_index. htm. Last accessed 3/26/06.

Gerrity, Peggy. "Sperm Cell." Photography.

"Get in the Know: 20 Questions About Pregnancy, Contraception and Abortion." 2006. Guttmacher Institute. http://www.guttmacher.org/in-the-know/index.html. Last accessed 8/11/06.

"Get in the Know: Questions About Pregnancy, Contraception and Abortion: Medical Abortion." 2006. Guttmacher Institute. http://www.guttmacher.org/in-the-know/medical.html. Last accessed 8/11/06.

Gewertz, Deborah. 1981. "A Historical Reconsideration of Female Dominance Among the Chambri of Papua New Guinea." *American Ethnologist*, 8: 94–106.

Giami, Alain. 2005. "Book Review: 'An Interpretation of Desire: Essays in the Study of Sexuality.' By John H. Gagnon." *Archives of Sexual Behavior*, 34(5): 583–584.

Gibbs, Nancy. 2006. "When is an Abortion Not an Abortion? *Time Online*. March 6. http://www.time.com/time/nation/article/0,8599,1170368,00.html. Last accessed 8/11/06.

Gill, Jan. 2000. "The Effects of Moderate Alcohol Consumption on Female Hormone Levels and Reproductive Function." *Alcohol and Alcoholism*, 35: 417–423.

Gilligan, Carol. 1982. *In a Different Voice*. Cambridge: Harvard University Press.

"Girls Maturing Slightly Earlier." 2001. *BBC News: Health*. May 3. http://news.bbc.co.uk/1/hi/health/1310280.stm. Last accessed 7/11/06.

Gis, Luk, and Louis Gooren. 1999. "Hormonal and Psychopharmacological Interventions in the Treatment of Paraphilias: An Update." *Journal of Sex Research*, 33: 273–291.

Gladue, Brian, Richard Green, and Ronald Hellman. 1984. "Neuroendocrine Responses to Estrogen and Sexual Orientation." *Science*, 225: 1496–1498.

Gleitman, Henry. 1987. *Basic Psychology*. 2nd ed. New York: W. W. Norton.

Glenmullen, Joseph. 1993. *The Pornographer's Grief and Other Tales of Human Sexuality*. New York: Harper Perennial.

"Global Challenges: Shortage of Health Workers in Developing Countries Impeding Fight Against HIV/AIDS, TB, Malaria, WHO Report Says." 2006. Kaiser Daily HIV/AIDS Report. http://www.kaisernetwork.org/daily_reports/rep_index.cfm?DR_ID=36483. Last accessed 4/7/06.

"Global Challenges: Brazil, Abbott Close to Deal To Lower Price on Antiretroviral Drug Kaletra." 2005. Kaiser Daily HIV/AIDS Report. October 5. http://www.kaisernetwork.org/daily_reports/rep_index.cfm?DR_ID=32926. Last accessed 2/9/2006.

Godziehen-Shedlin, Michelle. 1981. "Notes From a Field Log: Doña Bernarda at Work." *Medical Anthropology*, Winter, 5(1): 13–15.

Goffman, Erving. 1963. *Stigma: Notes on the Management of Spoiled Identity*. New York: Simon and Schuster.

Goldberg, Alisa B., Gillan Dear, M. -Sulc kang, Sarah Youssof, and Philip D. Darney. 2004. "Manual versus Electric Vacuum Aspiration for Early First-trimester Abortion: A Controlled Study of Complication Rates." *Obstetrics and Gynecology*, 103, (axel): 101–107.

Goldberg, D. C., B. Whipple, E. E. Fishkin, H. Waxman, P. Fink, and M. Weisberg. 1983. "The Grafenberg Spot and Female Ejaculation: A Review of Initial Hypothesis." *Journal of Sex and Marital Therapy*, 9: 27–37.

Goldberg, Herb. 1976. *The Hazards of Being Male: Surviving the Myth of Masculinity*. New York: Nash Publishers.

———. 1979. *The New Male: From Macho to Sensitive but Still All Male*. New York: New American Library.

———. 1980. *The New Male: From Self-destruction to Self-care*. New York: New American Library.

———. 1984. *The New Male-Female Relationship*. New York: New American Library.

———. 1985. "Sex at Cross-Purposes." *Human Sexuality 85/86*. Ollie Pocs, eds. Guilford: Dushkin Publishers. Pp. 147–149.

Golden, Arthur. 1997. *Memoirs of a Geisha*. New York: Alfred A. Knopf, Inc.

Goldenring, John. 2005. "Puberty and Adolescence." *MedlinePlus Medical Encyclopedia*. http://www.nlm.nih.gov/medlineplus/ency/article/001950.htm. Last accessed 5/12/06.

Goldman, Ronald and Juliette Goldman. 1982. *Children's Sexual Thinking*. Boston: Routledge and Kegan Paul.

Goldstein, David B. 1990. "Genetic and Biochemical Functioning in Human Sexual Behavior." Paper presented as AASECT XXII Annual Conference 16, February, Arlington, Virginia.

Goldstein, Melvyn. 1987. "When Brothers Share a Wife." *Natural History*, 96(3): 39–48.

Goldstein, Nancy. 1997 "Lesbians and the Medical Profession: HIV/AIDS and the Pursuit of Visibility." In *The Gender Politics of HIV/AIDS in Women: Perspectives on the Pandemic in the U.S.* Nancy Goldstein and Jennifer L. Manlowe, eds. New York: New York University Press. Pp. 86–110.

Goldstein, Nancy and Jennifer L. Manlowe, eds. 1997. *The Gender Politics of HIV/AIDS in Women: Perspectives on the Pandemic in the U.S.* New York: New York University Press.

Gomez, Cynthia A. 1995. "Lesbians at Risk for HIV. The Unresolved Debate." In *AIDS, Identity, and Community. The HIV Epidemic and Lesbian and Gay Men*. Gregory M. Herek and Beverly Greene, eds. Thousand Oaks: Sage Publications, Inc.

Gonzalo, I. T., R. S. Swerdloff, A. L. Nelson, B. Clevenger, R. Garcia, N. Berman and C. Wang. 2002. "Levonorgestrel Implant (Norplant II) for Male Contraception Clinical Trials: Combination with Trans-dermal and Injectable Testosterone." *Clinical Endocrinological Metabolism*, 87(3): 562–572.

Goodale, Jane. 1971. *Tiwi Wives: A Study of the Women of Melville Island, North Australia*. Seattle: University of Washington Press.

———. 1986. *The Chimpanzees of Gombe*. Cambridge: Belknap Press.

Goode, Erica. 2003. "AIDS Researchers Get Warning: Federal Health Officials Advise Them to Avoid Controversial Topics." *San Francisco Chronicle*, February 18.

Goodman, Raymond E. 1983. "Biology of Sexuality: Inborn Determinants of Human Sexual Response." *British Journal of Psychiatry*. September, 143: 216–220.

Gordon, Michael, ed. 1978a. *The American Family in Social-Historical Perspective*. New York: St. Martin's Press.

————. 1978b. "Demography: Births, Deaths, and Migration." *The American Family in Social-Historical Perspective*. Michael Gordon, ed. New York: St. Martin's Press. Pp. 13–15.

————. 1988. "College Coaches' Attitudes Toward Pregame Sex." *Journal of Sex Research*, 24: 256–62.

Gordon, N. 1978. *The Family in Social-Historical Perspective*. New York: St. Martin's Press.

Gordon, Sol and Craig W. Snyder. 1986. *Personal Issues in Human Sexuality*. Boston: Allyn and Bacon, Inc.

Gotz, Michael J. et al. 1999. "Criminality and Antisocial Behavior in Unselected Men with Sex Chromosomes Abnormalities." *Psychological Medicine*, July, 29(4): 953–962.

Grafenberg, Ernst. 1950. "The Role of the Urethra in Female Orgasm." *The International Journal of Sexology* 3: 145–148.

Green, Jamison. 2004. *Becoming a Visible Man*. Nashville: Vanderbilt University Press.

Green, Richard. 1974a. *Sexual Identity Conflict in Children and Adults*. New York: Basic Books.

————. 1974b. "Children Quest for Sexual Identity." *Psychology Today*, 7(9): 45–51.

————. 1978. "Sexual Identity of 37 Children Raised by Homosexual or Transsexual Parents." *American Journal of Psychiatry*, 135(6): 692–697.

————. 1979a. "Biological Influences on Sexual Identity." *Human Sexuality: A Comparative and Developmental Perspective*. Berkeley: University of California Press.

————. 1979b. "Childhood Cross-Gender Behavior and Subsequent Sexual Preference." *American Journal of Psychiatry*, 135: 692–697.

————. 1987. *The "Sissy Boy" Syndrome and the Development of Homosexuality*. New Haven: Yale University Press.

Green, Richard and John Money, eds. 1969. *Transsexualism and Sex Reassignment*. Baltimore: The Johns Hopkins University Press.

Greenberg, David F. 1988. *The Construction of Homosexuality*. Chicago: University of Chicago Press.

Greenberg, Jerrold S., Clint E. Bruess, and Kathleen D. Mullen. 1993. *Sexuality Insights and Issues*. Madison: W. C. Brown.

Greenspan, Jose D. and Stanley J. Bolanowski. 1996. "The Psychophysics of Tactile Perception and Its Peripheral Physiological Basis." In *Pain and Touch (Handbook of Perception and Cognition)*. Vol. 7. Lawrence Kruger, ed. Pp. 25–103.

Greer, Germaine. 1971. *The Female Eunuch*. New York: McGraw-Hill.

————. 1992. *The Change: Women, Aging and the Menopause*. New York: Alfred Knopf.

Gregerson, Edgar. 1983. *Sexual Practices: The Story of Human Sexuality.* 1st ed. New York: Franklin Watts.

————. 1992. *Sexual Practices: The Story of Human Sexuality.* 2nd ed. New York: Franklin Watts.

————. 1994. *The World of Human Sexuality: Behaviors, Customs and Beliefs.* New York: Irvington Publishers, Inc.

Griffin, R. Morgan. 2005. "HIV and Pregnancy." Aetna Intelihealth Medical Content. Harvard Medical School. http://www.intelihealth.com. Last accessed 2/9/2006.

Grimes, David A., James Benson, Susheela Singh, Mariana Romero, Bela Ganatra, Friday E. Okonofua, and Iqbal H. Shah. 2006. "Unsafe Abortion: The Preventable Pandemic." *The Lancet,* November, 1–20. http://www.thelancet.com/DO1: 10.1016/S0140–6736(06)69481–6. Last accessed 1/20/2007.

Grossman, Linda S., Brian Martis, and Christopher G. Fichtner. 1996. "Are Sex Offenders Treatable? A Research Overview." *Psychiatric Services,* 50: 349–361.

"Group Asks U.S. FDA to Stop Sales of Hormone Combo." 2006. *Medscape Today.* http://www.medscape.com/viewarticle/543550. Last accessed 11/5/06.

Gruenbaum, Ellen. 2001. *The Female Circumcision Controversy: An Anthropological Perspective.* Philadelphia: University of Pennsylvania Press.

————. 2005. "Female Genital Cutting: Culture and Controversy." In *Gender in Cross-Cultural Perspective.*" Caroline B. Brettell and Carolyn F. Sargent. Upper Saddle River: Pearson Prentice Hall. Pp. 481–494.

————. 2006. "Sexuality Issues in the Movement to Abolish Female Genital Cutting in Sudan." *Medical Anthropology Quarterly,* 20(1): 121–138.

Guylaya, N. M., V. M. Margitich, N. M. Govseeva, V. M. Klimashevsky, I. I. Gorpynchenko, and M. I. Boyko. 2001. "Phospholipid Composition of Human Sperm and Seminal Plasma in Relation to Sperm Fertility." *Archives of Andrology,* 46(7): 169–175.

Haeberle, Erwin J., ed.; Vern L. Bullough and Bonnie Bullough, original eds. 2006 [1994]. *Human Sexuality: An Encyclopedia.* http://www2.hu-berlin.de/sexology/GESUND/ARCHIV/SEN/INDEX.HTM. Last accessed 8/11/06.

Hall, Ed. 1989. "A Conversation with Clifford Grolo Stein and When Does Life Begin?" *Psychological Today,* 1989: 42–46.

Hall, Edward Twitchell. 1966. *The Hidden Dimension.* Garden City: Doubleday.

Hall, Edward T. and M. R. Hall. 1990. *Understanding Cultural Differences: Germans, French and Americans.* Yarmouth: Intercultural Press.

Halperin, Daniel. 1994. "HIV, STS, Anal Sex, and AIDS Prevention Policy in a Northeastern Brazilian City." *International Journal of STD and AIDS,* 9: 294–298.

————. 1999. "Heterosexual Anal Intercourse: Prevalence, Cultural Factors, and HIV Infection and Other Health Risks, Part I." *AIDS Patient Care and STDs,* 13: 717–730.

Halpern, Carolyn T., Kara Joyner, J, Richard Udry and Chirayath Suchindran. 1999–2000. "Smart Teens Don't Have Sex (or Kiss Much Either)." *Journal of Adolescent Health,* 26(3): 213–225.

Hamer, Dean and Peter Copeland. 1994. *The Science of Desire: The Search for the Gay Gene and the Biology of Behavior.* New York: Simon and Schuster.

Hamilton, Jean A. and Sheryle J. Gallent. 1990. "Problematic Aspects of Diagnosing Premenstrual Phase Dysphoria: Recommendations for Psychological Research and Practice." *Professional Psychology: Research and Practice*, 21(1): 60–68.

Hamilton, William D. and Marlene Zuk. 1982. "Heritable True Fitness and Bright Birds: A Role for Parasites?" *Science*, 218: 384–387.

Hammock, Georgina S. 2003. "Physical and Psychological Aggression in Dating Relationships: Similar or Different Processes?" *International Review of Social Psychology*, 16(3): 31–51.

Handy, Bruce. 1998. "The Viagra Craze." *Time*, 15(17): 50–57.

Harder, Ben. 2005. "Striking a Better Bargain with HIV: New Interventions Needed to Save Infants and to Spare Mothers." *Science News*, June 18.

Harlow, Harry F., Margaret K. Harlow, and E. W. Hansen. 1963. "The Maternal Affectional System of Rhesus Monkey." In *Maternal Behavior in Mammals*. Harriet L. Rheingold, ed. New York: Wiley.

Harlow, Harry F., Margaret K. Harlow, and Stephen J. Suomi. 1971. "From Thought to Therapy: Lessons from a Primate Laboratory." *American Scientist*, 59: 538–49.

Harman, S. Mitchell, E. Jeffrey Metter, Jordan D. Tobin, Jay Pearson and Marc R. Blackman. 2001. "Longitudinal Effects of Aging on Serum Total and Free Testosterone Levels in Healthy Men." *The Journal of Clinical Endocrinology and Metabolism*, 86(2): 724–731.

Harris, Marvin. 1974. *Cows, Pigs, Wars, and Witches: The Riddles of Culture*. New York: Random House.

———. 1989. *Our Kind*. New York: Harper Perennial.

———. 1993. *Culture, People and Nature*. New York: Harper Collins.

———. 1999. *Theories of Culture in Postmodern Times*. Walnut Creek: Altamira Press.

Harrison, Diane. 2004. "Opinion: Stealth War on Reproductive Rights." *American Sexuality Magazine*, 3(3): 1–3.

Hart, Charles William M. and Arnold R. Pilling. 1960. *The Tiwi of North Australia*. New York: Holt, Rinehart, and Winston.

Hart, Charles William Merton, Arnold R. Pilling, and Jane C. Goodale. 1988. *The Tiwi of North Australia*. Fort Worth: Holt, Rinehart, and Winston.

Harry Benjamin International Gender Dysphoria Association. 2001. *Harry Benjamin International Gender Dysphoria Association's Standards of Care for Gender Identity Disorders*. 6th version. http://www.hbigda.org/Documents2/socv6.pdf. Last accessed 6/9/06.

Hartley, Heather. 2005. "The Pinking of Viagra Culture: Drug Industry Efforts to Create and Repackage Sex Drugs for Women." *Sexualities*, 9(3): 363–378.

Hartmann, Katherine, Meera Viswanathan, Rachel Palmiere, Gerald Gartlehner, John Thorp, and Kathleen N. Lohr. 2005. "Outcomes of Routine Episiotomy: A Systematic Review." *Journal of the American Medical Association*, 293: 2141–2148.

Hatcher, Robert A. et al. 1986. *Contraceptive Technology 1986–1987*. 13th ed. New York: Irvington.

Hauspie, Ronald C., Martine Vercauteren, and Charles Susanne. 1996. "Secular Changes in Growth and Maturation: An Update." *Acta Paediatrica. Supplement*, 423: 20–27.

Haviland, William A. 1989. *Anthropology*. New York: Holt, Rinehart, and Winston.

Haviland, William A. and Robert J. Gordon, eds. 1993. *Talking About People: Readings in Cultural Anthropology*. Mountainview: Mayfield Publishing Company.

Hayes, James R. and James M. Henslin, eds. 1975. *Introducing Anthropology*. Boston: Holbrook Press, Inc.

Headland, Thomas N. and P. Bion Griffin. 2005. *SILEWP 1997–2004 Summary: A Bibliography of the Agta Negritos of Eastern Luzon, Philippines*. November 7. http://www.sil.org/silewp/1997/004/. Last accessed 3/27/06.

Health and Age. http://www.healthandage.com. Last accessed 1/20/2007.

"Healthy Youth Sexual Risk Behaviors." 2006. National Center for Chronic Disease Prevention and Health Promotion. http://www.cdc.gov/HealthyYouth/yrbs/pdf/trends/2005_YRBS_Sexual_Behaviors.pdf. Last accessed 8/14/06.

"Healthy Youth: Sexual Risk Behaviors 2006." 2006. Center for Disease Control. http://www.cdc.gov/HealthyYouth/sexualbehaviors/index.htm. Last accessed 7/11/06.

Henderson, William James. 1969. *Early History of Singing*. New York: AMS Press.

Hendrick, S. and C. Hendrick. 1987. "Multidimensionality of Sexual Attitudes." *Journal of Sex Research*, November, 23(4): 502–527.

Hengstschlager, Markus, Michael van Trotsenburg, Christa Repa, Erika Marton, Johannes C. Hubert and Gerhard Bernaschek. 2003. "Sex Chromosome Aberrations and Transsexualism." *Fertility and Sterility*, 79(3): 639–640.

Henshaw, Stanley K., A. M. Kenny, D. Somberg, and J. Van Vort. 1989. *Teenage Pregnancy in the United States: The Scope of the Problem and State Responses*. New York: Center for Population Options, Alan Guttmather Institute.

Henshaw, Stanley K., Susheela Singh and Taylor Haas. 1999. "Recent Trends in Abortion Rates Worldwide." *International Family Planning Perspectives*, January, 25(1): 44–48.

Herdt, Gilbert H. 1981. *Guardians of the Flute: Idioms of Masculinity*. New York: McGraw Hill.

——. 1982. *Rituals of Manhood: Male Initiation in Papua New Guinea*. Berkeley: University of California Press.

——. ed. 1984a. *Ritualized Homosexuality in Melanesia*. Berkeley: University of California Press.

——. 1984b. "Ritualized Homosexual Behavior in the Male Cults of Melanesia, 1862–1983: An Introduction in Ritualized Homosexuality in Melanesia." G. Herdt, ed. Los Angeles and Berkeley: University of California Press. Pp. 1–82.

——. 1987. *The Sambia: Ritual and Gender in New Guinea*. New York: Holt, Rinehart, and Winston.

——. 1988. "Cross-Cultural Forms of Homosexuality and the Concept 'Gay'." *Psychiatric Annal*, 18(1): 37–39.

——. ed. 1989. *Gay and Lesbian Youth*. New York: Harrington.

——. 1993. "Semen Transactions in Sambia Culture." In *Culture and Human Sexuality*. David Suggs and Andrew W. Miracle, eds. Belmont: Brooks/Cole Publishing Company. Pp. 298–327.

———. 1996. *Third Sex, Third Gender: Beyond Sexual Dimorphism in Culture and History*. New York: Zone.

———. 1999. "Clinical Ethnography and Sexual Culture." *Annual Review of Sex Research* 10: 100–120.

———. 2004. "A Welcome from the Editor." *Sexuality Research and Social Policy*, 1(1): 1–2

———. 2006. *The Sambia: Ritual, Sexuality, and Change in Papua New Guinea*. Belmont: Thomson Wadsworth.

Herdt, Gilbert, Francis Paine Conant, E. Michael Gorman, Stephanie Kane, Norris Lang, William Leap, Michael D. Quam, Ernest Quimby, Brooke Grundfest Schoepf, and Martha C. Ward. 1990. "AIDS on the Planet: The Plural Voices of Anthropology." *Anthropology Today*, June, 6(3): 10–15.

Herdt, Gilbert and Robert J. Stoller. 1989. "Commentary to the Socialization of Homosexuality and Heterosexuality in a Non-Western Society." *Archives of Sexual Behavior*, 18(1): 31–34.

———. 1990. *Intimate Communications: Erotics and the Study of Cutlure*. New York: Columbia University Press.

Herek, Gregory M. and Beverly Greene, eds. 1995. *AIDS, Identity, and Community. The HIV Epidemic and Lesbians and Gay Men*. Vol 2. Thousand Oaks: Sage Publications, Inc.

Herman, Judith and Lisa Hirschman. 1981. "Father-Daughter Incest." *Female Psychology*. Sue Cox, ed. New York: St. Martin's Press.

Herman-Giddens, Marcia E., Eric J. Slora, Richard C. Wasserman, et al. 1997. "Secondary Sexual Characteristics and Menses in Young Girls Seen in Office Practice: A Study from the Pediatric Research in Office Settings Network." *Pediatrics*, 99: 55–512.

Herrell, Richard, K. 1991. "Research and the Social Sciences." *Current Anthropology*, April, 32(2): 199–203.

Hewlett, Barry S. and Michael E. Lamb. 2005. *Hunter-Gatherer Childhoods: Evolutionary, Developmental and Cultural Perspectives*. New Brunswick: Transaction Press

Hicks, Karen. 2005. "The 'New View' Approach to Women's Sexual Problems." *Medscape Today*. http://www.medscape.com/viewprogram/4705. Last accessed 12/4/06.

Hickson, Mark L. III, Don W. Stacks, and Nina-Jo Moore. 2004. NONVERBAL COMMUNICATION: Studies and Applications. Los Angeles: Roxbury Publishing Co.

"High Rate of Return on Sexual and Reproductive Health Investment." 2005. Guttmacher Institute Media Kit. http://www.guttmacher.org/media/presskits/2005/03/14/index.html. Last accessed 8/11/06.

Hill, Willard W. 1935. "The Status of the Hermaphrodite and Transvestite in Navajo Culture." *American Anthropologist*, 37: 273–279.

———. 1938. "Note on the Pima Berdache." *American Anthropologist*, 40: 338–40.

Hinde, Robert A. 1983. *Primate Social Relationships*. Oxford: Blackwell.

Hirsch, Jennifer and Constance A. Nathanson. 2001. "Some Traditional Methods Are More Modern Than Others: Rhythm, Withdrawal and the Changing Meanings of Sexual Intimacy in Mexican Companionate Marriage." *Culture, Health and Sexuality*, 3(4): 413–428.

"Historical Information on Mifeprestone." 2006. U.S. Food and Drug Administration. http://www.fda.gov/cder/drug/infopage/mifepristone/default.htm. Last accessed 8/11/06.

Hite, Shere. 1976. *The Hite Report on Female Sexuality*. New York: Knopf.

————. 1981. *The Hite Report on Male Sexuality*. New York: Knopf.

————. 1987. *The Hite Report: Women and Love*. New York: Knopf.

"HIV and AIDS in China." 2005. AVERT.ORG. http://www.avert.org/aidschina.htm. Last accessed 2/9/06.

"HIV and AIDS in India." 2005. AVERT.ORG. http://www.avert.org/aidsindia.htm. Last accessed 2/9/06.

"HIV and AIDS—United States, 1981–2001." 2001. *Morbidity and Mortality Weekly Report*, 50: 430–434.

"HIV/AIDS Among African-Americans: Key Facts." 2001. Centers for Disease Control and Prevention. http://www.cdc.gov. Last accessed 6/9/06.

"HIV-Prevention Strategy Highlights Women." 1994. *The Female Patient*. 19(1): 26.

Hochschild, Arlie with Anne Machung. 1989. *Second Shift: Working Parents and the Revolution at Home*. New York: Viking Press.

Hoebel, E. Adamson. 1949. *Man in the Primitive World*. New York: McGraw Hill.

Hollander, Dore. 2005. "Many Young Teenagers Consider Oral Sex More Acceptable and Less Risky Than Vaginal Intercourse." In *Perspectives on Sexual and Reproductive Health*, 37(3), http://www.guttmacher.org/pubs/journals/3715505a.html. Last accessed 7/11/06.

Holmes, Lowell Don. 1987. *The Quest for the Real Samoa: The Mead/Freeman Controversy and Beyond*. South Hadley: Bergin and Garvey.

Holmes, Lowell P. and Ken Schneider. 1987. *Anthropology*. Prospect Heights: Waveland Press.

"Hormone Replacement Therapy." n.d. *Medline Plus*. http://www.nlm.nih.gov/medlineplus/hormonereplacementtherapy.html. Last accessed 1/1/2007.

"How Common Is Intersex?" n.d. Intersex Society of North America. http://www.isna.org/faq/frequency. Last accessed 6/26/06.

Howard, Jane. 1993. "Angry Storm Over the South Seas of Margaret Mead." *Smithsonian*, 14(1): 67–74.

Hrdy, Sarah Blaffer. 1981. *The Woman That Never Evolved*. Cambridge: Harvard University Press.

————. 1999. *Mother Nature: A History of Mothers, Infants, and Natural Selection*. New York: Pantheon Books.

Human Behavior and Evolution Society. 2006. http://www.hbes.com. Last accessed 6/8/06.

Human Biology Association. 2006. http://www.humbio.org/. Last accessed 6/8/06.

Human Rights Watch. 2004. http://www.hrw.org/reports/2004/dr0704/. Last accessed 2/9/2006.

Hurtado, A. Magdalena and Kim Hill. 1996. *Ache Life History: The Ecology and Demography of a Foraging* People. Hawthorne: Aldine de Gruyter.

Huxley, Aldous. 1946. *Brave New World*. New York: Harper and Brothers.

Hyde, Janet Shibley. 1982. *Understanding Human Sexuality*. New York: McGraw-Hill.

————. 1985. *Half the Human Experience*. Lexington: D. C. Heath and Company.

————. 1994. *Understanding Human Sexuality*. 5th ed. New York: McGraw-Hill.

Hyde, Janet. S. and Sara R. Jafee. 2000. "Becoming a Heterosexual Adult: The Experiences of Young Women." *Journal of Social Issues,* 56: 283–296.

ICPR (International Committee on Prostitutes' Rights). 1985. http://www.walnet. org/csis/groups/icpr_charter.html. Last accessed 2/9/06.

"IFPA Says Small Drop in Abortion Figures Is Due to Greater Numbers Accessing Services Outside Britain." 2005. Irish Family Planning Association. July 27. http://www.ifpa.ie/news/index.php?mr=110. Last accessed 1/20/2007.

Im-em, Wassana. 2002. "Changing Partner Relations in the Era of AIDS in Upper-North Thailand." In *Resistances to Behavioural Change to Reduce HIV/AIDS Infection in Predominantly Heterosexual Epidemics in Third World Countries.* John Caldwell, Pat Caldwell, John Anarfi, Kofi Awusabo-Asare, James Ntozi, I. O. Orubuloye, Jeff Marck, Wendy Cosford, Rachel Colombo, and Elaine Hollings, eds. Canberra: Health Transition Centre, Australian National University. Pp. 157–170.

Im-em, Wassana, Mark Van Landingham, John Knodel, and Chanpen Saengtienchai. 2002 "AIDS-Related Knowledge and Attitudes: A Comparison of Older Persons and Young Adults in Thailand." *AIDS Education and Prevention,* 14(3): 246–262.

"In the News: New Pill to Eliminate Menstrual Periods." 2006. *Sexual Science: The Official Newsletter of SSS,* 47(1): 6.

"Incidence of Abortion Worldwide: Abortion Statistics Compiled by the Alan Guttmacher Institute, The." 2005. The Alan Guttmacher Institute. http://www. mnstate.edu/gracyk/courses/phil%20115/Stats_on_abortion.htm. Last accessed 8/11/06.

Institute of Medicine. 2001a. *No Time to Lose: Getting More from HIV Prevention.* USA: National Academy of Sciences.

Institute of Medicine (IOM). 2001b. "Exploring the Biological Contributions to Human Health: Does Sex Matter?" http://www.nap.edu/books/ 0309072816/html/46.html. Last accessed 5/18/05.

International Academy of Sex Research. 2006. http://www.iasr.org. Last accessed 2/9/2006.

International Foundation for Gender Education. 2006. http://www.ifge.org. Last accessed 6/8/06.

International Journal of Men's Health. Men's Studies Press.

International Statistical Classification of Diseases and Related Health Problems, 2007. 10th revised version. World Health Organization. http://www.who.int/ classifications/icd/.

"Interpersonal Heterosexual Behaviors." 2006. http://www2.rz.hu-berlin.de/sex ology/GESUND/ARCHIV/IES/USA08.HTM. Last accessed 5/12/06.

Intersex Society of North America (INSA). http://www.isna.org. Last accessed 6/6/06.

"Irish Abortion Statistics." 2006. Irish Family Planning Association. http://www. ifpa.ie/abortion/hist.html. Last accessed 1/20/2007.

Irish Family Planning Association. 2006. http://www.ifpa.ie/news/index.php?mr= 124. Last accessed 8/11/06.

Irvine, Janice. 1990a. *Disorders of Desire: Sex and Gender in Modern American Sexology.* Philadelphia: Temple University Press.

———. 1990b. "From Difference to Sameness: Gender Ideology in Sexual Science." *The Journal of Sex Research,* 27(1): 7–24.

It's My Party. 1996. Directed by Richard Kleiser. USA: MGM.

"IUD." 2006. Planned Parenthood of America. http://www.plannedparenthood. org/utah/iud.htm. Last accessed 1/20/2007.

IXth International Conference on AIDS in Affiliation with the IVth STD World Congress. 1993. Programme. Berlin: International AIDS Society, WHO, Berline Medizinis, Che. Gesellschaft, Internation Union Against the Venereal Diseases and Treponematoses. Berlin, Germany. June 7–11.

J. 1969. *The Sensuous Woman*. New York: Dell.

Jackson, D. 1990. "Our Sexual Past, Our Sexual Future." *New Woman*. 20(10): 180–182, 184, 186.

Jacobs, Sue Ellen. 1994. "Native American Two Spirits." *Anthropology Newsletter*, 35(8): 7.

Jacobs, Sue Ellen and Christine Roberts. 1989. "Sex, Sexuality, Gender and Gender Variance." In *Gender and Anthropology: Critical Reviews for Research and Teaching*. Sandra Morgen, ed. Washington: American Anthropological Association. Pp. 438–462.

Jacoby, Susan. 1999. "Great Sex." *AARP/Modern Maturity Survey on Sexual Attitudes and Behavior*. September/October. http://www.aarpmagazine.org/lifestyle/relationships/great_sex.html. Last accessed 12/4/06.

———. 2005. "Sex in America" *AARP: The Magazine*. American Association of Retired People. www.aarpmagazine.org/lifestyle/relationships/sex_in_america. html. Last accessed 8/11/06.

"Jadelle" Implants: General Information." 2005. Population Council. http://www .popcouncil.org/biomed/jadellefaqgeninfo.html. Last accessed 1/20/2007.

Janssen, Diederik F. MD. 2002–5. "Growing Up Sexually." Magnus Hirschfeld Archive for Sexology, Berlin, Germany. http://www2.rz.hu-berlin.de/sexology/ GESUND/ARCHIV/GUS/GUS_MAIN_INDEX.HTM. Last accessed 8/2/06.

Janssen, Patricia A., Shook Lee, Elizabeth M. Ryan, Duncan J. Etches, Duncan F. Farquharson, Donlim Peacok, and Michael C. Klein. 2002. "Outcomes of Planned Homebirths Versus Planned Hospital Births after Regulation of Midwifery in British Columbia." *Canadian Medical Association Journal*, 166: 1–15.

Jarrett, Laura R. 1984. "Psychosocial and Biological Influences on Menstruation: Synchrony, Cycle, Length, Regularity." *Psychoneuroendocrinology*, 9: 21–28.

Jenkins, John B. 1990. *Human Genetics*. New York: Harper & Row.

Joannides, Paul. 2004. *Guide to Getting It On*. 4th ed. Berkeley: Publishers Group West.

Johanson, Richard, Mary Newburn, and Alison MacFarlane. 2002. "Has the Medicalization of Childbirth Gone too Far?" *British Medical Journal*, 324: 892–895.

Johansson, Warren, Wayne R. Dynes, and John Lauritsen. 1981/1985. "Homosexuality, Intolerance and Christianity. A Critical Examination of John Boswell's Work. Scholarship Committee of the Gay Academic Union." New York: Gay Academic Union, http://www.galha.org/ptt/lib/hic/. Last accessed 2/9/2006.

Johns Hopkins Children's Center, The. 2006. http://www.hopkinschildrens.org. Last accessed 2/10/06.

Johnsen, Jennifer and Deborah Friedman. 2002. "Nonoxyonol-9—Benefits and Risks." Planned Parenthood of America. http://www.plannedparenthood.org/ news-articles-press/politics-policy-issues/birth-control-access-prevention/nonox-yonol-9–6546.htm. Last accessed 1/20/2007.

Jolly, Alison. 1985. *The Evolution of Primate Behavior.* New York: Macmillan.

Jones, Rachel K. and Stanley K. Henshaw. 2002. "Mifepristone for Early Medical Abortion: Experiences in France, Great Britain and Sweden." *Perspectives on Sexual and Reproductive Health,* May/June, 34(3).

Jooma, Miriam Bibi. 2006. "Southern Africa Assessment. Food Security and HIV/AIDS." *Africa Watch,* 14(1): 1–8. http://www.iss.co.za/pubs/ASR/14No1/jooma.pdf. Last accessed 3/17/06.

Jordan, Brigitte. 1983. *Birth in Four Cultures.* Montreal: Eden Press.

———. 1992. *Birth in Four Cultures: A Cross-Cultural Investigation of Childbirth in Yucatan, Holland, Sweden, and the United States.* 4th ed. Long Grove: Waveland Press.

———. 1993. *Birth in Four Cultures.* 4th ed. Prospect Heights: Waveland Press.

Jordan, Brigitte and Robbie Davis-Floyd. 1993. *Birth in Four Cultures: A Cross-Cultural Investigation of Childbirth in Yucatan, Holland, Sweden and the United States.* Prospect Heights: Waveland Press.

Jost, Alfred. 1961. "Role of Hormones in Prenatal Development." *Harvey Lectures,* 55: 201.

———. 1972. "A New Look at the Mechanisms Controlling Sex Differentiation in Mammals." *Johns Hopkins Medical Journal,* 130: 38.

Jurmain, Robert, Lynn Kilgore, and Wenda Trevathan. 2005. *Introduction to Physical Anthropology.* 10th ed. Belmont: Thompson-Wadsworth.

Kahn, Shivananda. 2001. "Male Homosexualities in India and South Asia: Cultures, Sexualities and Identities: Men Who Have Sex with Men in India." *Journal of Homosexuality,* 40. http://www.globalgayz.com/g-india.html. Last accessed 2/9/2006.

Kaiser Family Foundation. 2005a. Fact Sheet: The Global HIV/AIDS Epidemic—2005 Update.www.kff.org. Last accessed 12/2/05.

Kaiser Family Foundation. 2005b. Fact Sheet: The HIV/AIDS Epidemic in the United States—2005 Update. www.kff.org. Last accessed 12/2/05.

Kaleidoscope. http://ww.uky.edu/Kaleidoscope/fall2003/meyer/page3.htm. Last accessed 2/16/06.

"Kama Sutra of Vatsayana." 1983. *Sexual Practices: The Story of Human Sexuality.* 1st ed. Edgar Gregerson, ed. New York: Franklin Watts.

Kamwendo, Francis, Lars Forslin, Lennart Bodin, and Dan Danielsson. 2000. "Epidemiology of Ectopic Pregnancy during a 28 Year Period and the Role of Pelvic Inflammatory Disease." *Sexually Transmitted Infections,* 78: 28–32.

Kaplan, Helen Singer. 1974. *The New Sex Therapy: Active Treatment of Sexual Dysfunctions.* New York: Brunner/Mazel.

———. 1979. *Disorders of Sexual Desire and Other New Concepts and Techniques in Sex Therapy.* New York: Brunner/Mazel.

———. 1983. *The Evaluation of Sexual Desires.* New York: Brunner/Mazel.

———. 1989. *PE: How to Overcome Premature Ejaculation.* New York: Brunner/Mazel.

Kaplan, Helen S. and Trude Owett. "The Female Androgen Deficiency Syndrome." *Journal of Sex and Marital Therapy,* 19(1): 3–24.

Kapp, Clare. 2004. "Health and Hunger in Zimbabwe." *Lancet,* 364: 1569–1572.

Kaschak, Ellyn and Leonore Tiefer, eds. 2001. *A New View of Women's Sexual Problems.* Binghamton: The Haworth Press.

Katchadourian, Herant A. 1979. *Human Sexuality: A Comparative and Developmental Perspective*. Berkeley: University of California Press.
———. 1985. *Fundamentals of Human Sexuality*. New York: Holt, Rinehart and Winston.
Katchadourian, Herant A. and Donald T. Lunde. 1975. *Fundamentals of Human Sexuality*. New York: Holt, Rinehart, and Winston.
Kay, Margarita Artschwager. 1981. *Anthropology of Human Birth*. Philadelphia: F. A. Davis.
Kehrl, Brian H. 2005. "States Abstain from Federal Sex Ed. Money." http://www.stateline.org. Last accessed 7/11/06.
Keizer-Schrama, S. M. P. F. de Muinck and D. Mul. 2001. "Trends in Pubertal Development in Europe." *Human Reproduction Update*, 7(3): 287–291.
Kelly, Gary F. 1988. *Sexuality Today: The Human Perspective*. Sluice Dock: Dushkin Publishers.
———. 1990. *Sexuality Today: The Human Perspective*. 2nd ed. Sluice Dock: Dushkin Publishers.
———. 1994. *Sexuality Today: The Human Perspective*. 4th ed. Sluice Dock: Dushkin Publishers.
———. 2005. *Sexuality Today: The Human Perspective*. 8th edition. New York: McGraw-Hill Publishing Company.
Kempadoo, Kamala and Jo Doezema, eds. 1998. *Global Sex Workers. Rights, Resistance, and Redefinition*. New York: Routledge Publishers.
Kendall. 1999. "Women in Lesotho and the (Western) Construction of Homophobia." *Same-Sex Relations and Transgender Practices Across Cultures*. Evelyn Blackwood and Saskia E. Wieringa, eds. New York: Columbia University Press. Pp. 157–180.
Kenkel, Sebastian, Rolf Claus, and Nieschlag Eberhard. 2001. "Occupational Risks for Male Fertility: An Analysis of Patients Attending a Tertiary Referral Center." *The International Journal of Andrology*, December, 24(6): 318–326.
Kessler, Suzanne. 2004. "The Medical Construction of Gender." In *Feminist Frontiers*. Laurel Richardson, Verta Taylor and Nancy Whittier, eds. Boston: McGraw Hill. Pp. 51–66.
Kessler, Suzanne J. and Wendy McKenna. 1978. *Gender: An Ethnomethodological Approach*. New York: John Wiley and Sons.
"Key Moments in NARAL Pro-Choice America's History Moments in NARAL Pro-Choice America's History." 2006. NARAL Pro-Choice America. http://www.prochoiceamerica.org/about-us/learn-about-us/history.html. Last accessed 8/11/06.
Kiefer, Alex. 2005. "Female Ejaculation-Just What Is It?" http://www.umkc.edu/sites/hsw/femejac. Last accessed 3/17/05.
Kilbride, Philip L 2005. "African Polynyny: Family Values and Contemporary Changes." In *Applying Cultural Anthropology*. Aaron Podlesfsky and Peter J. Brown, eds, Boston: McGraw Hill. Pp. 206–214.
Kilmartin, Christopher. 2000. *The Masculine Self*. Boston: McGraw-Hill.
———. 2007. *The Masculine Self*. Cornwall-on-Hudson: Sloan Publishing.
Kimball, Lindsay and Shawna Craig. 1988. "Women and Stress in Brunei." In *Women and Health: Cross-Cultural Perspectives*. Patricia Whelehan, ed. Granby: Bergin and Garvey Publishers. Pp. 170–183.
Kimmel, Michael S. 2000. *The Gendered Society*. New York: Oxford University.

King, Bruce M. 2005. *Human Sexuality Today.* 5th ed. Upper Saddle River: Pearson Prentice-Hall.

King, Bruce M., Cameron J. Camp, Ann M. Downey. 1991. *Human Sexuality Today.* Englewood Cliffs: Prentice Hall.

Kinsey, Alfred C., Wardell B. Pomeroy, and Clyde E. Martin. 1948. *Sexual Behavior in the Human Male.* Philadelphia: Saunders.

Kinsey, Alfred C., Wardell B. Pomeroy, Clyde E. Martin, and Paul H. Gebhard. 1953. *Sexual Behavior in the Human Female.* Philadelphia: N.B. Saunders Co.

Kinsey Institute for Research in Sex, Gender, and Reproduction. 2006. http://www.indiana.edu/~kinsey. Last accessed 3/28/06.

Kirby, Douglas. 1984. *Sexuality Education: An Evaluation of Programs and Their Effects.* Santa Cruz: Network Publications.

———. 2001. "Emergency Answers: Research Findings on Programs to Reduce Teen Pregnancy." *National Campaign to Prevent Teen Pregnancy.* http://www.teenpregnancy.org. Last accessed 1/20/07.

Kirby, D., W. J. Utz, and P. J. Parks. 2006. "An Implantable Ligation Device That Achieves Male Sterilization Without Cutting the Vas Deferens." *Urology,* 67(4): 807–811.

Kirk, Marshall and Hunter Madsen. 1989. *After the Ball.* New York: Doubleday.

Klaiber, Edward L., William Vogel, and Susan Rako. 2005. "A Critique of the Women's Health Initiative Hormone Therapy Study." *Fertility and Sterility,* December, 84(6): 1589–1601.

Klapper, Bradley S. 2006. "WHO Condemns Genital Cutting on Women." *Newsvine.com,* June 2. http://www.newsvine.com/_news/2006/06/02/240061-who-calls-for-end-to-genital-cutting.html. Last accessed 7/11/06.

Klee, Linnea. 1988. "The Social Significance of Elective Hysterectomy." *Women and Health: Cross-Cultural Perspective.* Pat Whelehan, ed. Granby: Bergin and Garvey Publishers.

Klein, Diane. 1981. "Interview: Helen Singer Kaplan." *Omni,* 3(11): 73–75.

Klein, Fred. 1978. *The Bisexual Option.* New York: Arbor House/Berkeley Books.

Kluckhohn, Clyde and Dorothea Leighton. 1962. *The Navaho.* New York: Doubleday.

Klugman, L. 1993. "The New Contraceptives." *New Body,* August: 58–59, 70.

Knauft, Bruce M. 2003. "Whatever Happened to Ritualized Homosexuality? Modern Sexual Subjects in Melanesia and Elsewhere." *Annual Review of Sex Research,* 14: 137–159.

Koch, Patricia B. 2004. "Abstinence-Only Sexuality Education." In *The Continuum Complete International Encyclopedia of Sexuality.* Robert T. Francoeur and Raymond J. Noonan, eds. New York: Continuum International Publishing Group, Inc.

Koch, Patricia Barthalow, Phyllis Kernoff Mansfield, Debra Thurau and Molley Carey. 2005. "'Feeling Frumpy': The Relationships Between Body Image and Sexual Response Changes in Midlife Women." *The Journal of Sex Research,* 42(3): 215–223.

Komarovsky, Mira. 1962. *Blue Collar Marriage.* New York: Vintage Books.

Konker, Claudia. 1992. "Rethinking Child Sexual Abuse: An Anthropological Perspective." *American Journal of Orthopsychiatry,* 62(1): 147–153.

Kopelman, Loretta M. 2002. "Yes: Female Circumcision/Genital Mutilation and Ethical Relativism." In *Taking Sides: Clashing Views on Controversial Issues in Human Sexuality*. William J. Taverner, ed. Guilford: McGraw-Hill/Dushkin. Pp. 50–57.

Kottak, Conrad P. 1991. *Anthropology*. New York: McGraw Hill.

————. 2002. *Anthropology: The Exploration of Diversity*. Boston: McGraw-Hill.

————. 2004. *Cultural Anthropology*. 8th ed. Boston: McGraw-Hill.

Kottak, Conrad Phillip and Kathryn Kozaitis. 1999. *On Being Different*. New York: McGraw-Hill.

Koutsky, Laura A., Kevin A. Ault, Cosette M. Wheeler, Darron R. Brown, Eliav Barr, Frances B. Alvarez, Lisa M. Chiacchierini, and Kathrin U. Jansen. 2002. "A Controlled Trial of a Human Papilloma Virus Type 16 Vaccine." *The New England Journal of Medicine*, November 21, 347(21): 1645–1651.

Krippendorf's Tribe. 1998. Directed by Todd Holland. United States: Touchstone Pictures.

Kroeber, A. L. 1953. *Handbook of the Indians of California*. Berkeley: University of California Press.

Kruger, Jill M., and L. M. Richter. 2003. "South African Street Children at Risk for AIDS." *Children, Youth and Environments*, Spring 13(1): 1–15.

Kulick, Don. 1998. *Travesti: Sex, Gender and Culture Among Brazilian Transgendered Prostitutes*. Chicago: University of Chicago Press.

Kumar, Narendar, Frederick Schmidt; Régine Sitruk-War and Irving Sivin. 2006. "Male Hormone Therapy: Comparing MENT with Testosterone." Population Council. http://www.popcouncil.org/projects/BIO_MaleHT_MENT.html. Last accessed 8/11/06.

Kunkel, Dale, Erica Bieley, Keren Eyal, Kirstie Cope-Farrar, Edward Donnerstein, Rena Fandrich. 2003. "Sex on TV: Part 3." The Henry J. Kaiser Family Foundation. November. http://www.kff.org/entmedia/upload/Sex-on-TV-3.pdf. Last accessed 8/14/06.

Kunkel, Dale, Keren Eyal, Keli Finnerty, Erica Bieley, and Edward Donnerstein. 2005. "Sex on TV: Part 4." The Henry J. Kaiser Family Foundation. November. http://www.kff.org/entmedia/upload/Sex-on-TV-4-Full-Report.pdf. Last accessed 8/14/06.

Kuriansky, Judy. 2005. "Healing Bodies: Eastern Sex Therapy Techniques Improve Performance—and Pleasure." *American Sexuality Magazine*, 3(4): 1–2. http://nsrc.sfsu.edu. Last accessed 8/11/06.

Kusz, Kyle. 2001. "I Want to Be the Minority: 'The Politics of Youthful White Masculinities in Sport and Popular Culture in 1990's America'." *Journal of Sport and Social Issues*, 25(4): 290–415.

Kwakwa, Helena, and Michel W. Ghobrial. 2003. "Female-to-Female Transmission of Human Immunodeficiency Virus." *Clinical Infectious Diseases*, February, 36(1): 40–41.

Lacayo, Richard. 1990. "Do the Unborn Have Rights?" *Time*, 13(19): 22–23.

Ladas, Alice Kahn, Beverly Whipple and John D. Perry. 1982. *The G-spot and Other Recent Discoveries about Human Sexuality*. New York: Dell.

LaFont, Suzanne, ed. 2003. *Constructing Sexualities: Readings in Sexuality, Gender and Culture*. Upper Saddle River: Prentice Hall.

LaLeche League. 2005. http://www.lalecheleague.org. Last accessed 2/9/06.

Lamb, Sarah. 2005. "The Making and Unmaking of Persons: Gender and Body in Northeast India." In *Gender in Cross-Cultural Perspective*. Caroline B. Brettell and Carolyn F. Sargent, eds. Upper Saddle River: Pearson Prentice Hall. Pp. 230–240.

Lambda Legal Defense Fund. 2005. http://www.lambdalegal.org/cgi-bin/iowa/index.html. Last accessed 2/9/2006.

Lancaster, Jane Beckham. 1985. "Evolutionary Perspectives on Sex Differences in the Higher Primates." In *Gender and the Life Course*. Alice S. Rossi, ed. Hawthorne: Aldine. Pp. 3–27.

Lancaster, Roger N. 2003. *The Trouble with Nature: Sex in Science and Popular Culture*. Berkeley: University of California Press.

Lang, Sabine 1998. *Men as Women as Men: Changing Gender in Native American Cultures*. Austin, TX: University of Texas Press.

Laumann, Edward. et al. 2002a. "Abstracts." Pfizer Global Study of Sexual Attitudes and Behaviors. http://www.pfizerglobalstudy.com/public/publications .asp. Last accessed 12/4/06.

Laumann, Edward, et al. 2002. "Selected Results." Pfizer Global Study of Sexual Attitudes and Behaviors. http://www.pfizerglobalstudy.com/study/study-results. asp. Last accessed 12/4/06.

———. et al. n.d. "A Cross-National Study of Subjective Sexual Well Being Among Older Men and Women: Findings from the Global Study of Sexual Attitudes and Behaviors." http://www-news.uchicago.edu/releases/06/images/ 060419.sex.pdf. Last accessed 1/20/2007.

———. 2002b. "Media Resources." Pfizer Global Study of Sexual Attitudes and Behaviors. http://www.pfizerglobalstudy.com/mediaresource/mediaresource .asp. Last accessed 12/4/06.

Laumann, Edward O., John H. Gagnon, Robert T. Michael, and Stuart Michaels. 1994. *The Social Organization of Sexuality: Sexual Practices in the United States*. Chicago: University of Chicago Press.

Laumann, Edward O. and Robert T. Michael, eds. 2000. *Sex, Love and Health in America: Private Choice and Public Policies*. Chicago: University of Chicago Press.

Laumann, Edward O., Anthony Paik, Dale B. Glasser, Jeong-Han Kang, Tianfu Wang, Bernard Levinson, Edson D. Moreira, Afredo Nicolosi, and Clive Gingell. 2006. "A Cross-National Study of Subjective Sexual Well-Being Among Older Women and Men: Findings from the Global Study of Sexual Attitudes and Behaviors." *Archives of Sexual Behaviors*, April, 35(2): 145–161. http://www-news.uchicago.edu/releases/06/images/060419.sex.pdf. Last accessed 8/11/06.

Laumann, Edward O., Anthony Paik, and Raymond C. Rosen. 1999. "Sexual Dysfunction in the United States: Prevalence and Predicators." *Journal of the American Medical Association*, 281(6): 537–544.

Lauzen, Martha M. and David M. Dosier. 2005. "Maintaining the Double Standard: Portrayals of Age and Gender in Popular Films." *Sex Roles*, 52(7/8): 437–446.

"Lawrence and Garner V. State of Texas: US Supreme Court Ruling." 2003. http://www.supremecourtus.gov/opinions/02pdf/02–102.pdf. Last accessed 3/28/06.

Lawrence, Anne A. 1998. "Men Trapped in Men's Bodies: An Introduction to the Concept of Autogynephilia." *Transgender Tapestry*, 85: 65–68.

Leahy, Elizabeth. 2006. "Mapping Supplies: Are Contraceptives Going Where They Are Most Needed?" *Population Action International*, March, 1(3). http://

www. populationaction.org/resources/researchCommentaries/ResearchComm_ v1i3_Mar06.pdf. Last accessed 8/11/06.

Leavitt, Judith Walzer. 2003. "What Do Men Have to Do With It? Fathers and Mid-Twentieth Century Childbirth." *Bulletin of the History of Medicine*, Summer, 77(2): 235–262.

Leavitt, Sarah. 2006. "A Private Little Revolution: The Home Pregnancy Test in American Culture." *Bulletin of the History of Medicine*, 80(2): 317–346.

LeClerc-Madlala, Suzanne. 2001. "Virginity Testing: Managing Sexuality in a Maturing HIV/AIDS Epidemic." *Medical Anthropology Quarterly*, 15(4): 533–552.

Lee, Richard. 1985. "Work, Sexuality, and Aging Among !Kung Women." *In Her Prime: A New View of Middle Aged Women.* Judith K. Brown and Virginia Kerns, eds. South Hadley: Bergin and Garvey Publishers.

"Legistative Update 2003." 2003. Population Connection. http://www.population connection.com/Action_Alerts/alert392.html#3. Last accessed 8/11/06.

Leo, John. 1984. "The Revolution Is Over." *Time*, 123(5): 74–78, 83.

Leone, Tiziana and Andrew Hinde. 2005. "Sterilization and Union Instability in Brazil." *Journal of Biosocial Science*, 37(4): 459–469.

Lepowsky, Maria. 1993. *Fruit of the Motherland: Gender in an Egalitarian Society.* Columbia: Columbia University Press.

Lett, James. 1987. *The Human Experience: A Critical Introduction to Anthropological Theory.* Boulder: Westview Press.

LeVay, Simon. 1991. "A Difference in Hypothalamic Structure Between Heterosexual and Homosexual Men." *Science*, 253: 1034–37.

LeVay, Simon and Sharon McBride Valente. 2002. *Human Sexuality.* Sunderland: Sinauer Associates, Inc.

Levine, Martin P. and Richard R. Troiden. 1988. "The Myth of Sexual Compulsivity." *The Journal of Sex Research*, 25(3): 347–363.

Levine, Nancy. 1988. *The Dynamics of Polyandry: Kinship, Domesticity, and Population in the Tibetan Border.* Chicago: University of Chicago Press.

Levine, Nancy and Walter Sangree. 1980. "Women with Many Husbands." *Journal of Comparative Family Studies*, 11(3).

Levy, Robert I. 1973. *Tahitians: Mind and Experience in the Society Islands.* Chicago: University of Chicago Press.

Lewin, Ellen, ed. 2006. *Feminist Anthropology: A Reader.* Malden: Blackwell Publishing, Pp. 333–357.

Lewin, Ellen and William Lelap, eds. 1996. *Out in the Field.* Urbana: University of Illinois Press.

Lewis, Oscar. 1941. "Manly-Hearted Women Among the Northern Piegan." *American Anthropologist*, 43: 173–187.

Lichtenstein, Bronwen and Amanda Crabb. 2004. "'The Woman's Right to Know' Act: The Atwood Principle and Abortion Law in Alabama." *American Sexuality Magazine*, 2(6): 1–3.

Lieblum, Sandra and Raymond C. Rosen, eds. 2000. *Principles and Practice of Sex Therapy.* 3rd ed. New York: Guilford Press.

Lieblum, Sandra and Judith Sachs. 2002. *Getting the Sex You Want: A Woman's Guide to Becoming Proud, Passionate, and Pleased in Bed.* New York: Crown Publishing.

Life's First Great Crossroad: Teens Make Choices That Affect Their Lives Forever. 2000. Centers for Disease Control. Pp. 1–32. http://www.cdc.gov/youth campaign/research/PDF/LifesFirstCrossroads.pdf.

Lightfoot-Klein, Hanny. 1989. "The Sexual Experience and Marital Adjustment of Genitally Circumcised and Infibulated Females in Sudan." *Journal of Sex Research*, August, 26(3): 375–393.

———. 1990. *Prisoners of Ritual: An Odyssey Into Female Genital Circumcision in Africa*. Binghamton, NY: The Haworth Press.

Lindsey, Linda. 2005. *Gender Roles*. Upper Saddle River: Pearson Prentice Hall.

Lippa, Richard A. 2005. *Gender, Nature, and Nurture*. 2nd ed. Mahwah: Lawrence Erlbaum Associates.

———. 2006. "Is High Sex Drive Associated with Increased Sexual Attraction to Both Sexes?" *Psychological Science*, 17: 46–52.

Lips, Hilary M. 1993. *Sex and Gender: An Introduction*. 2nd ed. Mountain View: Mayfield Publishing Co.

Lipscomb, Gary H., Thomas G. Stovell, and Frank W. Ling. 2000. "Nonsurgical Treatment of Ectopic Pregnancy." *Primary Care*, 343: 1325–1329.

Lish, Jennifer D., Heino F. L. Meyer-Bahlburg, Anke A. Ehrhardt, Bayla G. Travis, Norma Veridiano. 1992. "Prenatal Exposure to Diethylstibestrol (DES): Childhood Play Behavior and Adult Gender Role Behavior in Women." *Archives of Sexual Behavior*, 21: 423–441.

Lloyd, Elisabeth A. 2005. *The Case of the Female Orgasm: Bias in the Science of Evolution*. Cambridge: Harvard University Press.

Lock, Margaret. 1993. *Encounters with Aging: Mythologies of Menopause in Japan and North America*. Berkeley and Los Angeles: California University Press.

Long, Lynellen and E. Maxine Ankrah, eds. 1996. *Women's Experiences with HIV/AIDS: An International Perspective*. New York: Columbia University Press.

Love, Susan M. with Karen Lindsey. 1990/1991. *Dr. Susan Love's Breast Book*. Reading: Addison-Wesley Publishing Company.

Lubbock, John. 1870. *The Origin of Civilization and the Primitive Condition of Man: Mental and Social Condition of Savages*. New York: D. Appleton.

Luker, Kristin. 1977. "Contraceptive Risk Taking and Abortion: Results and Implications of a San Francisco Bay Area Study." *Studies in Family Planning* 8(8): 190–196.

Lurie, Nancy O., ed. 1973. *Mountain Wolf Woman, Sister of Crashing Thunder: The Autobiography of a Winnebago Indian*. Ann Arbor: University of Michigan Press.

Lydon, Christine. 2006 [2002]. "There is No Place Like Home." *Your Family*. July. http://umanitoba.fitdv.com/new/articles/article.html?artid=16. Last accessed 7/11/06.

Lyons, Andrew P. and Harriet Lyons. 2004. *Irregular Connections: A History of Anthropology and Sexuality*. Lincoln: University of Nebraska Press.

Mackie, Nick. 2005. "The Chinese Region with Women in Charge." *BBC News*. http://news.bbc.co.uk/2/hi/asia-pacific/4252552.stm. Last accessed 5/12/06.

Mah, Kenneth and Yitzchak M. Binik. 2005. "Are Orgasms in the Mind or the Body? Psychosocial Versus Physiological Correlates of Orgasmic Pleasure and Satisfaction." *Journal of Sex and Marital Therapy*, 31: 187–200.

Mahoney, E. Richard. 1983. *Human Sexuality*. New York: McGraw-Hill.

"Makassar." 2006. *Wikipedia: The Free Encyclopedia*. http://en.wikipedia.org/wiki/Macassan. Last accessed 2/9/06.

"Male Contraceptive Reversible." 2006. *BBC News: Health*. http://news.bbc.co.uk/ 1/hi/health/4948302.stm. Last accessed 8/11/06.

Males, Mike. 1992. "Adult Liaison in the Epidemic of 'Teenage' Birth, Pregnancy and Vernereal Disease." *Journal of Sex Research*, November, 29(4): 525–547.

Malinowksi, Bronislaw. 1929. *The Sexual Life of Savages in North-Western Melanesia: An Ethnographic Account of Courtship, Marriage and Family Life Among the Natives of Trobriand Islands, British New Guinea*. London: George Routledge.

———. 1961 [1927]. *Sex and Repression in Savage Society*. Cleveland: World.

———. ed. 1987. *The Sexual Life of Savages*. Boston: Beacon Press.

Malpani, Aniruddha. 2002. "Preimplantation Genetic Diagnosis For Gender Selection For Family Balancing: A View From India." *Reproductive Technologies*, 4: 7–9.

Maltz, Wendy. 1989. "Counter Points: Intergenerational Sexual Experience or Child Sexual Abuse?" *Journal of Sex Education and Therapy*, Spring, 15(1): 13–16.

Manderson, Lenore, Linda Rae Bennett, and Michelle Sheldrake. 1999. "Sex, Social Institutions and Social Structure: Anthropological Contributions to the Study of Sexuality." *Annual Review of Sex Research*, 10: 184–210.

Manfredi-Romanini, Maria Gabriella. 1994. "A Histological Approach to the Knowledge about the Neuron Nucleus: The 'Pre-Alarm' Chromatin." *Neurochemical Research*, 19: 783–787.

Mange, Arthur P. and Elaine Johansen Mange. 1980. *Genetics: Human Aspects*. Philadelphia: Saunders College.

"Manifesto: A New View of Women's Sexual Problems, The." 2002. FSD-Alert. http://www.fsd-alert.org/manifesto.html#1. Last accessed 1/20/2007.

March E-News. 2006. NARAL Pro-Choice America. Email: can@ProChoice America.org. http://www.prochoiceamerica.org. Last accessed 11/1/06.

Mariano, Esmeralda. 2005. "Clients' Perceptions of HIV/AIDS Voluntary Counseling and Testing (VCT) in Mozambique." *Training in Sexual Health Research*. *Geneva 2005*. WHO Scholarship: 1–6. http://www.gfmer.ch/Medical_education_En/PGC_SH_2005/csh_lectureplan2005.htm. Last accessed 4/8/06.

Marino. E. 1993. "The T Word." *Democrat and Chronicle*. 7/25.

Marins, Jose R., Kimberly Page-Shafer, Bertide de Azevedo, Marlisa Barros, Esther Hudes, Sanny Chen and Norman Hearst. 2000. "Seroprevalence and Risk Factors for HIV Infection Among Incarcerated Men in Sorocaba, Brazil." *AIDS and Behavior*, 4(1): 121–128.

Marmor, Judith A. 1988. "Health and Health-Seeking Behavior of Turkish Women in Berlin." In *Women and Health Cross-Cultural Perspectives*. Pat Whelehan, ed. Granby: Bergin and Garvey Publishers. Pp. 84–97.

"Married Teens: Early Marriage Is Still Common in Much of the World, Especially in Sub-Saharan Africa and South-Central Asia." http://www.guttmacher.org/ pubs/tgr/07/2/gr070201.pdf. Last accessed 1/20/2007.

Marshall, Barbara L. and Stephen Katz. 2002. "Forever Functional: Sexual Fitness and the Aging Male Body." *Body and Society*, 8(94): 43–70.

Marshall, Carolyn. 2004. "Dozens of Gay Couples Marry in San Francisco Ceremonies." *New York Times*, February 13, A: 24.

Marshall, Donald S. 1971. "Sexual Behavior on Mangaia." In *Human Sexual Behavior*. Donald S. Marshall and Robert C. Suggs, eds. New York: Basic.

———. 1993. "Sexual Aspects of the Life Cycle." In *Culture and Human Sexuality.* David N. Suggs and Andrew W. Miracle, eds. Pacific Grove: Brooks/Cole Publishing Company. Pp. 91–102.

Marshall, Donald S. and Robert C. Suggs, eds. 1971. *Human Sexual Behavior.* New York: Basic Books.

Martin, Emily. 1987. *The Woman in the Body.* Boston: Beacon Press.

Martin, Joyce A., Brady E. Hamilton, Fay Menacker, Paul D. Sutton, and T. J. Matthews. 2005. "Preliminary Births for 2004: Infant and Maternal Health." *National Center for Health Statistics.* CDC. http://www.cdc.gov/ nchs/products/ pubs/pubd/hestats/prelimbirths04/prelimbirths04health.htm.

Martin, M. Kay and Barbara Voorhies. 1975. *Female of the Species.* New York: Columbia University Press.

Mascia-Lees, Francis E. and Nancy Johnson Black. 2000. *Gender and Anthropology.* Prospect Heights: Waveland Press.

Mascia-Lees, Francis E. and Patricia Sharpe. 1992. *Tattoo, Torture, Mutilation and Adornment: The Denaturalization of the Body in Culture and Text.* Albany: State University of New York Press.

Masters, William H. and Virginia E. Johnson. 1966. *Human Sexual Response.* Boston: Little Brown and Company.

———. 1970. *Human Sexual Inadequacy.* Boston: Little, Brown and Company.

———. 1974. *The Pleasure Bond: A New Look at Sexuality and Commitment.* Boston: Little, Brown and Company.

Masters, William H., Virginia E. Johnson, Robert C. Kolodny. 1985. *Human Sexuality.* 2nd ed. Boston: Little Brown and Company.

———. 1982. *Human Sexuality.* Boston: Little Brown and Company.

Mathur, Sanyukta, Margaret Greene and Anju Malhotra. 2003. "Too Young to Wed: The Lives, Rights, and Health of Young Married Girls." International Center for Research on Women. http://www.icrw.org/docs/tooyoungtowed_ 1003.pdf. Last accessed 7/11/06.

Maticka-Tyndale, Eleanor, Jacqueline Lewis, and Megan Street. 2005. "Making a Place for Escort Work: A Case Study." *Journal of Sex Research,* 42: 46–53.

Matzner, Andrew. 2001. *'O Au No Keia: Voices from Hawai'i's Mahu and Trans gender Communities.* Philadelphia: Xlibris Corporation.

Mayer, Kenneth H., and Hank F. Pizer, eds. 2000. *The Emergence of AIDS: The Impact on Immunology, Microbiology, and Public Health.* Washington, DC: American Public Health Association.

Mazur, Allan and Allan Booth. 1998. "Testosterone and Dominance in Men." *Behavioral and Brain Sciences,* 21: 353–364.

Mazur, Allan, Alan Booth, and James M. Dabbs Jr. 1992. "Testosterone and Chess Competition." *Social Psychology Quarterly,* 55(1): 70–77.

McAnulty, Richard D. and M. Michelle Burnett. 2003. *The Fundamentals of Human Sexuality.* Boston: Pearson Education.

McCabe, M. 1987. "Desired and Experienced Levels of Premarital Affection and Sexual Intercourse During Dating." *Journal of Sex Research,* February, 23(1): 23–24.

McCammon, Susan, David Knox, and Caroline Schaat. 1993. *Choices in Sexuality.* St. Paul: West Publishers.

———. 2004. *Choices in Sexuality.* Cincinnatti: Atomic Dog Publishing.

McCarthy, P. 1990. "The Romance Factor: Fertility Clinic Sends Couples to the Bedroom." *American Health*, January/February, IX(1): 14.

McClintock, Martha K. 1971. "Menstrual Synchrony and Suppression." *Nature*, 229: 244.

McDaniel, Ed and Peter A. Andersen, 1998. "International Patterns of Interpersonal Tactile Communication: A Field Study." *Journal of Nonverbal Behavior*, 22(1): 59–73.

McGill, Michael E. 1987. *The McGill Report on Male Intimacy*. New York: Harper and Row.

McGrath, Janet W., Charles B. Rwabukwali, Debra A. Schumann, Jonnie Pearson-Marks, Sylvia Nakayiwa, Barbara Namande, Lucy Nakyobe, and Rebecca Mukasa. 1993. "Anthropology and AIDS: The Cultural Context of Sexual Risk Behavior Among Urban Baganda Women in Kampala, Uganda." *Social Science and Medicine*, 36(4): 429–439.

McKeganey, Neil, Samuel R. Friedman and Fabio Mesquita. 1998. "The Social Context of Injectors' Risk Behavior." In *Drug Injecting and HIV Infection: Global Dimensions and Local Responses*. Gary Stimson, Don DesJarlais, and Andrew L. Ball, eds. London, Bristol: UCL Press. Pp. 22–41.

McKinney, Kathleen and Susan Sprecher, eds. 1989. *Human Sexuality: The Societal and Interpersonal Context*. Norwood: Ablex Publishing Co.

McLennan, John. 1865. *Primitive Marriage*. Edinburgh: Adam and Charles Black.

McWhirter, David P. and Andrew M. Mattison. 1984. *The Male Couple: How Relationships Develop*. Englewood Cliffs: Prentice-Hall.

Mead, Margaret. 1949. *Male and Female*. New York: Morrow.

———. 1961 [1928]. *Coming of Age in Samoa*. New York: Morrow Quill Paperbooks.

———. 1963 [1935]. *Sex and Temperament in Three Primitive Societies*. New York: W. W. Morrow and Co.

Mead, Margaret and Niles Newton. 1967. "Cultural Patterning of Perinatal Behavior." In *Childbearing: Its Social and Psychological Aspects*. Stephen A. Richardson and Alan Frank Guttmacher, eds. Baltimore: Williams and Wilkins.

Mealey, Linda. 2004. *Sex Differences. Developmental and Evolutionary Strategies*. San Diego, CA: Academic Press.

Medical Aspects of Human Sexuality. 1991. July 14.

Meigs, Anna and Kathleen Barlow. 2002. "Beyond the Taboo: Imagining Incest." *American Anthropologist*, 104(1): 38–49.

Melnikow, Joy and Lori A. Boardman. "Abortion." *Medical Encyclopedia*. http://health.msn.com/encyclopedia/healthtopics/articlepage.aspx?cp-document id=100078473. Last accessed 1/1/2007.

"Menopause—Another Change in Life." 2006. Planned Parenthood of America. http://66.151.111.132/pp2/portal/files/portal/medicalinfo/femalesexualhealth/pub-menopause.xml. Last accessed 8/11/06.

"Menopause Management in Light of the Women's Health Initiative." 2006. The Hormone Foundation. www.hormone.org. Last accessed 8/11/06.

"Men's Shots Used as Contraceptive." 1990. *Syracuse Herald American*, October, 21: 1.

Menstuff. 2005. http://www.menstuff.org. Last accessed 2/9/06.

Mernissi, Fatima. 1975. *Beyond the Veil*. Cambridge: Schenkman Publishing Company, Inc.

————. 1994. *Dreams of Trespass: Tales of a Harem Girlhood*. Reading: Addison-Wesley

Messenger, John C. 1971. "Sex and Repression in an Irish Folk Community." In *Human Sexual Behavior: Variations in the Ethnographic Spectrum*. Donald S. Marshall and Robert C. Suggs, ed. New York: Basic Books. Pp. 3–38.

Meuleman, Eric J. H. and Jacques J. D. M. Van Lankveld. 2005. "Hypoactive Sexual Desire Disorder: An Underestimated Condition in Men." *British Journal of Urology International*, 95: 291–296.

Meyer-Bahlburg, Heino. 1977. "Sex Hormones and Male Homosexuality in Comparative Perspectives." *Archives of Sexual Behavior*, 6(4): 297–335.

————. 1979. "Sex Hormones and Female Homosexuality: A Critical Examination." *Archives of Sexual Behavior*, 8(2): 101–120.

Michael, Robert T., John H. Gagnon, Edward O. Laumann, and Gina Kolata. 1994. *Sex in America: A Definitive Survey*. New York: Warner Books Edition.

Michaelson, Karen L., ed. 1988a. *Childbirth in America*. Granby: Bergin and Garvey Publishers.

————. 1988b. "Childbirth in America: A Brief History and Contemporary Issues." In *Childbirth in America*. Karen Michaelson, ed. Granby: Bergin and Garvey Publishers. Pp. 1–32.

Michalski, Richard L. 2002. "American Sex in the Private and Public Sectors." *The Journal of Sex Research*, 39(2): 155–157.

"Midwives and Modernization." 1981. *Medical Anthropology*, Special Issues, Winter, 5(1).

"Mifeprestone." 2006. *Wikpedia*. http://en.wikipedia.org/wiki/RU-486. Last accessed 8/11/06.

Migeon, Claude V., M. A. Rivarola, and M. G. Forest. 1969. "Studies of Androgens in Male Transsexual Subjects: Effects of Estrogen Therapy." In *Transsexualism and Sex Reassignment*. Richard Green and John Money, eds. Baltimore: The John Hopkins University Press.

Miller, Patricia Y. and William Simon. 1980. "The Development of Sexuality in Adolescence." In *Handbook of Adolescence*. Joseph Adelson, ed. New York: John Wiley and Sons.

Miracle, Andrew W. and David N. Suggs. 1993. "On the Anthropology of Human Sexuality." In *Culture and Human Sexuality: A Reader*. David N. Suggs and Andrew W. Miracle, eds. Pacific Grove: Brooks/Cole Publishing Co.

Mitford, Jessica. 1992. *The American Way of Birth*. New York: Dutton.

Modern Maturity. 1999. September-October.

Mohammadi, Mohammad Reza, Kazem Mohammad, Farideh K. A. Farahani, Siamak Alikhani, Mohammad Zare, Fahimeh R. Tehrani, Ali Ramezankhani and Farshid Alaeddini. 2006. "Reproductive Knowledge, Attitudes and Behavior Among Adolescent Males in Tehran, Iran." *International Family Planning Perspectives*, March, 32(1). http://www.guttmacher.org/pubs/journals/3203506.html. Last accessed 8/11/06.

Money, John. 1986. *Lovemaps: Clinical Concepts of Sexual Erotic Health and Pathology, Paraphilia, and Gender Transposition in Childhood, Adolescence, and Maturity*. New York: Irvington.

————. 1988. *Gay, Straight, and In-Between*. New York: Oxford University Press.

Money, John and Anke Ehrhardt. 1972. *Man and Woman, Boy and Girl*. Baltimore: The Johns Hopkins Press.

Money, John and Dana Mathews. 1982. "Prenatal Exposure to Virilizing Progestins: An Adult Follow-Up Study of Twelve Women." *Archives of Sexual Behavior* 11(1): 73–83.

Money, John, and Herman Musaph, eds. 1978. *The Handbook of Sexology: History and Ideology*. Vol. 1. New York: Elseview.

Money, John and Anthony J. Russo. 1981. "Homosexual vs. Transvestite or Transsexual Gender-Identity/Role: Outcome Study in Boys." *International Journal of Family Psychiatry*, 2(1–2): 139–45.

Money, John and Claus Wiedeking. 1980. "Gender Identity Role: Normal Differentiation and Its Transpositions." In *Handbook of Human Sexuality*. Benjamin B. Wolman and John Money, eds. Englewood Cliffs: Prentice-Hall. Pp. 270–284.

Montagu, Ashley. 1978. *Touching: The Human Significance of the Skin*. 2nd ed. New York: Harper and Row.

Moore, Ann M. 2006. "Gender Role Beliefs at Sexual Debut: Qualitative Evidence from Two Brazilian Cities." *International Family Planning Perspectives*, March, 32(1). http://www.guttmacher.org/pubs/journals/3204506.html. Last accessed 8/11/06.

Moore, Lorna G., P. W. Van Arsdale, J. E. Glittenberg, and R. A. Aldrich. 1980. *The Biocultural Basis of Health*. Prospect Heights: The Waveland Press.

Morgan, Louis Henry. 1870. *Systems of Consanquinity and Affinity of the Human Family*. Washington: Smithsonian Institution.

Morgan, Lynn M. 1996. "When Does Life Begin: A Cross-Cultural Perspective on the Personhood of Fetuses and Young Children." In *Talking About People: Readings in Cultural Anthropology*. William A. Haviland and Robert J. Gordon, eds. Mountainview: Mayfield Publishing Company. Pp. 24–34.

"Morning Edition: Lesbian Mothers in Custody." 1994. National Public Radio (NPR). June.

Morris, Sandra, ed. 1989. *Critical Reviews for Research and Teaching*. Washington: American Anthropological Association.

Morrison, J. Stephen and Janet Fleishman. 2005. "Strengthening HIV/AIDS Programs for Women. Lessons for U.S. Policy from Zambia and Kenya. A Report of the CSIS Task Force on HIV/AIDS." http://www.csis.org/hivaids/0505_strengthening.pdf. Last accessed 2/9/06.

Mosher, William, Anjani Chandra, and Jo Jones. 2003. "Sexual Behavior and Selected Health Measures: Men and Women 15–44 Years of Age, United States, 2002." *Advance Data from Vital and Health Statistics*, September 15, 362: 21–26.

Moss, A. M. 1978. "Men's Mid-Life Crisis and the Marital-Sexual Relationship." *Medical Aspects of Human Sexuality*, 13(2): 109–110.

Muecke, Edward C. 1979. "The Embryology of the Urinary System." In *Campbell's Urology*. Meredith Campbell, ed. 4th ed. Vol. 2. Philadelphia: Saunders. Pp. 1286–1307.

Mukhopadhyay, Carol and Patricia Higgins. 1988. "Anthropological Studies of Women's Status Revisited: 1977–1987." *Annual Review of Anthropology*, 17: 461–495.

Munroe, Robert, John W. M. Whiting and David J. Hally. 1969. "Institutionalized Male Transvestism and Sex Distinctions." *American Anthropologist*, 71(1): 87–90.

Murdock, George Peter. 1949. *Social Structure*. New York: The Free Press.

———. 1965. *Social Structure*. New York: The Free Press.

Murdock, George Peter, C. Ford, A. Hudson, R. Kennedy, L. Simmons, and W. Whiting. 1964. *Outline of Cultural Materials*. 4th ed. New Haven: HRAF Press.

Murphy, Joseph J. and Scott Boggess. 1998. "Increased Condom Use Among Teenage Males, 1988–1995: The Role of Attitudes." *Family Planning Perspectives*, 30(6). http://www.guttmacher.org/pubs/journals/3027698.html. Last accessed 7/11/06.

Murphy, Yolanda and Robert Murphy. 1974. *Women of the Forest*. New York: Columbia University Press.

Musaph, Herman. 1978. "Sexology: A Multidisciplinary Science." *The Handbook of Sexology: History and Ideology*. Vol 1. John Money and Herman Musaph, eds. New York: Elsevier. Pp. 81–84.

Museum of Menstruation. http://www.mum.org. Last accessed February 8, 2006.

Mutisya, P. Masila. 2002. "No: A Symbolic Form of Female Circumcision Should Be Allowed for Those Who Want It." In *Taking Sides: Clashing Views on Controversial Issues in Human Sexuality*. William J. Taverner, ed. Guilford: McGraw-Hill/Dushkin. Pp. 58–67.

Nadeau, Kathleen. 2005. "Is Sex Trafficking in Asia Ancient or New?: Challenge to the Churches." http://eapi.admu.edu.ph/eapr003/kathleen.htm. Last accessed 6/13/06.

Nag, Moni. 1962. "Factors Affecting Human Fertility in Non-Industrial Societies: A Cross-Cultural Study." *Yale University Publications in Anthropology* 66. New Haven: HRAF Press.

Namu, Yang Erche and Christine Mathieu. 2003. *Leaving Mother Lake: A Girlhood at the End of the World*. Boston: Little, Brown.

Nanda, Serena. 1999. *Neither Man Nor Woman: The Hijras of India*. Belmont, CA: Wadsworth Publishing.

Nanda, Serena. 2000. *Gender Diversity: Cross-cultural Variations*. Prospect Heights: Waveland Press.

Nanda, Serena and Richard Warms. 2004. *Cultural Anthropology*. Belmont: Thomson Wadsworth.

———. 2007. *Cultural Anthropology*. Belmont: Thomson Wadsworth.

Nannup, Brett. n.d. Assistant curator of Berndt Museum. Personal communication.

NARAL Pro-Choice American. 2006. http://www.prochoiceamerica.org/index .html. Last accessed 8/29/06.

National Center for Complementary and Alternative Medicine: The National Institutes of Health, The. http://www.nccam.nih.gov/health/menopauseandcam/. Last accessed 1/20/2007.

"National Health and Social Life Survey ('The Sex Survey'): Summary, The." n.d. National Organization for Research (NORC), University of Chicago. http://cloud9.norc.uchicago.edu/faqs/sex.htm. Last accessed 8/14/06.

"National Institutes of Health Consensus Development Conference on Interventions to Prevent HIV Risk Behaviors: Statement of the American Anthropological Association on AIDS Research and Education January 24, 1997." 1997. American Anthropological Association. http://www.aaanet.org/stmts/nih.htm. Last accessed 5/12/06.

"National Politics and Policy. Merck's HPV Vaccine Gardasil To Receive FDA Priority Review." 2006. Kaiser Daily Women's Health Policy Report. http:// www.kaisernetwork.org/daily_reports/rep_index.cfm?DR_ID=35293. Last accessed 2/9/06.

National Sexuality Resource Center. 2006. http://www.nsrc.sfsu.edu. Last accessed 2/10/06.

"National Vulvodynia (NVA) Research Update Newsletter, The." 2005. December. www.nva.org. Last accessed 8/11/06.

"National Youth Risk Behavior Survey 1991–2005: Trends in the Prevalence of Sexual Behaviors." n.d. Department of Health and Human Services: Centers for Disease Control and Prevention. http://www.cdc.gov/HealthyYouth/yrbs/pdf/trends/2005_YRBS_Sexual_Behaviors.pdf. Last accessed 7/11/06.

Navarro, Mireya. 2004. "Genital Makeover Quietly Gains Notice." *Panorama. Taiwan News*. November 29. P. 8.

Nelson, Adie. 2000. "The Pink Dragon Is Female: Halloween Costumes and Gender Markers." *The Psychology of Women Quarterly*, 24(2): 137–144.

Nelson, Joan. 1989a. "Intergenerational Sexual Contact: A Continuum Model of Participants and Experiences." *Journal of Sex Education and Therapy*, Spring, 15(1): 3–13.

———. 1989b. "Joan Nelson's Rebuttal." *Journal of Sex Education and Therapy*, Spring, 15(1): 16.

Netter, Frank H. 1974. *The Ciba Collection of Medical Illustrations*: Vol. 2: *The Reproductive System*. Fifth printing. Summit: Ciba Pharmaceutical Products, Inc.

"New Study Shows Female Genital Mutilation Exposes Women and Babies to Significant Risk at Childbirth." 2006. MediaCentre New Releases. *LANCET*, June 1. http://www.who.int/mediacentre/news/releases/2006/pr30/en/index.html. Last accessed 7/11/06.

"New Study of Male Contraception." 2006. Planned Parenthood Affiliates of New Jersey. May 2. http://www.kten.com/Global/story.asp?S=4847515. Last accessed 8/11/06.

"'New View' of Women's Sexuality, The." 2006. www.fsd-alert.org. Last accessed 2/9/2006.

"New York/International Women's Anthropology Conference (NYWAC/IWAC), 1972–2002." 2002. http://homepages.nyu.edu/~crs2/index.html. Last accessed 3/28/06.

Newcomer, Susan F. and J. Richard Udry. 1985. "Oral Sex in an Adolescent Population." *Archives of Sexual Behavior*, 14: 41–46.

Newman, Amy L. and Christopher Peterson. 1996. "Anger of Women Incest Survivors." *Sex Roles*, 34: 463–474.

Newton, Niles. 1981. "Foreword." *Anthropology of Human Birth*. M. Kay, ed. Philadelphia: F. A. Davis. Pp. ix–xi.

Ng, Emil Man-Wu, Juan Jose Borras-Valls, Maria Perez-Concillo and Eli Coleman. 2000. *Sexuality in the New Millennium*. Bologna: Editrice Compositori.

"NIA Statement on IOM Testosterone Report." 2003. National Institution of Aging. November 12. http://www.nia.nih.gov/newsAndEvents/PressReleases/PR20031112NIAStatementonIOMTestosterone.htm. Last accessed 8/11/06.

"NIH News. Release. NHLBI Stops Trial of Estrogen Plus Progestin Due to Increased Breast Cancer Risk, Lack of Overall Benefit." 2002. National Institutes of Health (NIH). http://www.nih.gov. Last accessed 2/10/06.

Ninghua, Li, Ou Pinzhong, Zhu Hanmin, Yang Dingzhou, and Zheng Pinru. 2002. "Prevalence Rate of Osteoporosis in the Mid-Aged and Elderly in Selected Parts of China." *Chinese Medical Journal*, 115: 773–775.

Noonan, Raymond J. 2001. "Web Resources for Sex Researchers: The State of the Art, Now and in the Future." *The Journal of Sex Research*, 38(4): 348–351.

North American Menopause Society, The. http://www.menopause.org. Last accessed 1/20/2007.

Northrup, Christiane. 2001. *The Wisdom of Menopause.* New York: Dantam Books.

"No-Scalpel Vasectomy." 2006. School of Medicine, Department of Urology, State University of New York at Stonybrook. http://www.hsc.stonybrook.edu/som/urology/urology_cp_vasectomy.cfm. Last accessed 1/20/2007.

Notting Hill. Directed by Roger Mitchell. 1999. Hollywood, USA: MCA/Universal Pictures.

Nyboe, A., Andersen L. Gianaroli, and K. G. Nygren. 2004. "Assisted Reproductive Technology in Europe 2000. Results Generated from European Registers by ESHRE." *Human Reproduction*, 19(3): 490–503.

O'Brien, Denise. 1977. "Female Husbands in Southern Bantu Societies." In *Sexual Stratification: A Cross-Cultural View.* Alice Schlegel, ed. New York: Columbia University Press. Pp. 109–126.

O'Kelly, Charlotte G. and Larry S. Carney. 1986. *Women and Men in Society: Cross-Cultural Perspectives on Gender Stratification.* Belmont: Wadsworth Publishing Co.

O'Neill, Nena and George O'Neill. 1972. *Open Marriage: A New Lifestyle for Couples.* New York: M. Evans and Company.

Oboler, Regina S. 1980. "Is the Female Husband a Man? Woman/Woman Marriage Among the Nandi of Kenya." *Ethnology*, 19(1): 69–88.

Oesterling. Joseph. 1991. "The Role of PSA in Detecting Prostate Cancer." *Medical Aspects of Human Sexuality*, July: 22–27.

Offir, Carol Wade. 1982. *Human Sexuality.* New York: Harcourt Brace Jovanovich, Inc.

Ohm, M. 1980. "Female Circumcision." *Sexology Today*, June: 21–25.

Ohno, Susumu. 1979. *Major Sex-Determining Genes.* Berlin: Springer-Verlag.

Old Salem. 2006. http://www.oldsalem.org/about/sbh.htm. Last accessed 5/12/06.

"Old Salem Christmas, An." 2006. Mother Earth News.Com. http://www.motherearthnews.com/Homesteading_and_Self_Reliance/1988_November_December/An_Old_Salem_Christmas. Last accessed 5/12/06.

Olesen, Virginia L. and Nancy Fugate Woods, eds. 1986. *Culture, Society and Menstruation.* New York: Hemisphere Publishing Corp.

Olive-Miller, Shirley. 2004. "Papua New Guinea." *The Continuum Complete International Encyclopedia of Sexuality.* Robert T. Francouer and Raymond J. Noonan, eds. New York: Continuum International Publishing Group, Inc. Pp. 813–823.

"Opinion: U.S. Requirement That AIDS Groups Sign Pledge Against Sex Work, Trafficking is 'Manipulative, Dangerous,' Editorial Says." 2005. *Kaiser Daily AIDS Report*, July 14, http://www.kaisernetwork.org/daily_reports/rep_index.cfm?DR_ID=31377. Last accessed 2/9/06/.

Ortner, Sherry B. and Harriet Whitehead, eds. 1981. *Sexual Meanings: The Cultural Construction of Gender and Sexuality*. Cambridge: Cambridge University Press.

Orwell, George. 1950. *Nineteen Eighty-Four*. San Diego: Harcourt, Brace, Jovanovich, Inc.

Oswalt, Wendell H. 1986. *Lifecycles and Lifeways*. Palo Alto: Mayfield Publishing Company.

Outwater, Anne. 1996. "The Socioeconomic Impact of AIDS on Women in Tanzania." In Lynellen Long and E. Maxine Ankrah, eds. *Women's Experiences with HIV/AIDS: An International Perspective*. New York: Columbia University Press. Pp. 112–122.

Overview of Abortion in the United States, An. 2003. Physicians for Reproductive Choice and the Allan Guttmacher Institute. January. http://www.agi-usa.org/pubs/abslides/.

Padian, Nancy. 1998. "Prostitute Women and AIDS: Epidemiology." *AIDSCare*, 2: 413–419.

Padian, Nancy. 1987. "Male-to-Female Transmission of Human Immunodeficiency Virus." *Journal of the American Medical Association*, August 14, 258(6): 788–790.

Padian, Nancy, Stephen C. Shiboski and Nicholas P. Jewell. 1991. "Female to Male Transmission of Human Immunodeficiency Virus." *Journal of the American Medical Association*, 266(12): 1664–1667.

PAEG (Potsdam AIDS Education Group). 2006. http://www.potsdam.edu/content.php?contentID=E9CABAC13BFD227A43FF1BE205B2B184. Last accessed 8/7/06.

Parisot, Jeanette. 1985. *Johnny Come Lately: A Short History of the Condom*. London: The Journeyman Press.

Parker, Hilda and Seymour Parker. 1986. "Father-Daughter Sexual Abuse: An Emerging Perspective." *American Journal of Orthopsychiatry*, 56: 531–549.

Parker, Richard. 2000. "Sexuality and Culture." In *The Role of Theory in Sex Research*. John Bancroft, ed. Bloomington: Indiana University Press. Pp. 307–321.

———. 2001. "Sexuality, Culture and Power in HIV/AIDS Research." *Annual Review of Anthropology*, 30: 163–179.

Parker, Richard G. and Peter Aggleton, eds. 1997. *Culture, Society and Sexuality: A Reader*. London: UCL Press.

Parker, Richard G., Regina Maria Barbosa, and Peter Aggleton, eds. 1999. *Framing the Sexual Subject: The Politics of Gender, Sexuality, and Power*. Berkeley: University of California Press.

Parker, Richard G. and Anke A. Ehrhardt. 2001. "Through an Ethnographic Lens: Ethnographic Methods, Comparative Analysis, and HIV/AIDS Research." *AIDS and Behavior*, 5(2):105–114.

Parker, Richard G. and John H. Gagnon. 1995. *Conceiving Sexuality: Approaches to Sex Research in a Postmodern World*. New York: Routledge.

Parker, Richard G., Gilbert Herdt, and Manuel Carballo. 1991. "Sexual Culture, HIV Transmission, and AIDS Research." *The Journal of Sex Research*, February 28(1): 77–98.

Parker-Pope, Tara. 2006. "Personal Health (A Special Report): A Safer Prescription Menopause?" *The Wall Street Journal*, October 21: R1.

Parrinder, Geoffrey. 1996. *Sexual Morality in the World's Religions*. Oxford: Oneworld Publication.

Patterson, Mary. 2005. "Coming Too Close, Going Too Far: Theoretical and Cross-Cultural Approaches to Incest and Its Prohibitions." *Australian Journal of Anthropology*, April: 1–18.

Paul, Elizabeth L., ed. 2000. *Taking Sides: Clashing Views on Controversial Issues in Sex and Gender*. Guilford: Dushkin McGraw-Hill.

Paul, Jay. 1984. "The Bisexual Identity: An Idea Without Social Recognition." *Journal of Homosexuality*, 9: 45–63.

Pawlowski, Boguslaw. 1999. "Loss of Oestrus and Concealed Ovulation in Human Evolution." *Current Anthropology*, 40: 257–275.

Penis website, The. 2005. http://www.the-penis-website.com/shape.html. Last accessed 1/29/06.

Peris, Anna. 2005. "ART: ZIFT, GIFT, ICSI." *Fertilititext*. http://www.ferilititext.org/p2_doctor/art.html. Last accessed 5/18/05.

Perper, Timothy. 1985. *Sex Signals: The Biology of Love*. Philadelphia: ISI Press.

Perry, John D. and Beverly Whipple. 1981. "Pelvic Muscle Strength of Female Ejaculators: Evidence in Support of a New Theory of Orgasm." *The Journal of Sex Research*, February 17(1): 22–39.

Person, Ethel S. and Lionel Ovesey. 1974. "The Psychodynamics of Male Transsexualism." *Sex Differences in Behavior*. Richard. C. Friedman et al., eds. New York: Wiley. Pp. 315–331.

"Perspective from India: Homosexuality Stands Criminalized Because of Mid-19th Century Colonial Law, A." 2004. ILGA. http://www.ilga.org/news_results.asp? LanguageID=1&FileCategoryID=44&FileID=64&ZoneID=3. Last accessed 2/9/2006.

Pfafflin, Friedemann. 1981. "H-Y Antigen in Transsexualism." Paper presented at the 7th International Gender Dysphoria Association. March 4–8, in Lake Tahoe, Nevada.

Pfizer Global Study of Sexual Attitudes and Behaviors. 2002. www.PfizerGlobal Study.com

Phelan, Patricia. 1986. "The Process of Incest: Biologic Father and Stepfather Families." *Child Abuse and Neglect: The International Journal*, 10(4): 531–539.

Philadelphia. 1993. Directed by Jonathan Demme. USA: Clinica Estetico Ltd. and TriStar Pictures.

"Plan B: One Step Forward, Two Steps Back." 2006. National Women's Health Network. August 24. http://www.nwhn.org. Last accessed 1/20/2007.

Planned Parenthood of America. http://www.plannedparenthood.org. Last accessed 12/6/2006.

Pocs, Ollie. 1989. *Annual Editions: Human Sexuality, 1989–90*. Sluice Dock: Dushkin Publishers.

Podlesfsky, Aaron and Peter J. Brown, eds. 2005. *Applying Cultural Anthropology*. Boston: McGraw Hill.

Ponzetti, James J., ed. 2003. *International Encyclopedia of Marriage and Family*. Vol. 3. 3rd ed. New York: Macmillan Reference USA.

"Porn Stars Get HIV." 2004. *The Body: The Complete HIV/AIDS Resource.* April 16. http://www.thebody.com/cgi-bin/bbs/showthreaded.php?cat=&Board=infected&Number=95720&page=0&view=collapsed&sb=7&o=&fpart=1. Last accessed 2/10/06.

Potts, Malcolm. 2003. "The Unmet Need for Family Planning" *Scientific American,* 6(1): 88–93.

"Pragmatic Americans Liberal and Conservative on Social Issues: Most Want Middle Ground on Abortion." 2006. The Pew Research Center for the People and the Press. August 3. http://people-press.org/reports/display.php3?ReportID-283. Last accessed 1/20/2007.

"Pregnancy and Childbearing Among U.S. Teens." 2006. Planned Parenthood. www.plannedparenthood.org.

"Pregnancy & Childbirth: More Than One-Quarter of NYC Births in 2003 Were C-Sections, Public Advocate Report Says Findings Reflect National Trend." 2005. *Kaiser Daily Reproductive Health Report*, July 14. http://www.kaisernet work.org/daily_reports/rep_repro_recent_re-ports.cfm?dr_DateTime=07–14–5& show=yes#31368. Last accessed 7/3/06.

Prendergast, A. 1990. "Beyond the Pill." *American Health,* 9(8): 37–45.

Presley, Elvis. 1999 [1995]."Baby Let's Play House." *Artist of the Country*: RCA.

"Price of Homophobia, The." 2005. *New York Times*, January 20: Section A, p. 22.

Psychology of Gender Identity and Transgenderism. 2006. http://www.gender psychology.org/reproduction. Last accessed 6/8/06.

Public Anthropology. 2006. http://www.publicanthropology.org/index.htm. Last accessed 2/10/06.

"Public Health Women with an Unmet Need for Family Planning." 2006. Earth Trends: Institute Environmental Information. http://earthtrends.wri.org/search-able_db/index.php?theme=4&variable_ID=1271&action=select_countries. Last accessed 8/11/06.

"Putting the Pill (for Men) in Perspective." 1998. *Harvard Health Letter*, 23(8): 4–5.

"Quality of Midwifery Care Given Throughout the World: Report of the Fourth Coste." 2000. International Homebirth Conference, March 16, 17, 18. Amsterdam, The Netherlands." *Midwifery*, 16: 161–164.

Radin, Paul, ed. 1926. *Crashing Thunder: The Autobiography of an American Indian.* New York: D. Appleton.

Ragone, H. 1994. *Surrogate Motherhood: Conception in the Heart.* Boulder: Westview Press.

Raiders of the Lost Ark. 1981. Directed by Steven Speilberg. USA: Lucasfilm, Ltd. and Paramount Pictures.

Ramet, Sabrina Petea. 1996. *Gender Reversals and Gender Cultures: Anthropological and Historical Perspectives.* New York: Routledge.

Ramey, Estelle. 1973. "Sex Hormones and Executive Ability." *Annals of the NY Academy of Science*, 28: 237.

Raphael, Dana. 1988. "The Need for a Supportive *Doula* in an Increasingly Urban World." In *Women and Health: Cross-Cultural Perspectives.* Patricia Whelehan, ed. Granby: Bergin and Garvey Publishers.

Ray, Celeste. 2003. "'Thighibh!' Means 'Y'all Come!': Renegotiating Regional Memories Through Scottish Heritage Celebration." In *Southern Heritage on Display: Public Ritual and Ethnic Diversity Within Southern Regionalism.* Celeste Ray, ed. Tuscaloosa: University of Alabama Press. Pp. 251–282.

Reaves, Stanley. 1997. "Alternative Rites to Female Circumcision Spreading in Kenya." *Africa News Service.* November 19.

Reibel, Tracy. 2004. "Normal Birth: A Thing of the Past or the New Future for Primary Health Care?" *Primary Health Care Research and Development,* 5: 329–337.

Reid, Anthony. 1999. *Charting the Shape of Early Modern Southeast Asia.* Chiang Mai: Silkworm Books: 100–154. From Wikipedia, http://en.wikipedia.org/wiki/macassan. Last accessed 3/24/06.

Reiss, Ira. 1960. *Premarital Sexual Standards in America.* Glencoe, IL: The Free Press.

———. 1967. *The Social Context of Premarital Permissiveness.* New York: Holt, Rinehart and Winston.

———. 1980. *Family Systems in America.* New York: Holt, Rinehart, and Winston.

———. 1986. *Journey into Sexuality: An Exploratory Voyage.* Englewood Cliffs: Prentice-Hall.

Remland, Martha S., Tricia S. Jones and Heidi Brinkman. 1995. "Interpersonal Distance, Body Orientation, and Touch: Effects of Culture, Gender, and Age." *The Journal of Social Psychology,* 5(3): 81–297.

Renshaw, Domeena C. 1976. "Understanding Masturbation." *Journal of School Health,* 46(2): 98–101.

Renzetti, Claire M. and Daniel J. Curran. 2003. *Women, Men and Society.* Boston: A and B Pearson Education, Inc.

"Repeat Births to Teenagers Carry High Individual and Societal Costs." 2000. Alan Guttmacher Institute. April 22. www.guttmacher.org/media/nr/newsrelease_tgr0303.html. Last accessed 8/14/06.

Reynolds, Meredith A., Laura A. Schieve, Joyce A. Martin, Gary Jeng, and Maurizio Macaluso. 2003. "Trends in Multiple Births Conceived Using Assisted Reproductive Technology, United States, 1997–2000." *Pediatrics,* 111: 1159–1162.

Rheingold, Harriet L., ed. 1963. *Maternal Behavior in Mammals.* New York: Wiley.

Rice, Anne. 1982. *Cry to Heaven.* New York: Pinnacle Books.

Richardson, Laura. 1988. *The Dynamics of Sex and Gender: A Sociological Perspective.* New York: Harper Collins Publishers.

Richardson, Laurel, Verta Taylor, and Nancy Whittier, eds. 2004. *Feminist Frontiers.* Boston: McGraw Hill.

Richardson, Stephen A. and A. Guttmacher, eds. 1967. *Childbearing: Its Social and Psychological Aspects.* Baltimore: Williams and Wilkins.

Richters, J. M. A. 1997. "Menopause in Different Cultures." *Journal of Psychosomatic Obstetrics and Gynecology,* 18: 73–80.

Riddle, John M. 1992. *Contraception and Abortion from the Ancient World to the Renaissance.* Cambridge: Harvard University Press.

———. 1997. *Eve's Herbs: A History of Contraception and Abortion in the West.* Cambridge: Harvard University Press.

Riddle, John M., J. Worth Estes, and Josiah C. Russell. 1994. "Birth Control in the Ancient World." *Archaeology,* 47(2): 29–35.

Riessman, Catherine K. 1983. "Women and Medicalization: A New Perspective." *Social Policy,* 14: 3–18.

Riportella-Mueller, R. 1989. "Sexuality in the Elderly: A Review." *Human Sexuality: The Societal and Interpersonal Context.* Kathleen McKinney and Susan Sprecher, eds. Norwood: Ablex Publishing Corp.

"Risks and Disadvantages are Raised for Teenage Mothers." 2001. *Family Planning Perspectives*, November/December 33(6): 1–3. www.guttmacher.org/pubs/journals/3328501.html.

Robbins, Richard. 2005. *Global Problems and the Culture of Capitalism*. 3rd ed. Boston: Allyn and Bacon.

———. 2006. *Cultural Anthropology: A Problem-Based Approach*. Belmont: Thomson Wadsworth.

Robertson, Jennifer. 2005. *Same-sex Cultures and Sexualities: An Anthropological Reader*. Malden: Blackwell.

Rogers, Lesley. 2001. *Sexing The Brain*. New York: Columbia University Press.

Roman, Mar. 2005. "Spain Legalizes Gay Marriage." *Lincoln Journal Star*, July 1: A3.

Rosaldo, Michelle Zimbalist and Louise Lamphere. 1974. *Woman, Culture, Culture and Society*. Stanford: Stanford University Press.

Roscoe, Paul. 1994. "Amity and Aggression: A Symbolic Theory of Incest." *Man*, 29(1): 49–76.

Roscoe, Will. 1991. *The Zuni Man-Woman*. Albuquerque University of New Mexico Press.

Roscoe, Will. 1998. *Changing Ones: Third and Fourth Genders in Native North America*. London: Macmillian.

Rosen, Harold, ed. 1967. *Abortion in America*. Boston: Beacon Press.

Rosen, R. C. 2000. "Prevalence and Risk Factors of Sexual Dysfunction in Men and Women." *Current Psychiatry Report*, 2: 189–195.

Ross, Ellen and Rayna Rapp. 1983. "Sex and Society: A Research Note from Social History and Anthropology." In *Powers of Desire: The Politics of Sexuality*. Christine Stansell and Sharon Thompson, eds. New York: Monthly Review Press. Pp. 49–72.

Rossi, Alice S. 1985. *Gender and the Life Course*. Hawthorne: Aldine.

"RU 486 Non-Surgical/Medical Abortion NARAL." 2006. http://www.prochoiceamerica.org/issues/abortion/medical-abortion/. Last accessed 8/11/06.

Ruan, Fang Fu. 1988. *Sex in China: Studies in Sexology and Chinese Culture*. New York: Springer.

———. 1991. *Sex in China. Studies in Sexology in Chinese Culture*. New York: Plenum Press.

Ruan, Fang Fu and Vernon L. Bullough. 1989. "Males Transsexualism in Mainland China." *Journal of Sex Research*, 18: 517–522.

———. 1992a. "Lesbianism in China." *The Archives of Sexual Behavior*, June, 21(3): 217–226.

———. 1992b. "Sex in China." *Medical Aspects of Human Sexuality*, July: 59–62.

Ruan, Fang-fu and M. P. Lau. 2004. "China." In *The Continuum Complete International Encyclopedia of Sexuality*. Robert T. Francoeur, Raymond J. Noonan and Beldina Opi Yo-Omolo, eds. New York: Continuum International Publishing Group. Pp. 182–209.

Ruan, Fang Fu and Y.M. Tsai. 1988. "Male Homosexuality in Contemporary Mainland China." *The Archives of Sexual Behavior*, April, 17(2): 189–199.

Rubin, Gayle. 1975. "The Traffic in Women: Notes on the 'Political Economy of Sex'." In *Toward an Anthropology of Women*. Rayna R. Reiter, ed. New York: Monthly Review Press. Pp. 1557–2102.

Rubin, Lillian B. 1976. *Worlds of Pain*. New York: Basic Books.

Russell, Andrew, Elisa J. Sobo, and Mary S. Thompson, ed. 2000. *Contraception Across Cultures: Technologies, Choices, Constraints.* New York: Berg Press.

"Russia: Gay Pride Parade Should Not Be Banned." 2006. Human Rights Watch. http://hrw.org/english/docs/2006/02/27/russia12728.htm. Last accessed 5/12/06.

Rust, Paula C., ed. 1999. *Bisexuality in the United States: A Social Science Reader.* New York: Columbia University Press.

Salmon, Merrilee H. 2006. "Ethical Considerations in Anthropology and Archaeology, or Relativisim and Justice for All." In *Taking Sides: Clashing Views in Cultural Anthropology.* Robert L. Welsch and Kirk M. Endicott, eds. Dubuque: McGraw-Hill.

Sanday, Peggy Reeves. 1990. *Fraternity Gang Rape: Sex, Brotherhood and Privilege on Campus.* New York: New York University Press.

———. 2003. "Rape-Free versus Rape-Prone: How Culture Makes a Difference." In *Evolution, Gender and Rape.* Cheryl Brown Travis, ed. Cambridge: The MIT Press. Pp. 336–359.

Sargent, Carolyn and Nancy Stark. 1989. "Childbirth Education and Childbirth Models: Parental Perspectives on Control, Anesthesia, and Technological Intervention in the Birth Process." *Medical Anthropology Quarterly*, March, 3(1): 36–51.

Sarvis, Betty and Hyman Rodman. 1974. *The Abortion Controversy.* 2nd ed. Irvington: Columbia University Press.

Save the Children. 2006. "State of the World's Mothers 2006: Saving the Lives of Mothers and Newborns." www.savethechildren.org. Last accessed 11/9/07.

Saxton, Lloyd. 1993. *The Individual, Marriage, and the Family.* Belmont: Wadsworth.

Sayers, Janet. 1986. *Sexual Contradictions.* New York: Tavistock Publications.

Schenker, J. and S. Evron. 1983. "New Concepts in the Surgical Management of Tubal Pregnancy and the Consequent Postoperative Results." *Fertility and Sterility.* 40: 709–723.

Scheper-Hughes, Nancy, ed. 1987. *Child Survival.* Boston: D. Reidel.

Schlegel, Alice, ed. 1977. *Sexual Stratification: A Cross-Cultural View.* New York: Columbia University Press.

Schlegel, Alice and Herbert Barry III. 1980. "The Evolutionary Significance of Adolescent Initiation Ceremonies." *American Ethnologist*, 7(4): 696–718.

———. 1991. *Adolescence: An Anthropology Inquiry.* New York: The Free Press.

Schneider, David M. 1968. "Abortion and Depopulation on a Pacific Island." In *People and Cultures of the Pacific.* Andrew P. Vayda, ed. Garden City: The National History Press. Pp. 383–406.

Schoepf, Brooke. 2001. "International AIDS Research in Anthropology: Taking a Critical Perspective on the Crisis." *Annual Review of Anthropology.* 30: 335–361.

Schroeder, Elizabeth. 2004. "Nepal." In *The Continuum Complete International Encyclopedia of Sexuality.* Robert T. Francoeur and Raymond J. Noonan, eds. New York: Continuum. Pp. 714–724.

Schultz, Emily and Robert Lavenda. 1990. *Cultural Anthropology.* St. Paul: West Publishing Company.

———. 2001. *Anthropology: A Perspective of the Human Condition.* Mountain View: Mayfield.

Schultz, Willibrord Weijmar, Pek van Andel, Ida Sabelis, and Eduard Mooy-
aart. 1999. "Magnetic Resonance Imaging of Male and Female Genitals during Coitus and Female Sexual Arousal." *BMJ (British Medical Journal)*, 319:
1596–1600.

SciDev.Net. 2003. http://www.scidev.net/. Accessed 12/13/03.

Scupin, Raymond. 2003. *Cultural Anthropology: A Global Perspective.* 5th ed.
Upper Saddle River: Prentice Hall.

Scupin, Raymond and Christopher De Corse. 1992. *Anthropology: A Global
Perspective.* Englewood Cliffs: Prentice Hall, Inc.

———. 1998. *Anthropology: A Global Perspective.* Upper Saddle River: Prentice
Hall.

Seabrook, Jeremy. 2001. *Travels in the Skin Trade: Tourism and the Sex Industry.*
2nd edition. Sterling: Pluto Press.

Seaman, Barbara and Gideon Seaman. 1977. *Women and the Crisis in Sex
Hormones.* New York: Rawson Associates Publishing, Inc.

Segal, Edwin S. 2003. "Gender Transformation in Cross-Cultural Perspective." *The
Encyclopedia of Sex and Gender.* Vol.1. Carol Ember and Melvin Ember, eds.
New York: Kulwer Press for the Human Relations Area Files.

"Semen." 2005. *Menstuff.* http://www.menstuff.org/.

Semenic, Sonia E., Lynn Clark Callister, and Perle Feldman. 2004. "Giving Birth:
The Voices of Orthodox Jewish Women Living in Canada." *JOGNIN Clinical
Research*, Jan/Feb, 33(1): 80–87.

Service, Elman R. 1978. *Profiles in Ethnology.* 3rd ed. New York: Harper and Row.

Setel, Philip. 1999. *A Plague of Paradoxes: AIDS, Culture, and Demography in
Northern Tanzania.* Chicago: University of Chicago Press.

Setel, Philip and Eleuther Mwageni. 2004/2005. "Tanzania." *The Continuum
Complete International Encyclopedia of Sexuality.* Robert T. Francoeur and
Raymond Noonan. New York: Continuum International Publishing Group, Inc.
Pp. 1009–1020.

"Sex Quiz." 1991. *Wellness Letter.* Berkeley: UCB. P. 4.

"Sex Smarts: A Public Information Partnership." 2002. Henry J. Kaiser Family Foundation and *Seventeen.* http://www.kff.org/entpartnerships/upload/Teens-
and-Sexual-Health-Communication-Summary-of-Findings.pdf. Last accessed
8/14/06.

"Sex Workers." 2005. *Perspectives in Public Health and Human Rights*, Spring,
33(2).

"Sexual Assault of Young Children as Reported to Law Enforcement: Victim, Incident, and Offender Characteristics." 2000. Bureau of Justice Statistics. Electronic
document. http://www.ojp.usdoj.gov/bjs/abstract/saycrle.htm. 12/4/06.

"Sexuality at Midlife and Beyond: 2004 Update of Attitudes and Executive Summary" 2005. AARP Organization. http://assets.aarp.org/rgcenter/
general/2004_sexuality.pdf. Last accessed 12/4/06.

Seyfarth, Robert M. 1983. "Grooming and Social Competition in Primates."
In *Primate Social Relationships.* Robert A. Hinde, ed. Oxford: Blackwell.
Pp. 182–189.

Seyler, L. Everett, Ernesto Canalis, S. Spare, and Seymour Reichlin. 1978. "Abnormal Gonadotropin Secretory Responses to Luetinizing Releasing Hormone in
Transsexual Women After Diethylstilbestrol Priming." *Journal of Clinical Endocrinology and Metabolism*, 47: 176–183.

Shankman, Paul. 1994. "Sex, Lies and Anthropologists: Margaret Mead, Derek Freeman, and Samoa." In *Research Frontiers in Anthropology* . Carol R. Ember, Melvin Ember and Andrea Shaw, eds. Englewood Cliffs: Prentice Hall.

———. 1996. "The History of Samoan Sexual Conduct and the Mead-Freeman Controversy." *American Anthropologist*, 98(3): 555–567.

Shapiro, Harry L. 1958. *Man, Culture and Society*. New York: Oxford University Press.

Shapiro, Judith. 1979. "Cross-Cultural Perspectives on Sexual Differentiation." In *Human Sexuality: A Comparative and Developmental Perspective*. Herant Katchadourian, ed. Berkeley: University of California Press. Pp. 269–308.

Sharp, Henry S. 1981. "The Null Case: The Chipewayan." *Woman the Gatherer*. Frances Dahlberg, ed. New Haven: Yale University Press. Pp. 221–44.

Sherfey, Mary Jane. 1972. *The Nature and Evolution of Female Sexuality*. New York: Vintage Books.

Shih, Chuan-Kang. 2001. "The Genesis of Marriage among the Moso and Empire-Building in Late Imperial China." *The Journal of Asian Studies*, 60(2): 381–412.

Shilts, Randy. 1987. *And the Band Played On: People, Politics, and the AIDS Epidemic*. New York: St. Martin's Press.

Shiva Shakti Mandalam. 2006. http://www.religiousworlds.com/mandalam/ index. html. Last accessed 1/20/2007.

"SIECUS PEPFAR Country Profiles." 2005. SIECUS. http://www.siecus.org/ inter/pepfar/. Last accessed 2/10/06.

Silber, Sherman J. 1981. *The Male: From Infancy to Old Age*. New York: Charles Scribner's Sons.

Simons, Jeffrey S. and Michael P. Carey. 2001. "Prevalence of Dysfunctions: Results from a Decade of Research." *Archives of Sexual Behavior*, 30(2): 177–219.

Sinatra, Frank. 1966. "Strangers in the Night." Lyrics by Charles Singleton and Eddie Snyder. Music by Bert Kaempfert. Album: *Strangers in the Night*. Reprise/Wea.

Sinding, Steven W. 2005. "Does 'CNN' (Condoms, Needles, Negotiation) Work Better than 'ABC' (Abstinence, Being Faithful and Condom Use) in Attacking the AIDS Epidemic?" *International Family Planning Perspectives*, 31(1). http:// www.guttmacher.org/pubs/journals/3103805.html. Last accessed 7/11/06.

Singer, Josephine and Irving Singer. 1972. "Types of Female Orgasm." *Journal of Sex Research*, 8(4): 255–267.

Singer, Merrill. 2005. *Something Dangerous: Emergent and Changing Illicit Drug Use and Community Health*. Long Grove, IL: Waveland.

Singer, Merrill, Elsa Huertas, and Glenn Scott. 2000. "Am I My Brother's Keeper?: A Case Study of the Responsibilities of Research." *Human Organization*, Winter, 59(4): 389–400.

Singer, Milton. 1961. "A Survey of Culture and Personality Theory and Research." In *Studying Personality Cross-Culturally*. Bert Kaplan, ed. New York: Harper and Row Publishing: 9–90.

Singh, Andrew, et al. 2001. *Aboriginal Australia and the Torres Strait Islands: Guide to Indigenous Australia*. Footscray, Victoria: Lonely Planet.

Singh, Devendra. 1993. "Adaptive Significance of Female Physical Attractiveness: Role of Waist-to-Hip Ratio." *Journal of Personality and Social Psychology*, 65: 292–307.

Singh, Susheela, Deidre Wulf, Renee Samara and Yvette P. Cuca. 2000. "Gender Differences in the Timing of First Intercourse: Data from 14 Countries." *International Family Planning Perspectives*, 26(1): 1–19. http://www.guttmacher. org/pubs/journals/2602100.html. Last accessed 7/11/06.

Sinnott, Megan. 2004. "Toms and Dess: Transgender Identity and Female Same-Sex Relationships in Thailand." Honolulu: University of Hawaii Press.

Sittitrai, Werasit. 1990. "Research on Human Sexuality in Pattern III Countries." In *Human Sexuality: Research Perspectives in a World Facing AIDS*. A. Chouinard and J. Albert, eds. Ottawa: IDRC. Pp. 173–190.

Sivin, I., F. A. Sanchez, S. Diaz, P. Holma, E. Coutinho, O. McDonald, D. N. Robertson and J. Stern. 1983. "Three Year Experience with Norplant Subdermal Contraception." *Fertility and Sterility*, 39(6): 799–808.

Sizonenko, P. C. 2003. "Human Sexual Differentiation." *Geneva Foundation for Medical Education and Research*. http://www.gfmer.ch/Books/Reproductive_health/Human_sexual_differentiation.html. Last accessed 6/13/06.

Small, Meredith F. 1993. "The Gay Debate/Lesbianism: Less Is Known." *American Health*, March, XII(2): 70–77.

———. 1998.*Our Babies, Ourselves: How Biology and Culture Shape the Way We Parent*. New York: Anchor Books.

Smythers, Ruth. 1989 [1894]. "Instructions and Advice for the Young Bride on the Conduct and Procedures of the Intimate and Personal Relationship of the Marriage State for the Greater Spiritual Sanctity of This Blessed Sacrament and the Glory of God." *Transgender Views*, 3(9): 5–7.

Snitow, Ann Barr. 1983. *Powers of Desire: The Politics of Sexuality*. New York: Monthly Review Press.

Sobo, Elisa Janine and Sandra Bell. 2001. *Celibacy, Culture and Society: The Anthropology of Sexual Abstinence*. Madison: University of Wisconsin Press.

Society for the Scientific Study of Sexuality. 2006. http://www.sexscience.org. Last accessed 2/10/06.

Sodomy Laws. 2006. http://www.sodomylaws.org. Last accessed 3/28/06.

SOLGAN (Society of Lesbian and Gay Anthropology Newsletter). 1992. 14(2).

Somlai, Anton M., Jeffrey A. Kelly, Eric Benotsch, Cheryl Gore-Felton, Dmitri Ostrovski, Timothy McAuliffe and Andrei P. Zozlov. 2002. "Characteristics and Predictors of HIV Risk Behaviors Among Injection-Drug-Using Men and Women in St. Petersburg, Russia." In *AIDS Education and Prevention*, 14(4): 295–305.

Sommerville, C. John. 1990. *The Rise and Fall of Childhood*. New York: Vintage Books.

Sonefield, Adam. 2006. "Working to Eliminate the World's Unmet Need for Contraception." *Guttmacher Policy Review*, Winter, 9(1). http://www.guttmacher. org/pubs/gpr/09/1/gpr090110.html. Last accessed 8/11/06.

Sonenstein, Freya L., Joseph H. Pleck, Leighton C. Ku. 1989. "Sexuality Activity, Condom Use and AIDS Awareness Among Adolescent Males." *Family Planning Perspectives*, 21(4): 152–158.

Sorensen, Robert C. 1973. *Adolescent Sexuality in Contemporary America*. New York: World.

Speroff, Leon, Robert H. Glass, and Nathan G. Kase. 1978. *Clinical Gynecologic Endocrinology and Infertility*. 2nd ed. Baltimore: Williams and Wilkins.

Spiro, Melford. 1965. *Children of the Kibbutz*. New York: Schocken Books.

Spock, Benjamin and Robert Needlman. 2004. *Dr. Spock's Baby and Child Care.* 8th ed. New York: Pocketbooks.

Spock, Benjamin and Michael R. Rothenberg. 1985. *Dr. Spock's Baby and Child Care.* New York: Pocket Books.

Spradley, James. 1987a. *Conformity and Conflict.* Boston: Little, Brown and Co.

Spradley, James. 1987b. "Ethnography and Culture." In *Conformity and Conflict.* James Spradley and David McCurdy, eds. Boston: Little, Brown and Co. Pp. 17–25.

Spradley, James and David W. McCurdy, eds. 1987. *Conformity and Conflict: Readings in Cultural Anthropology.* Boston: Little, Brown and Company.

Sprecher, Susan, Kathleen McKinney, and Terri Orbuch. 1987. "Has the Double Standard Disappeared?: An Experimental Test." *Social Psychology Quarterly,* 50(1): 24–31.

Stack, Carol B. 1974. *All Our Kin.* New York: Harper & Row.

Stanford, Craig B., J. Walliz, H. Matama, and J. Goodall. 1994. "Patterns of Predation by Chimpanzees on Red Colobus Monkeys in Gombe National Park, Tanzania, 1982–1991." *American Journal of Physical Anthropology,* 94: 213–228.

Stansell, Christine and Sharon Thompson, eds. 1983. *Powers of Desire: The Politics of Sexuality.* New York: Monthly Review Press.

Starka, Lubos, I. Sipova and Joseph Hynie. 1975. "Plasma Testosterone in Male Transsexuals." *The Journal of Sex Research,* 1(2): 134–138.

"State of the World's Mothers 2006: Saving the Lives of Mothers and Newborns." 2006. Save the Children. http://www.savethechildren.org/publications/mothers/2006/SOWM_2006_final.pdf.

"State Policies in Brief: An Overview of Abortion Laws." 2006. Guttmacher Institute. http://www.guttmacher.org/statecenter/spibs/spib_OAL.pdf. Last accessed 1/20/2007.

"State Profiles: A Portrait of Sexuality Education and Abstinence-Only-Until Marriage Programs in the United States." 2004. SIECUS. http://www.siecus.org/policy/states/index.html. Last accessed 8/11/06.

Stein, Jonathan A. 2005. "Mitzvah: A Liberal Jewish Look at Human Sexuality." *American Sexuality Magazine,* August, 3(4): 1–3. http://nsrc.sfsu.edu. Last accessed 8/11/06.

Stewart, Elizabeth G. and Paula Spencer. 2002. *The V Book.* New York, NY: Bantam Books.

Stewart, Felicia Hance, F. Guest, Gary Stewart, and Robert Hatcher. 1979. *My Body, My Health: The Concerned Woman's Guide to Gynecology.* New York: John Wiley & Sons.

Stewart, Omer C. 1960. "Homosexuality Among the American Indians and Other Native Peoples of the World." *The Mattachine Review,* 6(1): 9–19.

Stimson, Gerry V. and Katchit Choopanya. 1998. "Global Perspectives on Drug Injecting." In *Drug Injecting and HIV Infection: Global Dimensions and Local Responses.* Gerry V. Stimson, Don C. DesJarlais, and Andrew Ball, eds. London; Bristol, PA: UCL Press: 1–21.

Stimson, Gerry V., Don C. DesJarlais, and Andrew Ball, eds. 1998. *Drug Injecting and HIV Infection: Global Dimensions and Local Responses.* Bristol: UCL Press.

Stine, Gerald. 1977. *Biosocial Genetics.* New York: MacMillan Publishing Co.

———. 1997. *Acquired Immune Deficiency Syndrome: Biological, Medical, Social and Legal Issues.* 3rd ed. Upper Saddle River: Prentice-Hall, Inc.

Stoddard, David Mitchell. 1990. *The Scented Ape*. Cambridge: Cambridge University Press.

Stoller, Robert J. 1968. *Sex and Gender: On the Development of Masculinity and Femininity*. New York: Science House.

Stone, Lawrence. 1977. *The Family, Sex and Marriage in England 1500–1800*. New York: Harper & Row.

Storms, Michael D. 1980. "Theories of Sexual Orientation." *Journal of Personality and Social Psychology*, 38: 783–792.

Strachey, James, ed. and tr. 1959 [1929]. *Group Psychology and the Analysis of the Ego*. London: Hogarth Press.

Stryker, Susan and Stephen Whittle, eds. 2006. *Transgender Studies Reader*. New York: Routledge.

"Submissions of the Irish Family Planning Association to the U.N. Committee on the Elimination of Discrimination Against Women, May 2005." 2005. http://www.ifpa.ie/download/ifpa-CEDAW-submission.doc. Last accessed 1/20/2007.

Suggs, David N. 1993. "Female Status and Role Transition in the Tswana Life Cycle." In *Culture and Human Sexuality*. David N. Suggs and Andrew W. Miracle, eds. Pacific Grove: Brooks/Cole Pub. Pp. 103–116.

Suggs, David N. and Andrew W. Miracle, eds. 1993. *Culture and Human Sexuality: A Reader*. Pacific Grove: Brooks/Cole Publishing.

———. 1999. *Culture, Biology, and Sexuality*. Athens: University of Georgia Press

Suggs, Robert. 1966. *Marquesan Sexual Behavior*. New York: Harcourt Brace & Jovanovich.

Sukkary, Soheir. 1981. "She is No Stranger: The Traditional Midwife in Egypt." *Medical Anthropology*, Winter, 5(1): 27–34.

Sullivan, K. 1998. "Gay Youths Struggle in Personal Hell." *San Francisco Examiner*, Sunday, July 26, D1: 4.

"Summary and Findings Kids Count Data Book, 2004." 2004. Annie Casey Foundation. http://www.aecf.org/kidscount/databook/pdfs_e/summary_e.pdf. Pp. 1–19. Last accessed 1/20/2006.

Sundahl, Deborah. 2002. *How to Female Ejaculate. Find Your G-Spot with Deborah Sundahl*. Santa Fe: Isis Media.

———. 2003a. *Female Ejaculation and the G-Spot*. Berkeley: Hunter House Publishers.

———. 2003b. *How to Female Ejaculate for Couples: Share Your G-Spot*. Santa Fe: Isis Media.

"Surveillance of Health Care Personnel with HIV/AIDS, as of December 2002." 2002. Centers for Disease Control and Prevention (CDC). http://www.cdc.gov/ncidod/dhqp/bp_hiv_hp_with.html. Last accessed 2/9/06.

Swaab, Dick F. 2004. "Sexual Differentiation of the Human Brain Identity: Relevant for Gender Identity, Transsexualism and Sexual Orientation." *Gynecological Endocrinology*, 19: 301–302.

Swain, Carolyne R., Lynn K. Ackerman, and Mark A. Ackerman. 2006. "The Influence of Individual Characteristics and Contraceptive Beliefs on Parent-Teen Sexual Communications: A Structural Model." *Journal of Adolescent Health*, 38(6): 753.e9–753.e18.

Symons, Donald. 1979. *The Evolution of Human Sexuality*. New York: Oxford University Press.

"Syndromes of Abnormal Sex Differentiation." 2005. The Johns Hopkins Children's Center. http://www.hopkinschildrens.org/specialities/categorypages/ intersex/sd2. html. Last accessed 2/10/06.

Tamkins, Theresa. 2004. "In Brazil, Women Who Lack Knowledge About Fertility Control Are Those Most Likely to Become Sterilized" Digest. *International Family Planning Perspectives*, June, 30(2). http://www.guttmacher.org/ pubs/journals/3010204.html.

Tan, Robert S. and J. W. Culbertson. 2003. "An Integrative Review on Current Evidence of Testosterone Replacement Therapy for the Andropause." *Maturitas* 45: 15–27.

Tanner, Deborah. 1995. *Gender and Discourse*. New York and Oxford: Oxford University Press.

————. 2001. *You Just Don't Understand: Women and Men in Conversation*. New York: Quill.

Tarín, Juan J. and Vanessa Gómez-Piquer. 2002. "Do Women Have a Hidden Heat Period?" *Human Reproduction*, 17(9): 2243–2248.

Taverner, William J. 2002. *Taking Sides: Clashing Views on Controversial Issues in Human Sexuality*. Guilford: McGraw-Hill/Dushkin.

Tavris, Carol. 1992. *The Mismeasure of Woman*. New York: Simon & Schuster.

Taylor, Jill McLean and Janie Victoria Ward. 1991. "Culture, Sexuality and School: Perspectives from Focus Groups in Six Different Cultural Communities." *Women's Studies Quarterly*, 1 and 2: 121–137.

Taylor, Shelley E., Laura Cousino Klein, Brian D. Lewis, Tara L. Gruenewald, A. R. Regan, and John A. Updegraff. 2000. "Biobehavioral Responses to Stress in Females: Tend-and-Befriend, Not Fight-or-Flight." *Psychol Rev*, 107(3): 411–429.

"Teen Sexual Activity Rises." 1991. *Parade Magazine*, February: 24, 25.

"Teenagers' Sexual and Reproductive Health: Developed Countries: Facts in Brief." 2004. Guttmacher Institute. http://www.guttmacher.org/pubs/fb_ teens.html. Last accessed 8/11/06.

Tew, Susan, and Rebecca Wind. 2002. "Differences in Contraceptive Use More Important Than Sexual Activity in Explaining Cross-Country Variations in Teen Pregnancy and Childbearing." http://www.guttmacher.org/media/nr/2002/01/ 02/nr_3306.html.

Thacker, Paul, D. 2004. "Medical Biology: Age of Fathers and Sperm Defects." *Journal of the American Medical Association*, 291(14): 1683.

The Body Pro. 2007. "New Jersey gives four cities approval for first needle exchanges." www.thebody pro.com. Accessed 11/09/07.

Thomas, John A. 2000. "Is the Sky Really Falling or Is It Just the Sperm Counts?" *International Journal of Toxicology*, January, 19(1): 1–4.

Thomas, Patricia. 2001. *Big Shot: Passion, Politics and the Struggle for an AIDS Vaccine*. New York: Public Affairs Press.

Thompson, W. M., J. M. Dabbs, Jr., and R. L. Friday. 1990. "Changes in Saliva Testosterone Levels During a 90-Day Shock Incarceration Program." *Criminal Justice and Behavior*, 17: 246–252.

Thornhill, Randy and Steven W. Gangestad. 1994. "Human Fluctuating Asymmetry and Sexual Behavior." *Psychological Sciences*, 2: 297–303.

Thornhill, Randy and Craig T. Palmer. 2000. *A Natural History of Rape: Biological Bases of Sexual Coercion*. Cambridge: The MIT Press.

Thuy, Nguyen Thi Than, Christine P. Landan, Nguyen Xuan Hoan, John Barclay and Ha Ba Ba Khiem. 2000. "Sexual Risk Behavior of Women in Entertainment Services, Vietnam." *AIDS and Behavior*, 4(1): 93–101.

Tiefer, Lenore. 1986. "In Pursuit of the Perfect Penis.: The Medicalization of Male Sexuality." *American Behaviorial Scientist*, 29: 579–599.

———. 2000. "Let's Look at Contexts." In *The Role of Theory in Sex Research*. John Bancroft, ed. Bloomington: Indiana University Press. Pp. 46–50.

———. 2004. *Sex Is Not a Natural Act and Other Essays*. 2nd ed. Boulder: Westview Press.

———. 2006a. "The 'New View' Approach to Men's Sexual Problems." *Medscape Today*. Pp. 1–23. http://www.medscape.com/viewprogram/5737. Last accessed 8/11/06.

———. 2006b. "The Viagra Phenomenon." *Sexualities*, 9(3): 273–294.

Tiefer, Leonore, Peggy Brick, and Meg Kaplan. 2003. *A New View of Women's Sexual Problems: A Teaching Manual*. New York: Campaign for a New View of Women's Sexual Problems.

Tielman, Rob, Manuel Carballo and Aart Hendriks, eds. 1991. *Bisexuality and HIV/AIDS: A Global Perspective*. Buffalo: Prometheus Books.

Timberake, Justin, 2002. "Rock Your Body". *Justified*. Jiv.

Tobach, Ethel and Betty Rosoff, eds. 1978. *Genes and Gender*. New York: Gordian Press.

Todosijević, Bojan, Snezand Ljubinkovic, and Aleksandra Arančić. 2003. "Mate Selection Criteria: A Trait Desirability Assessment Study of Sex Differences in Serbia." *Evolutionary Psychology*, June 23, 1: 116–126.

"Towards Ending Violence Against Women in South Asia." 2004. *Oxfam International*, August: 1–19.

Towle, Evan B. and Lynn M. Morgan. 2006. "Romancing the Transgender Native: Rethinking the Use of the 'Third Gender' Concept." *Transgender Studies Reader*. Susan Stryker and Stephen Whittle, eds. New York: Routledge. Pp. 666–684.

Transgender Views. 3(9): 5–7.

Travis, Cheryl Brown. 2003. *Evolution, Gender and Rape*. Cambridge: The MIT Press.

"Trends in Circumcisions Among Newborns." 2005. National Center for Health Statistics. http://www.cdc.gov/nchs/products/pubs/pubd/hestats/circumcisions/circumcisions.htm. Last accessed 2/10/06.

Trevathan, Wenda R. 1987. *Human Birth: An Evolutionary Perspective*. Hawthorne: Aldine de Gruyter.

Trevathan, Wenda R., E. O. Smith, and James J. McKenna, eds. 1999. *Evolutionary Medicine*. New York: Oxford University Press.

———. 2007. *Evolutionary Medicine: New Perspectives*. New York: Oxford University Press.

Troiano, L. 1990. "Verbal Birth Control." *American Health*, 9(4): 101.

———. 1924. *Primitive Culture: Researches into the Development of Mythology, Philosophy, Religion, Language, Art, Custom*. 7th ed. New York: Brentano's.

Turnbull, Colin M. 1972. *The Mountain People*. New York: Simon and Schuster.

———. 1961. *The Forest People*. New York: Simon and Schuster.

Turner, Victor W. 1969. *The Ritual Process: Structure and Anti-Structure*. Chicago: Aldine Press.

Tylor, Edward Burnett. 1897. *Anthropology: An Introduction to the Study of Man and Civilization.* New York: Appleton and Company.

Tylor, Edward Burnett. 1924. *Primitive Culture: Researches into the Development of Mythology, Philosophy, Religion, Language, Art, Custom.* 7th ed. New York: Bretano's.

Tyroler, Paula M. 1996. "The Recovered Memory Movement: A Female Perspective." *Institute Psychological Therapies,* 8 (2): n.p. http://www.ipt-forensics.com/journal/volume8/j8_2_toc.htm. Last accessed 5/12/06.

Ubeda, Alicia, Ramón Labastida, and Santiago Dexeus. 2004. "Essure®: A New Device for Hysteroscopic Tubal Sterilization in an Outpatient Setting." *Fertility and Sterility,* 82(1): 196–199.

UN AIDS. 2006. http://www.unaids.org/en/default.asp. Last accessed 8/7/06.

"UN AIDS Report on the Global AIDS Epidemic 2004." 2004. UNAIDS. http://www.unaids.org/bangkok2004/report_pdf.html. Accessed 2/10/06.

"UNFPA State of World Population." 2005. United Nations Population Fund. http://www.unfpa.org. Last accessed 11/18/07.

UNIFEM (2005). http://www.unifem.org. Last accessed 2/10/06.

United States Census 2000. 2000. http://www.census.gov/main/www/cen2000.html. Last accessed 2/10/06.

"Unmet Need for Family Planning, The." 2006. Planned Parenthood Federation of America. http://www.plannedparenthood.org/pp2/portal/international/global resource/resource-need-family.xml. Last accessed 8/11/06.

Unsafe Abortion: Global and Regional Estimates of the Incidence of Unsafe Abortion and Associated Mortality in 2000. 2004. 4th edition. Geneva: World Health Organization.

Urban, Hugh B. 2003. *Tantra: Sex, Secrecy, Politics and Power in the Study of Religion.* Berkeley: University of California Press.

U.S. Bureau of Labor Statistics. 1985. Washington: U.S. Dept. of Labor.

U.S. Census Bureau. 1980. United States Census, 1980.

U.S. Census Bureau. 2000. United States Census, 2000.

"U.S. Teenage Pregnancy Statistics: Overall Trends, Trends by Race and Ethnicity and State-by-State Information." 2004. Alan Guttmacher Institute. February 19. http://www.guttmacher.org/pubs/state_pregnancy_trends.pdf. Last accessed 8/14/06.

Utian, Wulf H., C. Cohen, J. H. Isacs, J. J. Mikuta, and L. Plouffe. 1993. "Doctor, Will HRT Cause Cancer?" *Menopause Management,* 11(7): 11–12, 14, 16.

"Vaginal Rejuvenation Surgery." 2003. Liberty Women's Health Care. http://www.libertywomenshealth.com/services.php?id=4. Last accessed 7/11/06.

Van Gennep, Arnold. 1960 [1909]. *The Rites of Passage.* M. B. Vizedom and G. I. Caffee, trs. London: Routledge and Kegan Paul.

Vance, Carol. 1983. "Gender Systems, Ideology and Sex Research." In *Powers of Desire: The Politics of Sexuality.* Ann Barr Snitow, Christine Stansell, and Sharon Thompson, eds. New York: Monthly Review Press. Pp. 371–384.

———. 1991. "Anthropology Rediscovers Sexuality: A Theoretical Account." *Social Science and Medicine,* 33: 875–884.

Vance, Carol S. and Carol A. Pollis. 1990. "Introduction: A Special Issue on Feminist Perspectives on Sexuality." *Journal of Sex Research,* 27(1): 1–5.

Varga, Christine, A. 1999. "South African Young People's Sexual Dynamics: Implications for Behavioural Responses to HIV/AIDS." In *Resistances to Behavioural*

Change to Reduce HIV/AIDS Infection. John C. Caldwell, ed. Canberra: Health Transition Center. Pp. 13–34.

Vatuk, Sylvia. 1985. "South Asian Cultural Conceptions of Sexuality." *In Her Prime: A New View of Middle-Aged Women.* Virginia Kerns and Judith K. Brown, eds. South Hadley: Bergin and Garvey Publishers, Inc.

Vayda, Andrew P. 1968. *People and Cultures of the Pacific.* Garden City: The Natural History Press.

Vernon, Irene S. 2001. *Killing Us Quietly.* Lincoln: University of Nebraska Press.

Vermeulen, Alex. 2000. "Andropause." In *Human Sexuality: Cross-Cultural Readings.* Brian J. du Toit, ed. New York: McGraw-Hill.

Verrilli, Adrienne. "Revamped Federal Abstinence-Only-Until-Marriage Program Go Extreme." 2006. SIECUS. http://65.36.238.42/media/press/press0124.html. Last accessed 11/21/06.

Vilet, Elizabeth. 1993. "New Insights on Hormones and Mood." *Menopause Management,* 11(6): 14–16.

Von Hollen, Cecilia. 2003. *Birth on the Threshold: Childbirth and Modernity in South India.* Berkeley: University of California Press.

Wade, Carole and Sarah Cirese. 1991. *Human Sexuality.* 2nd ed. San Diego: Harcourt Brace Jovanovich, Publishing

Walker, Bonnie L. and Donna Harrington. 2002. "Effects of Staff Training on Knowledge and Attitudes about Sexuality." *Educational Gerontology,* 28(8): 639–654.

Walley, Christine J. 2006. "Searching for 'Voices': Feminism, Anthropology, and the Global Debates over Female Genital Operations." In *Feminist Anthropology: A Reader.* Ellen Lewin, ed. Malden: Blackwell Publishing, Pp. 333–357.

Walter, Alex. 1990. "Putting Freud and Westermarck in Their Places: A Critique of Spain." *Ethos,* 18(4): 439–446.

Ward, Marths. 2002. *A World Full of Women.* Upper Saddle River: Allyn & Bacon.

———. 2006. *Nest in the Wind: Adventures in Anthropology on a Tropical Island.* Long Grove: Waveland Press.

Ward, Martha and Monica Edelstein. 2006. *A World Full of Women.* Boston: Pearson A and B.

Wattleton, Faye. 1990. "Teenage Pregnancy: The Case for National Action." *The Nation,* July 24/31: 138–141.

Waxman, Henry. 2004. "United States House of Committee on Government Reform Minority Staff Special Investigations Prepared for Henry Waxman: The Content of Federally Funded Abstinence-Only Education Programs." http://www.democrats.reform.house.gov. Last accessed 7/31/06.

———. 2006. "Letter to Michael O. Leavitt, Secretary of Health and Human Services." February 16. http://www.democrats.reform.house.gov. Last accessed 7/31/06.

Weber, Terry. 2005. "Canada Legalizes Same Sex Marriages." *San Francisco Chronicle,* July 21: A3.

Weil, Andrew. 1998. *Health and Healing.* Boston: Houghton-Mifflin Co.

———. 2004. *Health and Healing.* Boston: Houghton-Mifflin Co.

Weil, Mildred. 1990. *Sex and Sexuality: From Repression to Expression.* Lanham: University Press of America.

Weiner, A. B. 1987. "Introduction." In *The Sexual Life of Savages*. Bronislaw Malinowski, ed. Boston: Beacon Press.

Weinrich, James D. 1987. *Sexual Landscapes*. New York: Charles Scribner's and Sons.

Weiss, David. 2004a. "United States: Adolescent Sexuality." In *The Continuum Complete International Encyclopedia of Sexuality*. Robert T. Francoeur and Raymond J. Noonan, eds. New York, NY: Continuum. Pp. 1187–1188.

———. 2004b. "United States of America; Basic Sexological Premises." *The Continuum Complete International Encyclopedia of Sexuality*. Robert T. Francoeur and Raymond J. Noonan, eds. New York: Continuum. Pp. 1133–1139.

———. 2004c. "United States Interpersonal Heterosexual Behaviors: Childhood Sexuality." In *The Continuum Complete International Encyclopedia of Sexuality*. Robert T. Francouer and Raymond J. Noonan, eds. New York: Continuum. Pp. 1180–1188.

Weiss, David L. 2004. "United States of America." *The Continuum Complete International Encyclopedia of Sexuality*. Robert T. Francoeur and Raymond J. Nooran, eds. New York.

Weiss, Deborah. 2000. "Reducing Teenage Pregnancy." Planned Parenthood Federation of America. http://www.plannedparenthood.org/pp2/portal/files/portal/medicalinfo/teensexualhealth/fact-teen-pregnancy.xml. Last accessed 8/14/06.

———. 2006. "Pregnancy and Childbearing among US Teens." Planned Parenthood. http://www.plannedparenthood.org/pp2/portal/files/portal/medical info/teensexual health/fact-pregnancy-teens-us.xml. Last accessed 8/14/06.

Weiss, Jillian. 2007. "The Lesbian Community and FTMs: Détente in the Butch/FTM Borderlands." *The Journal of Lesbian Studies*, 11(3/4): 219–227. http://phobos.ramapo.edu. Accessed 8/9/05.

Weller, Aron, and Leonard Weller, 1998. "Prolonged and Very Intensive Contact May Not be Conducive to Menstrual Synchrony." *Psychoneuroendocrinology*, 23(1): 19–32.

Wells, Robert V. 1978. "Family History and Demographic Transitions." *The Family in Social-Historical Perspective*. N. Gordon, ed. New York: St. Martin's Press. Pp. 516–532.

Welsch, Robert L. and Kirk M. Endicott, eds. *Taking Sides: Clashing Views in Cultural Anthropology*. Dubuque: McGraw-Hill.

Westermarck, Edward. 1906–1908. *The Origin and Development of the Moral Ideas*. London: Macmillan and Co., Limited.

———. 1956 [1906]. "Homosexual Love." *Homosexuality: A Cross-Cultural Approach*. Donald Webster Corey, ed. New York: The Julian Press. Pp. 101–138.

Westheimer, Ruth. 2000. *Encyclopedia of Sex*. New York: Continuum Publishing Group Inc.

Westheimer, Ruth K. and Sanford Lopater. 2005. *Human Sexuality: A Psychosocial Perspective*. Philadelphia: Lippencott, Williams and Wilkins.

Wheeler, G. D., S. R. Wall, A. N. Belcastro and D. C. Cummings. 1984. "Reduced Serum Testosterone and Prolactin in Male Distance Runners." *Journal of the American Medical Association*, 252(4): 514–516.

Whelehean, Patricia. 1987. "Review of Labor More Than Once." *American Anthropologist*, March, 89(1).

———. 1988. *Women and Health: Cross-Cultural Perspectives*. Granby: Bergin and Garvey Publishers.

————. 2001a. *An Anthropological Perspective on Prostitution: Mellen Studies in Anthropology.* Vol. 4. Lewiston: Edwin Mellen Press.

————. 2001b. "Cross-Cultural Sexual Practices." In *The Encyclopedia of Women and Gender.* Judith Worell, ed. San Diego: Academic Press. Pp. 291–302.

————. n.d. Field notes.

Whelehan, Patricia with contributions by Thomas Budd. In press. *The Anthropology of AIDS: A Global Perspective.* Gainesville: University of Florida.

Whelehan, Patricia and James Moynihan. 1984. "Survey of Sexual Attitudes and Behaviors of Potsdam College Students." *College Student Personnel Association Journal*, 1.

Whipple, Beverly. 2006. "G-Spot and Female Pleasure." In *Human Sexuality: An Encyclopedia.* Erwin J. Haeberle, ed. Vern L. Bullough and Bonnie Bullough, original editors. http://www2.hu-berlin.de/sexology/GESUND/ARCHIV/SEN/INDEX.HTM. Last accessed 8/11/06.

Whipple, Beverly and B. R. Komisaruk. 1999. "Beyond the G Spot: Recent Research on Female Sexuality." *Psychiatric Annals*, 29(1): 34–37.

Whitaker, R. 1990. "Intolerance the Rule for Gay Teenagers." *Times Union* (Albany), May 27: G1-G2.

Whitam, Frederick L., Christophere Daskalos, Curt G. Sobolewski, and Peter Padilla. 1998. "The Emergence of Lesbian Sexuality and Identity Cross-Culturally: Brazil, Peru, the Philippines, and the United States." *Archives of Sexual Behavior*, 27(1): 31–56.

White, David Gordon. 2003. *Kiss of the Yogini: "Tantric Sex" in South Asian Contexts.* Chicago: University of Chicago.

White, Jacquelyn W. and Mary P. Koss. 1991. "Courtship Violence: Incidence in a National Sample of Higher Education Students." *Violence and Victims*, 6(4): 247–256.

White, Luise. 1990. *The Comforts of Home: Prostitution in Colonial Nairobi.* Chicago: University of Chicago Press.

Whitehead, Harriet. 1981. "Institutionalized Homosexuality in North America." *Sexual Meanings: The Cultural Construction of Gender and Sexuality.* Sherry B. Ortner and Harriet Whitehead, eds. Cambridge: Cambridge University Press. Pp. 80–115.

WHO Collaborating Centre on Adolescence Health. 2000. "A Portrait of Adolescent Health in the Caribbean." Pan American World Health Organization and Regional Office of the World Health Organization. http://www.paho.org/English/HPP/HPF/ADOL/monogra.pdf. Last accessed 7/11/06.

"Who gets Abortions." 1990. *Syracuse Herald American*, October 21, G1.

WHO Study Group on Female Genital Mutilation and Obstetric Outcome. 2006. "Female Genital Mutilation and Obstetric Outcome: WHO Collaborative Prospective Study in Six African Countries." *LANCET*, 367: 1835–41. http://www.who.int/reproductive-health/fgm/. Last accessed 7/11/06.

Wiegers, Therese A., Jouke van der Zee, Jan J. Kerssens, and Marc J.N.C. Keirse. 2000. "Variations in Home-Birth Rates between Midwifery Practices in the Netherlands." *Midwifery*, June, 16(2): 96–104.

Wierman, Margaret, Rosemary Basson, Susan R. Davis, Sundeep Khosla, Karen K. Miller, William Rosner, and Nanette Santoro. 2006. "Androgen Therapy in Women: An Endocrine Society Clinical Practice Guideline." *The Endocrine*

Society, 1–32. http://www.endo-society.org/quickcontent/clinicalpractice/clinical-guidelines/CG_AndroWomen.dfm. Last accessed 1/2006.

Wikan, Unni. 1977. "Man Becomes Woman: Transsexualism in Oman as a Key to Gender Roles." *Man*, 12(2): 304–319.

————. 2000. "Man Becomes Woman: Transsexualism in Oman." In *Human Sexuality: Cross-Cultural Readings*. 6th ed. Brian du Toit, ed. New York: McGraw-Hill. Pp. 132–146.

Wikipedia. 2006. www.en.wikipedia.org.

Williams, J. Whitridge, Jack Pritchard, Paul MacDonald, et al. 1985. *Williams' Obstetrics*. Norwalk: Appleton-Century-Crafts.

————. 1989. *Williams' Obstetrics*. 18th ed. Norwalk: Appleton and Lang.

Williams, Lena. 1989. "Inner City Under Siege: Fighting AIDS in Newark." *The New York Times*, February 6: 1, B-8.

Williams, Thomas R. 1966. "Cultural Structuring of Tactile Experience in a Borneo Society." *American Anthropologist*, 68: 27–39.

Williams, Walter L. 1986. *The Spirit and the Flesh*. Boston: Beacon Press.

Williams, Walter L. 1986. *The Spirit and the Flesh: Sexual Diversity in American Indian Culture*. Boston: Beacon Press.

Wilson, Jean D. 1979. "Embryology of the Genital Tract." In *Campbell's Urology*. Vol. 2. 4th ed. Meredith F. Campbell, ed. Philadelphia: Saunders. Pp. 1469–1483.

Wilson, Katherine K. 2000. "Gender as Illness: Issues of Psychiatric Classification." In *Taking Sides: Clashing Views on Controversial Issues in Sex and Gender*. Elizabeth L. Paul, ed. Guilford: Dushkin McGraw-Hill. Pp. 31–38.

Wind, Rebecca. 2005. "Research Often Misused for Political Ends: How Can Advocates and Policymakers Ensure the Evidence They Rely On Is Trustworthy?" *Guttmacher Institute*, November 7. http://www.guttmacher.org/media/nr/2005/11/04/index.html. Last accessed 8/14/06.

Winick, Charles. 1970. *Dictionary of Anthropology*. Totowa: Littlefield, Adams and Co.

Winn, Rhonda L. and Niles Newton. 1982. "Sexuality in Aging: A Study of 106 Cultures." *Archives of Sexual Behavior*, 11(4): 283–298.

Winters, Kelly. 2007. "Issues of GID Diagnosis for Transsexual Women and Men." Gender Identity Reform Advocates. http://gidreform.org/GID30285a.pdf. Last accessed 11/09/07.

Wolf, Arthur. 1966. "Childhood Association, Sexual Attraction and the Incest Tabu." *American Anthropologist*, 66: 883–898.

————. 1968. "Adopt a Daughter-in-Law, Marry a Sister: A Chinese Solution to the Problem of the Incest Taboo." *American Anthropologist*, 70: 864–874.

————. 1970. "Childhood Association and Sexual Attraction: A Further Test of Westermark Hypothesis." *American Anthropologist*, 72: 503–515.

Wolf, Eric. 1982. *Europe and the People Without History*. Berkeley: University of California Press.

Wolffers, Ivan and Mascha Bevers. 1997. *Sex Work, Mobility and AIDS in Kuala Lumpur, Malaysia*. Amsterdam: Caram-Asia and the Free University of Amsterdam.

Wolffers, Ivan and Fernandez I. Josie, eds. 1999. *Health Compromised. Two Preliminary Studies of Bangladeshi Female Migrant Workers. One in Malaysia and One in Bangladesh*. Kuala Lumpur: CARAM Asia.

Wolman, Benjamini B. and John Money, ed. 1980. *Handbook of Human Sexuality*. Englewood Cliffs: Prentice-Hall.

Womack, Mari and Judith Marti, eds. 1993. *The Other 50 Percent: Multi-Cultural Perspectives on Gender Relations*. Prospect Heights: Waveland Press, Inc.

"Woman and AIDS: Confronting the Crisis." 2004. UNAIDS/UNFPA/UNIFEM. http://www.unaids.org/. Last accessed 6/13/06.

"Women's Experiences with HIV Serodisclosure in Africa: Implications for VCT and PMTCT." 2003. Washington, D.C.: USAID Office of HIV/AIDS. The Synergy Project. http://www.synergyaids.com/documents/VCTDisclosureReport.pdf. Last accessed 11/21/06.

"Women's Health Information and Resources." 2006. *The National Women's Health Network*. http://www.nwhn.org/health/index.php. Last accessed 12/4/06.

"Women's Health Initiative." 2006. http://www.nhlbi.nih.gov/whi/. Last accessed 12/4/06.

"Women's Same-Sex Forum and African Women's Life History Project of Sex and Secrecy, The." 2004. The 4th Conference of the International Association for the Study of Sexuality, Culture and Society. *Sexuality Research and Social Policy*, 1(1): 104–107.

"Working Group on a New View of Women's Sexual Problems, The. 2002. The Manifesto: A New View of Women's Sexual Problems," http//www.fsdalert.org/manifesto.asp.

"World AIDS Day: Fighting HIV Discrimination in the Health Sector." 2003. Pan American Health Organization (PAHO). http://www.paho.org/English/DD/PIN/hiv_factsheet.htm. Last accessed 2/10/2006.

"World AIDS Day: Human Rights Central to Battle Against AIDS." 2002. Amnesty International. http://web.amnesty.org/library/index/ENGPOL300082002. Last accessed 2/9/06.

"World Charter for Prostitutes' Rights." 1985. International Committee for Prostitutes Rights. Amsterdam. http://www.walnet.org/csis/groups/icpr_charter.html. Last accessed 8/15/06.

"World Contraceptive Use 2001: Substantial use increase in 1990s." 2002. *United Nations Chronicle Online Edition*, XXXIX(3). http://www.un.org/Pubs/chronicle/2002/issue3/0302p44_world_contraceptive_use.html. Last accessed 8/11/06.

"World Contraceptive Use 2005." 2005. United Nations Department of Economic and Social Affairs Population Dvision. http://www. un.org/esa/population/publications/contraceptive2005/2005_World_Contraceptive_files/WallChart_WCU 2005.pdf. Last accessed 8/11/06.

World Health Organization (WHO). 2004a. http://www.who.int/en/. Last accessed 2/10/2006.

———. 2004b. XVth International AIDS Conference, Bangkok 2004. http://www.who.int/3by5/bangkok/en/. Last accessed 2/10/2006.

———. 2006. http://www.who.int/en/. Last accessed 8/7/06.

———. 2006. "Future of Sexual and Reproductive Health at the Tipping Point According to Global Study 2006." http://www.who.int/mediacentre/news/releases/2006/pr63/en/index.html. Last accessed 12/19/08.

World Health Statistics Annual. 1988. Geneva: World Health Organization.

World Population Prospectus: The 2004 Revision Volume 3 Analytical Report. 2004. United Nations. Executive Summary. Pp. xiii–xxii. http://www.un.org/esa/population/publications/WPP2004/2004EnglishES.pdf. Last accessed 8/11/06.

Worrell, Judith, ed. 2001. *The Encyclopedia of Women and Gender*. San Diego: Academic Press.

Wright, Victoria C., Laura A. Schieve, Meredith A. Reynolds, and Gary Jeng. 2003. "Assisted Reproductive Technology Suveillance-United States, 2000." *MMWR Surveillance Summaries*, August 29, 52(SS09): 1–16.

XVth International AIDS Conference (IAC). 2004. Electronic document. http://www.aids2004.org. Last accessed 8/29/06.

"XYY Syndrome." http://encyclopediaas.families.com. Last accessed 7/12/06.

"Yemen Training of Village Midwives at the Regional Hospital." 2005. Panos Pictures. http://www.panos.co.uk/. Last accessed 2/10/2006.

Yesterday. 2004. Directed by Darrell Roodt. South Africa: HBO.

Young, Frank W. 1965. *Initiation Rites: A Cross-Cultural Dramatization*. Indianapolis: Bobbs-Merrill.

"Young Mothers Disadvantage, Not Their Age Itself, Accounts for Their Children's Educational Problems." 2001. *Family Planning Perspectives*, November/December, 33(6): 1–3. www.guttmacher.org/pubs/journals/3328201.html. Last accessed 8/14/06.

"Youth Risk Behavior Surveillance—United States, 2005." 2006. *Morbidity & Mortality Weekly Report*, 55(SS-5): 1—108. http://www.cdc.gov/mmwr/PDF/SS/SS5505.pdf. Last accessed 8/14/06.

Yuan, Lu and Sam Mitchell. 2000. "Land of the Walking Marriage." *Natural History*, 109(19): 58–65.

Zaviacic, Milan. 1987. "The Female Prostate: Nonvestigal Organ of the Female: A Reappraisal. " *Journal of Sex and Marital Therapy*, 13(2): 148–52.

Zaviacic, Milan, Sylvia Dolezalova, Igor Karol Holoman, Alexandra Zaviacicova, MiroslavMikulecky, and Valer Brazdil. 1988. "Concentrations of Fructose in Female Ejaculate and Urine: A Comparative Biochemical Study." *Journal of Sex Research*, January, 24: 319–25.

Zelman, Elizabeth Crouch. 1977. "Reproduction, Ritual and Power." *American Ethnologist*, 4(4): 714–733.

Zhou, Jiang-Ning, Michel A. Hofman, Louis J. G. Gooren, and Dick F. Swaab. 1995. "A Sex Difference in the Human Brain and Its Relation to Transsexuality." *Nature*, 378(6552): 68–70.

Zilbergeld, Bernie. 1978. *Male Sexuality*. Boston: Little, Brown and Company.

———. 1992. *The New Male Sexuality*. 2nd ed. Boston: Little, Brown Company.

———. 1999. *The New Male Sexuality: The Truth about Men, Sex, and Pleasure*. 2nd ed. USA: Bantam.

Zubin, Joseph and Alfred N. Freedman, eds. 1970. *Psychopathology of Adolescence*. New York: Greene and Stratton.

Zucker, Kenneth J. and Susan J. Bradley. 1995. *Gender Identity Disorder and Psychosexual Problems in Children and Adolescents*. New York: Guilford Press.

Zverina, Jaroslav. 2004. "Czech Republic." In *The Continuum Complete International Encyclopedia of Sexuality*. Robert T. Francoeur and Raymond J. Noonan, eds. New York: Continuum. Pp. 320–328.

Index

Note: Page references in **bold** refer to terms defined in the Glossary

616   *Index*

624   *Index*